Benson and Hedges

Cricket Year

Benson and Hedges

Cricket Year

Twentieth Edition
September 2000 to September 2001

Edited by **Jonathan Agnew**

with additional contributions by
Qamar Ahmed
Charlie Austin
Mark Baldwin
Tony Cozier
Ralph Dellor
Jim Maxwell
Marcus Prior
Craig Ray
Telford Vice
Bryan Waddle

BLOOMSBURY

Edited by Jonathan Agnew
with additional contributions by
Qamar Ahmed
Charlie Austin
Mark Baldwin
Tony Cozier
Ralph Dellor
Jim Maxwell
Marcus Prior
Craig Ray
Telford Vice
Bryan Waddle
with special thanks to Ghaus Mohammed, R. Mohan,
Grant Shimmin, Utpal Shuvro, Jeff Thomson

First published in 2001 by
Bloomsbury Publishing Plc
38 Soho Square
London W1D 3HB

www.bloomsburymagazine.com

A copy of the CIP entry for this book is available from the
British Library.

ISBN 0 7475 5458 7

10 9 8 7 6 5 4 3 2 1

Project editor: Chris Hawkes
Design: Clive Dorman
Statistics: Wendy Wimbush
Pictures researched and supplied by David Munden at
Sportsline Photographic
www.sportsline.org.uk

Printed and bound in Great Britain
by Butler and Tanner, Frome

Contents

Sponsor's Message

The summer of 2001 will be remembered for the way in which the all-conquering Australian team showed England how to win Tests. In the lead up to the Ashes, England's hopes were high after series wins in the winter against Pakistan and Sri Lanka, which were then followed by a one-one draw against Pakistan in a shortened two-match series.

Mark Butcher's 173 not out at Headingley, which took England to victory in the fourth Test, was one of the few English highlights of the summer. Otherwise it was a tale of what might have been as both the summer and the Ashes once again belonged to the Australians.

However, the Aussies had not had it all their own way during the previous 12 months. After setting a world record of 16 consecutive Test victories, they were finally beaten by India at Eden Gardens, Calcutta in a Test never to be forgotten. Records tumbled from day one: Singh became the first Indian to take a hat-trick in Test cricket; Laxman became India's highest individual Test scorer with an unforgettable 281 in India's second innings; finally, India became only the third team to win a Test after following-on – the last time had been in 1981 when Ian Botham had inspired England's victory. All three victories were against Australia! India went on to win the third Test in Chennai and to take the newly-named Border-Gavaskar Trophy.

Australia also lost their crown as the Women's World Cup Champions when hosts New Zealand beat them in the final by four runs.

I also can't miss the opportunity of noting that Hampshire, who I have supported for many years, added to the Australians' list of defeats when they beat them by two wickets for the first time since 1912 at the Rose Bowl, their beautiful new ground, over a glorious three days in July!

On a more positive note, this the 20th edition of the *Benson and Hedges Cricket Year* has documented in great detail England's fantastic victories in the winter months. Firstly, in the gloom of Karachi, they beat Pakistan by six wickets, only their second overseas series win since 1986 (the other one was against New Zealand) and Pakistan's first-ever defeat in the 46-year history of the National Stadium in Karachi. Secondly, the much talked about series in Sri Lanka where the umpires occupied as much space in the newspaper columns as the cricket. After losing the first Test, England fought back to win the next two in Colombo and Kandy. The 5,000 travelling supporters in Kandy had much to cheer as England claimed their third Test win in one winter for the first time since the 1970s.

The first domestic trophy of the year, our own Benson and Hedges Cup brought Gloucestershire's unique run of success in Lord's finals over the past two years to an end when Surrey beat them by a convincing 47-run margin.

Other winners this summer have been Yorkshire and Sussex in the County Championship and Kent and Glamorgan in the Norwich Union Leagues. The Cheltenham & Gloucester Trophy was won by Somerset.

With Jonathan Agnew again at the helm, the 20th edition of the *Benson and Hedges Cricket Year* will once again bring back the memories of the last 12 months of cricket both on and off the field. From the losses of two greatly loved cricketers, Sir Donald Bradman and Lord Cowdrey, the lows of the pitch invasions at Headingley and the can-throwing incident at Lord's, to the highs of Australia's 16th Test victory when India were their victims and Bangladesh finally stepping into the world of Test cricket.

My thanks as always to Jonathan and all the other contributors to the book, as well as to Bloomsbury who work miracles to ensure that the *Benson and Hedges Cricket Year* is published just six weeks after the end of the domestic season in England.

When the winter months are upon us, I hope the *Benson and Hedges Cricket Year* brings back many happy memories of the last 12 months of cricket.

Barry Jenner
Managing Director, UK
Gallaher Ltd

INTRODUCTION

By Jonathan Agnew

INTRODUCTION
By Jonathan Agnew

These thoughts and reflections were made in the same week that many thousands of people died in the terrorist attacks on New York and Washington. How trivial sport now seems, and I wonder how many of us regret ever using the word 'disaster' to describe something as unimportant as an England batting collapse?

I pen these notes in the certain knowledge that life does go on and, one day, we will once again be focusing on Mark Butcher's technique outside the off stump and the value, or otherwise, of central contracts, however absurd and irrelevant those arguments appear today.

Such is the current uncertainty that England's winter plans hang in the balance. The proposed schedule includes a Test tour of India, the one senior representative of the subcontinent that England has not played – and defeated – in the past twelve months. That India dealt with Australia, coming back from one Test behind, shortly before the Aussies beat England so emphatically, says everything about Nasser Hussain's task. The captain, with the support of his coach, Duncan Fletcher, has endured a roller coaster of a year, which included unforgettable victories at Karachi, Kandy, Colombo and Headingley but crushing defeats at the hands of the Australians who retained the Ashes for a record sixth time. It is also necessary to mention that England lost 11 successive one-day internationals in that time and while they owed their well-deserved successes in the Test series in Pakistan and Sri Lanka to discipline and organization, their attempts at the shortened version of the game were shambolic and irresponsible.

That absolutely mirrored the manner in which the NatWest series was organized and marketed during the summer. Marred by pitch invasions, a serious injury to a steward which prompted England to concede the match and the first ever occasion in this country in which a team left the field because the players feared for their safety, the England and Wales Cricket Board must reconsider its approach to one-day international cricket. These matches have now been dumbed-down to an entirely unacceptable level; one at which bad behaviour and violence becomes part of the territory. It is unrealistic, on the one hand, to rev up spectators with deafening blasts of utterly irrelevant pop music and then expect them to behave in an orderly manner on the other. The loud horns that were available in and outside the grounds made both watching and listening an unbearable experience, and the decision to thrash out yet more music every time a batsman emerged from the pavilion backfired magnificently when England, foolishly, chose the theme to *The Great Escape*. Fleetingly it was funny, but it did not take long for the blood of sane and enthusiastic cricket lovers to boil: we used to stage these games so well.

Floodlit international cricket is now a proven failure in England and should be abandoned immediately. Unfortunately the Board has already signed an agreement with BskyB television that condemns us to a further four years of inadequate lights and unfavourable conditions. These matches are now not worth watching. Save your money and go to an open-air pop concert instead: overall it will be a similar experience except, crucially, the musicians will be able to perform to their best.

There is disquiet at county level, too. Nottinghamshire's players were so concerned about the poor quality of the floodlights before a day/night match against Yorkshire at Trent Bridge that they sought legal advice. In the event, no one lost their teeth and since the National League needs every ounce of assistance it can lay its hands on, I would continue with floodlit county matches, so long as the lighting is sufficient.

Besides, the quality of bowling in county cricket has now slumped to alarming proportions. It was not long ago that each team boasted a lightning-fast opening bowler and a couple of quality English seamers in support. There is now barely a fast bowler in the land and while our hearts went out to Scott Boswell, whose second and final over in the Cheltenham & Gloucester final contained 14 deliveries, it is inconceivable that he would have been opening the bowling in a Lord's showpiece only three years ago. Harsh, maybe, but true and an illustration of the problem England's selectors will face in the near future. Since England's best bowlers are withdrawn – far too often, in my view – from county cricket because of the central contracts, something must be done to fill the void because batsmen can only be as good as the bowling they face. There seems little option but to raise the limit of overseas players to two per county and although people will throw their hands up in horror at that suggestion, I can state quite categorically that I learned more from the experience of bowling at the other end to Andy

Previous page: Twilight starts to fall at Edgbaston during England's clash with Pakistan, but playing under the lights proved to be a huge disadvantage for those batting second.

Roberts than from any amount of coaching.

Rod Marsh, who has been chosen to head England's Academy, will have plenty on his hands when his new charges arrive in Adelaide. Hopefully he will offer something more important than coaching: a fresh approach. The last thing England's hopefuls need is more of the same dreary monotony and Mark Ramprakash was quite wrong when he suggested that an Englishman should have been appointed instead of Marsh.

Mike Atherton might reflect on the standard of bowling on offer from his new position in the commentary box. We pay tribute to him elsewhere in this edition of the *Benson and Hedges Cricket Year*, but his contribution to English cricket is worthy of a further mention here. A cussed, determined individual, Atherton was the batsman whose wicket was treasured most by the opposition throughout his 115 Tests and he will be hugely missed. We do not yet know if England has seen the last of Alec Stewart who, with Darren Gough, caused a furore by opting out of the Indian leg of the winter tour, but expected to be considered for the trip to New Zealand that immediately follows it. While one has every sympathy for senior cricketers who spend every winter away from home and decide to put family before duty for once, it is clearly not on for players to pick and choose what parts of a tour they undertake. The ECB has done everything possible, at the request of the players, to allow them home for Christmas this year and besides, part of this argument is being used by the more militant players to push for 12-month contracts, rather than the present arrangement of six-month central contracts. It does seem a little incongruous to argue to be bound to the Board for 12 months while arguing equally vociferously for a winter off. Besides, whose interests are protected by what amounts to guaranteeing selection for a whole year? Only those of the player.

The final word this year belongs to Australia, a proud and patriotic country that is setting new standards on the cricket field for others to follow. It is impossible for me to answer the question of where this current team stands in the history of the game, but I must confess to being somewhat surprised by the names contained in an 'all-time great XI' that was attributed to Sir Donald Bradman shortly after his death this year. The finest batsman the game has ever seen and, according to Richie Benaud, no less, a superb chairman of selectors. Yet this unbalanced outfit can only have been chosen on sentimental grounds if, indeed, the Don ever chose it at all. His prowess was the stuff of legends and it is a safe bet that no other batsman will ever have an average of 99.94 after 52 Tests. But Shane Warne, Glenn McGrath and, especially, Steve Waugh deserve their places in history, too, and we should all feel fortunate in the extreme to have seen them at their very best this summer.

Jonathan Agnew
Leicestershire, September 2001

Alec Stewart's decision not to tour with the England team to India this winter placed the England management in an awkward position. Should senior players be allowed to pick and choose when they play for their country?

THE YEAR IN PICTURES

(above) Twilight zone: Nasser Hussain reflects on an extraordinary last-day win for England in their first visit to Pakistan since the infamous trip in 1987.

(left) As dusk settled over Karachi, Nasser Hussain and Graham Thorpe defied the time-wasting tactics of Pakistan captain Moin Khan to lead England to an unlikely 1–0 series win.

(right) The victor's spoils. Another series win to follow those over Zimbabwe and the West Indies in the summer of 2000. Things were looking good for the England side.

INVESCO-INVESTS

(above) The banners in the crowd say it all. England's series win in Sri Lanka was marred by poor umpiring, histrionic appealing and bad sportsmanship.

(left) Nasser Hussain's fighting 109 in the first innings of the second Test at Kandy ended a terrible run of form for the England captain and helped lay the foundations for victory.

(left) Four out of four. Nasser Hussain is all smiles following England's remarkable four-wicket win inside three days at Colombo that secured the series.

(below) Craig White and Ashley Giles embrace after squaring the series against Sri Lanka with a three-wicket win at Kandy. The best was still to come.

(above) Chris Cairns hits the winning runs for New Zealand
to secure their victory over India in the final of the ICC
Knock-Out Trophy in Kenya. It was New Zealand's first
success in a major international tournament.

(right) A spectacular effort from Jimmy Adams in the Carlton One-Day Series. However, his team's 5–0 whitewash at the hands of the all-conquering Australians would cost him both the captaincy and his place in the side.

(below) Group huddle. The Australian players celebrate victory over the West Indies in the second Test at Perth. Their win took them past the West Indies' proud record of 11 consecutive wins.

(above) Australia's Test series in India started with the news of the death of the game's greatest-ever player, Sir Donald Bradman.

(left) Harbhajan Singh was one of the Indian heroes, taking an extraordinary 32 wickets in his side's 2–1 series win over the Australians.

(right) The hero of the greatest Test match ever played? Forced to follow on 274 runs in arrears, V.V.S. Laxman inspired India's recovery with a magnificent innings of 281 to lead the home side to an unlikely 171-run victory.

(right) In an unprecedented decision, England's stand-in skipper, Alec Stewart, was forced to concede the match against Pakistan at Headingley following a series of pitch invasions.

(below) An injured steward is led from the field of play following a pitch invasion at Headingley during England's NatWest series clash with Pakistan. It was one of a number of incidents that marred the tournament.

(above) The behaviour of the crowds throughout the NatWest series marred the tournament and should lead to a major rethink about the future of international one-day cricket in England.

(right) After a firecracker had been thrown dangerously close to Brett Lee, Australian captain Steve Waugh led his players from the field of play at Trent Bridge.

(left) Mark Butcher's inspired 173 not out that led England to a six-wicket victory in the fourth Test against Australia at Headingley was the highlight of the summer for the England team.

(right) Captain Courageous. Steve Waugh defied injury to smash an unbeaten 157 in the fifth and final Test at The Oval. It was an innings that said everything about the Australian captain's approach to the game.

(left) Steve Waugh holds a glass replica of the Ashes trophy. There can be little doubt that the English public were treated to some of the finest displays by a cricket team ever seen in this country.

(above) After acknowledging the crowd and raising his bat
(even though he had only scored nine runs), Mike Atherton
left the crowd in no doubt that the fifth Test was to be his
final appearance in an England shirt.

(below) Champagne time for Shane Warne, who took his 400th Test wicket in the final Test at The Oval – one of 31 wickets in the series.

(above) We're there. Yorkshire captain
David Byas helps his side past the winning
post against Glamorgan and eases the Tykes
to their first county championship success
since 1968.

(left) The glory days are back at Taunton. Somerset skipper Jamie Cox celebrates his county's first domestic success since 1983.

(below) Surrey's all-star side ended Gloucestershire's bid for a fifth-successive Lord's cup final victory with their triumph in the Benson and Hedges Cup final.

ENGLAND

Pakistan in England
NatWest Triangular Series
Australia in England
CricInfo County Championship
Norwich Union National League
Benson & Hedges Cup
Cheltenham & Gloucester Trophy
First-Class Averages

PAKISTAN IN ENGLAND
By Jonathan Agnew

British Universities v. Pakistanis
4–5 May 2001 at Trent Bridge
British Universities 74 and 155 (Mushtaq Ahmed 8 for 49)
Pakistanis 316 (Saeed Anwar 89, Salim Elahi 78, Waqar Younis 50*, TJ Murtagh 6 for 86)
Pakistanis won by an innings and 87 runs

Scheduled to last three days, this meeting of the British Universities and the Pakistan tourists at Trent Bridge was a mismatch and was over within two. Wasim Akram and Waqar Younis destroyed the students' first innings on the opening morning – James Pyemont's 18 being the top score in an all-out total of 74. Tim Murtagh bowled manfully to finish with career-best figures of six for 86, but the Pakistanis still managed to reach 316 in their first innings with Saeed Anwar (89) and Saleem Elahi (78) underlining the gulf in class. Mushtaq Ahmed then bamboozled the Universities side with his leg-spin, taking eight for 49 from 24 overs in their second-innings total of 155. Pakistan had thus completed victory by an innings and 87 runs.

Derbyshire v. Pakistanis
8–10 May 2001 at Derby
Derbyshire 166 (Saqlain Mushtaq 6 for 34) and 247 for 5 dec. (MP Dowman 145*)
Pakistanis 262 (Azhar Mahmood 80*, Faisal Iqbal 65) and 63 for 1
Match drawn

Rain showers blighted Pakistan's three-day match against Derbyshire at Derby, preventing a positive result. But there were still some eye-catching performances from the tourists, and a wonderful last-day 145 not out – on his 27th birthday – by Mathew Dowman, featuring two sixes and 20 fours. Dowman also top-scored in the Derbyshire first innings, but with just 36 as Saqlain Mushtaq (six for 34) routed the county for 166. Shoaib Akhtar took two for 31 from 12 overs just 24 hours after flying in from Lahore to join the tour following treatment for illness. Azhar Mahmood, with 80 not out, was helped by Shoaib to put on 80 for Pakistan's final wicket during their first-innings total of 262, in which 20-year-old local farmer, Nathan Dumelow

Previous page: The Yorkshire players celebrate the club's first county championship success since 1968.

impressed by taking four for 81 with his off spin on his first-class debut. After Derbyshire had declared their second innings on 247 for five, there was time only for Pakistan to reply with 63 for one.

Kent v. Pakistanis
12–14 May 2001 at Canterbury
Kent 313 for 5 dec. (RWT Key 119, MJ Walker 98) and 94 for 3
Pakistanis 307 for 1 dec. (Saeed Anwar 201, Salim Elahi 94*)
Match drawn – no play was possible on the third day

Rain washed away the scheduled third day of the match between Kent and the Pakistan tourists at Canterbury, but by then spectators had already seen some sparkling strokeplay from both sides. On the first day, which the county made an Open Day, Rob Key (119) and Matthew Walker (98) led the way to 313 for five declared, but their worthy effort was overshadowed on the next day by a truly scintillating 201 from just 225 balls from Saeed Anwar. The left-handed opener hit the suffering Min Patel for five sixes, and there were 27 fours from him besides, as Pakistan raced to 307 for one declared. Saleem Elahi finished on 94 not out, but Anwar's innings was the highest by a touring batsman against Kent since Graeme Pollock's sublime 203 for the South Africans in 1965.

FIRST TEST
17–20 May 2001 at Lord's

Three-match Test series are often unsatisfactory, but the combination of the new world championship and the ECB's scheduling handed Pakistan the cruellest cut there can ever have been – two Tests, both starting before May was out.

Clearly this is a nonsense, and while the conditions invariably favour England in these circumstances, the satisfaction gained through catching your opponents unprepared can only be superficial – unless, of course, it is Australia! Maybe that should be the ECB's next ploy.

Pakistan had absolutely no chance at Lord's. The spring weather had been so foul that they had scarcely been able to set foot on a cricket field since their arrival and, after the opening day was declared a complete washout at a quarter to two (Peter Willey never was one to mess about unnecessarily), the following day was the coldest ever recorded during a Test match in England. The mercury struggled to only 8°C – 46.4°F in old money – and Pakistan, by their own choice, were in the field. It was truly horrible.

That, however, is where one's sympathy for the visitors runs out. Their final selection, in which they decided to leave out Saqlain Mushtaq in favour of a fifth seamer, was bonkers. It is true that the conditions were barely conducive to spin bowling, but Saqlain is a master of his art and, importantly, bamboozles the lower order with his string of variations that do not depend entirely upon the pitch. Having omitted the spinner, Waqar had little choice but to field first, although his battery of seam and swing bowlers found little encouragement and

Nasser's unlucky break: Hussain's thumb is broken by Shoaib Akhtar at Lord's. The delivery reared from a good length.

by lunch, when England had rattled along to 92 for one, the decision was already looking flawed.

There was a brief tremor when England slipped to 114 for three. After a bright start, Michael Vaughan was caught down the leg side by Latif off Azhar Mahmood for 32, and Atherton then missed a completely straight ball from the same bowler for 42. This was to be Pakistan's best chance of the match, but they were denied by a fighting partnership of 132 between Nasser Hussain – who had taken the decision before the match to drop to number four – and Graham Thorpe who, therefore, was now at five. Just before the close of play, Thorpe surprised everyone by hooking Waqar Younis straight down fine leg's throat for 80, at which point the debutant Ryan Sidebottom crammed his thatch into a helmet and appeared as nightwatchman. England were 254 for four at the end of the first day of play.

Sidebottom – who is the tenth son of an England cricketer to appear for his country – did not hang about the following morning: he was caught at first slip off Wasim, who bowled with far greater hostility and intent than during the previous day. In fact, the entire Pakistani attack changed its policy and frequently banged the ball in short, rather than looking for swing and movement from a full length.

Shoaib Akhtar worked up a rapid pace and, during his first spell of the day, he made a delivery rear at Hussain and fractured his right thumb. It was yet another cruel blow for the England captain – his third broken digit in as many seasons, and this one was to keep him out of both the second Test and the NatWest series to boot. Alec Stewart played breezily for his 44 from 53 balls and Ian Ward, who made 39, looked the part in his first Test innings.

England's last three wickets added 74 precious runs before Waqar finished the innings at ten minutes to three on the third day. A positive result at this stage – exactly half way through the game – seemed inconceivable.

By the close of play, thanks to Yousuf Youhana and Younis Khan,

FIRST TEST – ENGLAND v. PAKISTAN
17–20 May 2001 at Lord's

ENGLAND

	First innings	
MA Atherton	b Azhar Mahmood	42
ME Trescothick	c Azhar Mahmood, b Abdur Razzaq	36
MP Vaughan	c Rashid Latif, b Azhar Mahmood	32
N Hussain (capt)	c Rashid Latif, b Azhar Mahmood	64
GP Thorpe	c Abdur Razzaq, b Waqar Younis	80
RJ Sidebottom	c Inzamam-ul-Haq, b Wasim Akram	4
*AJ Stewart	lbw b Shoaib Akhtar	44
IJ Ward	c Abdur Razzaq, b Waqar Younis	39
DG Cork	c Younis Khan, b Wasim Akram	25
AR Caddick	b Azhar Mahmood	5
D Gough	not out	5
	b1, lb5, w1, nb8	15
		391

	First innings			
	O	M	R	W
Wasim Akram	34	9	99	1
Waqar Younis	25	5	77	2
Shoaib Akhtar	19	4	64	1
Abdur Razzaq	21	2	68	1
Younis Khan	5	0	27	–
Azhar Mahmood	26	12	50	4

Fall of Wickets
1-60, 2-105, 3-114, 4-246, 5-254, 6-307, 7-317, 8-365, 9-385

PAKISTAN

	First innings		Second innings	
Saeed Anwar	c Atherton, b Gough	12	c Thorpe, b Caddick	8
Salim Elahi	c Atherton, b Caddick	0	c Thorpe, b Caddick	0
Abdur Razzaq	c Stewart, b Caddick	22	c Atherton, b Caddick	53
Inzamam-ul-Haq	c Stewart, b Caddick	13	c Stewart, b Cork	20
Yousuf Youhana	lbw b Gough	26	c Vaughan, b Cork	6
Younis Khan	b Cork	58	lbw b Cork	1
Azhar Mahmood	c Trescothick, b Caddick	14	c Stewart, b Caddick	24
*Rashid Latif	c Stewart, b Gough	18	c Stewart, b Gough	20
Wasim Akram	not out	19	c Thorpe, b Gough	12
Waqar Younis (capt)	c Thorpe, b Gough	0	c Stewart, b Cork	21
Shoaib Akhtar	b Gough	0	not out	2
	b1, lb7, nb13	21	lb6, nb6	12
		203		**179**

	First innings				Second innings			
	O	M	R	W	O	M	R	W
Gough	16	5	61	5	16	4	40	3
Caddick	17	3	52	4	18	3	54	4
Sidebottom	11	0	38	–	9	2	26	–
Cork	11	3	42	1	15.3	3	41	3
Trescothick	2	1	2	–				
Vaughan					1	0	12	–

Fall of Wickets
1-4, 2-21, 3-37, 4-60, 5-116, 6-153, 7-167, 8-203, 9-203
1-2, 2-30, 3-67, 4-84, 5-87, 6-121, 7-122, 8-147, 9-167

Umpires: P Willey & DB Hair
Toss: Pakistan
Test debuts: RJ Sidebottom and IJ Ward (England)

England won by an innings and 9 runs

Pakistan had recovered from 60 for four to 115 for four. Their top order batsmen had displayed enough uncertainty to suggest that they might struggle to avoid the follow-on. This feeling was strengthened by the fact that, since the first day was washed out, the follow-on was reduced to a deficit of 150 rather than the customary 200. This was to make all the difference.

Darren Gough celebrates as he captures his 200th Test wicket.

It was vital that England broke the partnership between Yousuf and Younis and, with only one run added on the fourth morning, Gough trapped Yousuf lbw for 26. Azhar Mahmood and young Younis battled away until, with 89 still required to avoid the follow-on, Caddick produced a real brute that flew off the shoulder of Mahmood's bat to Trescothick at second slip. On the stroke of lunch, Latif edged Gough to Stewart, to become the Yorkshireman's 200th Test wicket and, after the interval, Gough finished the job to complete a run of three wickets in four balls. Pakistan had lost five wickets for 88 runs and had fallen 39 runs short of avoiding the follow-on. With more than a day and a half in which to bat, they now knew that defeat was a real possibility.

What followed, however, was little short of a shambles as Gough, Caddick and Cork scythed the hapless visitors down within the day. Razzaq scored a pleasant half-century after Salim Elahi had bagged a pair and Inzamam seemed mortified when given out caught behind down the leg side. Replays showed that umpire Willey had made an excellent decision, which should have resulted in a heavy punishment for Inzy who had, quite deliberately, sought to make the umpire appear incompetent.

We have seen England in this mood before recently, and when they are on a roll, they can now be admirably clinical. Caddick took four for 54 and Gough three for 40, but there was no reward for Sidebottom who bowled earnestly but with no sign of bringing the ball into the right-handed batsman. Pakistan, meanwhile, were unhappy – and not without some justification – although even a lack of preparation could not entirely excuse their demise in the second innings. As far as England were concerned, however, this was a performance that merely heightened the growing excitement and anticipation for the Ashes.

Leicestershire v. Pakistanis
23 May 2001 at Leicester
Leicestershire 225 for 7 (50 overs) (BF Smith 105)
Pakistanis 228 for 3 (42.4 overs) (Salim Elahi 108*)
Pakistanis won by seven wickets

Leicestershire, rallying to 225 for seven from their 50 overs following a fierce new-ball spell of three for 14 in six overs by Shoaib Akhtar, gave Pakistan a decent work-out at Grace Road. Ben Smith included 12 boundaries in his 116-ball 105, while Iain Sutcliffe made 46 and Darren Maddy 40 on his 27th birthday. But Saleem Elahi, with an unbeaten 108, was joined

by Yousuf Youhana in a stand of 112 in just 19 overs as Pakistan emerged the victors by seven wickets and with more than seven overs in hand.

Leicestershire v. Pakistanis
24–25 May 2001 at Leicester
Leicestershire 96 (Waqar Younis 5 for 23, including a hat-trick) and 172
Pakistanis 294 (Faisal Iqbal 83, Yousuf Youhana 80)
Pakistanis won by an innings and 26 runs

The Pakistanis overpowered a weakened Leicestershire side in two of the three scheduled days, their innings-and-26-run victory merely underlining the massive gulf in class between a top international side and run-of-the-mill county professionals. The time for a drastic re-think about the sort of warm-up matches given to teams touring England must begin now. Surely, games between the tourists and an England 'A' team, or regional side, would provide better entertainment – and a relevant stage on which the best of up-and-coming Englishmen could test themselves. It would help to bridge the gap between the county and Test arenas.

In this game, on a good pitch, Pakistan dismissed Leicestershire for just 96 in their first innings on the opening morning – Waqar Younis taking a hat-trick with the last three deliveries of his second over. Waqar finished with five for 23, while his new-ball partner, Wasim Akram, picked up four for 19. It was like shelling peas for the two old maestros. Waqar's hat-trick victims were Neil Burns, Phil DeFreitas and Omari Banks. Burns was lbw to an in swinger, DeFreitas clean bowled in his first innings of the season, and the teenage Banks – an all-rounder from Anguilla – given no chance by a ball which started out on middle and leg but then swung away late to clip the top of his off stump.

By the close of day one, Pakistan were 201 for three in reply, with Faisal Iqbal on 81, but the youngster only made it to 83 the next morning as the Pakistanis fell away lethargically to 294 all out.

Yousuf Youhana underlined his class with 80, and in Leicestershire's second innings only Iain Sutcliffe and Ashley Wright, on his debut, resisted for long as the county were rolled over for 172. Sutcliffe, in fact, was the one Leicestershire player to emerge from the match with credit – in the first innings carnage he also made a brave 55 before being the last man out. Spinners Mushtaq Ahmed and Saqlain Mushtaq did the second-innings damage, sharing eight wickets as Pakistan skipper Waqar took the opportunity to give them a good work-out.

SECOND TEST
31 May–4 June 2001 at Old Trafford

It was clear that Old Trafford was to stage something out of the ordinary before a single ball had been bowled. As the hacks assembled the day before the start for the customary briefings with the two captains, a wild rumour began to sweep around the ground – the Pakistan team had gone to Blackpool for the day!

It is a difficult one to check but, surely, this was unprecedented. Even in the glory days of Compton and Edrich, Cowdrey and May, the players would have had some sort of a net the day before a Test match. Pakistan's players, one down with just one to play, were having a whale of a time on the roller coaster!

Next day, refreshed and relaxed, they caned England's attack all over Old Trafford. The close-of-play score of 370 for eight illustrates the extraordinary entertainment that owed as much to England's lack of discipline with the ball as Pakistan's positive approach. Gough and Caddick were out of sorts while Cork, worryingly, completely lost his ability to swing the ball. A stiff wind blowing straight down the ground did not help matters, but international bowlers should have made a better fist of it. 216 of those 370 came in boundaries and, while the stately Inzamam held centre stage, almost half of those came on the leg side. Inzy does like to work the ball from middle stump to mid-wicket but, even so, England's bowlers were extremely generous.

Inzamam's 114 was easily the highlight of the day. After he was caught behind off a no ball on 31, he added 141 in only 142 minutes with Younis Khan, who made 65. Rashid Latif hit his highest Test score, 71, before Pakistan were dismissed half an hour into the second day for 403.

England's reply was almost as vigorous. Atherton and Trescothick fell in successive overs to Waqar and Wasim and, at 15 for two, the horns and

A ride on Blackpool's Big Dipper clearly had an effect on Inzamam who scored a brilliant century at Old Trafford.

Michael Vaughan, the Lancashire-born Yorkshireman, reached his first Test century in bizarre circumstances.

claxons, that were to become just one of a number of blights in the one-day series, were blaring as loudly and as obtrusively as possible. Gradually they fell quiet, however, as Thorpe and Vaughan saw England into the third day with an outstanding partnership of 267 for the third wicket. Thorpe reached his century first and, moments later, Vaughan passed three figures for England for the first time in the most bizarre fashion. Setting off for an unlikely second to third man, Vaughan did not appear to see that Wasim's wild throw flew wide of the wicket-keeper and away to the boundary for four. It was only when Thorpe congratulated him that Vaughan glanced at the scoreboard and celebrated with a gloved punch in the air.

On they went until, first, Thorpe was run out for 138 and, one run later, Vaughan was caught behind

SECOND TEST – ENGLAND v. PAKISTAN
31 May–4 June 2001 at Old Trafford

PAKISTAN

	First innings		Second innings	
Saeed Anwar	c Atherton, b Caddick	29	c Thorpe, b Gough	12
Abdur Razzaq	b Caddick	1	c Cork, b Hoggard	22
Faisal Iqbal	c Vaughan, b Gough	16	c Stewart, b Caddick	14
Inzamam-ul-Haq	c Ward, b Hoggard	114	c Trescothick, b Hoggard	85
Yousuf Youhana	c Knight, b Caddick	4	c Atherton, b Caddick	49
Younis Khan	lbw b Hoggard	65	lbw b Cork	17
Azhar Mahmood	c Knight, b Hoggard	37	b Caddick	14
*Rashid Latif	run out (Trescothick)	71	c Atherton, b Hoggard	25
Wasim Akram	c Stewart, b Gough	16	b Gough	36
Saqlain Mushtaq	not out	21	c Stewart, b Gough	5
Waqar Younis (capt)	lbw b Gough	5	not out	14
	lb9, nb15	24	lb11, nb19	30
		403		**323**

	First innings				Second innings			
	O	M	R	W	O	M	R	W
Gough	23.4	2	94	3	22.5	2	85	3
Caddick	28	2	111	3	22	4	92	3
Hoggard	19	4	79	3	29	4	93	3
Cork	21	2	75	-	25	9	42	1
Trescothick	3	0	14	-				
Vaughan	2	0	21	-				

Fall of Wickets
1-6, 2-39, 3-86, 4-92, 5-233, 6-255, 7-308, 8-357, 9-390
1-24, 2-41, 3-63, 4-204, 5-208, 6-232, 7-241, 8-300, 9-306

ENGLAND

	First innings		Second innings	
MA Atherton	c Rashid Latif, b Waqar Younis	5	b Waqar Younis	51
ME Trescothick	b Wasim Akram	10	c Rashid Latif, b Wasim Akram	117
MP Vaughan	c Rashid Latif, b Waqar Younis	120	c Rashid Latif, b Abdur Razzaq	14
GP Thorpe	run out (Wasim Akram)	138	b Wasim Akram	10
*AJ Stewart (capt)	not out	39	lbw b Saqlain Mushtaq	19
IJ Ward	run out (Azhar Mahmood)	12	c Rashid Latif, b Saqlain Mushtaq	10
NV Knight	c Rashid Latif, b Abdur Razzaq	15	lbw b Wasim Akram	0
DG Cork	c Saeed Anwar, b Abdur Razzaq	2	lbw b Saqlain Mushtaq	4
AR Caddick	c Rashid Latif, b Saqlain Mushtaq	1	b Saqlain Mushtaq	0
D Gough	b Abdur Razzaq	0	c sub (Imran Nazir), b Waqar Younis	23
MJ Hoggard	b Saqlain Mushtaq	0	not out	0
	lb5, w2, nb8	15	b6, lb4, w1, nb2	13
		357		**261**

	First innings				Second innings			
	O	M	R	W	O	M	R	W
Wasim Akram	30	7	89	1	23	4	59	2
Waqar Younis	24	3	87	2	22.1	3	85	3
Azhar Mahmood	8	0	35	-				
Saqlain Mushtaq	30.2	7	80	2	47	20	74	4
Abdur Razzaq	19	2	61	3	13	5	33	1

Fall of Wickets
1-15, 2-15, 3-282, 4-283, 5-309, 6-348, 7-353, 8-354, 9-356
1-146, 2-174, 3-201, 4-213, 5-229, 6-230, 7-230, 8-230, 9-261

Umpires: DR Shepherd & EA Nicholls
Toss: Pakistan
Test debuts: nil

Pakistan won by 108 runs

off Waqar for 120. 282 for two had become 283 for four and the innings quickly subsided as Saqlain and Razzaq ran through the lower order. England's last six wickets fell for just 48 runs and, as Stewart faced just six deliveries, the last five fell for nine runs in 34 balls. We thought these cataclysmic collapses were things of the past.

Buoyed by an unlikely lead of 46, Pakistan's second innings got away to a furious start. Saeed Anwar was caught by Thorpe off Gough in the third over with the score already on 24 and it was 41 for two in the sixth when Razzaq drove Hoggard to mid-on. Inzamam added some much-needed circumspection, and although Faisal Iqbal was snared down the leg side off Caddick for 14, Pakistan closed the third day with a lead of 133 with seven wickets still in hand.

In the sixth over of the fourth morning, Inzamam – on 36 – received a crucial let-off. Knight, usually so secure, was having a nightmare of a match and he would normally catch this offering every time. Down it went, and England had to wait until the big man had reached 85 before Trescothick gratefully clung on to a catch at mid-wicket. Pakistan's lead was now 250. In the following over, Yousuf edged to Atherton at slip for 49, but by tea Wasim – who was smashing the ball all over the place – and Latif had extended the lead to 320. Gough wrapped up the innings shortly afterwards setting England 370 to win from 112 overs.

Had Atherton and Trescothick not made such a positive start that evening, any thoughts of an England victory would have been dismissed as madness. However, in the 22 overs that remained, they had breezed to 85 for no wicket, setting up the most fascinating of final days in which England needed 285 to win.

The final morning belonged to England as they added 64 runs and, importantly, lost only a single wicket – Atherton for 51. However, the aimless manner in which Trescothick and Vaughan approached the afternoon suggested that England had no real idea how they should be batting. Should they try and win, or settle for the draw that would be enough to secure the series? In 29 overs, England managed to score only 47 runs – it was inexplicably awful, but they seemed safe in the knowledge that, with eight wickets still in hand at tea, the series was theirs.

Pakistan had different ideas, however. Inspired by their captain Waqar Younis, who removed Thorpe in the second over with the new ball, they preyed on England's confused approach. Amidst hysterical

TEST MATCH AVERAGES
England v. Pakistan

ENGLAND

Batting	M	Inns	NO	HS	Runs	Av	100	50	c/st
GP Thorpe	2	3	0	138	228	76.00	1	1	5
MP Vaughan	2	3	0	120	166	55.33	1	–	2
ME Trescothick	2	3	0	117	163	54.33	1	–	4
AJ Stewart	2	3	1	44	102	51.00	–	–	10/-
MA Atherton	2	3	0	51	98	32.66	–	1	6
IJ Ward	2	3	0	39	61	20.33	–	–	1
D Gough	2	3	1	23	28	14.00	–	–	–
DG Cork	2	3	0	25	31	10.33	–	–	1
AR Caddick	2	3	0	5	6	2.00	–	–	–

Also batted in one Test: MJ Hoggard 0, 0*; N Hussain 64; NV Knight 15, 0 (2ct); RJ Sidebottom 4.

Bowling	Overs	Mds	Runs	Wkts	Av	Best	10m	5/inn
D Gough	78.3	13	280	14	20.00	5-61	–	1
AR Caddick	85	12	309	14	22.07	4-52	–	–
MJ Hoggard	48	8	172	6	28.66	3-79	–	–
DG Cork	72.3	17	200	5	40.00	3-41	–	–

Also bowled: RJ Sidebottom 20-2-64-0; ME Trescothick 5-1-16-0; MP Vaughan 3-0-33-0.

PAKISTAN

Batting	M	Inns	NO	HS	Runs	Av	100	50	c/st
Inzamam-ul-Haq	2	4	0	114	232	58.00	1	1	1
Younis Khan	2	4	0	65	141	35.25	–	2	1
Rashid Latif	2	4	0	71	134	33.50	–	1	9/-
Wasim Akram	2	4	1	36	83	27.66	–	–	–
Abdur Razzaq	2	4	0	53	98	24.50	–	1	2
Azhar Mahmood	2	4	0	37	89	22.25	–	–	1
Yousuf Youhana	2	4	0	49	85	21.25	–	–	–
Saeed Anwar	2	4	0	29	61	15.25	–	–	1
Waqar Younis	2	4	1	21	40	13.33	–	–	–

Also batted: Faisal Iqbal 16, 14; Salim Elahi 0, 0; Saqlain Mushtaq 21*, 5; Shoaib Akhtar 0, 2*.

Bowling	Overs	Mds	Runs	Wkts	Av	Best	10m	5/inn
Saqlain Mushtaq	77.2	27	154	6	25.66	4-74	–	–
Abdur Razzaq	53	9	162	5	32.40	3-61	–	–
Waqar Younis	71.1	11	249	7	35.57	3-85	–	–
Wasim Akram	87	20	247	5	49.40	2-59	–	–

Also bowled: Azhar Mahmood 34-12-85-4; Shoaib Akhtar 19-4-64-1; Younis Khan 5-0-27-0.

appealing – which clearly distracted the umpires who failed to call a number of no balls – wickets started to tumble. Replays suggested that David Shepherd should have called the deliveries from Saqlain that dismissed Ward, Caddick and Cork and it made for a convenient excuse. But the fact is that England lost their precious eight wickets for 65 runs in 25.1 overs after tea, with four going down for a single run in five overs. Saqlain, who was on a hat-trick, took four for five from 36 deliveries.

It was as awesome a collapse as you could ever see and the entire match was a triumph for the groundsman, Peter Marron. Before the Test, not a single ball had been bowled in county cricket all season. Somehow, Marron and his team managed to produce a superb pitch which, in turn, produced a sensational match. Suddenly, the Aussies might not have been so worried, after all.

NATWEST TROPHY TRIANGULAR SERIES
By Jonathan Agnew

The NatWest triangular series was ruined by the worse scenes of crowd disturbance ever seen on cricket grounds in this country. The perpetrators were those dressed in the colours of Pakistan's cricketers, and although a debate raged concerning which team this minority did in fact support, this was an irrelevance. Crowd trouble and hooliganism are not welcome on cricket grounds in England and we must not be intimidated and prevented from pointing the finger of blame at those who are culpable. As the tournament progressed, I have little doubt that the pitch invasions became pre-planned. The fact is that the searches conducted by the stewards were hopeless, the short-sighted policy of the ECB in dumbing down one-day cricket whipped up the spectators into a frenzy (or drove them away vowing never to return) and England was once again exposed as being completely inappropriate for staging floodlit cricket at international level. The combination of the above will soon have a serious impact on the enjoyment, and credibility, of cricket in this country unless the Board takes note.

The first of the problems occurred at the very first game. Edgbaston staged a day/night match between England and Pakistan – Graham Thorpe injured a calf muscle in the warm-up which was to prevent him from playing until the second Test against Australia – and the game followed a depressingly familiar script for a floodlit match in this country: the team batting second had no chance.

When England were 159 for nine in the 44th over – still 115 runs short of their target – some of the crowd, which had sat bored rigid throughout England's innings, lined the boundary rope in anticipation (or a desire to be put out of their misery) of the end of the match. An unsuccessful appeal sparked the invasion that had the players racing from the field, the stumps stolen and an unpleasant atmosphere of intimidation as Pakistan's 'supporters' celebrated a premature victory. Waqar Younis made a public appeal, the field was cleared and the match limped on for a further three overs until the final wicket was taken.

Two days later, Australia – helped by a fantastic innings from Ricky Ponting – romped to a seven-wicket win over Pakistan at Cardiff. No-one seemed to notice the crazy dash for the stumps at the end of play that resulted in a punch-up between Pakistan 'supporters', but when Australia narrowly triumphed over England in the best match of the tournament – and the first not involving Pakistan – not a solitary spectator ran on to the ground. It was an excellent match, effectively sealed by a spectacular six over extra-cover by Ian Harvey, and who knows what difference might have been made to the summer as a whole – if any – had England managed to have won.

They should have defeated Pakistan at Lord's. Trescothick scored a brilliant 137 as England chased 243 to win. However, as panic started to grip the lower order, Trescothick went for glory and holed

Inzamam gives England's bowlers a taste of what was to come in the NatWest series by scoring a rapid 79 in the opening match at Edgbaston which was marred by crowd trouble.

Ricky Ponting was in masterful form throughout the series. He was Man of the Match on three occasions.

The pitiful sight of stewards holding up temporary fencing in an attempt to avoid crowd trouble at Trent Bridge.

out in the deep. Three were required from the last ball, and Caddick was stumped.

Old Trafford staged one of the most one-sided one-day internationals there can ever have been. Australia batted first and scored 208 for seven, only for England, in the long twilight and under inadequate lights, to bomb to 40 for six. Mercifully, the crowd did not have so long to wait this time as England were bundled out in the 33rd over for a dismal 86.

So England were still without a win when they met Pakistan at Headingley. Here the collapse was even more extraordinary – 58 for seven – with Waqar taking the first seven wickets to fall. It was a magnificent performance, and although Ben Hollioake scored 53 and Gough 40, Pakistan romped towards their target with the minimum of fuss. However, with three runs required by Pakistan, several hundred of their 'supporters' dashed on to the field from the new Western Stand. A steward, whose job it was to protect the players, was beaten up on the square and had to be stretchered off. It was an appalling scene and, in an unprecedented move, Alec Stewart conceded the match that Pakistan had all but won.

England were now out of the running for the final, but there was still time for more mindless crowd behaviour at Trent Bridge. The authorities there went to the extent of installing some temporary fencing in an attempt to keep the crowd off the field. Indeed, the sight of grey-haired men holding up some orange-coloured garden netting against threatening, massed supporters is one of the most unsavoury memories of the summer. The match was also marred by the throwing of a firecracker dangerously close to the Australian fieldsman, Brett Lee. After a brief consultation, Steve Waugh took his players from the field until order, finally, was restored.

Waqar turned in another admirable performance – six for 59 – as Pakistan triumphed and Australia discovered that batting second in day/night matches in this country is a lottery.

There was time, before the much-awaited final between Australia and Pakistan, for England to be trounced once again. They were dismissed for 176 at The Oval and the Aussies knocked them off with 20 overs remaining – England's tournament: played six, lost six.

To put the seal on a thoroughly forgettable series, the final was equally disappointing. A re-run of the World Cup final, all the ingredients suggested a magnificent match. Pakistan, however, were every bit as disappointing as they had been in 1999: in fact they managed only 20 runs more than their 132 on that occasion. Australia, with one eye on grabbing every bit of psychological advantage for the Ashes that was on offer, swamped Pakistan and knocked off the target of 153 in 26.3 overs. Another yawn stifled: can't wait until next year.

Match One
7 June 2001 at Edgbaston (day/night)
Pakistan 273 for 6 (50 overs) (Inzamam-ul-Haq 79, Saeed Anwar 77)
England 165 (47.2 overs) (NV Knight 59*, Shahid Afridi 3 for 15)
Pakistan won by 108 runs
Man of the Match: Saeed Anwar

Match Two
9 June 2001 at Cardiff
Pakistan 257 (49.5 overs) (Yousuf Youhana 91*, Rashid Latif 66)
Australia 258 for 3 (45.4 overs) (RT Ponting 70, MG Bevan 56*, SR Waugh 54*)
Australia won by seven wickets
Man of the Match: RT Ponting

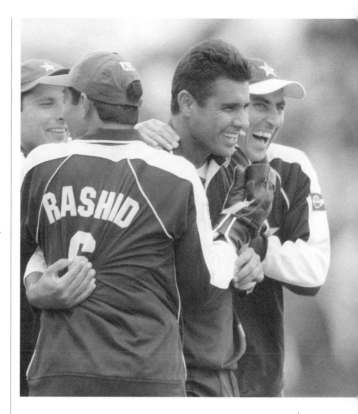

Waqar Younis produced a devastating spell of seven for 36 at Headingley where England were forced to concede the match after a pitch invasion.

Match Three
10 June 2001 at Bristol
England 268 for 4 (50 overs) (NV Knight 84, ME Trescothick 69)
Australia 272 for 5 (49.3 overs) (RT Ponting 102)
Australia won by 5 wickets
Man of the Match: RT Ponting

Match Four
12 June 2001 at Lord's
Pakistan 242 for 8 (50 overs) (Yousuf Youhana 81, Younis Khan 44)
England 240 (50 overs) (ME Trescothick 137, OA Shah 62)
Pakistan won by 2 runs
Man of the Match: ME Trescothick

Match Five
14 June 2001 at Old Trafford (day/night)
Australia 208 for 7 (48 overs) (SR Waugh 64, DR Martyn 51*, AD Mullally 3 for 50)

England 86 (32.4 overs) (JN Gillespie 3 for 20)
Australia won by 125 runs
Man of the Match: JN Gillespie

Match Six
16 June 2001 at Chester-le-Street
Australia v. Pakistan abandoned without a ball being bowled

Match Seven
17 June 2001 at Headingley
England 156 (45.2 overs) (BC Hollioake 53, D Gough 40*, Waqar Younis 7 for 36)
Pakistan 153 for 4 (39.5 overs) (Abdur Razzaq 75)
England conceded the match after a pitch invasion caused play to be abandoned
Man of the Match: Waqar Younis

Match Eight
19 June 2001 at Trent Bridge
Pakistan 290 for 9 (50 overs) (Salim Elahi 79)
Australia 240 (46.3 overs) (AC Gilchrist 70, SR Waugh 56, Waqar Younis 6 for 59)
Pakistan won by 36 runs
Man of the Match: Waqar Younis

Match Nine
21 June 2001 at The Oval
England 176 (43.2 overs) (NV Knight 48)
Australia 177 for 2 (30.1 overs) (AC Gilchrist 80, RT Ponting 70*)
Australia won by 8 wickets
Man of the Match: RT Ponting

Australia celebrate with the NatWest trophy shortly before a beer can was hurled at the balcony from the crowd below.

NATWEST TROPHY FINAL – AUSTRALIA v. PAKISTAN
23 June 2001 at Lord's

PAKISTAN

Saeed Anwar	c Bevan, b Harvey	27
Salim Elahi	c Gilchrist, b McGrath	10
Yousuf Youhana	run out (Ponting)	11
Inzamam-ul-Haq	lbw b Warne	23
Younis Khan	c Warne, b Lee	0
Abdur Razzaq	c Warne, b Lee	24
*Rashid Latif	b Warne	23
Azhar Mahmood	b Warne	1
Wasim Akram	b Gillespie	17
Waqar Younis (capt)	lbw b Harvey	0
Saqlain Mushtaq	not out	0
	b2, lb3, w8, nb3	16
	42.3 overs	**152**

	M	O	R	W
McGrath	10	2	28	1
Gillespie	7	1	25	1
Harvey	7.3	0	18	2
Lee	8	1	20	2
Warne	10	0	56	3

Fall of Wickets
1-28, 2-47, 3-60, 4-60, 5-92, 6-102, 7-110, 8-151, 9-152

AUSTRALIA

*AC Gilchrist	not out	76
ME Waugh	run out (Youhana/Latif)	36
RT Ponting	not out	35
MG Bevan		
SR Waugh (capt)		
DR Martyn		
IJ Harvey		
SK Warne		
B Lee		
JN Gillespie		
GD McGrath		
	b1, w8	9
	(for 1 wicket) 26.3 overs	**156**

	O	M	R	W
Wasim Akram	7	0	15	-
Waqar Younis	5	0	32	-
Saqlain Mushtaq	8	0	50	-
Abdur Razzaq	5	0	40	-
Azhar Mahmood	1.3	0	18	-

Fall of Wickets
1-78

Umpires: DR Shepherd & P Willey
Toss: Pakistan
Man of the Match: AC Gilchrist
Man of the Series: Waqar Younis

Australia won by nine wickets

AUSTRALIA IN ENGLAND
By Jonathan Agnew (with Jeff Thomson)

Worcestershire v. Australians
1-3 June 2001 at Worcester
Australians 351 (DR Martyn 108, SK Warne 68) and
360 for 8 dec. (ML Hayden 65, RT Ponting 65)
Worcestershire 163 (A Singh 62) and 188 (DA
Leatherdale 72)
Australians won by 360 runs

The Australians began their tour with the kind of positive – indeed, supercharged – cricket that acted as a clear marker for the way they intended to continue during the course of the summer. Worcestershire, their traditional first-up opponents, did their best to make a game of it in front of capacity crowds basking in the New Road splendour, but only Australia's own desire to get as much match practice as possible stretched the contest out over the full three days. The Aussies, in fact, were 178 for six on the opening day before Damien Martyn (108) and Shane Warne, with a belligerent 68, added 148. Martyn's second 50 took him just 51 balls and 88 of his runs came in boundaries. Warne also struck a six and 12 fours and, despite Anurag Singh's 62, Glenn McGrath's early dismissal of Graeme Hick on the second morning condemned Worcestershire to a big first-innings deficit when they folded to 163 all out. Opting to bat again, Australia this time ran up 360 for eight declared, with Matthew Hayden and Ricky Ponting contributing attractive 65s, before Warne again wielded the willow to great effect with an unbeaten 23-ball 41. Hick was then out first ball to Damien Fleming before McGrath, on his return to the county he served with such distinction in 2000, wrapped things up with four for 31. Only David Leatherdale (72) delayed the inevitable as Worcestershire, dismissed for 188, were beaten by 360 runs.

Middlesex v. Australians
5 June 2001 at Lord's
Australians 232 (44.2 overs) (IJ Harvey 84, RT Ponting 57)
Middlesex 233 for 4 (47.1 overs) (BL Hutton 73, OA Shah 50)
Middlesex won by six wickets

Middlesex won themselves a famous victory over the Australians at Lord's, winning by six wickets in a 50-over contest after bowling the tourists out for 232 in the 45th over. Ricky Ponting was the only top-order batsman to dominate, with 57 from 47 balls, but Ian Harvey then came in to hit 84 off just 65 deliveries. Middlesex, however, knew they were in with a chance – and a second-wicket stand of 113 between Ben Hutton (73) and Owais Shah (50) confirmed it. Robin Weston's unbeaten 36 was then influential in guiding the county home. It was a considerable feather in the cap of Paul Weekes, too, who accepted the acting captaincy in the absence of Angus Fraser, Stephen Fleming and Phil Tufnell, and then took three for 36 with his off breaks.

Northamptonshire v. Australians
7 June 2001 at Northampton
Australians 234 for 3 (50 overs) (DR Martyn 101*, ME Waugh 88*)
Northamptonshire 234 (50 overs) (ME Hussey 73)
Match tied

Northamptonshire failed to emulate Middlesex's achievement of beating the Australians two days earlier, when they somehow contrived to lose three wickets in a frenetic final over with the scores level. An exciting 50-over match at Northampton thus ended in a tie, with Northants all out for 234 in reply to the Australians' 234 for three. The tourists were boosted by Damien Martyn's 101 not out, plus an unbeaten 88 by Mark Waugh, but then another Australian, Mike Hussey, threatened to upstage them with a punchy 73. Largely due to his efforts, Northants went into the last 15 overs needing only 64 to win with seven wickets in hand. Batsmen came and went, however, until in that amazing final over – bowled by Ian Harvey – Lesroy Weekes was run out off the second ball, Darren Cousins caught behind off the fourth and Jason Brown run out from the very last delivery attempting a desperate bye to the wicket-keeper!

MCC v. Australians
25–27 June 2001 at Arundel
Australians 390 (SM Katich 168*, SK Warne 69) and
294 for 8 dec. (SR Waugh 105, DR Martyn 80)
MCC 124 (MH Richardson 64*) and 280 (JC Adams 81*, DM Ward 57)
Australians won by 280 runs

A brilliant, unbeaten 168 from Simon Katich on the opening day was the major highlight of Australia's comfortable 280-run victory over the MCC at Arundel. Katich rallied the Australians from a shaky

64 for four on the first morning, following a four-wicket, new-ball burst from 30-year-old Queenslander Joe Dawes, to underline his claims for a Test berth. The left-hander was later joined by Shane Warne (69) in a rollicking seventh-wicket stand of 190 in hot sunshine as the Aussies reached 390 all out in just 74.5 overs. By the close, the MCC were already 82 for six in reply, and Colin Miller picked up four for 41 as they were dismissed for 124. Steve Waugh (105) and Damien Martyn (80) then took advantage of some ideal batting practice, instead of enforcing the follow-on, and Australia eventually declared their second innings on 294 for eight. Miller took three for 87 as the MCC were

The Australian opener, Matthew Hayden warmed up for the first Test with 98 against Essex.

winkled out for 280, but not before David Ward (57) and Jimmy Adams, with 81 not out, had provided some defiance.

Essex v. Australians
29 June–1 July 2001 at Chelmsford
Australians 405 for 5 dec. (AC Gilchrist 150*, DR Martyn 114*, RT Ponting 63) and 569 for 9 dec. (ML Hayden 98, B Lee 79, RT Ponting 79, CR Miller 62, MJ Slater 58, PM Such 5 for 131)
Essex 231 (JS Foster 74, GR Napier 59, JN Gillespie 5 for 37)
Match drawn

Capacity crowds attended Essex's match against the Australians at Chelmsford on all three days – and ended up by jeering the touring team when they batted throughout the whole of the final day in a seemingly cynical attempt to prevent England captain Nasser Hussain, who was returning after injury, from having a second chance to bat. Large sections of the final-day, 5,000-strong crowd made their feelings known to the Australians, who were being led by Adam Gilchrist in the absence of Steve Waugh. The tourists began the last day on 188 for two in their second innings, having bowled out Essex for 231 in reply to their own first-innings total of 405 for five declared, and ended up on 569 for nine. Gilchrist, coming in at number 11 in a rejigged batting order, finished on 25 not out. 'They cheated the paying public and sponsors, all of whom paid good money to come along today,' said Essex's former England off spinner Peter Such. By the end, indeed, the Australians' overall lead was a ridiculous 743 – but Gilchrist defended his actions by insisting that batting practice for his men was all-important ahead of the opening Ashes Test. Matthew Hayden (98) and Michael Slater (58) had added 138 for the first wicket the previous evening, and Brett Lee made 79 from number four and Glenn McGrath 38 from number eight. Ricky Ponting added 79 to his first-innings score of 63, which included 13 fours, while Damien Martyn scored an unbeaten 46 from number ten in the order to go with his 114 not out on the first day. Gilchrist, however, was perhaps the star turn of the match – as well as its ultimate villain – by thrashing an unbeaten 150 from 149 deliveries, with three sixes and 21 fours, as he and Martyn had rallied their side from 154 for five with a breathtaking partnership. Jason Gillespie also warmed up for the Test series with five for 37, and although Hussain made an uncomfortable 16 against the Aussie quicks, there was a chink of light for

England's future in the form of 21-year-old wicket-keeper James Foster, whose superb 74 signalled his class.

FIRST TEST
5–8 July 2001 at Edgbaston

In order for this series to be competitive, it was widely believed that England should not lose the opening Test. A draw, a complete washout, even a mass pitch invasion – anything would do apart from an Australian victory. As things turned out, however, the match, apart from being astonishingly entertaining, was grotesquely one-sided.

England's build-up, far from being controlled, was a complete shambles. Graham Thorpe, who had torn a calf muscle before the first match in the forgettable NatWest series, was ruled out at the start of the week, only for his replacement, Mark Ramprakash, to aggravate a hamstring injury and join Thorpe on the physio's couch. Michael Vaughan was the next to go with a knee problem (which led to an operation during the first day of the match) and then Ashley Giles, who had missed much of the season with an Achilles injury, reported in with tonsillitis. Darren Gough had a troublesome stomach upset. What a great start and, as smug as you like, Australia announced their team – even down to the 12th man – three days before the off!

Still, some habits die hard and Nasser Hussain lost his seventh-consecutive toss. Steve Waugh, sensing his opportunity to expose England's hastily assembled batting line up – which now included a startled Mark Butcher and Nottinghamshire's Usman Afzaal. Mind you, if Butcher was surprised by his call-up, he woke up immediately when he found himself striding out to the middle in just the second over after Marcus Trescothick had been caught in the slips off Gillespie for a duck.

Any thoughts of 'here we go again' were rapidly dispelled, however, as Butcher and Mike Atherton set about the Australian attack with relish. Waugh set attacking fields that bordered on the outrageous, to such an extent that even the metronomic McGrath seemed a little fazed by it all. The lunch score, after only 25 overs, was 106 for two with

Andy Caddick flails another boundary during his extraordinary innings of 49 during the first Test at Edgbaston.

Steve Waugh added 133 with his brother, Mark, as Australia powered to an unassailable position in the first Test.

Butcher caught in the final over of the session at silly point off Warne's second delivery of the series.

Two hours and 27 overs later, England had added 85 runs, but at a cost of five further wickets. Atherton made 57, but was taken at second slip off Gillespie before a more controlled McGrath returned to rip out the middle-order. Hussain fell lbw offering no stroke for 13, Ian Ward – with a crooked bat – played on for 23. Afzaal, left-handed, received a massively turning leg break that ripped out of the rough and cleaned him up for four and White completed the misery when he was given out leg before, on the front foot, as he tried to sweep Warne for four.

Within minutes of the end of the tea break, England were 191 for nine and Caddick joined a beleaguered Stewart. The Aussies closed in for the

FIRST TEST – ENGLAND v. AUSTRALIA
5–8 July 2001 at Edgbaston

ENGLAND

	First innings		Second innings	
MA Atherton	c M Waugh, b Gillespie	57	c M Waugh, b McGrath	4
ME Trescothick	c Warne, b Gillespie	0	c M Waugh, b Warne	76
MA Butcher	c Ponting, b Warne	38	c Gilchrist, b Lee	41
N Hussain (capt)	lbw b McGrath	13	retired hurt	9
IJ Ward	b McGrath	23	b Lee	3
*AJ Stewart	lbw b McGrath	65	c Warne, b Gillespie	5
Usman Afzaal	b Warne	4	lbw b Gillespie	2
C White	lbw b Warne	4	b Gillespie	0
AF Giles	c Gilchrist, b Warne	7	c M Waugh, b Warne	0
D Gough	c Gillespie, b Warne	0	lbw b Warne	0
AR Caddick	not out	49	not out	6
	b10, lb8, nb16	34	b1, lb5, nb12	18
		294		**164**

	First innings				Second innings			
	O	M	R	W	O	M	R	W
McGrath	17.3	2	67	3	13	5	34	1
Gillespie	17	3	67	2	11	2	52	3
Lee	12	2	71	–	7	0	37	2
Warne	19	4	71	5	10.1	4	29	3
ME Waugh					1	0	6	–

Fall of Wickets
1-2, 2-106, 3-123, 4-136, 5-159, 6-170, 7-174, 8-191, 9-191
1-4, 2-99, 3-142, 4-148, 5-150, 6-154, 7-155, 8-155, 9-164
Hussain retired hurt at 117 for two

AUSTRALIA

	First innings	
MJ Slater	b Gough	77
ML Hayden	c White, b Giles	35
RT Ponting	lbw b Gough	11
ME Waugh	c Stewart, b Caddick	49
SR Waugh (capt)	lbw b Gough	105
DR Martyn	c Trescothick, b Butcher	105
*AC Gilchrist	c Caddick, b White	152
SK Warne	c Atherton, b Butcher	8
B Lee	c Atherton, b Butcher	0
JN Gillespie	lbw b Butcher	0
GD McGrath	not out	1
	b3, lb7, nb23	33
		576

	First innings			
	O	M	R	W
Gough	33	6	152	3
Caddick	36	0	163	1
White	26.4	5	101	1
Giles	25	0	108	1
Butcher	9	3	42	4

Fall of Wickets
1-98, 2-130, 3-134, 4-267, 5-336, 6-496, 7-511, 8-513, 9-513

Umpires: G Sharp & SA Bucknor (TV: KE Palmer)
Toss: Australia
Test debut: Usman Afzaal

Australia won by an innings and 118 runs

kill and bombarded Caddick – who they consider to be fragile – with bouncers. The tall number 11 retreated to leg and, as he resorted to swiping anything within reach through the covers, the runs started to flow at an astonishing rate. Stewart joined in the fun as frustration started to consume the Australians. 103 runs were plundered in only 12.4 overs of absolute mayhem that not only brought Edgbaston to its feet, but also lifted the flagging spirits in the England dressing room beyond measure.

How cruelly that was swept away when, with the cheers still ringing in their ears, England took to the field. Gough tore in from the City End like a man possessed and Michael Slater calmly drilled him for four boundaries. Add Gough's two no balls to the tally, and 18 runs came from the opening over. To a man, England's shoulders slumped.

Two wickets fell before the close, Hayden and Ponting, to complete a session in which no fewer than 236 runs were scored for the loss of five wickets! Can there ever have been a more productive session in Test cricket?

Slater fell before lunch on the second day, but the Waugh twins were together with Australia only 56 runs behind. England's task was to contain the inevitable lead to manageable proportions and Caddick accounted for Mark Waugh for 49 after a stand of 133 with his brother, Steve, who reached his century shortly before a storm ended play early with the loss of 31 overs.

It was on the third day that Australia grabbed the game by the scruff of the neck and all but condemned England to defeat. Waugh was dismissed in only the third over for 105, but Martyn, who was given two reprieves behind the stumps by Stewart, teamed up with Gilchrist. We had heard much of this fellow, and admired his aggression in the one-day game. But how would he bat in a Test, we wondered? The answer was thrashed out in the most uncompromising fashion. Having lost all control from his main bowlers, Hussain, in absolute desperation, turned to Mark Butcher. Suddenly the ball began to swing on its way to the batsman rather than towards the boundary boards. Martyn sliced a catch to point for 105 after hitting 15 fours, and before we knew it, Butcher had also snared Warne, Lee and Gillespie. At one point, for goodness sake, he was on a hat-trick!

And so it was that McGrath joined Gilchrist with the murderous left-hander still short of his century. In the unlikely partnership of 63 that followed, McGrath's contribution was a single while Gilchrist raced from 100 to 150 in only 23 deliveries. Poor

THOMMO'S VIEW

Who says Test cricket is boring? This was brilliant entertainment and, who knows, if England hadn't missed those chances – I reckon there were at least six – it might have been a very different story. That said, this was a disastrous start for the Poms because the last thing they wanted was to lose the first Test.

I have to be honest and say that there was little evidence, as far as I am concerned, of this great recovery we've been hearing about. Of course, injuries don't help anybody and, yes, the madness just before the match with blokes being called up from all over the place can't have helped. I can just imagine what it must have been like in the dressing room on the first morning with no-one sure who was going to walk in through the door next! The Aussies, on the other hand, had all their preparations in place long before the first ball was bowled. Call it luck if you like, but it's also the sign of a successful side.

Having said that, I was amazed that McGrath and Co. let Stewart and Caddick get away with that outrageous stand at the end of the first innings! It was great to watch but, come on, Caddick should have been cleaned up. I suspect the Aussies are right in thinking that he doesn't fancy the short stuff, but having got him backing away to leg, there's no need to keep bombarding him – get the yorker in there!

That was why Slater's little cameo at the start of Australia's reply was so important. England felt lifted by Stewart and Caddick's heroics, but Slats had other ideas and really handed it to them. You could almost see England's balloon bursting before your eyes. Slats softened them up, the Waugh boys played brilliantly and Gilchrist finished the job off spectacularly. But I come back to the point that they all gave chances and if anyone is going to beat this Aussie team, each and every catch and stumping has to be taken.

Just quietly, how well did Warne bowl? This is a guy who says that he's not a front-line bowler any more and he bowled 17 overs off the reel in the first dig to take five wickets. He's class and with the others all supporting each other, I can't see any respite for England in this series unless the injury bug hits the Aussies.

After this defeat, England desperately need Thorpe and Hussain back at Lord's. Thorpe is the lynchpin in the middle-order and he was dreadfully missed here. Even if he isn't quite 100 per cent, I would still urge him to get back on the park, because I haven't seen anything in the second-stringers that makes me feel that the second Test will be any different from the first – and I'm not just being a cocky Aussie in saying that. We all want to see a contest this summer – with Australia winning in the end, of course!

One of the catches of the summer: Mark Waugh dives to his left to dismiss Atherton off McGrath's bowling – again!

old Butcher was brought crashing down to earth as 22 were bludgeoned from his final over, and when Gilchrist finally holed out at long-on, he had smashed 152 from only 143 balls, including five sixes and 20 fours! It had been a breathtaking display of calculated hitting and Australia's lead – having been only 42 when their fifth wicket fell – was now 282.

The Aussies only had to bag Atherton before the close and victory would be assured on the fourth day. McGrath got him for the 14th time in Test cricket for four, and by 20 minutes after lunch the capitulation was complete. Trescothick made a heartening 76 and Butcher 41, but England lost nine wickets for 65 runs in a hapless performance that not merely gave Australia an early win and a day off, but made one wonder how on earth England could compete with the visitors for the remainder of the series. This was compounded by another injury to Hussain – a cracked finger resulting from a blow by Gillespie – that was certain to keep him out of the Lord's Test and, probably, the third match as well.

Somerset v. Australians
13–16 July 2001 at Taunton
Australians 348 for 3 dec. (RT Ponting 128, JL Langer 104*, ME Waugh 55*) and 335 for 4 dec. (DR Martyn 176*, WA Seccombe 76)
Somerset 267 (Aamir Sohail 50, DW Fleming 6 for 59) and 240 (M Burns 59, MJ Wood 51)
Australians won by 176 runs

The very future of the traditional county versus touring team match was once again brought into sharp relief as Somerset were forced by England to rest both Marcus Trescothick and Andy Caddick.

The home side then decided to stand down a handful of other first-choice players including Jamie Cox, the captain and overseas player, Mark Lathwell and Steffan Jones. In what was tantamount to an admission of their lack of strength, Somerset then hired two Pakistan Test cricketers, Aamir Sohail and Shoaib Akhtar, to beef up their line-up. The pair were reportedly paid £10,000 each by Boundary Sports, Somerset's kit sponsor, to play in the four-day match. Shoaib, bowling fast but sometimes also without control, eventually bowled Ricky Ponting via an inside edge on a first day on which the Australians ran up 348 for three in the 74 overs that were possible. Shoaib's 14 overs had cost 81 runs, and Ponting had smashed 128 from 130 balls, with two sixes and 20 fours. Justin Langer also made a century, finishing on 104 not out, while Mark Waugh chipped in with an unbeaten 55. An overnight declaration was followed by another truncated day, but in the 68.2 overs that the weather allowed, Somerset were bowled out for 267 with Sohail hitting 50 to justify some of the money spent on his services. On a full third day, the Australians at last came up against some opposition as Shoaib hurled himself into a new-ball spell of some ferocity. Simon Katich was beaten for pace while Langer was first struck in the midriff, then on the hand, before falling lbw to the very next delivery in a fearsome one-two-three. But, after taking two for nine from seven overs, Shoaib retired from the field of battle complaining of cramp in both legs. Normal, friendly service was resumed and Damien Martyn helped himself to an unbeaten 176, with 25 boundaries, while reserve wicket-keeper Wade Seccombe scored 76. Australia declared on 335 for four and by the close Somerset, set 417, were 52 for one. Sohail went on to 36 the next morning, Mike Burns batted well for his 59, and 20-year-old Matthew Wood impressed with 51 from 62 balls, but otherwise there was only token resistance as Australia dismissed the county for 240.

Second Test
19–22 July 2001 at Lord's

The highlight of the cricketing summer, the Lord's Test, was – from the English perspective – depressingly similar to Edgbaston. England lost the toss, again, and were skittled. Australia quickly amassed a lead and bowled England out for a second time. At least at Lord's Australia were required to bat again, albeit if they only had to score 14 to win.

After much debate, into which, once again, the Aussies entered uninvited, Mike Atherton was appointed as Hussain's replacement. Optimistically, Atherton reckoned on having to fill in for only one match but, from the outset, it was clear that he could pencil in Trent Bridge as well. The debate focussed on Stewart's unwillingness to take on the responsibility once again – this was where Steve Waugh entered the fray with his bemused observation that no Australian would ever refuse the opportunity to lead his country – and whether the selectors should turn to Trescothick. I felt, given the crisis facing England, that Atherton was the right

choice, and the fact that he accepted so readily after a three-year break suggested that he was also acutely aware of England's predicament.

So, for the 12th time in 13 attempts, England lost the toss. Waugh began to hint that England were making too much of this statistic and were now using it as a lame excuse, but he did not hesitate, even for a fraction of a second, as he put England into bat under cloudy skies.

Rain and bad light affected the first day, but England had limped to 121 for four at the close having lost Ramprakash to a snorter from Lee only five deliveries before the umpires called a premature halt to the day. Crucially, Thorpe – who had scarcely held a bat for six weeks – appeared reasonably comfortable, but England were swept away on the second morning, losing six wickets for 66 runs before lunch. McGrath was in superb form taking five for 54 – he loves Lord's – and England were cut

And he got him at Lord's, too, where Atherton was forced to take over the captaincy after a break of three years.

England's bowlers tried to unsettle Mark Waugh with a barrage of bouncers. He scored 108.

down at least 150 runs short of a par total.

It needed only 46 overs for Australia to sweep into the lead, they do score their runs at an astonishing rate, but they were helped by an inexplicable change of tactics by England's seamers. Having reduced Australia to 27 for two in helpful conditions, they then decided to hurl the ball half way down the pitch in an attempt to intimidate Mark Waugh. This was so successful that it required 165 deliveries for Waugh to reach his first century at Lord's in the most glorious display of timing and elegance. When the bowlers did not bowl short, they aimed at leg stump and were picked off time and time again. It required a run out to remove Waugh from the crease – a direct hit by Gough from mid-on – and at the end of play on the second day Australia were 255 for five, holding a slender advantage of 68 runs.

We had been here before, of course, barely a fortnight earlier, when Gilchrist ran amok at Edgbaston. Now, all the wiser for that experience, it was crucial that he was dismissed as quickly as possible, yet England managed to produce their worst cricket for 12 months. Gilchrist was dropped no fewer than four times in the morning session. He

was missed on 13, 33, 49 and 73 with the culprits being, in order, Butcher, Ward, Butcher, and Atherton. At lunch Gilchrist remained, somewhat shamefaced, on 87, but he was dismissed only three runs later when he feathered an edge to Stewart off the persevering Gough. I have never seen an Aussie walk so briskly for a catch behind!

Ably assisted by England, Gilchrist had, however, done more than enough. When Lee fell for 20, to give Caddick his fifth wicket, the Australian lead was now 214. As England left the field, Caddick triumphantly held the ball aloft in the new fashion, in order to receive a personal ovation from the crowd. Somehow this does not work when you leave the field having conceded such an imposing lead and can easily be interpreted as placing your own success before the team. Five for 40 is one thing – five for 105, in these circumstances, is quite another.

In just over an hour, England were 50 for three and Thorpe had sustained a broken hand! It is impossible to blame anything other than bad luck for these injuries and although Thorpe did not appear to appreciate the seriousness of his injury immediately – he was dismissed by the same bowler, Lee, shortly afterwards – it soon became clear that, like Hussain, he now faced another lengthy period on the sidelines.

England might have capitulated but, instead, Butcher and Ramprakash rallied them to 163 for four at the end of the third day. Rather than watch his son score his first Test century at Lord's, Alan Butcher was despatched to Guildford on Sunday morning in his capacity as Surrey's coach. In the event, Mark scored only ten more runs, falling to Gillespie for 83 as England collapsed yet again.

This time it was six for 64 in 13 overs before lunch, which left Australia needing to score 14 to win. England claimed the consolation wickets of Slater and Ponting – who had now scored only 29 runs from three Test innings – but there was little to

Alec Stewart lends a helping hand to Mike Atherton after he had dropped Adam Gilchrist – the fourth time that the Australian wicket-keeper had been let off the hook.

THOMMO'S VIEW

OK! So at least we had to bat twice, but this was still a good stuffing as far as I'm concerned. What worries me most is that England don't seem to have learned from their mistakes at Edgbaston. I made the point there that if England are to have any chance of competing this summer, they can't drop catches. Blow me if another stack didn't go down at Lord's.

I think it's true to say that you can only play as well as your opponent lets you, and these Aussies are very good indeed. What I like about them is that they never give up. Their opponents might be getting into a position when they're thinking: 'Wait a minute! We're in charge here', only for someone to step up from the Aussie ranks and crush them. McGrath is brilliant at this and his performance in England's first dig was typical of the man. 126 for four, 187 all out: no messing. That's what top-quality pace bowling is all about, and that's the best I've seen him bowl in a while.

I'm beginning to get a bit worried about Lee, however. Not about my speed record, but he's all over the place at the moment and well below top pace. He's had some injury worries, I know, but he's a shadow of the man who they reckon is the fastest bowler in the world right now.

England's batting still looks fragile to me. In fact, the way we're going with all these short games, I seriously think Headingley could be a one-dayer. Straight up! It was all over there in two days last year so why not? Trescothick has been worked out now because he doesn't move his feet enough outside the off stump. Twice they did him here and Ward's got some work to do on his technique, too. His bat doesn't come down straight, which explains why he played on twice at Birmingham. This is caused by a strong bottom hand on his handle and will also make him vulnerable to catches at slip because he's playing with an angled bat.

On the plus side, Butcher and Ramprakash battled away against Warne. He doesn't like to be frustrated by batsmen padding him away all the time, but that's what they have to do: it's all about patience. I thought Caddick and Gough ploughed on pretty well in the circumstances, but they've got no support. The selectors will have to make a change at Trent Bridge because Cork's lost his swing and control. I would plump for Mullally myself, because at least he offers you something different in taking the ball across the right-hander. Mind you, it doesn't really matter what they do because the chances are still going begging.

cheer in their dressing room as the Australians swept to within one more win of retaining the Ashes. They appeared unstoppable.

Hampshire v. Australians
28–30 July 2001 at Southampton Rose Bowl
Australians 97 (AD Mullally 5 for 18) and 389 for 9 dec. (ML Hayden 142, SM Katich 59)
Hampshire 354 (RA Smith 113, NC Johnson 88, DA Kenway 70) and 134 for 8
Hampshire won by two wickets

Hampshire won themselves £11,000 from the sponsors for a memorable, and thrilling, two-wicket win against the Australians at Southampton. The entire match, indeed, provided a terrific occasion early in the existence of the county's new ground at West End – with the drama set up by Hampshire's feat of bowling out the Aussies for a mere 97 on the first morning. Alan Mullally forced his way back into Test contention by taking five for 18, while James Schofield dismissed Matthew Hayden with his first ball in first-class cricket on his way to figures of three for 25. Hampshire were clearly aided by a long Australian tail which began with Shane Warne appearing at number six against the county he had served with such distinction the previous season, but it was still a fine effort. Moreover, by the close, they had reached 238 for three in reply, with Derek Kenway hitting 70 and Robin Smith and Neil Johnson already deep into a partnership which was finally worth 182. Smith rolled back the years with a superb 113 and Johnson made 88 as Hampshire totalled 354. Though under pressure, the Australians batted as positively as ever in their second innings with Hayden leading the way – also against his former county – with a powerful 142. Steve Waugh then underlined his reputation as a captain who likes constantly to challenge his men by declaring on 389 for nine. Hampshire had been set 133 to win in 26 overs and the crowd were literally on the edge of their seats as Brett Lee roared in with the new ball to take three for 17 in his opening burst. Johnson managed 37 off 29 balls to boost the Hampshire cause, but the county lost wickets regularly as they strived bravely for victory and, if Colin Miller had not dropped Iain Brunnschweiler in what proved to be the penultimate full over (the 23rd) then the Australians would probably have won. As it was, Brunnschweiler, the reserve wicket-keeper, hit the winning four off Miller to grab his little moment of glory in what was Hampshire's first victory against an Australian touring team for 89 years.

SECOND TEST – ENGLAND v. AUSTRALIA
19–22 July 2001 at Lord's

ENGLAND

	First innings		Second innings	
MA Atherton (capt)	lbw b McGrath	37	b Warne	20
ME Trescothick	c Gilchrist, b Gillespie	15	c Gilchrist, b Gillespie	15
MA Butcher	c ME Waugh, b McGrath	21	c Gilchrist, b Gillespie	83
GP Thorpe	c Gilchrist, b McGrath	20	lbw b Lee	2
MR Ramprakash	b Lee	14	lbw b Gillespie	40
*AJ Stewart	c Gilchrist, b McGrath	0	lbw b McGrath	28
IJ Ward	not out	23	c Ponting, b McGrath	0
C White	c Hayden, b McGrath	0	not out	27
DG Cork	c Ponting, b Gillespie	24	c Warne, b McGrath	2
AR Caddick	b Warne	0	c Gilchrist, b Gillespie	7
D Gough	b Warne	5	c ME Waugh, b Gillespie	1
	b7, lb8, w2, nb11	28	lb3, w2, nb9	14
		187		**227**

	First innings				Second innings			
	O	M	R	W	O	M	R	W
McGrath	24	9	54	5	19	4	60	3
Gillespie	18	6	56	2	16	4	53	5
Lee	16	3	46	1	9	1	41	1
Warne	5.3	0	16	2	20	4	58	1
ME Waugh	2	1	12	0				

Fall of Wickets
1-33, 2-75, 3-96, 4-121, 5-126, 6-129, 7-131, 8-178, 9-181
1-8, 2-47, 3-50, 4-146, 5-188, 6-188, 7-188, 8-193, 9-225

AUSTRALIA

	First innings		Second innings	
MJ Slater	c Stewart, b Caddick	25	(2) c Butcher, b Caddick	4
ML Hayden	c Butcher, b Caddick	0	(1) not out	6
RT Ponting	c Thorpe, b Gough	14	lbw b Gough	4
ME Waugh	run out (Gough)	108	not out	0
SR Waugh (capt)	c Stewart, b Cork	45		
DR Martyn	c Stewart, b Caddick	52		
*AC Gilchrist	c Stewart, b Gough	90		
SK Warne	c Stewart, b Caddick	5		
B Lee	b Caddick	20		
JN Gillespie	b Gough	9		
GD McGrath	not out	0		
	lb9, w1, nb23	33		
		401	(2 wickets)	**14**

	First innings				Second innings			
	O	M	R	W	O	M	R	W
Gough	25	3	115	3	2	0	5	1
Caddick	32.1	4	105	5	1.1	0	9	1
White	18	1	80	–				
Cork	23	3	84	1				
Butcher	3	1	12	–				

Fall of Wickets
1-5, 2-27, 3-105, 4-212, 5-230, 6-308, 7-322, 8-387, 9-401
1-6, 2-13

Umpires: JW Holder & SA Bucknor
Toss: Australia
Test debuts: nil

Australia won by eight wickets

THIRD TEST
2–4 August 2001 at Trent Bridge

The match was completed by teatime on the third day with Australia retaining the Ashes for the sixth time in only 11 days – a sorry record, indeed. And yet, this was the first glimpse of a contest we had seen in the series. Agreed, it was only a fleeting moment of excitement that bordered on English supremacy, but it was a moment nonetheless, occurring late on the first day.

England had been despatched for only 185 in less than 53 overs and Australia suddenly found themselves 80 runs behind with only three wickets left. That Gilchrist grabbed the game by the scruff of the neck the following morning was hardly a surprise, but it was the closest we had come to an upset.

Ironically, this was the only toss that England won throughout the series and, having chosen to bat first, the pitch turned out to be the least predictable of the summer. It is possible that Atherton, who was still deputizing for the injured Hussain, was still overcome with shock when he faced up to the first over from McGrath who nipped him out second ball. By lunch, England were 93 for three and although Stewart and Trescothick mustered 54 for the fourth wicket, McGrath returned and, finding spiteful bounce, blew away the lower order. Warne, as is his wont, confused the tail and everyone settled back to watch Australia build their lead.

Indeed, Hayden and Slater enjoyed their customary scampering start and quickly reached 48

If only he would show England's batsmen how he does it! McGrath leaves the field with another five wickets in the bag.

THIRD TEST – ENGLAND v. AUSTRALIA
2–4 August 2001 at Trent Bridge

ENGLAND

	First innings		Second innings	
MA Atherton (capt)	c ME Waugh, b McGrath	0	c Gilchrist, b Warne	51
ME Trescothick	c Gilchrist, b Gillespie	69	c Gilchrist, b Warne	32
MA Butcher	c Ponting, b McGrath	13	lbw b Lee	1
MR Ramprakash	c Gilchrist, b Gillespie	14	st Gilchrist, b Warne	26
*AJ Stewart	c ME Waugh, b McGrath	46	b Warne	0
IJ Ward	c Gilchrist, b McGrath	6	lbw b Gillespie	13
C White	c Hayden, b McGrath	0	c SR Waugh, b Warne	7
AJ Tudor	lbw b Warne	3	c Ponting, b Warne	9
RDB Croft	c Ponting, b Warne	3	b Gillespie	0
AR Caddick	b Lee	13	c Gilchrist, b Gillespie	4
D Gough	not out	0	not out	5
	b1, lb9, w1, nb7	18	b4, lb3, nb7	14
		185		**162**

	First innings				Second innings			
	O	M	R	W	O	M	R	W
McGrath	18	4	49	5	11	3	31	–
Lee	6.5	0	30	1	8	1	30	1
Gillespie	12	1	59	2	20	8	61	3
Warne	16	4	37	2	18	5	33	6

Fall of Wickets
1-0, 2-30, 3-63, 4-117, 5-142, 6-147, 7-158, 8-168, 9-180
1-57, 2-59, 3-115, 4-115, 5-126, 6-144, 7-144, 8-146, 9-156

AUSTRALIA

	First innings		Second innings	
MJ Slater	b Gough	15	(2) c Trescothick, b Caddick	12
ML Hayden	lbw b Tudor	33	(1) lbw b Tudor	42
RT Ponting	c Stewart, b Gough	14	c Stewart, b Croft	17
ME Waugh	c Atherton, b Tudor	15	not out	42
SR Waugh (capt)	c Atherton, b Caddick	13	retired hurt	1
DR Martyn	c Stewart, b Caddick	4	not out	33
*AC Gilchrist	c Atherton, b Tudor	54		
SK Warne	lbw b Caddick	0		
B Lee	c Butcher, b Tudor	4		
JN Gillespie	not out	27		
GD McGrath	c Butcher, b Tudor	2		
	lb3, w1, nb5	9	lb4, nb7	11
		190	(3 wickets)	**158**

	First innings				Second innings			
	O	M	R	W	O	M	R	W
Gough	15	3	63	2	9	1	38	0
Caddick	20	4	70	3	12.2	1	71	1
Tudor	15.5	5	44	5	7	0	37	1
White	2	1	8	–				
Croft	2	0	2	–	1	0	8	1

Fall of Wickets
1-48, 2-56, 3-69, 4-82, 5-94, 6-102, 7-102, 8-122, 9-188
1-36, 2-72, 3-88
SR Waugh retired hurt at 89 for three

Umpires: JH Hampshire & S Venkataraghavan
Toss: England
Test debuts: nil

Australia won by seven wickets

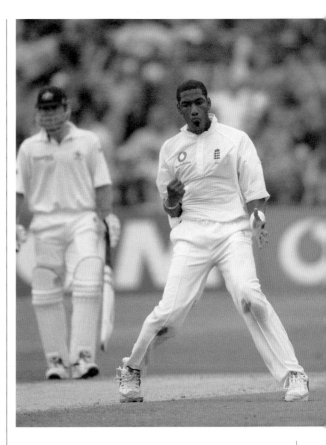

After much debate about his fitness, Alex Tudor returned at Trent Bridge. He took five wickets as, for a while, England were in the hunt.

before Alex Tudor stepped up.

This was a man who, it is fair to say, had enjoyed an unusual build-up to the Test. Recalled after injury, Tudor gave an impressive media conference on the Tuesday before the match in which he stated that his fitness problems were behind him, largely because he accepted that he had to put up with niggles and pain in order to be a fast bowler. 'Great,' everyone thought. However, normal service resumed on Wednesday when Tudor reported to be suffering from a minor ache in his left side. A harassed David Graveney hauled Somerset's Richard Johnson out of a championship match in Canterbury and, having thrashed his way up the M1, Johnson then discovered that Tudor had declared himself fit after all!

In fact, he bowled very well to take five for 44, and played his part in reducing Australia to an unbelievable 105 for seven at the close of the first day. Hayden was trapped lbw for 33, Gough nipped out Slater and Ponting, Tudor had Mark Waugh caught at slip for 15 and Caddick dismissed Steve Waugh, Martyn and, two balls later with the crowd roaring him on, Warne who was hit on the boot. The players were cheered from the field, but England were all too aware that the dangerous Gilchrist remained.

On the second morning, the wicket-keeper resumed with Lee. Seventeen runs were added before, in the seventh over, Lee edged Tudor to Butcher for four. Australia were still 63 runs behind – a margin that might have been crucial on this unpredictable pitch – and now only Gillespie and McGrath stood between England and the beginnings of an upset.

Their hopes were dashed, however, by the stubborn Gillespie, who supported Gilchrist for 74 minutes while 66 precious runs were added. Gilchrist finally edged Tudor to Atherton for 54 and McGrath fell to one of the catches of the series – by Butcher – in Tudor's next over. Although Australia's lead was only five, they had seized the initiative once again.

Despite this, Atherton and Trescothick put on 57 for the first wicket before Trescothick was dismissed in the most absurd manner. Sweeping Warne, the opener made good contact only for the ball to strike the massive figure of Hayden at short leg. Gilchrist dived to catch the rebound and, with a lot going on at once, the third umpire was called in to adjudicate on the fairness of the catch.

Imagine David Constant's horror when, on the first replay, it was clear that Warne had delivered a no ball – something on which the third umpire is not allowed to legislate. Worse still, the replay was shown on the giant screen and, soon, the entire crowd was booing. On seeing that the catch itself was taken cleanly, Constant had no choice but to despatch Trescothick for 32 and, once again, the scatterbrained use of technology had made an umpire look foolish.

Tea was taken at 57 for one and by the close, England had slumped to 144 for six, a lead of 139. The general feeling was that a further hundred runs, or so, would make a game of it, but the last four wickets added only 18 runs on the third morning with Warne taking six for 33, his best figures outside Australia.

England desperately needed quick wickets if they were to stand a chance. Slater made 12, Ponting 17 and Hayden 42, but, as Steve Waugh strode to the middle to join his brother, Mark, it seemed that the captain's dream of retaining the Ashes for the first

THOMMO'S VIEW

Well, that didn't last long did it? It's done nothing to change my view that Headingley could be done and dusted in a single day, either, although I've been ribbed a bit by my mates for making that suggestion.

The disappointing thing about this game was that England held the upper hand for a while but couldn't finish the job off. Again, you have to give the Aussies credit for that because they have strength in depth – and that is something England do not have.

So, with the Ashes gone, I really think England must start planning for the future. There are two dead games coming up and it might give them the chance to have a look at a few blokes. I'm afraid my first casualty would be Stewart. He's done a great job and he's a good guy, but he's 38 and should be looking to ease himself out. If he won't go, then it's time for someone else to hand over the bad news. I can't say I know who will replace him, but the selectors must have an eye on somebody in case Stewart came a cropper like everyone else.

I know people will be negative and say that youngsters shouldn't be exposed to this Aussie team because they'll make mincemeat of them, but, come on, be positive for once. There's absolutely nothing to be lost and, from what my spies tell me, Stewart doesn't want to tour India this winter, so a replacement has to be found then anyway. Sooner rather than later, I say.

Atherton is another target, but he's younger and I think it's up to him and his back. If he feels that he can carry on, then he must. But I think he should be straight with the selectors and if he's going to retire after The Oval Test, he might as well go now for the reasons I've just mentioned. It would be the end of an era, of course, but that's often a side effect of being thrashed.

We've got our problems too, mind you. Ponting looks all over the place at the moment – and this is the bloke who thrashed the ball all over the paddock in the one-day series. He's had a rotten year and there are others waiting to come in – men like Katich and Langer who are good players. Ponting might have a lifeline, though, as a result of Waugh's injury. I feel sorry for the captain because he deserved to be there at the end to enjoy the moment. I'm sure he'll stay around, though, because he's determined to beat England five-nil, and I reckon they'll do it, too.

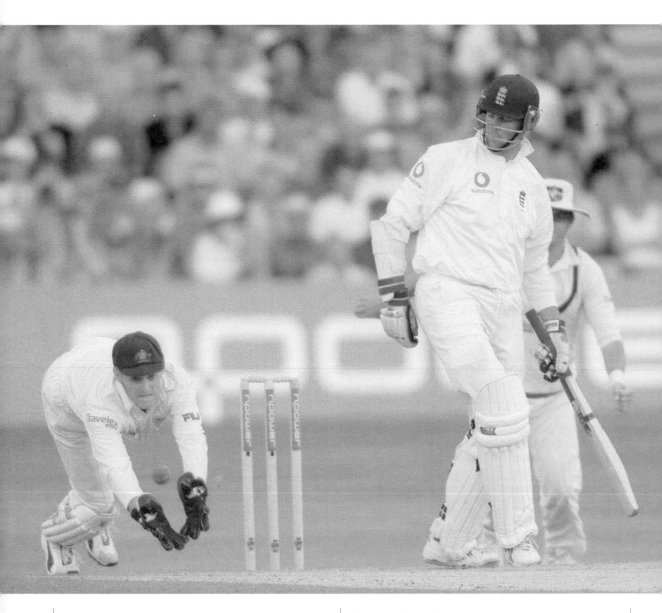

A freakish dismissal accounted for Trescothick. It should have been ruled a no ball, but the third umpire – who gave him out – was powerless.

time was merely a formality. Moments later, he was being stretchered from the field with a torn calf muscle and, as Mark and Martyn knocked off the remaining runs at a canter, Waugh learned of his team's victory – its 19th in 21 Tests – while being tended to in the local infirmary. His prospects of featuring again in the series seemed bleak, but his stated aim of accomplishing a five-nil whitewash was real enough.

Sussex v. Australians

8–10 August 2001 at Hove

Sussex 355 for 4 dec. (RR Montgomerie 157, MW Goodwin 105, CJ Adams 66*) and 67 for 5 dec.
Australians 86 for 2 dec. and 339 for 2 (RT Ponting 147*, AC Gilchrist 114)
Australians won by eight wickets

The Australians were victims of an act of petty theft before the final day of their match against Sussex at Hove, with £1,200 worth of equipment being taken from their dressing room. But that was nothing compared to the way Adam Gilchrist and Ricky

Ponting whipped this match from under the noses of Sussex with some blistering strokeplay on the last afternoon. Sussex, initially, had enjoyed much the best of the first-day exchanges – piling up 355 for four declared in their first innings and then reducing Australia to 19 for two in reply as Billy Taylor struck twice just before the close. Murray Goodwin (105) and Richard Montgomerie (157) had scored their sixth and seventh first-class centuries of the season, respectively, as they built an opening partnership of 202, while Brett Lee had endured a return of no wickets for 117 from his 23 overs. Rain allowed just 13 overs' play on the second day, however, in which time the Australians rallied to 86 for two through Michael Slater and Mark Waugh, leaving both captains with little alternative but to try to manufacture a result.

Sussex, in particular, had eyes on the sponsors' prize for a county beating the tourists and, after the Australians had declared at their overnight score, so did Sussex on 67 for five after giving their lower middle-order a bat. The Australians, though, set 337 to win from 68 overs, breezed home by eight wickets with more than five overs to spare as Gilchrist (114) and Ponting (147 not out) made short work of it.

Gilchrist's runs came from just 102 balls, with two sixes and 19 fours, while Ponting struck three sixes and 17 boundaries off the 170 deliveries he faced, and was joined in the end by Simon Katich who finished on 40 not out.

Ireland v. Australians
12 August 2001 at Belfast
Australia 86 for 1 (23.4 overs)
Ireland did not bat
Match abandoned due to persistent rain

Fourth Test
16–20 August 2001 at Headingley

It was inevitable that much of the pre-match build-up would include the rekindling of memories of perhaps the most famous Test match there has ever been, which occurred at Headingley exactly 20 years ago. Tributes to Ian

Botham were shown on television and even the reclusive Mike Brearley was tempted to appear in magazine articles. All of which served as a reminder that England were, once, capable of beating Australia. Little did we know it then, but Headingley 2001 produced a final day that was equally as uplifting – if not quite as dramatic – as the extraordinary events in 1981.

Ricky Ponting was close to losing his place, but he responded magnificently at Headingley, scoring 144 in Australia's first innings and 72 in the second.

Damien Martyn was enjoying the form of his life.

remaining on the fourth evening and with England requiring an unlikely 315 to win.

In fact, bad light ended play after only 15 deliveries had been bowled, so England were spared the potentially awkward period of batting under intense pressure. When play resumed in dry and sunny conditions the following morning, the match had been transformed into a one-day game. Australia were still fancied to win, not least because England had managed to score more than 300 in the fourth innings to win a match only twice before in their 785 Tests. That they managed to on this occasion was due to one of the most remarkable innings ever played in an Ashes Test.

It went without saying that Hussain, restored to the ranks once again, promptly lost his eighth-consecutive toss. That is never necessarily a bad thing at Headingley, where the conditions can change hour by hour, and although it did not appear to be a bad day to bowl first, Gilchrist elected to bat because he felt the unusually dry pitch would deteriorate.

England's victory was only made possible through a declaration by Australia's acting captain, Adam Gilchrist. Standing in for the injured Steve Waugh, Gilchrist called his batsmen in with 20 overs

Slater and Hayden both fell lbw to Caddick – Hayden was felled by a blow to the inside of the knee and was actually writhing in agony on all fours when umpire Venkat raised his finger – and Australia were quickly 42 for two with the out-of-form Ponting at the crease. Even before he had got off the mark, Ponting appeared to be caught low down by Ramprakash at slip. The fielder gestured that he had taken the catch cleanly, but it was referred to the third umpire. The replay was typical – grainy, fuzzy and impossible, therefore, to make a positive decision one way or the other. Neil Mallender had no option but to give Ponting the benefit of the doubt when, in fact, he was probably

Mark Butcher's innings, that won the match for England, will be remembered for years to come. Even he was not aware of just how well he had played.

THOMMO'S VIEW

Well, I did say that Headingley could be a one-day Test and, in many ways, it was! It was an amazing finish that will do wonders for cricket over here. We Aussies aren't supposed to heap much praise on you guys when you beat us, but this was one of those special moments that none of us could ever forget. Forget all this talk about generous declarations – England's victory was achieved the hard way and let's be honest, no-one gave them a prayer of scoring those runs.

That's particularly true when you consider all the terrible collapses we've seen throughout the summer – going right back to the second Test against Pakistan. No! Gilchrist's declaration was spot on and was only mucked up by the weather that closed in on the fourth evening. He reckoned he would have picked up three or four wickets by the close and that would have spelled the end for England the following day.

As it was, England could regroup and Gilchrist had to be much more wary of giving runs away because it had become a run-chase.

I hope Gilchrist doesn't cop too much stick back home. I believe him when he said that he made the decision by himself and I think the Aussies will all realize that they were on the receiving end of something really special. Let's face it, this talk of the declaration being generous and sporting is garbage – the Aussies had their hearts set on a whitewash. It had never been done before and they really fancied their chances this time. Now we'll have to wait for 18 months to have another go!

When I saw that ball take off and fly over Trescothick's head I thought England were going to be in real trouble – it could have killed him! But the ball softened up very quickly and that stopped it from happening again. I won't say that batting got a great deal easier as a result, but the ball certainly behaved itself more often.

Now we've got a humdinger to look forward to at The Oval. You can be sure that Steve Waugh will do all he can to be fit. If he isn't, I'll have a bet with you now that Gilchrist won't declare again!

out. The Tasmanian proceeded to score a blistering century and hastened the day when batsmen will never walk for anything again.

Ponting and Waugh added 221 for the third wicket, and such was Ponting's domination that he scored at double the rate of his partner. Ponting made 144 from only 154 balls before he was caught behind off Tudor, and Waugh was surprised by a delivery in the last over of the day from Caddick, that popped from short of a length and he was caught at point for 72.

Damien Martyn, who was enjoying the form of his life, dominated the second morning. For once, there were no fireworks from Gilchrist, who scored 19, but Martyn played with glorious panache as the lower order played sensibly in support until he was the last man out, after lunch, for 118. Australia had scored 447 and already people were talking of the tough prospect England faced in avoiding the follow-on.

In fact, due to a series of solid contributions, England made a reasonable fist of the first innings as the pitch started to show signs of wear. Butcher – who ran himself out in the most crazy of circumstances – Hussain and Ramprakash were all dismissed in the 40s and it was left to Stewart to rally the lower order with an amazing innings of 76. This, in truth, was little more than a slog and included a six over cover off McGrath.

It was difficult to work out Stewart's tactics since his first priority should have been to prolong England's innings as long as he possibly could. However, for sheer entertainment, it was a hoot and it could be argued – although Stewart was blissfully unaware of it at the time – that his strange approach contributed in some way to England's victory on the final day.

Australia's task was to build on their lead of 138, and then give England a stiff task to survive, but they were hampered by a weather-hit fourth day on which only 25 overs were bowled. Helped again by Ponting, who hit a six and ten fours in his 72, Australia quickly reached 176 for four and although the light threatened to disrupt play further, Gilchrist declared in the belief that his bowlers would make crucial inroads that evening.

After 14 deliveries, from which four runs had been scored, the umpires conferred about the light. This had an added interest for the crowd in that 24.5 overs had been bowled in the day. If the batsmen went off now, the spectators would be entitled to a 50 per cent refund. In fact, the umpires allowed one further delivery before offering the light, which the batsmen accepted, and to a chorus

FOURTH TEST – ENGLAND v. AUSTRALIA
16–20 August 2001 at Headingley

AUSTRALIA

	First innings		Second innings	
MJ Slater	lbw b Caddick	21	(2) b Gough	16
ML Hayden	lbw b Caddick	15	(1) c Stewart, b Mullally	35
RT Ponting	c Stewart, b Tudor	144	lbw b Gough	72
ME Waugh	c Ramprakash, b Caddick	72	not out	24
DR Martyn	c Stewart, b Gough	118	lbw b Caddick	6
SM Katich	b Gough	15	not out	0
*AC Gilchrist (capt)	c Trescothick, b Gough	19		
SK Warne	c Stewart, b Gough	0		
B Lee	c Ramprakash, b Mullally	0		
JN Gillespie	c Atherton, b Gough	5		
GD McGrath	not out	8		
	b5, lb15, w1, nb9	30	b5, lb7, nb11	23
		447	(for 4 wickets dec.)	**176**

	First innings				Second innings			
	O	M	R	W	O	M	R	W
Gough	25.1	4	103	5	17	3	68	2
Caddick	29	4	143	3	11	2	45	1
Mullally	23	8	65	1	7.3	2	34	1
Tudor	18	1	97	1	4	1	17	–
Butcher	1	0	7	–				
Ramprakash	4	0	12	–				

Fall of Wickets
1-39, 2-42, 3-263, 4-288, 5-355, 6-396, 7-412, 8-422, 9-438
1-25, 2-129, 3-141, 4-171

ENGLAND

	First innings		Second innings	
MA Atherton	c Gilchrist, b McGrath	22	c Gilchrist, b McGrath	8
ME Trescothick	c Gilchrist, b McGrath	37	c Hayden, b Gillespie	10
MA Butcher	run out (Lee)	47	not out	173
N Hussain (capt)	lbw b McGrath	46	c Gilchrist, b Gillespie	55
MR Ramprakash	c Gilchrist, b Lee	40	c Waugh, b Warne	32
Usman Afzaal	c Warne, b McGrath	14	not out	4
*AJ Stewart	not out	76		
AJ Tudor	c Gilchrist, b McGrath	2		
AR Caddick	c Gilchrist, b Lee	5		
D Gough	c Slater, b McGrath	8		
AD Mullally	c Katich, b McGrath	0		
	b2, lb3, nb7	12	b14, lb16, nb3	33
		309	(for 4 wickets)	**315**

	First innings				Second innings			
	O	M	R	W	O	M	R	W
McGrath	30.2	9	76	7	16	3	61	1
Gillespie	26	6	76	–	22	4	94	2
Lee	22	3	103	2	16	4	65	–
Warne	16	2	49	–	18.2	3	58	1
Waugh	1	0	7	–				

Fall of Wickets
1-50, 2-67, 3-158, 4-158, 5-174, 6-252, 7-267, 8-289, 9-299
1-8, 2-33, 3-214, 4-289

Umpires: DR Shepherd & S Venkataraghavan
Toss: Australia
Test debut: SM Katich (Australia)

England won by six wickets

of angry boos and shouts, play was abandoned for the day with the crowd deprived of its refund.

So to the historic final day, which began with England needing to score 311 from a minimum of 90 overs with all their second-innings wickets standing. Atherton was caught behind third ball by a beauty from McGrath that flicked the thumb of his glove and a tentative Trescothick, who had received a delivery from Gillespie that shot over his head and cleared the wicket-keeper from a good length, sliced a catch to gully for ten. It was 33 for two and England appeared to be destined for another defeat.

We will never know what it was that inspired Mark Butcher to play his extraordinary innings that day, but it would suffice to say that it matched anything I have ever seen from David Gower, Brian Lara or, for that matter, any other left-hander of recent times. He began awkwardly with much playing and missing, before emerging serenely to drive and cut the bowlers all over Headingley. As his innings blossomed, so Australia began to crack. The fielding became ragged and even McGrath lost his control. Hussain played bravely alongside Butcher, adding 181 before the captain was given out for 55.

Ramprakash's contribution of 32 in a stand of 75 was also important, but, all the time, it was Butcher who dominated the day.

Ramprakash fell to a brilliant diving catch by Waugh with 26 still needed, but Butcher then took 19 off Gillespie – including a six over cover point – to seal an astonishing victory with nearly 20 overs remaining. Butcher's innings of 173 was the third highest by an Englishman against Australia at Headingley. It came from 227 balls and included one six and 23 fours, and this from a man who, at the start of the season, found himself languishing in Surrey's 2nd XI.

FIFTH TEST
23–27 August 2001 at The Oval

The euphoria that swept the country after Mark Butcher's heroics at Headingley was quickly swept away as Australia responded with a crushing win that earned them a 4–1 series victory. It was as commanding a performance as Australia had produced throughout the summer and emphasized – had we temporarily forgotten – the chasm that exists between the two teams.

Steve Waugh announced that he was fit enough to play – although, in truth, it was a marginal decision – and he elected to bat first. James Ormond, the Leicestershire seamer, replaced Allan Mullally while,

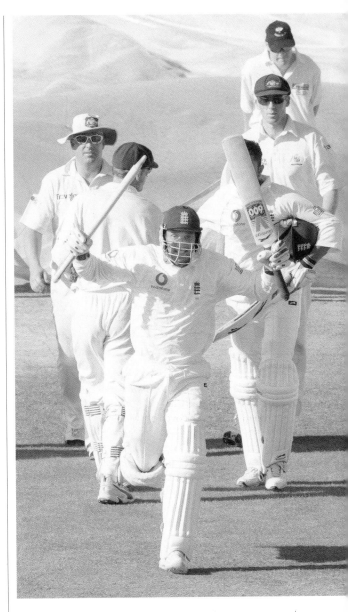

His expression says it all. Mark Butcher, undefeated on 173, runs from the field in triumph after England's astonishing victory at Headingley.

in response to the nation's call, Phil Tufnell was selected with an eye on the winter tour of India. However, both found the going tough and by the end of the first day, when the Australians were 324 for two, England were already struggling to stay in the game.

Justin Langer, who had controversially replaced Slater, dominated the day with a fine, determined

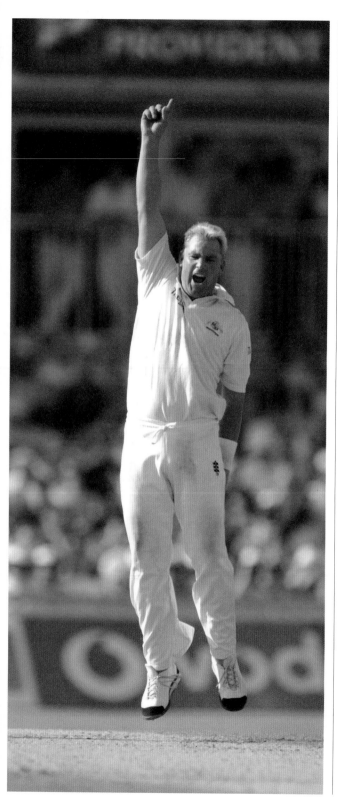

century, but he was forced to retire hurt on 102 when he was hit on the head by Caddick and despite every effort to return to the crease the following day, he appeared to be beaten to the dressing room door by his team-mates who could not wait to join in the fun.

The Waugh twins calmly and systematically tore England's attack apart. Mark, typically, was the more elegant of the two, while Steve, who damaged his injured calf early in his innings, was gradually reduced to little more than a hobble. After a partnership of 197, Mark was bowled as he backed away to slog Gough for 120.

Gilchrist was sent out to move things along, but made only 25 at which point Martyn appeared and, once again, batted magnificently. He managed to score his unbeaten 64 at more than a run a ball, despite the fact that his captain could do little more than limp singles. Waugh's discomfort was highlighted when he was stuck for 73 minutes in the nineties and it required 27 balls for him to move from 98 to 100. When he battled, gamely, down the pitch for his hundredth run, he was forced to dive for his ground and ended up raising his bat like a periscope as he lay, flat out, in the dust. It was a picture that said everything about an extremely brave innings.

After 152 overs, and with his score on 157, Waugh called it a day. He had faced 256 balls and Australia's total of 641 for four was impregnable. Worse still for England, they lost Atherton before the close as Warne ripped a leg-spinner from outside the leg stump to hit the top of the off. From that moment, realists knew that England were doomed.

Australia, and Warne in particular, chipped away throughout the third day. Afzaal emerged knowing that he was undoubtedly playing for a place on the winter tour and displayed admirable character – and flair – in recording his first half-century in Test cricket.

Unfortunately, on 55, Afzaal lofted McGrath to long leg and with him, it seemed, went England's hopes of avoiding the follow-on which was still 187 runs away. Stewart and Ramprakash added 58 for the sixth wicket, but, with the score on 313, Warne appealed successfully for a catch at the wicket against Stewart to claim his 400th Test wicket. Stewart refused to walk at first, a churlish decision for which he was fined by the referee, not merely because all available technology indicated that

Shane Warne took seven wickets in England's first innings and another four in the second to finish with a series tally of 31.

It was a typically unassuming farewell from Mike Atherton who announced his retirement from all cricket at the end of the season.

umpire Willey had made an excellent decision, but also because it unnecessarily spoiled Warne's moment.

Although England were really up against it, Ramprakash was in no mood for capitulation. He reached his second century in his 46th Test and was supported manfully, first, by Ormond, who made 18, and then by Gough.

As the fourth day dawned, England needed 33 more and while avoiding the follow-on did not necessarily guarantee safety, defeat would not have

THOMMO'S VIEW

I reckon 4–1 was about right. Australia were clearly the better team – the best in the world, in fact – so there's no shame being beaten and there were some encouraging signs here for England. I liked the look of Ormond. It's always interesting having a first sighter of a new quick bowler and while he's hardly express, he does at least swing the ball away from the bat and that's what gets good players out. I gather he's not the fittest bloke in the business, but if he knuckles down and works at it, there's no reason why he shouldn't add a yard to his pace and then he really could cause some problems.

Now, what do we make of Ramprakash? This is the same bloke who played the worst shot of the series up at Trent Bridge, which suggested to me that he hadn't got the bottle for this level, and now he produces an innings like this! I can't work him out. All I can say is that if this is finally the spur to make him get his act together, it'll be good news for England, because with Atherton retiring and Stewart unavailable for the tour this winter, you're going to need every bit of experience you can muster. Afzaal looked a class act, but the way he got out in the first dig was disappointing, and Butcher, who was only called up at Edgbaston because of injuries, turns out to be the player of the series with an average of 50.

All these blokes must prove that these performances were not simply a flash in the pan because then, even in defeat, England can build for the future and something positive can emerge.

I must end by paying tribute to the Aussies, though. I don't necessarily go along with this stuff about their being the best team ever, but they're damn good. What I like is the pace they play at – and that applies especially to their batting. If you can go along at four runs per over in Test cricket, you are giving yourself time to win and with a class attack like this, the opposition is exposed for longer. It's simple really – almost like an extended one-day game.

So we won't meet again for 18 months when the Ashes are up for grabs again. I wish I could say that I see a closer contest then, but I can't. It takes time to build a quality team and while I'm more optimistic about England's future now than I was three months ago, there's still a lot of ground to make up before you'll capture the Aussies' crown.

been a certainty. However, McGrath prised out Ramprakash for 133 with 18 still needed and although Tufnell threw himself behind the line, Gough perished for 24 and England had fallen ten runs short. Warne's seven for 167 was his 19th haul of five wickets in a Test match and his seventh against the old enemy.

The future of Mike Atherton had been widely discussed during the course of the match. The consensus of opinion was that he had decided to retire, but that he would not reveal his hand until after the match. He rather gave things away, however, when he edged McGrath to Warne – the 19th time that McGrath had dismissed him – and as he left the ground he waved his bat to the whole crowd.

This was entirely an un-Atherton gesture – particularly since he had scored just nine – and it signalled that a career spanning 115 Tests, 7,728

The Australians with a glass replica of the Ashes. Despite Steve Waugh's request, the real thing remains at Lord's!

runs and 16 centuries was at an end. The Australian fielders applauded as, at the entrance to the dressing room, Atherton's team-mates gathered and slapped him on the back. Rain then held up the Australians who needed to capture nine more wickets on the final day for victory.

The morning session was disastrous for England as they lost five for 78 including a spell of three wickets for ten runs that effectively sealed their fate. Stewart scored 34 before offering no stroke to Warne – there was no sign of a 'goodbye' gesture from the Gaffer as he departed – and although Gough entertained with 39 at the end, McGrath wrapped up the match at 3.30pm when he had Tufnell caught by Warne. It was a fitting end since McGrath had captured 32 wickets in the series and Warne 31, including 11 in this match. Steve Waugh, who had been so disappointed to miss the celebrations at Trent Bridge, led his team on a lap of honour, which gave the English public a final glimpse of one of the finest cricket teams there can ever have been.

FIFTH TEST – ENGLAND v. AUSTRALIA
23–27 August 2001 at The Oval

AUSTRALIA

	First innings	
ML Hayden	c Trescothick, b Tufnell	68
JL Langer	retired hurt	102
RT Ponting	c Atherton, b Ormond	62
ME Waugh	b Gough	120
SR Waugh (capt)	not out	157
*AC Gilchrist	c Ramprakash, b Afzaal	25
DR Martyn	not out	64
SK Warne		
B Lee		
JN Gillespie		
GD McGrath		
	b10, lb13, w1, nb19	43
	(for 4 wickets dec.)	641

	First innings			
	O	M	R	W
Gough	29	4	113	1
Caddick	36	9	146	-
Ormond	34	4	115	1
Tufnell	39	2	174	1
Butcher	1	0	2	-
Ramprakash	4	0	19	-
Usman Afzaal	9	0	49	1

Fall of Wickets
1-158, 2-292, 3-489, 4-534
JL Langer retired hurt at 236 for one

ENGLAND

	First innings		Second innings	
MA Atherton	b Warne	13	c Warne, b McGrath	9
ME Trescothick	b Warne	55	c & b McGrath	24
MA Butcher	c Langer, b Warne	25	c SR Waugh, b Warne	14
N Hussain (capt)	b ME Waugh	52	lbw b Warne	2
MR Ramprakash	c Gilchrist, b McGrath	133	c Hayden, b Warne	19
Usman Afzaal	c Gillespie, b McGrath	54	c Ponting, b McGrath	5
*AJ Stewart	c Gilchrist, b Warne	29	b Warne	34
AR Caddick	lbw b Warne	0	b Lee	17
J Ormond	b Warne	18	c Gilchrist, b McGrath	17
D Gough	st Gilchrist, b Warne	24	not out	39
PCR Tufnell	not out	7	c Warne, b McGrath	0
	b3, lb13, w1, nb5	22	lb2, nb2	4
		432		184

	First innings				Second innings			
	O	M	R	W	O	M	R	W
McGrath	30	11	67	2	15.3	6	43	5
Gillespie	20	3	96	-	12	5	38	-
Warne	44.2	7	165	7	28	8	64	4
Lee	14	1	43	-	10	3	30	1
Ponting	2	0	5	-	2	0	3	-
ME Waugh	8	0	40	1	1	0	4	-

Fall of Wickets
1-58, 2-85, 3-104, 4-166, 5-255, 6-313, 7-313, 8-350, 9-424
1-17, 2-46, 3-48, 4-50, 5-55, 6-95, 7-126, 8-126, 9-184

Umpires: P Willey & RE Koertzen
Toss: Australia
Test debut: J Ormond (England)
Men of the Series: MA Butcher (England) & GD McGrath (Australia)

Australia won by an innings and 25 runs

TEST MATCH AVERAGES
England v. Australia

ENGLAND

Batting	M	Inns	NO	HS	Runs	Av	100	50	c/st
MA Butcher	5	10	1	173*	456	50.66	1	1	4
MR Ramprakash	4	8	0	133	318	39.75	1	-	3
N Hussain	3	6	0	55	177	35.40	-	2	-
AJ Stewart	5	9	1	76*	283	35.37	-	2	13/-
ME Trescothick	5	10	0	76	321	32.10	-	3	4
MA Atherton	5	10	0	57	221	22.10	-	2	7
Usman Afzaal	3	6	1	54	83	16.60	-	1	-
AR Caddick	5	9	2	49*	101	14.42	-	-	1
D Gough	5	9	3	39*	82	13.66	-	-	-
IJ Ward	3	6	1	23*	68	13.60	-	-	-
C White	3	6	1	27*	38	7.60	-	-	1

Also batted: In two Tests: AJ Tudor 3, 9, 2. In one Test: DG Cork 24 & 2; RDB Croft 3 & 0;
AF Giles 7 & 0; AD Mullally 0; J Ormond 18, 17; GP Thorpe 20 & 2 (1ct); PCR Tufnell 7*, 0.

Bowling	Overs	Mds	Runs	Wkts	Av	Best	10m	5/inn
MA Butcher	14	4	63	4	15.75	4-42	-	-
AJ Tudor	44.5	7	195	7	27.85	5-44	-	1
D Gough	155.1	24	657	17	38.64	5-103	-	1
AR Caddick	177.4	24	748	15	49.86	5-101	-	1

Also bowled: Usman Afzaal 9-0-49-1; DG Cork 23-3-84-1; RDB Croft 3-0-10-1; AF Giles 25-0-
108-1; AD Mullally 30.3-10-99-2; J Ormond 34-5-115-1; MR Ramprakash 8-0-31-0; PCR Tufnell
39-2-174-1; C White 46.4-7-189-1.

AUSTRALIA

Batting	M	Inns	NO	HS	Runs	Av	100	50	c/st
SR Waugh	4	5	2	157*	321	107.00	2	-	2
ME Waugh	5	8	3	120	430	86.00	2	1	9
DR Martyn	5	7	2	118	382	76.40	2	2	-
AC Gilchrist	5	5	0	152	340	68.00	1	2	24/2
RT Ponting	5	8	0	144	338	42.25	1	2	7
ML Hayden	5	8	1	68	234	33.42	-	1	4
MJ Slater	4	7	0	77	170	24.28	-	1	1
JN Gillespie	5	4	1	27*	41	13.66	-	-	2
GD McGrath	5	4	3	8*	11	11.00	-	-	1
B Lee	5	4	0	20	24	6.00	-	-	-
SK Warne	5	4	0	8	13	3.25	-	-	6

Also batted in one Test: SM Katich 15, 0* (1ct); JL Langer 102rh (1ct).

Bowling	Overs	Mds	Runs	Wkts	Av	Best	10m	5/inn
GD McGrath	194.2	56	542	32	16.93	7-76	-	4
SK Warne	195.2	41	580	31	18.70	7-165	1	3
JN Gillespie	174	42	652	19	34.31	5-53	-	1
B Lee	120.5	18	496	9	55.11	2-37	-	-

Also bowled: RT Ponting 4-0-8-0; ME Waugh 13-1-69-1.

MIKE ATHERTON

It is always sad when an outstanding sportsman calls it a day and this is particularly true when the player is only 33. Mike Atherton was only entering the phase of his career that many of those who have gone before him have found to be their most successful. Batsmen like Graham Gooch, Geoff Boycott, Sunil Gavaskar and Colin Cowdrey all flourished in their mid- to late thirties, but none of them suffered from the crippling, degenerative back condition that has blighted much of Atherton's career. An operation ten years ago was the first warning of the trouble that lay ahead – there have been times when he could barely get out of bed in the morning – but these problems were always shrugged off and minimized: never were they used as an excuse.

Atherton has always had the ideal temperament for Test cricket. From the moment he made his debut in 1989, it was clear that he would quickly establish himself as one of England's most successful batsmen and, of course, there was always that unfortunate label of 'future England captain' hanging around his neck.

I remember the day he was appointed. Gooch had resigned at Leeds after the 1993 Ashes had been lost. A bright new dawn broke over English cricket that day as

It was uncomfortable for both of us as Mike Atherton tried to explain away the dirt in his pocket. We did not know it was being shown live on television!

Atherton, fresh-faced, outwardly innocent yet grimly determined, took the reins. Ted Dexter, his chairman of selectors, resigned during Atherton's first match in charge. England won the next at The Oval and the unlikely combination of Atherton and Ray Illingworth was soon running things.

It was the following summer, 1994, that everything changed. Atherton was caught on camera rubbing something – later confirmed to be dirt – onto the ball during a Test against South Africa. This split the press box so completely that, to this day, the scars still remain. I was one of those who believed that an England captain should not be involved in anything that could be construed as ball tampering and felt that he should resign. Some were not so strident, while others, blinkered in my view, could not see that what he had done was wrong.

Things were never the same again. Atherton's attitude towards the press changed largely to one of non-cooperation and he earned the rather unfair nickname of 'Captain Grumpy'. Atherton has never been grumpy and it was a great shame that the public only saw this side of him until, after a record 52 Tests, he gave up the captaincy following a traumatic, and quite unnecessary, series defeat in the West Indies.

Who could ever forget his brilliant innings of ten-and-three-quarter hours in Johannesburg in 1995 that thwarted the South Africans? I can vividly remember commentating high in the stand at the Corlett Drive End of the Wanderers as Allan Donald, Merrick Pringle, Brian MacMillan and a young Shaun Pollock began what appeared to be a formality in despatching England for a second time. Donald bowled at a furious pace while MacMillan – a big bully – snarled and swore. Thanks to television's pitch microphones, we could hear everything in our headphones and it was not pleasant listening as the South African fielders urged their bowlers on.

It was the following afternoon that the silence suddenly struck me. There was not a word from any of them as Atherton grimly and defiantly continued to grind them into the dirt. Even MacMillan became a spent force. I do not believe that I have ever seen Atherton more animated about anything than when the reality of what he had achieved actually hit him, and I do not believe that I will ever see an innings quite like it again.

Atherton bowed out of international cricket with a brief and simple statement after the final Test against Australia, and he did not play in Lancashire's final match of the season. He chose, quite deliberately, to deny himself the farewell he deserved from an admiring public. That, in itself, says much about the man who is now heading for a career behind a microphone where, I hope, the public will gain a more accurate view of a genial, humorous fellow with immense inner strength.

Atherton was at his best when blunting the fastest bowlers in the world and he enjoyed a special love-hate relationship with Allan Donald.

ENGLISH DOMESTIC SEASON INTRODUCTION
By Mark Baldwin

County cricket reaches a major staging post this winter. A thorough review of the English domestic game will recommend changes in structure to be implemented from 2003 onwards and, if accepted, these changes will have a marked bearing on how professional cricket in Britain plans to meet the many challenges of the 21st century.

Yet the last few years have seen massive change, too, with the introduction of two divisions in both the championship and one-day league, a proliferation of day-night matches around the country, a significant increase in the amount of international cricket played during a home summer, and the binding of a dozen leading players to centrally-controlled England contracts.

As a result of this year's review, by the England and Wales Cricket Board, it seems as if some sort of regional cricket, a scrapping of one of the one-day knockout cups, a reorganization of the fixture list, and even a 20-over per side evening league might emerge.

A tangible bridge between the county and Test arena is badly needed in England – and if regional teams are deployed to give touring teams more meaningful fixtures, then it will be an initiative both long overdue and to be applauded.

Some commentators have been pushing hard for the creation of an early-season regional tournament, before the start of the championship itself, in which the 44 best English players would play against each other in a series of Test-trial type matches. It is difficult, however, to see how these games would attract many spectators – and, more to the point, it is almost certain that the England management would keep their most valuable players away from such unnecessary action.

With seven Test matches and seven one-day internationals to be played each summer now, plus an increasingly 'full-time' winter schedule, contracted England players have – in effect – been taken outside of the domestic game. It is time to accept that as a new fact of life, and plan the domestic structure accordingly.

Regional selections, playing in a series of matches against the touring teams staged between the internationals, would also put an added strain on counties in terms of player availability.

The culling of one of the one-day cups could help to alleviate such a problem, but the counties operate on financially tight budgets as it is and any lessening

of the amount of cricket played would, naturally, be resisted. That is where the 'short-form' cricket might come in.

Personally speaking, the very idea of it is an abomination, but English cricket has got itself into such a fearful muddle over structure in recent years that to hear such ideas being bandied about on the circuit is not altogether surprising.

Look at the two-division championship, for a start. A three-up, three-down system for two nine-team leagues is palpable nonsense, and but for bad weather it could easily have resulted in Surrey, the star-studded 2000 champions, losing their first division status. Indeed, it was only by beating a seriously below-strength Yorkshire in the penultimate round of matches, when David Byas' side had already been crowned as new champions, that Surrey managed finally to pull away from the relegation zone.

How delicious it would have been (begging Surrey's pardon, of course) if the ECB had been forced to defend a system in which the most star-studded county in the game had found itself wallowing in division two next summer! Would Mark Ramprakash and others have immediately left in search of guaranteed division one cricket yet again?

An elite, however, is forming already even in spite of the uncertainty of existence which the three-up, three-down regulation imposes on the status of first-class counties. It is no surprise that the three promoted clubs from 1999 – Northamptonshire, Essex and Glamorgan – went straight back down again.

Four of the top-six championship sides – Yorkshire, Somerset, Kent and Leicestershire – are in the Norwich Union League elite too, and it is only a matter of time before Surrey and Lancashire join newly-promoted Warwickshire as big clubs with a top-six presence in both leagues.

Yet, how to square the ever-decreasing circle of the rich getting richer and the poor getting poorer with the ECB's proud boast of a game containing 18 separate but equally-valid 'centres of excellence'?

That, of course, is the powerful subtext of the current review of domestic cricket, especially with the Board's commitment to the creation of 18 county academies by September 2003 (six are already up and running) to underpin the recently launched National Academy. And, it seems to me, a very clear policy decision has to be made to ensure that all 18 counties and their academies can play a full and equal part in the raising of standards in English cricket.

Somehow, all 18 have to feel they are part of one big happy family committed to the cause of English cricket – and England. And the only way to do that is to prevent divisions in the structure. In other words, the elite must be 18. Otherwise, the elite must be nine, or six, or whatever, and everything else must follow from that.

Until now, I have believed that increased intensity, and competitiveness, could have been achieved by a return to a one-division championship – but with vastly increased prize money for the top-nine places. It puzzles, and even angers me, for instance, that in the current set-up Kent are given nothing at all for finishing third in the first division, but that Sussex and Hampshire receive £40,000 and £25,000 respectively for coming first and second in division two (effectively 10th and 11th).

Given the need for less than 17 first-class matches per club in the county calendar, however, my own solution to the current debate would be to agree how many championship matches, per county, form the ideal amount of first-class domestic cricket, and then create the number of conferences, out of the 18 clubs, which are needed to provide them. For instance, three conferences (plus play-off games) would produce 14 first-class matches. Play-offs in the final month of the season would determine the championship winners, and the prize-money positions, and would also – in effect – create an elite group of counties playing against each other for the biggest trophy. But, vitally, all 18 would start from the same gun every April and be running the same race.

I would also increase the numbers of overseas players available to each county – even if some of them are signed only to play in one-day cricket, which would be made up by a two-division league (as now) and one knock-out cup. Counties could organize some local derby challenge matches, with local sponsors, if they needed to fill a few 'holes' in the fixture list, but less official cricket would also allow players more time to prepare, rest or analyze their own games.

It is important to remember that the England cricket team was beginning to get stronger before the introduction of two divisions could have had any tangible effect – witness the run of results in 1999 and early 2000 and the emergence of players like Trescothick, Michael Vaughan, Craig White and Ashley Giles. Similarly, I haven't heard anyone blaming last summer's thrashing by Australia on the switch to two divisions!

Once again, however, 'soft' county cricket did find itself being offered up by lazy and uninformed commentators as a convenient scapegoat, yet England's real problem, in the Ashes series, was that they were trying to compete against one of the best teams ever to take to a cricket field without either confidence, sufficient firepower, or the maximum input from a core group of injury-plagued senior players in Graham Thorpe, Nasser Hussain, Vaughan, White and Giles.

As Surrey found to their cost in the championship, when you have too many valuable players taken away from you – whether by injury, loss of form or whatever – it is difficult even for the likes of the Saqlains or the Martin Bicknells that are left to do everything on their own. (Bicknell, by the way, did try to do just that with the outstanding all-round performance of 2001: 748 runs at 46.75 and 72 wickets at 21.36!) Gloucestershire, the one-day kings of 1999 and 2000, were also so badly hit by injuries and ill fortune that they even lost their place in the Norwich Union League's top division.

Yorkshire, who next to Surrey suffered the most from England calls, managed to win the championship because they had an exceptional and inspirational overseas player in Darren Lehmann, dependable support acts like skipper Byas and wicket-keeper Richard Blakey, and an extraordinary depth in pace bowling talent. Six of their fast, or fast-medium, bowlers have played Test cricket for England and a seventh, the fireball find of the season Steve Kirby, looks likely to join them in the near future. Also, making a mockery of the call for smaller professional staffs, Yorkshire used no fewer than 25 players in their quest for championship glory.

It remains to be seen what structure changes the ECB decree for the domestic game from 2003 onwards, and whether 2002 brings a resumption of the upturn in England's fortunes that were so rudely interrupted by Australia. But the performances in 2001 of young players like Kirby, James Kirtley, Ian Bell, Mark Wagh, Kevin Pietersen, Rob Key, Richard Johnson, Martin Saggers, Danny Law, Andrew Strauss, Ian Blackwell, Chris Taylor, Owais Shah, Nicky Peng, Dimitri Mascarenhas and the Matthew Woods of Yorkshire and Somerset (amongst others) show that emerging talent is still there in the English game.

The challenge for all of us who love English cricket is to make sure that such talent is not wasted.

(Mark Baldwin covered England and English cricket for the Press Association from 1986–98, and for the last three years has written on cricket for The Times *and* The Cricketer)

CRICINFO COUNTY CHAMPIONSHIP
By Mark Baldwin

ROUND ONE: 20–23 APRIL 2001

Division One

at The Oval
Kent 456 for 8 dec. (140 overs) (DP Fulton 111, MJ
Walker 105, RWT Key 101)
Surrey 473 (125.3 overs) (MR Ramprakash 146, AD
Brown 72, IJ Ward 70, JN Batty 59)
Match drawn – no play was possible on the fourth day
Surrey 11 pts, Kent 12 pts

at Taunton
Somerset 204 (61.5 overs) (J Cox 66, G Chapple 6 for
46) and 170 (PCL Holloway 74)
Lancashire 378 (101 overs) (NH Fairbrother 179*,
MJ Chilton 53, RL Johnson 5 for 107)
Lancashire won by an innings and 4 runs
Lancashire 19 pts, Somerset 4 pts

at Leicester
Essex 318 (124.1 overs) (RC Irani 87, WI Jefferson 69,
J Ormond 5 for 71)
Leicestershire 104 (49.2 overs) and (following on) 205
(DJ Marsh 61, RSG Anderson 5 for 50)
Essex won by an innings and 9 runs
Essex 18 pts, Leicestershire 3 pts

at Northampton
Glamorgan 548 for 6 dec. (161 overs) (A Dale 204, MJ
Powell 106, K Newell 103) and 65 for 1
Northamptonshire 446 for 7 dec. (117 overs)
(RJ Warren 175, AL Penberthy 132*)
Match drawn – no play was possible on the fourth day
Northamptonshire 10 pts, Glamorgan 11 pts

Champions Surrey were given a shock by Kent at
The Oval as they began their search for a third
successive championship title. After failing to take a
wicket on a rain-shortened opening day, when Kent
reached 176 without loss, the champions then saw
their opponents run up 456 for eight declared on
day two. Openers David Fulton and Rob Key, 86
and 88 not out respectively overnight, both
completed centuries, while Matthew Walker became
the third member of Kent's youthful top order to
reach three figures. Mark Ramprakash, on his debut
for Surrey following his acrimonious winter transfer
from Middlesex, batted sublimely in reply to reach
146 – leading a solid Surrey batting effort which

eventually enabled them to top the Kent first-
innings total. On reaching a 148-ball hundred,
Ramprakash took off his batting helmet and kissed
the badge on its front in a passionate gesture
directed towards The Oval pavilion. 'I did it because
I wanted people to know just how committed I am
to Surrey,' said Ramprakash. Alistair Brown's 89-ball
72 was also rich in entertainment, but rain meant
there was no play at all on the scheduled final day.

Lancashire, one of the counties with realistic
ambitions of toppling Surrey from their perch,
began their 2001 campaign with a heartening 19-
point win over Somerset at Taunton. No play at all
was possible on the third day, but by then Somerset

**Mark Ramprakash compiled a majestic 146 to complete a
memorable debut for Surrey following his winter move.**

DERBYSHIRE CCC

Home Ground:
Derby
Address:
County Ground, Nottingham Road,
Derby DE21 6DA
Tel: 01332 383211
Fax: 01332 290521
Email: derby@ecb.co.uk
Directions:
By road: From the south, exit M1 at junction 25,
follow A52 into Derby, take the fourth exit off
Pentagon Island. From the north, exit M1 at
junction 28, join A38 into Derby and then follow directional
signs.
Capacity: 4,000
Other grounds used: Chesterfield
Year formed: 1870

Chief Executive: John Smedley
Cricket Manager: Colin Wells
Other posts: Commercial Manager: Keith
Stevenson; County Development Officer: Colin
Davies; Head Groundsman: Neil Godrich;
Second XI coach: Adrian Pierson
Captain: Dominic Cork
County colours: Blue, brown and gold

HONOURS

COUNTY CHAMPIONSHIP
1936
SUNDAY LEAGUE
1990
BENSON & HEDGES CUP
1993
GILLETTE CUP/C&G TROPHY
1981

National Cricket League
nickname:
DERBYSHIRE SCORPIONS

Website:
www.dccc.org.uk

were already in deep trouble, and when the match resumed on the final morning it did not take Lancashire long to wrap up victory by an innings and four runs. Glen Chapple was Lancashire's first-day hero, taking six for 46 to send Somerset's first innings sliding to 204 all out. Then, after Mark Chilton had stroked ten fours in his 53, Neil Fairbrother took over to play the innings which did most of all to set up Lancashire's success. Dropped three times, the 37-year-old left-hander nevertheless batted magnificently to reach 179 not out. He hit a six and 27 fours, faced just 201 deliveries, and almost single-handedly steered Lancashire to 378. Richard Johnson picked up five for 107 on his Somerset debut, but the home side had slipped to 106 for six in their second innings by the end of the second day. There was some resistance from Piran Holloway (74) and Johnson (37), but Lancashire – runners-up in 2000 – soon completed the victory which gave them the perfect start to their championship season.

The other victors in Division One were Essex, who somewhat surprisingly trounced Leicestershire by an innings and nine runs at Leicester. Jimmy Ormond's five for 71 was not enough to prevent Essex from reaching 318 in their first innings, in which Ronnie Irani made 87 and Will Jefferson 69. Ricky Anderson (four for 21) and Mark Ilott (four for 27) then got to work on the home batsmen, silencing the Grace Road faithful by tumbling Leicestershire for just 104 in their first innings. Things hardly got better after they were asked to follow on, with Anderson picking up five for 50 as Leicestershire were dismissed for 205. Dan Marsh made 61, but the home side were also handicapped by the absence of Aftab Habib, who had been given compassionate leave following the death of his mother.

Runs, and lots of them, dominated proceedings at Northampton until rain arrived to wash away the final day of the match between Northants and Glamorgan. Adrian Dale, reaching three figures for the first time since July 1999, then turned his hundred into 204, while Michael Powell (106) and Keith Newell (103) also cashed in on an excellent surface produced by groundsman David Bates as Glamorgan piled up 548 for six declared.

Groundsmen all around the country, indeed, had worked minor miracles to get county grounds fit for play following perhaps the most horrendous winter of rain ever experienced. Then, when Northants batted, Russell Warren (175) and Tony Penberthy (132 not out) added a county-record sixth-wicket

stand against Glamorgan of 250 before the declaration came at 446 for seven.

Division Two

at Edgbaston
Warwickshire 455 (145.4 overs) (NV Knight 140, DP Ostler 119, NMK Smith 54)
Hampshire 170 (64.5 overs) and (following on) 285 for 7 (RA Smith 118, DA Kenway 52)
Match drawn
Warwickshire 12 pts, Hampshire 6 pts

at Chester-le-Street
Durham 242 (107.3 overs) (ML Love 61) and 255 for 7 dec. (PD Collingwood 68, ML Love 67)
Gloucestershire 198 (55.5 overs) (KJ Barnett 82*, JE Brinkley 6 for 32) and 6 for 1
Match drawn
Durham 8 pts, Gloucestershire 7 pts

at Lord's
Worcestershire 301 for 8 dec. (110.1 overs) (DA Leatherdale 93, GA Hick 81)
Middlesex 302 for 5 (112 overs) (AJ Strauss 125, MA Roseberry 63)
Match drawn – no play was possible on the fourth day
Middlesex 9 pts, Worcestershire 8 pts

Warwickshire were denied what looked like being a resounding victory at Edgbaston by a combination of bad weather and a stirring Hampshire rearguard action. All was going swimmingly for the home side as they totalled 455 in their first innings, with Nick Knight emulating his achievement of 12 months earlier by hitting a hundred on the opening day of the season. Dominic Ostler's 119 and 54 from Neil Smith also helped to put Warwickshire into a commanding position, and, by the end of the second day, Hampshire were in some disarray at 150 for eight – with Mo Sheikh picking up four for 36 from 20 overs. The Hampshire first innings was wrapped up quickly on the third morning, for 170, and they had slid to 114 for four after being asked to follow on when rain arrived in the afternoon. Warwickshire feared the worst, having lost more than 1,600 overs to the weather in 2000 – the equivalent of four complete matches – but although the final day was uninterrupted, they could not finish off the Hampshire second innings. Robin Smith made a fiercely-determined, six-hour 118, and John Stephenson (39 from 209 balls) hung around for a long time while 106 were added. In the end,

Warwickshire's Nick Knight emulated his feat of the previous year by hitting a century on the opening day of the season.

Hampshire were jubilant after forcing the draw at 285 for seven.

Martin Love, a 27-year-old from Queensland, hit ten fours in scoring 61 from 116 balls on his championship debut for Durham. He then made 67 in the second innings, but too many weather interruptions meant that Durham could not force a result against Gloucestershire at Chester-le-Street. The visitors were 44 runs behind after the first innings, despite Kim Barnett's unbeaten 82, and James Brinkley marked his return to championship action after a five-year absence by taking a career-best six for 32.

At Lord's most of the first day, and all of the fourth, were lost to rain – leaving Middlesex and Worcestershire to settle for a draw following some promising batting. Graeme Hick (81) and David Leatherdale (93) impressed for Worcestershire, while Andrew Strauss (125) and Mike Roseberry (63) put on 129 for the first wicket in Middlesex's reply of 302 for five.

ROUND TWO: 25–28 APRIL 2001

Division One

at Canterbury
Kent 142 (70.1 overs) (CEW Silverwood 5 for 45) and 318 (ET Smith 103*, RWT Key 98)
Yorkshire 285 (113 overs) (MP Vaughan 71, DS Lehmann 68) and 176 for 6
Yorkshire won by four wickets
Yorkshire 17 pts, Kent 3 pts

at Cardiff
Glamorgan 353 for 9 dec. (107.2 overs) (A Dale 64, MJ Powell 64, AD Shaw 62, RL Johnson 5 for 106)
Somerset 435 for 5 (133.4 overs) (ME Trescothick 147, J Cox 95*, PCL Holloway 78, M Burns 70)
Match drawn – no play was possible on the first day
Glamorgan 9 pts, Somerset 12 pts

at Chelmsford
Essex 206 (74.1 overs) (DDJ Robinson 61) and 257 for 8 dec. (SG Law 58, SD Peters 56*)
Northamptonshire 150 (62 overs) (RC Irani 5 for 43) and 199 for 7 (RJ Warren 55)
Match drawn
Essex 8 pts, Northamptonshire 7 pts

at Old Trafford
Lancashire v. **Surrey**
No play was possible on any of the four scheduled days

Lancashire 4 pts, Surrey 4 pts

Yorkshire squeezed home by four wickets, and with just three balls to spare, against Kent at Canterbury to post an important early victory in their championship season. The first two days were partly rain-affected, but at the halfway stage of the match Yorkshire seemed certain to be able to force victory at 208 for four in reply to Kent's first-innings slump to 142 all out. But, over the next five sessions, Kent fought back hard and – in the end – were perhaps unfortunate not to escape with a draw. First Yorkshire could reach only 285, despite Ryan Sidebottom's unbeaten 40, and then Rob Key initially led a rearguard action with the bat that was taken up superbly by Ed Smith. Key, 97 not out at

Marcus Trescothick continued his rich vein of early season form with a belligerent 147 for Somerset against Glamorgan.

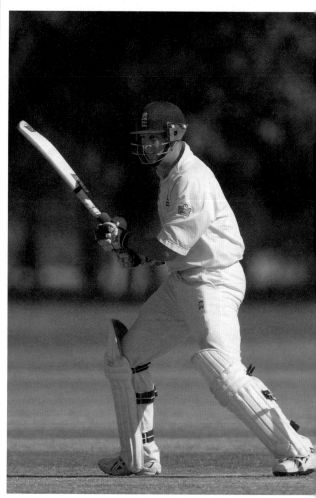

DURHAM CCC

Home Ground:
Chester-le-Street
Address:
County Ground, Riverside,
Chester-le-Street,
Co. Durham DH3 3QR
Tel: 0191 387 1717
Fax: 0191 387 1616
Email: marketing@durham-ccc.org.uk
Directions:
By rail: Chester-le-Street (approx. 5 minutes by taxi or a 10-minute walk).
By road: Easily accessible from junction 63 of the A1(M). Nearby car parking is available on match days.
Disabled access:
Viewing points for spectators in wheelchairs; Members' Lounge has induction loop system for members who are hard of hearing; guide dogs allowed into ground.
Capacity: 10,000
Other grounds used:
Darlington CC (Feethams); Hartlepool CC; Stockton CC 01642 672835.
Year formed: 1882

Chief Executive: David Harker
Director of Cricket: Geoff Cook
Director of Operations: Lesley Williamson
First Team Coach: Martyn Moxon
Captain: Jonathan Lewis
Second XI coach: Alan Walker
County colours:
Yellow, blue, burgundy

HONOURS

NONE YET

National Cricket League nickname:
DURHAM DYNAMOS

Website:
www.durham-ccc.org.uk

the end of the third day after four-and-a-half hours at the crease, could add only one run the following morning as Kent resumed their second innings on 192 for five. But Smith, batting at number seven because he had been unwell the previous day, and aided especially by Min Patel, went to 103 not out as Kent totalled 318. An ugly stroke from skipper Matthew Fleming apart, Kent had made their opponents battle for every wicket – and now the Yorkshiremen only had 38 overs to score 176 for victory. Kent sniffed a win themselves, of course, but Darren Lehmann's 41 and then a sparkling unbeaten 43 from Gary Fellows sneaked them home. Chris Silverwood's five for 45 had undone the Kent first innings, and Yorkshire's first-innings effort was based on high-class knocks of 71 from Michael Vaughan and 68 from Lehmann.

No play on the scheduled first day, combined with an excellent pitch, condemned the game between Glamorgan and Somerset at Cardiff to a high-scoring draw. England selectors David Graveney and Geoff Miller watched Michael Powell score 64 when the match finally got under way, and Glamorgan eventually declared early on the third day on 353 for nine after fine knocks from Adrian Dale and Adrian Shaw. The Somerset reply, however, featured some even better batting. Led by Marcus Trescothick, whose 147 came off 226 balls and contained a six and 23 fours, Somerset reached 435 for five before more bad weather halted things on the final day. Trescothick and Piran Holloway (78) put on 240 for the first wicket, and Jamie Cox (95 not out) and Mike Burns (70) also made the most of the favourable conditions.

Rain ruined the likelihood of an Essex victory at Chelmsford where Northants, set 314, were struggling on 199 for seven when the final 11 overs of the match were lost. The weather had brought constant interruptions throughout the four days, but a solid 61 from Darren Robinson had taken Essex to 206 in their first innings. Nasser Hussain, playing in his first championship match since August 12 the previous year, fell for just 15. Darren Cousins, who had endured three back operations in five years during his time at Essex, took four for 62 against his old county, but the Northants batting fell away badly against Ronnie Irani (five for 43). All out for 150, the visitors then found it difficult to restrain the strokemaking of Stuart Law (58) and Stephen Peters (56 not out) and, in the end, only 55 from Russell Warren and 47 from Alec Swann bought Northants the time which allowed them to claim the draw when the rain returned.

The match between Lancashire and Surrey at Old Trafford suffered a total washout, with the waterlogged state of the outfield, plus more rain, meaning that all four days were called off without a ball being bowled. Bad luck with the weather cannot be blamed on anyone, of course, but surely the administrators were unwise to schedule a game of this magnitude – the champions against last year's runners-up – in a late-April slot.

Division Two

at Worcester
Sussex 255 for 7 dec. (68.4 overs) (MW Goodwin 94) and 54 for 2 dec.
Worcestershire 14 for 1 dec. (6.2 overs) and 188 for 4 (WPC Weston 78*)
Match drawn – no play was possible on the first and second days
Worcestershire 6 pts, Sussex 6 pts

at Trent Bridge
Durham 284 (84.3 overs) (PD Collingwood 95, JJB Lewis 56)
Nottinghamshire 344 for 6 (105 overs) (GS Blewett 133)
Match drawn – no play was possible on the fourth day
Nottinghamshire 10 pts, Durham 8 pts

at Derby
Derbyshire 198 (98.4 overs)
Middlesex 146 for 5 (68 overs)
Match drawn – no play was possible on the first and fourth days
Derbyshire 5 pts, Middlesex 7 pts

All three division two matches ended in watery draws as the weather had the biggest say in the games at Worcester, Trent Bridge and Derby.

There was no play possible on each of the first two days at New Road, but a fine 116-ball 94 by Murray Goodwin breathed some life into proceedings on the third day and, after Sussex had declared their first innings on 255 for seven, two quick-fire declarations enabled Worcestershire to be set a target of 296. Despite Philip Weston's unbeaten 78, however, the weather had the final word.

Paul Collingwood's 95 was the highlight of Durham's first-innings total of 284, spread over almost the whole of the first two days, but Greg Blewett then struck a memorable 133 for Nottinghamshire to become only the second player from the county to score a hundred on his

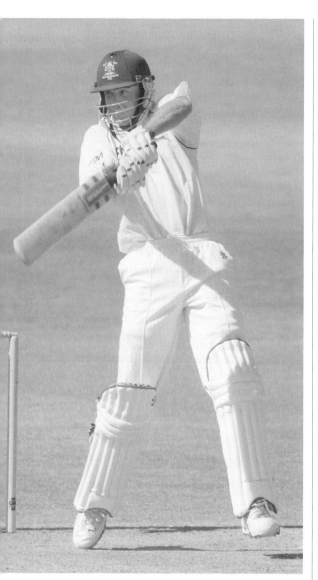

Greg Blewett's 133 made him only the second Notts player to hit a century on his county championship debut.

championship debut. Australian Blewett, who had managed only one century during a miserable season as Yorkshire's overseas player in 1999, hit 21 boundaries in a 237-ball effort, and there was also some good batting from Chris Read and Paul Franks as Notts reached 344 for six. No play, however, was possible on the last day.

There were washouts, too, on the first and final days at Derby. In between, Middlesex reached 146 for five in reply to Derbyshire's first innings 198. Despite the wet weather, though, veteran spinners

Phil Tufnell and Richard Illingworth enjoyed themselves. Tuffers picked up four for 42 while Illingworth claimed four for 37 on his Derbyshire debut.

ROUND THREE: 9–12 MAY 2001

Division One

at Headingley
Somerset 257 (99 overs) (MN Lathwell 65) and 327 for 8 dec. (PCL Holloway 85, J Cox 80, M Burns 50)
Yorkshire 231 (73.2 overs) (MP Vaughan 79, GM Fellows 63, AR Caddick 5 for 81) and 192 (DS Lehmann 77, AR Caddick 5 for 92)
Somerset won by 161 runs
Somerset 17 pts, Yorkshire 4 pts

at Leicester
Leicestershire 240 (72.3 overs) (DJ Marsh 71, G Chapple 5 for 40) and 169 (DJ Marsh 50*, PJ Martin 5 for 52)
Lancashire 199 (77 overs) (DE Malcolm 5 for 78) and 204 (JP Crawley 53)
Leicestershire won by 6 runs
Leicestershire 16 pts, Lancashire 3 pts

at Northampton
Northamptonshire 476 (149.1 overs) (AJ Swann 96, JW Cook 80, ME Hussey 75, AL Penberthy 75) and 304 for 1 (MB Loye 167*, ME Hussey 67, JW Cook 52*)
Surrey 607 (161.5 overs) (GP Thorpe 148, AD Brown 122, IJ Ward 79, MP Bicknell 56, AJ Hollioake 50)
Match drawn
Northamptonshire 11 pts, Surrey 11 pts

One of Andy Caddick's rare championship outings for Somerset resulted in a comprehensive 161-run victory against Yorkshire at Headingley. Mark Lathwell hit 65 as Somerset totalled 257 on the opening day before Caddick, operating in four spells, picked up five for 81 as Yorkshire were dismissed for 231 in reply, despite a classy 79 from Michael Vaughan and a championship-best 63 by Gary Fellows. Piran Holloway (85) and Jamie Cox (80) then spearheaded Somerset's second-innings drive to 327 for eight declared, with Vaughan picking up four for 47, and by the close of the third day, Caddick had already removed two of Yorkshire's first three wickets. Darren Lehmann offered a pugnacious 77, but Yorkshire were soon condemned to defeat on the final morning – Caddick finishing with five for 92 and Steffan

Jones again providing staunch support with four for 71 to add to his first-innings haul of three for 37. Nine of Caddick's ten victims were top-five batsmen.

Leicestershire won a thrilling six-run victory against Lancashire in a low-scoring affair at Grace Road. The home side looked to have wasted the advantage of batting first, slipping to 240 all out with some sloppy strokes, despite Dan Marsh's 71. Glen Chapple, due mainly to a fine second spell, finished with five for 40, but Leicestershire hit back themselves with the ball as Lancashire's first innings realized only 199. Devon Malcolm (five for 78) and Jon Dakin (three for 69) did most of the damage, but Leicestershire then failed to hammer home their advantage with the bat. Peter Martin (five for 52) and Muttiah Muralitharan (four for 56) were responsible for the slide to 169 all out, although an eighth-wicket stand of 56 between Marsh (50 not out) and Neil Burns (39) ultimately proved decisive. John Crawley scored 53, and Chapple 44 batting at number eight, but amid great tension Lancashire could only reach 204.

The bat totally dominated the ball at Northampton, meanwhile, with both the home side and the visitors Surrey picking up 11 points for the draw. The champions' attack looked a little ragged by the end of a weather-shortened first day in which Northants totalled 320 for four, with Mike Hussey and Jeff Cook both going well past 50. Alec Swann (96) and Tony Penberthy (75) then built a substantial fifth-wicket partnership and Northants eventually reached 476. In reply, however, the Surrey batsmen had even more of a ball. Graham Thorpe and Ally Brown both made hundreds, and with Ian Ward, Adam Hollioake and Martin Bicknell all hitting half-centuries, Surrey reached a mammoth 607 early on the final day. All that remained was for Northants to rattle up 304 for one in the 72 overs left, with Mal Loye ending on a brilliant unbeaten 167. He and Hussey (67) put on 189 for the opening wicket.

Division Two

at Bristol
Gloucestershire 272 (100.2 overs) (KJ Barnett 99) and 265 for 4 dec. (MGN Windows 106*)
Middlesex 245 (110 overs) (SP Fleming 52, DC Nash 50*) and 293 for 5 (SP Fleming 121*, BL Hutton 59, OA Shah 57)
Middlesex won by five wickets
Middlesex 16 pts, Gloucestershire 5 pts

Flying Dutchman Bas Zuiderent hit a maiden first-class century (122) as Sussex trounced Nottinghamshire.

at Southampton Rose Bowl
Hampshire 309 (100.5 overs) (AD Mascarenhas 104, JP Stephenson 51) and 159
Worcestershire 236 (84 overs) (GA Hick 120) and 108
Hampshire won by 124 runs
Hampshire 17.75 pts, Worcestershire 4 pts
Hampshire were fined .25 pt for their slow over-rate

at Hove
Sussex 404 (145.1 overs) (B Zuiderent 122, RSC Martin-Jenkins 55, GJ Smith 5 for 64) and 298 for 8 dec. (MH Yardy 68, RR Montgomerie 66, GJ Smith 5 for 37)
Nottinghamshire 332 (91.2 overs) (KP Pietersen 51, CMW Read 50, JD Lewry 5 for 95) and 208 (P Johnson 88*)

ESSEX CCC

Home Ground:
The County Ground, Chelmsford
Address:
County Cricket Ground, New Writtle Street,
Chelmsford, Essex CM2 0PD
Tel: 01245 252420
Fax: 01245 491607
Prospects of play: 01245 287921
Email: administration.essex@ecb.co.uk
Directions:
By rail: Chelmsford Station (8 minutes' walk away).
By road: M25 then A12 to Chelmsford.
Exit Chelmsford and follow AA signs
to 'Essex Cricket Club'.
Capacity: 6,000
Other grounds used: Castle Park, Colchester; Valentine's
Park, Ilford; Southchurch Park, Southend-on-Sea.
Year formed: 1876

Chief Executive: DE East
Commercial Manager: Dave Comley
Other posts: Manager/Coach Cricket School:
Norman Bambridge; Head Groundsman: SG Kerrison
Club Captain: Nasser Hussain
Team Captain: Ronnie Irani
County colours: Blue, gold and red

HONOURS

COUNTY CHAMPIONSHIP
1979, 1983, 1984, 1986,
1991, 1992
SUNDAY LEAGUE
1981, 1984, 1985
REFUGE ASSURANCE CUP
1989
BENSON & HEDGES CUP
1979, 1998
GILLETTE CUP/C&G TROPHY
1985, 1997

National Cricket League nickname:
ESSEX EAGLES

Website:
www.essexcricket.org.uk

Sussex won by 162 runs
Sussex 19 pts, Nottinghamshire 5 pts

at Edgbaston
Durham 329 (100.2 overs) (PD Collingwood 153,
A Pratt 52) and 102 (MM Betts 5 for 22)
Warwickshire 205 (55.3 overs) and 227 for 3
(MA Wagh 104)
Warwickshire won by seven wickets
Warwickshire 16 pts, Durham 6 pts

Wins for Middlesex, Hampshire, Sussex and
Warwickshire made this a significant round of
matches in terms of a pecking order beginning to be
established in the race for promotion from division
two.

Middlesex triumphed on a slow pitch at Bristol,
beating Gloucestershire by five wickets after being
asked to make 293 in 82 overs on the last afternoon.
Ian Harvey took four for 83, but Stephen Fleming
played the match-winning innings of 121 not out,
and the New Zealand Test captain was ably
supported by Owais Shah (57) and Ben Hutton (59).
Victory came with 3.1 overs to spare.

Gloucestershire had earlier gained a slender
first-innings lead of 27 after reaching 272, with
Kim Barnett being bowled by Phil Tufnell just one
run short of what would have been his 58th first-
class century, and then declaring their second
innings on 265 for four after Matt Windows had
reached 106 not out.

The 112th first-class hundred of Graeme Hick's
career, and his 82nd for Worcestershire, plus match
figures of eight for 100 from Alamgir Sheriyar,
could not prevent the county from slipping to a
124-run defeat against Hampshire at West End.
Hampshire, boosted on day one by a seventh-wicket
stand of 142 between a flamboyant Dimitri
Mascarenhas (104 from number eight) and an
obdurate John Stephenson (51), found that their
309 was enough to earn them a first-innings lead of
73, despite Hick's 120. Hampshire could make only
159 second time around, but Alex Morris then
followed first-innings figures of four for 39 with
four for 27 as Worcestershire folded to 108 all out
on the third day. For Hampshire, of course, victory
was especially sweet, as it came on their first
championship appearance at their new
headquarters.

Nottinghamshire, set 371 in 80 overs to beat
Sussex at Hove, were dismissed for 208 inside 53
overs with only Paul Johnson (88 not out) providing
any worthwhile resistance against the pace and

swing of Jason Lewry (four for 65) and James
Kirtley (four for 50). Lewry, in fact, had also taken
five for 95 in Notts' first-innings 332, a total that
condemned them to a sizeable first-innings deficit
following Sussex's march to 404. Bas Zuiderent hit a
maiden first-class hundred and there were several
useful contributions from the lower middle-order.
Sussex's solid second-innings total of 298 for eight
declared also contained Michael Yardy's maiden
first-class 50 – a knock of 68 – and only Greg Smith,
with match figures of ten for 101, emerged with any
credit in the visiting attack.

Warwickshire recovered from being 49 for five in
reply to Durham's first-innings total of 329 to beat
their visitors by seven wickets at Edgbaston. That
remarkable turnaround was achieved first on the
back of a gritty sixth-wicket stand of 78 between
Dougie Brown and Neil Smith, which enabled
Warwickshire to reach 205, and then by the seam
bowling of Brown and Mel Betts, who took five for
22 against his former county. With Brown picking
up three for 16, Durham were sent tumbling to 102
all out in their second innings, leaving the home
side a victory target of 227. By the close of the third
day they had already reached 176 for two, with
Mark Wagh unbeaten on 76 from 102 balls, and on
the final morning Wagh completed a deserved
hundred. Durham, missing five players through
injury, were left to reflect on what might have been
after they themselves had rallied from being 58 for
five on the first morning thanks to a career-best 153
from Paul Collingwood and a 108-run partnership
for the sixth wicket between him and Andy Pratt
(52).

ROUND FOUR: 16–19 MAY 2001

Division One

at Taunton
Kent 343 (99.5 overs) (DP Fulton 140, DJ Cullinan 57)
Somerset 184 (70.1 overs) and (following on) 334 for
7 (PD Bowler 87, J Cox 63, MN Lathwell 58)
Match drawn
Somerset 7 pts, Kent 10 pts

at Chelmsford
Yorkshire 403 for 9 dec. (114.2 overs) (JD Middlebrook
84, CEW Silverwood 70, D Byas 55)
Essex 249 (83 overs) (SG Law 53)
*Match drawn – no play was possible on the first and
second days*
Essex 8 pts, Yorkshire 12 pts

at The Oval
Leicestershire 246 (78.5 overs) (JM Dakin 69, ESH Giddins 5 for 48) and 94 for 5 dec.
Surrey 190 (63 overs)
Match drawn – no play was possible on the first and second days
Surrey 7 pts, Leicestershire 8 pts

at Old Trafford
Lancashire v. **Glamorgan**
No play was possible on any of the four scheduled days
Lancashire 4 pts, Glamorgan 4 pts

In a round of matches decimated by bad weather, Kent missed the chance of stealing a march on their rivals by failing to polish off Somerset at Taunton. In the only first division game to see play on all four scheduled days (albeit just 27 overs on the second day), Kent totalled 343 in their first innings on the back of David Fulton's 140 from 243 balls and then had Somerset following on. Martin Saggers and James Golding shared six wickets as the home side were dismissed for 184 in their first innings, but Jamie Cox led some stiffer resistance on the third evening, reaching 59 not out as Somerset closed on 109 for two. And, although Cox went early for 63 on the final day, Peter Bowler (87) was joined by Mark Lathwell (58) in an important stand of 135. With Pete Trego striking 43, Somerset finally finished on 334 for seven to defy the best efforts of Kent skipper Matthew Fleming, who took four for 74.

No play on either of the first two days at Chelmsford and The Oval left both Essex and Yorkshire, and Surrey and Leicestershire, to scrap for bonus points before draws were confirmed. Yorkshire emerged the best of the four in that respect, gaining the maximum eight by reaching 403 for nine declared and then bowling out Essex for 249 on the final afternoon. Yorkshire, in fact, had been 164 for six in their first innings before James Middlebrook, with a career-best 84, and Chris Silverwood, with a no-nonsense, 74-ball 70, added 126 in 24 overs. At The Oval some excellent seam and swing bowling from Ed Giddins (five for 48) and Martin Bicknell (four for 61) reduced Leicestershire to 246 all out but, after a fluent start, Surrey were themselves dismissed for 190. James Ormond and Carl Crowe, the off spinner, shared eight wickets to deny the champions a single batting point.

At Old Trafford, meanwhile, not a single ball was bowled in the match between Lancashire and Glamorgan – the second-successive championship washout at the ground.

David Fulton scored the second of his season's nine championship centuries against Somerset. It was a prolific year for the 29-year-old Kent opener.

Division Two

at Southampton Rose Bowl
Hampshire 350 for 4 dec. (109.2 overs) (DA Kenway 131, RA Smith 102*) and 55 for 6
Gloucestershire 133 (52.4 overs) (AD Mullally 5 for 41) and 272 (DR Hewson 89, JN Snape 73)
Match drawn
Hampshire 13 pts, Gloucestershire 5 pts

at Chester-le-Street
Middlesex 386 (128.2 overs) (OA Shah 190, SP Fleming 114, MA Gough 5 for 66) and 189 for 4 dec. (OA Shah 88)
Durham 274 (95.5 overs) (N Peng 101) and 226 for 6 (PD Collingwood 59)
Match drawn
Durham 9 pts, Middlesex 11 pts

at Worcester
Derbyshire 222 for 8 dec. (69 overs) (MJ Di Venuto 108)
Worcestershire 52 for 0 (15 overs)
Match drawn – no play was possible on the first, second and third days
Worcestershire 4 pts, Derbyshire 4 pts

at Trent Bridge
Nottinghamshire 402 for 6 dec. (103.1 overs) (DJ Bicknell 167, GS Blewett 99, Usman Afzaal 61)
Warwickshire did not bat
Match drawn – no play was possible on the second and third days
Nottinghamshire 9 pts, Warwickshire 6 pts

Hampshire threw away a gilt-edged opportunity to beat Gloucestershire at West End, batting with such recklessness in an exciting final hour that they failed by one run to reach their victory target of 56 from ten overs. The bowlers Jon Lewis and James Averis also held their nerve splendidly as Hampshire finished on 55 for six. The home side, however, did earn themselves a six-point bonus for the fact that the drawn game ended with scores level. Hampshire, in fact, had bossed the game right from the start, accelerating on to 350 for four declared early on the third morning after poor weather had allowed just 81.4 overs to be bowled on the first two days. Derek Kenway hit 131 and Robin Smith an unbeaten 102 to put Hampshire in charge, and, by the end of the third day, Gloucestershire were 36 for two in their second innings after being tumbled out for 133 with Alan Mullally (five for 41) and Shaun Udal (three for 30) doing most of the damage. Dominic Hewson, though, then held up Hampshire for five-and-three-quarter hours while amassing 89, and Jeremy Snape's combative 73 also meant that, in the end, Hampshire were left with their rather undignified scramble.

Two young batsmen with high talent shone out from Durham's drawn encounter with Middlesex at Chester-le-Street. Owais Shah dominated the match from the outset, scoring a career-best 190 in Middlesex's first-innings 386 and then hitting 88 as the visitors declared on 189 for four second time around. But Nicky Peng, too, left his mark on the game – the 18-year-old, 12 months on from his debut 98 against Surrey, hit his maiden first-class century in a Durham first-innings score of 269 and,

Heavy early season scoring propelled Middlesex's Owais Shah into the England one-day international team.

GLAMORGAN CCC

Home Ground:
Cardiff
Address:
Sophia Gardens, Cardiff CF1 9XR
Tel: 029 2040 9380
Fax: 029 2040 9390
Email: glam@ecb.co.uk
Directions:
By rail: Cardiff Central Train Station.
By road: From north, A470 and follow signs to Cardiff until
junction with Cardiff by-pass then A48 Port Talbot and City
Centre. Cathedral Road is situated off A48 for Sophia
Gardens. From east, M4 Junction 29 then A48.
Capacity: 4,000
Other grounds used: Pontypridd, Mid Glamorgan; St Helens,
Swansea; Rhos-on-Sea, Colwyn Bay; Pen-y-Pound Ground,
Abergavenny.
Year formed: 1888

Chief Executive: Mike Fatkin
Head Groundsman: Len Smith
Captain: Steve James
Vice-captain: Adrian Dale
County colours: Navy blue and yellow/gold

HONOURS

COUNTY CHAMPIONSHIP
1948, 1969, 1997
SUNDAY LEAGUE
1993

National Cricket League
nickname:
GLAMORGAN DRAGONS

Website:
www.glamorgancricket.com

on the final day, also batted attractively as the home side held on for a draw at 226 for six. Michael Gough took a career-best five for 66 with his off breaks during the Middlesex innings, which was built around a magnificent third-wicket stand of 248 between Shah and county captain Stephen Fleming (114).

No play for the first three days at New Road, where the outfield resembled a bog after heavy rains and the regular winter and spring flooding, left Worcestershire and Derbyshire to play out a meaningless final day. Michael Di Venuto, at least, enjoyed it by hitting 108 in Derbyshire's 222 for eight declared, and Worcestershire replied with 52 for no wicket.

The situation was almost as bad at Trent Bridge, where only 9.4 overs of play on the opening day prevented the match between Nottinghamshire and Warwickshire from being an exact replica of events at Worcester. Notts, having reached 41 for one on that truncated first day, then moved to 402 for six declared on the fourth afternoon with Darren Bicknell leading the way to maximum batting points with 167 and Greg Blewett reaching 99 before being bowled by Mo Sheikh.

ROUND FIVE: 25–28 MAY 2001

Division One

at Headingley
Yorkshire 374 (122.4 overs) (MP Vaughan 133, MJ Lumb 50, DM Cousins 8 for 102) and 77 for 6
Northamptonshire 195 (74.4 overs) (RJ Warren 65*, CEW Silverwood 5 for 58) and 255 (MB Loye 52, MJ Hoggard 5 for 82)
Yorkshire won by four wickets
Yorkshire 19 pts, Northamptonshire 3 pts

at The Oval
Surrey 498 (128.4 overs) (AJ Tudor 116, AJ Stewart 106, MA Butcher 52) and 206 for 5 dec. (MA Butcher 72, MR Ramprakash 52)
Essex 300 (94.4 overs) (SG Law 153) and 312 for 4 (AP Grayson 115, SG Law 57, RC Irani 51*)
Match drawn
Surrey 12 pts, Essex 10 pts

at Swansea
Kent 252 (81.5 overs) (MJ Walker 112*, DP Fulton 78)
Glamorgan 238 (92.2 overs) (MJ Saggers 5 for 70)
Match drawn – no play was possible on the third day
Glamorgan 8 pts, Kent 9 pts

Yorkshire moved to the top of the county championship with an efficient, yet ultimately tense, four-wicket win against Northamptonshire at Headingley. A first-innings total of 374 was built around a technically superb 133 from Michael Vaughan, who dealt with an awkward seaming pitch in the opening hour with aplomb. Useful knocks by Michael Lumb and Richard Blakey further boosted Yorkshire, who were then bowled into a position of power by Chris Silverwood's five for 58. Northants, dismissed for 195, with only Russell Warren's unbeaten 65 providing lengthy resistance, made it to 255 second time around in spite of Matthew Hoggard's five for 82. But Yorkshire, left with only 77 to win, struggled to get going against the fast-medium of John Blain (four for 34) and, in the end, it took skipper David Byas' determined 26 not out, plus no fewer than 27 extras, to edge them over the finishing line.

Surrey, the champions, fell further behind in the race for a third successive title when they paid a heavy price for not enforcing the follow-on against Essex at The Oval. Alex Tudor's maiden first-class century, 116 batting at number eight, was the highlight of Surrey's first-innings total of 498. Tudor and Alec Stewart, who made 106, doubled the Surrey total from 206 for six in a seventh-wicket stand that broke the 80-year-old county record against Essex. Stuart Law then waged a lone war against the home bowlers, the Australian's brilliant 153 almost single-handedly guiding Essex to 300. Batting again, Surrey ran up 206 for five declared, with Mark Butcher scoring his second half-century of the game, but Essex were 73 without loss by the close of the third day and, on the final day, went on to 312 for four with Paul Grayson (115) being ably supported by both Law (57) and skipper Ronnie Irani (51 not out).

Rain ruined the match at Swansea between Glamorgan and Kent, for whom Matthew Walker hit a third century of the season, an unbeaten 112. Walker and David Fulton (78) resuscitated a Kent first innings which was feeling a little groggy at 13 for three, and by the end of the first day Glamorgan were themselves reeling at 42 for four in reply to the visitors' 252. Martin Saggers, who on that first evening had figures of four for 15 from seven overs, eventually went on to claim five for 70 – but those figures were not completed until the final day. The bad weather allowed just 56 overs on the second day, and none at all on the scheduled third day. When play finally resumed at 3.50pm on the last afternoon, with both teams only interested in bonus

Michael Vaughan showed his Yorkshire team-mates how to cope with a seaming pitch with a knock of 133 against Northamptonshire.

and (following on) 215 (RK Illingworth 61*, MJ Di Venuto 52, SD Udal 7 for 74)
Hampshire won by nine wickets
Hampshire 20 pts, Derbyshire 5 pts

at Bristol
Worcestershire 326 (119.2 overs) (WPC Weston 83, AJ Bichel 76, J Lewis 5 for 71) and 256 for 8 dec. (WPC Weston 58)
Gloucestershire 175 (70.5 overs) (JN Snape 69, SR Lampitt 5 for 22) and 155 (AJ Bichel 6 for 44)
Worcestershire won by 252 runs
Worcestershire 18 pts, Gloucestershire 3 pts

at Hove
Warwickshire 395 (148 overs) (MJ Powell 93, MA Wagh 90, DR Brown 63) and 70 for 2
Sussex 208 (83 overs) and 253 (RR Montgomerie 116)
Warwickshire won by eight wickets
Warwickshire 19 pts, Sussex 3 pts

at Lord's
Nottinghamshire 467 (115.5 overs) (KP Pietersen 165*, PJ Franks 85, TF Bloomfield 5 for 133) and 252 for 8 dec. (GS Blewett 76, KP Pietersen 65*, PCR Tufnell 5 for 61)
Middlesex 370 (117.1 overs) (SJ Cook 93*, OA Shah 58, DC Nash 56, PN Weekes 50) and 197 for 8 (AJ Strauss 78)
Match drawn
Middlesex 11 pts, Nottinghamshire 12 pts

points, Glamorgan moved from 177 for eight to 238 all out before the elements closed in once again.

Division Two

at Derby
Hampshire 464 (143.2 overs) (WS Kendall 94, LR Prittipaul 84, AN Aymes 83*, DA Kenway 57, NC Johnson 53) and 49 for 1
Derbyshire 297 (102.4 overs) (SD Stubbings 93, RJ Bailey 52, NRC Dumelow 50*, AD Mullally 5 for 52)

Hampshire thrashed bottom club Derbyshire at Derby to push themselves to the head of the second division table. Their nine-wicket win was based on a solid first-innings total of 464, after Derbyshire had nonsensically put them in, and then penetrative bowling from Alan Mullally and Shaun Udal. Mullally's five for 52 broke up Derbyshire's first-innings resistance that had centred on Steve Stubbings' 93, Rob Bailey's 52 and an unbeaten 50 by Nathan Dumelow on his debut. Bowled out for 297, Derbyshire then followed on and ran into Udal's seven for 74, his best return for nine years. Only Richard Illingworth's unbeaten 61 made Hampshire bat again. Will Kendall top-scored with 94 in Hampshire's first innings, until he became

GLOUCESTERSHIRE CCC

Home Ground:
Bristol
Address:
The Sun Alliance Ground, Nevil Road,
Bristol BS7 9EJ
Tel: 0117 910 8000
Directions:
By road: M5, M4, M32 into Bristol: exit at second
exit (Fishponds/Horfield), then third exit – Muller
Road. Almost at end of Muller Road (bus station on right),
turn left at Ralph Road. Go to the top, turn left and then
right almost immediately into Kennington Avenue. Follow
the signs for County Cricket.
Capacity: 8,000
Other grounds used: College Ground, Cheltenham;
Kings School, Gloucester
Year formed: 1870

Chairman: John Higson
Director of Cricket: Andy Stovold
Other posts: Chief Executive: CL Sexstone; Youth
Development Officer: Richard Holdsworth
Captain: Mark Alleyne
Coaching contact: Andy Stovold, Director of Coaching
0117 910 8004
County colours: Blue, brown, gold, green and red,
sky blue

HONOURS

BENSON & HEDGES CUP
1977, 1999, 2000
GILLETTE CUP/C&G TROPHY
1973, 1999, 2000

**National Cricket League
nickname:
GLOUCESTERSHIRE GLADIATORS**

Website:
www.glosccc.co.uk

HAMPSHIRE CCC

Home Ground:
Southampton
Address:
The Hampshire Rose Bowl, Botley Road,
West End, Southampton SO30 3XH
Tel: 02380 472002
Fax: 02380 472122
Indoor school: 02380 472468
Email: enquiries.hants@ecb.co.uk
Directions:
By rail: Southampton Parkway – 4 miles.
By road: From M27, exit junction 7 and take the
A334 then the B3035 (Botley Road, West End).
Capacity: 9,950
Year formed: 1863

Chief Executive: Graham Walker
Marketing Manager: Mike Taylor
Director of Cricket: Tim Tremlett
Coach: Jimmy Cook
Other posts: Head Groundsman: Nigel Gray
Youth Development Officer: Alan Rowe
Cricket Development Coach: Raj Maru; Women's
Cricket Development Officer: Clair Slaney
Captain: Robin Smith
Vice-captain: Will Kendall
County colours: Navy blue, old gold

HONOURS

COUNTY CHAMPIONSHIP
1961, 1973
SUNDAY LEAGUE
1975, 1978, 1986
BENSON & HEDGES CUP 1988,
1992
GILLETTE CUP/C&G TROPHY
1991

National Cricket League nickname:
HAMPSHIRE HAWKS

Website:
www.hampshire.cricket.org

Karl Krikken's 500th first-class victim, and there were also half-centuries for Neil Johnson, Derek Kenway and 21-year-old Lawrence Prittipaul, whose 84 from 109 balls prompted rightful debate as to why he was making just his fifth championship appearance in two years.

Gloucestershire's players were kept behind closed dressing-room doors for an urgent team meeting after their heavy defeat against Worcestershire at Bristol. Jeremy Snape, with 69 and 42, was the only home batsman not to capitulate weakly, as

Kevin Pietersen, Notts' South-African-raised all-rounder, smashed an unbeaten 165 in a scintillating display of clean hitting that lit up the drawn match with Middlesex at Lord's.

Gloucestershire were bowled out for 175 and 155 – Stuart Lampitt (five for 22) doing the damage first time around and Andy Bichel (six for 44) cleaning up on the fourth day. Worcestershire's first innings 326 was based on a dedicated five-hour 83 by Philip Weston and a hard-hitting 76 by Bichel, while opener Weston also impressed with 58 in the visitors' second innings of 256 for eight declared.

Warwickshire took immediate control of their game against Sussex at Hove with a 115-run opening stand between Michael Powell (93) and Nick Knight, and didn't let up until victory had been confirmed by eight wickets. Mark Wagh's 90, with 16 fours, and Dougie Brown's 63, helped the visitors to reach 395 all out and, by the end of the second

day, Sussex had been condemned to following on after being bowled out for 208. Richard Montgomerie's brave 116 held them up until the fourth morning but, when Sussex were finally dismissed for 253, it left Warwickshire requiring only 65 for their fifth-successive championship win at Hove. Remarkably, it is still nine years since Sussex beat Warwickshire in any competition.

Scintillating batting from Kevin Pietersen, their 21-year-old, South African-raised, off-spinning all-rounder, lit up Nottinghamshire's draw at Lord's. The Middlesex attack were caned to the tune of 230 unbeaten runs as Pietersen set up the chance of victory, but, in the end, a determined innings from both Andrew Strauss (78) and Stephen Fleming (42) left Notts two wickets away from taking maximum points. Pietersen's 165 not out in Notts' first innings of 467 was his maiden century, and his 199-run stand with Paul Franks (85) broke a county seventh-wicket record against Middlesex which had stood since 1885. It was also Franks' highest first-class score, and the two youngsters both struck the ball with elan. Franks then picked up four for 65 as Middlesex made 370 in reply, thanks largely to Simon Cook's unbeaten 93, before Pietersen weighed in again with four sixes and four other boundaries in a 47-ball 65 not out in a Notts second innings of 252 for eight declared in which Greg Blewett top-scored with 76. Middlesex, who were nine for no wicket overnight, survived 104.5 overs in all to achieve the draw finishing on 197 for eight.

ROUND SIX: 30 MAY–2 JUNE 2001

Division One

at Swansea
Yorkshire 280 (99.1 overs) (DS Lehmann 75, D Byas 63, AG Wharf 5 for 63) and 277 for 7 dec. (D Byas 105, GM Fellows 61)
Glamorgan 104 (41.3 overs) (CEW Silverwood 5 for 20) and 125 (GM Hamilton 5 for 27)
Yorkshire won by 328 runs
Yorkshire 17 pts, Glamorgan 3 pts

at Tunbridge Wells
Kent 518 for 5 dec. (149.1 overs) (DP Fulton 179, MJ Walker 124, DJ Cullinan 63)
Essex 298 (117.1 overs) (SG Law 99, RC Irani 64, BJ Trott 5 for 65) and (following on) 68 (BJ Trott 6 for 13)
Kent won by an innings and 152 runs
Kent 20 pts, Essex 3 pts

at Northampton
Northamptonshire 398 (136.1 overs) (MB Loye 177, ME Hussey 70) and 194 (ME Hussey 82, G Chapple 5 for 60)
Lancashire 291 (90 overs) (MJ Chilton 104) and 305 for 7 (WK Hegg 107*, G Chapple 72*, DM Cousins 7 for 120)
Lancashire won by three wickets
Lancashire 16 pts, Northamptonshire 7 pts

at Leicester
Leicestershire 387 (99 overs) (DJ Marsh 138*, TR Ward 93, DI Stevens 63) and 390 for 7 dec. (TR Ward 119, VJ Wells 86, BF Smith 66, IJ Sutcliffe 58)
Somerset 374 (122.2 overs) (PD Bowler 138*, M Burns 60) and 268 for 8 (PCL Holloway 85, MN Lathwell 63)
Match drawn
Leicestershire 11 pts, Somerset 11 pts

Yorkshire continued to play like potential county champions as they crushed Glamorgan by 328 runs at Swansea. Their first-innings score of 280 on the opening day was a good effort on an uneven pitch, with Darren Lehmann hitting 75 and David Byas 63 in the face of some testing seam bowling from Alex Wharf and Steve Watkin. Then, on the second morning, genuinely fast outswing from Chris Silverwood, who took five for 20, shattered Glamorgan's first innings for 104. Byas, however, chose to bat again, no doubt wary of having to bat last in the conditions, and himself chalked up his first championship hundred since 1998, an unbeaten 105, before a second-innings declaration came at 277 for seven. Glamorgan, clearly short of match practice because of the poor weather in May, were tumbled out again for just 125 with Gavin Hamilton picking up five for 27 and Ryan Sidebottom fully deserving his four for 49.

Ben Trott was the Kent hero at Tunbridge Wells, taking 11 for 78 in the match as Essex were beaten by an innings and 152 runs – and then revealing the secret behind his sudden spring to prominence. Trott, 26, joined Kent from his native Somerset in 2000 because of the long-term injuries afflicting Dean Headley and Julian Thompson, but had taken only 12 wickets previously in first-class cricket. Now, acting on advice from Kent coach John Inverarity to lengthen his run-up by two strides, so as to improve his rhythm, Trott took five for 65 as Essex were bowled out for 298 in reply to Kent's imposing total of 518 for five declared and then a remarkable six for 13 from 9.5 overs as the visitors were blown away for just 68 on the third afternoon. A tall man at six foot five, he produced steep lift to go with disconcerting movement away from the right-handers, and only Jamie Foster and Mark Ilott made it into double figures as Essex were cut down for the lowest championship total of the season. David Fulton, with an eight-and-a-half hour 179, his fourth century of the campaign, was joined by the equally in-form Matthew Walker (124) in a stand of 212 for the fourth wicket, and Daryll Cullinan made 63. Essex, through Stuart Law, at first threatened to make a game of it, but their collapse was as startling as Trott's emergence from the shadows once Min Patel turned one just enough to bowl Law one run short of what would have been the Australian's 50th first-class century.

Northamptonshire threw away the chance at Wantage Road to kick-start their own championship season as well as condemning fancied Lancashire to bottom spot. As it was, flaccid batting by the home side on the third day gave Lancashire an escape route to victory – and, after much drama on the final afternoon, it was a journey accepted to the full by Warren Hegg and Glen Chapple. Their magnificent, unbroken, eighth-wicket stand of 136 eventually clinched a vital and unlikely three-wicket triumph for Lancashire. Hegg finished 107 not out, and Chapple 72 not out, as Lancashire rallied from being 169 for seven. Darren Cousins bowled his heart out to take seven for 120, but he received little worthwhile support from the rest of the Northants attack. Jason Brown, moreover, dropped a caught-and-bowled chance when Chapple was still to score. Yet Northants had only themselves to blame long before that incident, after earning a first-innings lead of 107 but then failing to bat their opponents out of the game. Mal Loye's superb 177 on the opening day, with two sixes off Muttiah Muralitharan and 22 fours besides, had put Northants in control. Loye had been joined in a first-wicket partnership of 159 by Mike Hussey, but the lower middle-order could not boost the total to something around 450 and Mark Chilton's dogged century, plus some late hitting from Chapple and Peter Martin, just about kept Lancashire in touch. Then came the poor batting in the Northants second innings with only Hussey, seventh out for 82, displaying the necessary resolve against Chapple (five for 60) and Martin (three for 49 off 33 overs). There was nothing too wrong with the pitch, as Hegg and Chapple proved on the last day, but Northants' lack of mental strength betrayed them.

Leicestershire captain Vince Wells opted to bat on for an extra half-hour on the final day at Grace Road, and surely lived to regret it when bad light in the last hour helped Somerset to survive for a draw at 268 for eight in their second innings. Devon Malcolm had bowled Leicestershire to within sight of victory on a belter of a pitch, but in the end Wells' indecisiveness, the light, and innings of 85 from Piran Holloway and 63 from Mark Lathwell combined to thwart them. Batsmen dominated the game, with Trevor Ward rediscovering his touch with 93 and 119 in his first championship appearance of the season, Dan Marsh also impressing with a forthright unbeaten 138, and then Peter Bowler exactly matching Marsh's score against one of his former counties as Somerset replied with 374 to Leicestershire's first-innings total of 387. Wells (86), Ben Smith (66) and Iain Sutcliffe (58) all profited in the home side's second innings of 390 for seven declared. But why did Wells not declare at 348 for six on the third evening?

Division Two

at Chester-le-Street
Nottinghamshire 371 (107 overs) (P Johnson 109, Usman Afzaal 89, SJ Harmison 5 for 100) and 219 for 5 dec. (GS Blewett 137*)
Durham 276 (83.1 overs) (PD Collingwood 91*) and 318 for 2 (ML Love 149*, JJB Lewis 112)
Durham won by eight wickets
Durham 17 pts, Nottinghamshire 7 pts

at Edgbaston
Gloucestershire 360 (132.4 overs) (MCJ Ball 68, THC Hancock 55, MW Alleyne 53) and 106 (VC Drakes 5 for 37)
Warwickshire 448 for 9 dec. (158 overs) (MJ Powell 133, DP Ostler 92, KJ Piper 55, IR Bell 52) and 22 for 0
Warwickshire won by ten wickets
Warwickshire 19 pts, Gloucestershire 6 pts

at Southgate
Middlesex 543 (160.1 overs) (OA Shah 203, BL Hutton 139)
Derbyshire 132 (63.4 overs) (PCR Tufnell 6 for 44) and (following on) 226 (NRC Dumelow 61)
Middlesex won by an innings and 185 runs
Middlesex 20 pts, Derbyshire 1 pt

at Southampton Rose Bowl
Sussex 500 for 7 dec. (166.3 overs) (MW Goodwin 195, RSC Martin-Jenkins 56*, RR Montgomerie 56) and 179 for 0 (RR Montgomerie 88*, MH Yardy 75*)
Hampshire 437 (157.5 overs) (GW White 141,

KENT CCC

Home Ground:
Canterbury
Address:
St Lawrence Ground,
Old Dover Road,
Canterbury,
Kent CT1 3NZ
Tel: 01227 456886
Fax: 01227 762168
Indoor school: 01227 473605
Email: kent@ecb.co.uk
Directions:
By rail: Canterbury East/West.
By road: AA roadsigns
Capacity: 10,000
Other grounds used: The Mote, Maidstone;
The Nevill, Tunbridge Wells
Year formed: 1870

Chief Executive: Paul Millman
First Team Coach: John Wright
Other posts: Head Groundsman: Mike Grantham;
Second Team Coach: Chris Stone; Marketing Manager: Adele
Aylwin
Captain: Matthew Fleming
County colours: Blue and white

HONOURS

COUNTY CHAMPIONSHIP
1906, 1909, 1910, 1913, 1970,
1977, 1978
SUNDAY LEAGUE
1972, 1973, 1976, 1995, 2001
BENSON & HEDGES CUP
1973, 1976, 1978
GILLETTE CUP/C&G TROPHY
1967, 1974

National Cricket League nickname:
KENT SPITFIRES

Website:
www.kentcountycricket.co.uk

AC Morris 65, NC Johnson 60)
Match drawn
Hampshire 8 pts, Sussex 10 pts

Durham were set 315 in 102 overs by
Nottinghamshire at Chester-le-Street, and romped to
victory with eight wickets and almost 17 overs to
spare. Martin Love's unbeaten 149 guided Durham
past the winning post, after the Queenslander had
been joined by skipper Jonathan Lewis (112) in a
match-winning partnership. Yet it had taken Paul
Collingwood's fighting 91 not out to keep the home
side in the game at all when they replied to a Notts
first-innings total of 371 that was based on a
buccaneering stand between Paul Johnson (109) and
Usman Afzaal (89). Thanks to Collingwood,
Durham reached 276. But no-one could have
foreseen the ease with which their second-innings
victory target was reached, even though Greg
Blewett batted serenely to 137 not out from 191
balls, before Notts declared second time around on
219 for five.

Warwickshire went second after destroying
Gloucestershire's second innings on the final day at
Edgbaston. Until then, a high-scoring draw seemed
likely, with Warwickshire declaring overnight on 448
for nine in reply to Gloucestershire's first-innings
total of 360. But Vasbert Drakes (five for 37) and
Mel Betts (three for 17) had other ideas and soon
the visitors had been shot out for just 106 despite a
blameless pitch. That left Warwickshire needing just
19 runs to wrap up victory by ten wickets. Martyn
Ball's 60-ball 68, with ten fours and a six, had been
the most entertaining aspect of Gloucestershire's
otherwise attritional first-innings effort, but Michael
Powell (133) led from the front when Warwickshire
replied, and there were other fine innings from
Dominic Ostler (92), Keith Piper (55) and Ian Bell,
whose 52 was a maiden first-class half-century in
only his second championship appearance.

Middlesex maintained their promising early-
season form by literally spinning Derbyshire into a
sticky web at Southgate. Phil Tufnell and Paul
Weekes were the spinners who did all the damage as
Derbyshire were bowled out for 132 and 226.
Tufnell, relishing conditions at his old club ground,
took six for 44 and four for 89 to prove yet again
that he remains the most accomplished slow bowler
in the land. The underrated Weekes, meanwhile,
picked up four for 37 and three for 70 with his off
breaks and only a forthright 61, containing ten
fours, from the promising Nathan Dumelow held up
Middlesex on the third afternoon after Derbyshire

had been forced to follow on. Middlesex, whose
first-innings 543 included a magnificent 203 from
Owais Shah and a maiden championship hundred
from Ben Hutton, won by an innings and 185 runs
to take maximum points. Shah, who hit 32 fours in
his 461-minute epic, took his season's first-class run
tally to 760 at an average of 69, while Hutton, who
had averaged less than 20 in his previous 24 first-
class matches, was understandably ecstatic at
reaching 139 with three sixes and 17 fours. The
second of those sixes, pulled off Richard
Illingworth, took him into three figures.

There was no such excitement at West End, where
Hampshire and Sussex played out one of the dullest
of draws. A career-best 195 by Murray Goodwin,
plus half-centuries from Richard Montgomerie and
Robin Martin-Jenkins, put Sussex in initial
command with a total of 500 for seven declared, but
then Giles White (141) led a Hampshire fightback
in which Neil Johnson (60) and Alex Morris (65)
also contributed. After Hampshire had been bowled
out for 437, all that remained on the final day was
for Sussex to saunter to 179 without loss against an
assorted attack.

ROUND SEVEN: 6–9 JUNE 2001

Division One

at Headingley
Kent 212 (73.2 overs) (ET Smith 84, RWT Key 58) and
250 (SP Kirby 7 for 50)
Yorkshire 413 (126.5 overs) (DS Lehmann 90,
MJ Wood 90, SA Richardson 69, RJ Blakey 59) and 53
for 1
Yorkshire won by nine wickets
Yorkshire 20 pts, Kent 4 pts

at Chelmsford
Glamorgan 370 (113.5 overs) (SD Thomas 138, A Dale
113, MC Ilott 5 for 85) and 367 for 4 (SP James 156,
MP Maynard 90)
Essex 193 (51.4 overs) (BJ Hyam 63) and (following on)
540 for 7 dec. (AP Grayson 189, DDJ Robinson 80,
SG Law 67, RC Irani 66)
Glamorgan won by six wickets
Glamorgan 19 pts, Essex 3 pts

at The Oval
Somerset 377 (130.1 overs) (MN Lathwell 99, PD
Bowler 73, RL Johnson 51) and 234 (IDK Salisbury
5 for 95)
Surrey 403 (114.1 overs) (MR Ramprakash 143,

MA Butcher 76, N Shahid 65) and 210 for 4
(MR Ramprakash 90)
Surrey won by six wickets
Surrey 20 pts, Somerset 7 pts

at Old Trafford
Leicestershire 202 (73.5 overs) (DL Maddy 57*) and
251 (M Muralitharan 6 for 74)
Lancashire 292 (83.2 overs) (NH Fairbrother 101,
WK Hegg 51) and 164 for 4 (JP Crawley 50)
Lancashire won by six wickets
Lancashire 17 pts, Leicestershire 6 pts

Steve Kirby, the 23-year-old fast bowler, provided
the performance of the week at Headingley – as well
as one of the most heart-warming of sports stories.
Kirby, a bustling redhead with a penchant for letting
batsmen know what he thinks of them, was brought
into Yorkshire's match against Kent as a special
replacement when Matthew Hoggard was suddenly
called up by England for the NatWest Series. He
ended up by taking seven for 50 in the Kent second
innings, with his dramatic first-class debut helping
the Tykes to an important victory. Hoggard, in fact,
had taken four for 48 in the Kent first innings of 212
on the opening day, before receiving his England
call. Kent had been 128 for two, with Ed Smith
making 84 and Rob Key 58, but their collapse
against Hoggard and Chris Silverwood (three for 38)
gave Yorkshire the chance to build a match-winning
lead. An opening partnership of 152 between the
uncapped duo Matthew Wood (90) and Scott
Richardson (69), his maiden first-class 50, launched
them towards an eventual total of 413, with Darren
Lehmann (90) and Richard Blakey (59) making sure
the fine start was not wasted. Then came Kirby. Two
wickets on the third afternoon were followed by a
magnificent five-wicket burst on the final morning
as Kent, 174 for five overnight, were dismissed for
250. That left Yorkshire needing just 50 to win and
Kirby, who had bowled with pace and genuine
hostility, said: 'I can't put into words what this
means. I thought my world had ended when
Leicestershire let me go in 1999.' Kirby, in fact, had
been troubled by a persistent back injury in his six
summers at Grace Road, but had worked hard to
remodel his action and, after seeing fellow ex-
Leicestershire player Richardson had been awarded
a contract at Yorkshire, wrote asking for a trial
himself. Two 2nd XI games brought him 12 wickets
and, armed with a two-year contract on the strength
of those performances, Kirby was ready and waiting
to take his chance. What a debut it was!

Glamorgan won a remarkable game at Chelmsford
to lighten their mood after a tough start to the
season, but their victory helped to deepen the gloom
that was starting to settle over Essex. The home
side, in fact, had fought back manfully from being
bowled out for just 193 in their first innings in reply
to Glamorgan's 370 – thus being condemned to the
follow-on. Paul Grayson reacted to the crisis by
playing one of the best innings of his long career, a
189 that contained 34 boundaries, and with Darren
Robinson (80), Stuart Law (67) and Ronnie Irani
(66) also getting stuck in, Essex were able to declare
midway through the final day's morning session at
540 for seven. Steve James and Matthew Maynard,
however, then took advantage of the flat pitch to
thrash 194 in 38 overs for the second wicket and set
up Glamorgan's win. James eventually made 156,
Maynard 90 and Adrian Dale a quick-fire, unbeaten
43 which guided the Welsh county to their 364-run
target for the loss of just four wickets. In the
Glamorgan first innings, by the way, Darren
Thomas' 138 was the highest score made by a
number eight in the county's championship history,
as well as being his maiden first-class hundred.
Thomas and Dale (113) put on 163 in 42 overs for
the seventh wicket to rally their side from 128 for
six, and then Thomas, who had celebrated wildly on
reaching his century, took four for 54 as the Essex
first innings crumbled around Barry Hyam's stout-
hearted 63.

After five draws, champions Surrey finally kick-
started their ambitions of a third successive
championship title by beating Somerset by six
wickets at The Oval. Mark Ramprakash was the star
of the show, following up his first-innings knock of
143 with a confident 99-ball 90 on the final day.
Somerset had looked fairly fireproof after totalling
377 in their first innings, thanks to a 140-run stand
for the fourth wicket between Peter Bowler and
Mark Lathwell, and then a combative 51 from
tailender Richard Johnson. Bowler made 73 and
Lathwell 99 before being caught at slip trying to cut
in the penultimate over of the opening day. Surrey,
however, led by Ramprakash and Mark Butcher's 76,
went quickly to 403, and by the end of the third day
Somerset were in some trouble at 190 for eight.
Their chief tormentor was leg-spinner Ian Salisbury,
who wrapped up the innings for 234 on the final
morning to finish with figures of five for 95.

Lancashire avenged their narrow, six-run defeat to
Leicestershire earlier in the season by romping home
by six wickets in this return fixture at Old Trafford.
Batting was never straightforward, but at least

Six second-innings wickets from Lancashire's Sri Lankan spin maestro, Muttiah Muralitharan, were enough to see off Leicestershire's challenge at Old Trafford.

championship cricket was played for the first time in the summer on the ground! It looked dodgy, however, on the opening day when yet more rain allowed only 40.1 overs to be bowled, but three wickets apiece for Peter Martin, Glen Chapple and Andy Flintoff sent back Leicestershire for 202 and, by the close of the second day, Lancashire were in charge at 191 for five. Neil Fairbrother, on 70 overnight, went on to 101 the next morning, and with Warren Hegg hitting 51, the home side earned themselves a useful 90-run first-innings lead. Leicestershire, 208 for six at the start of the last day, were then dismissed for 251 as Muttiah Muralitharan (six for 74) and Martin (four for 64) tightened the noose. Good innings from John Crawley and Flintoff made sure there were no hiccups for Lancashire on the way to their 162-run target.

Division Two

at Horsham
Sussex 137 (50.3 overs) and 372 (RR Montgomerie 112, MW Goodwin 109)
Worcestershire 183 (68.4 overs) (RJ Kirtley 5 for 60) and 293 (VS Solanki 89, MJG Davis 6 for 116)
Sussex won by 33 runs
Sussex 15 pts, Worcestershire 3 pts

at Trent Bridge
Gloucestershire 473 (129 overs) (CG Taylor 196, KJ Barnett 114) and 265 for 5 dec. (MGN Windows 73, DR Hewson 51)
Nottinghamshire 267 (76.2 overs) (Usman Afzaal 88) and 284 (KP Pietersen 72)
Gloucestershire won by 187 runs
Gloucestershire 20 pts, Nottinghamshire 5 pts

at Derby
Derbyshire 318 (108.3 overs) (KM Krikken 54, NC Phillips 5 for 64) and 267 (MJ Di Venuto 86, KM Krikken 75)
Durham 260 (91.2 overs) (ML Love 54) and 280 for 7 (N Peng 90)
Match drawn
Derbyshire 10 pts, Durham 9 pts

The great value of four-day championship cricket was underlined at lovely Horsham, where Sussex won a terrific match against Worcestershire by just 33 runs. Incredibly, the game went deep into the final day, despite 18 wickets tumbling on day one. But the umpires, John Holder and John Steele, were

LANCASHIRE CCC

Home Ground:
Old Trafford
Address:
Old Trafford, Manchester M16 0PX
Tel: 0161 282 4000 (switchboard)
       0161 282 4040 (ticket/membership office)
Fax: 0161 873 8353 (ticket office)
Indoor cricket centre: 0161 282 4039
Email: enquiries@lccc.co.uk
Directions:
By rail: Manchester Piccadilly or Victoria then
Metro link to Old Trafford (station alongside
ground).
By road: M63, Stretford slip road (junction 7) on to
A56; follow signs.
Capacity: 21,500
Other grounds used: Blackpool (Stanley Park);
Liverpool (Aigburth); Southport (Trafalgar Road);
Lytham (Church Road).
Year formed: 1864

Chairman: Jack Simmons MBE
Chief Executive: Jim Cumbes
Other posts: Cricket Secretary: David Edmundson; Head
Groundsman: Peter Marron; Sales & Marketing Manager:
Geoff Durbin
Captain: John Crawley
Vice-captain: Warren Hegg
County colours: Red, blue, green

HONOURS

COUNTY CHAMPIONSHIP
1881, 1897, 1927, 1928, 1930, 1934
JOINT CHAMPIONS
1878, 1882, 1889, 1950
NATIONAL LEAGUE
1999
BENSON & HEDGES CUP
1984, 1990, 1995, 1996
GILLETTE CUP/C&G TROPHY
1970, 1971, 1972, 1975, 1990,
1996, 1998

**National Cricket League
nickname:**
LANCASHIRE LIGHTNING

Website:
www.lccc.co.uk

Gloucestershire's Chris Taylor showed his promise with a career-best knock of 196 against Nottinghamshire.

polished off the innings to finish with five for 60 and Sussex's counter-attack then began with a 212-run opening partnership between Richard Montgomerie and Murray Goodwin. Both scored hundreds, Goodwin going for 109 before the close, but Montgomerie continuing on to 112 before being dismissed early on the third morning. An important unbeaten 43 by Mark Davis boosted Sussex to 372, and the off spinner then emerged as the main threat to Worcestershire in their chase for 327. At stumps on day three the visitors were 173 for three, but although Vikram Solanki went on to make 89, Sussex kept chipping away. In the end Davis took six for 116 and Worcestershire, despite Rhodes' determined 41 not out, came up short.

A tremendous, career-best 196 by Chris Taylor, off 297 balls and with 30 fours, proved the basis for Gloucestershire's much-needed 187-run victory against Nottinghamshire at Trent Bridge. Kim Barnett's 114, his 58th first-class ton, was another big factor – and the two centuries featured in a third-wicket stand of 111 as Gloucestershire totalled 473. Mike Cawdron then took four for 59 in a Gloucestershire attack missing Mike Smith, Jon Lewis, Ian Harvey and Ben Gannon as Notts were bowled out for 267, despite Usman Afzaal's 88. Mark Alleyne, the Gloucestershire captain, did not enforce the follow-on, however, and his decision to rest up his depleted attack paid off handsomely after the visitors had

quite right not to request an ECB pitch inspection after Sussex were skittled for 137 and Worcestershire had struggled to 133 for eight in reply. There had been some uneven bounce, but the way Steve Rhodes (46) guided Worcestershire to 183 the next morning showed there was nothing too wrong with the surface. James Kirtley finally scored 265 for five declared in their second innings, with Matt Windows top-scoring with 73. By the close of the third day, Notts were 61 for three and wickets continued to be shared around among the hard-working visiting bowlers as Notts were dismissed for 284. Kevin Pietersen's 71-ball 72 was the only real resistance as Gloucestershire claimed maximum points.

An attritional contest at Derby eventually ended in a draw, with Durham finishing on 280 for seven as they chased 328 to beat Derbyshire. Nicky Phillips picked up nine wickets in the match for Durham, but the home side ground out totals of 319 and 267 to keep ahead of the visitors throughout the four days. Karl Krikken's innings of 54 and 75 did much to keep Derbyshire ahead on points, but the best batting of a game played in sluggish conditions came on the last two days. First Michael Di Venuto hit 86 to inject some urgency into Derbyshire's second innings, and then 18-year-old Nicky Peng struck out courageously for the distant winning post with a fine knock of 90 that was only cut short by his run out.

ROUND EIGHT: 13–16 JUNE 2001

Division One

at Ilford
Surrey 198 (49.5 overs) (AJ Hollioake 77, RC Irani 5 for 58) and 306 (MR Ramprakash 61, GP Butcher 56, AJ Hollioake 52, RSG Anderson 5 for 79)
Essex 296 (106.3 overs) (RC Irani 119) and 153 for 2 (SG Law 66*, RS Clinton 58*)
Match drawn
Essex 9 pts, Surrey 7 pts

at Leicester
Northamptonshire 159 (48.4 overs) and 257 (RJ Warren 55, DL Maddy 5 for 67)
Leicestershire 185 (52.3 overs) (TR Ward 50) and 233 for 1 (TR Ward 160*, IJ Sutcliffe 55)
Leicestershire won by nine wickets
Leicestershire 15 pts, Northamptonshire 3 pts

at Maidstone
Kent 304 (102 overs) (RWT Key 97, ET Smith 74) and 358 (ET Smith 116, MK Walker 53)
Glamorgan 286 (97.3 overs) (MA Wallace 80*, SD Thomas 50) and 203 for 0 (JP Maher 123*, SP James 76*)
Match drawn
Kent 10 pts, Glamorgan 9 pts

at Bath
Somerset 553 for 5 dec. (143 overs) (M Burns 221, MN Lathwell 98*, J Cox 95, MJ Wood 71)
Yorkshire 589 for 5 (164 overs) (DS Lehmann 187*, MJ Wood 124, RJ Blakey 78*, SA Richardson 68, GM Fellows 63)
Match drawn
Somerset 10 pts, Yorkshire 10 pts

One of the great injustices, and inherent weaknesses, of the two-division system dealt Essex a cruel blow at Ilford. Rain, which prevented all but 15 overs on the final day, saved champions Surrey from a certain defeat – but, most pertinently, cost Essex a morale-boosting victory that might have changed the tone of their season. It is not beyond the bounds of possibility, moreover, that the points denied Essex by the weather here could, come September, be seen to be the difference between first division survival and the relegation which – in a two-tier structure – can bring devastating results in terms of player-retention and financial health. Indeed, should Essex go down as a result of this unfair draw, a sackful of protest letters from Chelmsford to Lord's might not be amiss.

As it was, Essex players and supporters alike had to drag themselves away from Valentine's Park bemoaning the frustration of seeing Surrey saved by the rain. The Essex captain, Ronnie Irani, was perhaps the most frustrated of all because, almost single-handedly, he had set up his side for a famous win by adding a dedicated 119 to the five for 58 with which he undermined the Surrey first innings. Seventeen wickets fell on the first day, with Surrey bowled out inside 50 overs for 198 and Essex limping to 145 for seven by the close in reply. But Irani, who was 55 not out overnight, then guided his side to 296 and a lead which Surrey had not quite wiped off in losing three second-innings wickets before the end of the second day. Mark Ramprakash, 49 overnight, could only reach 61 on the third morning before Mark Ilott, rediscovering his line and length after an unhappy time, won an lbw appeal and then celebrated with a madcap jig and several shrieks of sheer joy. Adam Hollioake, adding 52 to his first-innings 77, held up Essex a little in the company of Gary Butcher, who also batted well for the second time in the match. Ricky Anderson, however, was working his way methodically through the Surrey batting and his five for 79 made him the country's leading wicket-taker on 34. By the close of play on the third day, Essex were 65 for two and, with storm clouds gathering the next morning, Stuart Law and Richard Clinton, thumped 88 runs in the 15 overs that were possible. But, with Essex on 153 for two and just 56 away from a victory that would have taken them from third bottom in the table to fourth, and with Law on 66 and Clinton on 58, the weather and the system had their pitiless last laugh.

A violent electric storm came just too late to prevent Leicestershire from wrapping up a nine-wicket win over Northamptonshire midway through the third day of their match at Grace Road. An early finish had always looked likely after an amazing 20 wickets had fallen on the opening day – a clatter of timber, however, that did not bring censure from the ECB's pitch inspectorate due to a blameless surface. Swing did some of the damage on that first day, but poor batsmanship was more culpable with Leicestershire most disappointed to reply with only 185 to Northants' 159, despite Trevor Ward (50) taking them swiftly on to 92 for one. After more shoddy batting had condemned the visitors to 257 all out second time around, though, Ward decided to finish the job virtually on his own. Darren Maddy had claimed a career-best five for 67 with his medium-pacers on the second day, and Devon Malcolm had taken his match analysis to seven for 110 against the county he had left the previous winter, but opener Ward was the leading Leicestershire hero of this game. Continuing his dramatic upsurge in form, following a poor first season at the club in 2000, the former Kent batsman raced to an irresistible unbeaten 160, with a six and 28 fours, to sweep Leicestershire to their target. Iain Sutcliffe made 55 in an opening stand of 175, and then Ward's last 60 runs took him just 45 balls. What was the secret behind Ward's transformation? 'It's not that I am doing anything different, really. It's all about self-belief,' said Ward.

Rain interfered at Maidstone, too, with a potentially exciting final day being ruined when heavy showers prevented play from starting until 3.30pm. Glamorgan, who were resuming on 36 for no wicket as they chased 377 for victory, then showed what might have been by reaching 203 without loss in their second innings, with Jimmy Maher cruising to 123 not out and Steve James making an unbeaten 76 in support. The previous three days had seen some fascinating cricket, on yet another fine pitch at The Mote. It was the sort of contest, between bat and ball in top-quality conditions, that championship cricket should be all about. Kent were bowled out for 304 on the first day, with Darren Thomas taking four for 67 after

Robert Key (97) and Ed Smith (74) had added 121 for the second wicket. Glamorgan, seven for one overnight, slid further to 114 for six on the second morning before Mark Wallace rallied the lower-order with a battling 80 not out. Thomas weighed in with 50, but it was the 19-year-old Wallace who stole the headlines. Summoned as a late replacement for the ill Adrian Shaw, the former England Under 19 captain was withdrawn from a 2nd XI game at Abergavenny and only arrived in Maidstone midway through the first day. His efforts hauled Glamorgan up to 286, but Kent seemed to be taking command on day three when Smith (116) was batting with elegant ease. Matthew Walker and Matthew Fleming also made attractive contributions, but Thomas (four for 84) again chipped away and the home side were by no means overwhelming favourites – given the still-fine batting conditions – when the final day dawned. The rain, however, had the last word.

Yorkshire's decision to bowl first at Bath backfired badly when Somerset then ran up a massive 553 for five declared! But, in the end, a featherbed pitch and several weather interruptions condemned this match to a high-scoring draw, with Yorkshire replying with a mammoth 589 for five. Mike Burns made a career-best 221 in Somerset's total, and 20-year-old Devonian Matthew Wood impressed on debut with 71. But perhaps the best batting of the first two days came from Mark Lathwell, who continued his rehabilitation as a county batsman of class with a brilliant unbeaten 98 from 109 balls. Lathwell was denied a hundred only because his third six, to go with 12 fours, was propelled so far over the boundary ropes in the final over before lunch that it took too long to retrieve! Another over before the interval was therefore ruled out, and Somerset skipper Jamie Cox could not delay his declaration any longer. Rain, which began just before tea, cut short the second day and centuries from Yorkshire's Matthew Wood (124) and an unstoppable 187 not out from Darren Lehmann eventually took the visitors past the home score.

Division Two

at Arundel
Sussex 349 (104.5 overs) (CJ Adams 192, MJ Prior 66, B Zuiderent 58, G Welch 6 for 82)
Derbyshire 197 (74.5 overs) (SD Stubbings 67, MA Robinson 5 for 35) and (following on) 118 (RJ Kirtley 6 for 45)
Sussex won by an innings and 34 runs
Sussex 18 pts, Derbyshire 3 pts

LEICESTERSHIRE CCC

Home Ground:
Grace Road, Leicester
Address:
County Ground,
Grace Road,
Leicester LE2 8AD
Tel: 0116 283 2128
Fax: 0116 244 0363
Email: leicestershirecc@ukonline.co.uk
Directions:
By road: Follow signs from city centre, or from southern
ring road from M1 or A6.
Capacity: 5,500
Other grounds used: None
Year formed: 1879

Manager: Jack Birkenshaw
General Manager/Secretary: James Whitaker
Other posts: County coaches: Russell Cobb, John
Smith, Phil Whiticase, Lloyd Tennant; Administrative
Secretary: Kevin Hill
Captain: Vince Wells
Vice-captain: Ben Smith
County colours: Dark green and scarlet

HONOURS

COUNTY CHAMPIONSHIP
1975, 1996, 1998
SUNDAY LEAGUE
1974, 1977
BENSON & HEDGES CUP
1972, 1975, 1985

**National Cricket League
nickname:**
LEICESTERSHIRE FOXES

Website:
www.leicestershireccc.com

at Gloucester
Gloucestershire 417 (117.4 overs) (MW Alleyne 132, MCJ Ball 60*, CG Taylor 54, JN Snape 53, SJE Brown 6 for 70) and 159 for 4 dec. (MGN Windows 60*)
Durham 287 (84.2 overs) (ML Love 70) and 116 for 2 (ML Love 52*)
Match drawn
Gloucestershire 12 pts, Durham 9 pts

at Southgate
Hampshire 404 (135.1 overs) (AN Aymes 69, RA Smith 64, SD Udal 59, DA Kenway 58, NC Johnson 54, PN Weekes 5 for 90) and 61 for 0
Middlesex 380 (133.5 overs)
(RMS Weston 135*, DC Nash 77)
Match drawn – no play was possible on the fourth day
Middlesex 11 pts, Hampshire 10 pts

at Worcester
Warwickshire 277 (98.3 overs)
(KJ Piper 92*)
Worcestershire 347 for 7 (76.1 overs)
(GA Hick 124, WPC Weston 74)
Match drawn
Worcestershire 10 pts, Warwickshire 7.75 pts – no play was possible on the fourth day
Warwickshire were fined .25 pt for their slow over-rate

Sussex propelled themselves into the promotion race with an innings-and-34-run beating of hapless Derbyshire at Arundel. The home county's first-innings total of 349 was based on a sumptuous innings of 192 by Chris Adams – his best for Sussex and his first hundred against the county he left so acrimoniously in 1997. Bas Zuiderent's 58 and a maiden first-class 50 by the promising Matt Prior (66) helped Sussex into a position of strength and, despite initially reaching 82 for no wicket, Derbyshire were soon collapsing in familiar fashion to 197 all out. Following on, they folded for just 118 on the third morning with James

A commanding innings of 192 was Chris Adams' first century against his former county, Derbyshire.

Kirtley (six for 45) the chief executioner. Mark Robinson, with five for 35, had fulfilled that role the previous day.

Bad weather affected the other three games in the division, which all went into the soggy final day. Durham were perhaps let off the hook against Gloucestershire at Gloucester, reaching 116 for two in their second innings after play only began on the last day at 3.30pm. Earlier in the match, Gloucestershire's first-innings 417 had won them a sizeable lead when Durham were bowled out in reply for 287, with James Averis and Martyn Ball

sharing eight wickets. Gloucestershire had been rallied from 28 for three on the first morning by skipper Mark Alleyne, whose 132 contained 22 boundaries, and by chirpy half-centuries from Chris Taylor, Jeremy Snape and Ball. Simon Brown took six for 70, and then both Michael Gough and Martin Love hit 70s, but Durham were already up against it before Matt Windows' unbeaten 60 took Gloucestershire to 159 for four, and an overall lead of 289, by the close of the third day.

At Southgate a dull draw between Middlesex and Hampshire, again rain-affected, was illuminated by Robin Weston's unbeaten 135 – his first century for Middlesex since joining the county from Derbyshire the previous year. Weston would not have been playing but for Owais Shah's one-day international call-up by England, but he seized his chance magnificently and added 164 for the sixth wicket with David Nash (77) to help Middlesex recover from the depths of 117 for five in reply to a Hampshire total of 404 which included no less than five individual half-centuries, but no innings higher than Adrian Aymes' 69. Paul Weekes could also remember the match with some affection, as he took his first five-wicket haul since 1996, but more rain finally forced a lunchtime abandonment on the last day.

There was no play at all on the scheduled final day at Worcester, the sixth full day out of 12 so far lost to the elements at New Road. Warwickshire, having been 141 for eight, rallied to 277 in their first innings as Keith Piper hit 92 not out from number nine. Graeme Hick, however, then put a bad trot behind him to power to 124, and with Philip Weston scoring 74, Worcestershire had reached 347 for seven when more rain proved terminal. Hick, almost startlingly at county level, had made just 56 runs from his previous seven innings.

ROUND NINE: 19–23 JUNE 2001

Division One

at Old Trafford
Lancashire 431 (150.4 overs) (MA Atherton 160, WK Hegg 133) and 53 for 1
Essex 226 (113.5 overs) (SG Law 116*, M Muralitharan 6 for 53) and (following on) 257 (SG Law 123*)
Lancashire won by nine wickets
Lancashire 19 pts, Essex 3 pts

at Canterbury
Leicestershire 612 for 8 dec. (162 overs) (VJ Wells 138,

BF Smith 110, DJ Marsh 72, IJ Sutcliffe 64, PAJ DeFreitas 59*, Aftab Habib 55, ND Burns 51)
Kent 210 (61.2 overs) and (following on) 253 (DP Fulton 107, VJ Wells 5 for 36)
Leicestershire won by an innings and 149 runs
Leicestershire 20 pts, Kent 3 pts

at Northampton
Somerset 299 (95.3 overs) (ID Blackwell 103, KP Dutch 84) and 430 for 8 (ID Blackwell 122, MJ Wood 90, PD Bowler 60)
Northamptonshire 567 (162.1 overs) (MB Loye 197, D Ripley 95, AL Penberthy 80, RJ Warren 64, RL Johnson 5 for 127)
Match drawn
Northamptonshire 12 pts, Somerset 8 pts

Lancashire overcame heroic resistance from Stuart Law to see off Essex by nine wickets at Old Trafford. Law, perhaps the unluckiest cricketer of his generation with just one Australian Test cap to his name, became the first man since Hugh Morris in 1995 to score two undefeated hundreds in the same match. Law's unbeaten 116 held together the Essex first innings of 226, but it was not enough to prevent the follow-on after Lancashire had built a total of 431 on the back of Mike Atherton (160) and Warren Hegg (133), who added 143 for the sixth wicket. Essex's prolific Aussie even had few problems with the wiles of Muttiah Muralitharan, the Sri Lankan spinner taking six for 53 from 48 overs. And, when Essex followed on, Law again stood firm while Muralitharan whirled away to pick up four for 70. There were three sixes and 14 fours, in all, in Law's unbeaten 123, and his defiance was glorious. Unfortunately, after Essex had been bowled out for 257, Lancashire needed only 53 for victory and Atherton, whose seven-hour first-innings effort had been his 29th first-class hundred for Lancashire and 54th overall, guided them across the winning line.

Leicestershire's innings-and-149-run thrashing of Kent, at Canterbury, was a personal triumph for Vince Wells, their captain. Wells, 35, had spent four seasons with his native Kent from 1988–91 before being released, and now made all Kentish supporters wish he had not left by hitting 138 from 122 balls, with three sixes and 21 fours, before finishing off the home side by taking five for 36 as victory was wrapped up on the third day. Leicestershire's mammoth first-innings 612 for eight declared, was built first on unspectacular early batting and then dramatic, Wells-inspired

Devon Malcolm's pace and DeFreitas' canny experience seemed to be able to extract more life from a still-docile surface, and the veteran pair shared eight wickets as Kent's first innings folded for 210. Following on, the home side were then dismissed again for 253, with Wells doing most of the damage, but at least David Fulton gave Kent's supporters something to cheer with a stubborn and often attractive 107.

Somerset hung on gamely on the fourth day to force a draw with Northamptonshire at Wantage Road. The main thorn in Northants' side was Ian Blackwell, the combative all-rounder, who scored impressive hundreds in both Somerset's innings. On the first day, Blackwell's 103 and Keith Dutch's equally spirited 84 resuscitated Somerset from the despair of 35 for six, with the visitors eventually reaching 299. But this total still looked inadequate as Mal Loye, with a magnificent 197, led Northants to 567. Loye's seven-hour innings contained three sixes and 25 fours, and he received good early support from Russell Warren (64). Later in the innings, David Ripley (95) and Tony Penberthy (80) joined in a stand of 161 and Somerset looked down and out when they ended day three at 130 for four in their second innings. Blackwell, however, dug in to score 122 and with Matthew Wood (90) pushed Somerset up to 430 for eight and safety.

acceleration on the second day. It was the second highest score made against Kent at the St Lawrence Ground since 1847 – although Martin Saggers did especially well to emerge from the carnage with four for 94 from 34 overs. Ben Smith and a watchful Iain Sutcliffe (64) added 190 on the opening day, after another former Kent player, Trevor Ward, had departed to the first ball of the match, and Dan Marsh's 72 was initially responsible for improving a sluggish scoring rate. Then came Wells, Aftab Habib (55), Neil Burns (51) and Phil DeFreitas (59 not out), and by the end of the second day a weary Kent were already wobbling at 155 for seven in reply.

Division Two

at Derby
Gloucestershire 560 for 8 dec. (163 overs) (MW Alleyne 136, JN Snape 119, CG Taylor 83, KJ Barnett 73, RC Russell 53) and 177 for 0 dec. (DR Hewson 100*, KJ Barnett 72*)

MIDDLESEX CCC

Home Ground:
Lord's Cricket Ground
Address:
Lord's Cricket Ground,
St John's Wood, London NW8 8QN
Tel: 020 7289 1300
Fax: 020 7289 5831
Email: enquiries.middx@ecb.co.uk
Directions:
By underground: St John's Wood on Jubilee Line
(five minutes' walk).
By bus: 13, 82, 113 stop along east side of
ground; 139 at south-west corner; 274 at top
of Regent's Park
Capacity: 28,000
Other grounds used: Southgate; Richmond
Year formed: 1864

Chairman: Phil Edmonds
Secretary: Vinny Codrington
Head Coach: John Emburey
Assistant Coach: Jason Pooley
Captain: Angus Fraser
County colours: Navy

HONOURS

COUNTY CHAMPIONSHIP
1903, 1920, 1921, 1947,
1949 (JOINT), 1976, 1977 (JOINT),
1980, 1982, 1985, 1990, 1993
SUNDAY LEAGUE
1992
BENSON & HEDGES CUP
1983, 1986
GILLETTE CUP/C&G TROPHY
1977, 1980, 1984, 1988

National Cricket League nickname:
MIDDLESEX CRUSADERS

Website:
www.middlesexccc.co.uk

Derbyshire 432 for 5 dec. (156 overs) (CWG Bassano 186* – on first-class debut – SD Stubbings 126) and 297 for 9 (CWG Bassano 106, MP Dowman 50)
Match drawn
Derbyshire 9 pts, Gloucestershire 10 pts

at Southampton Rose Bowl
Hampshire 246 (70.3 overs) (AC Morris 59, DR Law 6 for 53) and 230 (NC Johnson 86*)
Durham 266 (82.2 overs) (ML Love 78, JJB Lewis 62) and 163
Hampshire won by 47 runs
Hampshire 16 pts, Durham 5 pts

at Trent Bridge
Sussex 354 (118.4 overs) (MW Goodwin 115, B Zuiderent 73, MH Yardy 50, AJ Harris 6 for 98) and 372 for 0 dec. (MW Goodwin 203*, RR Montgomerie 160*)
Nottinghamshire 280 (86 overs) (JE Morris 60) and 285 (DJ Bicknell 123, CMW Read 78)
Sussex won by 161 runs
Sussex 19 pts, Nottinghamshire 5 pts

at Edgbaston
Middlesex 273 (89.3 overs) (SP Fleming 67, MM Betts 5 for 88 and 359 for 6 dec. (RMS Weston 100, SP Fleming 92, PN Weekes 52)
Warwickshire 251 (85.4 overs) (DL Hemp 105) and 252 (MA Wagh 77, DL Hemp 61)
Middlesex won by 129 runs
Middlesex 17 pts, Warwickshire 5 pts

A fine game of cricket at Derby was particularly memorable for a remarkable debut performance from the home county's Chris Bassano. A 25-year-old, South African-born graduate of Tasmania University, who holds a British passport through his mother, Bassano carved his own little niche in the game's history by becoming the first player to score two hundreds on his debut championship appearance. His first-innings 186 not out, an eight-and-three-quarter hour epic which included two sixes and 27 fours, was also the highest score by a Derbyshire batsman on debut, and his 202-run stand with Steve Stubbings (126) for the second wicket was the first three-figure partnership recorded for Derbyshire in any competition this season. Their efforts enabled Derbyshire to declare on 432 for five in reply to Gloucestershire's huge first-innings total of 560 for eight declared, in which Mark Alleyne's 136 and Jeremy Snape's 119, his maiden first-class century in his 118th innings spread over ten years,

were the highlights. Declaration bowling on the final morning then allowed Gloucestershire to race to 177 for no wicket declared, in which Dominic Hewson made a rather unsatisfactory maiden first-class ton. Derbyshire, set 306 from 69 overs to win, were again inspired by Bassano. His 106, and Mathew Dowman's 50, took the home side to the brink of an unlikely win but, in the end, they were forced to hang on for the draw at 297 for nine.

Hampshire won a closely-fought encounter with Durham at West End by just 47 runs, bowling out their visitors for 163 on the third day. At one stage Durham were 120 for four, with Nicky Peng making 49, but Chris Tremlett took four for 34 as Hampshire turned the screw. Hampshire also had to thank Adrian Aymes (41) and Alex Morris (59 from 72 balls) for putting on 92 for the ninth wicket in their first-innings total of 246, and Neil Johnson for an invaluable unbeaten 86 in their second innings of 230. Durham, who totalled 266 in their first innings, with Jon Lewis (62) and Martin Love (78) impressing, had looked favourites to win before Johnson rode some luck to play his decisive knock.

Nottinghamshire, looking for a good performance ahead of their important Benson and Hedges Cup semi-final against Surrey, instead put in an uninspired display at Trent Bridge as they were beaten by Sussex by 161 runs. Sussex took control on the first day, having been put in to bat by Darren Bicknell, and reached 315 for six by the close with Murray Goodwin (115) and Bas Zuiderent (73) leading the way. Andy Harris knocked over the tail to finish with six for 98 the next morning, as Sussex were dismissed for 354, but Notts could not force themselves back into the match and needed a ninth-wicket stand of 65 in just ten overs between John Morris (60) and Greg Smith (44 not out from 34 balls) to get to 280 all out. The third day was all about Sussex openers Goodwin and Richard Montgomerie, who put the home bowlers to the sword as they clocked up 372 for no wicket declared in 97 overs. Goodwin finished 203 not out, and Montgomerie was unbeaten on 160. By the close, Notts were 16 for one, with the unfortunate Guy Welton continuing his wretched season as he was run out by a deflected drive as he backed up at the non-striker's end. Notts skipper Bicknell did his best to lead the resistance on the final day with 123, but only had support from Chris Read (78) in a seventh-wicket stand of 141. In the end Notts were bowled out for 285 with almost an hour to spare.

Middlesex were well worth their 129-run win against Warwickshire at Edgbaston, despite being

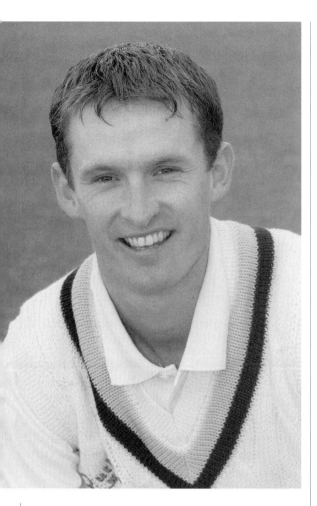

Derbyshire's Chris Bassano became the first player to score two hundreds on his first-class debut, 186 not out and 106 against Gloucestershire.

bowled out for 273 on the opening day with Mel Betts taking five for 88. By the close, Warwickshire were 33 for three in reply, thanks to three strikes with the new ball by Tim Bloomfield, and from that moment on Middlesex remained in command. A fine innings of 105 by David Hemp could not prevent the visitors from gaining a 22-run first-innings lead, and this small advantage was built on significantly by Robin Weston and Stephen Fleming, whose second-wicket partnership of 181 set Middlesex up for a third-day total of 359 for six declared. Warwickshire entered the last day on 33 for one, and although Mark Wagh (77) and Hemp (61) offered some defiance, Phil Tufnell's four for 57 enabled Middlesex to dismiss their opponents again for 252 with one session still remaining.

Round Ten: 29 June–2 July 2001

Division One

at Headingley
Yorkshire 500 (133.2 overs) (MJ Lumb 122, DS Lehmann 104, MJ Wood 102, DE Malcolm 5 for 123)
Leicestershire 174 (50.4 overs) (SP Kirby 6 for 46) and (following on) 99 (SP Kirby 6 for 26)
Yorkshire won by an innings and 227 runs
Yorkshire 20 pts, Leicestershire 2 pts

at The Oval
Surrey 248 (99.4 overs) (MR Ramprakash 59, MP Bicknell 50, M Muralitharan 5 for 81) and 320 for 9 dec. (MA Butcher 86, AJ Hollioake 73)
Lancashire 276 (95.3 overs) (WK Hegg 74*, JJ Haynes 57, Saqlain Mushtaq 6 for 89) and 170 for 2 (JP Crawley 84*)
Match drawn
Surrey 8 pts, Lancashire 8 pts

at Cardiff
Glamorgan 556 for 7 dec. (155.2 overs) (JP Maher 150, RDB Croft 93, MJ Powell 86, MP Maynard 69, SP James 62, A Dale 54)
Northamptonshire 344 (104.3 overs) (ME Hussey 159, MB Loye 73, RDB Croft 5 for 95) and (following on) 349 for 7 dec. (RJ Warren 77, ME Hussey 68, AS Rollins 65, AL Penberthy 60, RDB Croft 5 for 96)
Match drawn
Glamorgan 12 pts, Northamptonshire 8 pts

Steve Kirby acknowledged the huge debt of gratitude he owes Leicestershire's cricket manager Jack Birkenshaw after his six for 46 and six for 26 had destroyed his former county at Headingley. It was some way of saying thanks. Fast bowler Kirby had remodelled his action in his last months at Grace Road before leaving with Birkenshaw's blessing to try to kick-start his injury-plagued career in pastures new. 'I owe Jack a lot,' said Kirby, after taking his first-class wicket haul to 20 from three matches at an average of just 10.05. 'It is a roller coaster ride for me at the moment and I just don't want to get off!' Kirby almost single-handedly demolished Leicestershire, who were bowled out for 174 and 99, after Darren Lehmann, Matthew Wood and Michael Lumb had all plundered centuries in Yorkshire's first-innings total of 500. Lehmann's 104 included a square cut which killed a pigeon, Wood made 102 and Lumb 122. The last time three Yorkshire batsmen reached three figures in the same innings was in 1975 – the threesome then being Geoff Boycott, John Hampshire and Richard Lumb, Michael's father.

Surrey and Lancashire, champions and runners-up in 2000, fought out a cagey draw at The Oval – a result which suited Yorkshire! A classy 59 from Mark Ramprakash, and 50 from Martin Bicknell, helped Surrey to 248 on the opening day. Muttiah

Muralitharan took five for 81 from 39.4 overs, but Saqlain Mushtaq then went ahead on points in the battle of the spin maestros by replying with six for 89. Lancashire, however, reached 276 in their first innings, Warren Hegg compiling a determined 74 not out, and by the close of the third day Surrey had needed to scrap hard to reach 285 for eight in their second innings. Mark Butcher's 86 and Adam Hollioake's 73 enabled the Surrey captain to declare on 320 for nine midway through the final morning, but John Crawley showed no inclination to risk a run-chase and the Lancashire captain finished on 84 not out as his side batted out time to end the day on 170 for two from 71 overs.

At Cardiff, a marathon effort by off spinner Robert Croft ultimately failed to earn Glamorgan anything more than a high-scoring draw with Northants. Croft took five for 96 from 57 overs after Northants were forced to follow on, and finished with match figures of ten for 191 off 90.3 overs – all that after hitting 93 in an intimidating Glamorgan first-innings total of 556 for seven declared. Jimmy Maher's 150 was the base on which the imposing total was built, and not even a fine 159 by his fellow Australian Mike Hussey could prevent Croft from whittling out Northants for 344. Hussey (68), Adrian Rollins (65), Russell Warren (77) and Tony Penberthy (60), however, all combined to thwart Croft second time around as the visitors clawed their way to 349 for seven.

Yorkshire's Steve Kirby provided the comeback story of the season by taking 47 wickets at an average of 20.85.

NORTHAMPTONSHIRE CCC

Home Ground:
Northampton
Address:
The County Ground, Wantage Road,
Northampton NN1 4TJ
Tel: 01604 514455
Fax: 01604 514488
Email: post@nccc.co.uk (general enquiries) or
commercial@nccc.co.uk (commercial enquiries)
Directions:
By rail: Castle Station, three miles.
By road: M1 to J15, A508 and follow RAC signs.
RAC signs from all other areas. Parking on ground when
space permits otherwise ample local street parking.
By coach: regular service from Greyfriars coach station.
Capacity: 4,250
Other grounds used: Campbell Park, Milton Keynes.
Year formed: 1878

Chairman: Lynn Wilson
Chief Executive: Stephen Coverdale
Director of Excellence: David Capel
Director of Cricket: Bob Carter
Captain: David Ripley
Coaching contact: Ian Lucas 01604 632917
County colours: Claret and gold

HONOURS

BENSON & HEDGES CUP
1980
GILLETTE CUP/C&G TROPHY
1976, 1992

National Cricket League nickname:
STEELBACKS

Website:
www.nccc.co.uk

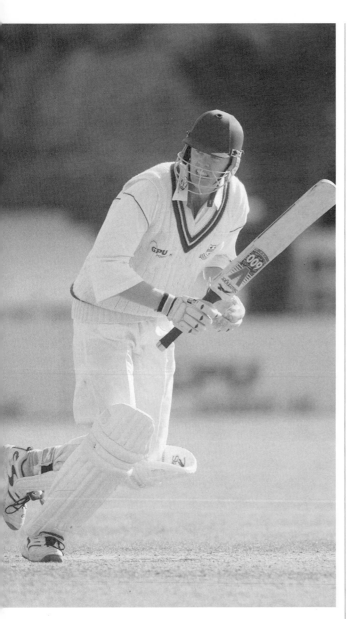

A fine innings of 192 by Worcestershire's Philip Weston was ultimately in vain as Nottinghamshire smashed 461 in the fourth innings to claim a dramatic victory.

Division Two

at Worcester
Worcestershire 248 (55.4 overs) (GA Hick 123, RJ Logan 5 for 96) and 369 (WPC Weston 192)
Nottinghamshire 160 (42.4 overs) (KP Pietersen 103*, AJ Bichel 5 for 45) and 461 for 3 (GS Blewett 134*, DJ Bicknell 104, JE Morris 94, Usman Afzaal 88)

Nottinghamshire won by seven wickets
Nottinghamshire 15 pts, Worcestershire 4 pts

at Southampton Rose Bowl
Hampshire 383 (114.1 overs) (SD Udal 81, AN Aymes 73, NC Johnson 59, TA Munton 5 for 85) and 6 for 0
Derbyshire 140 (48.3 overs) and (following on) 244 (RJ Bailey 98, AD Mascarenhas 6 for 60)
Hampshire won by ten wickets
Hampshire 19 pts, Derbyshire 3 pts

at Chester-le-Street
Warwickshire 310 (117.3 overs) (DP Ostler 121, NV Knight 75) and 324 for 6 dec. (MA Wagh 112, DP Ostler 86, DR Brown 67*)
Durham 231 (97.2 overs) (PD Collingwood 69, ML Love 66) and 284 for 8 (N Peng 70, MP Speight 67*)
Match drawn
Durham 8 pts, Warwickshire 10 pts

at Lord's
Sussex 323 (106.1 overs) (MW Goodwin 69, CJ Adams 59) and 315 for 6 dec. (RR Montgomerie 116, MW Goodwin 61, B Zuiderent 56)
Middlesex 326 (113.2 overs) (RMS Weston 83, DC Nash 50) and 135 for 4
Match drawn
Middlesex 10 pts, Sussex 10 pts

A quite remarkable victory by Nottinghamshire, at Worcester, provided the highlight of this round of games. Early on the fourth day, Notts completed their first win of the season when they reached 461 for three in their second innings with Greg Blewett unbeaten on 134. Darren Bicknell, with 104, and John Morris, with a belligerent 94 off 106 balls, had made the win possible with a magnificent opening stand, but Usman Afzaal's 88 was also invaluable as Notts built the biggest fourth-innings winning total in their history. It beat their previous best of 419 for six, made against Leicestershire in 1926, and was only 41 runs short of Middlesex's championship record. Yet what made Notts' achievement all the more memorable was that 20 – yes, 20 – wickets fell on the opening day alone before the batsmen of both sides began to master a pale-coloured surface of some variable bounce. Staggeringly, however, that dramatic first day also contained two individual hundreds, of cavalier brilliance, by Graeme Hick and Kevin Pietersen. Hick's 123 from 151 balls, with two sixes and 20 fours, enabled Worcestershire to reach 248 – Richard Logan capturing five for 96 – but then Pietersen responded with a 92-ball 103 not out. Notts were actually in desperate straits at 51 for seven before Pietersen, who also hit 20 boundaries, was joined by David Lucas in an eighth-wicket stand of 92. An eventual total of 160, however, still looked inadequate – especially when Philip Weston then put together a superb 192 to guide the home side to 369 in their second innings. By the third evening, though, Notts were 367 for two, and Worcestershire's shell-shocked bowlers were powerless again on the fourth morning as Blewett and Paul Johnson took Notts to their historic seven-wicket win.

Hampshire had a much more straightforward victory over struggling Derbyshire at West End. The visitors, tumbled out for just 140 in reply to Hampshire's first-innings 383, with Alan Mullally and Neil Johnson sharing eight wickets, could make only 244 second time around, despite Rob Bailey's defiant 98. Dimitri Mascarenhas picked up six for 60, but it was an eighth-wicket stand of 130 between Shaun Udal (81) and Adrian Aymes (73) that was perhaps the most important contribution in Hampshire's ten-wicket win.

Tailender Nicky Phillips survived an hour in the company of Martin Speight, who finished on 67 not out, as Durham earned a draw against Warwickshire at Chester-le-Street. The home side ended up at 284 for eight in their second innings, with Nicky Peng earlier having made 70 and featuring in a stand of 107 with Speight, who resisted in all for just short of four hours. Dominic Ostler's 121 had initially put Warwickshire in control, and Mel Betts had then taken four for 78 against his old county as Durham slipped to 231 all out in reply to the visitors' first-innings total of 310. Ostler again dominated the Durham bowlers, hitting 86 as Warwickshire ran up 324 for six declared in their second innings – Mark Wagh impressing with 112 and Dougie Brown weighing in with an unbeaten 67 from 64 balls.

A draw of some tediousness at Lord's was, however, enough for Middlesex to confirm their status as second division leaders. Sussex's first innings of 323 was entertaining only when Chris Adams was compiling 59, and Middlesex's reply of 326 was a workmanlike effort based on 83 from Robin Weston. Murray Goodwin then added a solid 61 to his equally well-crafted first-innings score of 69 and Bas Zuiderent contributed a well-made 56, but the Sussex second innings of 315 for six declared was built around a six-hour 116 from Richard Montgomerie. There was time, thereafter, only for Middlesex to reach 135 for four in their own second innings before the contest was laid to rest.

Round Eleven: 4–8 July 2001

Division One

at Leicester
Leicestershire 165 (43 overs) and 472 for 8 dec. (BF Smith 179, DJ Marsh 82, ND Burns 66*, Saqlain Mushtaq 5 for 172)
Surrey 102 (38 overs) (DE Malcolm 8 for 63) and 478 for 9 (AJ Tudor 86, MP Bicknell 85*, AJ Hollioake 64, BC Hollioake 59)
Match drawn
Leicestershire 7 pts, Surrey 7pts

at Canterbury
Kent 348 (115.4 overs) (PA Nixon 82, DP Fulton 65, MJ Saggers 61*) and 240 (RWT Key 83, ET Smith 59, M Muralitharan 6 for 70)
Lancashire 214 (53.2 overs) (MA Ealham 6 for 64) and 106 (BJ Trott 5 for 43)
Kent won by 268 runs
Kent 17pts, Lancashire 4 pts
Kent were deducted 1 pt for their slow over-rate

at Taunton
Somerset 415 (129.1 overs) (KP Dutch 118, RJ Turner 115*)
Essex 130 (42.2 overs) and 225 (RC Irani 57)
Somerset won by an innings and 60 runs
Somerset 20 pts, Essex 3 pts

at Northampton
Northamptonshire 253 (88.5 overs) (ME Hussey 64, MB Loye 50) and 298 (ME Hussey 122, GP Swann 55)
Yorkshire 309 (111 overs) (D Byas 110*, MJ Wood 55) and 10 for 1
Match drawn
Northamptonshire 9 pts, Yorkshire 10 pts

A ridiculously cautious approach by skipper Vince Wells cost Leicestershire the prized scalp of champions Surrey in a truly remarkable match at Grace Road. Surrey, seemingly set for a heavy defeat at 28 for one in their second innings on what was only the second evening of the game, then managed to bat out for a draw while compiling the highest fourth-innings score in their 156-year history! And, in finishing on 478 for nine, with Martin Bicknell unbeaten on 85 and Ian Salisbury not out on 30, despite a foot injury, Surrey were also only 57 runs short of what would have been one of the most amazing victories ever witnessed. Yet, for all Surrey's rearguard heroics, in which Alex Tudor (86) and

NOTTINGHAMSHIRE CCC

Home Ground:
Trent Bridge
Address:
Trent Bridge,
Nottingham NG2 6AG
Tel: 0115 982 3000
Fax: 0115 945 5730
Ticket line: 0870 168 88 88
Email: administration.notts@ecb.co.uk
Alternative website: www.nottsccc.co.uk
Directions:
By road: Follow signs from Ring Road, towards
city centre.
Capacity: 14,500 (16,000 during Test Matches/ODIs)
Other grounds used: Worksop
Year formed: 1841

Chief Executive: David Collier
Cricket Manager: Clive Rice
Other posts: Head Groundsman: Steve Birks Sales;
Marketing Manager: Lisa Pursehouse
Captain: Jason Gallian
County colours: Green and gold

HONOURS

COUNTY CHAMPIONSHIP
1907, 1929, 1981, 1987
SUNDAY LEAGUE
1991
BENSON & HEDGES CUP
1989
GILLETTE CUP/C&G TROPHY
1987

National Cricket League nickname:
NOTTS OUTLAWS

Website:
www.trentbridge.co.uk

NOTTS OUTLAWS

SOMERSET CCC

Home Ground:
Taunton
Address:
The Clerical Medical County Ground,
Taunton,
Somerset TA1 1JT
Tel: 01823 272 946
Fax: 01823 332 395
Centre of Cricketing Excellence: 01823 352266
Email: somerset@ecb.co.uk
Directions:
By road: M5 junction 25. Follow A358 to town centre.
Signposted from there.
Other grounds used: Bath
Year formed: 1875

Chief Executive: Peter Anderson
First XI Coach: Kevin Shine
Captain: Jamie Cox
Other posts: Head Groundsman: Phil Frost; Second
XI Coach: Julian Wyatt
County colours: Black, white and maroon

HONOURS

SUNDAY LEAGUE
1979
BENSON & HEDGES CUP
1981, 1982
GILLETTE CUP/C&G TROPHY
1979, 1983, 2001

National Cricket League nickname:
SOMERSET SABRES

unofficial **Website:**
www.somersetcountycricket.co.uk

Leicestershire's Ben Smith scored 179 against Surrey in an absorbing draw at Grace Road.

both Hollioake brothers also played major parts, Leicestershire only had themselves to blame. Time and again, in the Surrey second innings, edges flew through gaps in pathetically defensive fields – while, on the third evening, Wells opted not to take the extra half-hour despite Surrey being 281 for six. The only gripe Leicestershire could make at the end of it

all was that rain had taken 28 overs out of the final day, and had also interrupted the third day – although Surrey might also have wanted that extra time in the end! Incredibly, too, for such an ultimately high-scoring contest, the match had begun with 20 wickets falling on the opening day. On a blameless pitch, and under blue skies, Leicestershire were dismissed for 165, with Bicknell and Saqlain Mushtaq sharing eight wickets, but then fought back through the heroic Devon Malcolm to skittle Surrey for just 102. Malcolm, bowling 18 overs in two spells with just a short rest in between, showed astonishing stamina and sustained hostility for a 38 year old and was rewarded with his championship-best figures of eight for 63. Leicestershire, on 79 without loss by the close of that bizarre first day, sped on to 472 for eight declared on day two. Ben Smith made 179, adding 167 for the third wicket with Dan Marsh (82), while Saqlain wheeled away unchanged from 11am to the 6pm declaration – a continuous 47.2-over spell – to take five for 172.

Matthew Fleming was a frustrated man at the end of Kent's meeting with Lancashire at Canterbury, too, in spite of his side's three-day triumph by 268 runs. Fleming, the Kent captain, was fuming at the regulation which resulted in a point being docked for a slow over-rate. 'It's farcical,' said Fleming, 'How can you be penalized for slow play when you win with more than a day in hand? Sometimes the law's an ass.' Kent's win was, however, a perfect send-off for temporary coach John Inverarity, who was returning to his teaching post in Western Australia after a highly successful three-month term of office. Inverarity, in particular, had won widespread praise for his work with Kent's clutch of young batsmen – all of whom had blossomed under his tutelage. In this game, too, David Fulton's first innings 65 – containing ten fours – had kick-started Kent towards their eventual total of 348, as well as making him the first batsman to pass 1,000 runs for the season, and in their second innings a stand of 104 between Rob Key (83) and Ed Smith (59) was instrumental in them reaching 240 in the face of more magic from Muttiah Muralitharan. The Sri Lankan spinner took six for 70 in what could have been his last first-class appearance for Lancashire, lifting his championship wicket tally to 111 from 13 matches over two seasons. Kent were also indebted to Paul Nixon, who struck a six and 11 fours in his first-innings 82, while fast bowler Martin Saggers was awarded his county cap during a career-best innings of 61 not out. Mark Ealham then put the skids under the Lancashire first innings, claiming six for 64 as they were dismissed for 214 to leave Kent in charge. Nixon also hit an unbeaten 46 in the second innings, before Ben Trott (five for 43) and Ealham (three for 20) found too much cut and swing for the Lancashire batsmen. The visitors were tumbled out for 106 before Fleming could do anything to up the over-rate.

A seventh-wicket stand of 222 between Rob Turner and Keith Dutch knocked the stuffing out of Essex at Taunton and set up a Somerset win by an innings and 60 runs. Somerset were struggling on 158 for six when Turner and Dutch came together midway through day one but, mainly through their efforts, the home side eventually raised a total of 415. Turner's unbeaten 115 was his first century for more than a year, while Dutch hit 118. Richard Johnson then took four for 43 as Essex were skittled out for 130, and the match would have been over on the third evening but for a stubborn ninth-wicket partnership between Mark Ilott and Justin Bishop, which lasted throughout the claimed extra half-hour. The end came, however, inside ten overs after Essex had resumed the final day on 189 for eight, with Dutch taking four wickets with his off breaks.

Bad weather on the last day robbed both Northants and Yorkshire of an intriguing tussle for victory at Wantage Road. Mike Hussey had been the home star, scoring 64 and 122 in Northants' totals of 253 and 298. Graeme Swann also contributed 55 in the second innings, from just 48 balls. In between, Yorkshire had made a first-innings 309, largely thanks to skipper David Byas' unbeaten 110, but on the final morning they were ten for one when the rain had the last word.

Division Two

at Hove
Hampshire 81 (44.1 overs) (JD Lewry 6 for 37) and 108 (JD Lewry 7 for 42, including a hat-trick)
Sussex 302 (82.3 overs) (MH Yardy 87*, CJ Adams 71)
Sussex won by an innings and 113 runs
Sussex 18 pts, Hampshire 3 pts

at Derby
Worcestershire 496 (138.3 overs) (GA Hick 171, VS Solanki 109, A Singh 60)
Derbyshire 198 (58 overs) (SD Stubbings 75) and (following on) 295 (RJ Bailey 136*, SD Stubbings 53, A Sheriyar 5 for 68)
Worcestershire won by an innings and three runs
Worcestershire 20 pts, Derbyshire 2 pts

at Trent Bridge
Middlesex 527 (138.1 overs) (SP Fleming 151, OA Shah 144, BL Hutton 82, AJ Strauss 67, RJ Logan 5 for 118)
Nottinghamshire 314 (97.4 overs) (GS Blewett 79, BM Shafayat 72) and (following on) 215 for 8 (CMW Read 76*, DJ Bicknell 50, TF Bloomfield 5 for 58)
Match drawn
Nottinghamshire 9 pts, Middlesex 12 pts

at Bristol
Gloucestershire 145 (65.3 overs) (JN Snape 61) and
297 (RC Russell 91*, JN Snape 89)
Warwickshire 204 (76.1 overs) (MA Wagh 89,
MW Alleyne 5 for 50) and 113 for 2
Match drawn
Gloucestershire 7 pts, Warwickshire 8 pts

Jason Lewry produced the most memorable
individual performance of this round, finishing with
the remarkable match figures of 13 for 79 as Sussex
routed promotion rivals Hampshire by an innings
and 113 runs at Hove. The match was over inside
two days as Hampshire were dismissed for 81 and
108. Lewry, finding disconcerting swing with his
rapid left-armers, first took six for 37 on the
opening morning and then, after Sussex had
replied with 302, he soon had hapless
Hampshire reeling again at 42 for eight
following a first over hat-trick (Derek
Kenway, caught at short leg from the third
ball of the innings, and Will Kendall and
Robin Smith both lbw). Shaun Udal did at
least manage to delay the end with 40 not out,
but Lewry finished with second-innings
figures of seven for 42 to cap a remarkable
individual display. Chris Adams (71) and
Michael Yardy, with a career-best 87 not out,
showed that runs could be made in the
conditions.

Derbyshire's woes continued at Derby
where they were thrashed by an innings and
three runs by Worcestershire. Rob Bailey
fought hard with an unbeaten 136 in
Derbyshire's second innings, but the damage
was done when, in reply to Worcestershire's
496, the home side collapsed in their first
innings from an overnight 134 for one to 198
all out. Steve Stubbings, who made 75, then
added another 53, but despite his effort – and
that of Bailey and Graeme Welch, who added
115 for the sixth wicket – Derbyshire were
dismissed for 295. Alamgir Sheriyar picked
up five for 68 and Andy Bichel four for 53 in
Derbyshire's first innings, but the men who
built the base for Worcestershire's success
were Graeme Hick and Vikram Solanki.
Hick's 171 was his 115th first-class hundred
and Derby became the 45th ground to
witness a Hick ton, while Solanki's 109 –
which included four sixes and 12 fours – was
his first century of the season.

Nottinghamshire, helped by weather

interruptions on days three and four, escaped with a
draw after being forced to follow on by Middlesex
at Trent Bridge. Opener Andrew Strauss set the tone
for the Middlesex first innings by including 16
boundaries and only three singles in his 67, but then
Owais Shah and Stephen Fleming took total control
with a third-wicket stand of 206. Shah made 144,
and by the close of the first day Middlesex were
already 397 for three. On the resumption, Fleming
took his overnight 120 to 151 and Ben Hutton (82)
continued to plunder the home attack. Richard
Logan (five for 118) managed to emerge with some
credit, but Middlesex's 527 soon began to look like

Derby became the 45th county ground to witness a first-class
century from Graeme Hick. His 171 helped Worcestershire to
a comprehensive victory over struggling Derbyshire.

SURREY CCC

Home Ground:
The Fosters' Oval
Address:
The AMP Oval, Kennington,
London SE11 5SS
Tel: 020 7582 6660
Fax: 020 7735 7769
Email: enquiries@surreyccc.co.uk
Directions:
By rail: Vauxhall, SouthWest lines, five
minutes' walk away.
By underground: Northern Line, Oval Tube 100 yds
away; Victoria Line, Vauxhall is five minutes away.
By road: Situated on A202 near junction of A24 and A3
south of Vauxhall Bridge.
By bus: 36 and 185 from Victoria
Capacity: 16,500
Other grounds used: Guildford Cricket Club,
Woodbridge Road, Guildford.
Year formed: 1845

Chief Executive: Paul Sheldon
Chairman: Michael Soper
Captain: Adam Hollioake
County colours: Brown and silver

HONOURS

COUNTY CHAMPIONSHIP
1890, 1891, 1892, 1894, 1895,
1899, 1914, 1952–1958, 1971,
1999, 2000
SUNDAY LEAGUE
1996
BENSON & HEDGES CUP
1974, 1997, 2001
GILLETTE CUP/C&G TROPHY
1982

National Cricket League
nickname:
SURREY LIONS

Website:
www.surreyccc.co.uk

a match-winning score. Greg Blewett's 79 offered some resistance, but by the end of day two only an unbeaten 54 from the 16-year-old debutant Bilal Shafayat was holding them together. The lad from the local Bluecoat School kissed the pitch on reaching fifty, which apparently is something of a habit, but although he went on to 72 and played with the skill and assurance which suggested that many more English pitches will be receiving a Shafayat smacker, the Notts total of 314 left them facing an uphill struggle for survival. Darren Bicknell initially led the second-innings resistance, but rain breaks helped too, and in the end an unbeaten 76 from Chris Read, stoutly supported by Andrew Harris, was enough to frustrate the visitors.

Rain showers throughout the match also prevented any chance of a result on a seamer's pitch at Bristol, although it took a determined stand of 136 on the final morning between Jeremy Snape (89) and Jack Russell (91 not out) to thwart Warwickshire's attempts to force a win against Gloucestershire. Their efforts allowed Gloucestershire to reach the comparative safety of 297 for nine declared in their second innings, and Warwickshire only had time to reach 113 for two after being set an unrealistic run-chase. Snape had also bolstered a shaky Gloucestershire first innings, hitting 61 as the home side struggled to 145. Mark Alleyne and James Averis then shared nine wickets as Warwickshire replied with 204 – a total built around Mark Wagh's fine 89 batting at number six.

ROUND TWELVE: 18–22 JULY 2001

Division One

at Guildford
Northamptonshire 120 (44 overs) (AJ Tudor 5 for 54) and 193 (MP Bicknell 7 for 60)
Surrey 368 (98.5 overs) (AD Brown 103)
Surrey won by an innings and 55 runs
Surrey 20 pts, Durham 5 pts

at Southend
Essex 107 (59.5 overs) (MA Ealham 5 for 13) and 114 (AP Grayson 54, MJ Saggers 5 for 24)
Kent 353 for 7 dec. (116 overs) (RWT Key 123, DP Fulton 70)
Kent won by an innings and 132 runs
Kent 19 pts, Essex 2 pts

at Cardiff
Leicestershire 588 (132.5 overs) (IJ Sutcliffe 203,

BF Smith 117, TR Ward 109, Aftab Habib 72*)
Glamorgan 211 (71.3 overs) (RDB Croft 89, PAJ DeFreitas 6 for 65) and (following on) 287 (A Dale 89, SD Thomas 69, DE Malcolm 5 for 98, ND Burns 5ct)
Leicestershire won by an innings and 90 runs
Leicestershire 20 pts, Glamorgan 3 pts

at Old Trafford
Lancashire 324 (76.2 overs) (G Chapple 155, CP Schofield 58) and 126
Somerset 385 (126.3 overs) (RJ Turner 72, PD Bowler 65, ID Blackwell 64, M Burns 55, G Keedy 5 for 73) and 66 for 0
Somerset won by ten wickets
Somerset 19 pts, Lancashire 6 pts

Martin Bicknell, irked no doubt by his continued omission by England, showed just why he should have been playing in the Lord's Test by spearheading Surrey's much-needed win over Northamptonshire at his home ground of Guildford. Alex Tudor, too, gave the England selectors a healthy dig in the ribs by taking five for 54 as Northants were skittled out for 120 in their first innings on the opening day. Alistair Brown, with his 26th first-class century, ensured that Surrey had a sizeable first-innings lead, and the match was dramatically all but wrapped up by Bicknell on the second evening. Bicknell, who had taken 16 wickets on this ground the previous summer, took five for 35 in a 14-over spell with the new ball to leave Northants reeling on 99 for five at the close. The next morning saw Bicknell extend his figures to seven for 60 as the visitors were dismissed for 193 – all of which saw Surrey defeat the visitors by an innings and 55 runs.

Kent maintained their challenge for Surrey's title by whipping Essex by an innings and 132 runs at Southend. Mark Ealham, with five for 13, and Ben Trott (three for 27) began the rout by reducing Essex to 107 all out on day one – and by the close Kent were already ahead at 116 for no wicket. David Fulton fell to the very first ball of the next morning for 70, but his opening partner, Rob Key, batted throughout a rain-shortened day to reach three figures. Kent went on to score 353 for seven before declaring, with Key finally being dismissed for 123, and Essex quickly disintegrated again with the bat. They were all out for 114 in the second innings, with Martin Saggers (five for 24) this time linking up with Trott (three for 32) to illustrate just how big a gulf currently exists between these two fierce rivals.

Glamorgan were another struggling side who were trounced, this time by an innings and 90 runs at the hands of Leicestershire, who amassed the highest total ever made at Sophia Gardens when they posted 588 in their first innings. Trevor Ward, with 109 from 121 balls, tucked in hungrily against some poor home bowling and put on 198 for the first wicket with Iain Sutcliffe, who was on 86 not out at the end of a truncated opening day. Sutcliffe,

however, powered on to a career-best 203, with 26 fours, and added a further 229 for the second wicket with Ben Smith (117). Aftab Habib also tucked in, finishing on 72 not out, and on the third day Phil DeFreitas showed that advancing years had not yet affected his potency as a purveyor of swing and seam by taking six for 65 as Glamorgan

were bowled out for 211. The Welsh county, moreover, began the final day already at 15 for two after being asked to follow on, and although they put up more of a fight second time around, it was always likely that Leicestershire would complete a 20-point victory. Adrian Dale hit 89 from 109 balls, Robert Croft added a breezy 40 to his first-innings 89, and Darren Thomas also played spiritedly for 69, but the star of the last day was 38-year-old Devon Malcolm. The former England fast bowler became the first bowler to pass 50 wickets for the season, and hurled himself into the fray like a teenager as he picked up five for 98.

The death of John Crawley's mother, which forced the Lancashire captain out of the match, cast a shadow over the contest at Old Trafford, which Somerset won by ten wickets. The visitors, to their credit, supported Lancashire's request that Graham Lloyd be allowed to take Crawley's place and bat in the second innings – but Lord's ruled against it.

Martin Bicknell was enjoying a magnificent season with both bat and ball, but he still could not command a place in the England set-up.

Lancashire collapsed to 82 for six on the first morning before Chris Schofield and Glen Chapple launched a thrilling counter-attack to take the home side to 324 all out. Schofield went for 58, but number eight Chapple was inspired as he drove and hooked his way to 155 from 164 balls, hitting five sixes and 15 fours and dominating a last-wicket stand of 129 with Gary Keedy, who contributed just 20. Somerset, however, batted solidly all the way through their order to reach 385 and gain a handy first-innings lead, and on the third morning Lancashire's second innings crumbled to 126 all out, with Richard Johnson (four for 40) and Ian Blackwell (three for 47) doing much of the damage. That left Somerset with a straightforward victory target, which was gratefully accepted to keep the West Countrymen snapping at the heels of leaders Yorkshire.

Division Two

at Chester-le-Street
Sussex 442 (139.3 overs) (RR Montgomerie 156, UBA Rashid 106, CJ Adams 53, SJ Harmison 6 for 111) and 253 for 9 dec. (CJ Adams 90, RR Montgomerie 71)
Durham 360 (113 overs) (JJB Lewis 99, A Pratt 51*) and 202
Sussex won by 133 runs
Sussex 20 pts, Durham 5 pts

at Southampton Rose Bowl
Hampshire 347 (104 overs) (AN Aymes 112*) and 352 for 8 dec. (DA Kenway 166)
Nottinghamshire 209 (55.3 overs) (CMW Read 76*, RD Stemp 66) and 152 (AD Mullally 5 for 68)
Hampshire won by 338 runs
Hampshire 18 pts, Nottinghamshire 4 pts

at Edgbaston
Derbyshire 165 (66.3 overs) (TA Munton 50) and 435 for 5 dec. (LD Sutton 110*, MJ Di Venuto 109, G Welch 64, SD Stubbings 62)
Warwickshire 204 (71 overs) (G Welch 5 for 53)
Match drawn – no play was possible on the first day
Warwickshire 8 pts, Derbyshire 7 pts

at Worcester
Gloucestershire 222 (68.3 overs) (KJ Barnett 54, CG Taylor 50, AJ Bichel 6 for 54) and 87 (Kabir Ali 5 for 22)
Worcestershire 240 (71.5 overs) and 73 for 3
Worcestershire won by seven wickets
Worcestershire 16 pts, Gloucestershire 4 pts

The form of Richard Montgomerie was one of the reasons that Sussex found themselves at the top of division two come the end of July.

Sussex went to the top of division two with a hard-working, 133-run win over Durham at Chester-le-Street. Richard Montgomerie, breezing past his 1,000 runs for the season with a magnificent 156, set Sussex on their way after Jon Lewis, the Durham captain, had lost his seventh-successive championship toss. Chris Adams scored 53 and Sussex were further boosted as Umer Rashid completed a fine innings of 106, full of powerful strokes. Steve Harmison, taking five for 31 on the second day, finished with career-best figures of six for 111, but the Sussex total of 442 put them in a position of strength. Durham replied determinedly, however, with Lewis playing especially well, until he got himself out on 99. Andrew Pratt ended up on 51 not out, steering Durham to 360. Adams, though, had chipped away with his occasional medium-pacers to pick up a career-best four for 28, and now the Sussex captain hit out strongly, making 90. With Montgomerie continuing his prolific form with 71, Sussex were able to declare their second innings on

SUSSEX CCC

Home Ground:
Hove
Address:
County Ground, Eaton Road, Hove,
East Sussex BN3 3AN
Tel: 01273 827100
Fax: 01273 771549
Membership: 01273 827133
Scoreline (home games only): 01273 827145
Email: fwatson@btconnect.com
Directions:
By rail: Hove station is a ten-minute walk.
By road: Follow AA signs. Street parking at no cost.
Capacity: 5,500
Other grounds used: Eastbourne, Horsham, Arundel
Year formed: 1839

Chief Executive: tba
Captain: Chris Adams
Vice-captain: James Kirtley
Head Groundsman: Derek Traill
County colours: Dark blue, light blue and gold

HONOURS

SUNDAY LEAGUE
1982
GILLETTE CUP/C&G TROPHY
1963, 1964, 1978, 1986

National Cricket League nickname:
SUSSEX SHARKS

Website:
www.sccc.demon.co.uk

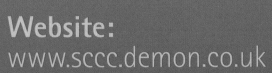

253 for nine before lunch on the final day. Durham, under pressure again, were bowled out for 202 with Rashid capping his own fine match by taking four for nine in 9.1 overs of slow left-arm spin.

A calculated gamble by Robin Smith, the Hampshire captain, was ultimately rewarded by a thumping 338-run victory against Nottinghamshire at Southampton. Smith was worried about how the West End pitch might play after heavy overnight rain but, on winning the toss, he decided to trust the new ground's efficient draining system and bat first anyway. By the close of the first day, Hampshire were 292 for eight, and they went on to reach 347 with Adrian Aymes completing a worthy unbeaten 112. Notts, in reply, were seemingly down and out at 74 for nine before Chris Read was joined by last man Richard Stemp in a rollicking final-wicket stand which raised 137 in 27 overs. Read ended on 76 not out, hitting 11 boundaries, while Stemp enjoyed himself hugely with ten fours as he reached a career-best 66 from 80 balls. Notts' 211 just about kept them in the game, but Derek Kenway then took the match well out of their reach on day three with a majestic 166. It enabled Hampshire to declare their second innings on 352 for eight, and by the end of the third day Notts were truly without hope, trailing at 113 for seven. Just one hour was required on the final morning for Hampshire to wrap up the win, Alan Mullally taking five for 68 and Chris Tremlett three for 15 in Notts' eventual 152 all out.

Wooden spoon candidates Derbyshire had much the better of a draw against Warwickshire at Edgbaston – but that should come as little comfort after a match which left both sides without credit. The first day was washed away by rain, but there was still a good chance of a positive result when the final day dawned with Derbyshire 165 runs ahead at 204 for two in their second innings. Neither side, however, seemed willing to risk the chance of defeat in a bid to force a win – a particularly strange decision since both counties were desperate to turn around poor seasons. As it was, after more weather interruptions, Luke Sutton batted on to complete a maiden first-class hundred worthy of only muted celebration, while Graeme Welch made 64 against his former county. Tim Munton, too, made satisfying runs against his old teammates by scoring only the fourth first-class fifty of his 17-year career on the opening day. Welch also took five for 53 as Warwickshire were dismissed for 204 in reply to Derbyshire's first-innings total of 165, and the second half of the third day belonged to the visitors

as Michael Di Venuto (109) and Steve Stubbings (62) put on 170 for the first wicket in a positive manner which suggested that Derbyshire were determined to press for a rare win. Some hope.

Gloucestershire coach John Bracewell, meanwhile, slammed the quality of the New Road pitch after Worcestershire had won by seven wickets in little more than two days. It was, ironically, the last surface produced by long-serving groundsman Roy McLaren before his retirement, and Bracewell attacked its uneven, and sometimes alarmingly inconsistent, bounce, adding that it was the poorest he could remember in his time in English cricket. Gloucestershire did manage to reach 222 on the opening day, with half-centuries from Kim Barnett and Chris Taylor, and although Andy Bichel's six for 54 highlighted the inconsistencies in the pitch, Worcestershire replied with a largely untroubled 84 for no wicket by the close. Mark Alleyne, however, spearheaded a fightback in the field taking four for 30 and Worcestershire were bundled out for 240. Suddenly, though, the contest was decided as Gloucestershire's second innings fell apart. Alleyne completed a king pair, nicking another Bichel lifter, and the Australian's four for 32 was surpassed by Kabir Ali's impressive five for 22 as the visitors were shot out for 87. Worcestershire knocked off the runs early on day three, with Philip Weston finishing on 38 not out off 48 balls.

ROUND THIRTEEN: 27–30 JULY 2001

Division One

at Northampton
Northamptonshire 633 for 6 dec. (162 overs) (ME Hussey 329*, AL Penberthy 101, MB Loye 52) and 96 for 0 (ME Hussey 70*)
Essex 430 (134 overs) (AP Grayson 173, JS Foster 79, DDJ Robinson 63) and (following on) 297 (AP Grayson 149, JF Brown 5 for 107)
Northamptonshire won by ten wickets
Northamptonshire 19 pts, Essex 5 pts
Note: ME Hussey was on the field for the entire match

Lancashire 373 (107.4 overs) (WK Hegg 76, JP Crawley 73, JC Scuderi 56, CP Schofield 55) and 314 (JP Crawley 113, PJ Martin 51*)
Yorkshire 531 (134.2 overs) (DS Lehmann 252, D Gough 96, MJ Wood 86, G Chapple 5 for 83) and 158 for 3 (MJ Wood 51)
Yorkshire won by seven wickets
Yorkshire 20 pts, Lancashire 7 pts

at Leicester
Leicestershire 425 (117.1 overs) (Aftab Habib 153, BF Smith 111, ND Burns 60, MJ Saggers 6 for 92) and 365 for 7 dec. (DL Maddy 111, TR Ward 110, ND Burns 64*)
Kent 390 (101.1 overs) (MJ Walker 120*, MV Fleming 59) and 403 for 7 (A Symonds 125, ET Smith 107)
Kent won by three wickets off the last ball of the match
Kent 19 pts, Leicestershire 8 pts

at Taunton
Glamorgan 169 (47.1 overs) (JP Maher 62, AR Caddick 5 for 84) and 364 (JP Maher 98, MP Maynard 80, SP James 77rh)
Somerset 600 for 8 dec. (127 overs) (PD Bowler 164, ID Blackwell 102, M Burns 81, KP Dutch 69*, MN Lathwell 53)
Somerset won by an innings and 67 runs
Somerset 20 pts, Glamorgan 2 pts

A round of matches rich in individual achievement saw Mike Hussey, perhaps, take pride of place as Northants beat Essex by ten wickets to raise hopes that they might escape relegation to Division Two come September. Hussey, the county's opener from Western Australia, was on the field for the whole match and contributed an unbeaten aggregate of 399 runs. It all started with Hussey reaching 200 not out on the opening day, already a career-best, out of a Northants overnight total of 378 for three, and he went on to add 210 for the fourth wicket with Tony Penberthy (101) before the declaration finally arrived after the home side had reached a mammoth 633 for six. Hussey, by this time, was 329 not out, and then spent two-and-a-half days fielding as Essex, bowled out in their first innings for 430, were

forced to follow on. Paul Grayson, however, also found the Northampton pitch to his liking and – on the final day – added 149 to his first-innings 173 to lead Essex to the brink of safety. But Paul Taylor, by this stage tossing up some probing left-arm spin instead of his usual seamers, had Grayson lbw and Essex suddenly lost their last five wickets for 14 runs in nine overs. Jason Brown finished with five for 107 and Northants, who had bowled out their visitors for 297, now needed 95 to win from the 15 overs

A career-best 329 not out from Northamptonshire's overseas opener Mike Hussey helped his side to victory over Essex.

WARWICKSHIRE CCC

Home Ground:
Edgbaston
Address:
County Ground,
Edgbaston,
Birmingham, B5 7QU
Tel: 0121 446 4422
Fax: 0121 446 4949
Ticket Hotline: 0121 446 5506
Indoor cricket centre: 0121 446 3633
Email: info@thebears.co.uk
Alternative website: www.warwickccc.org.uk
Directions:
By rail: New Street station, Birmingham
By road: M6 to A38M, to city centre, then follow signs to
County Ground.
Capacity: 20,000
Other grounds used: None
Year formed: 1882

Chairman: MJK Smith OBE
Chief Executive: Dennis Amiss MBE
Director of Coaching: Bob Woolmer
Other posts: 2nd XI Coach: Steve Perryman; Marketing
Manager: Peter Thompson; Indoor cricket centre coach:
RN Abberley
Captain: Michael Powell
County colours: Blue and white

HONOURS

COUNTY CHAMPIONSHIP
1911, 1951, 1972, 1994, 1995
SUNDAY LEAGUE
1980, 1994, 1997
BENSON & HEDGES CUP
1994
GILLETTE CUP/C&G TROPHY
1989, 1993, 1995

National Cricket League
nickname:
THE BEARS

Website:
www.thebears.co.uk

WORCESTERSHIRE CCC

Home Ground:
Worcester
Address:
New Road, Worcester WR2 4QQ
Tel: 01905 748474
Fax: 01905 748005
Ticket office: 01905 422694
Cricket Development Admin Officer (Allan Scrafton): 01905 429147
Directions:
By rail: Worcester Foregate Street Station (city centre), half a mile from ground. Worcester Shrub Hill Station, one mile from ground.
By road: From the north, M5 junction 6 then follow signposted route to Worcester and city centre, then take A44 for New Road.
By bus: Midland Red West Nos 23–6.
Disabled access: designated viewing area for disabled visitors; free admission for carers; disabled toilet facilities.
Capacity: 4,500
Other grounds used: Kidderminster CC, Chester Road North, Kidderminster
Year formed: 1865

Chairman: John Elliott
Chief Executive: Mark Newton
Director of Cricket: Tom Moody
2nd XI Coach: Damian D'Oliveira
Captain: Graeme Hick
Vice-captain: Steve Rhodes
County colours: Green, black and white

Website:
www.wccc.co.uk

HONOURS

COUNTY CHAMPIONSHIP
1964, 1965, 1974, 1988, 1989
SUNDAY LEAGUE
1971, 1987, 1988, 1991
BENSON & HEDGES CUP
1991
GILLETTE CUP/C&G TROPHY
1994

National Cricket League nickname:
WORCESTERSHIRE ROYALS

remaining in the match. Enter, again, Hussey. The left-hander, footsore but far from weary, smashed the bowling to all parts while racing to an unbeaten and triumphant 70 from just 33 balls. He hit a six and 11 fours, with Mal Loye supporting him sensibly with 21 not out, as Northants reached their victory target with four overs still in hand.

Darren Lehmann, another Australian left-hander, was the man of the moment in the Roses match at Headingley, which Yorkshire won by seven wickets in a pivotal result for the seasons of the two trans-Pennine rivals. Indeed, in years to come, the game will be remembered as 'Lehmann's Match' for the brilliance of his first-innings aggregate of 252, which enabled Yorkshire to go so far and so quickly past Lancashire's 373 that a positive result was possible. Darren Gough took four for 65 during Lancashire's solid first-innings effort that saw John Crawley (73) and Warren Hegg (76) as the top-scorers, but by the end of day two Yorkshire were already three runs ahead with five first-innings wickets remaining. One of those, too, was Lehmann's and, on a remarkable third morning, he converted his overnight 222 not out into the highest individual score ever made in 236 Roses contests going back to 1863. Lehmann faced only 288 balls, hitting a six and 35 fours, and his magnificent effort certainly inspired Gough who, suddenly displaying the talent with the bat that has for too long remained hidden both at county and Test level, careered to a wonderful 96 from 101 deliveries with a six and 14 boundaries. Steve Kirby, the fast-emerging paceman, then sent back Mike Atherton cheaply for the second time in the match, but Crawley, the Lancashire captain, responded to the crisis with a technically-superb innings of 113. Wickets continued to fall at the other end, though, and by the close of the third day Lancashire were in trouble at 280 for eight. Peter Martin reached a defiant, unbeaten 51 to lift Lancashire's second innings to 314, but Yorkshire still had plenty of time to score the 157 they required for an important 20-point victory. Lehmann, needless to say, was on hand to speed them to the finishing line. As Matthew Wood added 51 to his fine first-innings 86, Lehmann thumped 48 off a mere 24 balls with two sixes and seven fours to see the Tykes to victory.

At Leicester, too, it was yet another Australian who provided the spark for one of the most red-hot finishes ever seen in a county championship match. Kent, set an imposing 401 from 84 overs by Leicestershire on the final afternoon of a high-scoring and fiercely contested game, were ignited in their chase by Andrew Symonds' 125 off 134 balls.

Symonds struck a six and 17 fours while adding 235 in 47 overs for the third wicket with Ed Smith, whose 107 was no less important to the Kentish cause. Eventually, with Paul Nixon emerging to thrash an unbeaten 29 from 18 balls against his old county, Kent won a great victory by three wickets from the very last ball of the game. With 14 required off the last over, bowled by Darren Maddy, Nixon hit four twos and then two boundaries to mid-wicket. It was Kent's second-highest fourth-innings winning total. Leicestershire had scored 425 in their first innings, with Aftab Habib (153) and Ben Smith (111) the first to take advantage of a lovely batting pitch in a stand worth 151. Martin Saggers, however, plugged away manfully to finish with six for 92 and Matthew Walker then hit an unbeaten 120, his fourth championship hundred of the campaign, as Kent replied with 390. Leicestershire's second innings of 365 for seven declared, was mostly notable for Trevor Ward's 110 against his former county, after which he was awarded his county cap during the tea interval, a 22-ball 42 from Shahid Afridi which included three sixes and five fours, and a fine 111 by Maddy.

Somerset welcomed back Andy Caddick and Marcus Trescothick for only their second championship appearance of the season, and the first since May, and it was Caddick who provided the inspiration for their innings-and-67-run win over Glamorgan at Taunton. His five for 84, coupled with Richard Johnson's four for 33, broke the back of the Glamorgan first innings and, dismissed for 169, the Welsh county were already staring defeat in the face by the end of the opening day as Somerset cruised to 246 for three. Mike Burns, with 81 from 66 balls, provided early impetus and, on the second day, Peter Bowler took his overnight 63 to 164, the 42nd hundred of his first-class career, while Mark Lathwell made a pleasant 53 and Ian Blackwell an altogether more rumbustious 102 off just 110 deliveries. With Keith Dutch chipping in with 69 not out, Somerset were able to declare well before the close on 600 for eight. In 31 overs that evening, Jimmy Maher and Steve James took Glamorgan to 152 without loss, but their resistance was shattered the following morning by Caddick. Not only did the England paceman take two wickets, including that of Maher for 98, in an 11-over spell costing only 19 runs, but he also broke a bone in James' left hand – forcing the Glamorgan captain to retire hurt on 77. Matthew Maynard offered a fighting 80, but Glamorgan were bowled out for 364 as Somerset methodically wrapped things up.

Division Two

at Cheltenham
Gloucestershire 520 (138 overs) (CG Taylor 140,
JN Snape 131, KJ Barnett 79) and 23 for 0
Sussex 167 (75.5 overs) and (following on) 375
(CJ Adams 123, RR Montgomerie 107, IJ Harvey
5 for 33)
Gloucestershire won by ten wickets
Gloucestershire 20 pts, Sussex 2 pts

at Lord's
Middlesex 424 (134.4 overs) (AJ Strauss 176,
BL Hutton 120, DR Law 5 for 94)
Durham 187 (74.5 overs) (ML Love 64) and
(following on) 163 (N Peng 66, PCR Tufnell 5
for 46, including his 1,000th first-class wicket)
Middlesex won by an innings and 74 runs
Middlesex 20 pts, Durham 2 pts

at Derby
Nottinghamshire 526 (118.2 overs)
(JE Morris 170, Usman Afzaal 138) and 557 for
5 (KP Pietersen 218*, JE Morris 136*, GS
Blewett 52, GE Welton 50)
Derbyshire 572 (149.1 overs) (DG Cork 128, SD
Stubbings 127, KM Krikken 93*,
MJ Di Venuto 59)
Match drawn
Derbyshire 12 pts, Nottinghamshire 11 pts

Gloucestershire upset the division's form
book when they crushed Sussex by ten
wickets at Cheltenham – although visiting
captain Chris Adams handed the home side
the initiative by nonsensically choosing to
bowl first at a venue where batting
traditionally becomes more difficult as the
pitch wears. The result of Adams' generosity
was a Gloucestershire first-innings total of
520, and an end-of-first-day scoreboard
which read 415 for five. Kim Barnett kicked
things off with a fluent 79, Chris Taylor then
underlined his burgeoning talent with 140
and Jeremy Snape weighed in with 131.
When Sussex were dismissed in reply for just
167, there was only one likely winner – hard
though Richard Montgomerie (107) and
Adams himself (123) tried to overcome the

odds. Ian Harvey was the Gloucestershire bowling
hero, the Australian all-rounder bowling his sharp
seamers with a wonderful variation of pace and also
with tight control to add five for 33 from 23 overs to

After waiting for ten years to record a maiden
championship century, Jeremy Snape's 131 against
Sussex was his second ton of the season.

his first-innings three for 13 off 18.5 overs (13 of which were maidens). With Sussex bowled out for 375 in their second innings early on the fourth day, Gloucestershire were left with the simple task of knocking off the 23 runs they required for an invaluable 20-point haul.

Middlesex maintained their push for promotion by thrashing Durham by an innings and 74 runs at Lord's and moving to the top of the division. Andrew Strauss (176) and Ben Hutton (120) were the batsmen mainly responsible for pushing Middlesex up to a first-innings total of 424, and, by the close of the second day, Durham were in trouble at 186 for nine against the Middlesex spinners. Following on after being bowled out for 187, Durham were then quickly dismissed again for 163. Nicky Peng (66) offered the only real resistance, and Phil Tufnell's five for 46 included his 1,000th first-class wicket.

Derbyshire's season of torture found relief of sorts in a high-scoring draw against neighbours and fierce rivals Nottinghamshire at Derby. The home side even had a sniff of victory early on the final day, as Kevin Dean took three wickets in 27 balls to leave Notts at 185 for five in their second innings, only 139 in front with a minimum of 84 overs left in the day. But then Kevin Pietersen, with 218 not out, and John Morris, with his second hundred of the match against his former county, closed out the match with an unbroken 372-run stand. Derbyshire's bowling was increasingly friendly as the contest petered out, allowing Pietersen to strike nine sixes and 23 fours in his 255-ball innings. Morris added 136 not out to his first-innings 170, taking his first-class hundreds tally to 52, but to the credit of both batsmen they merely blocked out the last half-hour or so rather than continuing to plunder easy runs. Morris' first-innings century, from 208 balls and with three sixes and 22 fours, was the knock he will want to remember most – especially as before the game he had announced his intention to retire at the end of the season – and his 316-run stand for the fourth wicket with Usman Afzaal (138) was only 53 short of the county record. Nottinghamshire eventually totalled 526, but the Derbyshire reply was even better. Steve Stubbings (127) added 124 with Michael Di Venuto (59) before Dominic Cork, striding in at number six, struck an aggressive 128. Karl Krikken's unbeaten 93 allowed Derbyshire to reach 572, which earned the 46-run first-innings lead that helped them to put Notts under that little bit of pressure the following morning.

ROUND FOURTEEN: 1–6 AUGUST 2001

Division One

at Headingley
Surrey 278 (80.2 overs) (IDK Salisbury 58) and 281 (BC Hollioake 68, RKJ Dawson 6 for 98)
Yorkshire 206 (65.4 overs) (DS Lehmann 52) and 244 for 2 (DS Lehmann 106*, MJ Wood 85*)
Match drawn
Yorkshire 8 pts, Surrey 9 pts

at Canterbury
Kent 451 for 7 dec. (DP Fulton 208*, MJ Walker 81, A Symonds 56, RWT Key 50, PS Jones 5 for 115) and 205 for 3 dec. (DP Fulton 104*, A Symonds 59)
Somerset 336 (104.2 overs) (KP Dutch 75*, MN Lathwell 63, J Cox 50, MN Patel 8 for 119) and 113 for 8
Match drawn – only 11 balls were possible on the second day
Kent 12 pts, Somerset 9 pts
Note: DP Fulton was on the field for the entire match

at Chelmsford
Leicestershire 559 (153.5 overs) (IJ Sutcliffe 165, Aftab Habib 124, DL Maddy 55, ND Burns 50*, JE Bishop 5 for 148)
Essex 356 (117.1 overs) (SG Law 115, DDJ Robinson 102, Shahid Afridi 5 for 84) and (following on) 236 for 5 (DDJ Robinson 118*)
Match drawn
Essex 9 pts, Leicestershire 12 pts

at Colwyn Bay
Glamorgan 479 (134.2 overs) (MP Maynard 143, A Dale 140, JP Maher 60, G Keedy 5 for 98) and 220 for 7 dec. (K Newell 73*)
Lancashire 402 for 9 dec. (89.4 overs) (NH Fairbrother 158, G Chapple 64) and 225 for 7 (MJ Chilton 83, A Flintoff 68)
Match drawn
Glamorgan 12 pts, Lancashire 11 pts

Champions Surrey were hoping to cut back Yorkshire's lead in the championship race when the two counties met at Headingley, and for a time it did look as if they would be able to force the victory they craved. But, on the final day, the 22 overs lost to rain in the morning session probably cost Yorkshire the chance of winning as Darren Lehmann and Matthew Wood then joined in a third-wicket stand that was still unbroken on 190

YORKSHIRE CCC

Home Ground:
Headingley
Address:
Headingley Cricket Ground,
Leeds LS6 3BU
Tel: 0113 278 7394
Fax: 0113 278 4099
Email: cricket@yorkshireccc.org.uk
Other grounds used: Scarborough
Year formed: 1863

Chairman: Keith H Moss
Chief Executive: Chris Hassell
Secretary: David Ryder
Coach: Arnie Sidebottom
Captain: David Byas
County colours: Oxford blue, Cambridge blue and gold

HONOURS

COUNTY CHAMPIONSHIP
1893, 1896, 1898, 1900, 1901,
1902, 1905, 1908, 1912, 1919,
1922, 1923, 1924, 1925, 1931,
1963, 1966, 1967, 1968, 2001
BENSON & HEDGES CUP
1987
SUNDAY LEAGUE
1983
GILLETTE CUP/C&G TROPHY
1965, 1969

National Cricket League nickname:
YORKSHIRE PHOENIX

Website:
www.yorkshireccc.org.uk

when the overs ran out and the draw was confirmed. Yorkshire had begun that last day on 50 for one as they chased 354 for victory, by far the highest total of the match on a surface taking spin, but Saqlain Mushtaq and Ian Salisbury were powerless to prevent Lehmann (106 not out) and Wood (85 not out) taking their side to 244 for two. Salisbury and Saqlain, in fact, had enjoyed more success with the bat on the opening day when they scored 58 and 34 respectively to rally Surrey from 189 for eight to 278 all out. That was enough to earn the visitors a handy first-innings lead when Yorkshire were bowled out for 206 in reply, with Lehmann making 52 and Ed Giddins picking up four for 52. A solid 46 from Michael Carberry, 44 from Alistair Brown and a mature 68 from Ben Hollioake then took Surrey to 281 in their second innings – although off spinner Richard Dawson, on the eve of his 21st birthday, finished with six for 98 to suggest that Yorkshire's batsmen might struggle. They didn't.

Kent and Somerset, two of the other counties making a firm challenge for the championship title, ended up with different emotions after an exciting finish at Canterbury. The match ended up drawn, but although Somerset were relieved and grateful to escape with the four extra points for the draw as they closed on 113 for eight, Kent were left to rue a missed opportunity at the conclusion of a weather-interrupted match in which they had also spilled several important catches in the Somerset first innings. Kent captain Matthew Fleming might also have declared earlier on the final afternoon, instead of waiting to set Somerset a purely theoretical target of 321 in a minimum of 41 overs. In the end, Kent bowled 48, with spinners Min Patel and Andy Symonds whistling through their overs as they destroyed the Somerset middle-order, but they did not quite have time enough as Richard Johnson and Steffan Jones stayed firm for the last 20 minutes. The match was memorable, however, for Kent opener David Fulton who became only the 43rd batsman in the history of first-class cricket worldwide to score a double hundred and a hundred in the same game. Fulton's first innings 208 not out, supported by 81 from Matthew Walker and half-centuries from Rob Key and Symonds, enabled Kent to post 451 for seven declared in their first innings. He faced 313 balls, hitting two sixes and 25 fours, and in Kent's second innings of 205 for three declared, Fulton added an unbeaten 104 as he and Symonds (59) scored at almost seven runs per over. In between those two efforts, Somerset totalled 336

with Keith Dutch resisting gamely for 75 not out and Johnson thumping 46 from just 34 balls to further frustrate the home team. Patel bowled with great control and self-discipline to finish up with eight for 119. Unfortunately for Kent, however, he was not given enough time to bowl out Somerset again – despite taking four for 35 in that dramatic last session.

Two hundreds in the match by Darren Robinson helped Essex to draw their contest against Leicestershire at Chelmsford, despite following on, and put behind them a run of six defeats in seven matches. Rain interruptions on the second and final days also came to Essex's aid after Leicestershire had run up a total of 559 with Iain Sutcliffe (165) and Aftab Habib (124) putting on 233 for the third wicket. On the opening day, in fierce sunshine and sweltering temperatures, 47-year-old umpire Jeff Evans – in his first season on the county list – fainted while standing at square leg, although he emerged from the pavilion a little later on to resume his duties wearing a hat! Robinson (102) and the unsettled Stuart Law (115) added 204 for the second wicket in Essex's first-innings total of 356, and then opener Robinson scored an unbeaten 118 as the home side reached 236 for five on the final day.

At Colwyn Bay, a determined Lancashire fightback wrested back the initiative from Glamorgan, who then needed an unbeaten eighth-wicket stand of 85 between Keith Newell (73 not out) and Darren Thomas (44 not out), plus rain early on the final day, to keep their visitors at bay and secure the draw. Glamorgan began strongly enough, with Matthew Maynard (143 from 191 balls) hitting his 48th first-class hundred, with two sixes and 23 fours, and Adrian Dale continuing his fine season with the bat by converting his overnight unbeaten 92 into 140. Gary Keedy toiled bravely to take five for 98, but Glamorgan's 479 put them in control. Lancashire, however, replied with 402 as Neil Fairbrother (158 off 199 balls) was joined late on by spirited innings from both Chris Schofield (40) and Glen Chapple, whose 99-ball 64 contained two sixes off Dean Cosker and nine other boundaries. By the close of day three, moreover, Glamorgan's second innings had been reduced to 85 for five, but then Newell and Thomas rallied the home side on the final day to allow a declaration at 220 for seven. Lancashire, though, never really got into contention, although they batted brightly to reach 225 for five with Mark Chilton (83) and Andy Flintoff (61) providing much of the entertainment.

Division Two

at Hove
Sussex 351 for 8 dec. (114.1 overs) (MW Goodwin 127)
and 210 for 7 dec. (MH Yardy 72, CJ Adams 54)
Middlesex 208 (73 overs) (PN Weekes 64) and 161
(AJ Strauss 51)
Sussex won by 192 runs
Sussex 19 pts, Middlesex 3 pts

at Kidderminster
Worcestershire 227 (65.3 overs) and 147 (A Singh 57,
DR Law 5 for 52)
Durham 260 (61 overs) (DR Law 64, ML Love 50,
A Sheriyar 6 for 88) and 118 for 3 (ML Love 58)
Durham won by seven wickets
Durham 17 pts, Worcestershire 7 pts

at Edgbaston
Warwickshire 373 (108 overs) (DR Brown 104,
IR Bell 103, DL Hemp 52) and 257 for 3 dec.
(DL Hemp 105, NV Knight 98*)
Nottinghamshire 350 for 6 dec. (109.5 overs)
(GS Blewett 97, Usman Afzaal 86,
KP Pietersen 71) and 141
Warwickshire won by 139 runs
Warwickshire 18 pts, Nottinghamshire 7 pts

at Cheltenham
Gloucestershire 334 (102.3 overs) (MGN Windows 91,
CG Taylor 56) and 245 for 6 dec. (KJ Barnett 93)
Hampshire 230 (56 overs) (NC Johnson 72,
JS Laney 52*) and 40 for 1
Match drawn – no play was possible on the second day
Gloucestershire 10 pts, Hampshire 8 pts

Sussex won a crucial meeting with Middlesex at
Hove by 192 runs, and the manner of their victory
not only underlined their own strength of purpose
in their bid for promotion, but also exposed the
frailty of their opponents' resolve. Only 31 overs
were possible on the first day due to bad weather,
but that was enough time for Murray Goodwin and
Richard Montgomerie – surely the star opening
partnership of the county summer – to put together
their fifth century stand of the campaign.

Montgomerie made just 39 of the 116 they added,
but Goodwin was 73 not out at the close, which
Sussex reached at 118 for one, and went on the next
morning to 127 before the home side ground on to
an eventual total of 351 for eight declared. In 19
overs before the close, Middlesex slipped to 48 for
two, and on the next day, only Paul Weekes resisted

for long with 64 as the visitors were bowled out for
208. Goodwin and Montgomerie both actually failed
in the Sussex second innings, but Michael Yardy
(72) joined his captain Chris Adams (54) in a gritty
third-wicket century stand which ultimately allowed
Adams to declare at 210 for seven after just under
an hour's batting on the final morning. Andrew
Strauss made 51 and Weekes 41, but otherwise the
Middlesex resistance was almost negligible as Robin
Martin-Jenkins (four for 18 from 17 overs) and
Mark Robinson (four for 34) combined to dismiss
the visitors for 161.

Danny Law and Martin Love provided much of
the inspiration behind Durham's seven-wicket
triumph over Worcestershire at Kidderminster.
Graeme Hick chose to bat first on winning the toss,
but on a rain-hit opening day he fell for a first-ball
duck to six foot seven inch tall paceman Nicky
Hatch as Worcestershire struggled to 149 for seven.
The home side battled to 227 all out the next day,
but by the close Durham had earned themselves a
handy first-innings lead of 33, thanks mainly to Love
(50), Paul Collingwood (47) and Law, who hit hard
and handsomely with a six and 11 fours in his 81-
ball 64 while dominating a match-turning, last-
wicket stand of 84 with Hatch. Alamgir Sheriyar
finished with six for 88, but his figures were even
better before Law took the attack to him. Only
Anurag Singh, with 57 to add to his first-innings 45,
then held up Law (five for 52) and James Brinkley
(three for 19) for long as Durham bowled out
Worcestershire for 147 in their second innings.
Love's classy innings of 58 made sure Durham did
not stumble over their modest victory target of 115.

Ian Bell, at 19 years and 115 days old, became the
youngest first-class century-maker in Warwickshire's
history when he square drove a ball from off spinner
Kevin Pietersen to the boundary early on the second
day of his county's 139-run victory over
Nottinghamshire at Edgbaston. Bell had ended the
opening day on 80 not out, after figuring in a fifth-
wicket stand with Dougie Brown (104) which almost
trebled the Warwickshire score after they had
slipped to 94 for four, despite David Hemp's 52.
Bell was eventually out for 103, in a Warwickshire
first-innings total of 373, but the match looked
evenly balanced when Notts replied with 350 for six
declared – Greg Blewett hitting 97, Usman Afzaal
86 and Pietersen 71. Jason Gallian, the Notts
captain, suffered yet more terrible luck when – in
his first game back after a chronic knee injury – he
had a finger broken on his left hand and had to
retire hurt on 23. Gallian later learned he would

Ian Bell's 103 for Warwickshire against Nottinghamshire made him the youngest century-maker in the county's history at 19 years and 115 days.

miss the rest of the season. Aggressive batting on the third evening by Hemp, with two sixes and 18 fours in his 105, took Warwickshire to an overnight score of 214 for three in their second innings. Then, despite the rain which prevented a start until 1.30pm, some gentle declaration bowling by Chris Read and John Morris allowed Nick Knight to reach 98 not out and Warwickshire to declare on 257 for three. Notts clearly fancied their chances of making 281 from 62 overs, but soon that ambition was in tatters. Neil Smith and Mark Wagh both took three wickets with their off breaks as Notts tumbled to 141 all out.

A washed-out second day, more rain on the final morning and a cautious second-innings declaration by Gloucestershire captain Mark Alleyne all contributed to a tepid draw with Hampshire at Cheltenham. Gloucestershire had batted attractively to total 334 on the first day, with Matt Windows top-scoring on 91, and after the lost day the home side managed to bowl out Hampshire for 230,

despite Neil Johnson's 72 and an unbeaten 52 from Jason Laney on a fine pitch offering bounce, pace and some turn. By the close, Kim Barnett had raced to 70 not out in a Gloucestershire second innings of 104 for one, but any thoughts of an exciting last day were ruined by the weather. Alleyne also chose not to open up the game by offering Hampshire a juicy target, and the match petered out into a draw with Barnett falling for 93 in Gloucestershire's eventual 245 for six declared and Hampshire then replying with 40 for one.

ROUND FIFTEEN: 7–11 AUGUST 2001

Division One

at Old Trafford
Yorkshire 467 for 9 dec.(100 overs) (C White 186, MJ Wood 115)
Lancashire 242 (53.3 overs) (WK Hegg 78, A Flintoff 52) and (following on) 188 (MJ Chilton 74)
Yorkshire won by an innings and 37 runs – no play was possible on the first day
Yorkshire 20 pts, Lancashire 4 pts

at The Oval
Surrey 281 (75 overs) (MA Butcher 145*) and 141
Glamorgan 223 (73.3 overs) (MA Wallace 63*, SD Thomas 57, MP Bicknell 6 for 69) and 201 for 7 (IJ Thomas 59, MJ Powell 51, MP Bicknell 5 for 48)
Glamorgan won by three wickets – no play was possible on the second day
Glamorgan 16 pts, Surrey 5 pts

at Northampton
Northamptonshire 355 (104 overs) (RJ Warren 84, AL Penberthy 77) and 13 for 0
Kent 464 for 4 dec. (107.1 overs) (DP Fulton 197, A Symonds 131, ET Smith 91)
Match drawn
Northamptonshire 9 pts, Kent 12 pts

at Taunton
Leicestershire 277 (69.1 overs) (Shahid Afridi 69, DE Malcolm 50, M Burns 6 for 54) and 400 for 4 (BF Smith 180*, Aftab Habib 149)
Somerset 298 (70 overs) (RJ Turner 93, RL Johnson 68)
Match drawn – no play was possible on the third day
Somerset 9 pts, Leicestershire 9 pts

Lancashire cricket was plunged into crisis, according to the *Manchester Evening News* and the vast majority of its followers, after a spineless innings-

and-37-run defeat in the Roses encounter with Yorkshire at Old Trafford. The fact that Yorkshire's 20-point haul strengthened their challenge for a first championship title since 1968 merely served to heighten Lancastrian anguish at the continued failings of a team now under a very real threat of relegation. David Lloyd, the former coach of both Lancashire and England, summed up the feelings of many in the Red Rose county by speaking of how 'appalled and angry' he was at the capitulation against the oldest enemy. Remarkably, all this happened after the first day had been washed away by rain. But, the next day, Yorkshire's openers Craig White and Matthew Wood tore the Lancashire attack apart with a partnership of 309 which allowed the visitors to race to 358 for two in the 76 overs permitted. Wood made 115, but White, recapturing the batting form England would have wanted from him in the Ashes series, was 179 not out at the close and went on to hit 186. Yorkshire declared at 467 for nine, after batting on for another 24 overs on day three, and then bowled out Lancashire for 242, despite Warren Hegg's 78 and 52 from Andy Flintoff. Following on, they began the final day on 74 for one in their second innings, but from 100 for one and after an 87-run stand between Mark Chilton (74) and Flintoff (43), they fell apart so badly that Hegg (26) was the only other batsman to reach double figures. Richard Dawson, the emerging off spinner, took four for 29 and Gavin Hamilton picked up three for 33.

Champions Surrey, meanwhile, were another high-profile county receiving a bloody nose – and also on home territory. Glamorgan, the visitors to The Oval, held their nerve at the end of a tense contest to win by three wickets and inflict upon Surrey their first defeat of the championship summer. Moreover, for a Surrey side boasting 11 internationals, it was their first home loss in the competition since the last match of the 1998 season. Only two Surrey players could hold their heads high at the end – Mark Butcher, for carrying his bat with a magnificent 145 not out in a first-innings total of 281, and Martin Bicknell for his match analysis of 11 for 117. Butcher made his runs from only 75 overs, striking 21 fours from 215 deliveries, but his brilliance also exposed the shortcomings of the other Surrey batsmen. Then, after a second-day washout, Bicknell took six for 69 to go past 50 wickets for the season for the tenth time in his 16 seasons with the club, to give Surrey the upper hand. Glamorgan, who at one point were struggling on 83 for six, recovered to reach 223 through the efforts of seventh-wicket pair

Craig White rediscovered his batting form with 186 during Yorkshire's triumph over their cross-Pennine rivals. The manner of the result left Lancashire cricket in despair.

Mark Wallace (63 not out) and Darren Thomas (57), but when the Surrey second innings began, the visitors were favourites to lose the game. Two wickets apiece, however, for Steve Watkin, Simon Jones and Andrew Davies reduced the home side to 129 for seven by the close and, the next morning, Watkin took his figures to four for 28 as Surrey were quickly dismissed for 141. Glamorgan were cruising to their victory target of 200 at 163 for three, following a chancy 59 from Ian Thomas and a solid 51 by Mike Powell, but then the evergreen Bicknell returned to grab four wickets in seven balls. At 166 for seven, things did not look quite so straightforward, but once again the 19-year-old Wallace showed the quality of his temperament by dropping anchor and making sure he was still there at the end. Fast bowler Davies also played his part, with a few fine blows, and Glamorgan's hopes of escaping relegation were soon being boosted with the 16-point victory.

Yet another century by David Fulton – and almost

his second double-hundred in three innings at that – was the main talking point of an otherwise dull and weather-hit draw between Kent and Northamptonshire at Wantage Road. Following his 208 not out and 104 not out against Somerset in the previous match, Fulton built another fine innings of 197 to lift his wonderful season's first-class run tally to 1,662. It was his eighth century of the campaign, and Kentish fans were beginning to believe that the 29-year-old opener – who had made just seven hundreds in his entire nine-year career before this season – could match the county record of ten made by Frank Woolley in both the 1928 and 1934 summers. Andy Symonds (131 from 129 balls) and Ed Smith (91) also enjoyed themselves as Kent replied with 464 for four declared to Northants' first-innings 355. The gathering of bonus points was the only relevance to the final day – such was the amount of time lost over all four days.

There was a similar story at Taunton, where a completely blank third day spoilt what, even after two truncated days, was the prospect of an interesting contest between Somerset and Leicestershire. In the 48.3 overs possible on day one, Leicestershire had reached 200 for eight with some reckless batting and an unbeaten 62 off 57 balls from Shahid Afridi. The Pakistani, who had come in at 100 for five, was dismissed for 69 the next morning but then, in an hour of sometimes pure comedy, Devon Malcolm struck a blow for all natural number 11s by blasting a six and seven fours in a 50-ball 50. Malcolm's unlikely assault hauled Leicestershire's total up to 277 and, at 84 for six in reply, Somerset were in some bother. Rob Turner (93) and Richard Johnson (68), however, added 109 for the eighth wicket to earn their side an eventual first-innings lead of 21 and, at the halfway mark, Leicestershire were 19 for one in their second innings. Then, frustratingly, came the whole day of rain and, on a largely academic final day, Ben Smith (180 not out) and Aftab Habib (149) put on 300 for the third wicket as Leicestershire totalled 400 for four to ensure the draw.

Division Two

at Chester-le-Street
Durham 125 (43.2 overs) (G Welch 6 for 30, MJ Di Venuto 5 catches) and 193 (A Pratt 68*, KJ Dean 6 for 73)
Derbyshire 95 (27 overs) (JE Brinkley 6 for 14) and 224 for 6 (MJ Di Venuto 111 rh, CWG Bassano 70*)
Derbyshire won by four wickets – no play was possible

on the first day
Derbyshire 15 pts, Durham 3 pts

at Trent Bridge
Nottinghamshire 149 (51.3 overs) (JE Morris 51) and 423 (GS Blewett 108, KP Pietersen 86, CMW Read 65, Usman Afzaal 53)
Worcestershire 252 (62.3 overs) (A Singh 88, AJ Bichel 53, GJ Smith 5 for 59) and 259
Nottinghamshire won by 61 runs
Nottinghamshire 15 pts, Worcestershire 5 pts

at Lord's
Gloucestershire 400 for 3 dec. (111 overs) (IJ Harvey 130*, MGN Windows 123, DR Hewson 77)
Middlesex 222 (85.3 overs) (JMM Averis 5 for 55, RC Russell 5 catches) and (following on) 119
Gloucestershire won by an innings and 59 runs – no play was possible on the second day
Gloucestershire 20 pts, Middlesex 2 pts

at Southampton Rose Bowl
Warwickshire 308 (109 overs) (IR Bell 98, MJ Powell 83, DR Brown 50, AD Mullally 8 for 90)
Hampshire 26 for 1 (10.1 overs)
Match drawn – no play was possible on the third and fourth days
Hampshire 7 pts, Warwickshire 7 pts

Joy at last for Derbyshire who, boosted by a fine hundred by acting captain Michael Di Venuto, overcame the trauma of being bowled out for just 95 on an opening day which saw the fall of 24 wickets to beat Durham by four wickets. It was the bottom club's first championship win of the summer and also featured some excellent swing and seam bowling by Kevin Dean and Graeme Welch, plus another innings of great promise by Chris Bassano. Rain washed out the scheduled opening day, but there were veritable fireworks when the contest began the following morning. Jon Lewis, the Durham captain, was one of the few batsmen who managed to survive for long as – on a hot and humid, almost thundery day – the ball swung alarmingly. Welch (six for 30) and Dean (four for 32) exploited the conditions gratefully as Durham were bowled out for 125, but their efforts paled in comparison to the bowling of James Brinkley, whose mastery of line and length – allied to controlled swing – brought him figures of 10-4-14-6 as the Derbyshire first innings crumbled too. By the close of a dramatic day, Durham were already 73 for four in their second innings, having at first slipped to 11

Ian Harvey smashed an unbeaten 130 for Gloucestershire at Lord's, before the home side capitulated to hand the visitors victory.

batting easing, Di Venuto took full advantage. His 111, brought to an end only by a groin strain which forced him to retire hurt, was full of exquisite cover drives and hearty swings to leg and, after he limped from the field, Bassano stayed to calm nerves with 70 not out as several wickets tumbled around him.

Nottinghamshire's meeting with Worcestershire at Trent Bridge was fortunate to escape much of the bad weather which plagued other games in this round, and the result was a fine game of cricket which swayed one way and then the other. Notts won by 61 runs in the end, but for the first half of the match it was the visitors who held the upper hand. Alamgir Sheriyar's four for 51 spearheaded the dismissal of Notts for just 149 on the opening day, with John Morris top-scoring on 51, and then a superb 88 by Anurag Singh, plus a beefy 38-ball half-century from Andy Bichel (53), gave Worcestershire a handy first-innings lead of 103 as they reached 252 all out. Greg Smith's five for 59 had hinted, however, that Notts still had some fight in them, and so it proved during their second innings as Greg Blewett and Kevin Pietersen led the charge to 423 all out. Blewett's 108 was his fourth

for three, with Martin Speight counter-attacking with gusto and good sense on 43 not out. Speight, however, failed to add to his overnight score and it took a final-wicket stand of 46 between Andrew Pratt (68 not out) and Nicky Hatch to lift the Durham total to 193. That left Derbyshire needing to make 224 for victory, and with conditions for

championship century of the season, while Pietersen's 86 off 100 balls was a by now familiar exhibition of clean hitting as he struck a six and 14 fours. In addition, Usman Afzaal made 53 and Chris Read a good 65 with two sixes and eight fours. Needing 321, Worcestershire began the final day at nine without loss but, although four players got into the forties, none could go on to make the big score which their county so badly required and Smith's three for 42 helped to dismiss the visitors for 259.

Gloucestershire recorded a remarkable innings-and-59-run victory at Lord's when Middlesex crumbled shockingly on the final day. The match had seemed to be heading for a rain-affected draw, especially as the bad weather had washed away almost half of the opening day and the entire second day. The visitors had reached 198 for two in the 60 overs possible on day one, with Dominic Hewson playing well for his 77, but then Matt Windows (123) and Ian Harvey, with an attractive unbeaten 130, stepped up the pace on the third day to take Gloucestershire to their initial objective of maximum batting points at 400 for three declared. At the close, Middlesex were 141 for four in reply, but there was no suggestion of the surrender to come. Bowled out just before lunch for 222, with James Averis finishing with five for 55, Middlesex were then asked to follow on and proceeded to slide ignominiously to 119 all out. Robin Weston (40) and David Alleyne (44), who put on 80 for the fifth wicket, were the only batsmen to make double figures as Ian Harvey (four for 20) led the destruction.

Rain, unfortunately, seeped under the covers at West End to leave the match between Hampshire and Warwickshire abandoned as a draw. Bad weather had already interrupted proceedings on each of the first two days, on which Warwickshire had totalled 308 and Hampshire had replied with 26 for one, but then heavy storms washed out the third day and also led to the problems which caused the final day to be called off too. Notable performances in the play possible came from 19-year-old Ian Bell, who made 98, and Alan Mullally, who led a Hampshire fightback in the field by taking eight for 90.

ROUND SIXTEEN: 15–20 AUGUST 2001

Division One

at Canterbury
Surrey 258 (86.2 overs) (MP Bicknell 78) and 193 for 8

(MP Bicknell 110*)
Kent 301 (118.2 overs) (RWT Key 79, PA Nixon 66*)
Match drawn – no play was possible on the fourth day
Kent 10 pts, Surrey 9 pts

at Leicester
Yorkshire 230 (96.5 overs) (MP Vaughan 82, ND Burns 6 catches) and 429 for 8 dec. (DS Lehmann 193, D Byas 100, J Ormond 5 for 146)
Leicestershire 121 (35 overs) and 370 (VJ Wells 133, PAJ DeFreitas 97)
Yorkshire won by 168 runs
Yorkshire 16 pts, Leicestershire 3 pts

at Old Trafford
Lancashire 600 for 6 dec. (JP Crawley 280, JC Scuderi 89, WK Hegg 75*, NH Fairbrother 51) and 243 for 7 dec. (JP Crawley 68, JC Scuderi 61*)
Northamptonshire 495 for 8 dec. (128.5 overs) (RJ Warren 194, ME Hussey 93, GP Swann 54) and 13 for 1
Match drawn
Lancashire 11 pts, Northamptonshire 10 pts

at Cardiff
Essex 327 (110.4 overs) (SG Law 91, AP Cowan 68, JS Foster 57, SL Watkin 6 for 67) and 64 for 0
Glamorgan 546 for 8 dec. (137.5 overs) (JP Maher 217, MJ Powell 108, SD Thomas 68)
Match drawn – no play was possible on the fourth day
Glamorgan 12 pts, Essex 9 pts

Champions Surrey avoided a humiliating defeat by Kent at Canterbury solely because of the all-round talents and fighting spirit of Martin Bicknell. In the end, thanks to Bicknell's magnificent performance with the bat, a last-day washout enabled Surrey to escape with a draw. Though consistently overlooked by England, Bicknell has become the rock on which Surrey's increasingly desperate battle to stay in the championship top flight is founded. Here, coming in to bat with Surrey on 95 for six on the opening morning, Bicknell made 78 to lead a recovery to 258 all out. And then, after Kent had replied with 301, Bicknell was required to march out again with Surrey fading fast at 44 for six on a rain-shortened third day. The Surrey lead was just one run, Martin Saggers and Ben Trott had each taken three wickets, and Kent knew that if Bicknell went early then a famous victory would be theirs inside three days. Bicknell, however, dug in again by playing straight and using his no-frills method to frustrate the bowlers. Even at 129 for eight, he refused to panic or throw his wicket away and, with Saqlain Mushtaq now giving him solid support, the total grew ever larger. By the close Bicknell was 110 not out, and rarely has a maiden first-class century been more deserved. With Saqlain sitting tight on 13, Surrey at 193 for eight had a lead of 150 – but the prospect of an interesting final day was ruined by heavy rain. Bicknell ended this match as Surrey's top wicket-taker in the championship with 60 at 20 runs apiece and, more remarkably, also the county's top run-getter with 660 at an average of 50. And a two-fingered salute to the England selectors, as well? Yes, we might write that, but he couldn't

Keeping Surrey afloat ... another big effort from Martin Bicknell in the match at Canterbury.

possibly comment!

Yorkshire, meanwhile, drove on towards claiming Surrey's title by beating Leicestershire by 168 runs at Grace Road. Michael Vaughan made 82 and 47 in his first first-class match since June 4, bolstering a Yorkshire first innings of 230, but perhaps the most telling contribution of the match came from Steve Kirby. The fiery young fast bowler took two quick wickets on the first evening, as Leicestershire closed on 23 for three, and was so whipped up that he once sledged Trevor Ward by literally bending close to his helmet to make sure his words hit their target. Kirby was told to cool down by the umpires, but in his next over he had Ward caught at first slip. Craig White then took three for 11 the next morning and, at 121 all out, Leicestershire's challenge was fading. A stand of 186 for the fourth wicket between Darren Lehmann (193) and David Byas (100) then ensured a huge overall lead for Yorkshire – although Byas still delayed his declaration until 429 for eight to make certain that Leicestershire could not win. At 132 for seven, chasing their nominal target of 529, it seemed as if the home side were coming quietly, with Kirby picking up three more wickets, but then a cavalier century partnership between Vince Wells (133) and Phil DeFreitas (97) took the match well into the final day. Eventually, with Jimmy Ormond 39 not out, Leicestershire reached 370 and – moreover – Byas was beginning to look increasingly anxiously at approaching rain clouds as victory was clinched.

Storm clouds of a different nature were gathering over Old Trafford, with captain John Crawley going into Lancashire's home match against Northamptonshire with the threat of relegation afflicting his team, stinging words of criticism from high-profile former players ringing in his ears, and the added pressure of playing one of the counties also fighting to avoid the drop. His personal response was heroic. Crawley won the toss, opened the Lancashire innings himself and batted all day to reach 208 not out in a total of 444 for three. Then, the next morning, he batted on to 280 – just six runs short of his career best – before his eight-and-a-half hour epic, containing a six and 39 fours, was brought to an end. Joe Scuderi, with 89, and Warren Hegg, whose unbeaten 75 took only 84 balls, also cashed in on a fine batting surface – but the Lancashire first-innings total of 600 for six declared was all about Crawley's statement of character. 'There are certain fundamental things in the way the team is dealt with, the captain and coach in particular, which need to be addressed,' said

Crawley, in a clear reference to the public criticism of media pundit Paul Allott, who is also a member of the Lancashire committee, and the recent decision of Bobby Simpson to leave his coaching post at the end of the season – an action which was seen by many to be a case of jumping before being pushed. Northants, meanwhile, fought back grittily with the bat themselves as the prolific Mike Hussey hit 93 off 116 balls to leave them at 218 for three at the halfway mark. Russell Warren then converted his overnight 63 into a superb 194, including a six and 26 fours, before being bowled as he missed a sweep off Chris Schofield. Lancashire had hoped their three spinners might tip the balance their way as the pitch dried and dusted still further, but none of them was Muralitharan and Northants were able to declare at 495 for eight as they tried to get something more out of the match themselves. Crawley, in effect, was challenged to set them a target on the last afternoon, but the Lancashire skipper was in no mood for generosity, and hit 68 himself as his side batted on to 243 for seven in their second innings. Northants, left a token 349 in 140 minutes, were 13 for one when rain brought an early finish to a draw which suited Lancashire most.

Bad weather – this time steady drizzle – washed away the final day at Cardiff, and denied Glamorgan the chance to put pressure on an Essex side who were due to resume their second innings still 155 runs adrift at 64 for no wicket. Steve Watkin had taken six for 67 as Essex were dismissed for 327 in their first innings, with Stuart Law stroking 91 and adding 119 for the fifth wicket with James Foster (57), before Ashley Cowan made the tail wag with a hard-hit 68. Glamorgan, however, were soon in command of the contest as left-handed opener Jimmy Maher struck another blow for Australian cricket's dominance by compiling a career-best 217. Maher hit 32 boundaries, and added 284 for the third wicket with Mike Powell (108). Darren Thomas (68) then put on another 98 with Andrew Davies (40) as Glamorgan racked up 546 for eight declared.

Division Two

at Derby
Sussex 280 (112.3 overs) (MW Goodwin 67, MJG Davis 52) and 230 (CJ Adams 59)
Derbyshire 263 (97.5 overs) (LD Sutton 140*) and 117 (LD Sutton 54, MA Robinson 5 for 38)
Sussex won by 130 runs
Sussex 17 pts, Derbyshire 5 pts

at Chester-le-Street
Durham 323 (96 overs) (DR Law 103, JE Brinkley 65) and 202 (ML Love 52, AC Morris 5 for 39)
Hampshire 312 (103.1 overs) (AD Mascarenhas 76, AC Morris 52, GD Bridge 6 for 84) and 216 for 3 (GW White 74, JS Laney 60, WS Kendall 54)
Hampshire won by seven wickets
Hampshire 18 pts, Durham 6 pts

at Bristol
Nottinghamshire 322 (96.4 overs) (P Johnson 149, GE Welton 61, DJ Bicknell 50) and 166 (JE Morris 54)
Gloucestershire 608 for 8 dec. (146 overs) (MGN Windows 174, CG Taylor 148, JN Snape 100*, MW Alleyne 72)
Gloucestershire won by an innings and 120 runs
Gloucestershire 20 pts, Northamptonshire 4 pts

at Edgbaston
Worcestershire 524 (134.1 overs) (GA Hick 201, VS Solanki 112, NM Carter 5 for 78, KJ Piper 4ct/1st) and 233 for 2 dec. (WPC Weston 102*, VS Solanki 56)
Warwickshire 447 for 6 dec. (137 overs) (DL Hemp 186*, DR Brown 85, MA Wagh 83) and 77 for 4
Match drawn
Warwickshire 12 pts, Worcestershire 11 pts

Sussex kept up their momentum at the top of the second division table with a win over Derbyshire at Derby, but they were made to work harder than they might have anticipated by the championship whipping boys. Half-centuries from Murray Goodwin and Mark Davis helped Sussex to reach 280 in the face of some testing seam and swing from Kevin Dean (four for 72) and Trevor Smith (four for 61), but in an equally attritional first innings, Derbyshire made 263 thanks to a remarkable effort by Luke Sutton. The opener carried his bat for a six-and-a-half hour 140, and the match was in the balance as Sussex fought their way to 230 in a second innings pepped up by Chris Adams (59) and Davis again (44). Derbyshire however, needing 248 to win, finally fell away to 117 all out with only Sutton (54) providing any real resistance as Mark Robinson (five for 38) swept away the middle-order following new-ball incisions from Jason Lewry and James Kirtley.

Hampshire moved into second place with a hard-working, seven-wicket win over Durham at Chester-le-Street. There was only an over of the match remaining when Hampshire reached their second-innings target of 214, following an opening stand of 110 between Jason Laney (60) and Giles White (74), but the visitors were always comfortable in their run-chase on the final afternoon as they kept up with an asking rate of four runs per over. Hampshire, in fact, had been 11 runs adrift after the first innings, replying with 312 to Durham's 323, but then took control when Alex Morris – with a career-best five for 39 – had inspired the dismissal of the home side for 202 in their second innings. Nicky Peng suffered concussion when he missed a hook at Neil Johnson during the Durham first innings, and needed a hospital check-up, but the home side recovered from 92 for five as Danny Law (103) hit a maiden championship hundred and added 127 for the seventh wicket with James Brinkley (65). Brinkley then took four for 67 in Hampshire's reply, while Graeme Bridge's promising slow left-arm brought him six for 84, but spirited efforts from Dimitri Mascarenhas (76) and Morris (52) kept Hampshire – crucially – in the game.

Gloucestershire maintained their championship revival by beating Nottinghamshire by an innings and 120 runs at Bristol. Paul Johnson struck a brilliant and typically combative 149 on the opening day – his 40th first-class hundred bringing him to within striking distance of 20,000 career runs – but it was all one-way traffic after Notts had been bowled out for 322. By the close of the second day Gloucestershire were 305 for two, and on the following day Matt Windows (174) and Chris Taylor (148) took their third-wicket partnership to 306 as Gloucestershire surged on to 608 for eight declared. Jeremy Snape finished on 100 not out, with his second fifty taking just 34 balls, and Mark Alleyne chipped in with 72, and Notts were clearly demoralized by their five sessions in the field when they emerged to bat again. By the end of the third day they were already down and out at 139 for nine as the Gloucestershire seamers ran amok, but Notts almost then escaped with an undeserved draw when rain prevented any play on the final day until 5pm. After eight-and-a-half tense overs, James Averis at last removed Stephen Randall to give Gloucestershire a 20-point maximum.

The West Midlands derby between Warwickshire and Worcestershire at Edgbaston ended in a high-scoring draw. Worcestershire ran up 524 in their first innings, with Graeme Hick's 201 anchoring it and giving the skipper the 116th century of his first-class career. Vikram Solanki's 166-ball 112, with three sixes and 15 fours, was perhaps the more

beguiling innings, while Neil Carter did well to emerge with figures of five for 78. A career-best 186 not out from David Hemp then underpinned the Warwickshire reply of 447 for six declared, although Mark Wagh (83) and Dougie Brown (85) also made significant contributions. In the limited time remaining, Worcestershire declared at 233 for two in their second innings, with Philip Weston scoring 102 not out, and Warwickshire limped to 77 for four as Chris Liptrot did some damage with the new ball.

Nottinghamshire's Paul Johnson moves toward his 40th first-class hundred against Gloucestershire at Bristol.

Round Seventeen: 21–26 August 2001

Division One

at Scarborough
Glamorgan 223 (88.1 overs) (A Dale 59, RKJ Dawson
6 for 82) and 245
Yorkshire 580 for 9 dec. (164.5 overs) (C White 183,
MJ Wood 124, D Byas 104, RJ Blakey 54)
Yorkshire won by an innings and 112 runs
Yorkshire 20 pts, Glamorgan 3 pts

at Northampton
Northamptonshire 469 (113.5 overs) (ME Hussey 232)
and 302 for 8 dec. (AJ Swann 113, ME Hussey 82,
RJ Warren 52*, RP Davis 6 for 73)
Leicestershire 484 (138 overs) (Shahid Afridi 164 –
including the to-date fastest hundred of 2001 from 74
balls, Aftab Habib 74*, ND Burns 69, ID Sutcliffe 64,
RP Davis 51) and 85 (GP Swann 5 for 34)
Northamptonshire won by 202 runs
Northamptonshire 19 pts, Leicestershire 8 pts

at Colchester
Lancashire 423 (134.3 overs) (NH Fairbrother 132,
MJ Chilton 98, CP Schofield 80*, RC Irani 6 for 79)
Essex 236 (97.1 overs) and (following on) 334 for 8
(AP Grayson 186*)
Match drawn
Essex 7 pts, Lancashire 12 pts

at Taunton
Somerset 373 (109.4 overs) (ID Blackwell 120, J Cox
76, Saqlain Mushtaq 6 for 107) and 311 for 6 dec.
(M Burns 70, ID Blackwell 67)
Surrey 278 (71.2 overs) (BC Hollioake 56, RL Johnson
5 for 62) and 294 for 6 (AJ Hollioake 83, AD Brown 64,
BC Hollioake 56)
Match drawn
Somerset 11 pts, Surrey 9 pts

Yorkshire's long wait for championship glory ended
just as drizzle began to fall at Scarborough on Friday
24 August when, 19 overs into the final day,
Glamorgan's last second-innings wicket fell to a
catch by David Byas. The Welsh county had fought
hard to resist, none more so than their unbeaten
captain Adrian Dale, on 45, and last man Simon
Jones – whose 46 in a final-wicket stand of 56 had,
remarkably, contained six sixes. But, fittingly,
Yorkshire captain Byas snaffled another attempted
big hit by Jones and – as his county celebrated their
first championship title since Brian Close's great

team won in 1968 – the normally taciturn Byas said:
'I am very emotional. If you had wanted to write a
fairytale it would have been like this. I'm here on my
home ground, in my home town, I have scored a
century in the match, and we have won the
championship!' Byas' 104 came as Yorkshire built a
match-winning, first-innings lead following the
dismissal of Glamorgan for 223 on the opening day.
Richard Dawson, the fast-emerging, 21-year-old, off
spinner, had taken six for 82 and only Dale (59) had
made much of an impression against the Yorkshire
attack. Glamorgan's cause had not been helped
when Matthew Maynard twisted an ankle during the
warm-up and pulled out of the game, but now it was
the turn of their bowlers to suffer as Yorkshire
constructed a massive 580 for nine declared.
Matthew Wood, struck by a ball from Jones, had
been taken to hospital for checks and needed
stitches in a cut over his left eye after retiring hurt
for 15 on the first evening, but he was able to
resume following the fall of nightwatchman Steve
Kirby the next morning and responded with a fine
124. Wood hooked the second ball he faced on
resuming, from Jones, for six. Craig White, too, was
in prime form as he strode on to 183 and, between
them, the pair added 243 for the second wicket.
Then came Byas' hundred, and a supporting 54
from Richard Blakey, as a third successive big crowd
of around 5,000 were made to wait for the
declaration. Ever cautious, Byas wanted to grind his
opponents down before allowing them to bat again,
and his tactics seemed to be justified when
Glamorgan struggled to reach 142 for six by the
close of day three. Pettily, the ECB refused to allow
an official trophy presentation ceremony, because of
the possibility of points deductions for poor pitches,
but the Yorkshire players opened the champagne
anyway and the joyous Yorkshire public began to
party the moment this innings-and-112-run victory
was complete.

Northamptonshire kept their hopes of avoiding
relegation alive with a dramatic 202-run win against
Leicestershire at Northampton. For almost three-
and-a-half days, however, this contest looked
destined to be a high-scoring draw, despite help for
the spinners on a dry, dusting surface. But then,
having declared their second innings at 302 for
eight, just after lunch, Northants skittled out their
neighbours and close rivals for just 85 to earn
themselves a priceless 19-point success. The heroes
of the last afternoon were the three-pronged spin
attack of Graeme Swann, Jason Brown and Monty
Panesar – with 19-year-old slow left-armer Panesar

Ian Blackwell hit 187 runs in total against Surrey to propel Somerset towards second position in the championship.

producing, on first-class debut, the most eye-catching figures of 20-16-11-4. Swann was not as phenomenally accurate as the Luton-born, Bedford School-educated Sikh, but he constantly switched his line of attack imaginatively to pick up five for 34 with his off breaks. Brown, the senior off spinner,

was accurate and testing too, but only had the wicket of Vince Wells to show for his labours. Trevor Ward, with a 32-over 20, was the only Leicestershire batsman to resist for long, but what a contrast such a struggle was after the run-fest of the previous three innings. Mike Hussey was the first player to get stuck in, reaching 150 not out in a rain-shortened opening day, and then going on to make 232 as Northants totalled 469. Leicestershire, though, hit back thrillingly and hard through the explosive strokeplay of Shahid Afridi. After completing the fastest first-class hundred of the season from 74 balls, the Pakistani rushed on to 164 off a mere 121 balls – hitting, overall, six sixes and 22 fours. Iain Sutcliffe made 64 in an opening stand of 233 and, on the third day, Leicestershire won themselves a slight first-innings lead by going on to 484. Neil Burns (69), Aftab Habib (74 not out) and Richard Davis (51) all contributed significantly and, although the Northants spin trio had captured all ten wickets between them, they conceded more than 100 runs apiece. How different it was all to be on the final day, after Northants had batted well again through the remarkable Hussey (82), Alec Swann (113) and Russell Warren (52 not out). Davis, a 35-year-old slow left-arm spinner making his debut for a fifth county, after being signed on a special registration the day before the match, ended up with six for 73 but was about to be completely outshone.

A magnificent innings of 186 not out by Paul Grayson allowed Essex to escape with a hard-earned draw against Lancashire at Colchester. Essex had followed on after being bowled out for 236 in reply to Lancashire's 423 – a total built around Mark Chilton's 98 and the evergreen Neil Fairbrother's 132, but also featuring a career-best 80 not out from Chris Schofield. Ronnie Irani's six for 79 was a fighting performance, but his Essex team seemed to be facing almost certain defeat when they slid to 110 for three second time around by the close of the third day. Grayson, however, who had opened the innings, held firm throughout a total of 129 overs – and 87 on the final day – to guide Essex to 334 for eight. The best of the support he received came from Ashley Cowan, with 32.

Somerset had much the better of a draw with Surrey at Taunton, but will perhaps look back on this game as one they could have won if they had been prepared to gamble more with the prospect of defeat. Caution, however, is fast becoming the watchword of the two-division championship – and Jamie Cox, the Somerset skipper, certainly erred on the side of it when he decided to bat on for another

11 overs on the fourth morning to set Surrey a win target of 407 in what turned out to be 84 overs. Surrey finished on 294 for six, after the attacking natures of Adam Hollioake (83), Ally Brown (64) and Ben Hollioake (56) had tempted them to go for glory, but at no stage did Somerset feed those temptations with some easy runs in a bid to lead Surrey on to the rocks. Ian Blackwell had another good match with the bat for Somerset, scoring 120 in the first innings of 373, and then 67 off 75 balls before the second-innings declaration came at 311 for six. Other performances of note were Jamie Cox's first-day 76, Saqlain Mushtaq's tenacious six for 107, and the five for 62 with which Richard Johnson caused Surrey's first-innings slide to 278 all out.

Division Two

at Hove
Durham 254 (105 overs) (JA Daley 89, RJ Kirtley 5 for 48) and 199 (ML Love 82, RJ Kirtley 5 for 47, MA Robinson 5 for 59)
Sussex 117 (35.4 overs) and 265 (RSC Martin-Jenkins 94, MW Goodwin 65)
Durham won by 71 runs
Durham 17 pts, Sussex 3 pts

at Trent Bridge
Derbyshire 320 (101.1 overs) (MJ Di Venuto 165, CWG Bassano 56, RJ Logan 6 for 93) and 221 (MJ Di Venuto 93, MN Malik 5 for 57)
Nottinghamshire 322 (77.2 overs) (KP Pietersen 150, KJ Dean 5 for 89) and 223 for 3 (GS Blewett 106*, P Johnson 65)
Nottinghamshire won by seven wickets
Nottinghamshire 18 pts, Derbyshire 6 pts

at Worcester
Worcestershire 247 (81 overs) and 306 (AJ Bichel 78, GA Hick 76, SJ Rhodes 52)
Hampshire 247 (97.1 overs) (NC Johnson 103) and 194 (AJ Bichel 5 for 62)
Worcestershire won by 112 runs
Worcestershire 16 pts, Hampshire 4 pts

at Lord's
Middlesex 502 for 7 dec. (153.5 overs) (PN Weekes 107, EC Joyce 104, DC Nash 103*, SP Fleming 102) and 167 for 6 (SP Fleming 65)
Warwickshire 631 for 9 dec. (167.4 overs) (MA Wagh 315, IR Bell 98, DR Brown 53)
Match drawn
Middlesex 10 pts, Warwickshire 10 pts

Durham upset Sussex's progress at the top of the division, defeating them by 71 runs on their home patch at Hove. Sussex's fate was sealed when, in reply to a Durham first-innings total of 254 based on Jimmy Daley's excellent 89, they were tumbled out for just 117. Their lowest total of the season, in which Steve Harmison took four for 52 to exploit cloudy and murky second-morning conditions, put them in big trouble, and, by the end of the day, Martin Love had increased Durham's stranglehold by hitting 16 fours in a superb 82. Resuming the next day on 179 for five, however, Durham slid sloppily to 199 all out as James Kirtley added five for 47 to his

Mark Wagh cuts on his way to 315 against Middlesex

first-innings haul of five for 48 and Mark Robinson took five for 59. Needing 337 for victory, there was still an outside chance of a home victory, but no-one could stay with Murray Goodwin (65) early on and in the end it took a brave 94 from Robin Martin-Jenkins to get Sussex up to 265 all out.

Michael Di Venuto did his best to inspire Derbyshire against their keen rivals Nottinghamshire at Trent Bridge, but ultimately the Tasmanian left-hander's 165 and 93 were not enough to prevent a comfortable seven-wicket win for the home side. Di Venuto began the match by racing to a 43-ball fifty, and in all he struck 20 boundaries as Derbyshire totalled 320 in their first innings. Chris Bassano hit 56, but Richard Logan's six for 93 was instrumental in keeping Notts in the game. Kevin Pietersen then took command of the stage, underlining his enormous talent by smashing six sixes and 19 fours in a brilliant 150. Kevin Dean took five for 89 to try and hold him down, but Pietersen's mastery was such that he plundered 73 of the last 75 runs scored in the innings of 322. With honours even, however, by the close of the second day as Derbyshire moved to 51 without loss, a close contest seemed in store. Di Venuto certainly did his best, with his 93, but Derbyshire's batting otherwise fell away and, with Nadeem Malik picking up five for 57, they were bowled out for 221. By the day's end, Notts were already within touching distance of their target at 172 for three, Paul Johnson stroking 11 fours in his 65 from 88 balls to lend Greg Blewett just the support he wanted. Blewett went on from an overnight 76 to 106 not out as Notts quickly wrapped things up on the fourth morning.

Hampshire's batting fell away badly against Worcestershire at New Road as their promotion aims were undermined by a 112-run defeat. Neil Johnson's 103, containing two sixes and 14 fours, had enabled Hampshire to match exactly Worcestershire's first-innings total of 247, in which seven batsmen scored between 22 and 35, but none managed to go on. But, after Worcestershire had totalled 306 second time around, with Graeme Hick (76), Andy Bichel (78) and Steve Rhodes (52) all playing important knocks, Hampshire dissolved worryingly to 194 all out. Bichel completed his fine match by taking five for 62.

Perhaps the individual performance of this round of games should go, however, to Warwickshire's Mark Wagh. The 24-year-old, at last beginning to fulfill this season the prophecies of greatness which surrounded his youth, hit an epic 315 – unsurprisingly a career-best – in a high-scoring draw with Middlesex at Lord's. Replying to Middlesex's first-innings total of 502 for seven declared, in which there were four different century-makers for the county for the first time since 1923, Warwickshire slipped initially to six for two. Then, though, Wagh took complete control as, first in the company of 19-year-old Ian Bell, he anchored a mammoth reply of 631 for nine declared. Bell was disappointed to fall for 98, but Dougie Brown hung around for 53 and Wagh – who had been on 81 at the match's halfway point – finished the third day on 266 after nine hours at the crease. Amazingly, after he had finally been caught off Tim Bloomfield after batting for 630 minutes and facing 449 balls, Wagh took two for 29 from 18 overs of off breaks as Middlesex wobbled uncertainly for a while before holding out for the draw at 167 for six. In their own first innings, though, there had been centuries for Stephen Fleming (102), Ed Joyce (104), Paul Weekes (107) and David Nash (103 not out). Joyce, a 22-year-old left-hander from Dublin, became, in his tenth first-class match, the only born-and-bred Irishman to score a championship hundred.

ROUND EIGHTEEN: 5–10 SEPTEMBER 2001

Division One

at The Oval
Yorkshire 235 (114.4 overs) (A McGrath 116*, MJ Wood 51) and 235 (A McGrath 73, MP Vaughan 61, Saqlain Mushtaq 7 for 58)
Surrey 516 for 9 dec. (130.4 overs) (MR Ramprakash 131, BC Hollioake 118, MA Butcher 90, IJ Ward 63)
Surrey won by an innings and 46 runs
Surrey 20 pts, Yorkshire 3 pts

at Chelmsford
Somerset 391 (118.2 overs) (J Cox 186, RJ Turner 70) and 64 for 1
Essex 172 (59.2 overs) (DDJ Robinson 89, RL Johnson 5 for 40) and (following on) 282 (SG Law 66, GR Napier 56)
Somerset won by nine wickets
Somerset 19 pts, Essex 3 pts

at Leicester
Leicestershire 372 (85.2 overs) (ND Burns 111, BF Smith 68, VJ Wells 67) and 20 for 0
Glamorgan 146 (49.5 overs) (SA James 61*) and (following on) 245 (JP Maher 100)
Leicestershire won by 10 wickets
Leicestershire 19 pts , Glamorgan 3 pts

at Canterbury
Kent 108 (25 overs) (JAR Blain 6 for 42) and 576 for 8 dec. (DP Fulton 196, MA Ealham 153*)
Northamptonshire 357 (115.4 overs) (RJ Warren 104, AL Penberthy 73, AJ Swann 61, JW Cook 50, BJ Trott 5 for 89) and 199 for 9 (D Ripley 62*)
Match drawn
Kent 7 pts, Northamptonshire 11 pts

Surrey's fears of relegation were eased by their innings-and-46-run thrashing of Yorkshire at The Oval, but the rest of the division had every right to be irked by the make-up of the new champions' line-up for this high-profile match. No less than six members of what would be Yorkshire's strongest XI were missing: Craig White (barred by the England management), Darren Gough (resting a slight niggle), Darren Lehmann (resting a bad knee), and three other senior fast bowlers in Chris Silverwood, Ryan Sidebottom and Gavin Hamilton (all carrying an injury). By contrast, Surrey were fielding all their heavyweights bar Graham Thorpe. No doubt had Yorkshire needed points from this match to tie up the championship, at least three of those absent six would have played – a fact that meant that yet again the aim of the two-division system (raising standards and higher 'intensity') was compromised by reality. Matthew Wood made 51 and Anthony McGrath battled long and hard to remain 116 not out, but Yorkshire's first-innings 235 soon allowed Surrey to move into a position of authority against their much-weakened attack. Mark Butcher (90) and Ian Ward, with a more circumspect 63, set the tone for the rest of the match by adding 164 for the first wicket and, although Surrey wobbled slightly to 222 for five, by the close of the second day they were already 56 runs in front as Mark Ramprakash and Ben Hollioake settled into a decisive partnership. Matthew Hoggard and Steve Kirby both bowled with fire in an effort to dislodge them, but Ramprakash and Hollioake eventually took their sixth-wicket stand to a massive 215 as Surrey totalled 516 for nine declared. Ramprakash scored a high-class 131 while Hollioake finally added a maiden championship century to the two first-class hundreds he had made in Sri Lanka with England 'A'. Hollioake's 118 included three sixes and 16 fours. Yorkshire's second-innings resistance came solely in a century third-wicket stand between Michael Vaughan (61) and the impressive McGrath (73). They were still together on the third evening, with Yorkshire on 171 for two, but both fell early the next day as Saqlain Mushtaq (seven for 58)

teamed up with Martin Bicknell to send Yorkshire tumbling to their second total of 235 all out in the match. Surrey's maximum haul of 20 points virtually assured them of staying up and, although the 1999 and 2000 champions are clearly too good a side to be outside the top division, the manner of their survival left a rather unpleasant taste in the mouth.

Somerset made sure of the runners-up position, the highest championship finish in the club's 126-year history, by beating Essex by nine wickets at Chelmsford. Jamie Cox, the captain, underpinned Somerset's first-innings 391 with a superb 186. Rob Turner (70) joined Cox in a 176-run stand which rallied their side from an unpromising 139 for five. The value of their runs was soon apparent as Essex slumped to 172 all out, despite Darren Robinson's 89, with Richard Johnson (five for 40) and Keith Dutch (four for 32) combining to good effect. Essex, following on, then totalled just 282, with the ever-improving Johnson and Ian Blackwell picking up three wickets apiece and Dutch this time chipping in with two. Stuart Law, in his last appearance as an Essex player at Chelmsford, scored 66 and received a generous hand on his return to the dressing room. A good number of his team-mates, too, stood and applauded a player who has given much to Essex cricket over six years – a welcome sight, given the personality clashes which soured his final months at the club. Somerset were left needing just 64 runs for victory – a task which took them little more than nine overs. As for Essex, their only consolation as a dreadful season drew to a close was the news that Graham Gooch, the former England captain, was to return to his native county as head coach. Gooch said he was prepared to put on hold a burgeoning career as a media pundit to come to the aid of his former county, for whom he scored 30,701 first-class runs in 25 seasons between 1973 and 1997.

Glamorgan were relegated as a result of their ten-wicket defeat by Leicestershire at Grace Road, with the victory confirming the home side's first-division status for 2002. It was a disappointing moment for the Welsh county, who were promoted with such hope the previous year, but they can have few complaints. Poor bowling, their most obvious deficiency, was all too apparent once more as Leicestershire racked up 372 in their first innings, with Neil Burns hitting a fine 111 after Ben Smith (68) and Vince Wells (67) had done much of the early spadework to resuscitate their side following initial collapses to 28 for three and then 93 for five. Jimmy Ormond's four for 43 was then instrumental in undermining Glamorgan's first innings, with only

Man of Kent ... all-rounder Mark Ealham scored an unbeaten 153 against Northamptonshire.

skipper Steve James standing firm as they were bundled out for 146. James carried his bat for an unbeaten 61, but by the close of the second day, Glamorgan were 126 for two as they followed on. Jimmy Maher, the left-handed Australian, took his overnight 78 to 100, from 112 balls, but soon Adrian Dale was left high and dry on 32 not out as the tail subsided. Ormond, Devon Malcolm and Darren Maddy shared nine wickets.

Northamptonshire remained prime candidates to join Glamorgan and Essex in division two after their abject failure to beat Kent at Canterbury – despite dismissing them for just 108 on the opening morning. John Blain took six for 42, almost doubling his first-class wicket tally for the season, and only a spirited 32 by Min Patel hauled Kent up into three figures on a damp pitch. As it dried out, however, a batting paradise was revealed, and Northants took advantage of the improving conditions to total 357 in their first innings. Alec Swann and Jeff Cook compiled worthy half-centuries on the second half of that dramatic first day, and then Russell Warren (104) was joined by Tony Penberthy (73) in an unflashy but sensibly solid stand of 167 for the fourth wicket that seemingly put the match out of Kent's reach. Yet, from 308 for three, Northants fell away alarmingly as Ben Trott (five for 89) spearheaded a determined Kentish comeback and, by the halfway mark in the game, the home side were 158 for three in their second innings and sniffing half a chance of an escape route. David Fulton, indeed, had no intention of giving up his wicket carelessly – especially as he had been dropped on 37 by Northants' wicket-keeper David Ripley. Fulton began the third day on 80, and as it wore on, Ripley's error began to assume a major significance. From 202 for five, Kent flourished in the form of a sixth-wicket partnership of 219 between Fulton and Mark Ealham, with 29-year-old opener Fulton finally falling for 196 only when he hit a short ball straight to cover. His eight-hour epic had brought him alongside Arthur Fagg in Kent's record books – Fagg having scored nine first-class hundreds in the 1938 season – and just behind Frank Woolley, who hit ten in both 1928 and 1934. At the start of the final day Kent were 214 runs in front at 463 for six, with Ealham unbeaten on 109, but Matthew Fleming adopted uncharacteristic caution by not declaring until lunch at 576 for eight. Ealham finished on a career-best 153 not out, but the fact that he could not bowl due to a muscle strain probably persuaded Fleming to act conservatively. Northants, set 328 in what turned out to be 76 overs as the spinners wheeled away in poor light, looked devastated by Kent's magnificent comeback as they slipped to 96 for seven. But then Ripley, no doubt straining to atone for his missed catch two days earlier, rallied the lower-order with a gutsy unbeaten 62. In the end, with Kent appealing unsuccessfully for an extra over just as the clock ticked to 6pm, Northants held out at 199 for nine for the draw that was not really much good to them.

Division Two

at Southampton Rose Bowl
Middlesex 101 (50 overs) (AJ Strauss 56,
AD Mascarenhas 6 for 26) and 253 (AJ Strauss 112*
(carried his bat), SP Fleming 74)
Hampshire 191 (70.2 overs) (SD Udal 62,
AN Aymes 57*) and 166 for 5 (NC Johnson 74)
Hampshire won by five wickets
Hampshire 15 pts, Middlesex 3 pts

at Edgbaston
Sussex 321 (105.5 overs) (MW Goodwin 150) and 376
for 5 dec. (CJ Adams 139, RR Montgomerie 121,
TR Ambrose 52)
Warwickshire 248 (86.3 overs) (IR Bell 80, VC Drakes
50) and 240 for 3 (MA Wagh 74*, NV Knight 59)
Match drawn
Sussex 10 pts, Warwickshire 8 pts

at Bristol
Gloucestershire 508 (130 overs) (DR Hewson 168,
IJ Harvey 104, MCJ Ball 59)
Derbyshire 210 (61.4 overs) (SD Stubbings 62,
MJ Di Venuto 61, MCJ Ball 6 for 23) and (following on)
278 (SD Stubbings 120, IJ Harvey 5 for 89)
Gloucestershire won by an innings and 20 runs
Gloucestershire 20 pts, Derbyshire 4 pts

at Chester-le-Street
Durham 369 (132.3 overs) (JJB Lewis 129,
 PD Collingwood 103) and 237 for 7 dec.
(PD Collingwood 68, ML Love 62)
Worcestershire 356 for 9 dec. (93.2 overs)
(GA Hick 200*, WPC Weston 55) and 85 for 7
Match drawn
Durham 11 pts, Worcestershire 11 pts

Hampshire clinched promotion after out-punching
close rivals Middlesex in what effectively was an
eliminator at Southampton. It was, however, a tense
contest in which 17 wickets fell on the opening day
and which only fully swung Hampshire's way on the
third and final morning. Dimitri Mascarenhas made
the first significant contribution to Hampshire's
cause with six for 26 as Middlesex's first innings
distintegrated to 101 all out on the opening day.
Andrew Strauss, the left-handed opener, batted well
to score 56, but the ball was swinging and, on a
pitch with a little bit of uneven bounce, a succession
of batsmen found survival difficult. By the close,
indeed, Hampshire were 99 for seven in reply
themselves – with Angus Fraser sweating buckets in

the Middlesex cause as he took three for 34 in an
unbroken spell of 22 overs. Chad Keegan went on to
pick up four for 54, as well, but Hampshire's eighth-
wicket pair of Adrian Aymes (57 not out) and Shaun
Udal (62) produced a stand of 102 which boosted
the total to 191 all out. Back, though, came
Middlesex again with Strauss being joined by
Stephen Fleming (74) in a third-wicket partnership
of 127. At the end of day two, Middlesex were 232
for five in their second innings, with Strauss having
just completed a very fine hundred, and the match
seemed to be in the balance. On the third morning,
however, the Hampshire bowlers made the decisive
move, taking the remaining five wickets for just 21
runs and leaving Strauss high and dry on 112 not
out, and the first Middlesex player to carry his bat
for six years. At 27 for three, Hampshire's target of
164 seemed a way off, but just when home fans
feared yet another swing in fortune, Neil Johnson
arrived to join Will Kendall in a match-winning
stand of 91. Kendall's 38 was invaluable, but it was
Johnson's more aggressive 74 which provided
Hampshire with the conviction they required at such
a critical moment. John Francis, too, played well to
see Hampshire home by five wickets with an
unbeaten 29.

Sussex also made sure of their promotion to
division one by taking the ten points they needed
from a draw with Warwickshire at Edgbaston. So
determined were Sussex to avenge their
disappointment of 2000, when they led the second
division for a time before collapsing in the final
weeks of the season and finishing last, that Chris
Adams even delayed his declaration on the final day
to ensure that the risk of defeat was taken out of the
equation. Adams, the captain, made 139 in a Sussex
second innings of 376 for five declared – and that
after his side had gained a first-innings lead of 73 by
bowling out the home side for 248 in reply to their
own 321. It was another case of two divisions
breeding excessive caution, but in this case Sussex's
reasons were entirely valid – even if the match then
fell away as a contest with Warwickshire jogging
along to 240 for three in the 79 overs remaining.
Murray Goodwin underlined his magnificent
contribution to Sussex's success with a first-innings
150, and his similarly prolific opening partner
Richard Montgomerie scored 121 as he helped
Adams add 199 for the third wicket during the
Sussex second innings. Robin Martin-Jenkins took
four for 75 in the Warwickshire first innings, in
which Ian Bell again impressed with 80. Eighteen-
year-old Tim Ambrose caught the eye on debut with

52 in the Sussex second innings, and both Nick Knight and Mark Wagh cashed in with half-centuries on the final afternoon.

Gloucestershire moved into the third promotion place, seven points ahead of Middlesex, by trouncing bottom-of-the-table Derbyshire by an innings and 20 runs at Bristol. The home side's first-innings 508 was based on an elegant 168 from opener Dominic Hewson, featuring 29 fours, and an explosive 104 from Ian Harvey. The Australian all-rounder smashed his runs in a stand of 115, from only 65 balls, and his assault contained six sixes and 12 boundaries. Poor Derbyshire simply could not halt him as he completed the fastest first-class hundred of the season in 61 deliveries with unorthodox brilliance. By the end of the day Gloucestershire were 418 for five and, on the second

morning, Martyn Ball enjoyed himself with 13 fours in a sparkling 59. It was with his off spin, however, that Ball really increased Derbyshire's suffering. He caused havoc among the visitors' seven left-handers and, in 18 controlled overs, took six for 23 as Derbyshire plunged from 121 without loss to 210 all out. Steve Stubbings made 62 and Michael Di Venuto 61 in that opening stand, but by the close Di Venuto was out again as Derbyshire, following on, slipped to 33 for two in their second innings. Stubbings, a well-built left-hander of much promise, continued to lead the resistance the next day with 120 – during which he passed 1,000 runs for the season – but Gloucestershire's bowlers kept taking wickets at the other end. Nathan Dumelow did swing four sixes and three fours in a 56-ball 48, but the last word went to Harvey (five for 89) and Ball (three for 67) as Derbyshire were dismissed for 278. Better news for Derbyshire, however, came during this latest defeat when it was confirmed that Dominic Cork had agreed a new contract to stay at the club until the end of the 2004 season – and to stay on as captain for 2002.

The latest run-scoring achievement of Graeme Hick dominated proceedings at Chester-le-Street where, in the end, despite his first-innings 200 not out off 238 balls, Worcestershire were forced to hang on grimly for a draw. After Durham had built a first-innings total of 369, with Jon Lewis (129) and Paul Collingwood (103) doubling their score in a third-wicket stand of 138, Hick set about the bowling with his familiar, clinical efficiency. He was 68 not out by the end of day two, and then cruised on to his double century after becoming the first batsman to complete a first-class hundred against all 17 other counties. Phil Mead, of Hampshire, and Wally Hammond, of Gloucestershire, were the only previous batsmen to have made a 'full set' for their counties against the (then) 16 others. It was also Hick's 117th first-class ton, bringing him level with Sir Donald Bradman in the all-time list, and after hitting 26 boundaries he brought up his 200 with a straight six off Graeme Bridge. Hick's last fifty occupied only 23 balls, and his mastery allowed Worcestershire to declare at 356 for nine. Durham then ran up 237 for seven declared in their second innings,

The Plunderer. Graeme Hick clocks up another batting record at Chester-le-Street.

with Martin Love (62) and Collingwood (68) batting attractively, and they were then left wishing they had declared a little earlier as Worcestershire, set 251, struggled to bat out the remaining 55 overs and finished on 85 for seven.

ROUND NINETEEN: 12–15 SEPTEMBER

Division One

at Taunton
Northamptonshire 463 for 9 dec. (134 overs)
(ME Hussey 208, RJ Warren 144, RJ Turner 7ct) and
432 for 9 dec. (AL Penberthy 101, JW Cook 88,
GP Swann 61, JP Taylor 53, ID Blackwell 5 for 122)
Somerset 650 (137.3 overs) (KA Parsons 139,
MJ Wood 122, MN Lathwell 92, J Cox 82,
ID Blackwell 77) and 250 for 6 (J Cox 86, MJ Wood 65)
Somerset won by four wickets
Somerset 20 pts, Northamptonshire 7 pts

at Old Trafford
Kent 377 (103.5 overs) (RWT Key 132, PA Nixon 87*,
M Muralitharan 5 for 130)
Lancashire 21 for 1 (12.4 overs)
Match drawn – no play was possible on the second and fourth days)
Lancashire 7 pts, Kent 8 pts

at Scarborough
Essex 250 (77.3 overs) (MJ Hoggard 6 for 51) and 172
for 8 dec. (RC Irani 51*)
Yorkshire 104 for 5 dec. (33.3 overs) and 267
(MP Vaughan 113, A McGrath 70, AP Grayson 5 for 20)
Essex won by 51 runs – no play was possible on the second day
Essex 15 pts, Yorkshire 3 pts

at Cardiff
Glamorgan 258 (74.4 overs) (RDB Croft 70*, MJ Powell
56) and 69 for 1
Surrey 701 for 9 dec. (191.3 overs) (MA Butcher 230,
AD Brown 115, AJ Hollioake 97, MA Carberry 84,
IJ Ward 63)
Match drawn
Glamorgan 7 pts, Surrey 12 pts

Northamptonshire, needing to beat Somerset at Taunton to go above fellow relegation candidates Lancashire and avoid the drop, ultimately failed in a brave bid to win a game of 1,795 runs. Only one other championship match in history – Sussex v. Essex at Hove in 1993 – has produced more

aggregate runs, 1,808, and Northants began by posting a formidable 463 for nine declared. On the first evening they had already run up 382 for five with Mike Hussey and Russell Warren putting on 287 in 77 overs for the third wicket. Hussey took his overnight 192 not out to 208 the next morning, and during his innings the prolific West Australian became the first Northants player since Allan Lamb in 1981 to top 2,000 championship runs for the season. There was also a county-record seven dismissals for Somerset wicket-keeper Rob Turner in the Northants first innings. If the visitors thought they were on top, however, they were sadly mistaken. Somerset, in reply, scored at five runs per over on Taunton's wonderful batting surface to whistle up 650 all out – their highest total at their headquarters. Jamie Cox made 82 in an opening stand worth 163 with 20-year-old Matt Wood, who was then joined by fellow Devonian Mark Lathwell in a lovely stand between two highly-watchable strokemakers. Wood finally went for 122, a maiden first-class hundred, and Lathwell's 92 from 111 balls was a joy. Then came the butchery, as Keith Parsons smote two sixes and 20 fours in his 139 while Ian Blackwell included two sixes and 11 boundaries in his 83-ball 77. By the close of the third day, Northants were 89 for one in their second innings and still almost 100 runs behind. Nevertheless, they went for their strokes on the final morning and into the afternoon, and in 65.2 further overs had managed to lift their total to 432 for nine declared. Jeff Cook's 88 set the tone early on, and Tony Penberthy (101) played another innings of substance. Graeme Swann, with 61 from 48 balls, and Paul Taylor, with a violent 32-ball fifty, provided a late burst of acceleration and, set 246 from 42 overs, there was still time for Somerset to lose the match in a run-chase that went wrong. Unhappily for Northants, and despite the best efforts of their spinners, Somerset made no such error. Cox (86) and Wood (65) put on 147 for the first wicket, and there were enough wickets in hand to cope with an asking rate first of 100 off 12 overs and then 49 from the final six. Parsons, in the end, was the man who swept Somerset to the victory which rounded off their best-ever championship season in style. His 36 not out, from 19 balls, included the winning hit – a six swung off Monty Panesar from the third delivery of the last over.

Meanwhile, at Old Trafford, Lancashire were mightily relieved when confirmation of Northants' defeat came through. Rain had all but obliterated their match against Kent, with the second and fourth days being washed away completely to take the tally of total washouts to 13 for the summer. In what play there was, Kent reached 117 for three in the 28 overs possible on day one, and going on to total 377 when the contest resumed on the third day. Rob Key underlined the strides he had taken during the season to compile a career-best 132, with two sixes and 19 fours, and Paul Nixon finished on 87 not out. The Kent wicket-keeper even reverse-swept Muttiah Muralitharan for one extraordinary six, the Sri Lankan spinner having been flown back from Asia especially for this match as Lancashire revealed just how desperate they were to stay in division one. Murali's five for 130 from 38 overs took his season's tally to 50 from seven matches. Lancashire had time only to reach 21 for one in their own first innings before the third day, and subsequently the match, ended.

Champions Yorkshire looked like finishing their triumphant season on a fitting note, after two positive declarations set up an exciting final afternoon at Scarborough. But relegated Essex found in Paul Grayson an unlikely demon bowler as Yorkshire collapsed from 204 for two to 267 all out, and defeat by 51 runs. The match began with Darren Gough the only absentee from the group of 25 players who had represented Yorkshire in their championship campaign – a group which had been gathered together at Scarborough for the official presentation of the trophy, and commemorative photographs. Gough had a prior engagement at a golf day, but his absence merely fuelled still further strong local rumours that he was about to leave a club he had represented just twice in the championship during the summer. Just 36 overs were possible on day one, Essex reaching 99 for three, and then the second day was washed out completely. Matthew Hoggard, in only his seventh first-class match of the season because of foot problems, took a career-best six for 51 as Essex were bowled out for 250, and Yorkshire captain David Byas then declared his team's first-innings reply at 104 for five. The challenge was accepted by Essex, who declared their second innings on 172 for eight shortly before lunch on the final day. Yorkshire lost both their openers without a run on the board, but Michael Vaughan also tried to put an injury-troubled season behind him with a blissful 113 from just 89 balls, with four sixes and 16 fours, while Anthony McGrath was scarcely less impressive with 70. Their 204-run stand for the third wicket required just 26 overs, but when they were parted,

Mark Butcher, England's newest cricket hero, hits Glamorgan for 230 at Cardiff.

Grayson stepped in with his slow left-arm spinners to claim five for 20 from ten overs and change the course of the innings.

Another rain-hit match, at Cardiff, brought no such enterprise from Surrey captain Adam Hollioake. His side had already run up 572 for three in reply to Glamorgan's first-innings 258 after three stop-start days, but when play began late on the final day he decided not to declare, and set Glamorgan 314 in what would have been around 67 overs to avoid an innings defeat, but to bat on instead to a huge, but meaningless, 701 for nine declared. In the short time that then remained, Glamorgan scored 69 for one off 14 overs with 20-year-old debutant Jonathan Hughes hitting out to add 49 to his first-innings 38. Robert Croft's unbeaten 70 was

Glamorgan's best score in their first innings, but then England Test hero, Mark Butcher, began to dwarf all other efforts by putting together a superb 230, the second double-hundred of his career and packed full of beautifully timed strokes all around the wicket. Michael Carberry (84), Ian Ward (63), Hollioake, whose quickfire 97 in 47 overs helped add 199 for the third wicket with Butcher, and Alistair Brown, with 115, all enjoyed themselves. The Glamorgan supporters were less than amused, however.

Division Two

at Derby
Derbyshire 106 (42.2 overs) (CE Dagnall 6 for 50) and 194 (DR Brown 6 for 60)
Warwickshire 400 for 6 dec. (85.4 overs) (IR Bell 135, NV Knight 124, DR Brown 53*)
Warwickshire won by an innings and 100 runs
Warwickshire 20 pts, Derbyshire 2 pts

at Hove
Sussex 384 (112.5 overs) (RSC Martin-Jenkins 113, RJ Kirtley 51*, RJ Sillence 5 for 97) and 18 for 0
Gloucestershire 228 (60.1 overs) (IJ Harvey 71) and (following on) 173 (DR Hewson 79, RJ Kirtley 6 for 34)
Sussex won by ten wickets
Sussex 19 pts, Gloucestershire 4 pts

at Worcester
Middlesex 349 (94.3 overs) (RMS Weston 106, AJ Strauss 92, PN Weekes 63, A Sheriyar 5 for 121) and 368 for 4 dec. (EC Joyce 108*, AJ Strauss 83, SP Fleming 55)
Worcestershire 434 (113 overs) (A Singh 168, WPC Weston 71) and 179 for 4 (GA Hick 59*)
Match drawn
Worcestershire 12 pts, Middlesex 11 pts

at Trent Bridge
Nottinghamshire 245 (76.3 overs) (Usman Afzaal 91, AD Mullally 5 for 74, AC Morris 5 for 108) and 314 for 7 dec. (KP Pietersen 87, BM Shafayat 75, DJ Bicknell 62)
Hampshire 259 for 4 dec. (75 overs) (NC Johnson 105*, JD Francis 72*) and 245 for 6 (GW White 112, WS Kendall 72)
Match drawn
Nottinghamshire 6 pts, Hampshire 9 pts

Warwickshire seized on the opportunity presented to them by playing hapless Derbyshire in their final

Warwickshire's Ian Bell underlined his enormous potential with a sumptuous innings of 135 against Derbyshire.

match, duly completing a maximum 20-point victory by an innings and 100 runs and confirming their promotion to division one by finishing in third place. Seconds after Mel Betts finished off the Derbyshire second innings, following a 65-run, last-wicket stand between Tom Lungley and Lian Wharton, it began to rain – but, overall, Warwickshire always looked in control of this game once they had tumbled out the home side for 106 on a first day at Derby shortened to just 43 overs by the weather. Charlie Dagnall, with six for 50 from 21 unchanged overs, and Dougie Brown (four for 20) did that early damage, and despite reaching only 69 for three in reply on an even shorter rain-hit second day, Warwickshire were soon in total command as Nick Knight and Ian Bell racked up a brilliant 245-run stand for the fourth wicket on day three. Knight made 124, but it was 19-year-old Bell who really caught the eye with 135 from 178 balls. Compact, classy, patient, but with a welcome desire to punish hard anything loose, Bell took his run aggregate from his last six matches to 597 at an average of 85. Perhaps the Warwickshire management might find such a comment churlish, but why on earth did a batting talent like Bell have to wait, first for Knight to be called up into the England one-day squad and then for Dominic Ostler to sustain an elbow injury, before being given his chance in the championship side? Brown's 41-ball unbeaten 53 quickly lifted Warwickshire to 400 for six declared, and by the close of the third day Derbyshire were down and almost out at 91 for five. Brown's six for 60 was the feature of the final day, despite the resistance led by Lungley's 47.

At Hove, meanwhile, Sussex's ten-wicket victory confirmed them as second division champions and prevented Gloucestershire from challenging Warwickshire for that third and final promotion berth. In fairness, Gloucestershire's wretched season-long luck with injuries finally caught up with them at this last hurdle: they just did not have the strength to leap it. Ian Harvey, Mike Smith and Jon Lewis were all out of their first-choice attack – and although Harvey was able to play as a batsman, Gloucestershire were also wounded by the absence through injury of Jack Russell, Jeremy Snape and Chris Taylor. In addition, after bowling 14 overs on the first day, James Averis limped out of the attack, too, with a groin strain. Roger Sillence, a reserve seamer, did well to finish with five for 97, but Sussex's first-innings 384 was more of a triumph for Robin Martin-Jenkins, who completed a forthright maiden century to lead a late middle-order rally from 164 for six. His watching father Christopher, covering the match for *The Times*, wrote with scarcely concealed joy that 'there was even the clink of glasses in the press box' as Sussex supporters celebrated Martin-Jenkins' 113. James Kirtley (51 not out) and Jason Lewry (47) then punished a wilting Gloucestershire with a ninth-wicket stand of 82 and, by the close of the second day, Sussex captain Chris Adams was deliberating whether or not to enforce the follow-on after the dispirited visitors had been bowled out for 228.

Gloucestershire, who had actually reached 171 for four thanks mainly to a 54-ball 71 from Harvey, featuring two sixes and 11 fours, fell apart against Kirtley (four for 59) and Mark Robinson (four for 39). Adams, by the next morning, had chosen to send in Gloucestershire again, and with Kirtley rampant they duly slid to 173 all out. Dominic Hewson resisted for a while with 79, but the waspish Kirtley (six for 34) was well supported by Martin-Jenkins and Robinson, who took two final wickets to end his 15-year career on a high. Fittingly, too, the prolific Sussex opening pair of Richard Montgomerie and Murray Goodwin were able to emerge to knock off the 18 runs required for victory – and Sussex, already preparing for the challenge of joining the first division elite, announced that Yorkshire's 24-year-old, left-arm paceman Paul Hutchison was joining them on a three-year contract.

Warwickshire's win was also bad news for Middlesex, who had begun their final match, against Worcestershire at New Road, also harbouring hopes that they could squeeze themselves into the third promotion place. An opening stand of 143 between Andrew Strauss (92 off just 107 balls) and Robin Weston, whose 106 was his third hundred of the season, gave Middlesex a fine start, but thereafter only Paul Weekes (63) flourished as they totalled 349. Worcestershire, moreover, looked to be in fine fettle themselves with the bat as, led by Anurag Singh, they ran up 434 in reply. Singh's 168 was his maiden championship century, and he did a jubilant little jig of sheer elation when he went into three figures. Phil Weston, no doubt roused by his younger brother's ton, hit 71. Middlesex then scored 368 for four declared in their second innings, with Strauss again impressing with 83 and Ed Joyce finishing on 108 not out, but by then all hope of promotion had passed and, on the last afternoon, Worcestershire batted out time on 179 for four with Graeme Hick unbeaten with 59 when the draw was agreed.

A rain shower, in mid-chase, spoiled the chance of a good finish at Trent Bridge where Hampshire, already promoted, had been set 301 to win from 63 overs by Nottinghamshire. Giles White (112) and Will Kendall (72) looked equal to the challenge, but the rain break took ten overs out of the equation at a crucial stage, and on their return to the field Hampshire had little option but to settle for the draw at 245 for six. Earlier in the day, Notts had reached 314 for seven in their second innings as Hampshire captain Robin Smith fed them some declaration bowling in the shape of Adrian Aymes (two for 101 from 11 overs) and Derek Kenway (one for 66 from eight). The first three days had been well contested, with Alan Mullally and Alex Morris each taking five wickets as Notts totalled 245 in their first innings. Usman Afzaal hit 91, but Hampshire were interested only in securing the third bowling point that made sure of their elevation to division one. In reply, they declared on 259 for four, having been 76 for four, with Neil Johnson (105 not out) being joined by the promising John Francis (72 not out) in an unbroken stand of 183. Darren Bicknell's half-century (62) kept Notts afloat on the third evening, before Kevin Pietersen (87) and Bilal Shafayat (75) waded into the declaration dross.

DIVISION ONE FINAL RESULTS

	P	W	L	D	Bat	Bowl	Pts
Yorkshire	16	9	3	4	50	45	219.00
Somerset	16	6	2	8	55	44	203.00
Kent	16	4	3	9	48	44	175.00
Surrey	16	3	1	12	43	43	169.50
Leicestershire	16	5	6	5	38	47	165.00
Lancashire	16	4	5	7	38	39	153.00
Northamptonshire	16	2	5	9	52	36	148.00
Glamorgan	16	2	5	9	36	37	133.00
Essex	16	2	7	7	28	36	116.00

Slow Over-rate Fines
Kent   1.00 pt   v Lancashire (Canterbury) 4-6 July
Surrey   0.50 pt   v Glamorgan (Oval) 8-11 August

DIVISION TWO FINAL RESULTS

	P	W	L	D	Bat	Bowl	Pts
Sussex	16	9	3	4	42	42	208.00
Hampshire	16	7	2	7	34	44	192.00
Warwickshire	16	5	1	10	46	40	185.75
Gloucestershire	16	5	5	6	46	43	173.00
Middlesex	16	4	3	9	46	42	172.00
Worcestershire	16	4	5	7	35	41	151.75
Nottinghamshire	16	3	7	6	44	38	141.25
Durham	16	3	6	7	32	44	140.00
Derbyshire	16	1	9	6	20	37	92.25

Hampshire gained two additional points from the drawn match v Gloucestershire at Southampton Rose Bowl (16-19 May) where the scores finished level.

Slow Over-rate Fines
Warwickshire   0.25 pt   v Worcestershire (Worcester)   13-16 June
Worcestershire   0.25 pt   v Hampshire (Southampton Rose Bowl)   9-11 May
Nottinghamshire   0.25 pt   v Warwickshire (Edgbaston)   3-6 August
Nottinghamshire   0.50 pt   v Derbyshire (Trent Bridge) 22-25 August
Derbyshire   0.75 pt   v Warwickshire (Derby)   12-15 September

FIRST-CLASS AVERAGES

BATTING

	M	Inns	NO	HS	Runs	Av	100	50
DR Martyn	9	14	5	176*	942	104.66	5	3
DS Lehmann	13	19	2	252	1416	83.29	5	5
AC Gilchrist	8	10	2	152	663	82.87	3	2
ME Hussey	16	30	4	329*	2055	79.03	5	9
DP Fulton	18	27	2	208*	1892	75.68	9	3
ME Waugh	9	15	6	120	644	71.55	2	2
SG Law	13	23	3	153	1311	65.55	4	8
SR Waugh	7	11	2	157*	583	64.77	3	-
IR Bell	11	16	3	135	836	64.30	3	4
NH Fairbrother	12	19	4	179*	939	62.60	4	1
MW Goodwin	17	32	5	203*	1654	61.25	7	5
RT Ponting	9	15	1	147*	844	60.28	3	5
RR Montgomerie	18	33	4	160*	1704	58.75	8	5
MA Wagh	16	24	2	315	1277	58.04	3	6
KP Pietersen	15	26	4	218*	1275	57.95	4	6
J Cox	15	25	3	186	1264	57.45	1	9
MA Butcher	15	25	2	230	1300	56.52	3	6
GA Hick	17	28	3	201	1409	56.36	6	3
MB Loye	12	21	3	197	1003	55.72	3	4
RJ Warren	16	26	2	194	1303	54.29	4	7
PJ Franks	5	8	4	85	217	54.25	-	1
JP Maher	14	23	2	217	1133	53.95	4	3
PD Collingwood	13	24	3	153	1108	52.76	3	6
MP Vaughan	9	16	0	133	839	52.43	3	4
SP Fleming	14	23	2	151	1091	51.95	4	6
CJ Adams	15	23	2	192	1086	51.71	3	7
A Dale	15	23	3	204	1026	51.30	3	4
ML Love	15	29	2	149*	1364	50.51	1	13
MR Ramprakash	13	22	0	146	1094	49.72	4	4
DL Hemp	17	25	5	186*	987	49.35	4	2
ID Blackwell	11	17	0	122	839	49.35	4	3
AP Grayson	16	29	3	189	1275	49.03	6	1
WK Hegg	13	20	4	133	782	48.87	2	5
JN Snape	14	21	3	131	868	48.22	3	5
MJ Wood (Y)	14	23	1	124	1060	48.18	4	6
GS Blewett	16	30	3	137*	1292	47.85	5	5
RSC Martin-Jenkins	9	15	4	113	524	47.63	1	3
SP James	9	15	3	156	568	47.33	1	4
DP Ostler	10	12	1	121	520	47.27	2	2
A Symonds	8	12	0	131	563	46.91	2	2
MP Bicknell	15	22	6	110*	748	46.75	1	4
CG Taylor	12	20	0	196	930	46.50	3	4
DJ Marsh	9	16	3	138*	600	46.15	1	5
TR Ward	12	21	2	160*	872	45.89	4	2
RWT Key	18	28	0	132	1281	45.75	4	7
JE Morris	8	16	2	170	640	45.71	2	4
MJ Di Venuto	14	25	1	165	1082	45.03	4	5
D Byas	16	24	5	110*	853	44.89	4	2
AJ Strauss	17	28	1	176	1210	44.81	3	6
MJ Walker	17	25	3	124	985	44.77	4	3
KJ Barnett	14	25	2	114	1029	44.73	1	7
NC Johnson	17	27	3	105*	1073	44.70	2	8
NV Knight	13	19	2	140	759	44.64	2	3
MJ Wood (Sm)	7	12	0	122	529	44.08	1	4
J Lewis	5	8	7	15*	44	44.00	-	-
BF Smith	17	30	2	180*	1222	43.64	5	2
CWG Bassano	8	14	2	186*	523	43.58	2	2
RMS Weston	10	17	1	135*	672	42.00	3	1
WPC Weston	18	31	4	192	1132	41.92	2	7
OA Shah	15	25	0	203	1040	41.60	3	4
PD Bowler	14	22	2	164	827	41.35	2	4
ME Trescothick	10	17	0	147	700	41.17	2	3
ND Burns	17	28	7	111	862	41.04	1	6
Aftab Habib	13	21	2	153	779	41.00	3	3
AL Penberthy	15	24	1	132*	942	40.95	3	5
AN Aymes	16	19	5	112*	572	40.85	1	4
IJ Harvey	10	15	2	130*	531	40.84	2	1
JP Crawley	14	24	2	280	898	40.81	2	5
AJ Holioake	13	20	1	97	758	39.89	-	7
ML Hayden	10	17	1	142	636	39.75	1	3
BL Hutton	14	22	2	139	786	39.30	3	2
DR Brown	16	20	3	104	666	39.17	1	6

FIRST-CLASS AVERAGES

BATTING

	M	Inns	NO	HS	Runs	Av	100	50
ET Smith	18	28	1	116	1054	39.03	3	4
AJ Stewart	12	18	3	106	581	38.73	1	2
PA Nixon	18	24	7	87*	651	38.29	-	4
Usman Afzaal	16	28	1	138	1011	37.44	1	8
RC Russell	10	12	2	91*	373	37.30	-	2
A Singh	18	31	2	168	1054	36.34	2	4
KA Parsons	5	8	1	139	254	36.28	1	-
DJ Bicknell	16	29	0	167	1050	36.20	3	3
Shahid Afridi	6	9	0	164	325	36.11	1	1
M Burns	17	28	1	221	961	35.59	1	7
KJ Piper	15	17	5	92*	426	35.50	-	2
DR Hewson	14	25	2	168	816	35.47	2	4
MN Lathwell	13	21	1	99	702	35.10	-	4
MGN Windows	16	27	3	174	840	35.00	3	3
MH Yardy	17	29	6	87*	796	34.60	-	5
DA Kenway	16	30	3	166	932	34.51	2	4
SJ Rhodes	15	20	7	52	442	34.00	-	1
N Hussain	6	10	1	64	306	34.00	-	3
SD Stubbings	17	31	0	127	1047	33.77	3	6
IJ Sutcliffe	17	31	1	203	1004	33.46	2	5
RJ Turner	17	26	3	115*	761	33.08	1	3
DDJ Robinson	18	31	2	118*	955	32.93	3	4
K Newell	7	11	2	103	296	32.88	1	1
DC Nash	15	19	5	103*	458	32.71	1	4
PN Weekes	17	27	5	107	719	32.68	1	5
CP Schofield	9	14	2	80*	390	32.50	-	4
MA Atherton	11	21	1	160	649	32.45	1	3
A McGrath	9	15	2	116*	417	32.07	1	2
C White	12	21	2	186	605	31.84	2	-
AJ Tudor	9	14	1	116	413	31.76	1	1
JL Langer	6	11	2	104*	285	31.66	2	-
GR Napier	10	16	0	104	506	31.62	1	2
RL Johnson	13	15	3	68	379	31.58	-	2
AD Brown	13	20	0	122	630	31.50	3	2
MJ Powell (Wa)	17	24	0	236	755	31.45	2	2
JJB Lewis	17	32	0	129	1000	31.25	3	3
MW Alleyne	16	26	3	136	718	31.21	2	2
A Flintoff	14	23	1	120	686	31.18	1	2
MA Carberry	6	10	0	84	311	31.10	-	1
P Johnson	13	24	2	149	684	31.09	2	2
G Chapple	13	19	3	155	497	31.06	1	2
MP Maynard	13	20	0	145	621	31.05	1	3
BC Holioake	12	19	0	118	586	30.84	1	4
CMW Read	16	27	5	78	666	30.27	-	5
VJ Wells	13	22	1	138	628	29.90	2	2
MJ Chilton	14	24	1	104	684	29.73	1	4
SK Warne	8	10	2	69	237	29.62	-	2
MJ Powell (Gm)	15	25	2	108	681	29.60	2	4
JC Scuderi	12	17	2	89	444	29.60	-	3
SD Thomas	15	21	2	138	562	29.57	1	4
SJ Cook	10	11	3	93*	236	29.50	-	1
KP Dutch	16	22	4	118	530	29.44	1	3
MCJ Ball	12	16	3	68	379	29.15	-	3
RC Irani	17	29	2	119	779	28.85	1	6
LD Sutton	15	27	3	140*	688	28.66	2	1
JA Daley	9	16	1	128*	428	28.53	1	1
GM Fellows	12	17	1	63	455	28.43	-	3
MJ Slater	8	13	1	77	341	28.41	-	2
PCL Holloway	12	21	1	85	567	28.35	-	4
PR Pollard	10	12	1	131rh	309	28.09	1	-
MA Roseberry	11	17	2	87	420	28.00	-	2
VS Solanki	18	29	0	112	803	27.65	3	2
RDB Croft	10	15	2	93	353	27.15	-	3
RJ Blakey	15	21	6	78*	405	27.00	-	4
JS Foster	16	25	0	103	664	26.56	1	4
IJ Ward	16	27	1	79	690	26.53	-	4
GW White	17	32	4	141	739	26.39	2	1
N Peng	13	23	7	101	551	26.23	1	3
AJ Bichel	16	24	0	78	627	26.12	-	3
JW Cook	9	16	1	88	391	26.06	-	4
IDK Salisbury	15	21	4	54	440	25.88	-	1
SR Lampitt	10	13	5	42*	205	25.62	-	-

FIRST-CLASS AVERAGES

BATTING

	M	Inns	NO	HS	Runs	Av	100	50
MJ Brown	5	10	2	60*	203	25.37	-	2
MP Speight	8	15	3	67*	304	25.33	-	1
D Ripley	15	25	6	95	481	25.31	-	2
GP Butcher	4	8	1	56	175	25.00	-	1
RA Smith	16	26	2	118	598	24.91	3	1
AC Morris	16	19	2	65	423	24.88	-	3
AD Mascarenhas	15	23	5	104	447	24.83	1	1
MJG Davis	15	22	4	52	439	24.38	-	1
SA Richardson	7	11	2	69	215	23.88	-	2
JID Kerr	8	12	5	36	167	23.85	-	-
DG Cork	7	11	0	128	262	23.81	1	-
B Zuiderent	17	27	1	122	619	23.80	1	3
AS Rollins	6	10	1	65	214	23.77	-	1
DA Leatherdale	17	27	3	93	570	23.75	-	2
WS Kendall	17	30	3	94	638	23.62	-	3
DR Law	16	26	1	103	586	23.44	1	1
SD Udal	16	20	2	81	414	23.00	-	3
MA Ealham	12	15	2	153*	299	23.00	1	-
MP Dowman	14	26	1	145*	567	22.68	1	1
JWM Dalrymple	5	10	1	70	203	22.55	-	1
MA Wallace	10	16	3	80*	290	22.30	-	2
SD Peters	15	26	3	56*	508	22.08	-	1
D Gough	9	15	5	96	219	21.90	-	1
MV Fleming	17	23	5	59	393	21.83	-	1
AJ Swann	13	22	0	113	479	21.77	1	2
KM Krikken	14	25	5	93*	435	21.75	-	3
Yousuf Youhana	6	8	0	80	174	21.75	-	1
GP Swann	15	25	0	61	543	21.72	-	3
NRC Dumelow	9	15	1	61	304	21.71	-	2
DI Stevens	8	14	2	63	259	21.58	-	1
RJ Bailey	14	25	1	136*	515	21.45	1	2
BJ Hyam	6	9	2	63	150	21.42	-	1
NMK Smith	14	14	2	54	254	21.16	-	1
THC Hancock	6	11	0	55	230	20.90	-	1
VC Drakes	14	13	3	50	209	20.90	-	1
CEW Silverwood	8	9	1	70	167	20.87	-	1
JP Pyemont	5	9	1	70	167	20.87	-	1
RS Clinton	8	15	1	58*	283	20.21	-	1
RJ Cunliffe	5	8	1	48	141	20.14	-	-
A Pratt	16	28	4	68*	476	19.83	-	3
PAJ DeFreitas	9	14	1	97	256	19.69	-	2
MJ Prior	16	24	2	66	433	19.68	-	1
MA Gough	13	23	0	79	450	19.56	-	1
JP Taylor	12	17	3	53	273	19.50	-	1
IJ Thomas	6	11	1	59	194	19.40	-	1
J Ormond	12	18	5	42	251	19.30	-	-
JM Dakin	7	11	0	69	211	19.18	-	1
G Welch	16	29	2	64	511	18.92	-	1
SL Watkin	15	17	7	38	188	18.80	-	-
PJ Martin	9	12	3	51*	169	18.77	-	1
DL Maddy	17	29	1	111	521	18.60	1	2
UBA Rashid	14	21	1	106	367	18.35	1	-
LR Prittipaul	7	9	0	84	165	18.33	-	1
PJ Prichard	7	11	0	111	201	18.27	1	-
DS Lucas	5	8	0	41	145	18.12	-	-
ID Hunter	8	14	3	37	199	18.09	-	-
RK Illingworth	5	8	1	61*	125	17.85	-	1
GJ Smith	15	20	9	44*	195	17.72	-	-
Nadeem Shahid	7	12	0	65	208	17.33	-	1
AP Cowan	15	24	3	68	360	17.14	-	2
MC Ilott	10	12	1	34	186	16.90	-	-
JJ Haynes	5	8	0	57	133	16.62	-	1
CT Tremlett	7	9	4	26	83	16.60	-	-
RJ Sidebottom	9	9	4	40*	82	16.40	-	-
PS Jones	16	16	5	29*	180	16.36	-	-
NG Hatch	9	16	8	24	129	16.12	-	-
JN Batty	10	16	1	59	239	15.93	-	1
DA Cosker	11	15	4	35	175	15.90	-	-
JN Gillespie	8	9	3	27*	94	15.66	-	-
MM Patel	17	19	3	38	247	15.43	-	-
T Lungley	6	11	4	47	108	15.42	-	-
GE Welton	12	22	0	61	337	15.31	-	2

FIRST-CLASS AVERAGES

BATTING

	M	Inns	NO	HS	Runs	Av	100	50
JM Golding	5	8	2	30	90	15.00	-	-
JD Lewry	17	18	4	47	202	14.42	-	-
J Wood	8	10	1	35	127	14.11	-	-
RSG Anderson	8	11	0	45	154	14.00	-	-
JB Hockley	7	13	1	29	166	13.83	-	-
Saqlain Mushtaq	13	18	6	38	164	13.66	-	-
RCJ Williams	5	9	0	33	123	13.66	-	-
JAR Blain	5	9	4	34	66	13.20	-	-
MJ Rawnsley	15	21	5	39	210	13.12	-	-
CG Liptrot	12	14	4	22	128	12.80	-	-
GM Hamilton	8	9	0	34	114	12.66	-	-
RJ Logan	10	15	2	37*	162	12.46	-	-
NC Phillips	7	11	4	30	87	12.42	-	-
DM Cousins	8	10	3	27	87	12.42	-	-
ARC Fraser	13	12	0	41	149	12.41	-	-
MJ Saggers	17	20	5	61*	185	12.33	-	1
MR Strong	9	13	4	34	110	12.22	-	-
TA Munton	9	13	1	50	145	12.08	-	1
MJ Cawdron	6	9	2	29	82	11.71	-	-
KJ Dean	8	12	2	23	117	11.70	-	-
RC Driver	5	8	0	35	93	11.62	-	-
G Keedy	13	15	8	20*	81	11.57	-	-
MM Betts	12	11	3	19	92	11.50	-	-
GD Bridge	7	13	2	39*	125	11.36	-	-
AR Caddick	9	15	4	49*	122	11.09	-	-
RJ Kirtley	16	24	6	51*	196	10.88	-	1
PM Such	15	20	9	25	117	10.63	-	-
AD Mullally	14	13	5	36	82	10.25	-	-
JE Brinkley	10	13	2	65	111	10.09	-	1
P Aldred	8	13	1	35	120	10.00	-	-
TJ Phillips	6	8	0	27	80	10.00	-	-
M Muralitharan	7	8	1	21	70	10.00	-	-

Qualification: 8 innings, average 10.00

BOWLING

	O	M	Runs	W	Av	Best	10m	5i
GD McGrath	234.5	74	624	40	15.60	7-76	-	4
AD Mullally	477.4	151	1184	64	18.50	8-90	-	6
SK Warne	263	56	784	42	18.66	7-165	1	3
IJ Harvey	288.4	92	773	41	18.85	5-33	-	2
MA Robinson	415.4	126	1083	56	19.33	5-35	-	3
M Muralitharan	484.5	159	971	50	19.42	6-53	1	5
CEW Silverwood	209.1	42	644	33	19.51	5-20	-	3
RSG Anderson	231.1	54	699	35	19.97	5-21	-	3
CT Tremlett	131.2	37	401	20	20.05	4-34	-	-
DW Fleming	138	32	390	19	20.52	6-59	-	1
Saqlain Mushtaq	567.2	157	1286	62	20.74	7-58	-	5
SP Kirby	280.3	60	980	47	20.85	7-50	1	3
MP Bicknell	541.5	132	1538	72	21.36	7-60	1	3
JE Brinkley	222.1	61	663	31	21.38	6-14	-	2
J Lewis	175.4	56	454	21	21.61	5-71	-	1
G Chapple	379.2	87	1174	53	22.15	6-46	-	4
Waqar Younis	119.1	23	399	18	22.16	5-23	-	1
MJ Hoggard	240	58	733	32	22.90	6-51	-	2
GD Bridge	172	48	413	18	22.94	6-84	-	1
MA Ealham	226.5	68	574	25	22.96	6-64	-	2
RJ Kirtley	566.3	135	1749	75	23.32	6-34	2	5
RL Johnson	463.2	89	1474	62	23.77	5-40	-	5
MJ Saggers	509.3	118	1544	64	24.12	6-92	-	3
GJ Smith	446.2	103	1256	50	25.12	5-37	1	3
A Sheriyar	536.1	125	1795	71	25.28	6-88	-	3
AD Mascarenhas	399.3	112	1015	40	25.37	6-26	-	2
Wasim Akram	153	44	385	15	25.66	4-18	-	-
MCJ Ball	348.4	90	876	34	25.76	6-23	-	2
GM Hamilton	211.2	43	672	26	25.84	5-27	-	1
KJ Dean	250.5	58	888	34	26.11	6-73	1	2
JD Lewry	512.1	126	1548	59	26.23	7-42	1	3
DR Law	351	70	1103	42	26.26	6-53	-	2
BJ Trott	372.5	68	1235	47	26.27	6-13	1	4

FIRST-CLASS AVERAGES

BOWLING

	O	M	Runs	W	Av	Best	10m	5i
RJ Sidebottom	277.5	75	710	27	26.29	4-49	-	-
MW Alleyne	374.4	87	1079	41	26.31	5-50	-	1
MM Betts	308.2	70	979	37	26.45	5-22	-	2
JM Dakin	122.3	23	427	16	26.68	4-53	-	-
A Richardson	395.5	111	983	36	27.30	5-89	-	1
AJ Bichel	555.5	137	1804	66	27.33	6-44	1	4
PAJ DeFreitas	303	66	934	34	27.47	6-65	-	1
CG Liptrot	308.4	80	966	35	27.60	3-12	-	-
JN Gillespie	228	52	801	29	27.62	5-37	-	2
VJ Wells	181	47	498	18	27.66	5-36	-	1
SR Lampitt	203.2	49	669	24	27.87	5-22	-	1
AC Morris	472	106	1428	51	28.00	5-39	-	2
DE Malcolm	546.1	94	1948	68	28.64	8-63	1	4
PCR Tufnell	690	166	1721	60	28.68	6-44	1	3
DL Maddy	237.3	45	804	28	28.71	5-67	-	1
J Ormond	485.4	114	1417	49	28.91	5-71	-	2
AR Caddick	351.2	53	1376	47	29.27	5-81	1	4
PJ Martin	322.3	86	969	33	29.36	5-52	-	1
SD Udal	566.1	143	1660	54	29.81	7-74	-	1
PN Weekes	439.5	100	1198	40	29.95	5-90	-	1
DR Brown	472.1	123	1284	42	30.57	6-60	1	1
DS Lehmann	139.1	33	368	12	30.66	3-13	-	-
MM Patel	524.2	158	1228	40	30.70	8-119	1	1
D Gough	321.4	55	1212	39	31.07	5-61	-	2
RSC Martin-Jenkins	248	63	764	24	31.83	4-18	-	-
RJ Logan	329.1	53	1375	43	31.97	6-93	-	3
MA Gough	157.3	34	449	14	32.07	5-66	-	1
RC Irani	354.5	97	1040	32	32.50	6-79	-	3
NMK Smith	314	75	813	25	32.52	4-76	-	-
SL Watkin	472.4	113	1400	43	32.55	6-67	-	1
CR Miller	157.2	37	586	18	32.55	4-41	-	-
NM Carter	120	12	456	14	32.57	5-78	-	1
DM Cousins	333.4	54	1176	36	32.66	8-102	-	2
CB Keegan	170	38	588	18	32.66	4-54	-	-
A Symonds	106.2	23	333	10	33.30	3-28	-	-
GM Fellows	156	43	398	12	33.16	3-23	-	-
NG Hatch	248.4	43	867	26	33.34	3-42	-	-
RKJ Dawson	315.5	69	1014	30	33.80	6-82	-	2
MC Ilott	287	65	921	27	34.11	5-85	-	1
PS Jones	560	100	2015	59	34.15	5-115	-	1
TF Bloomfield	479.4	79	1709	50	34.18	5-58	-	2
TA Munton	242.1	61	659	19	34.68	5-85	-	1
SJ Cook	218.1	47	696	20	34.80	3-10	-	-
TM Smith	91.3	15	383	11	34.81	4-61	-	-
C White	214.1	52	599	17	35.23	4-57	-	-
AJ Tudor	251.1	53	927	26	35.65	5-44	-	2
Abdur Razzaq	105.3	19	359	10	35.90	3-61	-	-
SJ Harmison	419.5	86	1262	35	36.05	6-111	-	2
AN Bressington	120.4	31	397	11	36.09	3-42	-	-
UBA Rashid	134.2	38	398	11	36.18	4-9	-	-
KP Dutch	367	64	1268	35	36.22	4-32	-	-
DA Leatherdale	158	39	580	16	36.25	4-70	-	-
MA Wagh	184	37	473	13	36.38	3-3	-	-
VC Drakes	505.2	107	1537	42	36.59	5-37	-	1
ESH Giddins	352.5	83	1102	30	36.73	5-48	-	1
G Welch	502.3	108	1631	44	37.06	6-30	-	3
ARC Fraser	469.4	140	1204	32	37.62	3-46	-	-
JMM Averis	462.1	112	1621	43	37.69	5-55	-	1
GR Napier	104.1	15	453	12	37.75	3-55	-	-
JE Bishop	224	39	915	24	38.12	5-148	-	1
RDB Croft	328.3	86	927	24	38.62	5-95	1	2
A Flintoff	245.3	48	736	19	38.73	3-36	-	-
AJ Harris	330.4	84	1097	28	39.17	6-98	-	1
JAR Blain	153	16	673	17	39.58	6-42	-	1
NC Johnson	252.5	42	911	23	39.60	4-20	-	-
MJG Davis	349.3	82	956	24	39.83	6-116	-	1
AL Penberthy	339.2	70	1019	25	40.76	4-39	-	-
NC Phillips	285.5	60	939	23	40.82	5-64	-	1
G Keedy	387.1	76	1150	28	41.07	5-73	-	2
MV Fleming	302.4	59	910	22	41.36	4-53	-	-
MJ Cawdron	168	50	498	12	41.50	4-79	-	-

FIRST-CLASS AVERAGES

BOWLING

	O	M	Runs	W	Av	Best	10m	5i
DA Cosker	423.5	84	1390	33	42.12	4-48	-	-
IDK Salisbury	396.2	72	1151	27	42.62	5-95	-	1
ID Hunter	181.3	27	700	16	43.75	4-55	-	-
Shahid Afridi	166.1	41	569	13	43.76	5-84	-	1
T Lungley	115.4	14	527	12	43.91	3-58	-	-
RD Stemp	244.4	51	708	16	44.18	3-39	-	-
B Lee	186.5	30	752	17	44.23	3-17	-	-
ID Blackwell	291.4	72	896	20	44.80	5-122	-	1
MJ Rawnsley	446.2	122	1211	27	44.85	3-55	-	-
M Burns	138.5	23	539	12	44.91	6-54	-	1
GP Swann	422.3	87	1365	30	45.50	5-34	-	1
AP Cowan	461.5	104	1522	33	46.12	3-64	-	-
JP Taylor	379.2	49	1345	29	46.37	4-100	-	-
JF Brown	473.5	102	1407	28	50.25	5-107	-	1
SD Thomas	420.1	56	1668	33	50.54	4-54	-	-
DG Cork	206.5	44	618	12	51.50	4-122	-	-
NRC Dumelow	185.5	34	723	14	51.64	4-81	-	-
SP Jones	198.2	29	887	17	52.17	3-36	-	-
MR Strong	256.3	46	992	19	52.21	3-98	-	-
CP Schofield	252.1	52	757	14	54.07	3-53	-	-
PM Such	433	98	1358	24	56.58	5-131	-	1
P Aldred	189.3	30	742	13	57.07	3-102	-	-
JWM Dalrymple	203.3	47	578	10	57.80	4-86	-	-
Usman Afzaal	158.2	29	579	10	57.90	3-88	-	-
AC McGarry	148	19	637	10	63.70	3-77	-	-

Qualification: 10 wickets in 8 innings

The following bowlers took 10 wickets in fewer than 8 innings:

	O	M	Runs	W	Av	Best	10m	5i
CJ Adams	40.2	6	111	10	11.10	4-28	-	-
Mushtaq Ahmed	69.2	18	176	14	12.57	8-49	1	1
Kabir Ali	84	19	253	14	18.07	5-22	-	1
N Killeen	89	29	222	11	20.18	3-14	-	-
JEK Schofield	89.1	17	285	13	21.92	4-51	-	-
CE Dagnall	83	16	279	12	23.25	6-50	-	1
SJE Brown	115	29	333	14	23.78	6-70	-	1
AKD Gray	92	23	281	10	28.10	4-128	-	-
TC Hicks	143	30	394	13	30.30	5-77	-	1
RK Illingworth	126.4	39	316	10	31.60	4-37	-	-
AG Wharf	127.4	19	448	14	32.00	5-63	-	1
MS Panesar	101.3	28	358	11	32.54	4-11	-	-
PJ Franks	149.1	33	429	13	33.00	4-65	-	-
AF Giles	154.5	41	429	12	35.75	5-46	-	1
JP Hewitt	83	8	386	10	38.60	3-72	-	-
MN Malik	104	21	414	10	41.40	5-57	-	1
JP Pyemont	146	31	512	10	51.20	4-101	-	-

LEADING FIELDERS

68 – ND Burns (65ct,3st); 59 – RJ Turner; 56 – A Pratt (49ct,7st); 54 – RJ Blakey (49ct,5st); 52 – SJ Rhodes (51ct,1st); 48 – PA Nixon (44ct,4st), D Ripley (45ct,3st); 45 – AN Aymes (43ct,2st); 44 – CMW Read (43ct,1st), RC Russell (42ct,2st); 43 – DC Nash (39ct,4st); 41 – MJ Prior (39ct,2st); 40 – KJ Piper (39ct,1st); 39 – JS Foster (31ct,8st); 38 – D Byas, WK Hegg (35ct,3st); 37 – AJ Stewart (36ct,1st); 34 – KM Krikken (33ct,1st); 32 – AC Gilchrist (28ct,4st); 28 – CJ Adams, JN Batty (26ct,2st), NC Johnson, MA Wallace (27ct,1st); 27 – DP Fulton; 24 – GS Blewett; 22 – SP Fleming, DP Ostler; 21 – MCJ Ball, BJ Hyam (20ct,1st), ML Love; 20 – BL Hutton; 19 – KP Dutch, GA Hick, ME Hussey, BF Smith, GW White (17ct,2st); 18 – BC Hollioake, NV Knight, SG Law, B Zuiderent; 17 – MA Atherton, A Flintoff, VS Solanki; 16 – DR Brown, NH Fairbrother, DA Kenway, RR Montgomerie, Rashid Latif (15ct,1st), RCJ Williams (15ct,1st); 15 – MA Butcher, MJ Di Venuto, AJ Hollioake, DL Maddy, KP Pietersen, PN Weekes; 14 – PD Bowler, MJ Powell (Wa), OA Shah; 13 – MW Alleyne (12ct,1st), M Burns, JP Maher, DJ Marsh, A Symonds, SK Warne; 12 – DL Hemp, MJ Powell (Gm), ME Waugh; 11 – IR Bell, WS Kendall, AL Penberthy, RT Ponting, DDJ Robinson, AD Shaw, WPC Weston; 10 – KJ Barnett, MJ Chilton, PD Collingwood, DA Cosker, DR Law, AC Morris, WA Seccombe (8ct,2st), JN Snape, MJ Wood (Y)

Qualification: 10 catches or more

FEATURES OF 2001 FIRST-CLASS SEASON

+ denotes 2nd innings

TOTALS OVER 600

701-9 dec.	Surrey v. Glamorgan	at Cardiff
650	Somerset v. Northamptonshire	at Taunton
633-6 dec.	Northamptonshire v. Essex	at Northampton
631-6 dec.	Worcestershire v. Durham UCCE	at Worcester
631-9 dec.	Warwickshire v. Middlesex	at Lord's
612-8 dec.	Leicestershire v. Kent	at Canterbury
608-8 dec.	Gloucestershire v. Nottinghamshire	at Bristol
607	Surrey v. Northamptonshire	at Northampton
600-6 dec.	Lancashire v. Northamptonshire	at Old Trafford
600-8 dec.	Somerset v. Glamorgan	at Taunton

TOTALS UNDER 100

67	Durham UCCE v. Durham	at Chester-le-Street
68+	Essex v. Kent	at Tunbridge Wells
74	British Universities v. Pakistanis	at Trent Bridge
81	Hampshire v. Sussex	at Hove
87+	Gloucestershire v. Worcestershire	at Worcester
95	Derbyshire v. Durham	at Chester-le-Street
96	Leicestershire v. Pakistanis	at Leicester
97	Australians v. Hampshire	at Southampton Rose Bowl
99+	Leicestershire v. Yorkshire	at Headingley

INDIVIDUAL SCORES OVER 200

329*	ME Hussey	Northamptonshire v. Essex	at Northampton
315	MA Wagh	Warwickshire v. Middlesex	at Lord's
280	JP Crawley	Lancashire v. Northamptonshire	at Old Trafford
252	DS Lehmann	Yorkshire v. Lancashire	Headingley
232	ME Hussey	Northamptonshire v. Leicestershire	at Northampton
230	MA Butcher	Surrey v. Glamorgan	at Cardiff
221	M Burns	Somerset v. Yorkshire	at Bath
218*+	KP Pietersen	Nottinghamshire v. Derbyshire	at Derby
217	JP Maher	Glamorgan v. Essex	at Cardiff
208*	DP Fulton	Kent v. Somerset	at Canterbury
208	ME Hussey	Northamptonshire v. Somerset	at Taunton
204	A Dale	Glamorgan v. Northamptonshire	at Northampton
203*+	MW Goodwin	Sussex v. Nottinghamshire	at Trent Bridge
203	OA Shah	Middlesex v. Derbyshire	at Southgate
203	IJ Sutcliffe	Leicestershire v. Glamorgan	at Cardiff
201	Saeed Anwar	Pakistanis v. Kent	at Canterbury
201	GA Hick	Worcestershire v. Warwickshire	at Edgbaston
200*	GA Hick	Worcestershire v. Durham	at Worcester

FEATURES OF 2001 FIRST-CLASS SEASON

PLAYERS WHO CARRIED THE BAT

SAA Block 56* (129)	Cambridge UCCE v. Kent	at Cambridge
MH Richardson 64* (124)	MCC v. Australians	at Arundel
MK Floyd 128* (325)	Cambridge Uni v. Oxford Uni	at Cambridge
MA Butcher 145* (281)	Surrey v. Glamorgan	at The Oval
SD Sutton 140* (263)	Derbyshire v. Sussex	at Derby
AJ Strauss +112* (253)	Middlesex v. Hampshire	at Southampton
SP James 61* (146)	Glamorgan v. Leicestershire	at Leicester

TWO HUNDREDS IN THE SAME MATCH

116* & 123*	SG Law	Essex v. Lancashire	at Old Trafford
103 & 122	ID Blackwell	Somerset v. Northamptonshire	at Northampton
186* & 106	CWG Bassano	Derbyshire v. Gloucestershire	at Derby
115 & 203*	MW Goodwin	Sussex v. Nottinghamshire	at Trent Bridge
173 & 149	AP Grayson	Essex v. Northamptonshire	at Northampton
170 & 136*	JE Morris	Notts v. Derbyshire	at Derby
208* & 104*	DP Fulton	Kent v. Somerset	at Canterbury
102 & 118*	DDJ Robinson	Essex v. Leicestershire	at Chelmsford

HUNDRED & 0 IN THE SAME MATCH

0 & 106*	MGN Windows	Gloucestershire v. Middlesex	at Bristol
0 & 136*	RJ Bailey	Derbyshire v. Worcestershire	at Derby
0 & 218*	KP Pietersen	Nottinghamshire v. Derbyshire	at Derby
140 & 0	A Dale	Glamorgan v. Lancashire	at Colwyn Bay
127 & 0	MW Goodwin	Sussex v. Middlesex	at Hove
0 & 193	DS Lehmann	Yorkshire v. Leicestershire	at Leicester
149 & 0	P Johnson	Nottinghamshire v. Gloucestershire	at Bristol
0 & 147*	RT Ponting	Australians v. Sussex	at Hove
0 & 121	RR Montgomerie	Sussex v. Warwickshire	at Edgbaston
150 & 0	MW Goodwin	Sussex v. Warwickshire	at Edgbaston

FEATURES OF 2001 FIRST-CLASS SEASON

MOST FIRST-CLASS RUNS

2055	ME Hussey (Northamptonshire)

FIRST PLAYER TO 1000 FIRST-CLASS RUNS

DP Fulton	(Kent)	4 July 2001

FIRST PLAYER TO 2000 FIRST-CLASS RUNS

ME Hussey	(Northamptonshire) 13 September 2001

FASTEST FIRST-CLASS HUNDRED

Ian Harvey	61 balls	Gloucestershire v Derbyshire	at Bristol

EIGHT WICKETS IN AN INNINGS

8-49+	Mushtaq Ahmed	Pakistanis v. British Universities	at Trent Bridge
8-63	DE Malcolm	Leicestershire v. Surrey	at Leicester
8-90	AD Mullally	Hampshire v. Warwickshire	at Southampton
8-102	DM Cousins	Northants v. Yorkshire	at Headingley
8-119	MM Patel	Kent v. Somerset	at Canterbury

TEN WICKETS IN A MATCH

13-79	JD Lewry	Sussex v. Hampshire	at Hove
12-72	SP Kirby	Yorkshire v. Leicestershire	at Headingley
12-144	MM Patel	Kent v. Somerset	at Canterbury
11-78	BJ Trott	Kent v. Essex	at Tunbridge Wells
11-117	MP Bicknell	Surrey v. Glamorgan	at The Oval
11-229	SK Warne	Australia v. England	at The Oval
10-51	Mushtaq Ahmed	Pakistanis v. British Universities	at Trent Bridge
10-80	DR Brown	Warwickshire v. Derbyshire	at Derby
10-86	AJ Bichel	Worcestershire v. Gloucestershire	at Worcester
10-93	RJ Kirtley	Sussex v. Gloucestershire	at Hove
10-95	RJ Kirtley	Sussex v. Durham	at Hove
10-101	GJ Smith	Nottinghamshire v. Sussex	at Hove
10-115	KJ Dean	Derbyshire v. Durham	at Chester-le-Street
10-123	M Muralitharan	Lancashire v. Essex	at Old Trafford
10-133	PCR Tufnell	Middlesex v. Derbyshire	at Southgate
10-173	AR Caddick	Somerset v. Yorkshire	at Headingley
10-187	DE Malcolm	Leicestershire v. Surrey	at Leicester
10-191	RDB Croft	Glamorgan v. Northamptonshire	at Cardiff

FEATURES OF 2001 FIRST-CLASS SEASON

HAT-TRICK

Waqar Younis	Pakistanis v. Leicestershire	at Leicester
JD Lewry	Sussex v. Hampshire	at Hove

MOST FIRST-CLASS WICKETS

75	MP Bicknell (Surrey)

SIX DISMISSALS IN AN INNINGS

7ct	ND Burns	Leicestershire v. Somerset	at Leicester
7ct	RJ Turner	Somerset v. Northamptonshire	at Taunton
6ct	CMW Read	Nottinghamshire v. Middlesex	at Trent Bridge
6ct	ND Burns	Leicestershire v. Yorkshire	at Leicester
6ct	RJ Turner	Somerset v. Surrey	at Taunton
6ct	ND Burns	Leicestershire v. Glamorgan	at Leicester

EIGHT DISMISSALS IN A MATCH

9ct	ND Burns	Leicestershire v. Somerset	at Leicester
8ct/1st	ND Burns	Leicestershire v. Yorkshire	at Leicester
9ct	RJ Turner	Somerset v. Surrey	at Taunton
8ct	JN Batty	Surrey v. Northamptonshire	at Guildford
8ct	KM Krikken	Derbyshire v. Sussex	at Derby

MOST DISMISSALS

68 (65ct/3st)	ND Burns (Leicestershire)

MOST FIELD CATCHES

28	CJ Adams (Sussex), NC Johnson (Hampshire)

NORWICH UNION NATIONAL LEAGUE
By Mark Baldwin

Division One: 29 April 2001
at Leicester
Gloucestershire 116 (38.4 overs)
Leicestershire 117 for 8 (40.3 overs)
Leicestershire (4 pts) won by two wickets

at Canterbury
Kent v. **Warwickshire**
No play – 2 pts each

Leicestershire toppled champions Gloucestershire in an exciting, low-scoring contest at Grace Road, limping to 76 for eight in reply to the visitors' 116 all out before Jon Dakin and Jimmy Ormond hauled them past the winning post. Ian Harvey's spell of 9-4-7-2 did much to bring Gloucestershire back into the game, but Dakin and Ormond were up to the task of scoring 41 from the final nine overs. In the end, six were required from the last over – and Dakin went to 36 not out by striking each of the first three balls of the over for twos.

There was no play in the other scheduled division one match, between Kent and Warwickshire at Canterbury, because of rain. Frustrated spectators were, however, given some excellent impromptu entertainment in the main pavilion with Kent officials staging a 'question-and-answer' hour with Bob Woolmer, Brian Luckhurst and Matthew Fleming. Well over 500 people attended, and memory lane was most pleasantly strolled down.

Division Two: 29 April 2001
at Derby
Glamorgan 138 (44.4 overs) (G Welch 5 for 22)
Derbyshire 140 for 6 (41.4 overs) (DG Cork 83*)
Derbyshire (4 pts) won by four wickets

at Kidderminster
Sussex 154 for 9 (45 overs) (B Zuiderent 53, SR Lampitt 4 for 37)
Worcestershire 155 for 5 (40.4 overs) (GA Hick 61*)
Worcestershire (4 pts) won by five wickets

at Old Trafford
Lancashire v. **Hampshire**
No play – 2 pts each

at Lord's
Middlesex v. **Durham**
No play – 2 pts each

A magnificent unbeaten 83 by Dominic Cork, from 99 balls, ably supported in an unbroken stand of 55 by Richard Illingworth, swept Derbyshire to an exciting four-wicket win over Glamorgan at Derby. Earlier Graeme Welch had taken five for 22 in Glamorgan's 138, with Adrian Dale (37) and Keith Newell (47 not out) the only batsmen to get into double figures.

Worcestershire's decision to switch their league match against Sussex to Kidderminster, because of the waterlogged state of the New Road outfield, paid off handsomely with a fine five-wicket win. When Graeme Hick was joined by Steve Rhodes at 73 for five, however, in reply to a Sussex total built around Bas Zuiderent's 53, the equation was 82 needed from 17 overs. So well did Hick (61 not out) and Rhodes (39 not out) bat that the game was won with 26 balls to spare!

Rain at Old Trafford and Lord's meant that the games between Lancashire and Hampshire, and Middlesex and Durham, were both abandoned.

Division One: 13 May 2001
at Northampton
Gloucestershire 222 for 5 (45 overs) (KJ Barnett 101)
Northamptonshire 108 for 3 (31 overs) (ME Hussey 53)
Gloucestershire (4 pts) won by 20 runs (DL Method: Northamptonshire needed to have 129 from 31 overs when rain stopped play)

at The Oval
Nottinghamshire 233 for 8 (45 overs) (GS Blewett 69, DJ Bicknell 50)
Surrey 216 for 9 (45 overs) (BC Hollioake 70*)
Nottinghamshire (4 pts) won by 17 runs

at Headingley
Somerset 154 (44 overs) (GD Rose 58)
Yorkshire 158 for 5 (35 overs) (A McGrath 58)
Yorkshire (4 pts) won by five wickets

It was a memorable day for Kim Barnett who, during his innings of 101 for Gloucestershire against Northants at Northampton, overtook Graham Gooch as the one-day league's highest-ever run scorer. Gooch's record was 8,573 runs, but Barnett fittingly set the new mark as he completed his 100th run. Moreover, Barnett's 101 helped Gloucestershire to reach a 45-over total of 222 for five and eventual victory by 20 runs, under the Duckworth/Lewis

Kim Barnett ... one-day league record-breaker.

system, when Northants were reduced to 108 for three from 31 overs in reply.

Darren Bicknell was yorked by his younger brother Martin at The Oval, but not before the Nottinghamshire opener had made 50. Greg Blewett's 80-ball 69 and 49 from Usman Afzaal also boosted Notts to 233 for eight, and there was further satisfaction for the elder Bicknell, on his return to his old county, when Surrey could only reach 216 for nine in reply – despite Ben Hollioake's unbeaten 70 off just 66 balls.

Another batting record fell at Headingley, where Yorkshire captain David Byas eclipsed Geoff Boycott's previous county-record tally of 5,051 runs in one-day league competition. Byas made 48 and Anthony McGrath 58 as Yorkshire waltzed past Somerset's inadequate 154 all out with ten overs to spare.

Division Two: 13 May 2001
at Derby
Derbyshire 198 for 6 (45 overs) (RJ Bailey 94)
Essex 131 (35.2 overs) (T Lungley 4 for 28)
Derbyshire (4 pts) won by 67 runs

at Southampton Rose Bowl
Worcestershire 183 for 7 (45 overs)
Hampshire 186 for 7 (44.4 overs)
Hampshire (4 pts) won by three wickets

Rob Bailey, bowled for 94 by the last ball of the innings, inspired Derbyshire to victory by 67 runs against Essex on an awkward pitch at the Racecourse Ground. Bailey hit seven fours in his 153-ball innings to push Derbyshire up to 198 for six. Tom Lungley's four for 28 then wrecked the Essex reply, and the visitors were eventually all out for 131.

Hampshire had a solid middle-order batting effort to thank for their exciting three-wicket win against Worcestershire at Southampton. The visitors made 183 for seven from their 45-over allocation, but then Robin Smith, Will Kendall and the 21-year-old Lawrence Prittipaul all hit 40s as Hampshire reached their target with just two balls remaining.

Division One: 20 May 2001
at Bristol
Yorkshire 158 (44.5 overs) (DS Lehmann 56)
Gloucestershire 161 for 5 (44.2 overs) (MGN Windows 51)
Gloucestershire (4 pts) won by five wickets

at Trent Bridge
Warwickshire 202 for 7 (45 overs) (MA Wagh 50)
Nottinghamshire 203 for 6 (44.4 overs) (U Afzaal 94*)
Nottinghamshire (4 pts) won by four wickets

at Taunton
Kent 180 for 7 (45 overs) (DJ Cullinan 70)
Somerset 149 (42.4 overs)
Kent (4 pts) won by 31 runs

at The Oval
Surrey 230 for 4 (45 overs) (AD Brown 111*, BC Hollioake 64*)
Leicestershire 231 for 6 (44.3 overs) (DJ Marsh 97*)
Leicestershire (4 pts) won by four wickets

Champions Gloucestershire overcame Yorkshire at Bristol thanks to another tight performance in the field. Only Darren Lehmann broke the shackles with

The man Surrey call 'Lord' ... another one-day hundred for Alistair Brown.

56 from 78 balls as Yorkshire totalled 158, and then Matt Windows' 51 helped Gloucestershire to a five-wicket win with four balls to spare.

An unbeaten 94 off 105 balls by Usman Afzaal swept Nottinghamshire to a four-wicket victory against Warwickshire at Trent Bridge – this time with just two deliveries remaining. Mark Wagh's 50 had been the highlight of Warwickshire's 45-over total of 202 for seven.

Daryll Cullinan, the South African Test batsman, played the decisive innings at Taunton where Kent outfought Somerset on a seaming pitch to win by 31 runs. Cullinan's 70, in a Kent total of 180 for seven, included a six into the River Tone off Keith Dutch's off spin and, at 15 for four, Somerset were left with too much to do. The run-outs of Peter Bowler and Ian Blackwell did not help their cause either, and Martin Saggers impressed with three for 19.

Alistair Brown hit an unbeaten 111 from 129 balls and put on an unbroken 127 with Ben Hollioake, whose 64 not out took him only 63 deliveries. But the Surrey men still finished on the losing side at The Oval as Leicestershire, inspired by their

Australian Dan Marsh, overhauled the home side's 230 for four with just three balls remaining. Marsh's 97 not out, from 102 balls, included a six and nine fours while Darren Maddy's 46 was also an important contribution.

Division Two: 20 May 2001
at Chester-le-Street
Middlesex 182 for 8 (45 overs) (BL Hutton 77)
Durham 186 for 8 (44.5 overs) (CB Keegan 4 for 43)
Durham (4 pts) won by two wickets

at Chelmsford
Sussex 243 for 6 (45 overs) (RR Montgomerie 91)
Essex 242 for 9 (45 overs) (SD Peters 66)
Sussex (4 pts) won by 1 run

at Old Trafford
Lancashire 147 for 6 (45 overs) (NH Fairbrother 62)
Glamorgan 148 for 6 (40.5 overs)
Glamorgan (4 pts) won by four wickets

at Worcester
Derbyshire 168 for 6 (45 overs)
Worcestershire 172 for 7 (42.2 overs) (VS Solanki 52, TA Munton 4 for 31)
Worcestershire (4 pts) won by three wickets

Durham's thrilling two-wicket victory over Middlesex at Chester-le-Street included an extraordinary incident in the 43rd over when Danny Law was bowled but the delivery was declared a no ball because Middlesex did not have enough fielders inside the 30-yard circle. The ball ricocheted off the stumps and flew for four! Law, thus reprieved, stayed to make 31 not out and hit the winning runs off the penultimate ball! Paul Collingwood also made 47 while, for Middlesex, Ben Hutton top-scored with 77 in the visitors' total of 182 for eight.

Sussex triumphed by just one run in another contest of high drama at Chelmsford, with Bas Zuiderent's run out of Essex's Stuart Law for a 41-ball 40 perhaps the biggest turning-point. Richard Montgomerie hit his highest one-day league score, 91, in an opening stand of 106 with Murray Goodwin as Sussex raced to 243 for six from their 45 overs. But then Stephen Peters (66), Law and Paul Grayson, with an unbeaten 48 from 40 balls, took Essex to the very brink.

After three washed-out games – and a total of nine abandoned days – Lancashire finally got on to the field of play at Old Trafford. Perhaps they wished they hadn't, however, when Glamorgan beat them by four wickets with Matthew Maynard's unbeaten 39 guiding the Welsh county past a Lancashire total of 147 for six built around Neil Fairbrother's 62 on an understandably sluggish pitch.

It was hard work for batsmen, too, on a seamer-friendly pitch at Worcester, but in the end Vikram Solanki's 52 proved decisive for the home side after Derbyshire had totalled 168 for six. Tim Munton's four for 31 was ultimately in vain as Worcestershire scraped home by three wickets in the final over.

Division Two: 27 May 2001
at Chester-le-Street
Durham 211 for 6 (45 overs)
Lancashire 187 for 8 (45 overs) (MA Atherton 62, G Chapple 52, NC Phillips 4 for 21)
Durham (4 pts) won by 24 runs

Nicky Phillips, the Durham off spinner, outbowled the celebrated Sri Lankan, Muttiah Muralitharan, at Chester-le-Street to earn his side a 24-run win against Lancashire. Phillips took four for 21 from his nine overs as Lancashire fell away alarmingly following a belligerent 52 from just 48 balls by makeshift opener Glen Chapple. Mike Atherton scored 62, but took 124 deliveries to do so, and Neil Fairbrother was left on 39 not out as Lancashire finished on 187 for eight in reply to a Durham total of 211 for six which was built around an opening partnership worth 85 from Nicky Peng and Danny Law.

Division One: 29 May 2001
at Edgbaston (floodlit)
Warwickshire 248 for 4 (45 overs) (DP Ostler 134*)
Gloucestershire 209 (44.4 overs)
Warwickshire (4 pts) won by 39 runs

A wonderful unbeaten 134 of increasing violence from Dominic Ostler overwhelmed Gloucestershire at Edgbaston, eventually bringing Warwickshire victory by 39 runs. Ostler, however, had the advantage of batting in daylight as he struck his runs from just 114 balls, with three sixes and 12 fours. His half-century had taken 70 balls, but his second 50 came off only 31 deliveries and his last 34 runs from a mere 13. Trevor Penney also smote 30 not out from 17 balls and the last ten overs of the innings brought 118 runs including 23 from the final over, bowled by James Averis. Gloucestershire fought hard to total 209 in reply, in front of an 8,000 crowd, but batting was always going to be more difficult under the evening lights.

Division One: 3 June 2001
at Tunbridge Wells
Kent 181 for 9 (45 overs)
Somerset 181 for 8 (45 overs) (RJ Turner 56*)
Match tied – 2 pts each

at Oakham School
Nottinghamshire 204 (43.2 overs) (P Johnson 75, DJ Marsh 4 for 44)
Leicestershire 207 for 4 (36 overs) (DJ Marsh 67*, JM Dakin 65)
Leicestershire (4 pts) won by six wickets

at Northampton
Northamptonshire 213 for 6 (45 overs) (ME Hussey 80)
Surrey 217 for 6 (43 overs) (MR Ramprakash 85*, MA Butcher 55)
Surrey (4 pts) won by four wickets

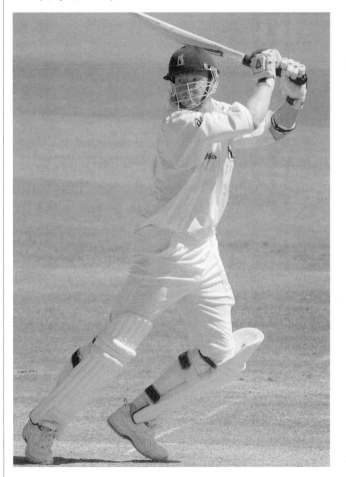

Dominic Ostler ... a wonderful 134 to see off Gloucestershire.

Imaginative and inspired stroke play by Rob Turner earned Somerset an unlikely tie against Kent at Tunbridge Wells. James Hockley's 31-ball 41 had launched Kent towards their eventual 181 for nine and Somerset's hopes seemed to be fading when they reached the final over needing 15 runs to win. Matthew Fleming was the bowler, but Turner struck out bravely to leave his side requiring four for the tie from the very last delivery. With wicket-keeper Paul Nixon standing up (a mistake?), Turner gambled that the ball would be full and from the sweep position flicked the ball up past Nixon's head and through to the boundary. Turner finished on 56 not out.

A fine all-round performance by Daniel Marsh spearheaded Leicestershire's six-wicket win over Nottinghamshire at Oakham School. Marsh first took four for 44 with his left-arm spin as Notts, boosted by Paul Johnson's 75 off 74 balls, totalled 204, and then struck an unbeaten 67 from just 61 deliveries. Jon Dakin, with 65 off 55 balls, was just as destructive, and Leicestershire strolled home with nine overs in hand.

Surrey needed 70 from the final ten overs to overhaul Northamptonshire's 213 for six at Wantage Road, but with Mark Ramprakash in splendid form it proved little problem. Ramprakash finished on 85 not out, from 100 balls, as Surrey romped to victory by four wickets and with two full overs to spare. Mark Butcher also played well for his 63-ball 55 while, for Northants, Mike Hussey (80) and Jeff Cook (47) added 96 for the second wicket.

Division Two: 3 June 2001
at Southampton Rose Bowl
Essex 216 for 7 (45 overs)
Hampshire 208 (44.1 overs)
Essex (4 pts) won by 8 runs

at Southgate
Middlesex 233 for 6 (45 overs) (RMS Weston 80*, DC Nash 57*, AJ Strauss 55)
Derbyshire 217 for 9 (45 overs) (RJ Bailey 71, BL Hutton 5 for 45)
Middlesex (4 pts) won by 16 runs

at Swansea
Sussex 224 for 4 (45 overs) (RR Montgomerie 68, CJ Adams 61*, MW Goodwin 51)
Glamorgan 228 for 4 (42 overs) (JP Maher 71, SP James 52*)
Glamorgan (4 pts) won by six wickets

A brave last-wicket stand between Lawrence Prittipaul and Chris Tremlett almost pulled off an unexpected victory for Hampshire at West End. When Ronnie Irani, the Essex captain, began the final over, the pair had already put on 39 and required just another nine runs to win. But Irani then bowled Prittipaul for 45 and Hampshire were all out for 208. Essex's 216 for seven was based on Stuart Law's 45 and an unbeaten 47 from Jamie Foster.

Career-best one-day figures of five for 45 from Ben Hutton helped Middlesex to a 16-run win against Derbyshire at Southgate. Earlier, despite 55 by Andrew Strauss, Middlesex had stumbled to 109 for six before an unbroken stand of 124 between Robin Weston, with 80 not out against his former county, and David Nash (57 not out) rallied them to 233 for six. Rob Bailey's 71 and 31 from 29 balls by Nathan Dumelow took Derbyshire close ... but not close enough.

Glamorgan put an unhappy few weeks behind them with a comfortable six-wicket victory over Sussex at Swansea that did much for their confidence. Chris Adams blasted 61 not out from 56 balls, and there were half-centuries too for Richard Montgomerie and Murray Goodwin as Sussex ran up 224 for four from their 45 overs. But Jimmy Maher replied with a fine 71, and with Robert Croft hitting 35 from 44 balls and skipper Steve James an unbeaten 52, Glamorgan eased home with three overs to spare.

Division One: 10 June 2001
at Headingley
Yorkshire 189 for 8 (45 overs) (MJ Lumb 66, VJ Craven 55, MJ Walker 4 for 24)
Kent 191 for 6 (44 overs) (DP Fulton 82)
Kent (4 pts) won by four wickets

at Trent Bridge
Gloucestershire 228 for 8 (44 overs) (JN Snape 104*, MA Hardinges 65)
Nottinghamshire 228 for 4 (43.2 overs) (P Johnson 88*, DJ Bicknell 64, KP Pietersen 57)
Nottinghamshire (4 pts) won by six wickets (DL Method: Nottinghamshire needed to have 228 from 43.2 overs when rain stopped play)

at Northampton
Northamptonshire 216 for 4 (45 overs) (MB Loye 90)
Warwickshire 219 for 5 (44.1 overs) (MJ Powell 78, DR Brown 73)
Warwickshire (4 pts) won by five wickets

at The Oval
Surrey 68 for 5 (10 overs)
Somerset 69 for 2 (6.3 overs)
Somerset (4 pts) won by eight wickets

David Fulton's prolific season continued apace at Headingley when his limited-overs best of 82 helped Kent to step up their league challenge by beating Yorkshire by four wickets. Fulton finally fell in the penultimate over, but by then Kent needed only another four runs to surpass Yorkshire's 189 for eight. That total was built around a stand of 108 for the fourth wicket by two youngsters, Michael Lumb (66) and Vic Craven (55). The 21-year-old Lumb once hit Martin Saggers for six over mid-wicket, but then Matthew Walker pegged the home side back again by taking four for 24 with his little medium-pace trundlers.

Nottinghamshire joined Kent and Leicestershire at the head of the first division table by defeating Gloucestershire by six wickets at Trent Bridge. However, Gloucestershire's famed resilience shone out for all to see before the home side triumphed thanks to the batting efforts of Darren Bicknell (64), Paul Johnson (a controlled 88 not out) and Kevin Pietersen (a violent 40-ball 57). Earlier in the game, though, Gloucestershire were 52 for six before recovering to 228 for eight through a partnership of 164 from 155 balls between Jeremy Snape and Mark Hardinges. Snape's 104 not out, from 119 deliveries, was his first century in any form of county cricket, while Hardinges hit two sixes and six fours in a 68-ball 65 in his first competitive one-day county fixture. Their stand was also the highest for the seventh wicket in English one-day cricket, beating the 160 put on by Jack Richards and Ian Payne for Surrey against Lincolnshire in the 1983 NatWest Trophy.

Northamptonshire remained stuck at the bottom of the table, pointless, after being undone by a stand of 132 in 20 overs between Warwickshire's Dougie Brown and Michael Powell at Wantage Road. Mal Loye's 90, containing 12 fours, and a belligerent 37 not out by Alec Swann had lifted Northants to 216 for four from their 45 overs, but then Brown (73) and Powell (78 from 62 balls) rallied Warwickshire from 82 for three to the very brink of their eventual five-wicket victory.

A ten-over slog match at The Oval, which began at 5.45pm, was won at a canter by Somerset after Surrey had only managed to reach 68 for five. Ian Blackwell's 18-ball 33 not out gave Somerset their first league win of the season.

Division Two: 10 June 2001
at Derby
Derbyshire 179 for 7 (45 overs) (MJ Di Venuto 71)
Durham 180 for 6 (44.3 overs)
Durham (4 pts) won by four wickets

at Horsham
Worcestershire 210 for 6 (45 overs) (VS Solanki 63, GA Hick 50)
Sussex 140 (40.1 overs)
Worcestershire (4 pts) won by 70 runs

at Chelmsford
Essex 243 for 6 (34 overs) (R Irani 108*)
Glamorgan 254 for 2 (31.5 overs) (K Newell 97, MP Maynard 87*)
Glamorgan (4 pts) won by eight wickets (DL Method: Glamorgan target 254 runs from 34 overs)

at Old Trafford
Middlesex 184 for 9 (45 overs)
Lancashire 185 for 3 (29.2 overs) (G Chapple 56)
Lancashire (4 pts) won by seven wickets

Durham went to the top of the second division when Andy Pratt's spirited 42 not out, from 36 balls, took them past Derbyshire's 179 for seven at Derby with three balls to spare. Until Pratt and Michael Gough added 65 in 11 overs for the sixth wicket, however, Durham looked as if they would fall just short of a home total based on a classy 71 from Michael Di Venuto

Worcestershire also moved into the promotion places with a 70-run win over Sussex at Horsham. Vikram Solanki's silky 63 was the highlight of their 210 for six, and Sussex fell away alarmingly to 140 all out, losing five wickets in six overs as Stuart Lampitt and Matthew Rawnsley turned the screw.

Glamorgan set the seal on a profitable week at Chelmsford by beating Essex by eight wickets in a high-scoring, rain-affected contest. Ronnie Irani's superb 108 not out from 61 balls, which included four sixes and 13 fours, swept Essex to an intimidating 243 for six from their 34 overs. But Glamorgan, incredibly, still romped home with 13 balls to spare thanks to a stunning 97 by Keith Newell and a beautifully played unbeaten 87 by Matthew Maynard. Newell swung five sixes and ten fours in his 53-ball assault, while Maynard's runs came from 77 balls as he added 100 in ten overs with Newell, and then an unbroken 95 with Michael Powell.

Lancashire totally outplayed Middlesex at Old

Bad luck, Big Ron ... 108 from 61 balls by Irani against Glamorgan is in vain.

Trafford, first restricting them to 184 for nine from their 45 overs and then rattling to their victory target with no fewer than 15.4 overs remaining and seven wickets in hand. Glen Chapple took three for 29 and then hit a 50-ball 56 when sent in first with Mike Atherton to launch the Lancashire reply. Andrew Flintoff also impressed with both bat and ball, with a 28-ball 40 following his haul of three for 27, while Muttiah Muralitharan contributed a magical spell of one for 18 from his nine overs.

Division One: 17 June 2001
at Gloucester
Gloucestershire 152 for 9 (45 overs) (MW Alleyne 68)
Warwickshire 156 for 5 (42.2 overs) (DP Ostler 70*, DR Brown 61)
Warwickshire (4 pts) won by five wickets

at Leicester
Northamptonshire 172 for 9 (45 overs
Leicestershire 173 for 7 (38 overs) (ND Burns 90*)
Leicestershire (4 pts) won by three wickets

at Maidstone
Kent 188 for 6 (30 overs) (JB Hockley 70*)
Nottinghamshire 133 (28.1 overs) (DJ Bicknell 59)

Kent (4 pts) won by 60 runs (DL Method: Nottinghamshire target 194 from 30 overs)

at Bath
Somerset 259 for 7 (45 overs) (PD Bowler 97, ID Blackwell 76)
Yorkshire 244 for 6 (45 overs) (D Byas 81, DS Lehmann 75*, PS Jones 4 for 40)
Somerset (4 pts) won by 15 runs

Gloucestershire's hold on the one-day league title was loosened considerably by a five-wicket loss to Warwickshire at Gloucester's Archdeacon Meadow – the champions' fourth defeat from six matches this season. The home side never really recovered from finding themselves at ten for four on a well-grassed pitch, with Dougie Brown taking three for eight in his six-over new-ball spell. Mark Alleyne's fighting 68 and some late hitting from Mike Cawdron (29) raised Gloucestershire's total to 152 for nine, but it never looked remotely enough as Brown (61) and Dominic Ostler (70 not out) put on 115 for the third wicket.

Leicestershire, meanwhile, took their 100 per cent record into a fourth game with a remarkable three-wicket win against Northamptonshire at Grace Road. Northants totalled 172 for nine from their 45 overs, with Alec Swann top-scoring with 47, but then Leicestershire tumbled dramatically to 30 for six against the seam and swing of Darren Cousins and Lesroy Weekes, who took three wickets apiece. Soon, indeed, it was 57 for seven as Kevin Innes bowled Darren Stevens, but then Phil DeFreitas joined Neil Burns and the match underwent a stunning transformation. With Burns reaching 90 not out, from 96 balls, and DeFreitas a careful unbeaten 33, the Leicestershire tailenders established a new county eighth-wicket record of 116 for the competition and swept their side home with seven overs outstanding. Fittingly, wicket-keeper Burns was awarded his county cap at the end of the match.

Kent maintained their challenge at the top of the division with a 60-run win over Nottinghamshire at Maidstone. Rain reduced the match to a 30-over-per-side affair, but Kent batted well to reach 188 for six with opener James Hockley anchoring the innings with an unbeaten 70 from 79 deliveries. Defending 193 under the Duckworth/Lewis system, Kent then bowled out their visitors for just 133 with the wickets shared out among six bowlers. Darren Bicknell, the Notts captain, did his best to hold things together with 59, but to no avail.

Somerset won a high-scoring contest at Bath, running up 259 for seven and then holding Yorkshire to 244 for six in reply. Peter Bowler hit 97 from 129 balls to provide the solid base for the Somerset effort, but it was Ian Blackwell's bludgeoning 76 from just 54 deliveries, including four sixes and five fours, which provided the rapid acceleration in a fifth-wicket partnership of 112 that took only 88 balls. Similarly, Yorkshire's response was built on skipper David Byas' 118-ball 81, but their mid-innings acceleration was not quite swift enough. The last five overs began with 63 runs still required and not even Darren Lehmann, who finished unbeaten on 75 from 67 balls with three sixes and four fours, could respond to a final over task of scoring 19.

Division Two: 17 June 2001
at Ilford
Durham 264 for 3 (45 overs) (N Peng 112*, JJB Lewis 63*)
Essex 240 (43 overs) (RS Clinton 56)
Durham (4 pts) won by 24 runs

at Worcester
Worcestershire 99 (34.5 overs)
Lancashire 89 (29.2 overs)
Worcestershire (4 pts) won by 10 runs

at Southgate
Hampshire 171 for 9 (45 overs) (DA Kenway 65, CB Keegan 5 for 17)
Middlesex 154 for 9 (45 overs) (JRC Hamblin 4 for 29)
Hampshire (4 pts) won by 17 runs

at Arundel
Sussex 209 for 9 (45 overs) (B Zuiderent 65, MW Goodwin 63)
Derbyshire 201 for 8 (45 overs)
Sussex (4 pts) won by 8 runs

Nicky Peng, one of the rising stars of English cricket, hit a maiden one-day century of both power and poise as Durham defeated Essex by 24 runs at Ilford to stay on top of the second division. The 18-year-old Peng's 112 not out, from just 116 balls, helped to lift Durham's total to an intimidating 264 for three and it was an innings beautifully paced and full of particularly eye-catching offside strokes. Danny Law, opening up with a hard-hit 47, and Jon Lewis, coming in at number five to score 63 not out from 58 deliveries and join Peng in an unbroken stand of 128, both enjoyed themselves hugely against

their former county. Essex, however, maintained a determined response, led by Paul Grayson's 33-ball 43 and a promising 56 from Richard Clinton, and in the end it took three late wickets from Law, who only conceded 28 runs from his seven overs, to wrap things up for Durham.

Worcestershire went into second place with a truly remarkable ten-run win against Lancashire. On a New Road pitch that helped the seamers immensely, and was clearly not ideal for a limited-overs game, Worcestershire managed to delight their supporters by defending a seemingly inadequate total of just 99. Andy Flintoff, in particular, was a fearsome prospect as he moved the ball around at pace to take three

A maiden one-day hundred for Nicky Peng.

for 16, but the home seamers – led by Andy Bichel and Alamgir Sheriyar, who both took three for 23 – were also difficult to play and Lancashire lost wickets steadily to be bowled out for 89 in the 30th over. The Worcestershire team marched off at the end to a standing ovation for their magnificent effort. But throughout the match, good length balls were just about unplayable and was it what limited-overs cricket is supposed to be about?

Derek Kenway's battling 65, at a cold and damp Southgate, ultimately proved to be enough for Hampshire to withstand a burst of five for 17 from Chad Keegan and defeat Middlesex by 17 runs. Hampshire's 45-over total of 171 for nine was always going to be competitive on a strip hastily prepared after a day's rain, and so it proved as James Hamblin (four for 29) and Chris Tremlett (two for 28) spearheaded a bowling effort which restricted Middlesex to 154 for nine.

Good innings of 65 and 63 by Bas Zuiderent and Murray Goodwin respectively, enabled Sussex to build a big enough total to withstand a spirited Derbyshire reply at lovely Arundel. Zuiderent drove Trevor Smith for six and Goodwin pulled Richard Illingworth for another as the pair put on 120 for the third wicket. Mathew Dowman (45) threatened initially, and then Karl Krikken helped Chris Bassano (45) add 67 in 12 overs for the sixth wicket. But after Chris Adams ran out Krikken and Bassano was bowled by Billy Taylor, the Derbyshire innings fell away to 201 for eight. Sussex's eight-run win lifted them into sixth place, level on points with Derbyshire who remained one place ahead of them.

Division Two: 23 June 2001
at Old Trafford (floodlit)
Lancashire 254 for 6 (45 overs) (NH Fairbrother 101, JP Crawley 63)
Essex 217 (41.4 overs) (SG Law 108, CP Schofield 4 for 41)
Lancashire (4 pts) won by 37 runs

A stand of 151 between the evergreen Neil Fairbrother (101) and John Crawley (63) formed the basis of Lancashire's 254 for six and eventual 37-run win over Essex at Old Trafford. Stuart Law scored 108 in reply, following his two centuries in the preceding championship fixture, but once again the rest of the Essex batting could not match up to their Australian star. Chris Schofield picked up four for 41 to ensure that the 7,000-strong crowd went home happy.

Getting better with age? Another one-day century for Lancashire's Neil Fairbrother.

Division One: 24 June 2001
at Trent Bridge
Somerset 232 for 9 (45 overs) (ID Blackwell 59, KA Parsons 58*, RD Stemp 4 for 25)
Nottinghamshire 235 for 4 (44.1 overs) (U Afzaal 94*, GS Blewett 89)
Nottinghamshire (4 pts) won by six wickets

at The Oval
Surrey 154 (44.2 overs)
Kent 158 for 8 (39.3 overs) (AJ Tudor 4 for 36)
Kent (4 pts) won by two wickets

at Edgbaston
Warwickshire 221 for 7 (45 overs) (DP Ostler 54)
Leicestershire 225 for 5 (43 overs) (BF Smith 65*)
Leicestershire (4 pts) won by five wickets

at Headingley
Yorkshire 204 for 6 (45 overs) (D Byas 52)

Northamptonshire 188 for 9 (45 overs) (AJ Swann 55, RJ Warren 54)
Yorkshire (4 pts) won by 16 runs

A classy 94 not out by Usman Afzaal, plus a fine 89 from Greg Blewett in a third-wicket stand between the pair of 161 in 31 overs, swept Nottinghamshire to a morale-boosting six-wicket win over Somerset at Trent Bridge that took them into third place in the table. Earlier, Richard Stemp had equalled his competition-best by taking four for 25 in a controlled nine-over spell. Somerset, boosted initially by Ian Blackwell's 59, fell away against Stemp before Keith Parsons guided them to 232 for nine with an unbeaten 58.

Reserve wicket-keeper Geraint Jones, making his league debut as a stand-in batsman, emerged as the unlikely hero of Kent's two-wicket win against Surrey at The Oval. Jones went in with Kent struggling at 59 for five in reply to Surrey's modest 154, but hit 39 from 39 deliveries to dominate a stand of 54 with Matthew Fleming. Fleming then remained on 26 not out as, with Martin Saggers, he saw Kent home on a poor one-day pitch.

Leicestershire, however, stayed ahead of Kent at the top of the division by virtue of a fifth-successive victory. This time their victims were Warwickshire at Edgbaston, who must have thought they had chances themselves after totalling 221 for seven and then reducing the visitors to 135 for five. Ben Smith and Darren Maddy played themselves in coolly, though, and were so unfazed by the task of scoring 74 from the final ten overs that Leicestershire's win was achieved with 12 balls to spare. Smith ended up on 65 not out as the pair added an unbroken 90.

At the bottom of the table there was a fifth defeat out of five for struggling Northamptonshire, who went down to Yorkshire at Headingley by 16 runs. David Byas' 52 laid the base for Yorkshire's total of 204 for six, and then the home side's pace attack – with both Chris Silverwood and Craig White taking three wickets – proved to be too potent for the Northants batting. Russell Warren and Alec Swann played well to score 54 apiece, but the last six Northants wickets tumbled for 18 runs as the pressure told.

Division Two: 24 June 2001
at Cardiff
Glamorgan 305 for 6 (45 overs) (JP Maher 94, RDB Croft 59, A Dale 52*)
Worcestershire 194 (34.3 overs)
Glamorgan (4 pts) won by 111 runs

at Derby
Derbyshire 196 for 7 (45 overs) (RJ Bailey 55)
Middlesex 154 (40.2 overs)
Derbyshire (4 pts) won by 42 runs

at Southampton Rose Bowl
Hampshire 222 for 7 (45 overs)
Durham 158 (39.1 overs)
Hampshire (4 pts) won by 64 runs

Glamorgan moved into second place in the division by thrashing Worcestershire by 111 runs at Cardiff. Jimmy Maher's 76-ball 94, with 18 fours, set the tone of the Glamorgan innings – and both Robert Croft (59) and Adrian Dale (62 not out) weighed in with quick-fire half-centuries as the carnage continued. Graeme Hick's dismissal for 25 signalled the end of Worcestershire's hopes, and Croft also took three cheap wickets as the visitors declined to 194 all out.

Derbyshire's difficult season took a rare turn for the best when Middlesex were beaten by 42 runs at Derby. Rob Bailey's 55, on a slow and low pitch, enabled Derbyshire to reach 196 for seven from their 45 overs, and Middlesex were not helped by the fact that Stephen Fleming, their New Zealander, could not bat until number eight after dislocating a finger in the field. But the Derbyshire out-cricket was sharp, and of particular pleasure to the home supporters was the sight of Lian Wharton and Nathan Dumelow, the two young spinners, sharing five wickets as Middlesex were bowled out for 154.

Hampshire kept the upward momentum of their season going with a 64-run victory against top-of-the-table Durham at Southampton. The home side's total of 222 for seven, in which Derek Kenway's aggressive 41-ball 46 stood out, was always going to be a challenging one for Durham and, against disciplined seam bowling on a Rose Bowl pitch offering more than a hint of uneven bounce, the visitors soon slipped to 55 for five. They eventually made 158, but Hampshire's five seamers were in complete control and, fittingly, shared out the ten wickets to fall equally.

Division One: 1 July 2001
at Taunton
Gloucestershire 219 for 9 (45 overs) (KJ Barnett 94)
Somerset 211 for 8 (45 overs) (PD Bowler 60, IJ Harvey 4 for 42)
Gloucestershire (4 pts) won by 8 runs

Kim Barnett, county cricket's oldest player, was the shining star of Gloucestershire's narrow eight-run victory in the West Country derby with Somerset at Taunton. Barnett, nearing his 41st birthday, hit 94 in Gloucestershire's 45-over total of 219 for nine – and then bowled six tight overs at a crucial stage as Somerset were held to 211 for eight in reply. Ian Harvey took four for 42, in addition, and in the end the efforts of Peter Bowler (60) and Mike Burns, with 32 not out from 30 balls, came to naught.

Division Two: 3 July 2001
at Derby (floodlit)
Worcestershire 288 for 6 (45 overs) (WPC Weston 134, VS Solanki 63, GA Hick 53)
Derbyshire 150 (38.4 overs) (Kabir Ali 4 for 22)
Worcestershire (4 pts) won by 138 runs

Worcestershire crushed Derbyshire by 138 runs at Derby after Philip Weston's 141-ball 134 had sent them charging to 288 for six. Graeme Hick made 53 and Vikram Solanki 63 in 38 balls while adding 135 in just 12 overs with Weston. But it was the tall opener who dominated proceedings, striking five sixes and 11 fours in his highest limited-overs score. Kabir Ali then took four for 22 as Derbyshire were tumbled out for 150 inside 39 overs.

Division Two: 4 July 2001
at Southampton Rose Bowl (floodlit)
Hampshire 231 for 7 (45 overs) (DA Kenway 76)
Sussex 152 (43.2 overs)
Hampshire (4 pts) won by 79 runs

A crowd of 5,500 at West End enjoyed themselves hugely under the lights as Hampshire thumped neighbours Sussex by 79 runs. Derek Kenway launched Hampshire towards their eventual total of 231 for seven with a cleanly-struck 76, while Robin Smith's 34-ball 38 not out provided the late burst of scoring. Will House managed 39 in reply, but otherwise Sussex were quite unable to mount a challenge. Chris Tremlett (three for 22) and Shaun Udal (three for 23) both bowled their nine overs with aplomb.

Division One: 8 July 2001
at Leicester
Leicestershire 240 (45 overs) (DI Stevens 63)
Surrey 112 (35.4 overs)
Leicestershire (4 pts) won by 128 runs

at Canterbury
Kent 114 (29.2 overs) (KJ Barnett 4 for 12)
Gloucestershire 86 (27 overs) (MJ Saggers 5 for 22)

Kent (4 pts) won by 31 runs (DL Method: Gloucestershire target 118 from 33 overs)

at Taunton
Somerset 248 for 8 (45 overs) (PD Bowler 98)
Nottinghamshire 252 for 7 (44 overs) (DJ Bicknell 79, P Johnson 67)
Nottinghamshire (4 pts) won by three wickets

at Northampton
Yorkshire 161 for 8 (45 overs) (GM Fellows 67, MR Strong 4 for 28)
Northamptonshire 165 for 7 (41.1 overs) (MB Loye 65*)
Northamptonshire (4 pts) won by three wickets

Leicestershire's sixth-consecutive win, a 128-run humbling of Surrey, kept them flying high at the top of the table with their proud 100 per cent record intact. A ragged effort in the field by Surrey betrayed their position at the bottom of the division, and allowed Leicestershire to reach an imposing 240. Darren Stevens made 63 from 72 balls, Darren Maddy's 44 took just 33 deliveries and the

A competition-best by Martin Saggers against Gloucestershire kept the Spitfires soaring.

Leicestershire innings was further boosted by Aftab Habib emerging at number nine and bludgeoning an unorthodox 26 not out. James Ormond and Scott Boswell both bowled their nine overs straight through, kept runs at a premium and claimed an early wicket apiece – thus putting real pressure on the Surrey middle-order to increase the scoring rate. And, after Phil DeFreitas had removed Adam Holliake with his first ball, Surrey subsided meekly to 112 all out.

Kent, having played a game more than Leicestershire, stayed in second place by virtue of a 31-run victory against Gloucestershire at Canterbury in a game shortened to 33 overs per side by rain. With the Duckworth/Lewis system also kicking in, Gloucestershire were required to score 118 to beat Kent, after bowling them out for just 114 on a seaming pitch. Kim Barnett's four for 12 was his best bowling analysis in 313 league matches spread over 23 seasons, but Martin Saggers outdid him to win the game for Kent with a competition-best five for 22. Ian Harvey hit James Golding for three sixes to raise Gloucestershire hopes, despite their initial plunge to 32 for six, but then Saggers returned to have him caught on the mid-wicket boundary for a 40-ball 39 and the visitors were soon all out for 86.

An unfortunate run out incident involving Darren Bicknell, the Nottinghamshire captain, and Peter Robinson, the stand-in umpire, failed to prevent a Notts victory against Somerset in a high-scoring affair at Taunton. Somerset totalled 248 for eight, with Peter Bowler hitting two sixes and ten fours, but Notts were cruising towards their target with Bicknell in irresistible form when the incident occurred. David Shepherd, the umpire, had to leave the field with a pulled calf muscle and Robinson, the former Somerset coach who is now the county's security officer, replaced him to stand at square leg. Almost immediately, he upheld a run-out appeal against Bicknell, who had raced to 79 from only 70 balls, and the opener showed marked dissent at the decision. Notts, however, overcame Bicknell's loss and with Paul Johnson (67), 16-year-old Bilal Shafayat (31) and Chris Read (30 not out) all making significant contributions, they swept home by three wickets and with an over to spare.

Northamptonshire, meanwhile, could heave a huge collective sigh of relief after overcoming Yorkshire by three wickets at Wantage Road – it was their first win of the season in either one-day or four-day league cricket! Michael Strong's four for 28, and a tight spell from Jason Brown, was largely responsible for restricting Yorkshire to 161 for eight,

and Mal Loye's unbeaten 65 was the rock on which the run-chase towards a long-overdue victory was built. Mike Hussey was awarded his county cap during the tea interval.

Division Two: 8 July 2001
at Chester-le-Street
Glamorgan 145 (40.2 overs) (RDB Croft 67)
Durham 146 for 8 (43.3 overs)
Durham (4 pts) won by two wickets

at Southgate
Essex 120 (42.5 overs) (JWM Dalrymple 4 for 14)
Middlesex 120 (43 overs) (OA Shah 52*, AP Cowan 5 for 14)
Match tied: 2 pts each

Durham moved to the head of the second division table with a hard-fought, two-wicket win over Glamorgan in a tense, low-scoring contest on a dampish pitch at the Riverside. Glamorgan, struggling at 15 for four, were rescued initially by Robert Croft's mature 67, but Durham, though themselves wobbling early at ten for three in reply to the Welsh county's 145, were also rallied as skipper Jon Lewis battled to an unbeaten 46. Paul Collingwood must take great credit, too, for launching the counter-attack with three sixes in his 31-ball 25, while the Durham lower-order supported Lewis stoutly.

Middlesex and Essex tied their match at Southgate, in another low-scoring affair, but not even a thrilling finish could overshadow the drama taking place off the field. Stuart Law, Essex's prolific Australian batsman, was missing the match with a finger injury, but his comments in a local radio interview left his future with the county in grave doubt. 'There's very little respect for me. It's a shame there are some players who are sticking the knife into me,' said Law, revealing the depth of dressing-room disharmony. David East, the Essex chief executive, said no decision on Law's contract situation would be made until the end of the season, but the wounds at the club looked deep on Law's evidence. At least, on the field, there was some succour for Essex, with Justin Bishop defeating Tim Bloomfield's timid forward push to bowl him with the last ball of the 43rd over and clinch the tie. That was rough luck on Owais Shah, who remained on 52 not out but stranded at the other end. Ashley Cowan was the other Essex star, taking five for 14 in Middlesex's total of 120 all out, while off spinner Jamie Dalrymple had done much of the damage in the Essex innings by taking four for 14.

Division One: 15 July 2001
at Scarborough
Leicestershire 247 for 9 (45 overs)
Yorkshire 231 for 7 (45 overs) (DS Lehmann 103)
Leicestershire (4 pts) won by 16 runs

at Trent Bridge
Kent 196 (44.5 overs)
Nottinghamshire 195 for 7 (45 overs) (DJ Bicknell 64)
Kent (4 pts) won by 1 run

at Edgbaston
Northamptonshire 158 for 8 (45 overs) (RJ Warren 80*)
Warwickshire 159 for 6 (38.2 overs) (MR Strong 4 for 39)
Warwickshire (4 pts) won by four wickets

Table-toppers Leicestershire withstood a 108-ball innings of 103 from Australian left-hander Darren Lehmann to beat Yorkshire by 16 runs at Scarborough and extend their 100 per cent record in

the competition to seven matches. The absence of the 'rested' Darren Gough caused much consternation among Yorkshire supporters, especially when coach Wayne Clark said he thought Gough had looked tired. Gough had bowled, at this stage of the season, only 248 overs for county and country, and England were due to play Australia in the second Ashes Test at Lord's later the same week. But many also understood Clark's reasoning that to ask Gough to drive five hours from his Buckinghamshire home, and then five hours back, just to bowl a maximum of nine overs, was foolish anyway. Whatever, Yorkshire's attack could not prevent Leicestershire from reaching 247 for nine from their 45 overs, despite Iain Sutcliffe's 48 being the highest individual score. Again, Aftab Habib, batting low down the order at number eight, made an important late contribution with 37 not out from 48 balls.

Kent stayed hard on the heels of the leaders with an exciting, one-run victory against Nottinghamshire at Trent Bridge. Kevin Pietersen, having played wonderfully well for 48 to keep the Notts challenge alive, despite a stuttering middle-order, was run out by Andrew Symonds' throw from long-on as he tried to complete the second run that would have produced a tie. Notts, however, had been seemingly coasting at 116 for two in reply to Kent's 196, in which only David Fulton got past 30. Darren Bicknell made 64 and Paul Johnson became the eighth player to reach 7,000 one-day league runs when he got to 26, but Notts then lost momentum as Kent fought back tigerishly in the field and it was only due to Pietersen that they came so close to making the 45 required from the last five overs.

Nick Knight and Dominic Ostler used all their one-day know-how to guide Warwickshire to a four-wicket win against Northamptonshire at Edgbaston. In conditions that always offered something to the bowlers, Northants reached 158 for eight from their 45 overs, largely due to the efforts of Russell Warren, whose 80 contained eight of only ten boundaries struck in the whole innings. Neil Carter picked up three for 28 and Charlie Dagnall was equally impressive with the new ball, despite going wicketless. Warwickshire experienced a wobble at 18 for three, with Mark Wagh and Dougie Brown both out for ducks, but Knight's 47 and Ostler's 49 restored calm and eventually thwarted the efforts of Michael Strong (four for 39).

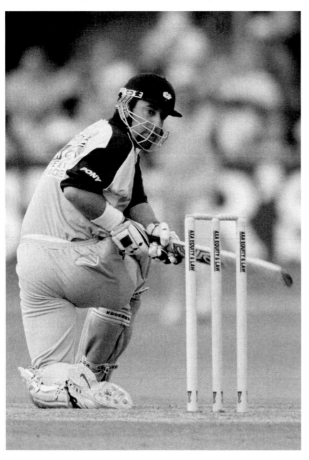

Darren Lehmann sweeps ... but his 103 was not enough for Yorkshire as Leicestershire took the spoils.

Division Two: 15 July 2001
at Worcester
Middlesex 128 (43.1 overs)
Worcestershire 129 for 5 (37.4 overs) (DA Leatherdale 55*)
Worcestershire (4 pts) won by five wickets

at Southampton Rose Bowl
Hampshire 155 for 9 (45 overs)
Derbyshire 139 (44.2 overs)
Hampshire (4 pts) won by 16 runs

at Old Trafford
Lancashire v. **Durham**
No play – 2 pts each

Worcestershire moved back to the top of the second division as a highly competent unbeaten 55 from the often-underestimated David Leatherdale guided them to a five-wicket victory against Middlesex on another slow, low seamer at New Road. Middlesex's 128 was never likely to be enough – despite Worcestershire having successfully defended 99 on this ground against Lancashire in their previous match – but at least Angus Fraser made them fight hard for their win by taking three for 13 from his nine-over, new-ball spell.

A pitch of uneven bounce made for another low-scoring affair at West End, where Hampshire's 155 for nine ultimately proved to be too much for Derbyshire, who lost by 16 runs. Accumulation, rather than brazen hitting, was the only answer to the conditions, but once Derbyshire lost Rob Bailey, who top-scored with 40, they subsided.

There was no play at Old Trafford, due to rain, with Lancashire and Durham both collecting two points apiece.

Division Two: 16 July 2001
at Hove (floodlit)
Sussex 241 for 3 (45 overs) (RR Montgomerie 108, MW Goodwin 87)
Essex 214 for 7 (45 overs) (JS Foster 56*, AP Grayson 52)
Sussex (4 pts) won by 27 runs

Essex were beaten far more heavily than their 27-run defeat at Hove suggests, after Sussex had run up a demanding total of 241 for three. Losing four wickets in the first 15 overs, and falling well below the required scoring rate in the process, left Essex with damage limitation as their only realistic target – something which Paul Grayson (52) and James

Foster (56 not out) were happy to live with. Earlier, well before the Hove floodlights were switched on, Richard Montgomerie and Murray Goodwin had put on a county record one-day league opening partnership of 176, in 34 overs. Montgomerie finished with 108 and Goodwin 87, with both innings full of delightful strokes all around the wicket as Essex's bowlers wilted.

Division One: 17 July 2001
at Bristol (floodlit)
Gloucestershire v. **Somerset**
No play – 2 pts each

The two points Gloucestershire and Somerset received for their abandoned floodlit match at Bristol pushed both a little further away from the relegation zone – although the three teams below them all had games in hand at this stage.

Division Two: 18 July 2001
at Old Trafford (floodlit)
Worcestershire 236 for 5 (45 overs) (A Singh 80)
Lancashire 127 (35.4 overs)
Worcestershire (4 pts) won by 109 runs

An impressive all-round performance by Worcestershire destroyed Lancashire by 109 runs at Old Trafford. First, the visitors piled up 236 for five with Anurag Singh hitting a classy 80 before Vikram Solanki (45) and Andy Bichel (36 not out off just 24 balls) led the acceleration. Then, against some testing and accurate seam bowling, Lancashire slid to 127 all out in reply.

Division One: 22 July 2001
at Leicester
Kent 144 (43.3 overs)
Leicestershire 145 for 5 (27 overs) (Shahid Afridi 70)
Leicestershire (4 pts) won by five wickets

at Guildford
Surrey 195 (41.1 overs) (AJ Hollioake 66)
Northamptonshire 176 for 2 (30.2 overs) (ME Hussey 96*, MB Loye 70*)
Northamptonshire (4 pts) won by eight wickets (DL Method: Northamptonshire needed to have 176 from 37 overs when rain stopped play)

Shahid Afridi, Leicestershire's overseas replacement for the injured Dan Marsh, made one of the most explosive one-day league debuts in history with a 32-ball 70 which included five sixes and six fours.

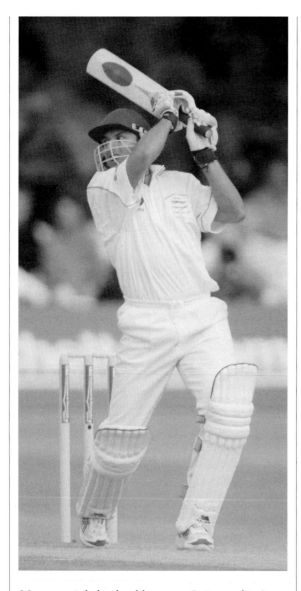

Shahid Afridi made an explosive debut for Leicestershire, smashing his way to 70 off a mere 32 balls.

did at last manage to have the whirling dervish caught as he top-edged a sweep, and Mark Ealham did take three good wickets, but, overall, Kent were simply swept aside.

Northants won a bottom-of-the-table meeting with a depleted Surrey side at Guildford by eight wickets to leave Adam Hollioake's team rooted to the foot of the division. Hollioake himself hit 66 in a Surrey total of 195, but Mike Hussey and Mal Loye made short work of a target further reduced to 176 after the second of the weather interruptions that had initially made this a 42-over contest. Hussey, coming in at number four with his team struggling on six for two following two strikes from Martin Bicknell, stroked 96 not out from just 88 balls with a six and 11 fours. Loye also batted with style to finish up unbeaten on 70, and together the pair put on 170 in 26 overs. The 176-run target was reached with almost seven overs to spare, such was their dominance.

Division Two: 22 July 2001
at Chester-le-Street
Sussex 144 (44.3 overs) (AM Davies 4 for 13)
Durham 145 for 3 (34 overs) (ML Love 75*)
Durham (4 pts) won by seven wickets

at Southend
Hampshire 213 for 6 (45 overs) (NC Johnson 105*, AD Mascarenhas 53)
Essex 128 (38.4 overs)
Hampshire (4 pts) won by 85 runs

at Cardiff
Derbyshire 199 for 8 (45 overs) (MP Dowman 64, SD Stubbings 60)
Glamorgan 200 for 4 (40.4 overs) (K Newell 59, IJ Thomas 53)
Glamorgan (4 pts) won by six wickets

Durham's promotion ambitions were boosted when they trounced Sussex by seven wickets at Chester-le-Street. Mark Davies, the young seamer, soon had the visitors staggering at 24 for four and his seven-over, new-ball spell earned him the memorable figures of four for 13. Richard Montgomerie ground out 29 singles in his 47, as he tried to lead a rally in testing conditions for batting, but Sussex's eventual 144 was clearly not enough. Martin Love then ensured there would be no hiccups, striking 13 boundaries in his

Moreover, it helped to blow away Leicestershire's nearest challengers Kent by five wickets at Grace Road and establish Afridi's new county a clear lead at the head of the Norwich Union League table. The 21-year-old Pakistani, with an astonishing 131 one-day internationals already under his belt, warmed up by taking one for 33 in his nine overs of fizzing leg-breaks as Kent struggled to 144 all out. Jimmy Ormond was the home side's main bowling hero, his three for 16 including a spell of three for four in five overs, but there was no doubting Afridi's status as top of the bill when he began to thrash the Kent attack to all parts. Min Patel, who had been swung for three fours and a six from consecutive deliveries,

75 not out as victory arrived with no fewer than 11 overs in hand.

As Hampshire's season continued to get better, so Essex's continued to get worse. Defeat by 85 runs at Southend left Essex rock bottom of the league, while Hampshire strengthened their promotion claims by first reaching 213 for six from their 45 overs and then dismissing Essex for 128 with commendable efficiency. Neil Johnson batted through the Hampshire innings to reach 105 not out, completing his hundred with a big six over long-on in the final over off Ashley Cowan, but Dimitri Mascarenhas also caught the eye with an 81-ball 53 as he and Johnson put on 113 for the third wicket.

Glamorgan also stayed in the promotion shake-up by breezing past Derbyshire by six wickets at Cardiff. The visitors could total only 199 for eight from their 45 overs, despite a stand of 109 for the third wicket between Steve Stubbings (60) and Mathew Dowman (64), and Glamorgan recorded their victory with more than four overs remaining. Half-centuries from both openers, Keith Newell and Ian Thomas, set them on their way, while Matthew Maynard's unbeaten 40 swept them across the finishing line with plenty to spare.

Division One: 23 July 2001
at Headingley (floodlit)
Yorkshire 234 for 6 (45 overs) (MJ Wood 68)
Warwickshire 59 (15.2 overs) (CEW Silverwood 4 for 21)
Yorkshire (4 pts) won by 175 runs

Warwickshire were humiliated under the Headingley floodlights, plunging first to 12 for six and then to 59 all out as Yorkshire beat them by 175 runs. Ironically, Warwickshire began the game with hopes of climbing above Nottinghamshire into third place, but when Chris Silverwood and Steve Kirby had them six wickets down during dramatic new-ball spells, it seemed as if the visitors could even be dismissed for the lowest total in the history of the one-day league. Small consolation came when they eased past Middlesex's 23 all out, made also against Yorkshire on this same ground in 1974, without further loss. Nevertheless, their rout – in just 15.2 overs – brought them their lowest total in the competition. Silverwood finished with four for 21 and Kirby three for 35, while Ryan Sidebottom helped to wrap things up clinically with two wickets that cost just one run. It was a good job, for the sake of the crowd, that Yorkshire had batted first,

although the early finish came before the lights were really needed. Matthew Wood anchored the innings of 234 for six with 68, before Gary Fellows (40 off 24 balls) and Darren Lehmann (39 off 32) laid into the Warwickshire attack.

Division One: 29 July 2001
at Edgbaston
Surrey 136 (42.2 overs) (BC Hollioake 52*)
Warwickshire 137 for 7 (37.3 overs) (DR Brown 63)
Warwickshire (4 pts) won by three wickets

Warwickshire won a tense, low-scoring affair at Edgbaston by three wickets to push Surrey closer to relegation. Ben Hollioake's unbeaten 52 was the only innings of substance in a Surrey total of 136 all out – in which Mark Butcher had to retire hurt when hit on the head by a short ball from Neil Carter. Warwickshire, in reply, were a nervous 55 for four before Dougie Brown (63) and Trevor Penney (35) added 73.

Division One: 31 July 2001
at Cheltenham
Gloucestershire 286 for 8 (45 overs) (KJ Barnett 100, DR Hewson 52)
Nottinghamshire 170 (39 overs)
Gloucestershire (4 pts) won by 116 runs

Gloucestershire put an uncharacteristic run of three successive one-day defeats behind them by thumping Nottinghamshire by 116 runs at Cheltenham. Kim Barnett's accomplished 100, from 112 balls, was the basis of their imposing total of 286 for eight, but Dominic Hewson also played well for his 52 in an opening stand of 124 while Ian Harvey came in at number three to thrash two sixes and six fours in his 36-ball 46. Late hitting was provided by Mark Hardinges and Martyn Ball, who added 47 in just over four overs for the eighth wicket, and it was all too much for Notts who lost their top four batsmen inside 21 overs and were finally dismissed for 170.

Division Two: 31 July 2001
at Worcester (floodlit)
Durham 274 for 7 (45 overs) (N Peng 121)
Worcestershire 275 for 3 (42.2 overs) (VS Solanki 91*, GA Hick 87, PR Pollard 62)
Worcestershire (4 pts) won by seven wickets

Vikram Solanki and Graeme Hick set a new record for floodlit cricket as Worcestershire triumphed by seven wickets after being set 275 to win by a Durham side inspired by the precocious talents of 18-year-old Nicky Peng. Solanki and Hick put on 160 in 27 overs to take Worcestershire to victory in front of a jubilant 4,500 crowd at New Road, as the home side reached 275 for three with a remarkable 16 balls to spare. Traditionally, batting under lights is more difficult, but this was, by 27 runs, the highest total made in floodlit league encounters by a side batting second. It was all a bit hard to take for Peng, whose 121 from 113 balls was an astonishingly dominant and assured innings for one so young. Peng hit a six and 19 fours in his highest one-day score, and Durham's 274 for seven looked to be a winning total. Paul Pollard, however, included only because Philip Weston was resting a sore knee, rushed to 62 in 44 balls, with a six amongst his 11 boundaries, and set the tone for Hick and Solanki to follow. Hick was bowled late on by Danny Law for 87, made from 94 balls, but Solanki ended on 91 not out from 104 deliveries when victory was clinched.

Vikram Solanki continued his fine one-day form for Worcestershire with an unbeaten 91 against Durham.

Division Two: 1 August 2001
at Hove (floodlit)
Sussex 161 for 7 (45 overs) (MW Goodwin 68)
Middlesex 154 for 9 (45 overs) (PN Weekes 55)
Sussex (4 pts) won by 7 runs

The first implementation of six penalty runs caused a minor flutter of excitement at the end of a routine, low-scoring, floodlit affair at Hove. Sussex, despite the penalty awarded against them for not being in a position to start the final over by 10.20pm, still beat Middlesex in relative comfort by seven runs. Murray Goodwin, quickly realizing that pitch conditions were not ideal for stroke play, grafted a valuable 68 with exemplary technique and liberal use of the quick single. Tim Bloomfield bowled his nine-over new-ball spell for just 12 runs, but did not take a wicket, and Sussex were able to reach 161 for seven from their 45 overs. Middlesex, by contrast, could not withstand the Sussex new ball and were soon in dire trouble at 38 for five. Acting skipper Paul Weekes responded with a brave 55, including the only six of the contest, and he was supported by Ben Hutton's 26 in a sixth-wicket stand that was eventually worth 88. But the asking rate had inevitably mushroomed, and Sussex held their nerve to close out their opponents. Robin Martin-Jenkins and Billy Taylor each took three wickets.

Division One: 2 August 2001
at Edgbaston (floodlit)
Nottinghamshire 105 for 3 (20.2 overs)
Warwickshire did not bat
Match abandoned – 2 pts each

Rain delayed the start and eventually caused the abandonment of Warwickshire's floodlit encounter with Nottinghamshire at Edgbaston. In a match initially reduced to 30 overs per side, Charlie Dagnall grabbed two quick wickets with the new ball, but Notts were rallied to 105 for three from 20.2 overs by Greg Blewett (44) and Usman Afzaal, who was on 40 not out when the bad weather closed in fatally.

Division One: 5 August 2001
at Canterbury
Leicestershire 236 for 9 (45 overs) (DI Stevens 51)
Kent 222 for 9 (45 overs) (RWT Key 59, PA Nixon 55)
Leicestershire (4 pts) won by 14 runs

at Cheltenham
Gloucestershire 344 for 6 (45 overs) (MGN Windows

117, IJ Harvey 67, CG Taylor 63rh)
Northamptonshire 261 (40.5 overs) (AL Penberthy 52, JMM Averis 5 for 56)
Gloucestershire (4 pts) won by 83 runs

at Headingley
Yorkshire 230 for 7 (45 overs) (GM Hamilton 57)
Surrey 163 (40 overs) (MR Ramprakash 58, CJ Elstub 4 for 25)
Yorkshire (4 pts) won by 67 runs

Leicestershire subdued a large crowd at Canterbury by completing a second victory over their chief title rivals Kent in a fortnight – and thereby taking a massive step towards bringing the one-day league's top prize to Grace Road. Kent actually did quite well to restrict Leicestershire to 236 for nine from their 45 overs, after Darren Stevens (51), Iain Sutcliffe, Vince Wells and Shahid Afridi had all contributed to a six-runs-per-over dash to 155 for two. In reply, however, Kent slid to 32 for three and then 84 for four when David Fulton was lbw to Wells in the 18th over. Rob Key (59) and Paul Nixon (55) resuscitated the chase with a fifth-wicket stand of 79 – with Nixon the chief aggressor – but they could not prevent the asking rate from spiralling upwards until 34 was required from the last two overs. That was beyond even Nixon and Matthew Fleming, and Kent's effort fizzled out at 222 for nine.

Gloucestershire, the reigning champions but now almost certain to be deposed, gave a glimpse of a power so often dissipated by injury this season when they crushed Northamptonshire by sheer weight of runs at Cheltenham. Ian Harvey provided the catalyst with a 34-ball 67, which included three sixes and eight fours, and both Matt Windows (117 off 94 balls, with five sixes and 10 fours) and Chris Taylor (63 off 50 balls) ensured there would be no mercy. Gloucestershire's final total of 344 for six was the third highest in the 33-year history of the one-day league and Michael Strong's analysis of 9-0-99-1 was a competition record in terms of runs conceded. Northants' hopes of matching Gloucestershire's pyrotechnics seemed to disappear with key batsman Mike Hussey's departure for just four, but the rest of the order did their best to entertain a big crowd – reaching a creditable 261 to bring a fitting end to a much-loved festival.

Only the ever-reliable Martin Bicknell (three for 20 from his nine overs) escaped punishment as Yorkshire ran up 230 for seven against Surrey at Headingley en route to a comfortable 67-run victory over the bottom club. Gavin Hamilton (57) and

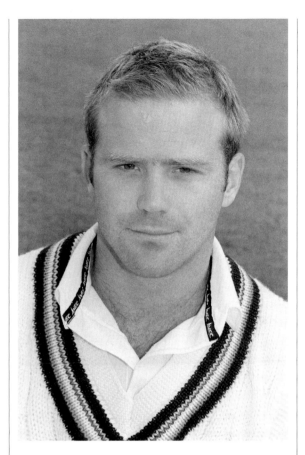

Matt Windows led the slaughter of the Northants attack at Cheltenham with a hard-hitting 117.

Matthew Wood (47) provided a solid launching pad with an opening partnership of 94, and Surrey's reply was tame apart from the classy 58 offered by Mark Ramprakash, and a final flurry of 38 not out by Saqlain Mushtaq.

Division Two
at Derby
Derbyshire 184 for 5 (44 overs)
Hampshire 186 for 1 (35.3 overs) (DA Kenway 93*, JS Laney 62*)
Hampshire (4 pts) won by nine wickets

at Colwyn Bay
Glamorgan 266 (43.5 overs) (RDB Croft 64)
Lancashire 220 (41.5 overs) (GD Lloyd 51)
Glamorgan (4 pts) won by 46 runs

Hampshire made almost embarrassingly light work of overhauling Derbyshire's 184 for five at Derby, winning by nine wickets with over eight overs to spare in a contest reduced to 44 overs per side by a light pre-match shower. Derbyshire were 100 for five and in deep trouble before Luke Sutton and Karl Krikken, both with 42 not out, at least gave them something to defend. But, although the dangerous Neil Johnson was lbw to Paul Aldred for 23, Derek Kenway joined Jason Laney to speed Hampshire to their target in an unbroken stand of 144. Kenway included two sixes and ten fours in his 93 not out, while Laney finished on 62 not out.

Robert Croft had hurried away from England's Test defeat at Trent Bridge in need of some kit to play in Glamorgan's meeting with Lancashire in front of a sun-soaked crowd of 4,500 at Colwyn Bay. His number 19 shirt bore the name of Simon Jones, but there was no mistaking Croft's determined batting style as he hit 64 from 90 balls, with a six and eight fours, to spearhead Glamorgan's rapid progress to a challenging target of 266. Croft then did his bit with the ball, too, taking the wicket of Mark Chilton for 34 and conceding only 37 runs from his nine overs as Lancashire were restricted to 220. Graham Lloyd top-scored for the visitors with 51.

Division One: 12 August 2001
at The Oval
Gloucestershire 176 (40.1 overs) (MGN Windows 70)
Surrey 180 for 8 (40.4 overs) (AJ Hollioake 56)
Surrey (4 pts) won by two wickets

at Northampton
Northamptonshire v. Kent
Match abandoned without a ball bowled – 2 pts each

A stand of 76 in 16 overs by the Hollioake brothers, Adam and Ben, who scored 56 and 42 respectively, was enough to earn Surrey their first win in seven league matches as they beat Gloucestershire by two wickets at The Oval. Any final and already fading hopes Gloucestershire had of being able to defend their one-day league title successfully disappeared as they were bowled out for 176 and then upstaged by the Hollioakes. Ben took three for 24, too, from his seven overs to cut short a rally from Matt Windows (70) and Jeremy Snape (49), who added 109 in 22 overs for the fifth wicket after Gloucestershire had stumbled to 48 for four against the new-ball attack of Ed Giddins and Carl Greenidge.

There was little luck for title challengers Kent, however, who saw their match against Northamptonshire at Northampton abandoned because of rain. The two points they received

enabled Kent to cut Leicestershire's lead at the top of the division to six points, but the leaders had played two games less.

Division Two
at Chelmsford
Essex 200 (39.2 overs) (GR Napier 73, AJ Bichel 5 for 21)
Worcestershire 167 (38.2 overs) (A Singh 61, GR Napier 6 for 29)
Essex (4 pts) won by 33 runs

at Chester-le-Street
Durham 269 for 8 (45 overs) (A Pratt 86, N Peng 50)
Derbyshire 134 for 5 (28.5 overs)
Durham (4 pts) won by 33 runs (DL Method: Derbyshire needed to have 168 runs from 28.5 overs when rain stopped play)

at Southampton Rose Bowl
Hampshire 120 (38.5 overs) (AP Davies 4 for 18)
Glamorgan 121 for 4 (27.5 overs)
Glamorgan (4 pts) won by six wickets

A remarkable all-round performance from Graham Napier inspired Essex to the victory over

Graham Napier inspired Essex to victory over Worcestershire, hitting 73 and then taking six for 29.

Worcestershire at Chelmsford which took them off the bottom of the table and gave their beleaguered supporters a rare chance to smile. Much attention was on England captain Nasser Hussain, who opened the Essex batting in an attempt to get some desperately needed batting practice before making his second Test comeback from injury of the summer three days later. But, despite figuring in a stand of 51 for the second wicket, Hussain made just seven before being bowled leg stump as he tried to drive. By then, Napier was well on the way to grabbing all the limelight and his eventual 73 off 60 balls included four sixes and six fours. Worcestershire, however, had reached 122 for two in the 29th over of their reply to Essex's 200 before the 21-year-old Napier stepped in to wreak havoc with his medium pacers. As Worcestershire attempted to strike out for victory, he took six for 29 and led Essex to a 33-run win.

Andy Pratt was another cricketer to underline his immense promise as Durham defeated Derbyshire by 33 runs at Chester-le-Street, courtesy of the Duckworth/Lewis system, to maintain their promotion push. Wicket-keeper Pratt, 26, struck a six and 13 fours in a one-day best 86 and dominated an opening stand of 128 with Nicky Peng (50). A final total of 269 for eight was only 13 runs short of Durham's competition-best, and Derbyshire's chances were sinking fast at 134 for five when the weather intervened to end their struggle.

Andrew Davies recorded his one-day best figures with the ball, four for 18 from his nine overs, as Glamorgan bowled out Hampshire for 120 at the Rose Bowl in Southampton and then raced to victory by six wickets with Matthew Maynard unbeaten on 41. Defeat brought to an end six successive Hampshire wins in the competition, but boosted Glamorgan's own chances of promotion to division one.

Division One: 13 August 2001
at Trent Bridge (floodlit)
Nottinghamshire 244 for 7 (45 overs) (Usman Afzaal 53)
Yorkshire 246 for 7 (44.2 overs) (C White 73, DS Lehmann 71)
Yorkshire (4 pts) won by three wickets

Richard Blakey drove the second ball of the final over through the covers for four to settle a tremendous contest Yorkshire's way at Trent Bridge. A weakened Yorkshire attack did well to restrict Nottinghamshire to 244 for seven, with 16-year-old

paceman Tim Bresnan impressing with figures of two for 31 on his senior debut as Usman Afzaal (53) and Kevin Pietersen (49) threatened to run amok. But, when Yorkshire slipped to 31 for four, the game looked up. Craig White, however, joined Darren Lehmann in a magnificent stand of 113 and, when the Australian left-hander was bowled off an inside edge for a 75-ball 71, White (73) was joined in a 68-run alliance by David Byas, the Yorkshire captain.

Division One: 14 August 2001
at Canterbury (floodlit)
Kent 207 (42 overs) (A Symonds 74, GJ Batty 4 for 36)
Surrey 164 (38.1 overs) (IJ Ward 51, MW Fleming four run outs)
Kent (4 pts) won by 43 runs

at Taunton
Somerset 263 for 7 (45 overs) (PD Bowler 104, ID Blackwell 86)
Leicestershire 262 for 9 (45 overs) (Shahid Afridi 68, ND Burns 59*)
Somerset (4 pts) won by 1 run

Four direct-hit run-outs by Matthew Fleming, including, remarkably, three in the space of four balls, fatally undermined Surrey at Canterbury and roused a near-capacity floodlit crowd to joyous celebration. Kent's 43-run triumph, which had seemed so unlikely when Surrey reached 147 for three in the 31st over in reply to the home side's underachieving 207, boosted their title aspirations in tandem with Leicestershire's one-run loss at Somerset earlier in the day. Kent certainly needed Fleming's inspiration, but they also needed a contentious decision from third umpire Trevor Jesty to help them back into the match. In the over after Ian Ward became Fleming's first run-out victim, for 51, Ben Hollioake was adjudged stumped by Jesty for momentarily lifting his back foot. If the Sky TV cameras had not been covering the game, however, there is little doubt that the square leg umpire would have given a considerable amount of benefit of the doubt to the batsman. Andy Symonds, the successful bowler, then had Nadeem Shahid caught at the wicket and – suddenly – Kent had the match won as Fleming swooped to run out Jon Batty, Saqlain Mushtaq and Martin Bicknell amid ecstatic scenes. Earlier, Symonds' brilliant 68-ball 74 had taken Kent to 151 for four with 20 overs still remaining – only for the lower middle-order to underperform with some careless strokes.

Playing the anchor role to perfection. Peter Bowler hit 104 to help Somerset to a one-run victory over Leicestershire.

The Taunton dress rehearsal for the Cheltenham & Gloucester Trophy final on September 1 became another showcase for the extraordinary batting talents of Shahid Afridi, but in the end not even the Pakistani's 30-ball 68, with three sixes and 12 fours, could prevent Leicestershire from defeat by a single run in a magnificent contest. In a match which would grace a Lord's showpiece, Somerset reached 263 for seven from their 45 overs, but were then forced to defend desperately as Afridi launched the Leicestershire reply with a fusillade of boundaries. To show that he was not all bludgeon, Afridi late cut one of his fours with delightful delicacy – off an attempted bouncer from Jamie Grove! Most of his runs, though, came from fierce drives to long-off and long-on and, once again, the trueness of the Taunton pitch enabled batsmen from both sides to get full value from their shot-making. Afridi, having been dropped at 22 and then 55, finally perished to

a catch on the deep mid-wicket boundary, and from 82 for one in the tenth over Leicestershire lost their way somewhat in the middle-order. Aftab Habib and Neil Burns did add 69 for the seventh wicket to revive their side's hopes, but when Habib fell for 44 Burns, playing against his old county, was left to battle on almost alone as he made a brave attempt to match an asking rate of 40 from the last five overs. Burns' 59 not out, from 61 balls, included a six swung to mid-wicket off the game's penultimate delivery from Jason Kerr – but, with four runs still needed for victory, the wicket-keeper could only manage a two to long-on. Somerset's innings was based on a fine opening stand of 163 between Peter Bowler, who played the anchor role to perfection with 104 off 128 balls, and Ian Blackwell, whose powerful 86 required a mere 69 deliveries. It was not in the Afridi class, but it was still – in the end – just enough.

Division Two: 14 August 2001
at Lord's
Lancashire 205 for 8 (45 overs)
Middlesex 206 for 7 (44.5 overs) (AJ Strauss 54)
Middlesex (4 pts) won by three wickets

Lancashire's woes continued when they were defeated by three wickets at Lord's, with Middlesex making the unlikely 16 runs they needed for victory from the final over. Until then, Lancashire had seemed on course for a morale-boosting win following their humblings in the Roses Match and the Cheltenham & Gloucester Trophy semi-final. A good recovery from 85 for five had produced a 45-over total of 205 for eight, and then they twice fought back well in the field after Andrew Strauss' 54 had given Middlesex a fine start and then a fifth-wicket stand of 69 between Owais Shah (49) and Paul Weekes had lifted the home side at one stage to 181 for four. But, with that 16 still required from the last over, bowled by Glen Chapple, Lancashire were overwhelming favourites. Chapple's first ball, however, disappeared over mid-wicket off the bat of Jamie Dalrymple, and the next flew to the third man boundary off an outside edge. A scrambled leg bye, and then a swept four by Chad Keegan, left only a single needed from the two remaining balls. Keegan pushed into the off side, called for a suicidal run, and saw Neil Fairbrother's throw at the stumps miss its intended target.

Division Two: 15 August 2001
at Chester-le-Street (floodlit)

Durham 259 for 6 (45 overs) (ML Love 89,
PD Collingwood 84)
Hampshire 188 for 6 (38 overs) (GW White 50)
*Durham (4 pts) won by 17 runs (DL Method: Hampshire
needed to have 206 runs from 38 overs when rain
stopped play)*

Rain eventually decided the outcome of this floodlit
match at Chester-le-Street, the Duckworth/Lewis
system ruling in favour of Durham after Hampshire
had struggled to 188 for six from 38 overs in reply
to the home side's 259 for six. Martin Love hit 89
from 91 balls and Paul Collingwood 84 off 90 balls,
but one of the main problems of night cricket in
England became apparent in the Hampshire innings,
as the combination of dusk and plainly inadequate
lighting from the four temporary pylons gave the
Durham bowlers an unfair advantage. James
Brinkley, with two for 19 from his six overs, made
the most of the conditions and Giles White's 50 was
Hampshire's top-score.

Division One: 19 August 2001
at Leicester
Yorkshire 176 for 8 (42 overs) (VJ Wells 4 for 30)
Leicestershire 178 for 9 (41.5 overs)
*Leicestershire (4 pts) won by one wicket (DL Method:
Leicestershire target 178 runs from 42 overs)*

at Trent Bridge
Nottinghamshire 267 for 6 (42.2 overs) (DJ Bicknell
115, GS Blewett 71)
Northamptonshire 185 (36.4 overs) (ME Cassar 58)
Nottinghamshire (4 pts) won by 82 runs

at Edgbaston
Somerset 120 (42.4 overs)
Warwickshire 120 for 0 (17.5 overs) (MA Wagh 70*)
*Warwickshire (4 pts) won by ten wickets (DL Method:
Warwickshire target 119 runs from 43 overs*

Leaders Leicestershire won themselves a thrilling
tenth victory of the campaign, out of 11 matches,
when their last-wicket pair of Scott Boswell and
Jimmy Ormond put on an unlikely 36 from 33 balls
to confound Yorkshire at an ecstatic Grace Road.
Defeat looked certain when Neil Burns was ninth
out for 29, yorked by Ryan Sidebottom, to leave
Leicestershire 142 for nine in reply to Yorkshire's
176 for eight. The talismanic Shahid Afridi had
fallen, earlier, for a first-ball duck as he mishit 16-
year-old seamer Tim Bresnan to mid-on, and no
home batsman had looked capable of playing a

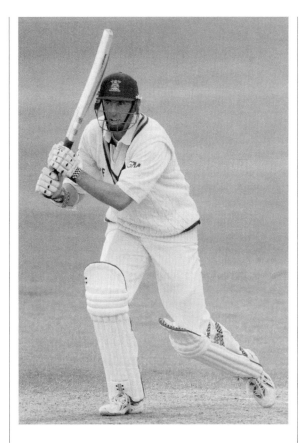

Outlaw chief ... Darren Bicknell leads from the front for
Notts with a battling 115 against Northamptonshire.

match-winning innings in unhelpful batting
conditions. Enter, however, last man Boswell to hit
23 not out – including a magnificent on-driven six
off Sidebottom in the penultimate over and then a
streaky inside-edge for four in the last, bowled by
Craig White.

A fine 115 from 120 balls by Darren Bicknell, the
captain, spearheaded Nottinghamshire to a
comfortable 82-run win over Northamptonshire at
Trent Bridge. Bicknell added 166 in 26 overs with
Greg Blewett (71) for the second wicket, powering
Notts on to 267 for six when rain interrupted play in
the 43rd over. Northants, initially set 281 from 42
overs under the Duckworth/Lewis formula, were
then asked to score 267 after another rain shower, but
they were never in the hunt and were eventually
bowled out for 185 in the 37th over. Nadeem Malik,
an 18-year-old, Nottingham-born pace bowler,
showed up well with two early wickets, and the only
consolation for the visitors was a successful return to
action for Matt Cassar, the all-rounder who joined the

club from Derbyshire during the winter. A long-standing groin injury had prevented him from making his first-team debut until now, and he hit five fours in a 78-ball 58 before having his leg-stump removed by former Northants seamer, Richard Logan.

Somerset were thrashed by ten wickets by Warwickshire at Edgbaston after struggling horribly to score just 120 all out. There were no less than 12 maidens in the innings, with Alan Richardson and Neil Smith both picking up three cheap wickets, but when Warwickshire batted it looked a completely different game. Mark Wagh included 15 fours in his unbeaten 70 and he and fellow opener Nick Knight (40 not out) needed just 17.5 overs to finish the game.

Division Two: 19 August 2001
at Cardiff
Glamorgan 289 for 6 (41 overs) (RDB Croft 92, K Newell 65)
Essex 111 (24.2 overs) (AP Davies 5 for 39)
Glamorgan (4 pts) won by 178 runs

at Lord's
Middlesex v. **Worcestershire**
Match abandoned without a ball bowled – 2 pts each

Glamorgan annihilated the second division's bottom club, Essex, by 178 runs at Cardiff to maintain their own push for promotion. Robert Croft, batting at number three, provided the early impetus for Glamorgan with an 83-ball 92. No doubt he worked off some of his frustration at again being surplus to Test match requirements – despite making the Headingley squad – by belting two sixes and five fours as he figured in stands worth 65 with Keith Newell (65) and 101 with Mike Powell (46). A total of 289 for six, from just 41 overs, was well beyond Essex as Andrew Davies enjoyed himself by picking up five for 39 as the visitors were tumbled out for just 111.

Rain prevented any play at all in the match between Middlesex and Worcestershire at Lord's.

Division Two: 20 August 2001
at Old Trafford (floodlit)
Lancashire 200 for 8 (45 overs) (GD Lloyd 56, JP Crawley 54)
Sussex 178 (44.1 overs) (RR Montgomerie 76)
Lancashire (4 pts) won by 22 runs

A floodlit Old Trafford crowd of more than 6,000 were happy to see an improved performance from Lancashire, who produced some tight out-cricket

against Sussex to defend successfully their 45-over total of 200 for eight, in which both John Crawley and Graham Lloyd had made half-centuries. Sussex's reply was based on Richard Montgomerie's 76, but the opener was capable only of playing an anchor role and in the end the visitors were bowled out in the last over for 178.

Division One: 21 August 2001
at Taunton
Surrey 236 for 8 (45 overs) (AD Brown 98, AJ Hollioake 70)
Somerset 237 for 6 (41 overs) (PD Bowler 86, M Burns 53)
Somerset (4 pts) won by four wickets

Somerset withstood a barrage of boundaries from Ally Brown and Adam Hollioake to beat Surrey by four wickets in front of a 5,000 floodlit crowd at Taunton and step up their bid to avoid relegation. Brown and Hollioake had added 155 in 24 overs for the third wicket to set up a truly big score, but when Hollioake was stumped for 70 and Brown caught and bowled for 98, the Surrey innings dried up against the spin of Ian Blackwell (three for 16). Only 38 runs were taken from the last 12 overs, for the loss of five wickets, and Surrey's eventual 236 for eight was not as challenging a score as it should have been. Nevertheless, Somerset had to bat well to get them – especially under the lights and with some drizzle falling – and a fine innings of 86 by opener Peter Bowler put them on their way. Mike Burns also made 53 in a fourth-wicket stand of 87, and in the end the home fans were able to celebrate a victory achieved with four overs to spare.

Division One: 22 August 2001
at Northampton
Northamptonshire 231 for 8 (45 overs) (GP Swann 83, AL Penberthy 50)
Leicestershire 232 for 3 (40.3 overs) (DI Stevens 68*, TR Ward 56)
Leicestershire (4 pts) won by seven wickets

A 5,000 Wantage Road crowd saw a floodlit spectacular in terms of stroke play as Leicestershire overtook Northamptonshire's 45-over total of 231 for eight with the loss of just three wickets and with four-and-a-half overs to spare. The catalyst of Leicestershire's successful assault was, once again, Shahid Afridi, who plundered 36 from 18 balls in a merciless first-wicket stand with the equally aggression-minded Trevor Ward (56). Darren

Stevens, with 68 not out from 93 balls, and Ben Smith (44 not out off 68 balls) were then left with the comparatively straightforward task of jogging to victory after the sprint to 159 for three. Graeme Swann, who earlier had included two sixes off Afridi in his 70-ball 83, added 99 in 19 overs with Tony Penberthy (50) to boost the Northants total.

Division One: 26 August 2001
at Scarborough
Yorkshire 352 for 6 (45 overs) (DS Lehmann 191)
Nottinghamshire 173 (43.3 overs) (DJ Bicknell 50)
Yorkshire (4 pts) won by 179 runs

Descriptive words were almost insufficient at Scarborough to portray the brilliance of Darren Lehmann's 191 against a shell-shocked Nottinghamshire. With 11 sixes and 20 fours, Lehmann tore apart the visiting bowlers in an innings spanning just 103 deliveries. It was the highest score made in the Norwich Union League,

Brilliance beyond words. Darren Lehmann's 191 against a shell-shocked Notts was the second-highest score in the 33-year history of the competition.

and the second highest in the 33 years of this competition in all its various guises. It was also the highest individual one-day score made for Yorkshire, and it also produced the biggest limited-overs total (352 for six) in the county's history. The next best score in the Yorkshire innings was Anthony McGrath's 38. For the Yorkshire supporters, who came in their thousands to celebrate the championship success of two days before, it was a memory to cherish. Lehmann then took two wickets for 38 in his nine-over stint of slow left-arm as Notts, unsurprisingly, found they could not compete with Yorkshire's total and slipped quietly to 173 all out and defeat by 179 runs.

Division Two: 26 August 2001
at Worcester
Worcestershire 141 for 5 (32 overs) (VS Solanki 65*)
Hampshire 166 for 8 (32 overs) (JD Francis 78*)
Hampshire (4 pts) won by two wickets (DL Method: Hampshire target 166 from 32 overs)

at Colchester
Lancashire 32 for 2 (11 overs)
Essex did not bat
Match abandoned – 2 pts each

at Lord's
Glamorgan 100 for 3 (21 overs)
Middlesex did not bat
Match abandoned – 2 pts each

at Hove
Sussex v. **Durham**
Match abandoned without a ball bowled – 2 pts each

John Francis, a 20-year-old left-hander, inspired Hampshire to a nerve-jangling, last-ball win against Worcestershire at New Road. Francis hit an unbeaten 78 from 81 balls to take them to a two-wicket victory in a match that was important to the promotion ambitions of both counties. Seven runs were needed from the final over, bowled by Andy Bichel, and it came down to Francis scampering a single off the very last delivery. Hit to mid-on, Francis was a relieved man when Anurag Singh's throw at the stumps missed. Hampshire's target had been 166, under the Duckworth/Lewis regulations, after Worcestershire had reached 141 for five in a match reduced to 32 overs per side by the rain which arrived when the home side were on 76 for three. Vikram Solanki, with 65 not out, was then largely responsible for 65 runs being taken from the

45 deliveries Worcestershire were granted following the resumption.

The matches at Colchester and Lord's were abandoned due to rain, after 11 and 21 overs of play respectively, but the game between Sussex and Durham at Hove was washed out completely. At Colchester two early wickets by Essex's Ashley Cowan had reduced Lancashire to 32 for two, while at Lord's, Jimmy Maher's unbeaten 35, from number four, had launched a Glamorgan recovery to 100 for three following a superb new-ball spell of 8-3-15-3 from Angus Fraser.

Division One: 27 August 2001
at Leicester
Somerset 250 for 6 (45 overs) (PD Bowler 77, ID Blackwell 75)
Leicestershire 240 for 9 (45 overs) (Shahid Afridi 58, ND Burns 55)
Somerset (4 pts) won by 10 runs

at Canterbury
Kent 200 (43.5 overs) (MV Fleming 58, JMM Averis 5 for 40)
Gloucestershire 199 for 9 (45 overs) (MV Fleming 5 for 40)
Kent (4 pts) won by 1 run

at Edgbaston
Yorkshire 137 for 9 (45 overs) (MA Sheikh 4 for 17)
Warwickshire 138 for 3 (26.5 overs) (NV Knight 53)
Warwickshire (4 pts) won by seven wickets

Somerset won a second league victory in a fortnight over Leicestershire to improve their own chances of avoiding relegation, further dent Leicestershire's title hopes, and give themselves a massive psychological boost ahead of the Cheltenham & Gloucester Trophy final at Lord's. In truth, this was a worryingly witless performance by Leicestershire, at a crucial stage of their season. Somerset's 250 for six, based on an opening stand of 138 between Peter Bowler (77) and Ian Blackwell (75), was a challenging score, but after just nine overs Leicestershire were 96 for no wicket following yet another thrilling assault by Shahid Afridi, who got off the mark with such a big hit for six over the Grace Road indoor school that the ball was never found. The Pakistani all-rounder, supported in no small way by Trevor Ward, launched a total of six sixes and four boundaries in a 25-ball 58 until being bowled by a slower ball from Steffan Jones. Suddenly, Somerset could regain some sort of control, and with Ward being run out by Jamie Grove's throw for 43,

the pressure began to build as the home side slipped to 134 for five amid some rash strokes. When Darren Maddy was lbw playing across the line, Leicestershire still required 94 from 18 overs with just four wickets in hand. Neil Burns and Aftab Habib revived hopes with a partnership of 71, but after Burns was run out for 55 the asking rate became 21 runs off 11 balls and it proved too much. Leicestershire ended up on 240 for nine and lost by ten runs.

Kent, meanwhile, cashed in on Leicestershire's defeat by pulling off a thrilling one-run victory against Gloucestershire at Bristol and closing to within six points of the leaders at the top of the division. In blazing sunshine, Kent captain Matthew Fleming produced an equally sizzling individual display to keep alive his side's title aspirations. First, Fleming's 58 got Kent off to a fine start on their way to 200 all out, a total which was lower than it should have been thanks to James Averis' five for 40. Then, after Gloucestershire had looked likely to overhaul it, Fleming strangled the home middle-order to take five for 40 himself. Min Patel's bowling of the dangerous Ian Harvey, for a 25-ball 45, was a key moment – but it came down to Fleming bowling the final over with seven runs required. He bowled Jack Russell, and in the end Gloucestershire could reach only 199 for nine.

Yorkshire, their energy no doubt spent by their championship title celebrations, and the thrashing of Nottinghamshire in the league on the previous day, slumped to 137 all out and defeat by seven wickets against Warwickshire at Edgbaston. In contrast to their 352 for six against Notts, the Yorkshire batting was poor – but perhaps they should not even

Five wickets for Gloucestershire's James Averis could not prevent his side from falling to Kent.

have been asked to travel and play again less than 24 hours afterwards. Only Anthony McGrath (38) got going and, in reply, Warwickshire's Nick Knight (53) and David Hemp (43 not out) simply strolled to their target with more than 18 overs remaining.

Division Two: 27 August 2001
at Cardiff
Glamorgan 250 for 9 (45 overs) (MP Maynard 54, SJ Harmison 4 for 43)
Durham 226 (43.5 overs) (N Peng 92, JJB Lewis 57)
Glamorgan (4 pts) won by 24 runs

at Derby
Derbyshire 206 for 3 (45 overs) (SD Stubbings 96*)
Sussex 209 for 3 (41 overs) (RR Montgomerie 94, MW Goodwin 53*)
Sussex (4 pts) won by seven wickets

at Southampton Rose Bowl
Lancashire 212 for 5 (45 overs) (JP Crawley 84*, A Flintoff 78)
Hampshire 169 (41 overs) (NC Johnson 67)
Lancashire (4 pts) won by 43 runs

Glamorgan moved above Durham to the top of the second division with a highly competent 24-run win at Cardiff. A solid batting display, with Matthew Maynard's 54 the top-score, enabled Glamorgan to reach 250 for nine from their 45 overs, and in reply, Durham's hopes rested on 18-year-old Nicky Peng. The former schoolboy prodigy, fast maturing into a batsman with an international future, hit 11 fours and a six in a 103-ball 92 – out of 149 – before being caught at deep mid-wicket. Jon Lewis (57) and Jimmy Daley (32) tried their best to keep up the scoring rate, but Andrew Davies returned to remove both and the rest of the Durham order could only take the eventual total to 226.

Sussex out-batted Derbyshire on a sluggish surface at Derby to win by seven wickets and keep their outside chance of promotion alive. Steve Stubbings anchored the Derbyshire innings of 206 for three with an unbeaten 96, but Sussex overhauled it with four overs to spare, as Richard Montgomerie opened up with 94 and Murray Goodwin finished things off with a 45-ball 53 not out.

Hampshire's own promotion hopes took a knock at Southampton when Lancashire totalled 212 for five and then ran out winners by 43 runs as the home side fell away from 81 for two to 169 all out. Andy Flintoff (78) and John Crawley (84 not out) put on 151 for the Lancashire third wicket, but Neil

Johnson (67) could find no-one to stay with him once Robin Smith had departed for 29.

Division Two: 28 August 2001
at Colchester (floodlit)
Middlesex 173 for 7 (45 overs) (AJ Strauss 59)
Essex 174 for 6 (38.3 overs) (RC Irani 56*, SG Law 51)
Essex (4 pts) won by four wickets

Essex attempted to put a little gloss on a wretched season as they defeated Middlesex by four wickets under the Castle Park lights at Colchester. Ronnie Irani, the Essex captain, contributed a typically whole-hearted all-round performance – first removing dangermen Owais Shah and Stephen Fleming with the new ball as Middlesex were held to 173 for seven, and then coming in at 53 for four to hit an unbeaten 56. Irani put on 70 with Stuart Law (51) to decide the outcome. Andrew Strauss (59) had earlier top-scored for the visitors.

Division One: 29 August 2001
at Canterbury
Kent 216 for 8 (45 overs) (JB Hockley 66)
Yorkshire 208 for 8 (45 overs) (A McGrath 102)
Kent (4 pts) won by 8 runs

Kent increased the pressure on leaders Leicestershire with a tigerish eight-run victory against Yorkshire in front of 3,500 fans at Canterbury. Defending 216 for eight, based on a third-wicket stand of 86 between James Hockley (66) and Andy Symonds (37), Kent were in need of inspiration as Anthony McGrath (102) was joined by Craig White (44) in a fourth-wicket partnership of 108 in 21 overs. But then Min Patel held on to a skier from White, after running in from long-off, and with 20 runs needed from three overs Kent had a chance. Great overs from Mark Ealham and Matthew Fleming meant that 13 were still required from the last. McGrath had been run out in Fleming's penultimate over, and Martin Saggers then took three wickets in four balls to send Kentish supporters into raptures. Their side were now just two points behind Leicestershire, while Yorkshire slipped nearer to the relegation places.

Division Two: 29 August 2001
at Cardiff
Glamorgan 244 for 6 (45 overs) (MP Maynard 116*)
Hampshire 193 (40.2 overs) (NC Johnson 66, RDB Croft 4 for 33)
Glamorgan (4 pts) won by 51 runs

Scintillating stroke play from Matthew Maynard, whose unbeaten 116 took just 103 balls and included two sixes and 12 fours, provided the basis of Glamorgan's 51-run floodlit win over Hampshire at Cardiff. A fine crowd, on a humid evening, then gloried in the spin partnership of Robert Croft and Dean Cosker, after James Hamblin (37 off 22 balls) had opened up with Neil Johnson to get Hampshire off to a flier. Johnson's 67-ball 66, with 13 fours, ended when he was bowled by Croft, and the England off spinner ended with four for 33 from his nine overs as he and Cosker turned the screw. Hampshire were eventually dismissed in the 41st over for 193.

Division One: 30 August 2001
at Northampton
Northamptonshire 214 (45 overs) (RJ Warren 93, KP Dutch 6 for 40)
Somerset 155 for 1 (24.4 overs) (J Cox 76*, ME Trescothick 72)
Somerset (4 pts) won by 70 runs (DL Method: Somerset needed to have 86 runs from 24.4 overs when rain stopped play)

at Whitgift School
Surrey 231 (45 overs) (AD Brown 116, DR Brown 4 for 56)
Warwickshire 108 (29.5 overs) (AJ Murtagh 4 for 31)
Surrey (4 pts) won by 123 runs

Somerset's relegation fears were eased by a straightforward win over Northamptonshire on another belter of a pitch at Wantage Road. With Andy Caddick and Marcus Trescothick both allowed to play by the England management, in a bid to warm up for the Cheltenham & Gloucester Trophy final, Somerset were even able to give both Richard Johnson and Steffan Jones a rare day off. Caddick, in fact, claimed the important scalp of Mike Hussey in a tight opening spell of one for 21 from nine overs, and despite good innings from Russell Warren (93) and Graeme Swann (41), the Northants innings underachieved at 214. Jamie Cox and Trescothick then set about the home bowling with relish, and Cox was 76 not out when Trescothick was caught off a top-edged sweep for a 65-ball 72. Rain then began to fall, forcing the players off, but at 155 for one in the 25th over Somerset had already done more than enough to win the match by 70 runs on a Duckworth-Lewis calculation. There was one bright note for Northants, however, in the appearance of David Sales for his first match of the summer. The

powerful young batsman had expected to be out for the whole season after severely damaging cruciate knee ligaments during England A's tour of the West Indies on New Year's Day.

The lordly Alistair Brown was the difference between the two sides at the picturesque natural amphitheatre of Whitgift School, as Surrey beat Warwickshire by 123 runs. Brown, coming in at 15 for three, batted with a majesty that no-one on either side could even approach to score 116 from just 108 balls. He hit four sixes and 14 fours and dominated stands of 77, 64 and 56 with Alec Stewart, Ben Hollioake and Gareth Batty, to lift Surrey to 231. Nick Knight and Mark Wagh gave Warwickshire a sprightly start by adding 44 in eight overs, but soon the visitors' innings became a procession as Hollioake junior (three for ten from eight overs) and Tim Murtagh (four for 31) got amongst them.

Division Two: 30 August 2001
at Hove (floodlit)
Sussex 229 for 5 (45 overs) (TR Ambrose 87, RR Montgomerie 53)
Lancashire 91 (31.3 overs)
Sussex (4 pts) won by 138 runs

Keith Dutch's six for 40 helped Somerset to a storming 70-run win over Northamptonshire.

Tim Ambrose, an 18-year-old Anglo-Aussie, caught the eye of many sound judges with a fine 87 in only his second appearance for Sussex. He struck only six boundaries, but played with such self-confidence and pugnacity that his runs came from just 117 deliveries. Sussex, with Richard Montgomerie (53) helping Ambrose add 99 for the first wicket, reached 229 for five and then overwhelmed Lancashire in the field to bowl out their visitors for 91. The Sussex seamers, with Mark Robinson (three for 17) and Billy Taylor (two for 16) in particularly miserly mood, never let Lancashire get going – and Ambrose also contributed two catches and a quicksilver legside stumping off Robinson. Carl Hopkinson, 19, took a late wicket with his third ball in senior cricket.

Division One: 2 September 2001
at Northampton
Nottinghamshire 182 (43.2 overs) (KP Pietersen 58)
Northamptonshire 185 for 6 (37.1 overs)
(GP Swann 56)
Northamptonshire (4 pts) won by four wickets (DL Method: Northamptonshire needed to have 182 runs from 37.1 overs when rain stopped play)

David Ripley fittingly marked his final appearance at Northampton by helping to guide his Northants side to a comfortable four-wicket win over Nottinghamshire. Only Kevin Pietersen, with a 62-ball 58, made a significant contribution to Nottinghamshire's innings of 182, which, although inadequate, still represented a marked recovery from the trouble they were in after they had slumped to 44 for five. Graeme Swann launched the Northants reply with a bright 56, off 61 balls, and, after a mini-collapse to 117 for five, Ripley joined Alec Swann (34 not out) to steer his side to the brink of victory with a sturdy partnership of 55. Yorkshireman Ripley made his debut for Northants in 1984, as a 17-year-old, and had announced his intention to retire at the end of the season to take up a coaching post with the county. He was warmly applauded both on and off the field, and his innings of 24 was both typically unfussy and tailored exactly to the needs of his team.

Division Two: 2 September 2001
at Worcester
Glamorgan 254 for 6 (43 overs) (MP Maynard 71, RDB Croft 61)
Worcestershire did not bat
Match abandoned – 2 pts each

at Chester-le-Street
Durham 178 (44.4 overs)
Essex 179 for 7 (41.5 overs) (DDJ Robinson 64, NC Phillips 4 for 36)
Essex (4 pts) won by three wickets

at Richmond
Middlesex 109 (37.1 overs) (MJG Davis 4 for 24)
Sussex 110 for 2 (28.1 overs)
Sussex (4 pts) won by eight wickets

Glamorgan clinched promotion to the first division with the two points they received from the abandonment of their match against Worcestershire at New Road. Having scored 254 for six from 43 overs when the rain came, Glamorgan would have been confident of winning the match – but, when the umpires called it off at 4.40pm, the Welsh county were not too bothered. A fourth-wicket partnership of 111 between Matthew Maynard (71) and Robert Croft (61) provided the main thrust of Glamorgan's imposing total.

Paul Grayson, a surprise call-up to England's winter one-day squad, took three for 23 from nine impressive overs as Essex upset promotion hopefuls Durham at Chester-le-Street. Grayson's first delivery bowled Martin Love for a fluent 36 – and from then on Durham struggled to build on a promising start and were all out for 178 in the 45th over. Darren Robinson, straight driving with aplomb, then hit 64 from 58 balls to make an Essex win look a formality, but the Durham spinners, Nicky Phillips (four for 36) and Graeme Bridge, who bowled Robinson, reduced the visitors to 141 for seven. However, the composure of James Foster, also picked by England earlier in the week as their new wicket-keeper/batsman, saw Essex home by three wickets.

A poor pitch at Old Deer Park in Richmond, plus some dreadful Middlesex batting, resulted in a low-key and decidedly one-sided victory for Sussex. Owais Shah took 73 balls over his top-score of 23 in a Middlesex slide to 109 all out, but the Sussex batsmen did not find the conditions quite as harrowing as they completed the eight-wicket win in the 29th over. Off spinner Mark Davis, with a competition-best four for 24, was the pick of an impressively efficient Sussex attack.

Division One: 3 September 2001
at Bristol
Gloucestershire 232 for 7 (45 overs) (THC Hancock 67)
Leicestershire 186 (35.1 overs) (BF Smith 53)
Gloucestershire (4 pts) won by 28 runs (DL Method:

Leicestershire target 215 from 38 overs)

at The Oval (floodlit)
Yorkshire 214 for 8 (45 overs)
Surrey 188 for 3 (33.2 overs) (GJ Batty 83*,
MA Butcher 50)
*Surrey (4 pts) won by seven wickets (DL Method: Surrey
target 186 from 34 overs)*

at Taunton
Somerset 190 for 8 (45 overs)
Warwickshire 191 for 2 (30.4 overs) (NV Knight 84*,
DR Brown 59*)
Warwickshire (4 pts) won by eight wickets

Gloucestershire, so injury-hit that they were literally
down to their last 11 fit players, still proved too
potent a force for faltering Leicestershire, beating
the league leaders by 28 runs under the
Duckworth/Lewis regulations at Bristol. The
champions, battling to avoid relegation, totalled 232
for seven from their 45 overs with Tim Hancock –
one player, at least, freeing himself of long-standing
injury problems – hitting 67 from 68 balls.
Leicestershire, needing 215 from 38 overs when a
rain shower necessitated a recalculation, batted with
a startling lack of resolve before being bowled out
for 186 in the 36th over. Ben Smith (53) and Darren
Stevens (46 not out) were the only exceptions.

Yorkshire, meanwhile, slipped into the relegation
zone as a result of their seven-wicket defeat – again
on Duckworth/Lewis – against Surrey at The Oval.
Darren Lehmann's 47 was just one of the solid
contributions towards a Yorkshire score of 214 for
eight, but the home side always looked favourites to
reach their revised target of 186 from 34 overs once
Mark Butcher (50) had given them a fine start.
Gareth Batty, with ten fours in an unbeaten 83 off
78 balls, then played with maturity and increasing
confidence to steer Surrey home with four balls
remaining.

Somerset, perhaps too busy celebrating their
Cheltenham & Gloucester Trophy success in front
of an adoring Taunton public, played well below
themselves to lose by eight wickets to Warwickshire.
Yet it did not seem to matter too much, after the
Lord's triumph, as Somerset reached only 190 for
eight and then saw Nick Knight spearhead
Warwickshire's breezy progress to victory. Knight
drove successive balls from Jamie Grove over the
sightscreen in his 84 not out, while Vasbert Drakes
struck 43 from 35 balls and Dougie Brown an even
brisker unbeaten 59 off 44 deliveries.

*Putting Derbyshire in a
spin ... Chris Schofield.*

**Division Two:
3 September 2001**
at Old Trafford
(floodlit)
Lancashire 210 for 6
(45 overs) (NH
Fairbrother 78)
Derbyshire 150 (39.2
overs) (CP Schofield 5
for 31)
*Lancashire (4 pts) won
by 60 runs*

Lancashire gave a
floodlit Old Trafford
crowd a morsel of
satisfaction, towards
the end of a miserable
season, by seeing off
Derbyshire by 60
runs. Given
Derbyshire's own
plight, however, it
was only a little
offering. Chris
Schofield, one of
many underachieving
Lancastrians, took
five for 31 to hasten Derbyshire to defeat. His spin
partner, Gary Yates, also impressed with two for 21
from his nine overs as the visitors were dismissed for
150 in reply to Lancashire's 210 for six. Neil
Fairbrother, at almost 38 still Lancashire's most
consistent and dependable batsman, made 78.

Division Two: 4 September 2001
at Hove (floodlit)
Sussex 225 for 2 (45 overs) (CJ Adams 100*,
MW Goodwin 67*)
Glamorgan 191 (42.5 overs) (JP Maher 54)
Sussex (4 pts) won by 34 runs

Sussex's fourth win in eight days strengthened still
further their late bid for promotion, while for
Glamorgan it meant a wait to be confirmed as
division two champions. This floodlit contest at
Hove began with Richard Montgomerie falling to
the very first ball of the match, but soon Tim
Ambrose, the exciting 18-year-old newcomer, was
flourishing alongside his captain Chris Adams.

When Ambrose was out for 46, Adams was joined by Murray Goodwin, and the pair added an unbroken 145 for the third wicket. Adams finished on 100 not out, from 122 balls, while Goodwin's share of a Sussex total of 225 for two was an unbeaten 73-ball 67. Jimmy Maher made 54, but otherwise Glamorgan were uninspired as they fell away to 191 all out.

Division One: 5 September 2001
at Leicester (floodlit)
Leicestershire 9 for 2 (3.5 overs)
Warwickshire did not bat
Match abandoned – 2 pts each

Bad weather enabled nervy Leicestershire to put one hand on to the Norwich Union League trophy – with Vince Wells' side quite happy to take two points from their rain-hit match against Warwickshire at Leicester. The home side were already up against it having lost two wickets for just nine runs after just 3.5 overs, following a 5pm start and a reduction to 40 overs per side, when the weather closed in again. Trevor Ward and Shahid Afridi were the two men out.

Division One: 9 September 2001
at Canterbury
Kent 284 for 5 (45 overs) (MV Fleming 125)
Northamptonshire 258 for 9 (45 overs) (GP Swann 61, JW Cook 55)
Kent (4 pts) won by 26 runs

at Trent Bridge
Nottinghamshire 277 for 7 (45 overs) (JE Morris 102, KP Pietersen 61*, Usman Afzaal 50)
Surrey 279 for 5 (43 overs) (AD Brown 130, GJ Batty 63, AJ Harris 4 for 42)
Surrey (4 pts) won by five wickets

Matthew Fleming produced a real tour de force at Canterbury to keep alive Kent's hopes of pipping Leicestershire to the title. Fleming first hit a one-day best 125, from just 107 balls, to spearhead Kent's rapid progress to 284 for five, and then took three key wickets for only 20 runs in a seven-over spell which turned the game Kent's way. Seldom can a captain have led quite so markedly from the front, but Fleming then capped his marvellous day by

Officer class ... Matthew Fleming, formerly of the Royal Green Jackets, keeps Kent on title alert with a brilliant 125 against Northants.

diving spectacularly at extra-cover to catch a drive from Paul Taylor as the Northants reply came up 26 runs short at 258 for nine. The win drew Kent level on 46 points with Leicestershire at the head of the table, with one match to go. David Fulton helped Kent get off to a flying start, on a splendid pitch, hitting 39 from 35 balls before being out with the score on 98 in the 13th over. James Hockley, Andy Symonds and Mark Ealham all made punchy contributions and Kent's attack, led of course by Fleming, held their nerve first when Graeme Swann (61 off 44 balls) and Russell Warren (40) flourished, and then when Toby Bailey helped Jeff Cook (55) add a quick 60 for the sixth wicket.

Dropped by the inconsolable Richard Logan on 12, Alistair Brown proceeded to thrash the Nottinghamshire bowlers to all parts of Trent Bridge in an explosive innings of 130 which helped Surrey to a five-wicket win. Defeat still left Notts with a chance of relegation, but it had all looked rosy earlier in the afternoon when John Morris (102), Usman Afzaal (50) and Kevin Pietersen (61 not out from 34 balls) were speeding them to a total of 277 for seven. Brown, though, hit five sixes and 13 fours

in his 97-ball masterclass – adding 189 with Gareth Batty (63) for the second wicket. Adam Hollioake's unbeaten 43 then saw Surrey safely home, and it was not a bad effort by the visitors who were missing a total of ten Test players!

Division Two: 9 September 2001
at Chester-le-Street
Durham 212 for 5 (41 overs) (JJB Lewis 76*, A Pratt 56)
Worcestershire 198 for 8 (39 overs) (A Singh 58)
Durham (4 pts) won by 9 runs (DL Method: Worcestershire target 208 from 39 overs)

at Southampton Rose Bowl
Hampshire 220 for 9 (45 overs) (GW White 59, JD Francis 57*)
Middlesex 224 for 6 (44.1 overs) (OA Shah 69)
Middlesex (4 pts) won by four wickets

at Chelmsford
Derbyshire 164 (44.2 overs) (AP Cowan 4 for 22)
Essex 165 for 5 (31.2 overs)
Essex (4 pts) won by five wickets

Durham clinched their place in next season's Norwich Union League first division by beating Worcestershire by ten runs under the Duckworth/Lewis formula. It was a tense affair, with Worcestershire knowing that victory would also have guaranteed them promotion. As it was, they were left needing to beat Essex in their last match to join Durham and Glamorgan in the top three. Durham's 212 for five, from 41 overs, was built around an innings of 56 from Andy Pratt, 43 from Martin Love, and in particular a 66-ball 76 not out by Jon Lewis, the captain. Anurag Singh (58) and Philip Weston (43) launched the Worcestershire reply with an opening stand of 83, but the key moment came when Graeme Hick, on just two, missed a legside flick at Danny Law and – after an agonizing wait for the third umpire to study the video replay – was given out brilliantly stumped by Pratt as he lifted a toe. Law's three for 28 was a timely burst, and in the end Worcestershire could not keep up with the asking rate as regularly falling wickets held them to 198 for eight from the 39 overs that weather interruptions allowed.

A glorious 65-run stand in just six overs by Simon Cook (46 not out) and Jamie Dalrymple cost Hampshire dear at Southampton. The home side, aiming for the win which would have boosted their promotion hopes, looked on course to defend a total

of 220 for nine, in which Giles White (59) and John Francis (57 not out) had impressed. But then Middlesex, for whom Owais Shah (69) and Ed Joyce (38) had already put on 98 for the third wicket, found a sting in the tail to reach 224 for six and a four-wicket victory, with five balls to spare. One of the Hampshire bowlers stung most nastily was Alan Mullally, who conceded 19 runs in the 43rd over.

Essex won the basement battle with Derbyshire at Chelmsford, by five wickets, and then confirmed the behind-the-scenes changes which they believe will revive the club's fortunes in 2002 and beyond. Graham Gooch's appointment as new head coach was announced officially, and John Childs is to become his assistant. Keith Fletcher moves to a development role and Geoff Arnold leaves his full-time coaching job. Essex also announced that five players would be released: Peter Such, Paul Prichard, Stuart Law, Tim Mason and Michael Davies. Law made just nine in his last innings for Essex, but received an ovation from the crowd anyway. Ronnie Irani, with 45 not out, saw his side home after Graham Napier's 24-ball 47 had got them off to a flyer in pursuit of Derbyshire's 164. That had represented something of a recovery from 78 for seven, mainly thanks to Tom Lungley's determined 45, before he became a fourth victim for Ashley Cowan.

Division One: 10 September 2001
at Scarborough
Yorkshire 161 for 8 (45 overs) (DS Lehmann 69, RJ Blakey 52, JMM Averis 4 for 42)
Gloucestershire 91 (36.5 overs)
Yorkshire (4 pts) won by 70 runs

Yorkshire, the county champions, gave themselves a chance of avoiding a drop to the second tier of the one-day league by beating Gloucestershire at Scarborough by 70 runs. A rare Yorkshire outing for Darren Gough brought him a useful 13 runs, as Yorkshire recovered from 38 for four to reach 161 for eight from their 45 overs, and then superb figures of 9-3-15-3 as a below-strength Gloucestershire were bowled out for just 91. Darren Lehmann (69) was joined by Richard Blakey (52) in a fifth-wicket stand of 73, but Yorkshire were perhaps fortunate not only that Ian Harvey was missing for Gloucestershire because of a rib injury, but also that Jack Russell had to pull out of the game after being hit in the face during the pre-match warm-up. Mark Alleyne took over the gloves, but that left the visitors' bowling attack even more threadbare. Yorkshire's victory completed their programme, but Gloucestershire themselves, together with Somerset and Nottinghamshire, could still send them down if they all manage to win their final game.

Division One: 16 September 2001
at Edgbaston
Kent 216 for 6 (40 overs) (JB Hockley 90, RWT Key 50)
Warwickshire 208 for 9 (40 overs) (MA Wagh 58, A Symonds 5 for 18)
Kent (4 pts) won by 9 runs (DL Method: Warwickshire target 218 from 40 overs)

at Trent Bridge
Leicestershire 185 for 9 (45 overs) (AJ Harris 4 for 24)
Nottinghamshire 186 for 5 (38.3 overs) (JE Morris 57, CD Crowe 4 for 30)
Nottinghamshire (4 pts) won by five wickets

at Bristol
Surrey 157 for 8 (45 overs) (GJ Batty 54)
Gloucestershire 121 (42 overs) (AJ Hollioake 4 for 19)
Surrey (4 pts) won by 36 runs

at Taunton
Somerset 255 for 4 (45 overs) (M Burns 101*, J Cox 68)
Northamptonshire 243 (43.5 overs) (ME Hussey 91, RJ Warren 59)
Somerset (4 pts) won by 12 runs

In an exciting climax to the season, Kent snatched the Norwich Union League title out of choking Leicestershire's grasp as Andy Symonds inspired them to a nerve-tingling nine-run victory against Warwickshire at Edgbaston. With news of Leicestershire's defeat at Nottingham filtering through, Symonds took a remarkable five for 18 from six overs to halt Warwickshire's seemingly solid progress towards a revised target of 218. In a match reduced to 40 overs per side, Kent's 216 for six was an adequate total, based on a fine innings of 90 from 102 balls by the unsung James Hockley and a timely 35-ball 50 by Rob Key. However, Mark Wagh (58) and Ian Bell (48) combined to put on 89 for Warwickshire's second wicket and, with ten overs remaining, the home side had closed to within 60 runs of their target with seven wickets still standing. Bowling his nippy seamers, Symonds rose to the occasion and Warwickshire were eventually bowled out for 208 as Kent regained control and kept up the pressure. Kentish celebrations went on all night in Birmingham, and Matthew Fleming, the captain, paid tribute to Symonds' outstanding contribution before adding: 'We have not made it easy for ourselves in this competition, and I don't think there has been one game in which there has been clear daylight between us and the opposition. But we hung in there every time, and showed great character and determination.'

Leicestershire's sad capitulation at Trent Bridge brought happiness, though, to their opponents Nottinghamshire, who confirmed with their five-wicket win their membership of the first division for 2002. Leicestershire's 45-over total of 185 for nine, in which Andrew Harris took four for 24, was never enough to embarrass a Notts side who were given the perfect start by John Morris, in his last county appearance. The 37-year-old former England batsman included 11 fours in his superb 48-ball 57 to bow out of senior cricket in some style. Greg Blewett, in his last match for Notts after not being retained as overseas player, hit 48 and, despite Carl Crowe's four for 30, the home side cruised to their target with more than six overs remaining.

Champions Gloucestershire, meanwhile, ended a season full of injuries and struggle with a 36-run defeat at home

Kent ... Norwich Union League champions 2001.

to Surrey and a demeaning drop into the second division. Surrey's 157 for eight did not look like an imposing score, but Gloucestershire lost three top-order batsmen in the space of six balls to Tim Murtagh (three for 15) and only Matt Windows (37) looked capable of leading a recovery. In the end, with Adam Hollioake bottling up the tail to take four for 19 from eight overs, Gloucestershire subsided to 121 all out. Gareth Batty was the game's outstanding performer, adding two for 20 with his off breaks to his earlier innings of 54.

Somerset made sure of their survival in the one-day league's top division by beating Northamptonshire by 12 runs at Taunton. On yet another fine batting pitch Somerset totalled 255 for four, Jamie Cox leading off with 68 and then Mike Burns (101 not out from 112 balls) and Rob Turner (41 not out) adding an unbroken 129. Northants made a brave stab at getting the runs, with Mike Hussey (91) and Russell Warren (59) adding 113 for the second wicket. But, from 159 for one, they slipped to 243 all out as Somerset defended their score determinedly to cap a memorable season with another significant result.

Division Two: 16 September 2001
at Worcester
Worcestershire 166 for 6 (30 overs) (WPC Weston 68)
Essex 97 (24.2 overs)
Worcestershire (4 pts) won by 96 runs (DL Method: Essex target 194 from 30 overs)

at Hove
Sussex 142 (37 overs)
Hampshire 143 for 3 (22.5 overs) (JRC Hamblin 61)
Hampshire (4 pts) won by seven wickets

at Cardiff
Glamorgan 272 for 4 (45 overs) (RDB Croft 114*, SP James 93)
Middlesex 232 for 8 (45 overs) (SJ Cook 50)
Glamorgan (4 pts) won by 40 runs

at Derby
Lancashire 159 for 5 (25 overs) (TW Roberts 55, JC Scuderi 50*)
Derbyshire 162 for 4 (24.2 overs) (MJ Di Venuto 56)
Derbyshire (4 pts) won by six wickets

Worcestershire finally made sure of the last available promotion place by trouncing Essex by 96 runs under Duckworth/Lewis regulations at New Road. Several weather interruptions left Worcestershire

with 166 for six from 30 overs – Phil Weston hitting 68 and Graeme Hick 46 – and, chasing 194 from their 30-over allocation, Essex crumbled to 97 all out in front of the celebrating Worcester faithful. Andy Bichel, the popular Australian all-rounder, was confirmed as overseas player for a second season in 2002, and the news capped a memorable final day of an otherwise frustrating season for Worcestershire's supporters.

The win by Hick's side at Worcester meant that the result of the Sussex-Hampshire match at Hove became largely academic. At the start of play, both sides knew that victory would earn them promotion should Worcestershire slip up – but Sussex fell away alarmingly to 142 all out once Dimitri Mascarenhas had nipped out both Richard Montgomerie and Murray Goodwin in a new-ball burst of 9-1-18-2. Robin Martin-Jenkins (38) attempted to fashion some sort of recovery, but James Hamblin's cleanly struck 61 off just 42 balls quickly settled the outcome. Fifty of Hamblin's first 54 runs came through boundaries and, in all, he hit a six and ten fours. Neil Johnson (41) also batted briskly in an opening stand of 103, and Hampshire's seven-wicket winning margin was confirmed as early as the 23rd over. Robin Smith, the Hampshire captain of four years, said, after what was probably his last match in charge, that the disappointment of missing out on Norwich Union League promotion was amply compensated by his county's success in reaching the championship elite.

Robert Croft hit a maiden one-day century at Cardiff as the second division champions celebrated by overpowering Middlesex by 40 runs. Croft's 114 not out came off just 111 balls, and contained three sixes and ten fours. It was largely as a result of his 181-run stand in 29 overs with Steve James (93) that Glamorgan amassed an imposing 272 for four, and this indeed proved too much for Middlesex who finished up on 232 for eight.

And last, but this time not least, came Derbyshire. Their miserable season, in which they took the wooden spoon in both the championship and one-day league, ended on a brighter note of hope for the future as they defeated the once-mighty Lancashire by six wickets at Derby. In a match reduced to 25 overs per side, Derbyshire overhauled Lancashire's 159 for five, in which Tim Roberts made 55 and Joe Scuderi 50, with four balls to spare. Michael Di Venuto launched the chase with 56 from 46 balls, adding a decisive 82 in 11 overs with Steve Selwood (30), before Chris Bassano clinched a rare win by cover-driving Glen Chapple triumphantly to the boundary.

Division One Final Results

	P	W	L	Tie	NR	Pts
Kent	16	11	2	1	2	50
Leicestershire	16	11	4	–	1	46
Warwickshire	16	8	5	–	3	38
Somerset	16	7	7	1	1	30
Nottinghamshire	16	7	8	–	1	30
Yorkshire	16	7	9	–	–	28
Gloucestershire	16	6	9	–	1	26
Surrey	16	6	10	–	–	24
Northamptonshire	16	3	12	–	1	14

Division Two

	P	W	L	Tie	NR	Pts
Glamorgan	16	11	3	–	2	48
Durham	16	9	4	–	3	42
Worcestershire	16	9	5	–	2	40
Hampshire	16	9	6	–	1	38
Sussex	16	8	7	–	1	34
Lancashire	16	5	8	–	3	26
Essex	16	5	9	1	1	24
Middlesex	16	3	9	1	3	20
Derbyshire	16	4	12	–	–	14

FEATURES OF NATIONAL LEAGUE 2001

HIGHEST TOTAL

352-6 (45 overs)   Yorkshire v. Nottinghamshire at Scarborough   26 August

HIGHEST TOTAL BATTING SECOND

279-5 (43 overs)   Surrey v. Nottinghamshire at Trent Bridge   9 September

LOWEST TOTAL

59 (15.2 overs)   Warwickshire v. Yorkshire at Headingley   23 July

HIGHEST INDIVIDUAL SCORE

191 DS Lehmann   Yorkshire v. Nottinghamshire at Scarborough   26 August
27 centuries were scored in the competition

SIX WICKETS IN AN INNINGS

6-29   GR Napier   Essex v. Worcestershire at Chelmsford   12 August
6-40   KP Dutch   Somerset v. Northamptonshire at Northampton   30 August
There were 50 instances of four wickets in an innings

TIED MATCHES

Kent tied with Somerset at Tunbridge Wells   3 June
Middlesex tied with Essex at Southgate   8 July

WINNING BY TEN WICKETS

Warwickshire beat Somerset at Edgbaston   19 August

WINNING BY ONE WICKET

Leicestershire beat Yorkshire at Leicester   19 August

WINNING BY 150 RUNS

179   Yorkshire beat Nottinghamshire at Scarborough   27 August
178   Glamorgan beat Essex at Cardiff   19 August
There were nine instances of a side winning by more than 100 runs

WINNING BY ONE RUN

Sussex beat Essex at Chelmsford   20 May
Kent beat Nottinghamshire at Trent Bridge   15 July
Leicestershire beat Somerset at Taunton   14 August
Kent beat Gloucestershire at Bristol   27 August

NO PLAY POSSIBLE

Kent v. Warwickshire at Canterbury   28 April
Lancashire v. Hampshire at Old Trafford   28 April
Middlesex v. Durham at Lord's   28 April
Lancashire v. Durham at Old Trafford   15 July
Gloucestershire v. Somerset at Bristol   17 July
Northamptonshire v. Kent at Northampton   12 August
Middlesex v. Worcestershire at Lord's   19 August
Sussex v. Durham at Hove   26 August

NATIONAL LEAGUE AVERAGES

DERBYSHIRE

Batting	M	Inns	NO	HS	Runs	Av	100	50	c/st
RJ Bailey	14	14	2	94	402	33.50	–	3	4
MJ Di Venuto	12	12	0	71	342	28.50	–	2	2
T Lungley	8	3	1	45	55	27.50	–	–	1
CWG Bassano	8	8	1	45	180	25.71	–	–	2
KM Krikken	14	12	4	42*	203	25.37	–	–	14/8
SA Selwood	3	3	0	37	75	25.00	–	–	–
SD Stubbings	13	13	1	96*	254	21.16	–	2	3
NRC Dumelow	10	9	2	33	145	20.71	–	–	1
MP Dowman	15	15	0	64	309	20.60	–	1	4
WG Khan	4	4	1	30	58	19.33	–	–	2
LD Sutton	10	10	2	42*	139	17.37	–	–	5/1
P Aldred	9	5	1	37	63	15.75	–	–	3
AD Edwards	7	3	1	17	18	9.00	–	–	1
G Welch	15	13	0	26	89	6.84	–	–	–

Also batted: DG Cork (2 matches) 83*, 4 (3ct); KJ Dean (6 matches) 2, 7 ; RK Illingworth (6 matches) 21*, 10*, 14* (2ct); TA Munton (6 matches) 3, 1*; JP Pyemont (2 matches) 7, 2; TM Smith (1 match) 6*; LJ Wharton (10 matches) 9*, 1*, 5*, 3*.
Did not bat in one match: ARK Pierson.

Bowling	O	M	Runs	W	Av	Best	4i
T Lungley	60	6	265	16	16.56	4-28	1
TA Munton	51	12	166	10	16.60	4-31	1
P Aldred	58	4	298	14	21.28	3-17	–
RK Illingworth	47.1	0	209	9	23.22	3-52	–
G Welch	121.4	17	473	16	29.56	5-22	1
NRC Dumelow	65	3	345	11	31.36	3-32	–
LJ Wharton	85	7	337	10	33.70	3-23	–

Also bowled: RJ Bailey 46-0-227-4; DG Cork 18-2-60-3; KJ Dean 40.3-4-232-4; MJ DiVenuto 5-0-30-0; MP Dowman 4-0-38-0; AD Edwards 45-1-242-3; WG Khan 2-1-7-1; SA Selwood 0.2-0-8-0; TM Smith 4-0-37-0.

DURHAM

Batting	M	Inns	NO	HS	Runs	Av	100	50	c/st
JJB Lewis	13	12	3	76*	373	41.44	–	3	1
N Peng	13	13	1	121	495	41.25	2	2	4
ML Love	13	13	1	89	431	35.91	–	2	8
A Pratt	13	11	2	86	287	31.88	–	2	14/7
JA Daley	5	5	1	35	124	31.00	–	–	–
MA Gough	8	6	2	35	115	28.75	–	–	1
PD Collingwood	11	11	0	84	294	26.72	–	1	6
DR Law	13	13	2	47	233	21.18	–	–	1
ID Hunter	6	4	1	21	47	15.66	–	–	1
MP Speight	5	5	1	30	59	14.75	–	–	2
NC Phillips	8	4	2	13*	23	11.50	–	–	3
GD Bridge	7	5	3	14*	20	10.00	–	–	3
SJ Harmison	7	3	1	11*	18	9.00	–	–	1
AM Davies	5	3	0	10	14	4.66	–	–	–
JE Brinkley	9	3	2	1*	2	2.00	–	–	3

Also batted: NG Hatch (5 matches) 5, 8*.
Did not bat: N Killeen (2 matches).

Bowling	O	M	Runs	W	Av	Best	4i
AM Davies	34	5	134	7	19.14	4-13	1
NG Hatch	33	3	144	7	20.57	3-26	–
NC Phillips	67.4	3	297	13	22.84	4-21	2
ID Hunter	38	5	186	8	23.25	3-47	–
PD Collingwood	57.5	1	293	11	26.63	3-21	–
DR Law	77.5	6	368	13	28.30	3-28	–
JE Brinkley	56.3	5	234	8	29.25	2-19	–
SJ Harmison	45	3	248	8	31.00	4-43	1
MA Gough	53	3	247	7	35.28	2-27	–
GD Bridge	51	1	218	6	36.33	2-42	–

Also bowled: N Killeen 17-0-73-1; ML Love 2-0-7-0

ESSEX

Batting	M	Inns	NO	HS	Runs	Av	100	50	c/st
RC Irani	16	15	3	108*	402	33.50	1	1	5
RS Clinton	9	6	2	56	125	31.25	–	1	–
SG Law	11	10	0	108	300	30.00	1	1	5
JS Foster	14	13	5	56*	207	25.87	–	1	17/1

ESSEX cont.

Batting	M	Inns	NO	HS	Runs	Av	100	50	c/st
SD Peters	13	12	1	66	253	23.00	–	1	4
AP Grayson	16	15	1	52	320	22.85	–	1	6
DDJ Robinson	16	15	0	64	304	20.26	–	1	2
BJ Hyam	3	3	1	30*	40	20.00	–	–	1/-
GR Napier	12	11	0	73	174	15.81	–	1	1
AP Cowan	16	15	0	31	204	13.60	–	–	4
TJ Mason	8	6	3	12	33	11.00	–	–	–
RSG Anderson	5	5	0	22	35	7.00	–	–	–
JE Bishop	11	7	2	14	28	5.60	–	–	3
MC Ilott	4	3	2	3*	5	5.00	–	–	1
AJ Clarke	10	5	1	5	10	2.50	–	–	1

Also batted: N Hussain (2 matches) 21, 7; WI Jefferson (1 match) 2; AC McGarry (5 matches) 1 (1ct); ML Pettini (2 matches) 14 (1ct); TJ Phillips (1 match) 2; PJ Prichard (1 match) 13.

Bowling	O	M	Runs	W	Av	Best	4i
GR Napier	32.2	0	151	7	21.57	6-29	1
AP Cowan	129.1	10	568	22	25.81	5-14	2
JE Bishop	79	2	411	15	27.40	3-33	–
AP Grayson	116	3	501	18	27.83	3-23	–
RC Irani	115.5	13	527	16	32.93	3-51	–
AJ Clarke	54	3	284	7	40.57	2-39	–

Also bowled: RSG Anderson 33.4-1-159-2; RS Clinton 3-0-25-0; MC Ilott 28-0-189-3; AC McGarry 12-0-71-2; TJ Mason 35.2-0-183-1; TJ Phillips 5-1-12-0.

GLAMORGAN

Batting	M	Inns	NO	HS	Runs	Av	100	50	c/st
MP Maynard	16	16	6	116*	527	52.70	1	3	7/2
RDB Croft	15	15	1	114*	570	40.71	1	5	3
AP Davies	10	3	2	24	35	35.00	–	–	3
JP Maher	15	15	1	94	453	32.35	–	3	1
K Newell	16	16	1	97	476	31.73	–	3	1
MJ Powell	16	14	5	46	271	30.11	–	–	8
SP James	9	8	1	93	210	30.00	–	2	2
IJ Thomas	7	7	0	53	194	27.71	–	1	1
A Dale	16	9	1	52*	221	27.62	–	1	3
SD Thomas	16	11	5	25*	131	21.83	–	–	3
DA Cosker	12	4	1	14*	22	7.33	–	–	6
OT Parkin	13	3	1	2*	2	1.00	–	–	2

Also batted: AW Evans (1 match) 4 (1ct); AD Shaw (4 matches) 6, 9* (2st); SL Watkin (8 matches) 3, 2.
Did not bat in two matches AG Wharf.

Bowling	O	M	Runs	W	Av	Best	4i
AP Davies	68.5	1	301	21	14.33	5-39	2
AG Wharf	16	1	76	5	15.20	3-23	–
A Dale	59.2	1	254	12	21.16	3-22	–
RDB Croft	102.2	5	363	16	22.68	4-33	1
SD Thomas	88.3	5	418	18	23.22	3-27	–
DA Cosker	85	5	391	14	27.92	3-40	–
OT Parkin	78.5	7	418	13	32.15	3-37	–

Also bowled: K Newell 4-0-23-1; SL Watkin 66-8-289-4.

GLOUCESTERSHIRE

Batting	M	Inns	NO	HS	Runs	Av	100	50	c/st
KJ Barnett	15	15	0	101	473	31.53	2	1	3
MGN Windows	15	15	0	117	458	30.53	1	2	5
JN Snape	12	12	4	104*	223	27.87	1	–	4
IJ Harvey	9	9	0	67	226	25.11	–	1	1
RJ Cunliffe	6	6	1	32	118	23.60	–	–	4
THC Hancock	11	11	0	67	223	20.27	–	1	1
MA Hardinges	8	8	2	65	114	19.00	–	1	1
MCJ Ball	14	12	5	38	132	18.85	–	–	11
MJ Cawdron	5	4	2	29*	36	18.00	–	–	1
MW Alleyne	15	15	2	68	211	16.23	–	–	8
CG Taylor	9	9	2	63rh	111	15.85	–	1	1
DR Hewson	8	8	0	52	120	15.00	–	1	5
JMM Averis	15	8	3	17*	51	10.20	–	–	3
RC Russell	10	9	1	24	65	8.12	–	–	6/4

Also batted: AN Bressington (3 matches) 5, 15 (2ct); APR Gidman (1 match) 7;

NATIONAL LEAGUE AVERAGES

GLOUCESTERSHIRE cont.

J Lewis (3 matches) 2*, 12; AM Smith (2 matches) 3*, 0; RCJ Williams (4 matches) 5, 28 (5ct,2st).

Bowling	O	M	Runs	W	Av	Best	4i
J Lewis	26	7	74	6	12.33	3-20	-
JN Snape	38.3	3	187	10	18.70	3-30	-
JMM Averis	121.3	8	546	27	20.22	5-40	3
KJ Barnett	30.2	2	130	6	21.66	4-12	1
MCJ Ball	111	2	518	21	24.66	3-15	-
IJ Harvey	64.1	7	261	10	26.10	4-42	1
MJ Cawdron	39.2	6	168	5	33.60	2-43	-
MW Alleyne	105	5	395	10	39.50	2-17	-

Alao bowled: AN Bressington 23-3-96-1; THC Hancock 2-0-13-0; MA Hardinges 32-1-169-3; AM Smith 18-6-37-4.

HAMPSHIRE

Batting	M	Inns	NO	HS	Runs	Av	100	50	c/st
JD Francis	5	5	2	78*	178	59.33	-	2	1
NC Johnson	15	15	1	105*	481	34.35	1	2	15
DA Kenway	14	14	2	93*	404	33.66	-	3	14/-
GW White	6	5	0	59	160	32.00	-	2	2
RA Smith	15	13	3	46	260	26.00	-	-	2
JS Laney	13	13	1	62*	259	21.58	-	1	2
JRC Hamblin	14	8	2	61	129	21.50	-	1	5
LR Prittipaul	13	12	1	45	201	18.27	-	-	6
SD Udal	15	11	3	28*	117	14.62	-	-	8
AD Mascarenhas	15	13	1	53	167	13.91	-	1	4
WS Kendall	11	9	0	47	108	12.00	-	-	8
CT Tremlett	12	9	3	15*	59	9.83	-	-	3
AD Mullally	11	4	2	5*	8	4.00	-	-	2
ZC Morris	3	3	1	7*	7	3.50	-	-	-

Also batted: AN Aymes (1 match) 9*; SRG Francis (1 match) 11*.
Did not bat in one match: JEK Schofield.

Bowling	O	M	Runs	W	Av	Best	4i
CT Tremlett	95.3	1	364	22	16.54	3-15	-
AD Mascarenhas	125	17	441	21	21.00	2-11	-
AD Mullally	90.1	13	311	14	22.21	3-19	-
JRC Hamblin	86	3	431	17	25.35	4-29	1
SD Udal	123.5	12	480	15	32.00	3-23	-
NC Johnson	66	1	362	10	36.20	2-13	-

Also bowled: ZC Morris 25-2-102-3; LR Prittipaul 3-0-18-0; JEK Schofield 6-0-22-1.

KENT

Batting	M	Inns	NO	HS	Runs	Av	100	50	c/st
MV Fleming	13	13	3	125	345	34.50	1	1	3
JB Hockley	14	14	1	90	403	31.00	-	3	6
MA Ealham	10	10	4	34	177	29.50	-	-	3
RWT Key	10	9	1	59	201	25.12	-	2	2
A Symonds	9	9	0	74	221	24.55	-	1	2
DP Fulton	14	14	0	82	334	23.85	-	1	10
PA Nixon	14	14	1	55	259	19.92	-	1	13/6
MJ Walker	14	14	1	34	205	15.76	-	-	3
GO Jones	4	4	0	39	59	14.75	-	-	-
JM Golding	5	5	2	15	42	14.00	-	-	-
MJ Saggers	13	8	4	21*	54	13.50	-	-	1
MM Patel	13	9	2	15	58	8.28	-	-	7
ET Smith	4	4	0	10	20	5.00	-	-	-
BJ Trott	13	6	4	2*	5	2.50	-	-	2

Also batted in two matches: DJ Cullinan 70, 30 (1ct); MJ McCague 5, 4 (1ct).

Bowling	O	M	Runs	W	Av	Best	4i
MJ Walker	19.3	0	77	9	8.55	4-24	1
MJ Saggers	94.4	10	414	25	16.56	5-22	1
A Symonds	46	3	170	9	18.88	5-18	1
MA Ealham	85	10	359	16	22.43	3-19	-
MM Patel	89	6	406	15	27.06	2-27	-
MV Fleming	83	4	354	13	27.23	5-40	1
BJ Trott	99	14	431	15	28.73	2-19	-

Also bowled: JM Golding 34-2-139-4; MJ McCague 12.1-1-55-2.

NATIONAL LEAGUE AVERAGES

LANCASHIRE

Batting	M	Inns	NO	HS	Runs	Av	100	50	c/st
NH Fairbrother	12	11	3	101	390	48.75	1	2	4
JP Crawley	13	13	3	84*	357	35.70	-	3	9
GD Lloyd	10	9	1	56	249	31.12	-	2	1
MA Atherton	4	4	0	62	107	26.75	-	1	6
JC Scuderi	8	6	1	50*	122	24.40	-	1	1
TW Roberts	3	3	0	55	68	22.66	-	1	-
A Flintoff	13	13	0	78	269	20.69	-	1	2
G Chapple	13	11	0	56	204	18.54	-	2	2
WK Hegg	10	9	2	29	105	15.00	-	-	11/6
G Yates	8	4	2	16	28	14.00	-	-	2
CP Schofield	14	11	4	20	96	13.71	-	-	4
MJ Chilton	9	8	1	34	84	12.00	-	-	2
J Wood	10	5	2	19*	33	11.00	-	-	2
PJ Martin	6	3	1	6	14	7.00	-	-	-
MP Smethurst	5	3	2	2*	4	4.00	-	-	1

Also batted: RC Driver (2 matches) 0, 9; JJ Haynes (4 matches) 11, 0 (2ct/1st); G Keedy (1 match) 2; M Muralitharan (5 matches) 1.
Did not bat: JM Anderson (1 match); ID Austin (1 match); KW Hogg (2 matches) (1ct).

Bowling	O	M	Runs	W	Av	Best	4i
CP Schofield	72.1	1	362	23	15.73	5-31	2
M Muralitharan	40	10	92	5	18.40	2-24	-
A Flintoff	60.5	4	271	12	22.58	3-16	-
G Chapple	93.1	5	403	17	23.70	3-19	-
JC Scuderi	46	4	196	8	24.50	3-28	-
PJ Martin	48.5	8	216	7	30.85	2-24	-
J Wood	66	8	319	8	39.87	2-20	-

Also bowled: JM Anderson 4-0-33-1; ID Austin 6.5-1-32-1; RC Driver 3-0-23-0; KW Hogg 9-1-36-1; G Keedy 4-0-37-1; TW Roberts 3-0-14-0; MP Smethurst 25-6-106-2; G Yates 53-3-201-4.

LEICESTERSHIRE

Batting	M	Inns	NO	HS	Runs	Av	100	50	c/st
DJ Marsh	5	5	2	97*	206	68.66	-	2	3
ND Burns	16	12	3	90*	376	41.77	-	3	14/4
Shahid Afridi	8	8	0	70	276	34.50	-	3	-
DI Stevens	14	12	2	68*	343	34.30	-	3	6
IJ Sutcliffe	5	5	0	48	166	33.20	-	-	2
Aftab Habib	12	9	3	44	183	30.50	-	-	1
JM Dakin	12	10	1	65	262	29.11	-	1	1
DL Maddy	16	14	4	46*	279	27.90	-	2	4
BF Smith	16	16	4	65*	323	26.91	-	2	4
TR Ward	11	11	0	56	180	16.36	-	1	4
VJ Wells	16	16	1	39	191	12.73	-	-	7
PAJ DeFreitas	10	7	1	33*	68	11.33	-	-	1
J Ormond	13	7	3	13*	42	10.50	-	-	1
SAJ Boswell	13	7	4	23*	27	9.00	-	-	3

Also batted: CD Crowe (2 matches) 5 (2ct); DE Malcolm (6 matches) 2*, 0; WF Stelling (1 match) 10.

Bowling	O	M	Runs	W	Av	Best	4i
DL Maddy	92.3	0	464	21	22.09	3-1	-
Shahid Afridi	56	2	266	11	24.18	3-45	-
VJ Wells	86	5	394	15	26.26	4-30	1
J Ormond	104	13	403	15	26.86	3-16	-
DJ Marsh	34.4	0	171	6	28.50	4-44	1
SAJ Boswell	89.3	9	398	12	33.16	3-32	-
JM Dakin	60.3	3	237	7	33.85	3-14	-
DE Malcolm	33	2	177	5	35.40	3-34	-
PAJ DeFreitas	74.3	7	324	6	54.00	2-29	-

Also bowled: CD Crowe 7.3-0-30-4; WF Stelling 8-1-20-2; DI Stevens 0.3-0-1-0.

MIDDLESEX

Batting	M	Inns	NO	HS	Runs	Av	100	50	c/st
AJ Strauss	13	12	0	59	326	27.16	-	3	1
OA Shah	12	11	1	69	244	24.40	-	2	5
BL Hutton	8	8	0	77	187	23.37	-	1	3
JWM Dalrymple	9	8	3	38*	114	22.80	-	-	2
PN Weekes	14	13	1	55	273	22.75	-	1	8
RMS Weston	8	8	1	80*	135	19.28	-	1	3

NATIONAL LEAGUE AVERAGES

MIDDLESEX cont.

Batting	M	Inns	NO	HS	Runs	Av	100	50	c/st
DC Nash	13	12	3	57*	161	17.88	-	1	7/4
SJ Cook	11	9	2	50	111	15.85	-	1	1
ARC Fraser	7	3	1	17	29	14.50	-	-	1
MA Roseberry	6	6	0	35	85	14.16	-	-	2
EC Joyce	6	5	0	38	63	12.60	-	-	3
JP Hewitt	4	4	2	11*	24	12.00	-	-	1
SP Fleming	10	9	0	28	107	11.88	-	-	2
CB Keegan	14	11	3	16	72	9.00	-	-	2
TF Bloomfield	10	4	1	2	6	2.00	-	-	2

Also batted: D Alleyne (1 match) 8 (2ct); AJ Coleman (3 matches) 4*, 11* (1ct);
MS Compton (1 match) 6; JK Maunders (2 matches) 6, 49 (1ct); PCR Tufnell
(2 matches) 0*.

Bowling	O	M	Runs	W	Av	Best	4i
ARC Fraser	61	12	159	15	10.60	3-13	-
CB Keegan	106.5	7	461	25	17.73	5-17	2
JWM Dalrymple	37.3	3	157	7	22.42	4-14	1
BL Hutton	44	2	188	8	23.50	5-45	1
PN Weekes	102	5	450	11	40.90	3-28	-
SJ Cook	72.3	4	366	8	45.75	2-33	-
TF Bloomfield	81	11	295	5	59.00	2-16	-

Also bowled: AJ Coleman 13.1-1-61-0; JP Hewitt 22-2-108-3; PCR Tufnell 17.2-1-85-2

NORTHAMPTONSHIRE

Batting	M	Inns	NO	HS	Runs	Av	100	50	c/st
RJ Warren	11	11	1	93	411	41.10	-	4	4
MB Loye	9	9	2	90	284	40.57	-	3	2
ME Hussey	15	15	1	96*	510	36.42	-	4	3
AJ Swann	12	12	4	54	280	35.00	-	1	1
GP Swann	13	12	0	83	348	29.00	-	3	3
AS Rollins	3	3	1	29	55	27.50	-	-	-
D Ripley	11	8	2	40*	153	25.50	-	-	9/5
ME Cassar	4	4	0	58	99	24.75	-	1	2
AL Penberthy	12	11	1	52	190	19.00	-	2	2
JW Cook	8	8	0	55	129	16.12	-	1	5
KJ Innes	8	6	2	19	61	15.25	-	-	2
MR Strong	7	4	2	11	27	13.50	-	-	1
DJG Sales	4	4	0	26	52	13.00	-	-	-
TMB Bailey	6	4	0	22	49	12.25	-	-	2/1
JP Taylor	11	9	1	19	51	6.37	-	-	2
LC Weekes	8	5	2	10*	19	6.33	-	-	2
JF Brown	15	7	3	5	12	3.00	-	-	3

Also batted: JAR Blain (3 matches) 0*, 3* (2ct); DM Cousins (5 matches) 3, 5* (1ct).

Bowling	O	M	Runs	W	Av	Best	4i
MR Strong	56.2	2	371	14	26.50	4-28	2
KJ Innes	53.2	5	294	9	32.66	3-60	-
AL Penberthy	99.3	7	453	12	37.75	3-43	-
JF Brown	108.4	3	461	13	35.46	3-25	-
JP Taylor	90	5	403	11	36.63	3-28	-
LC Weekes	62	3	353	7	50.42	3-34	-
GP Swann	68.1	2	349	6	58.16	2-35	-

Also bowled: JAR Blain 18-0-122-3; ME Cassar 6.3-0-52-0; JW Cook 18-2-81-3;
DM Cousins 43-2-226-4; AJ Swann 2-0-16-0.

NOTTINGHAMSHIRE

Batting	M	Inns	NO	HS	Runs	Av	100	50	c/st
Usman Afzaal	12	12	3	94*	449	49.88	-	4	2
JE Morris	5	5	0	102	204	40.80	1	1	2
DJ Bicknell	16	15	0	115	592	39.46	1	6	7
KP Pietersen	16	16	4	61*	386	32.16	-	3	7
GS Blewett	16	16	0	89	501	31.31	-	3	6
P Johnson	15	14	1	88*	384	29.53	-	3	5
GE Welton	8	7	0	38	115	19.16	-	-	-
CMW Read	15	13	3	36	180	18.00	-	-	17/3
BM Shafayat	5	5	0	31	76	15.20	-	-	3
RJ Logan	9	7	3	24	58	14.50	-	-	3
GD Clough	13	8	2	24	73	12.16	-	-	2
GJ Smith	15	5	1	8	19	4.75	-	-	1
AJ Harris	9	3	0	8	9	3.00	-	-	3

NOTTINGHAMSHIRE cont.

Also batted: PJ Franks (3 matches) 1*, 4*, 4*; JER Gallian (1 match) 1; CJ Hewison
(1 match) 20 (1ct); MN Malik (5 matches) 1, 3*; WM Noon (1 match) 17 (2ct,1st);
SJ Randall (2 matches) 15*, 13*; RD Stemp (8 matches) 0, 1* (5ct).
Did not bat in one match: DS Lucas.

Bowling	O	M	Runs	W	Av	Best	4i
AJ Harris	72	4	397	17	23.35	4-24	2
GJ Smith	112.5	13	495	21	23.57	3-25	-
RD Stemp	63	3	280	11	25.45	4-25	1
GD Clough	86.1	1	429	13	33.00	2-33	-
MN Malik	40	3	205	5	41.00	2-34	-
RJ Logan	65.2	1	420	10	42.00	2-37	-
KP Pietersen	88	1	480	11	43.63	3-39	-

Also bowled: Usman Afzaal 25-1-128-3; GS Blewett 41-1-272-3; PJ Franks 24-1-119-3;
P Johnson 0.4-0-2-1; SJ Randall 13-0-86-3.

SOMERSET

Batting	M	Inns	NO	HS	Runs	Av	100	50	c/st
PD Bowler	11	11	0	104	560	50.90	1	5	4
M Burns	14	13	4	101*	331	36.77	1	1	3
ID Blackwell	15	14	1	86	433	33.30	-	4	2
J Cox	12	12	1	76*	331	30.09	-	2	4
RJ Turner	14	13	5	56*	209	26.12	-	1	10/3
KA Parsons	10	9	1	58*	201	25.12	-	1	2
PS Jones	14	7	5	17*	41	20.50	-	-	2
RL Johnson	7	5	1	24*	69	17.25	-	-	-
MJ Wood	6	5	0	29	86	17.20	-	-	1
MN Lathwell	6	5	0	30	85	17.00	-	-	1
KP Dutch	15	13	3	28	159	15.90	-	-	8
PD Trego	5	4	1	21	44	14.66	-	-	-
JID Kerr	12	8	3	16	53	10.60	-	-	1
JO Grove	12	3	1	6	9	4.50	-	-	3
PCL Holloway	6	5	0	11	19	3.80	-	-	-

Also batted: GD Rose (1 match) 58; ME Trescothick (2 matches) 27, 72 (1ct).
Did not bat in one match: MPL Bulbeck; AR Caddick; I Jones.

Bowling	O	M	Runs	W	Av	Best	4i
PS Jones	111.4	8	560	22	25.45	4-40	1
ID Blackwell	71.5	2	329	12	27.41	3-16	-
KP Dutch	96	2	452	16	28.25	6-40	1
RL Johnson	57	4	290	8	36.25	3-51	-
KA Parsons	40	1	197	5	39.40	2-32	-
JID Kerr	85	3	493	12	41.08	2-33	-
JO Grove	80	2	437	9	48.55	3-24	-

Also bowled: MPL Bulbeck 2-0-22-0; M Burns 15-0-70-1; AR Caddick 9-2-21-1;
I Jones 2-0-14-3; GD Rose 1-0-2-0; PD Trego 15-1-81-3.

SURREY

Batting	M	Inns	NO	HS	Runs	Av	100	50	c/st
AD Brown	13	13	1	130	565	47.08	3	1	7
BC Hollioake	12	11	3	70*	368	46.00	-	3	2
MR Ramprakash	6	6	1	85*	214	42.80	-	2	1
GJ Batty	12	11	2	83*	317	35.22	-	3	2
AJ Hollioake	15	15	2	70	399	30.69	-	3	6
MA Butcher	8	8	1	55	147	21.00	-	2	-
IJ Ward	9	9	0	51	153	17.00	-	1	2
Nadeem Shahid	12	12	1	43	143	13.00	-	-	-
AJ Tudor	4	3	0	21	37	12.33	-	-	1
GP Butcher	7	6	1	17	61	12.20	-	-	-
TJ Murtagh	7	5	4	4*	12	12.00	-	-	1
MP Bicknell	11	8	2	23*	70	11.66	-	-	2
JN Batty	14	10	2	21*	83	10.37	-	-	19/2
Saqlain Mushtaq	10	9	2	38*	67	9.57	-	-	1
MA Carberry	5	5	0	20	33	6.60	-	-	1
ESH Giddins	15	6	1	3	4	0.80	-	-	5
CG Greenidge	4	3	1	1	1	0.50	-	-	3

Also batted: RR Clarke (2 matches) 0, 7 (1ct); JJ Porter (1 match) 23; IDK Salisbury
(3 matches) 2, 13 (1ct); AJ Stewart (2 matches) 0, 19 (3ct); SA Newman (2 matches) 0, 10.
Did not bat in one match: RM Amin; PJ Sampson.

Bowling	O	M	Runs	W	Av	Best	4i
BC Hollioake	81	8	384	21	18.28	3-10	-

NATIONAL LEAGUE AVERAGES

SURREY cont.

Bowling	O	M	Runs	W	Av	Best	4i
AJ Hollioake	56.4	2	278	15	18.53	4-19	1
AJ Tudor	34	6	136	7	19.42	4-36	1
CG Greenidge	20	2	112	5	22.40	2-17	-
GJ Batty	54.3	4	256	11	23.27	4-36	1
MP Bicknell	84	8	310	13	23.84	3-20	-
TJ Murtagh	52.5	5	262	10	26.20	4-31	1
ESH Giddins	109.5	14	519	15	34.60	3-31	-
Saqlain Mushtaq	71	3	348	6	58.00	3-44	-

Also bowled: RM Amin 3-0-21-0; AD Brown 8-0-54-1; GP Butcher 16-0-94-2; MR Ramprakash 3.3-0-23-0; IDK Salisbury 20-0-103-1; PJ Sampson 9-0-25-1.

SUSSEX

Batting	M	Inns	NO	HS	Runs	Av	100	50	c/st
RR Montgomerie	15	15	1	108	673	48.07	1	5	1
TR Ambrose	4	4	0	87	164	41.00	-	1	3/3
MW Goodwin	15	15	3	87	484	40.33	-	6	4
CJ Adams	12	11	2	100*	322	35.77	1	1	3
RSC Martin-Jenkins	7	5	2	38	82	27.33	-	-	5
WJ House	15	13	3	39	240	24.00	-	-	4
B Zuiderent	10	9	0	65	202	22.44	-	2	1
MJG Davis	14	8	1	27	87	12.42	-	-	1
RJ Kirtley	15	7	3	11	48	12.00	-	-	3
MH Yardy	5	5	0	24	56	11.20	-	-	-
UBA Rashid	6	6	2	28	41	10.25	-	-	1
JR Carpenter	5	3	0	18	28	9.33	-	-	1
BV Taylor	10	6	2	19	34	8.50	-	-	5
MJ Prior	11	8	1	25	50	7.14	-	-	6/1
MA Robinson	15	7	4	4	8	2.66	-	-	1

Also batted: PA Cottey (1 match) 0 (1ct); CD Hopkinson (2 matches) 10* (5ct); JD Lewry (2 matches) 0. Did not bat in one match: PM Havell.

Bowling	O	M	Runs	W	Av	Best	4i
BV Taylor	75	13	282	14	20.14	3-29	-
MA Robinson	131.5	16	416	19	21.89	3-17	-
RSC Martin-Jenkins	49	4	202	8	25.25	3-20	-
RJ Kirtley	116	9	493	18	27.38	2-8	-
MJG Davis	105.1	6	523	12	43.58	4-24	1

Also bowled: CJ Adams 27-0-147-4; PM Havell 4-0-20-0; CD Hopkinson 2-0-2-1; WJ House 22-0-112-2; JD Lewry 18-2-78-2; UBA Rashid 42-1-234-3; MH Yardy 19-0-78-2.

WARWICKSHIRE

Batting	M	Inns	NO	HS	Runs	Av	100	50	c/st
DP Ostler	6	6	2	134*	320	80.00	1	2	6
NV Knight	12	10	2	84*	301	37.62	-	2	4
DR Brown	15	11	1	73	320	32.00	-	4	7
VC Drakes	8	4	2	43	64	32.00	-	-	1
MJ Powell	15	11	1	78	248	24.80	-	1	4
TL Penney	15	10	3	35	171	24.42	-	-	5
MA Wagh	12	10	1	70*	201	22.33	-	3	1
DL Hemp	12	8	1	43	121	17.28	-	-	2
KJ Piper	13	4	2	17	30	15.00	-	-	14/3
AF Giles	5	5	3	23	27	13.50	-	-	1
NMK Smith	13	8	0	38	97	12.12	-	-	2
MA Sheikh	15	5	3	12*	17	8.50	-	-	3

Also batted: IR Bell (1 match) 48; NM Carter (4 matches) 13, 0; CE Dagnall (12 matches) 2, 3*; A Richardson (6 matches) 0*, 8* (1ct). Did not bat in one match: T Frost.

Bowling	O	M	Runs	W	Av	Best	4i
NM Carter	29	2	119	7	17.00	3-28	-
DR Brown	116.4	16	529	29	18.24	4-56	1
CE Dagnall	88.5	13	301	13	23.15	2-18	-
A Richardson	39.4	3	167	7	23.85	3-17	-
NMK Smith	71.4	2	343	14	24.50	3-19	-
MA Sheikh	120	13	383	15	25.53	4-17	1
AF Giles	45	1	228	8	28.50	2-41	-
VC Drakes	70.4	11	279	9	31.00	3-35	-

Also bowled: MJ Powell 12-0-58-0; MA Wagh 3-0-26-0.

NATIONAL LEAGUE AVERAGES

WORCESTERSHIRE

Batting	M	Inns	NO	HS	Runs	Av	100	50	c/st
SJ Rhodes	14	11	9	39*	139	69.50	-	-	18/6
VS Solanki	15	14	2	91*	502	41.83	-	5	5
WPC Weston	11	10	0	134	313	31.30	1	1	1
GA Hick	15	14	1	87	406	31.23	-	4	8
DA Leatherdale	15	14	2	55*	319	26.58	-	1	9
PR Pollard	8	7	1	62	154	25.66	-	1	1
SR Lampitt	15	8	6	27*	45	22.50	-	-	5
A Singh	14	14	0	80	299	21.35	-	3	4
AJ Bichel	15	12	1	36*	148	13.45	-	-	7
MJ Rawnsley	14	3	2	4*	8	8.00	-	-	1
NR Boulton	3	3	0	20	22	7.33	-	-	-
A Sheriyar	15	3	0	9	9	3.00	-	-	-

Also batted: DC Catterall (1 match) 0 (1ct); Kabir Ali (7 matches) 6, 4; DJ Pipe (1 match) 26 (1st). Did not bat in two matches: CG Liptrot (1ct).

Bowling	O	M	Runs	W	Av	Best	4i
AJ Bichel	115.4	22	428	27	15.85	5-21	1
Kabir Ali	45.5	6	210	13	16.15	4-22	1
SR Lampitt	116	11	448	23	19.47	4-37	1
GA Hick	27.4	1	145	7	20.71	3-41	-
A Sheriyar	108.2	11	507	22	23.04	3-23	-
DA Leatherdale	62.5	2	263	10	26.30	3-11	-
MJ Rawnsley	93	1	446	15	29.73	3-28	-

Also bowled: DC Catterall 4-0-31-0; CG Liptrot 10-0-59-1; VS Solanki 8-0-51-0.

YORKSHIRE

Batting	M	Inns	NO	HS	Runs	Av	100	50	c/st
CEW Silverwood	4	4	3	27*	63	63.00	-	-	1
DS Lehmann	15	15	1	191	753	53.78	2	4	9
A McGrath	9	9	0	102	344	38.22	1	1	1
RJ Sidebottom	8	6	5	17*	38	38.00	-	-	3
RJ Blakey	16	16	8	52	280	35.00	-	1	20/4
MJ Lumb	7	6	1	66	124	24.80	-	1	4
VJ Craven	3	3	0	55	66	22.00	-	1	-
C White	10	10	0	73	219	21.90	-	1	4
D Byas	16	16	0	81	347	21.68	-	2	11
GM Fellows	14	14	1	67	261	20.07	-	1	3
MJ Wood	13	13	0	68	256	19.69	-	1	5
GM Hamilton	10	10	1	57	171	19.00	-	1	3
TT Bresnan	3	3	1	7	12	12.00	-	-	2
MP Vaughan	3	3	0	24	30	10.00	-	-	2
RKJ Dawson	10	7	1	10	25	4.16	-	-	4

Also batted: CJ Elstub (6 matches) 0*, 0*; ID Fisher (2 matches) 0; D Gough (2 matches) 16*, 13; ADK Gray (2 matches) 2, 19* (1ct); MJ Hoggard (11 matches) 2, 5* (2ct); SP Kirby (4 matches) 4* (1ct); PM Middlebrook (3 matches) 7, 10* (1ct). Did not bat: TM Baker (1 match) (1ct); PM Hutchison (3 matches) (1ct).

Bowling	O	M	Runs	W	Av	Best	4i
CEW Silverwood	29	4	102	9	11.33	4-21	1
PM Hutchison	23	2	102	7	14.57	3-26	-
CJ Elstub	41	5	161	10	16.10	4-25	1
RJ Sidebottom	51.2	7	204	12	17.00	3-38	-
DS Lehmann	89.5	3	336	16	21.00	3-31	-
GM Hamilton	47	3	221	9	24.55	3-14	-
SP Kirby	27	1	158	6	26.33	3-35	-
C White	72.5	5	281	10	28.10	3-30	-
RKJ Dawson	57	4	266	9	29.55	3-28	-
GM Fellows	36	1	185	6	30.83	3-34	-
MJ Hoggard	74.3	11	329	9	36.55	2-14	-

Also bowled: TM Baker 5-1-22-1; TT Bresnan 23-3-86-4; ID Fisher 15-0-86-1; D Gough 16-3-53-4; ADK Gray 9.1-0-49-1; A McGrath 0.3-0-1-1; JD Middlebrook 19-0-99-2.

BENSON AND HEDGES CUP
By Mark Baldwin

NORTH DIVISION

30 April 2001
at Trent Bridge
Leicestershire 170 (48.5 overs) (BF Smith 51)
Nottinghamshire 174 for 2 (30.3 overs) (GE Welton 71, GS Blewett 59*)
Nottinghamshire (2 pts) won by eight wickets
Gold Award: GE Welton

at Headingley
Derbyshire 200 for 8 (50 overs)
Yorkshire 203 for 5 (44.2 overs) (DS Lehmann 103)
Yorkshire (2 pts) won by five wickets
Gold Award: DS Lehmann

Nottinghamshire overpowered Leicestershire by eight wickets at Trent Bridge with Greg Smith, the 29-year-old British passport-holding South African paceman, taking four for 34 and Richard Logan also

Darren Lehmann's 103 powered Yorkshire to victory over Nottinghamshire with over five overs to spare.

impressing with two for 19 following his winter transfer from Northants. Ben Smith's 51 enabled Leicestershire to reach 170, but it was never enough as Guy Welton (71) and the in-form Greg Blewett (59 not out) added 78 in just 11 overs.

Tom Baker, a 19-year-old seamer from Dewsbury, took the wicket of Steve Stubbings with his first legitimate ball in senior cricket as Yorkshire beat Derbyshire by five wickets at Headingley. The visitors totalled 200 for eight and Darren Lehmann's superb 103 from 114 balls made Yorkshire's chase a straightforward one.

1 May 2001
at Liverpool
Durham 193 for 7 (50 overs) (JA Daley 70)
Lancashire 139 (40.4 overs)
Durham (2 pts) won by 54 runs
Gold Award: N Killeen

Competition bests from Jimmy Daley (70) and Neil Killeen (four for 18 from eight overs) spearheaded Durham's fine win over Lancashire at Liverpool. Muttiah Muralitharan's ten overs cost just 19 runs on the slow Aigburth surface, even though eight were taken from his first, but Durham's 193 for seven proved to be ample when Lancashire's much-vaunted top-order crumbled against Killeen's medium pace. Leg-cutters accounted for international trio Mike Atherton, John Crawley and Andy Flintoff, and Killeen later picked up the Gold Award for his efforts. Lancashire might have known it was not going to be their day when Peter Martin, their leading fast bowler, dislocated a finger during the warm-ups.

2 May 2001
at Derby
Durham 204 for 6 (50 overs) (PD Collingwood 89)
Derbyshire 175 (47.2 overs) (RJ Bailey 50)
Durham (2 pts) won by 29 runs
Gold Award: PD Collingwood

at Headingley
Yorkshire 194 for 7 (50 overs)
Nottinghamshire 198 for 4 (39.4 overs)
(GS Blewett 84, P Johnson 71*)
Nottinghamshire (2 pts) won by six wickets
Gold Award: GS Blewett

at Leicester
Leicestershire 193 for 7 (50 overs)
Lancashire 90 (20.2 overs)

Leicestershire (2 pts) won by 27 runs
(DL Method: Lancashire target 118 from 21 overs)
Gold Award: DE Malcolm

Paul Collingwood's 89, from 129 balls, boosted Durham to an eventual 50-over total of 204 for six at Derby – and victory by 29 runs. Rob Bailey hit 50 for Derbyshire, who had to bat through steady drizzle for much of their reply of 175.

At Headingley, meanwhile, the Nottinghamshire pair of Greg Blewett and Paul Johnson defied the miserable conditions to produce batting more suited to the sunny Caribbean. Blewett continued his fine early-season form with 84, while Johnson's 71 not out included strokes of equal class – together, the pair put on 150 in just 24 overs to make mincemeat of Yorkshire's earlier 50-over total of 194 for seven. Victory for Notts, by six wickets, arrived with more than ten overs to spare.

Afternoon showers at Grace Road meant that Lancashire were given a revised target of 118 from 21 overs in reply to Leicestershire's 50-over score of 193 for seven, in which Dan Marsh's 42 and Jon Dakin's unbeaten 31 were the most significant contributions. Mike Atherton, however, took 18 balls to get off the mark, and then immediately lost his off bail to a rip-snorter from Devon Malcolm. The former England paceman, now aged 38 and with his third county, finished with three for 13 as Lancashire crumbled to 90 all out, and was presented with only his second Benson and Hedges Gold Award in his 17-year career.

3 May 2001
at Leicester
Leicestershire 224 for 8 (50 overs) (VJ Wells 76, BF Smith 50)
Yorkshire 210 (48.3 overs) (MP Vaughan 92)
Leicestershire (2 pts) won by 14 runs
Gold Award: J Ormond

There was another exciting affair at Leicester, where Yorkshire's seemingly comfortable pursuit of Leicestershire's 224 for eight dissolved dramatically in the face of some inspired home bowling and catching. The key moment, perhaps, came when Dan Marsh flung himself goalkeeper-fashion at backward point to cling on to a fierce cut by Michael Vaughan off Devon Malcolm. Vaughan had stroked 92 from only 88 balls, with 15 fours, and had added 90 for the second wicket with Anthony McGrath (46). Yorkshire, from 137 for one, and needing just 88 from the last 20 overs, now fell away

against the cut and swing of a half-fit James Ormond. He had actually left the field earlier in the Yorkshire innings for treatment, but Ormond's four for 25 was later enough to win him the Gold Award as the visitors tumbled to 210 all out midway through the 49th over. Vaughan, no doubt sick at the result, also missed out on the individual award even though he had also taken four for 46 with his off breaks. Vince Wells (76) and Ben Smith (50) had provided the base of the Leicestershire innings with a second-wicket partnership of 119.

4 May 2001
at Chester-le-Street
Durham 252 for 3 (50 overs) (JA Daley 92, ML Love 59)
Nottinghamshire 253 for 5 (49.1 overs)
(GE Welton 75, DJ Bicknell 62)
Nottinghamshire (2 pts) won by five wickets
Gold Award: GE Welton

at Liverpool
Derbyshire 117 (47.1 overs)
Lancashire 121 for 0 (33.3 overs) (MA Atherton 77*)
Lancashire (2 pts) won by 10 wickets
Gold Award: M Muralitharan

Nottinghamshire came out on top after a run-filled contest at Chester-le-Street, in which Durham had first totalled 252 for three from their 50 overs. Jimmy Daley (92) and Michael Gough put on 116, and Martin Love hit 59, but the Notts reply was given initial momentum by an opening stand of 131 between Guy Welton and Darren Bicknell. Kevin Pietersen's 35 not out kept Notts up with the required rate, and victory came in the end by five wickets and with five balls to spare.

Lancashire thrashed Derbyshire by ten wickets at Liverpool, Mike Atherton cantering to 77 not out from 111 balls after the visitors had been dismissed for a dismal 117. Muttiah Muralitharan mesmerized the Derbyshire batsmen, allowing just three scoring strokes in a remarkable ten-over spell that cost him only four runs.

5 May 2001
at Chester-le-Street
Leicestershire 200 for 7 (50 overs) (DI Stevens 54)
Durham 202 for 3 (42.4 overs) (PD Collingwood 95*, JJB Lewis 59*)
Durham (2 pts) won by seven wickets
Gold Award: PD Collingwood

Fine batting by Paul Collingwood (95 not out) and

Jon Lewis (59 not out) took Durham to a satisfying and comfortable seven-wicket win over Leicestershire at Chester-le-Street. Neil Killeen was the pick of the Durham bowlers as Leicestershire were initially restricted to 200 for seven, and then the home side's fourth-wicket pair made sure of victory with more than seven overs in hand.

6 May 2001
at Derby
Nottinghamshire 231 for 5 (50 overs)
(Usman Afzaal 50)
Derbyshire 233 for 4 (49.2 overs) (MP Dowman 76*, RJ Bailey 62)
Derbyshire (2pts) won by six wickets
Gold Award: MP Dowman

at Liverpool
Lancashire 170 for 9 (50 overs) (MA Atherton 60, JP Crawley 52)
Yorkshire 171 for 5 (46.4 overs) (D Byas 55)
Yorkshire (2 pts) won by five wickets
Gold Award: DS Lehmann

Mathew Dowman enjoyed sweet revenge on the county that had released him in 1999 when, at Derby, he inspired Derbyshire to a six-wicket win over Nottinghamshire. The visitors posted a challenging 231 for five from their 50 overs, but Rob Bailey (62) and Michael Di Venuto put on 88 for the first wicket, and then Dowman added a further 74 for the second wicket with Bailey, before going on to finish with 76 not out from 96 balls.

A 4,000 crowd basked in the sunshine at Liverpool's historic Aigburth ground to see Lancashire totally outplayed by Roses rivals Yorkshire. Mike Atherton (60) and John Crawley (52) did put on 110 for the second wicket, but Chris Silverwood (three for 30) spearheaded a top-class Yorkshire bowling and fielding effort and the home side could eventually reach only 170 for nine from their 50-over allocation. Yorkshire then cruised to their target with 20 balls to spare and Lancashire, who had failed to reach the quarter-finals of this competition for only the third time since 1988, also saw Andy Flintoff break down with a side strain.

Michael Di Venuto crashed 108, but lack of support from his Derbyshire team-mates meant that his efforts were in vain as Leicestershire won by 21 runs.

7 May 2001
at Trent Bridge
Lancashire 203 for 6 (50 overs) (JC Scuderi 73*)
Nottinghamshire 207 for 3 (43.4 overs)
(DJ Bicknell 89, Usman Afzaal 56*)
Nottinghamshire (2 pts) won by seven wickets
Gold Award: DJ Bicknell

at Headingley
Yorkshire 257 for 7 (50 overs) (DS Lehmann 88)
Durham 227 for 4 (50 overs) (MA Gough 58, DR Law 57*)
Yorkshire (2 pts) won by 30 runs
Gold Award: DS Lehmann

at Leicester
Leicestershire 267 (49.5 overs) (VJ Wells 57, DL Maddy 56)
Derbyshire 246 (48.1 overs) (MJ Di Venuto 108)
Leicestershire (2 pts) won by 21 runs
Gold Award: MJ Di Venuto

Nottinghamshire made sure of their qualification for the quarter-finals by beating Lancashire by seven wickets at Trent Bridge. Skipper Darren Bicknell hit 13 fours in his 89, while Usman Afzaal finished on 56 not out as Notts cruised past Lancashire's inadequate total of 203 for six.

Durham also made it into the last eight despite losing by 30 runs to Yorkshire at Headingley. Darren Lehmann earned himself a third Gold Award inside eight days for his 76-ball 88 in Yorkshire's 257 for seven while, in reply, Danny Law (57 not out) and Jon Lewis (45 not out) were content merely to make sure Durham's net run rate stayed high enough, as the visitors made it to 227 for four. Yorkshire's reward, meanwhile, was to become one of the two third-placed teams to make it into the quarter-final draw.

Leicestershire were frustrated in their efforts to qualify, despite beating Derbyshire by 21 runs in a tightly-fought contest at Grace Road. The home side made 267, but Michael Di Venuto put together the day's outstanding innings with 108. With more support it would have been a match-winning effort, too.

MIDLANDS/WEST/WALES DIVISION

30 April 2001
at Kidderminster
Worcestershire 227 for 7 (50 overs) (PR Pollard 69, DA Leatherdale 58)
Northamptonshire 131 (37.2 overs)
Worcestershire (2 pts) won by 96 runs
Gold Award: PR Pollard

Denis Jones, the Kidderminster groundsman, did a great job in producing a highly-acceptable pitch for a second unscheduled one-day fixture. As on the previous day, Worcestershire were rewarded for their decision to switch the game from waterlogged New Road by trouncing Northants by 96 runs. Darren Cousins (four for 23) was the only visiting bowler to impress as Worcestershire reached 227 for seven, thanks mainly to Paul Pollard (69) and David Leatherdale (58), and the less said about the Northants batting the better.

1 May 2001
at Edgbaston
Warwickshire 213 for 9 (50 overs) (DP Ostler 77, MJ Powell 55, IJ Harvey 5 for 32)
Gloucestershire 213 for 6 (50 overs) (RJ Cunliffe 75)
Gloucestershire (2 pts) won by losing fewer wickets
Gold Award: IJ Harvey

at Cardiff
Glamorgan 232 for 6 (50 overs) (MJ Powell 67)
Somerset 233 for 4 (47 overs) (ME Trescothick 113, KP Dutch 55)
Somerset (2 pts) won by six wickets
Gold Award: ME Trescothick

A mad moment by Vasbert Drakes, the West Indian all-rounder, cost Warwickshire their chance of toppling holders Gloucestershire at Edgbaston. With two balls remaining, Gloucestershire needed six runs to win – a task which seemed beyond them in the split second in which Drakes fired in a penultimate-ball yorker at Reggie Williams that the batsman could only just dig out. But, adrenalin pumping no doubt, Drakes continued his follow-through, seized the ball as it rolled harmlessly up the pitch and – seeing non-striker Chris Taylor struggling to get back – hurled it at the bowlers' stumps. It missed, and Gloucestershire gratefully scrambled an overthrow. Now Taylor was facing the final ball of the match, requiring a four to tie the match – or so he thought. Cover driving it thunderously for four, Taylor walked off merely thinking he had clinched a share of the spoils. But, on entering the pavilion, he was told that Gloucestershire had triumphed because they had lost fewer wickets than the home side! It was a dramatic end to a hard-fought contest in which Warwickshire totalled 213 for nine, despite Ian Harvey's Gold Award winning performance of five for 32. Dominic Ostler (77) and Michael Powell (55) made sure

An inspired 113 by Marcus Trescothick eased Somerset past the winning post against Glamorgan.

Warwickshire posted a defendable total, but then Rob Cunliffe anchored the Gloucestershire reply with 75 and figured in stands of 77 with Kim Barnett and 87 with Matt Windows, who hit 42 from 56 balls. Mark Alleyne then provided late acceleration with a vital 26 from 17 balls but, until Drakes' rush of blood, Warwickshire looked like edging it.

At Cardiff, a magnificent 113 by Marcus Trescothick swept Somerset to a comfortable six-wicket win against Glamorgan – even though the Welsh county had managed what they reckoned to be a decent 50-over total of 232 for six. Trescothick, however, timed the ball with an ease which belied the sluggishness of the pitch and the chill of the day, reaching his hundred from just 105 balls and dominating a second-wicket stand of 121 with Keith Dutch, who was happy just to chug along in the England opener's slipstream and make 55.

2 May 2001
at Cardiff
Glamorgan 228 for 9 (50 overs) (MP Maynard 63)
Worcestershire 229 for 5 (47.3 overs) (AJ Bichel 100)
Worcestershire (2 pts) won by five wickets
Gold Award: AJ Bichel

at Bristol
Gloucestershire 202 for 7 (50 overs) (MGN Windows 108*)
Northamptonshire 193 for 9 (50 overs) (AJ Swann 83*)
Gloucestershire (2 pts) won by 9 runs
Gold Award: MGN Windows

at Taunton
Somerset 174 (49.2 overs) (KA Parsons 72)
Warwickshire 178 for 6 (49.1 overs) (TL Penney 73*)
Warwickshire (2 pts) won by four wickets
Gold Award: MM Betts

Andy Bichel hit 100 off 116 balls after being sent in early to drive Worcestershire towards an eventual five-wicket victory against Glamorgan in Cardiff. The Australian fast bowler, who had had some success batting in the top-order for Queensland in one-day cricket the previous winter, needed just 34 deliveries to complete his second fifty – a bout of hitting which included a six and ten fours. Vikram Solanki's 44 gave him solid support and earlier Bichel had taken two for 34 from ten overs in his more usual guise of opening bowler, as Glamorgan reached 228 for nine thanks mainly to Matthew Maynard's 64-ball 63. Graeme Hick, with some well-directed flat off spin into the blockhole, picked up

three for 23 towards the end of the Glamorgan innings.

A brilliantly-paced 108 not out from Matt Windows inspired Gloucestershire's nine-run win against Northants at Bristol. Rallying his side after a poor start, Windows accelerated so well after completing a 110-ball 50 that his last 58 runs occupied just 40 balls and included the plunder of 17 of the 20 runs taken from the final over of the innings, bowled by Jason Brown. Alec Swann, with 83 not out, did his best to haul Northants beyond Gloucestershire's 202 for seven after the visitors' innings had suffered a bad start too. But Northants could only finish on 193 for nine as Gloucestershire defended their score with typical tenacity. Jon Lewis took three for 13 from his ten overs.

Warwickshire made the most of winning a good toss at Taunton, with Mel Betts in particular exploiting the seam movement available to take four for 22. As the pitch dried, batting became a little easier with Richard Johnson helping Keith Parsons

A clinical 108 not out from Matt Windows saw Gloucestershire triumph over Northants.

(72) to turn 115 for eight into a Somerset total of 174. But it was not quite enough as Trevor Penney, with a calm unbeaten 73, guided Warwickshire home by four wickets and with five balls to spare.

4 May 2001
at Bristol
Glamorgan 236 for 6 (50 overs) (JP Maher 142*)
Gloucestershire 240 for 5 (48.3 overs) (MW Alleyne 79*)
Gloucestershire (2 pts) won by five wickets
Gold Award: MW Alleyne

at Northampton
Warwickshire 263 for 7 (50 overs) (NV Knight 101)
Northamptonshire 264 for 3 (47.4 overs)
(ME Hussey 93, JW Cook 86, GP Swann 51*)
Northamptonshire (2 pts) won by seven wickets
Gold Award: ME Hussey

at Worcester
Somerset 179 (49.3 overs) (ID Blackwell 64)
Worcestershire 159 (47.3 overs) (DA Leatherdale 55)
Somerset (2 pts) won by 20 runs
Gold Award: ID Blackwell

A re-run of last year's Benson and Hedges Cup final also went Gloucestershire's way when, at Bristol, the home side maintained their impressive two-year record of not being beaten in a 50-over contest with a five-wicket win over Glamorgan. Jimmy Maher's magnificent unbeaten 142 swept the Welsh county towards their eventual total of 236 for six, but Gloucestershire, despite being 66 for four, rallied through Matt Windows (40) and were then accelerated towards their target thanks to an unbroken stand of 97 between skipper Mark Alleyne (79 not out) and the ever-dependable Jeremy Snape (46 not out).

Despite an electrical failure in the Ken Turner Stand, Northamptonshire still had enough power to see off Warwickshire at Wantage Road. Nick Knight's 101 included a second 50 from just 30 balls, but Northamptonshire had seven wickets and 14 balls remaining when they overhauled the visitors' total of 263 for seven. Mike Hussey (93) and Jeff Cook (86) added 90 before Graeme Swann's 30-ball unbeaten 51 hurried Northants past the winning line.

Worcestershire returned to New Road for the visit of Somerset – and probably wished they had decided to stay at their temporary home of Kidderminster! Worcester's battering by the weather left a pitch offering seam movement and occasional

steep lift, and Ian Blackwell's 64 from 74 balls, containing a six and six fours, was always likely to be a decisive innings on a low-scoring day. In the end Somerset's 179 was too much for Worcestershire, who folded to 154 all out in spite of David Leatherdale's 55 and some spirited hitting from Andy Bichel. Jamie Cox, the Somerset captain, handled his bowlers with aplomb and kept up the pressure on the home batsmen superbly.

5 May 2001
at Northampton
Northamptonshire 219 for 6 (50 overs)
(AL Penberthy 58, AJ Swann 54*)
Somerset 221 for 2 (39.1 overs) (ME Trescothick 109*, J Cox 72)
Somerset (2 pts) won by eight wickets
Gold Award: ME Trescothick

at Edgbaston
Warwickshire 227 for 8 (50 overs) (NV Knight 107*)
Glamorgan 172 (45.5 overs)
Warwickshire (2 pts) won by 55 runs
Gold Award: NV Knight

Marcus Trescothick maintained his enviable early-season form with a brilliant unbeaten 109 at Northampton. His stand of 145 for the second wicket with Jamie Cox (72) brought Somerset home by eight wickets and made Northants' 219 for six, which featured half-centuries from both Tony Penberthy and Alec Swann, look very inadequate.

Another likely England one-day selection, Nick Knight, played the match-winning innings at Edgbaston, where Warwickshire's 227 for eight was too much for Glamorgan. Knight hit 107 not out to anchor the innings, and then Mo Sheikh's three for 27 contributed much to Glamorgan's demise to 172 all out.

6 May 2001
at Bristol
Gloucestershire 263 for 8 (50 overs) (IJ Harvey 92, KJ Barnett 85)
Worcestershire 242 for 7 (50 overs) (A Singh 83, WPC Weston 65)
Gloucestershire (2 pts) won by 21 runs
Gold Award: IJ Harvey

Ian Harvey's highest one-day innings, a violent 92 from just 64 balls, was the highlight of Gloucestershire's 21-run success against Worcestershire at Bristol. Alamgir Sheriyar produced his competition-best four for 19 from ten overs, but Gloucestershire still ran up a forbidding 263 for eight with Kim Barnett (85) sharing in a fourth-wicket stand of 126 with Harvey, who struck three sixes and 11 fours. Anurag Singh (83) and Philip Weston (65) put together an opening stand of 150 in reply, but then Worcestershire could not break Gloucestershire's familiar iron grip in the field and, needing 55 from the last five overs, ended on 242 for seven.

7 May 2001
at Worcester
Worcestershire 138 for 9 (50 overs)
(DA Leatherdale 55)
Warwickshire 142 for 9 (45.1 overs)
Warwickshire (2 pts) won by one wicket
Gold Award: CE Dagnall

at Taunton
Somerset 262 for 9 (50 overs) (ME Trescothick 112,
PD Bowler 53)
Gloucestershire 154 (38.2 overs)
Somerset (2 pts) won by 108 runs
Gold Award: ME Trescothick

at Cardiff
Glamorgan 237 for 6 (50 overs) (A Dale 98*,
MP Maynard 59)
Northamptonshire 238 for 2 (ME Hussey 114*,
MB Loye 77)
Northamptonshire (2 pts) won by eight wickets
Gold Award: ME Hussey

Charlie Dagnall was the unlikely batting hero for Warwickshire at New Road where, thanks to a dramatic one-wicket win, they squeezed through to the Benson and Hedges Cup quarter-finals as one of the two best third-placed teams. Dagnall, marching in at number 11 with his side 105 for nine in reply to Worcestershire's 138 for nine on a difficult pitch, somehow managed to contrive an unbeaten 21 and hit the winning boundary. Mo Sheikh, with 19 not out, was the other hero of the last-wicket stand of 37, but he was known to be able to handle a bat! Dagnall, on the other hand, an unconventional character who glories in being a part-time model and singer in his brother's soul tribute band, had not batted in a serious match for over a year! Earlier, too, he had taken two for 18 from his ten-over stint while fellow paceman Vasbert Drakes had finished with figures of 10-6-14-2. That's how difficult batting was – until Dagnall wielded his willow to considerable effect!

Somerset and Gloucestershire, who had both qualified for the last eight, met at Taunton in a match totally dominated by Marcus Trescothick. Rarely can the Gold Award have been such an obvious choice, with Trescothick first hitting 112 from 99 balls – his third Benson and Hedges Cup century in eight days – as well as taking three for 30 with his medium-pacers and also picking up a sharp slip catch. Somerset's 262 for nine was always going to be too much for a severely-weakened Gloucestershire side missing the injured Smith, Russell, Alleyne and Harvey.

The bat dominated at Cardiff, with Mike Hussey (114 not out) and Mal Loye (77) adding 158 for Northamptonshire's first wicket to trump the earlier efforts of Glamorgan's Adrian Dale (98 not out) and Matthew Maynard (59). Glamorgan's 237 for six was not enough to prevent Northants from completing an eight-wicket victory.

SOUTH DIVISION

1 May 2001
at Hove
Sussex v. **Essex**
Match abandoned without a ball bowled – 1 pt each

at Canterbury
Hampshire 19 for 0 (4 overs)
Kent did not bat
Match abandoned – 1 pt each

at The Oval
Surrey 146 for 2 (35 overs) (IR Ward 71*)
Middlesex did not bat
Match abandoned – 1 pt each

Rain wrecked the opening round of matches in this division, causing a complete washout at Hove, where Sussex were due to take on Essex, and also bringing abandonments at Canterbury and The Oval.

Hampshire had reached just 19 without loss after four overs against Kent when the rain swept in at Canterbury, while Ian Ward's unbeaten 71 was ultimately a wasted effort as Surrey were cut short at 146 for two from 35 overs in the London derby against Middlesex.

2 May 2001
at Southampton Rose Bowl
Hampshire v. **Essex**
Match abandoned without a ball bowled – 1 pt each

at The Oval
Surrey v. **Sussex**
Match abandoned without a ball bowled – 1 pt each

Rain again obliterated the scheduled games in this division, with Hampshire against Essex at Southampton and Surrey against Sussex at The Oval both being abandoned without a ball being bowled.

3 May 2001
at Lord's
Middlesex 146 for 9 (31 overs) (AJ Strauss 61)
Kent 145 for 9 (31 overs)
Middlesex (2 pts) won by 1 run
Gold Award: PN Weekes

The weather-hit division finally got under way with a thriller at Lord's – Middlesex defeating Kent by just one run in a match reduced to 31 overs per side. Kent, however, only had themselves to blame as they chased a Middlesex total of 146 for nine based almost exclusively on Andrew Strauss' 61 and 48 from Owais Shah. After a solid start, Matthew Walker was seemingly guiding Kent towards the winning post but, on 36, the left-hander suddenly slogged across the line at Paul Weekes' off spin, and sparked a collapse which brought the overall loss of three wickets in four balls during a fateful penultimate over. Martin McCague swatted back a full toss to the bowler, and James Hockley was stumped off a legside wide. Now Kent needed nine off the final over and, although James Golding swung one boundary, he was then run out by Chad Keegan's throw from fine leg as he tried to compete a second run from the last ball of the match from Angus Fraser. Weekes, the unlikely hero, finished with four for 17.

4 May 2001
at Chelmsford
Essex 255 for 6 (50 overs) (DDJ Robinson 69, N Hussain 58)
Kent 257 for 7 (49.1 overs) (MJ Walker 106*)
Kent (2 pts) won by three wickets
Gold Award: MJ Walker

at Hove
Sussex 243 for 7 (50 overs) (MW Goodwin 108, MH Yardy 59)
Middlesex 181 for 8 (50 overs) (BL Hutton 52)
Sussex (2 pts) won by 62 runs
Gold Award: MW Goodwin

at Southampton Rose Bowl
Surrey 194 (50 overs)
Hampshire 171 for 9 (50 overs)
Surrey (2 pts) won by 23 runs
Gold Award: BC Hollioake

A wonderful, unbeaten 106 from Matthew Walker inspired Kent to victory against the odds at Chelmsford. In reply to Essex's 255 for six, in which Nasser Hussain and Darren Robinson had put on 129 for the first wicket, Kent were struggling at 102 for five at the halfway stage. But then Walker counter-attacked with both vigour and great self-belief, and was eventually joined by James Golding (33 not out) in a stand of 78 from 63 balls that swept Kent home with five deliveries to spare.

It had been 28 years and 12 matches since Sussex had beaten Middlesex in the Benson and Hedges Cup. Now, thanks to Murray Goodwin's 108 from 116 balls, and a confident 59 from Mike Yardy, their 243 for seven proved too hot for Middlesex to handle at Hove. The visitors, 15 for three early on, rallied slightly through Stephen Fleming and Ben Hutton, but were never really in the hunt and finished on 181 for eight.

A crowd of 1,200 were rewarded with some watery sunshine at the Rose Bowl, but they were denied the sight of a Hampshire victory in the county's first match at their new ground. Surrey's 194 proved too stiff a challenge for Hampshire, who could reach only 171 for nine in reply on a pitch which, although never easy, was still a tribute to groundsman Nigel Gray, considering the appalling weather conditions he had to contend with.

5 May 2001
at The Oval
Essex 222 for 8 (50 overs) (N Hussain 63, SG Law 55)
Surrey 223 for 4 (47 overs) (MR Ramprakash 97*, AJ Stewart 59)
Surrey (2 pts) won by six wickets
Gold Award: MR Ramprakash

A partnership of 151 for the second wicket between Mark Ramprakash (97 not out) and Alec Stewart (59) eased Surrey to a six-wicket win over Essex at The Oval. Nasser Hussain made 63 and Stuart Law 55, but Essex were then pegged back to 222 for eight by Adam Hollioake's four for 36.

6 May 2001
at Lord's
Middlesex 225 for 5 (50 overs) (OA Shah 118*)

Hampshire 200 for 8 (50 overs)
Middlesex (2 pts) won by 25 runs
Gold Award: OA Shah

at Hastings
Kent 175 (48.2 overs) (MJ Walker 52)
Sussex 180 for 5 (48.4 overs)
Sussex (2 pts) won by five wickets
Gold Award: MA Robinson

Owais Shah hit his first century for Middlesex since August 1999 to spearhead victory by 25 runs against Hampshire at Lord's. Shah's unbeaten 118 enabled Middlesex to reach 225 for five and Chad Keegan's three for 39 helped to restrict Hampshire to 200 for eight in reply.

Mark Robinson took the Gold Award at Hastings for his competition-best four for 29, which undermined Kent and held them to just 175 all out. Bas Zuiderent and Will House, against his former county, then figured in a decisive stand of 61 in 13 overs as Sussex claimed victory by five wickets.

7 May
at Canterbury
Kent 265 for 9 (50 overs) (PA Nixon 65*, JB Hockley 55)

Owais Shah's unbeaten 118 against Hampshire was his first century for Middlesex for nearly two years.

Surrey 264 (49.1 overs) (AJ Stewart 92, BC Hollioake 50*)
Kent (2 pts) won by 1 run
Gold Award: PA Nixon

at Southampton Rose Bowl
Sussex 255 for 7 (50 overs) (B Zuiderent 102*, MW Goodwin 87)
Hampshire 195 (46.2 overs) (RA Smith 77*)
Sussex (2 pts) won by 60 runs
Gold Award: B Zuiderent

at Chelmsford
Essex 232 (50 overs)
Middlesex 161 (42 overs) (SP Fleming 73)
Essex (2 pts) won by 71 runs
Gold Award: AP Grayson

Surrey qualified for the last eight despite losing by just one run in a thrilling finish at Canterbury. Kent's 265 for nine was built on a second wicket stand of 102 between James Hockley and Rob Key, and then a 56-ball 65 not out from Paul Nixon, which included two sixes and six fours. Alec Stewart launched the Surrey reply with 92 from 98 balls, but even Ben Hollioake's unbeaten 50 from 45 deliveries could not deny Kent their satisfying victory.

102 not out from the in-form Bas Zuiderent saw Sussex to a comfortable 60-run victory over Hampshire.

Sussex also clinched their quarter-final spot with a convincing 60-run win against Hampshire at Southampton. The in-form Bas Zuiderent (102 not out) and Murray Goodwin (87) led the way to 255 for seven, and not even Robin Smith's unbeaten 77 could get Hampshire close.

Middlesex, however, knowing that a win would have got them through from this group ahead of Sussex, fell to a humbling 71-run defeat against Essex at Chelmsford. Ashley Cowan's big-hitting 45 off 47 balls late in the innings boosted Essex to 232 and Stephen Fleming (73) was the only batsman to thrive in Middlesex's disappointing reply of 161 all out.

QUARTER-FINALS

22 May 2001
at Bristol
Gloucestershire 199 (49.5 overs)
Durham 133 (42.3 overs)
Gloucestershire won by 66 runs
Gold Award: J Lewis

Gloucestershire, the holders, overpowered Durham at Bristol with their traditional tactics on another slow, low surface. Batting first, they were given early impetus by Ian Harvey who, promoted to number three, thrashed 43 from 37 balls. An eventual total of 199 then proved easy enough against a Durham side who struggled from the start and were bowled out for just 133 in the 43rd over.

23 May 2001
at Trent Bridge
Warwickshire 212 for 7 (50 overs) (NV Knight 103)
Nottinghamshire 214 for 4 (46.1 overs)
(DJ Bicknell 117*)
Nottinghamshire won by six wickets
Gold Award: DJ Bicknell

at Taunton
Somerset 210 for 7 (50 overs) (PD Bowler 62, J Cox 62)
Yorkshire 213 for 2 (36.4 overs) (MP Vaughan 125*, DS Lehmann 51*)
Yorkshire won by eight wickets
Gold Award: MP Vaughan

at Hove
Surrey 239 for 7 (50 overs) (AD Brown 108*, MR Ramprakash 53)
Sussex 186 (47.2 overs) (RR Montgomerie 83)

Surrey won by 53 runs
Gold Award: AD Brown

An unbeaten 117 by Darren Bicknell trumped the 103 scored for Warwickshire by Nick Knight and gave Nottinghamshire a six-wicket win at Trent Bridge. Despite Knight's hundred, Warwickshire could reach only 212 for seven from their 50 overs, largely due to Greg Smith's four for 18 off his ten-over allocation. Led by opener Bicknell's 140-ball effort, Notts eased home with almost four overs to spare.

Incredibly, Michael Vaughan hit his first one-day century for Yorkshire in almost 150 limited-overs appearances as the Tykes thrashed Somerset at Taunton. But it was well worth the wait, for Vaughan's 125 not out came from just 128 balls and featured a six and 18 fours. Darren Lehmann's unbeaten 51 also helped Yorkshire cruise past Somerset's 210 for seven as early as the 37th over and, while Vaughan outshone his England colleague Marcus Trescothick, so Darren Gough outbowled his international new-ball partner Andy Caddick. Gough, in fact, took one for 18 from his ten overs and only Peter Bowler and Jamie Cox, who added 108 for Somerset's second wicket, made any headway against the Yorkshire attack.

A well-paced 108 not out by Alistair Brown, from 147 balls, and a more explosive 53 from Mark Ramprakash, enabled Surrey to set Sussex a stiff test at Hove. And, although Richard Montgomerie battled hard with 83, the visitors' total of 239 for seven proved too stern an examination for the home county, who were eventually all out for 186 in the 48th over.

SEMI-FINALS

25 June 2001
at Headingley
Gloucestershire 239 for 7 (50 overs)
(MGN Windows 54)
Yorkshire 142 (37.5 overs)
Gloucestershire won by 97 runs
Gold Award: MGN Windows

at The Oval
Surrey 361 for 8 (50 overs) (MA Butcher 84, AJ Stewart 67, IJ Ward 58)
Nottinghamshire 187 (31.5 overs) (KP Pietersen 78*)
Surrey won by 174 runs
Gold Award: MA Butcher

Holders Gloucestershire marched confidently into their fifth-successive Lord's final, demolishing

Yorkshire by 97 runs at Headingley with a typically energetic all-round performance. For Yorkshire, it was merely more confirmation of their unwanted tag as 'the bridesmaids of domestic one-day cricket' as they lost their seventh semi-final in ten years. Gloucestershire openers Tim Hancock and Kim Barnett gave their team a good, if more than occasionally fortunate, start with a stand of 48 and then Matt Windows (54) played the solid anchor role while others batted more aggressively around him. A total of 239 for seven was certainly competitive, but the real drama of the day was still to unfold. Remarkably, on a dry but blameless pitch, Yorkshire crumbled to 25 for five against the fast-medium pace bowling of James Averis and Ian Harvey, who two days earlier had helped Australia to beat Pakistan in the NatWest Series final at Lord's. Each took two wickets as Yorkshire's top-order paid dearly for being too ambitious too early with their strokeplay. Perhaps the biggest moment, though, came when Darren Lehmann was bizarrely run out for eight when Jack Russell whipped off the bails following a seemingly harmless return from Chris Taylor at mid-off, and the third umpire confirmed that the Australian batsman was standing just outside his crease. In the end, as Gloucestershire chipped away, Yorkshire were bowled out for 142 in the 38th over.

Irresistible batting by Surrey swept them past a disappointing Nottinghamshire challenge in the other semi-final at The Oval. Every member of the Surrey top-six weighed in as the county charged to 361 for eight from their 50 overs – the highest total that a county has made against another in the 30-year history of the competition. The ball was changed three times because its condition became so ragged under an assault led initially by Mark Butcher. The opener included 12 fours in his 86-ball 84, but his innings was in fact the slowest in terms of runs per balls faced. Ian Ward's 58 took just 50 deliveries, in a first-wicket stand of 112, and then came Nadeem Shahid (32 off 21), Alec Stewart (67 off 67), Ally Brown (49 off 37) and Ben Hollioake (39 not out from just 23 balls, with two sixes and two fours). In reply, Nottinghamshire could not match such a display, although Paul Johnson was very unfortunate in being given out lbw to a ball that clearly cannoned into his pads off a thick inside edge. Kevin Pietersen's unbeaten 78 from 67 balls, and a spirited 29 from last man Richard Stemp salvaged some Notts pride, but in the end Surrey romped home by 174 runs, despite missing both Mark Ramprakash and Graham Thorpe through injury.

FINAL – SURREY v. GLOUCESTERSHIRE
14 July 2001 at Lord's

SURREY

Batting

MA Butcher	lbw b Harvey	0
IJ Ward	c Russell, b Hardinges	54
MR Ramprakash	c Taylor, b Alleyne	39
*AJ Stewart	c Snape, b Alleyne	8
AD Brown	c Harvey, b Alleyne	3
AJ Hollioake (capt)	lbw b Ball	39
BC Hollioake	c Alleyne, b Averis	73
AJ Tudor	lbw b Ball	1
MP Bicknell	b Harvey	19
Saqlain Mushtaq	not out	1
ESH Giddins	b Harvey	0
	lb4, w3	7
	(49.5 overs)	244

Bowling

	O	M	R	W
Harvey	9.5	2	43	3
Averis	10	1	65	1
Allyene	10	1	51	3
Ball	10	0	39	2
Hardinges	7	0	31	1
Barnett	3	0	11	-

Fall of Wickets
1-7, 2-71, 3-89, 4-97, 5-118, 6-202, 7-204, 8-242, 9-244

GLOUCESTERSHIRE

Batting

*RC Russell	c Stewart, b Tudor	62
KJ Barnett	b Giddins	7
DR Hewson	c Bicknell, b Saqlain Mushtaq	11
IJ Harvey	lbw b Giddins	1
MGN Windows	b Giddins	10
MW Alleyne (capt)	c & b Saqlain Mushtaq	26
JN Snape	c Stewart, b Tudor	22
CG Taylor	b Saqlain Mushtaq	12
MA Hardinges	c Stewart, b Bicknell	12
MCJ Ball	not out	3
JMM Averis	b Tudor	1
	lb16, w14	30
	(45.5 overs)	197

Bowling — First innings

	O	M	R	W
Bicknell	10	1	38	1
Tudor	9.5	3	28	3
Giddins	8	1	31	3
Saqlain Mushtaq	8	0	37	3
BC Hollioake	10	0	47	-

Fall of Wickets
1-35, 2-68, 3-71, 4-89, 5-131, 6-133, 7-161, 8-190, 9-194

Umpires: JH Hampshire & KE Palmer (TV: B Leadbeater)
Toss: Surrey
Gold Award: BC Hollioake

Surrey won by 47 runs

BENSON AND HEDGES CUP FINAL: 14 JULY 2001 at Lord's

Ben Hollioake's mercurial talent lit up Lord's as Surrey's team of all-stars ended Gloucestershire's glorious run of cup final successes. Victory by 47 runs was a fitting reward for a hard-nosed and thoroughly professional Surrey performance, in which Hollioake junior provided the inspiration.

Gloucestershire were seeking a fifth-successive cup final triumph, after their Lord's 'doubles' of 1999 and 2000, but they never got back into contention once the Hollioake brothers joined forces with their side struggling at 118 for five and took the game away from them. Adam Hollioake played a supporting role with 39, while Ben added an impressively mature 73 to the two one-day Lord's innings of 1997 that made his name. But while the 63 for England against Australia and the 98 to help Surrey beat Kent to take the Benson and Hedges Cup were chiefly innings of attacking abandon, this was a knock that revealed skill and steely resolve as well as the ability to play sublime strokes.

After playing himself in with a sense of responsibility which has not always been his hallmark, Hollioake hit just one four in the first half of his innings. With his elder brother and captain, Hollioake added 84 in 104 balls, and then 38 off 34 deliveries with Martin Bicknell. Two sixes and three more fours flew from Hollioake's bat and it enabled Surrey to post a demanding total of 244 – meaning that Gloucestershire had to score as many runs as any side ever had to win this trophy batting second. 'Ben played fantastically,' said Adam, 'when we came together it could have gone one of two ways because we were looking down the barrel. But Ben showed how much he has come on this year. I was a bystander in the partnership: when it's his day you just let him go.'

Despite a gutsy 62 from makeshift opener Jack Russell, and defiant 20s from Mark Alleyne and Jeremy Snape, it was a task which proved beyond them after Bicknell and Alex Tudor had slowed the initial scoring rate with tight new-ball spells. Ed Giddins' removal of Ian Harvey, for just one, was a bitter blow to Gloucestershire's hopes and Giddins went on to claim three wickets alongside Tudor and the ever-reliable Saqlain Mushtaq. All in all, it was a

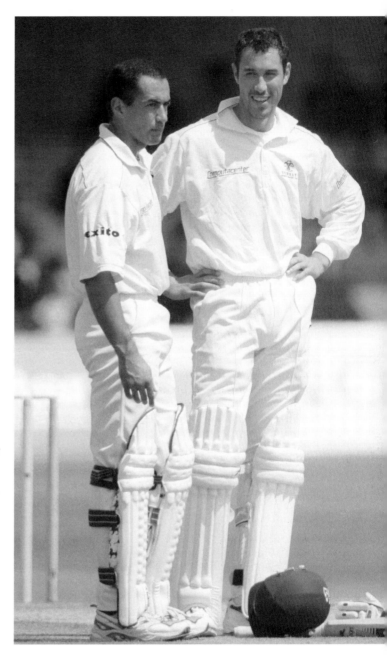

Brothers in arms: Adam and Ben Hollioake combined to thwart Gloucestershire's bid for a fifth-successive Lord's cup final success.

memorable day for Surrey, who imposed their great strength on their opponents from the start, with Ian Ward (54) and Mark Ramprakash (with an attractive 39) putting on 64 following the early loss of Mark Butcher.

CHELTENHAM & GLOUCESTER TROPHY

First Round: 1 and 2 May 2001

at Challow & Childrey CC
Huntingdonshire 252 for 5 (50 overs) (W Larkins 73)
Oxfordshire 175 (46 overs)
Huntingdonshire won by 77 runs
Man of the Match: W Larkins (Huntingdonshire)

at Shrewsbury
Shropshire 196 for 8 (50 overs)
Devon 189 for 7 (50 overs)
Shropshire won by 7 runs
Man of the Match: GJ Bryan (Shropshire)

at Sleaford
Lincolnshire 223 for 6 (50 overs) (JC Harrison 71)
Suffolk 227 for 6 (49 overs) (CWJ Athey 71)
Suffolk won by four wickets
Man of the Match: ID Graham (Suffolk)

at Luton
Nottinghamshire Cricket Board XI 210 for 8
(50 overs) (AFD Jackman 73)
Bedfordshire 212 for 7 (49.4 overs) (DR Clarke 93,
OJ Clayson 56*)
Bedfordshire won by three wickets
Man of the Match: DR Clarke

at Nelson
Yorkshire Cricket Board XI 160 for 6 (50 overs)
Lancashire Cricket Board XI 83 (42 overs)
Yorkshire Cricket Board XI won by 77 runs
Man of the Match: SJ Foster (Yorkshire CB XI)

at Wolstanton
Staffordshire 78 (36.3 overs) (J Wright 5 for 21)
Worcestershire Cricket Board XI 79 for 2 (15.4 overs)
Worcestershire Cricket Board XI won by eight wickets
Man of the Match: M Hodgkiss (Worcestershire CB XI)

at Chippenham
Derbyshire Cricket Board XI 193 for 5 (50 overs)
(JR Benstead 61)
Wiltshire 144 (46.4 overs) (IC Parkin 5 for 24)
Derbyshire Cricket Board XI won by 49 runs
Man of the Match: IC Parkin

at North Perrott Park CC
Wales Minor Counties 159 for 8 (50 overs)
Somerset Cricket Board XI 139 (47.1 overs)
Wales Minor Counties won by 20 runs

Man of the Match: AD Towse (Wales)

at Maidstone
Hampshire Cricket Board XI 29 for 2 (10 overs)
Kent Cricket Board XI did not bat
Match abandoned – no play possible on the second day
Kent Cricket Board XI won a bowl-out by 3–1

at Southgate
Middlesex Cricket Board XI v. **Northumberland**
No play was possible on either day
Middlesex Cricket Board XI won a bowl-out by 5–4

Second Round: 15 May 2001

at March
Derbyshire Cricket Board XI 146 (46.3 overs)
(BL Spendlove 55)
Cambridgeshire 147 for 2 (35.1 overs)
(M Mohammed 54*)
Cambridgeshire won by eight wickets
Man of the Match: M Mohammed

at Bournemouth
Dorset 197 for 9 (50 overs) (M Keech 73)
Bedfordshire 199 for 3 (45 overs) (S Young 78*,
JA Knott 66*)
Bedfordshire won by seven wickets
Man of the Match: S Young

at Brockhampton
Gloucestershire Cricket Board XI 169 for 9 (50 overs)
Herefordshire 172 for 5 (38.3 overs)
Herefordshire won by five wickets
Man of the Match: AR Adams (Herefordshire)

at Welwyn Garden City
Durham Cricket Board XI 172 (47.2 overs)
(A Worthy 72)
Hertfordshire 172 for 8 (50 overs) (I Fletcher 60)
Hertfordshire won by losing fewer wickets
Man of the Match: I Fletcher

at Maidstone
Buckinghamshire 221 for 7 (50 overs)
(MH Richardson 62, RP Lane 55)
Kent Cricket Board XI 222 for 5 (49.5 overs)
(JC Tredwell 71, JDP Bowden 60)
Kent Cricket Board XI won by five wickets
Man of the Match: JC Tredwell

at Richmond
Middlesex Cricket Board XI 218 for 7 (50 overs)

(PE Wellings 60, AGJ Fraser 57*)
Berkshire 219 for 2 (43.1 overs) (TD Fray 87*,
JR Wood 53*)
Berkshire won by eight wickets
Man of the Match: TD Fray

at Hellsdon
Wales Minor Counties 186 for 8 (50 overs)
Norfolk 151 (46.3 overs)
Wales Minor Counties won by 35 runs
Man of the Match: CJ Rogers (Norfolk)

at Northampton
Northamptonshire Cricket Board XI 225 for 7
(50 overs) (TE Coleman 82, DJ Capel 57)
Yorkshire Cricket Board XI 195 for 9 (50 overs)
(MA Wolstenholme 5 for 41)
Northamptonshire Cricket Board XI won by 30 runs
Man of the Match: TE Coleman

at Mildenhall
Essex Cricket Board XI 134 (47.2 overs)
Suffolk 135 for 4 (43.1 overs)
Suffolk won by six wickets
Man of the Match: DJ Callaghan (Suffolk)

at Cheam CC
Surrey Cricket Board XI 246 for 8 (50 overs)
(Z de Bruyn 113*)
Huntingdonshire 187 (46.1 overs)
Surrey Cricket Board XI won by 59 runs
Man of the Match: Z de Bruyn

at Hastings
Sussex Cricket Board XI 307 for 4 (50 overs)
(GRA Campbell 141, PJ Stevens 62)
Shropshire 271 (46.5 overs) (JT Ralph 73,
AN Johnson 62, Asif Din 60)
Sussex Cricket Board XI won by 36 runs
Man of the Match: GRA Campbell

at Coventry
Warwickshire Cricket Board XI 181 (49.4 overs)
(NV Humphrey 58, NJ Pullen 5 for 41)
Leicestershire Cricket Board XI 114 (44 overs)
Warwickshire Cricket Board XI won by 67 runs
Man of the Match: DAT Dalton (Warwickshire CB XI)

at Camborne
Cheshire 256 for 5 (50 overs) (A Hall 66,
RG Hignett 61)
Cornwall 258 for 7 (49.1 overs) (TG Sharp 61,
T Edwards 53*)

Cornwall won by three wickets
Man of the Match: T Edwards

at Kidderminster
Cumberland 111 for 6 (38.4 overs)
Worcestershire Cricket Board XI did not bat
Match abandoned – no play was possible on the first day
Cumberland won a bowl-out by 3–2

Third Round: 27 June 2001

at Luton
Bedfordshire 211 for 9 (50 overs)
Yorkshire 212 for 6 (46.3 overs) (DS Lehmann 88)
Yorkshire won by four wickets
Man of the Match: DS Lehmann

at Reading
Essex 218 for 9 (50 overs) (RC Irani 55)
Berkshire 149 (47.4 overs) (JR Wood 54)
Essex won by 69 runs
Man of the Match: RC Irani

at March
Somerset 271 for 9 (50 overs) (MN Lathwell 101)
Cambridgeshire 221 (49.1 overs) (Ajaz Akhtar 78,
SA Kellett 67)
Somerset won by 50 runs
Man of the Match: Ajaz Akhtar

at Truro
Sussex 253 for 6 (50 overs) (CJ Adams 89*,
MW Goodwin 66)
Cornwall 220 for 8 (50 overs)
Sussex won by 33 runs
Man of the Match: CJ Adams

at Barrow
Cumberland 72 (33.3 overs) (BJ Trott 5 for 18)
Kent 74 for 1 (10.2 overs)
Kent won by nine wickets
Man of the Match: BJ Trott

at Chester-le-Street
Hampshire 262 for 5 (50 overs) (NC Johnson 113*)
Durham 263 for 3 (40.2 overs) (N Peng 119,
PD Collingwood 59*, ML Love 51)
Durham won by seven wickets
Man of the Match: N Peng

at Cardiff
Derbyshire 195 for 9 (50 overs) (DG Cork 50)
Glamorgan 199 for 7 (47.2 overs)

Glamorgan won by three wickets
Man of the Match: DG Cork

at Luctonians CC, Kingsland
Middlesex 278 for 6 (50 overs) (DC Nash 58)
Herefordshire 279 for 7 (49.5 overs) (HV Patel 68, NW Round 66)
Herefordshire won by three wickets
Man of the Match: HV Patel

at Hertford
Worcestershire 336 for 8 (50 overs) (GA Hick 155, A Singh 79)
Hertfordshire 69 (25.5 overs) (DJ Pipe 8ct as wicket-keeper)
Worcestershire won by 267 runs
Man of the Match: GA Hick

at Canterbury
Kent Cricket Board XI 237 for 2 (50 overs) (PS Lazenbury 88*, JC Tredwell 57)
Warwickshire 238 for 3 (39.3 overs) (DP Ostler 82*, DR Brown 70)
Warwickshire won by seven wickets
Man of the Match: PS Lazenbury

at Northampton
Northamptonshire Cricket Board XI 277 for 6 (50 overs) (DE Paynter 104, TE Coleman 68)
Northamptonshire 278 for 1 (41.2 overs) (MB Loye 124*, RJ Warren 70*, ME Hussey 59)
Northamptonshire won by nine wickets
Man of the Match: MB Loye

at Mildenhall
Suffolk 87 (32.3 overs) (RJ Logan 5 for 24)
Nottinghamshire 89 for 1 (21.5 overs)
Nottinghamshire won by nine wickets
Man of the Match: RJ Logan

at Guildford
Surrey Cricket Board XI 158 (45.1 overs)
Surrey 160 for 0 (27.1 overs) (MA Butcher 73*, IJ Ward 70*)
Surrey won by ten wickets
Man of the Match: ESH Giddins

at Horsham
Gloucestershire 238 for 9 (50 overs) (MGN Windows 82)
Sussex Cricket Board XI 143 (39.2 overs)
Gloucestershire won by 95 runs
Man of the Match: MGN Windows

at Swansea
Leicestershire 332 for 4 (50 overs) (JM Dakin 179, BF Smith 64*)
Wales Minor Counties 199 for 8 (50 overs) (RW Sylvester 73)
Leicestershire won by 133 runs
Man of the Match: JM Dakin

at Blackpool
Warwickshire Cricket Board XI 163 (47 overs) (GF Shephard 73*, PJ Martin 5 for 16)
Lancashire 165 for 3 (34.5 overs) (JJ Haynes 59*)
Lancashire won by seven wickets
Man of the Match: GF Shephard

There was little doubt about the shock result of cricket's equivalent to FA Cup third round day – the thrilling three-wicket victory by Herefordshire against Middlesex at the home of Luctonians Cricket Club.

Overhauling Middlesex's 50-over total of 278 for six with just one ball to spare, Herefordshire became only the 11th minor county team to beat first-class opponents in 38 years. What is more, their great triumph earned them a fourth-round tie against close neighbours Worcestershire.

In retrospect, Middlesex might have chosen to bowl first rather than to bat after winning the toss, because an otherwise easy-paced pitch perhaps offered a little bit more to the bowlers in the morning. Nevertheless, Middlesex posted a decent score and were stunned when Harshad Patel and Nathan Round, the Herefordshire openers, began to make a mockery of it by thrashing 79 from the first ten overs of the reply. The 20-year-old Round's 93-ball 66 included ten fours, while Patel was scarcely slower to his 68. Ismael Dawood's 34 kept up the momentum, despite a worthy spell of one for 15 from ten overs by Phil Tufnell, and in the end it was Nick Davies' dashing unbeaten 39, off just 27 deliveries, which swept Herefordshire to their target. Nine runs had been needed from the final over, but the part-timers were not to be denied their little niche in cricketing history.

Elsewhere, there were brave performances from Bedfordshire, Berkshire, Cambridgeshire, Cornwall, and both the Northamptonshire and Kent County Board teams – but there were no further surprises.

Bedfordshire scored 211 for nine against Yorkshire at Luton, and then kept the first-class county waiting until the 47th over of their reply before victory was confirmed. Shaun Rashid took four for 54 and Yorkshire might have been in some bother but for an innings of 88 from Darren Lehmann.

Berkshire held Essex to 218 for nine at Reading and were then 109 for three in reply, with skipper Julian Wood hitting 54, before slumping to 149 all out. Cambridgeshire bravely scored 221 at March, after Mark Lathwell's 103-ball 101 had pushed Somerset up to a total of 271 for nine, with Simon Kellett (67) and Ajaz Akhtar (78) leading the resistance.

At Truro, Cornwall came within 33 runs of Sussex's 253 for six, and there was good batting too from the Northants and Kent Board XIs at Northampton and Canterbury respectively. David Paynter, the great grandson of Eddie Paynter, cracked 104 from 106 balls in the 'local derby' against Northamptonshire, and with Tim Coleman (68) added 159 for the first wicket in an eventual total of 277 for six. The county side, however, knocked off the runs with just one wicket lost, and Mal Loye ended on 124 not out. At Canterbury it was Paul Lazenbury, with an unbeaten 88 from 93 balls, who caught the eye as the Kent Board totalled

Jon Dakin smashed 179 off just 145 balls as Leicestershire cruised to victory against Wales Minor Counties.

237 for two against Warwickshire. James Tredwell, aged 19, also impressed with 57, but Dominic Ostler (82 not out) and Dougie Brown (70) made light work of the Board XI's bowling.

Other noteworthy performances came from Jon Dakin, who hit 179 off 145 balls, with ten sixes and 15 fours, as Leicestershire defeated Wales by 133 runs at Swansea, and from Graeme Hick, whose 155 helped Worcestershire crush Hertfordshire by 267 runs.

In the two all-county ties, Glamorgan beat Derbyshire, despite 50 and four for 35 from Dominic Cork, while Durham's Nicky Peng hit a brilliant 119 to trump an earlier innings of 113 not out by Hampshire's Zimbabwean Neil Johnson. With both Paul Collingwood and Martin Love hitting fifties, Durham breezed past Hampshire's 262 for five with almost ten overs remaining.

Fourth Round: 11 and 12 July 2001

at Worcester
Herefordshire 210 (47 overs) (R Nagra 105)
Worcestershire 214 for 3 (37.1 overs) (GA Hick 101*)
Worcestershire won by seven wickets
Man of the Match: R Nagra

at Taunton
Glamorgan 269 for 6 (50 overs) (MP Maynard 93*, MJ Powell 52)
Somerset 270 for 3 (41.4 overs) (ME Trescothick 121, J Cox 63*)
Somerset won by seven wickets
Man of the Match: ME Trescothick

at Canterbury
Northamptonshire 200 (49.1 overs) (JP Taylor 57, A Symonds 5 for 21)
Kent 204 for 4 (47.5 overs) (DP Fulton 63)
Kent won by six wickets
Man of the Match: A Symonds

at Bristol
Durham 232 (49.2 overs) (JJB Lewis 65*)
Gloucestershire 229 for 9 (50 overs) (MGN Windows 56)
Durham won by 3 runs
Man of the Match: GD Bridge (Durham)

at Edgbaston
Essex 160 (49.3 overs)
Warwickshire 161 for 5 (43.1 overs) (DR Brown 52*)
Warwickshire won by five wickets
Man of the Match: NM Carter (Warwickshire)

at Headingley
Surrey 243 (50 overs) (IJ Ward 81, MR Ramprakash 51)
Yorkshire 244 for 4 (48.1 overs) (GM Fellows 80*,
C White 73*)
Yorkshire won by six wickets
Man of the Match: GM Fellows

at Old Trafford
Sussex 151 (45.1 overs)
Lancashire 155 for 3 (35.2 overs) (A Flintoff 65*)
Lancashire won by seven wickets
Man of the Match: A Flintoff

at Trent Bridge
Nottinghamshire 176 (40.4 overs)
Leicestershire 179 for 4 (42.1 overs) (VJ Wells 54*)
Leicestershire won by six wickets
Man of the Match: VJ Wells

Herefordshire's brave run in the competition was
ended by the broad blade of Graeme Hick's bat at
New Road – but not before the minor county had
grabbed some more glory for themselves. Ravi
Nagra, in particular, a 22-year-old pharmacy student

at Brighton University, made a brilliant century off
93 balls to claim a little place for himself in the 38-
year history of the competition. Nagra, moreover,
was called up only the previous day when Andre
Adams pulled out with a wrist injury, and responded
to his big chance by striking two sixes and 12 fours
in his 105 off 107 deliveries. Nathan Round, the 20-
year-old opener, also added to his growing
reputation with a well-made 41, and Herefordshire's
total of 210 was disappointing only in the way they
fell away from being 179 for four. Round then ran
out Philip Weston, the Worcestershire opener, when
just ten was on the board, but Hick – first with
Anurag Singh and then with Vikram Solanki – made
sure there were no more upsets by striding to 101
not out off just 94 balls.

A belligerent 121 from Marcus Trescothick at
Taunton, containing 20 boundaries and compiled
from only 83 balls, swept Somerset into the quarter-
finals at the expense of Glamorgan. Such was the
brilliance of Trescothick's assault that Somerset had
more than eight overs in hand when they went past
Glamorgan's total of 269 for six. The supporting
acts, Peter Bowler and Jamie Cox, were no slouches
either with 43 and 63 not out respectively – Cox
including three sixes in his 55-ball effort. Earlier,
Glamorgan had been boosted by a 93-run, fifth-
wicket stand between Matthew Maynard (93 not
out) and Mike Powell (52).

Andrew Symonds was the star turn at Canterbury
as Kent brushed aside Northamptonshire by six
wickets. Symonds, brought in as the injured Daryll
Cullinan's replacement as overseas player, first took
five for 21 with his whippy medium-pacers and then
eased himself to 39 not out from 40 balls as Kent
sauntered past Northants' total of 200. It was
temporary coach John Inverarity's final match in
charge before returning to his teaching job in
Western Australia, and he left the county in rude
health after a highly successful three-month sojourn.
Northants only recovered from 92 for seven thanks
to Paul Taylor's maiden one-day fifty and an equally
defiant 35 from skipper David Ripley, but Kent were
set on their way by David Fulton's 63 at the head of
a solid batting effort.

Holders Gloucestershire were put out of the
competition by Durham at Bristol, their surprise
three-run defeat much the result of a skilful ten-over
spell of slow left-arm bowling by young Graeme

An innings of 121 off a mere 83 balls by Marcus Trescothick
saw Somerset ease past Glamorgan's challenging target of
269 with plenty to spare.

Bridge in his first senior one-day match. Bridge took three for 44, taking his wickets at vital times, while Mark Davies was another youngster to perform above expectations – conceding just 31 runs from his ten-over stint and sending back Gloucestershire's top-scorer Matt Windows (56) in the process. Windows and Chris Taylor had seemed to be setting up a Gloucestershire victory as they added 74 in 17 overs, taking their side to 179 for three in reply to Durham's 232. But then Davies struck, and with Bridge dismissing both Jeremy Snape and Jack Russell, the holders suddenly found that needing 33 from the last five overs with five wickets in hand was not a straightforward task. Martyn Ball tried to rescue the situation with some lusty swings, but in the end he could manage only a single from the final ball when a boundary was required.

Unhappy Essex slipped out of the competition at Edgbaston, where Neil Carter inspired Warwickshire to a five-wicket win. Carter, yet another South African with a British passport, took four for 21 with his left-arm fast-medium and then opened the batting too, striking 40 from 43 balls. Essex's 160 was totally inadequate, and a fifth-wicket stand of 63 between Ronnie Irani and James Foster was the only time they looked like making a game of it. Dougie Brown finished on 52 not out as he and Trevor Penney rallied Warwickshire to victory from a shaky 93 for five.

Yorkshire's fifth-wicket pair of Craig White and Gary Fellows added an unbroken 160 to upset Surrey, who had posted a decent total of 243 at Headingley. At 84 for four the Yorkshire cause looked to be a fading one, but Fellows and White fought their way through some murky light on the first evening of the weather-affected game before emerging in the sunshine of the reserve day to make short work of the target. Fellows took the Man of the Match award for his unbeaten 80, while White finished up on 73 not out. Surrey's total had been based on a second-wicket partnership of 92 between Ian Ward (81) and Mark Ramprakash (51).

Lancashire swept aside Sussex at Old Trafford to make sure of their place in the last eight. A gusty wind made batting difficult on the first day of another match to go over into a second day, and Sussex's 151 was always going to be too little once Andy Flintoff got going the next morning. John Wood did a useful job as a pinch-hitter, with 25 off 24 balls to add to his three wickets, but it was Flintoff's unbeaten 65 – including pulls for six off both Jason Lewry and Chris Adams – which powered Lancashire home.

Leicestershire became the first side in almost a year to beat Nottinghamshire in a one-day match on their home patch at Trent Bridge, bowling them out for 176 and then knocking off the runs with some comfort in a highly competent all-round display. Unsettled weather meant there were ten interruptions to play before the match was finished shortly before midday on the reserve day, with Vince Wells guiding his Leicestershire side home by six wickets with an unbeaten 54.

QUARTER-FINALS: 24 AND 25 JULY 2001

at Leicester
Leicestershire 297 for 9 (50 overs) (Shahid Afridi 67)
Worcestershire 179 (44.5 overs) (SJ Rhodes 56*)
Leicestershire won by 118 runs
Man of the Match: Shahid Afridi

at Canterbury
Somerset 263 for 8 (50 overs) (M Burns 71, ID Blackwell 50)
Kent 211 (46.2 overs) (RWT Key 58)
Somerset won by 52 runs
Man of the Match: M Burns

at Headingley
Yorkshire 188 (46.3 overs) (A McGrath 82)
Warwickshire 189 for 6 (44.1 overs) (TL Penney 58*)
Warwickshire won by four wickets
Man of the Match: TL Penney

at Blackpool
Durham 198 for 8 (50 overs) (PD Collingwood 60)
Lancashire 199 for 3 (38.4 overs) (NH Fairbrother 73, A Flintoff 72*)
Lancashire won by seven wickets
Man of the Match: A Flintoff

Leicestershire, with the remarkable Shahid Afridi again to the fore, demolished Worcestershire at New Road to march into the Cheltenham & Gloucester Trophy semi-finals with the 17th win from their last 19 games of limited-overs cricket. Afridi, with another devastating display of hitting, struck four sixes and six fours in his 67 as Leicestershire raced to 150 for two by the 20th over. From then on, the result was never seriously in doubt. Leicestershire's deep batting order ensured that the early momentum was not lost, despite the lack of any other major contribution, and in the end Worcestershire could only muster 179 in reply to Leicestershire's 50-over total of 297 for nine.

More than 3,000 of the Kent faithful trooped away disconsolately from Canterbury after seeing their team outplayed by a solid-looking Somerset side. From the moment that Marcus Trescothick was dropped at slip on 12, before accelerating on to 43, Kent were always playing catch-up as Somerset reached 263 for eight with Mike Burns top-scoring with 71 and Ian Blackwell offering a hard-hit 50 from 49 balls. Andy Caddick then plucked out Kent's two openers and Keith Parsons tore out the middle-order in a spell of three for 38. Rob Key tried his best to swim against the tide, with 58, and both Matthew Fleming and Min Patel hit out bravely. In the end, though, Kent were dismissed for 211 and defeated by 52 runs.

Yorkshire followers were even more disgruntled as they left Headingley after witnessing a four-wicket defeat to a Warwickshire side that had been humiliated in a Norwich Union League match at the same venue two days before. The return of Test players Darren Gough and Craig White to the team had little effect, and their presence simply added to Yorkshire's sense of disappointment. Poor cricket, however, was the root source of their problems on the day, against a team they had shot out for just 59 in that previous match. Batting first, Yorkshire seemed to have been put into a match-winning position by Anthony McGrath's fine 82 – especially as the pitch was not a straightforward one to bat on. But then, from 173 for five, Yorkshire lost their last five wickets for just 15 runs – with three run outs – and also committed the cardinal one-day sin of leaving 3.3 of their overs allocation unbowled. Warwickshire, in reply, stuttered somewhat to 100 for five, before Keith Piper helped Trevor Penney add 30, after which Ashley Giles stayed to the end while Penney picked off the loose balls and scampered gleefully between the wickets to fashion a match-clinching 58 not out.

Lancashire switched their quarter-final against Durham to Blackpool because of a three-day Robbie Williams concert at Old Trafford. That decision drew initial criticism, but all that was forgotten when Lancashire eased the worries of a troubled season by completing an emphatic seven-wicket victory in the sunshine in front of a 5,000-strong full house. Only Paul Collingwood, with 60, looked capable of breaking out of the straitjacket that Lancashire's excellent out-cricket put on Durham, and a total of 198 for eight never looked like being sufficient. So it proved, despite the early exit of Mike Atherton, as Andrew Flintoff (72 not out) and Neil Fairbrother (73) added 136 for the third wicket

to set the seal on what Fairbrother called 'our best performance of the season'.

SEMI-FINALS: 11–13 AUGUST

at Taunton
Warwickshire 228 for 8 (50 overs)
Somerset 230 for 6 (46 overs) (KP Dutch 61*)
Somerset won by four wickets
Man of the Match: KP Dutch

at Leicester
Lancashire 190 for 9 (50 overs) (WK Hegg 60)
Leicestershire 194 for 3 (29.5 overs) (Shahid Afridi 95, VJ Wells 64*)
Leicestershire won by seven wickets
Man of the Match: Shahid Afridi

A daring and unbroken partnership of 100 between Keith Dutch and Rob Turner swept Somerset dramatically and thrillingly past Warwickshire's challenge in their Cheltenham & Gloucester Trophy semi-final at Taunton. The home crowd were in raptures as Dutch, with 61 not out from 54 balls, and Turner (42 not out) raised hopes of a first Somerset trophy since 1983. Warwickshire's 50-over

A murderous innings of 95 off just 58 balls propelled Leicestershire into the final at the expense of Lancashire.

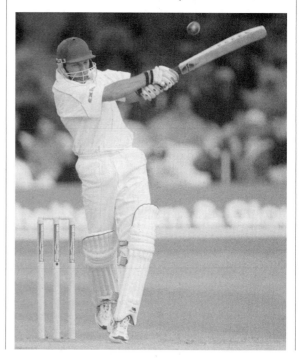

total of 228 for eight, based on a 101-run opening stand between Nick Knight and Mark Wagh, looked a match-winning score as Somerset first slumped to six for three against the new ball and then to 130 for six after a mini-revival launched by Jamie Cox (47) and Keith Parsons (31). Ian Blackwell had also contributed with a useful 30, but the target still seemed a long way off when Dutch marched in to join Turner. The former Middlesex all-rounder, however, grabbed the glory in the first semi-final appearance of his career – and soon the cider was flowing in the Taunton bars.

Lancashire captain John Crawley was vilified by both the national and local press after deciding to bat first in seam-friendly conditions and then seeing his side collapse to 38 for five against the swing and movement of Scott Boswell (four for 44) and Jimmy Ormond (two for 16). But, after rallying to 190 for nine through the plucky efforts of Warren Hegg (60) and Chris Schofield (42), in a match which spilled over into the reserve day because of a late start at 3.15pm, Lancashire were blown away by an astonishing assault from Shahid Afridi. The Pakistani, playing without inhibition and few glances at the coaching manual, trusted to both eye and luck as he swung six sixes and eight fours in an amazing 58-ball 95. That his one-man blitz came after he had seen both Trevor Ward and Darren Stevens depart with just nine runs on the board was even more remarkable. 'I thought I should start to play my own game,' said Afridi afterwards, with classic *sang froid*. When he finally departed, caught on the mid-wicket boundary as he tried to complete his hundred with yet another six, the total was 161 and all that remained was for Vince Wells, the Leicestershire captain, to go to 64 not out and complete the formality of leading his side into an eagerly-anticipated Lord's final with Somerset.

FINAL: 1 SEPTEMBER 2001 at Lord's

Somerset secured their first domestic trophy since the days of Botham, Richards and Garner in 1983 when they overpowered Leicestershire by dint of controlled aggression in their batting and a steadier bowling display than their opponents. Keith Parsons, a 28-year-old journeyman all-rounder born in Taunton, had the greatest day of his cricketing life as he boosted Somerset's total to 271 for five with three sixes and three fours in his unbeaten 52-ball 60. He then took the wickets of both Trevor Ward, for a hard-hit 54, and Leicestershire captain Vince Wells, for three. Shahid Afridi, whose manic hitting at the top of the order Somerset so feared, managed three fours in a ten-ball 20 before being caught off a steepling leading edge. Darren Maddy (49) then batted well in the company of Ward to set up Leicestershire, at 105 for one, for a determined assault on the day's prize – but wickets began to fall with regularity as Somerset seized a control that they never relinquished. Leicestershire were bowled out for 230 in the 46th over, to lose by 41 runs, but perhaps they had known it was not to be their day when the unfortunate Scott Boswell sent down a nightmarish 14-ball second over that, sadly for the bowler, will go down in the annals of cup final

Celebration time for Somerset as they secured their county's first trophy success since 1983.

A 52-ball innings of 60 from Keith Parsons powered Somerset to a daunting total of 271.

incidents. Boswell, with his strange round-arm action, could not control either the ball's swing or his own nerves and there were eight wides in his fateful over – five of them in succession. After two overs costing 23 runs, including three boundaries and nine wides, he was never seen again. Peter Bowler and Jamie Cox batted sensibly, after the early loss of Marcus Trescothick, and built the base on which Parsons and Rob Turner (37 not out) flourished in a 95-run, match-winning partnership in little more than 13 overs. For Somerset, it was a great relief after their 1999 defeat to Gloucestershire in the then NatWest Trophy final; that it also came without major contributions from either Trescothick or Andy Caddick, whose ten steady overs for 33 runs were wicketless, merely added to the warm pleasure felt in the cider county.

FINAL – SOMERSET v. LEICESTERSHIRE
1 September 2001 at Lord's

SOMERSET

Batting

ME Trescothick	c Shahid Afridi, b Ormond	18
PD Bowler	b Shahid Afridi	42
J Cox (capt)	b Shahid Afridi	44
ID Blackwell	b Shahid Afridi	15
M Burns	c Maddy, b Wells	21
KA Parsons	not out	60
*RJ Turner	not out	37
KP Dutch		
RL Johnson		
AR Caddick		
PS Jones		
	lb19, w15	34
	(for 5 wickets) 50 overs	**271**

Bowling

	O	M	R	W
Ormond	10	2	38	1
Boswell	2	0	23	-
DeFreitas	10	1	57	-
Wells	10	1	40	1
Maddy	8	0	47	-
Shahid Afridi	10	0	47	3

Fall of Wickets
1-40, 2-107, 3-132, 4-149, 5-176

LEICESTERSHIRE

Batting

TR Ward	b Parsons	54
Shahid Afridi	c Turner, b Johnson	20
DL Maddy	c & b Dutch	49
VJ Wells (capt)	c Turner, b Parsons	3
BF Smith	c Trescothick, b Dutch	15
DI Stevens	lbw b Jones	23
*ND Burns	c Turner, b Jones	6
Aftab Habib	c Dutch, b Blackwell	15
PAJ DeFreitas	b Johnson	14
J Ormond	not out	18
SAJ Boswell	b Jones	2
	lb3, w2, nb6	11
	(45.4 overs)	**230**

Bowling

	O	M	R	W
Caddick	10	2	33	-
Johnson	8	0	39	2
Jones	7.4	0	40	3
Parsons	6	0	40	2
Dutch	10	0	50	2
Blackwell	4	0	25	1

Fall of Wickets
1-20, 2-105, 3-111, 4-142, 5-156, 6-171, 7-182, 8-194, 9-225

Umpires: B Dudleston & G Sharp
Toss: Somerset
Man of the Match: KA Parsons

Somerset won by 41 runs

PAKISTAN

England in Pakistan
Pakistan Domestic First-Class Season
Pakistan Domestic One-Day Season
First-Class Averages

ENGLAND IN PAKISTAN
By Jonathan Agnew

Governor's XI v. England XI
20 October 2000 at National Stadium,
Karachi (floodlit)
England XI 323 for 7 (50 overs) (ME
Trescothick 102, GA Hick 82)
Governor's XI 242 (46.4 overs) (Salim
Elahi 120, D Gough 5 for 32)
England XI won by 81 runs

A pleasant, gentle opening game for England's players who had been kicking their heels following their defeat in the ICC Knock-Out competition in Kenya. Marcus Trescothick gave an early indication that he would enjoy the slow, flat pitches of the subcontinent by scoring 102 as he and Hussain (44) added 126 for the second wicket. Graeme Hick clubbed two sixes and nine fours in his 82.

Darren Gough warmed up for the serious action to follow, taking five wickets for only 32 runs.

Pakistan 'A' v. England XI
22 October 2000 at National Stadium, Karachi
Pakistan 'A' 169 for 7 (50 overs) (Naumanullah 64)
England 170 for 0 (29.4 overs) (ME Trescothick 59rh,
AJ Stewart 50rh)
England XI won by ten wickets

This was hardly a serious test, which was illustrated by the fact that both English openers – Stewart and Trescothick – retired once they had completed their half centuries. Ashley Giles and Andy Caddick both claimed three wickets as the easiest of victories was completed with 20 overs to spare.

ONE-DAY INTERNATIONALS

The subcontinent is home to the most passionate cricket followers on the planet, so it came as something of a surprise to learn that, up to this moment, floodlit cricket in Pakistan had never been played outside of Lahore. It was there, in the 1996 World Cup final, that Sri Lanka overcame the Australians; not least because the evening dew made

Marcus Trescothick started the tour in tremendous form with a century and a half-century in the opening two matches.

fielding second an absolute lottery. That, and swarms of insects that literally choked and blinded the players, was also to blight this series of three one-day internationals; so much so that it leaves one to wonder quite how much further the administrators can trivialize this version of the game – and the floodlit version in particular – in the interest solely of making money. The public will eventually have enough of putting up with second-grade cricket.

England's victory in the first match was

Pakistan relied on their attacking batsmen, Shahid Afridi and Saeed Anwar, to recover from their defeat in the first international to take the series 2–1.

Previous page: The victorious England team celebrate after their remarkable victory in Karachi.

England captain Nasser Hussain put his miserable form of the previous summer behind him, hitting 73 to lead England's charge to victory in the first one-day international.

burly Lancastrian could not see England all the way to their target – he was caught with just three runs required – but he had made a strong point and, more importantly, England held an early lead in the series.

On to Lahore, and a sensible anti-dew measure in starting the match early. Moin Khan won the toss and, having learned a painful lesson in Karachi, decided to field first. In fact, the dew hardly came into it as Pakistan successfully chased England's meagre 211 for nine. This time, it was swarming insects – attracted to the floodlights – that created the problems for the fielders.

They did not bother Shahid Afridi, however. The unorthodox, medium-paced leg-spinner nipped out five Englishmen for only 40 runs on a pitch that gave him some assistance. This gave rise to more fears about the quality of the Test tracks to come, as all 11 wickets in the match were taken by spinners.

At least the series was now level with just the decider to play in Rawalpindi. The excitement proved to be too much for many of the locals, however, and a riot amongst the spectators had to be broken up with a serious cloud of tear gas which then drifted slowly across the ground and into the players' eyes! On another pitch that allowed sharp spin, it was Saqlain's turn to get amongst the wickets. After Nasser Hussain fell to a ghastly leg before decision, the off spinner took five for 20 as England were bowled out in only 43 overs. Once again Inzamam came to the fore, making 60, as Pakistan romped home with six wickets and more than six overs to spare. The problems caused by Pakistan's spinners on wearing surfaces was to be the main talking-point as England turned their minds to the Test series.

remarkable. In chasing 305 to win, they recorded the fourth-highest score ever to win a one-day international when batting second – and that after having been 13 for two. The pitch was an absolute belter – wonderful for this form of the game – but Pakistan's bowlers and fielders were so hampered by the wet, dewy ball that the game was on the verge of becoming a farce. In no way should that understate England's achievement, but the hopelessness of Pakistan's predicament was somewhat buried beneath the avalanche of praise heaped upon Nasser's troops.

It was a day for the big men. First Inzamam led the way for Pakistan as England fielded in temperatures exceeding 40 degrees C. Inzy plundered six fours in his 87-ball innings of 71, but the fireworks were provided by young Abdur Razzaq – an all-rounder of huge potential – whose 75 not out came from only 40 deliveries. England came close to wilting under the onslaught and that probably accounted for the early loss of both Stewart and Trescothick. Happily, after a miserable summer with the bat, the recovery was led by Hussain, whose 73 provided a foundation for the stroke players to build upon. Hick made 56, but it was Andrew Flintoff who truly rose to the occasion hitting back at those who had tormented him about his weight and fitness problems. True, he may have been unable to bowl because of injury, but he swung the bat to awesome effect, hitting three sixes and six fours on his way to a swashbuckling 84 that came off just 60 deliveries. It was a desperate shame that the

Match One
24 October 2000 at National Stadium, Karachi (floodlit)
Pakistan 304 for 9 (50 overs) (Abdur Razzaq 75*, Inzamam-ul-Haq 71)

England 306 for 5 (47.2 overs (A Flintoff 84, N Hussain 73, GP Thorpe 64*, GA Hick 56)
England won by five wickets
Man of the Match: A Flintoff

Match Two
27 October 2000 at Gaddafi Stadium, Lahore (floodlit)
England 211 for 9 (50 overs) (ME Trescothick 65, N Hussain 54, Shahid Afridi 5 for 40)
Pakistan 214 for 2 (44.2 overs) (Shahid Afridi 61, Salim Elahi 58*)
Pakistan won by eight wickets
Man of the Match: Shahid Afridi

Matthew Hoggard, the young Yorkshire fast bowler, impressed in the warm-up matches in Pakistan, but failed to gain Test selection.

Match Three
30 October 2000 at Pindi Stadium, Rawalpindi (floodlit)
England 158 (42.5 overs) (Saqlain Mushtaq 5 for 20)
Pakistan 161 for 4 (43.3 overs) (Inzamam-ul-Haq 60*)
Pakistan won by six wickets
Man of the Match: Saqlain Mushtaq

Pakistan Cricket Board's Patron XI v. England XI
1–4 November 2000 at Pindi Stadium, Rawalpindi
PCB Patron's XI 237 (Qaiser Abbas 71, MJ Hoggard 5 for 62) and 169
England XI 433 (C White 120, GP Thorpe 88, GA Hick 81)
England XI won by an innings and 27 runs

Matthew Hoggard's seam bowling dominated a match that was played in ideal, English conditions: hardly similar to those England could expect to play on in the Test series. With the ball nipping about sharply, Hoggard claimed nine wickets for 102 in a match that England won with consummate ease. Thorpe and Hick both scored half-centuries, but the 120 scored by Craig White, as England rattled up 433, will have pleased the selectors more than anything else.

Governor's XI v. England XI
8–11 November 2000 at Arbab Niaz Stadium, Peshawar
Governor's XI 224 (Mohammad Hussain 65, Yasir Hameed 57) and 170 (Akhtar Sarfraz 53, Naumanullah 50)
England XI 315 (ME Trescothick 93, AJ Stewart 59) and 80 for 2
England XI won by eight wickets

First Test
15–19 November 2000 at Gaddafi Stadium, Lahore

It had been 13 years since England had last played a Test match in Pakistan. Their previous visit had been marred by controversy, culminating in an ugly bust-up between the umpire, Shakoor Rana, and Mike Gatting in Faisalabad. After such a long interlude, it was inevitable that diplomacy would play almost as important a part in England's mission as the cricket itself.

Even after such a long time, the major talking points remained the same. Nasser Hussain had been the victim of a couple of poor umpiring decisions in the build-up to the opening Test, and there was the suspicion that Pakistan would deliberately attempt to derail the tourists by producing specially

Yousuf Youhana was Pakistan's Man of the Series, scoring two centuries and a fifty in the three Tests. England simply could not get him out!

prepared, dusty pitches for their wealth of experienced spinners. Indeed, there was a widely held belief that the match at the Gaddafi Stadium would barely last four days.

In fact, England confounded the critics by controlling the game from the outset. Pakistan came to within a whisker of following on – at one stage they were eight runs short with only two wickets in hand – but Yousuf Youhana's magnificent century swept them to safety and ensured that the opening match ended in a stalemate.

If it was entertainment you were seeking, this was not a match to sit and watch. Even the Barmy Army was silent virtually throughout – although a ban on alcohol might also have had a welcome effect. The outfield was green and lush – it was also stupefyingly slow, which made the boundary rope virtually out of reach to all but the cleanest strikers of the ball. The over rate slowed to a crawl at times as Pakistan, in this case, knew that bad light would invariably stop play at the end of the day.

As is usually the case in this part of the world, the toss was crucial. Had Hussain called incorrectly, he would have condemned his team to batting last on the wearing strip. Who knows: the outcome of this series might have been very different had that been the case. Instead, however, Hussain won the toss and batted first. Midway through the first afternoon, Mike Atherton and Marcus Trescothick had posted their second successive opening stand of 100 or more – the last time that happened for England was ten years ago.

At tea, England were magnificently placed on 148 for one, but, helped by some rash strokes, Saqlain Mushtaq took four for 19 in 15 overs to reduce the visitors to 195 for four. Both openers fell to the sweep: Trescothick for 71 and Atherton for 73. Stewart was completely deceived by Saqlain's quicker ball and was leg before for just three, and although Hussain had been short of luck throughout the year, he could blame no-one but himself for the grotesque attempt to hit Saqlain over the top that produced a catch for Wasim in the covers. England were left to reflect on a wasted opportunity to put Pakistan under real pressure.

The next day, however, Graham Thorpe – who had been dropped on two – rescued the situation with an innings of consummate concentration. He lost Graeme Hick early – again to Saqlain – but Craig White strode confidently to the middle and confirmed his rapid development as a genuine Test all-rounder. Thorpe's approach was largely to nudge

Mike Atherton narrowly escapes a caught and bowled chance to Saqlain Mushtaq, who bowled 74 overs in England's first innings in Lahore and took all eight wickets to fall.

and run, while White hit two sixes and nine fours in the partnership of 166 in 60 overs. Try as hard as he could, Thorpe simply could not find the boundary – so much so that he struck just one boundary in his century. In 1,513 previous Tests, no hundred by anybody had ever contained such few boundaries. After seven hours, Saqlain finally removed him for 118 – another victim of the sweep stroke – and, seven runs later, White was snaffled up at short leg by Yousuf Youhana again off the bowling of Saqlain, just seven runs short of his century. Salisbury and Giles added a further 70 on the third morning, enabling Hussain to declare on 480 for eight and thus depriving Saqlain, who took eight for 164, of the opportunity to take all ten wickets.

Pakistan's first target was the 281 they needed to avoid the follow-on. Both openers are natural stroke-players, however, and Saeed Anwar raced to 40 before offering no shot to Hick's speculative second delivery and, shortly before the close, Shahid Afridi came down the pitch and launched Giles into Gough's waiting hands at long on for a 68-ball 52. Saleem Elahi and Inzamam-ul-Haq dominated the first hour of the fourth day, but with 82 still required to avoid the follow-on, Elahi was bowled off the inside edge by White for 44 and, three overs later, Giles deceived Inzamam with a slower ball and bowled him for 63.

Now the Pakistanis were under pressure. Qaiser Abbas sliced White to Hick in the gully and, irony of ironies, Moin Khan – Pakistan's captain – picked up the roughest leg before decision of the match from the home umpire, his departure leaving his side 38 runs short of the follow-on target with just four wickets remaining. As the tension mounted, Razzaq and Yousuf brought Pakistan to within nine runs of safety, before Razzaq fatally shouldered arms to White. Wasim Akram was immediately caught at short midwicket off the bowling of Giles.

Tea was taken with Pakistan at 276 for eight – five runs away from avoiding the follow-on – and the atmosphere was electric. Yousuf re-emerged, however, to dismiss the possibility of such an ignominy and with that, the match was inevitably destined to be a draw.

In fact, Saqlain – who failed to score from his first 41 balls – and Yousuf extended their partnership to 127 on a subdued final day. Yousuf, the only Christian in the Pakistan team, crossed his chest when he reached his hundred after five hours and 20 minutes at the crease. He was eventually caught by Stewart for 124 off a ball from Giles that spun sharply, and when Mushtaq Ahmed was immediately

FIRST TEST – PAKISTAN v. ENGLAND
15–19 November 2000 at Gaddafi Stadium, Lahore

ENGLAND

	First innings		Second innings	
MA Atherton	c Yousuf Youhana, b Saqlain Mushtaq	73	lbw b Mushtaq Ahmed	20
ME Trescothick	c Salim Elahi, b Saqlain Mushtaq	71	lbw b Wasim Akram	1
GP Thorpe	c & b Saqlain Mushtaq	118	(4) c Abdur Razzaq, b Saqlain Mushtaq	5
*AJ Stewart	lbw b Saqlain Mushtaq	3	(5) not out	27
N Hussain (capt)	c Wasim Akram, b Saqlain Mushtaq	7	(3) retired hurt	0
GA Hick	lbw b Saqlain Mushtaq	16	b Shahid Afridi	14
C White	c Yousuf Youhana, b Saqlain Mushtaq	93		
IDK Salisbury	lbw b Saqlain Mushtaq	31		
AF Giles	not out	37		
AR Caddick	not out	5		
D Gough				
	b3, lb13, nb10	26	lb7, nb3	10
	(for 8 wickets dec.)	480	(for 4 wickets dec.)	77

	First innings				Second innings			
	O	M	R	W	O	M	R	W
Wasim Akram	22.5	8	40	-	6	5	1	1
Abdur Razzaq	22	6	55	-	7	0	21	-
Saqlain Mushtaq	74	20	164	8	10	2	14	1
Mushtaq Ahmed	44	6	132	-	8	0	32	1
Shahid Afridi	18	6	38	-	1.1	0	2	1
Qaiser Abbas	16	3	35	-				

Fall of Wickets
1-134, 2-169, 3-173, 4-183, 5-225, 6-391, 7-398, 8-468
1-4, 2-29, 3-39, 4-77

Nasser Hussain retired hurt at 13 for one in the second innings

PAKISTAN

	First innings	
Saeed Anwar	lbw b Hick	40
Shahid Afridi	c Gough, b Giles	52
Salim Elahi	b White	44
Inzamam-ul-Haq	b Giles	63
Yousuf Youhana	c Stewart, b Giles	124
Qaiser Abbas	c Hick, b White	2
*Moin Khan (capt)	lbw b Caddick	17
Abdur Razzaq	lbw b White	10
Wasim Akram	c White, b Giles	1
Saqlain Mushtaq	not out	32
Mushtaq Ahmed	lbw b White	0
	b3, lb5, nb8	16
		401

	First innings			
	O	M	R	W
Gough	17	6	45	-
Caddick	24	4	68	1
Giles	59	20	113	4
Salisbury	31	5	71	-
Hick	8	0	42	1
White	24.3	5	54	4

Fall of Wickets
1-63, 2-101, 3-199, 4-203, 5-210, 6-236, 7-272, 8-273, 9-400

Umpires: Riazuddin & DB Hair
Toss: England
Test debut: Qaiser Abbas (Pakistan)

Match drawn

leg before to give White his fourth wicket, England were left the rest of the afternoon to bat out time.

Wasim roared in as if his place depended on it, dismissing Trescothick and forcing Hussain to retire hurt with a blow on the wrist. Atherton and Hick were also despatched, but the game was finally laid to rest when England did the noble thing and declared with ten minutes remaining.

Pakistan Cricket Board XI v. England XI
23–25 November 2000 at Bagh-e-Jinnar Stadium, Lahore
PCB XI 117 and 71 for 6
England XI 237 (ME Trescothick 50rh)
Match drawn – no play was possible on the second day

This was a forgettable practice match, which, once the weather closed in, was always destined for a draw. Matthew Hoggard could not believe his luck to discover another green and lively pitch on which to press his claims, which, in Pakistan at least, were unrealistic. Trescothick hit six fours in his half century before retiring to give someone else a go.

SECOND TEST
29 November–3 December at Iqbal Stadium, Faisalabad

Finally, England returned to the Iqbal Stadium where, 13 years ago, their relations with Pakistan were ruined by the argument between captain Mike Gatting and the umpire, Shakoor Rana. If Nasser Hussain's men arrived in Faisalabad feeling trepidation at the manner in which they would be received, they would have been more than just pleasantly surprised by the enthusiastic response by the locals.

They turned out in force, strolling into the ground via the newly-laid thoroughfare while the small Serena Hotel – just a short walk from the ground – was packed with players, officials and a healthy number of England supporters who all mingled happily during the evening barbeques.

Faisalabad school children were given time off to attend the match – the girls separated from the boys – and Wasim Akram, who was making his 100th Test appearance for Pakistan, was given a riotous welcome.

Mindful of their inability to trouble England's batsmen unduly in Lahore, Pakistan's selectors called up the teenager, Danish Kaneria who became only the second Hindu ever to represent his country. Striking a remarkable likeness to Tiger Woods, the leg spinner demonstrated a full range of variations in the nets beforehand, and looked extremely promising.

Once again, the pitch would be the talking point prior to the match – two strips were prepared for the match and after much debate, the Pakistani management settled for the one most likely to break up during the course of the game. If they felt any unease about this very obvious policy of 'pitch-fixing', England – wisely – were most diplomatic.

Pakistan won the toss this time, giving them the ideal opportunity to post a large, intimidating, first-innings total. Shahid Afridi fell to Gough in the seventh over, Saeed Anwar flicked Giles to midwicket for 53, but it was the bizarre departure of Inzamam on the stroke of lunch – the ball dribbled between his legs and bowled him second ball – that gave

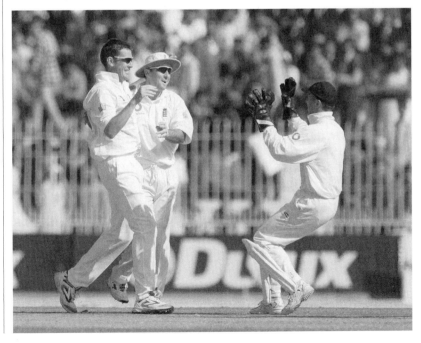

Alec Stewart rushed to congratulate Ashley Giles after the spinner dismissed Inzamam-ul-Haq in the most bizarre fashion.

England the edge. As Giles chipped away, Pakistan subsided to 151 for five, only for Yousuf Youhana to frustrate them once again. This time Moin was his ally and, on the second morning, they extended their partnership to 120 before Youhana hooked Gough to Thorpe at long leg. In the very next over, Moin edged a sharp-turner from Giles to Hussain for 65, and although Saqlain made another valuable contribution, Pakistan's total of 316 was at least 150 runs fewer than they would have liked.

The spinners were quickly in operation as England started their reply. Trescothick gave young Kaneria his first wicket when he charged a googly and was stumped for 30. Atherton and Hussain added 56 before the opener fell to Saqlain and, four overs later, the England captain was on the wrong end of what must rate as one of umpire Bucknor's worst mistakes. Bucknor failed to detect a thick inside edge and despatched a disbelieving Hussain to leave England sweating overnight on 110 for three.

It was crucial that the nightwatchman Ian Salisbury – whose bowling had been largely ignored by his captain – frustrated Pakistan for as long as possible on the third morning. In fact, he stayed at the crease for three-and-a-quarter hours, enabling Thorpe to rebuild the innings. Following Salisbury's departure for 33, there was a moment of mid-afternoon madness. First Stewart slogged a catch off Kaneria for 13, then Thorpe fell leg before to the new ball for 79 and, next ball, a leaden-footed Hick edged Razzaq to Yousuf Youhana for 17. England were 275 for eight when Giles was caught at slip, again off Razzaq, for a duck and the visitors were in danger of handing Pakistan a small lead and, importantly, time in which to press on. However, White hit 41 from only 46 balls to give England an advantage of 26 shortly before lunch on the fourth day.

If Pakistan were to make use of the deteriorating pitch, they had to score quickly. Razzaq, a rapidly improving all-rounder, was promoted to number three and played quite beautifully. He added 98 with Elahi, before the opener gloved a sweep to Stewart for 72. Then Inzamam joined in the fun. A further 148 runs were added as, once more, Hussain appeared deliberately to ignore Salisbury. Finally, as a declaration was inevitable, the captain turned to his leg spinner and Inzamam obligingly slogged him to long off for 71. It was to be Salisbury's sole wicket of a series in which he bowled only 69 overs to Giles' 182. Moin called his batsmen in with a lead of 175, and a minimum of 44 overs in which to bowl England out.

In fact, Pakistan managed to deliver 57 overs and

SECOND TEST – PAKISTAN v. ENGLAND

29 November–3 December 2000 at Iqbal Stadium, Faisalabad

PAKISTAN

	First innings		Second innings	
Saeed Anwar	c Thorpe, b Giles	53		
Shahid Afridi	c Thorpe, b Gough	10	c Giles, b Gough	10
Salim Elahi	c Atherton, b Giles	41	(1) c Stewart, b Giles	72
Inzamam-ul-Haq	b Giles	0	c Hick, b Salisbury	71
Yousuf Youhana	c Thorpe, b Gough	77		
Abdur Razzaq	b White	9	(3) not out	100
*Moin Khan (capt)	c Hussain, b Giles	65		
Wasim Akram	st Stewart, b Giles	1	(5) not out	4
Saqlain Mushtaq	c Trescothick, b Gough	34		
Arshad Khan	c Thorpe, b White	2		
Danish Kaneria	not out	8		
	b1, lb12, nb3	16	b6, lb5, nb1	12
		316	(for 3 wickets dec.)	**269**

	First innings				Second innings			
	O	M	R	W	O	M	R	W
Gough	23.1	2	79	3	10.2	1	32	1
Caddick	15	3	49	-	18	1	49	-
White	25	6	71	2	19	3	55	-
Giles	35	13	75	5	26	3	90	1
Salisbury	10	0	29	-	7	0	32	1

Fall of Wickets
1-33, 2-96, 3-96, 4-130, 5-151, 6-271, 7-271, 8-276, 9-283
1-13, 2-111, 3-259

ENGLAND

	First innings		Second innings	
MA Atherton	c Yousuf Youhana b Saqlain Mushtaq	32	not out	65
ME Trescothick	st Moin Khan, b Danish Kaneria	30	b Saqlain Mushtaq	10
N Hussain (capt)	lbw b Saqlain Mushtaq	23	c Moin Khan, b Arshad Khan	5
IDK Salisbury	c Yousuf Youhana, b Arshad Khan	33		
GP Thorpe	lbw b Wasim Akram	79	(4) b Arshad Khan	0
*AJ Stewart	c Abdur Razzaq, b Danish Kaneria	13	(5) c Yousuf Youhana, b Shahid Afridi	22
GA Hick	c Yousuf Youhana, b Abdur Razzaq	17	(6) b Shahid Afridi	0
C White	b Saqlain Mushtaq	41	(7) not out	9
AF Giles	c Shahid Afridi, b Abdur Razzaq	0		
AR Caddick	c Moin Khan, b Abdur Razzaq	5		
D Gough	not out	19		
	b4, lb14, nb32	50	lb4, nb10	14
		342	(for 5 wickets)	**125**

	First innings				Second innings			
	O	M	R	W	O	M	R	W
Wasim Akram	26	6	69	1	5	1	13	-
Abdur Razzaq	20	0	74	3	1	1	-	-
Danish Kaneria	34	9	89	2	7	0	30	-
Saqlain Mushtaq	30.4	8	62	3	19	4	26	1
Arshad Khan	25	12	29	1	13	4	31	2
Shahid Afridi	1	0	1	-	12	3	21	2

Fall of Wickets
1-49, 2-105, 3-106, 4-203, 5-235, 6-274, 7-274, 8-275, 9-295
1-44, 2-57, 3-57, 4-108, 5-110

Umpires: Mian Mohammad Aslam & SA Bucknor
Toss: Pakistan
Test debut: Danish Kaneria (Pakistan)

Match drawn

England survived, but not without experiencing some discomfort. Hussain failed again, making only five before falling to another poor umpiring decision and, in the next over, Thorpe shouldered arms and was bowled by Arshad Khan.

Stewart was caught at silly point by Yousuf Youhana off Afridi while the wicket of Hick was one of those dismissals predicted from the distance – and safety – of the press box: a couple of tantalizing leg-

Pakistan's young and exciting all-rounder Abdur Razzaq celebrates his first century in the second Test against England in Faisalabad. Despite Razzaq's promotion, the match ended in a tame draw.

spinners, followed by the arrow-like quicker ball. Feet nowhere, leg before, thank you very much indeed!

Only Atherton stood firm, offering nothing to the Pakistanis for nearly three-and-a-half hours. His 65 may not have been pretty, but it thwarted Moin who called the game off leaving it with all to play for in the final Test in Karachi.

THIRD TEST
7–11 December 2000 at National Stadium, Karachi

This was the most stirring, rousing and remarkable finale to a Test series that it has been my pleasure to watch. After four days of, largely, forgettable cricket, the match came to life on the final afternoon as England, batting in almost total darkness, successfully chased 176 to win their first Test in Pakistan for 39 years. So dark was it at the end that those locals who were observing the holy month of Ramadan had broken their fast some ten minutes before the winning runs were scored – in other words, the sun had officially set.

With Pakistan's strategy apparently in turmoil, no fewer than three pitches were prepared for the match: a green-top, a turner and something in-between. Two days before the start of play, I witnessed a lengthy discussion in the middle between the coach, Javed Miandad, and Wasim Akram. I do not know what was said, but the spinners' track was preferred and, controversially, Wasim was omitted from the team in favour of his old sparring partner, Waqar Younis. Much of the next two days were spent laying Wasim's career to rest, only for him immediately to gain reselection for Pakistan's tour of New Zealand.

Pakistan had never lost a Test in Karachi, and when the captains tossed and Moin chose to bat first, it hardly seemed likely that they would relinquish their proud record. However, throughout the series, his batsmen – Youhana apart – had shown surprisingly scant responsibility, bearing in mind that, in the main, the pitches were all comfortable to bat on. It was that recklessness that was to cost them this game – that and Moin's tactics on the final afternoon.

At the close of the opening day, Pakistan looked well set to bat England out of the game. They were 292 for three, with Inzamam and Youhana both undefeated with hundreds to their names. This after England had reduced Pakistan to 64 for three – it had been a long, hot afternoon in the sun.

Three quarters of an hour into the second morning, however, the wheels began to fall off

Pakistan's innings. Youhana was brilliantly caught, right-handed and low by Giles off his own first ball of the day. The partnership was a record: 259 in 78 overs and, as is so often the case, both batsmen were dismissed in quick succession. It was three overs later that a lazy Inzy carved White to Trescothick at point for 142. Pakistan were 325 for five and Gough and Giles – who took four for 42 that morning – finished off the innings between them for a further 80 runs.

Far from the 550, or so, that England could well have been facing, Atherton and Trescothick strode to the middle with England only 405 behind. Trescothick made 13, but Atherton – who had completely dug in – and Hussain put on 134 with the captain scoring his first half-century of the year for England. His miserable 2000 season is put into perspective by the fact that he passed 200 Test runs during the course of this innings.

Hussain was finally caught at slip by Inzamam off the bowling of Afridi for 51 and with Thorpe and Stewart both chipping in, the follow-on was avoided and the game appeared to be heading for a stalemate. Atherton's remorseless approach only reinforced this. On and on he went. He batted throughout the third day, ending it on 117 with England – who had started batting before tea the previous day – having crawled to 277 for seven, still 128 in arrears.

The following morning, however, Pakistan fought back as England lost three wickets for ten runs in seven overs, and six for 111 in all. Hick was caught hooking Waqar in the first over and Atherton's marathon ended after nine-and-a-half hours when he was caught by Moin off Razzaq for 125 off 430 deliveries. By the time England were all out for 388, Pakistan's lead was a mere 17. With time drifting on and an apparent lack of urgency from either team, the draw was still comfortably the favourite. At the close of the fourth day, Pakistan had lost three wickets and their lead stood at 88.

So to the extraordinary events of the final day of the tour. I read from my notes made at the time: 'England are the only team that could realistically win the game, but only if Pakistan suffer a serious collapse first thing.' Perhaps I should have taken more notice of the pressure being heaped on the home team by its media – infuriated by the lack of drive and intensity of the players. Whatever the reason, Pakistan's batsmen – far from simply batting out time in order to make the game safe – came out devoid of any plan or confidence. Possibly the most important wicket was the first: the obdurate

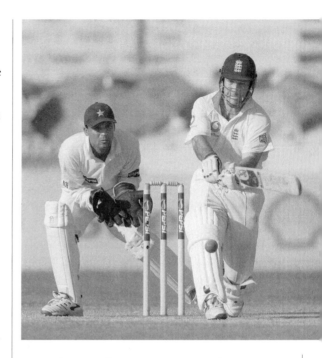

Graham Thorpe sweeps Saqlain Mushtaq during his masterful innings of 64 in England's historic second innings.

nightwatchman, Saqlain, who was trapped leg before by Gough in the fourth over of the morning. Ten minutes before lunch, they gained another important blow when Youhana gloved a pull off White to Stewart for 23 and, in the next over, Elahi was caught at silly point by Thorpe off the bowling of Giles. At the interval Pakistan led by 145 runs with four wickets in hand. In the press box, there was only a minimal increase in interest.

Suddenly, the Pakistan innings crumbled. Moin was as guilty as anybody, drilling a full toss off White to mid off, and when Waqar was absurdly run out in a mix up with Afridi, the home team appeared to be panic-stricken. Gough promptly cleaned up Kaneria to leave England chasing 176 to win from a minimum of 44 overs. Pakistan had lost their last six wickets for 30 in only 17 overs.

The fading light was always going to be an issue. Although it would hit their pockets, Pakistan could slow the over rate as much as they liked. However, with so much at stake, it was reasonable to expect at least an early attempt from them to win the match themselves. Instead, Moin was interested in nothing more than frustrating England by running out of daylight. The time-wasting reached absurd, totally cynical proportions which resulted in two warnings from Steve Bucknor. England, on the other hand, made a brisk reply – helped by the generous gaps in the field left by Moin who appeared too preoccupied by posting men on the fence. After 19 overs, England had 65 on the board, but had lost Atherton, Trescothick and Stewart on the way. Now it really was make or break.

Hick had endured a miserable series and had largely been written out of England's future plans by the media. Now, in a one-day situation, he looked a new man and, with Thorpe, scampered singles in a bustling partnership worth 91. When they were parted, with Hick making 40 from 66 balls, darkness was already falling with England still 20 runs away from victory.

As Moin protested about the light to umpire Bucknor, England knew they could not lose. If they lost a couple more wickets, they could – successfully – appeal themselves. As Hussain joined Thorpe, the captain gave the order to 'swing at everything'. Mind you, facing Waqar Younis in that light must have been terrifying.

With six required, Thorpe drove Saqlain into the covers and set off. Not a single fielder moved as, high in the stands, commentators also failed to see the ball at all. Over the boundary it went – the hammer blow. Next ball, an inside edge and a mad dash for the two runs that brought the most incredible victory with 15 balls to spare. It was a triumph for a team that had never lost sight of winning.

Nasser Hussain and Graham Thorpe head for the England dressing room having completed England's victory that clinched the series.

THIRD TEST – PAKISTAN v. ENGLAND
7–11 December 2000 at National Stadium, Karachi

PAKISTAN

	First innings		Second innings	
Saeed Anwar	lbw b Gough	8	c Thorpe, b Caddick	21
Imran Nazir	c Giles, b Trescothick	20	c Stewart, b Gough	4
Salim Elahi	b Caddick	28	c Thorpe, b Giles	37
Inzamam-ul-Haq	c Trescothick, b White	142	b Giles	27
Yousuf Youhana	c & b Giles	117	(6) c Stewart, b White	24
Abdur Razzaq	c Hussain, b Giles	21	(7) c Atherton, b Giles	1
*Moin Khan (capt)	c Hick, b Giles	13	(8) c Hussain, b White	14
Shahid Afridi	b Giles	10	(9) not out	15
Saqlain Mushtaq	b Gough	16	(5) lbw b Gough	4
Waqar Younis	b Gough	17	run out (Stewart)	0
Danish Kaneria	not out	0	lbw b Gough	0
	b3, lb3, nb7	13	b3, lb5, nb3	11
		405		**158**

	First innings				Second innings			
	O	M	R	W	O	M	R	W
Gough	27.4	5	82	3	13	4	30	3
Caddick	23	1	76	1	15	2	40	1
Trescothick	14	1	34	1				
White	22	3	64	1	12	4	30	2
Salisbury	18	1	49	–	3	0	12	–
Giles	35	7	94	4	27	12	38	3

Fall of Wickets
1-8, 2-44, 3-64, 4-323, 5-325, 6-340, 7-359, 8-374, 9-402
1-24, 2-26, 3-71, 4-78, 5-128, 6-128, 7-139, 8-143, 9-149

ENGLAND

	First innings		Second innings	
MA Atherton	c Moin Khan, b Abdur Razzaq	125	c Saeed Anwar, b Saqlain Mushtaq	26
ME Trescothick	c Imran Nazir, b Waqar Younis	13	c Inzamam-ul-Haq, b Saqlain Mushtaq	24
N Hussain (capt)	c Inzamam-ul-Haq, b Shahid Afridi	51	(6) not out	6
GP Thorpe	lbw b Waqar Younis	18	not out	64
*AJ Stewart	c Yousuf Youhana, b Saqlain Mushtaq	29	(3) c Moin Khan, b Saqlain Mushtaq	5
GA Hick	c Shahid Afridi, b Waqar Younis	12	(5) b Waqar Younis	40
C White	st Moin Khan, b Danish Kaneria	35		
AF Giles	b Waqar Younis	19		
IDK Salisbury	not out	20		
AR Caddick	c Moin Khan, b Danish Kaneria	3		
D Gough	c Yousuf Youhana, b Saqlain Mushtaq	18		
	b12, lb9, nb24	45	b8, lb2, w1	11
		388	(for 4 wickets)	**176**

	First innings				Second innings			
	O	M	R	W	O	M	R	W
Waqar Younis	36	5	88	4	6	0	27	1
Abdur Razzaq	28	7	64	1	4	0	17	–
Shahid Afridi	16	3	34	1	11	1	40	–
Saqlain Mushtaq	52.1	17	101	2	17.3	1	64	3
Danish Kaneria	47	17	80	2	3	0	18	–

Fall of Wickets
1-29, 2-163, 3-195, 4-256, 5-278, 6-309, 7-339, 8-345, 9-349
1-38, 2-51, 3-65, 4-156

Umpires: Mohammad Nazir & SA Bucknor
Toss: Pakistan
Test debuts: nil

England won by six wickets

TEST MATCH AVERAGES
Pakistan v. England

PAKISTAN

Batting	M	Inns	NO	HS	Runs	Av	100	50	c/st
Yousuf Youhana	3	4	0	124	324	85.50	2	1	8
Inzamam-ul-Haq	3	5	0	142	303	60.60	1	2	2
Salim Elahi	3	5	0	72	222	44.40	-	1	1
Abdur Razzaq	3	5	1	100*	141	35.25	1	-	2
Saeed Anwar	3	4	0	53	122	30.50	-	1	1
Saqlain Mushtaq	3	4	1	34	86	28.66	-	-	1
Moin Khan	3	4	0	65	109	27.25	-	1	5/2
Shahid Afridi	3	5	1	52	97	24.25	-	1	2
Danish Kaneria	2	3	2	8*	8	8.00	-	-	-
Wasim Akram	2	3	1	4*	6	3.00	-	-	1

Also batted in one Test: Arshad Khan 2; Imran Nazir 20, 4 (1ct); Mushtaq Ahmed 0; Qaiser Abbas 2; Waqar Younis 17, 0.

Bowling	Overs	Mds	Runs	Wkts	Av	Best	10m	5/inn
Waqar Younis	42	5	115	5	23.00	4-88	-	-
Saqlain Mushtaq	203.2	52	431	18	23.94	8-164	-	1

Also bowled: Abdur Razzaq 82-15-231-4; Arshad Khan 38-16-60-3; Danish Kaneria 91-26-217-4; Mushtaq Ahmed 52-6-164-1; Qaiser Abbas 16-3-35-0; Shahid Afridi 59.1-13-136-4; Wasim Akram 59-20-123-2.

ENGLAND

Batting	M	Inns	NO	HS	Runs	Av	100	50	c/st
MA Atherton	3	6	1	125	341	68.20	1	2	2
C White	3	4	1	93	178	59.33	-	1	2
GP Thorpe	3	6	1	118	284	56.80	1	2	6
IDK Salisbury	3	3	1	33	84	42.00	-	-	-
AF Giles	3	3	1	37*	56	28.00	-	-	3
ME Trescothick	3	6	0	71	149	24.83	-	1	2
N Hussain	3	6	2	51	92	23.00	-	1	3
AJ Stewart	3	6	1	29	99	19.80	-	-	4/1
GA Hick	3	6	0	40	99	16.50	-	-	3
AR Caddick	3	3	1	5*	13	6.50	-	-	-

Also batted: D Gough (3 Tests) 19*, 18 (1ct).

Bowling	Overs	Mds	Runs	Wkts	Av	Best	10m	5/inn
AF Giles	182	55	410	17	24.11	5-75	-	1
D Gough	91.1	18	268	10	26.80	3-30	-	-
C White	102.3	21	274	9	30.44	4-54	-	-

Also bowled: AR Caddick 95-11-282-3; GA Hick 8-0-42-1; IDK Salisbury 69-8-193-1; ME Trescothick 14-1-34-1.

PAKISTAN DOMESTIC FIRST-CLASS SEASON
By Qamar Ahmed

For the Pakistan Cricket Board (PCB) and the cricketing public, the cancellation of the India tour to Pakistan came as a huge disappointment. They were scheduled to tour for the first time since 1989. Tension on each side of the border due to the dispute over Kashmir had caused cancellations of tours earlier by both countries.

Despite threats by Bal Thackeray, the Shiv Sena's Hindu extremist, Pakistan had toured India in 1999 and the tour was one of the most successful that Pakistan had ever undertaken to the neighbouring country. The return visit would have been more than welcomed, but it was not to be.

For Pakistan, therefore, England's first visit after a gap of 13 years was a big winner and it was the highlight of the season in which exactly 100 first-

Wasim's international future seemed uncertain, but he led the Lahore Blues to victory in the Quaid-e-Azam Trophy.

class matches were played, including the Tests and the representative games against the England tourists. The domestic tournaments had reverted to the previous format with the Grade 1 and 2 tournaments returning to the circuit once again and the Patron's Trophy, which was relegated to second grade the previous year, regaining its first-class status.

To popularize the game in the remote corners of the country, nine teams from the various districts were allowed to play at various levels. Sialkot, Sheikhupura, Naseerabad, Azad Jammu and Kashmir, Northern Areas, Rahimyar Khan, Federally Administered Tribal Areas, Okara and Sahiwal were all inducted into the domestic scene.

Sialkot won the Grade II Quaid-e-Azam Trophy and qualified with Hyderabad for the next season's Grade 1 championship. The Patron's Trophy Grade 2 was won by Public Works Department (PWD) who beat the Sui Gas team in the final.

The Lahore Blues took the Grade 1 Quaid-e-Azam Trophy, narrowly beating the Karachi Whites by one wicket in the final. Lahore's Wasim Akram grabbed nine wickets for 103 and Abdur Razzaq ten for 133 as Karachi (297 and 104) succumbed to Lahore's (218 and 185) Test pace duo – despite all-rounder Shahid Afridi's magnificent innings of 102.

The Patron's Trophy Grade 1 was won by the Customs team which defeated the National Bank by four wickets to win the trophy for the first time. Only two batsmen, Naved Latif (1,352 at 46.62) of Sargodha & Customs and Zahoor Elahi (1,225 at 49.00) of Lahore Whites and ADBP scored over 1,000 runs in the season. Naved Latif hit 394 for Sargodha in a Quaid-e-Azam Trophy match against Gujranwala, which was

Abdur Razzaq combined with international team-mate Wasim Akram to lead the Lahore Blues to domestic glory.

the tenth highest individual score in first-class history. Asif Mujtaba (987), Humayun Frahat (977), Mohammad Wasim (972), Sargodha's Misbah-ul-Haq (953) with four hundreds and Hasan Raza (969) were other successful batsmen of the season.

As many as 14 bowlers took 50 wickets or more. Sheikhupura's and Custom's 23-year-old medium-pacer Naved-ul-Hasan took 91 wickets at 22.93 apiece. Yasir Arafat of Rawalpindi and Rao Iftikhar of Islamabad bagged 73 wickets each and wrist spinner Danish Kaneria, who was to make his Test debut against England, finished with 61 wickets at 22.00 apiece. Mohammad Sami, Karachi White's fast bowler had a tally of 44 wickets in only seven matches at 16.95 per wicket.

Wicket-keeper Atiq-uz-Zaman created a new national record with 76 dismissals (70 ct, 6 st) in eight matches for Karachi.

PAKISTAN DOMESTIC ONE-DAY SEASON
By Qamar Ahmed

After losing the sponsorship of Tissot, the Pakistan Cricket Board (PCB) wasted no time in initiating their own national one-day tournaments, one involving the Department teams and the other with the teams from various Associations.

The National One-Day tournament for the departments was won by Habib Bank, who defeated the National Bank by eight wickets in the final game at Sheikhupura. Habib Bank, chasing a modest 193, raced to victory with 21 overs to spare. Salim Elahi who, in earlier matches had made an unbeaten 170 and 115, blasted 61 runs with 12 fours and shared an opening stand of 108 runs with left-hander Taufiq Umar who made an unbeaten 71 as Habib Bank cruised home.

Besides Habib Bank seven other teams, National Bank, PIA, WAPDA, KRL, Allied Bank, ADBP and Customs had participated in the tournament. Habib Bank, National Bank, PIA & WAPDA finished as the top four teams.

The tournament played between the Associations was won by Karachi Whites who beat Sheikhupura by 79 runs in the final. Karachi, led by Test discard Moin Khan, ran up a total of 278 for five and then bowled their opponents out for 199 in the 46th over. Moin hit five fours and two sixes in his 67 and held three catches behind the stumps.

It had not been a memorable season for Pakistan's captain, Moin Khan, but he had the consolation of scoring 67 as Karachi Whites beat Sheikhupura in the Association one-day tournament.

FIRST-CLASS AVERAGES

BATTING

	M	I	NO	HS	Runs	Av	100	50
Faisal Iqbal	7	11	1	200	558	55.80	1	3
Mohammad Ramzan	9	17	4	205	719	55.30	3	1
Ali Naqvi	8	15	3	119	628	52.33	2	2
Humayan Farhat	11	20	1	188	977	51.42	3	5
Imran Farhat	9	17	1	200	816	51.00	2	3
Misbah-ul-Haq	12	20	1	142	953	50.15	4	4
MA Atherton	5	9	1	125	399	49.87	1	2
Asif Mujtaba	17	25	5	202*	987	49.35	2	5
Zahoor Elahi	18	29	4	203	1225	49.00	4	5
Usman Tariq	11	16	3	106*	620	47.69	1	6
Naved Latif	18	29	0	394	1352	46.62	2	7
Mohammad Masroor	11	19	5	171*	611	43.64	1	4
Akhtar Sarfraz	15	25	4	142	903	43.00	2	6
Farhan Adil	14	24	1	211	952	41.39	1	5
Fida Hussain	9	14	3	116*	450	40.90	1	3
Afsar Nawaz	7	13	0	165	531	40.84	2	1
Majid Saeed	7	11	1	124	402	40.20	1	1
Naeem Ashraf	6	10	1	106	356	39.55	1	2
Adil Nisar	7	14	2	171*	474	39.50	1	1
Wajahatullah Wasti	12	20	4	162*	626	39.12	2	1
Mansoor Rana	5	8	0	117	312	39.00	1	1
Younis Khan	8	13	0	221	501	38.53	1	3
Saeed Bin Nasir	5	9	0	124	342	38.00	1	2
Mohammad Tariq	11	17	1	134	606	37.87	1	4
Rashid Latif	9	15	4	72	415	37.72	-	5
Nadeem Abbasi	8	12	2	102	373	37.30	1	2
Mohammad Wasim	15	27	0	147	1005	37.22	3	4
Ijaz Ahmed, jr	13	22	1	138	760	36.19	2	4
Taufiq Umar	14	27	2	120	898	35.92	1	7
Shahid Afridi	10	18	1	108	594	34.94	2	3
Hasan Raza	19	33	5	100*	969	34.60	2	7
ME Trescothick	6	10	1	93	311	34.55	-	3
Hasan Adnan	8	15	2	99	447	34.38	-	3
Maisam Hasnain	6	10	1	67	309	34.33	-	3
Wasim Haider	9	14	1	88*	446	34.30	-	5
Asim Munir	6	10	2	114	274	34.25	1	1
Fareed Butt	8	15	3	166*	404	33.66	1	1
Tariq Aziz	9	16	1	93	502	33.46	-	3
Zeeshan Parvez	11	18	0	115	595	33.05	1	3
Bilal Asad	9	17	0	112	561	33.00	1	4
Zaheer Abbasi	8	14	0	127	457	32.64	1	3
Qaisar Abbas	16	26	1	84	808	32.32	-	6
Aamer Bashir	8	14	1	97	420	32.30	-	3
Imran Nazir	7	12	2	111	317	31.70	1	1
Aamer Sohail, jr	7	11	1	72*	316	31.60	-	2
Aamer Iqbal	6	9	0	129	280	31.11	1	1
Yasir Hameed	15	25	0	103	766	30.64	1	7
Mohammad Shahbaz	10	19	3	108	490	30.62	1	1
Kamran Akmal	17	26	5	174	640	30.47	1	1
Mohammad Hafeez	10	16	0	82	484	30.25	-	6
Shahid Javed	6	12	2	82	302	30.20	-	3
Shadab Kabir	10	17	1	116	478	29.87	2	1
Naumanullah	18	28	1	91	802	29.70	-	9
Pervez Aziz	13	23	2	154	617	29.38	1	3
Abdur Razzaq	5	9	1	100*	235	29.37	1	1
Tariq Mahmood	6	11	1	66*	290	29.00	-	2
Atiq-ur-Rehman	7	11	0	71	317	28.81	-	2
Imran Abbas	14	24	2	108	628	28.54	2	2
Ata-ur-Rehman	5	9	1	71	224	28.00	-	1
Asim Kamal	9	14	1	86	364	28.00	-	3
Mohammad Javed	5	9	1	59*	224	28.00	-	1
Mohammad Javed	11	17	1	90	446	27.87	-	2
Ghulam Ali	9	15	1	98	387	27.64	-	3
Naseer Ahmed	16	30	2	126	771	27.53	1	4
Hafiz Khalid	9	16	3	73	357	27.46	-	2
Mujahid Jamshed	14	24	0	104	659	27.45	1	4
Mohammad Hussain	11	19	0	69	521	27.42	-	4
Sajid Ali	8	14	1	77	354	27.23	-	3
Iqbal Imam	12	22	3	62	515	27.10	-	4
Majid Majeed	10	17	0	116	458	26.94	1	2
Zahid Fazal	9	15	1	121	377	26.92	1	1
Taimur Khan	14	25	4	69*	564	26.85	-	3
Faisal Naveed	7	13	0	121	349	26.84	2	-

FIRST-CLASS AVERAGES

BATTING

	M	I	NO	HS	Runs	Av	100	50
Bazid Khan	9	18	1	104	450	26.47	1	1
Manzoor Akhtar	7	13	0	92	344	26.46	-	2
Tahir Usman	5	8	0	98	208	26.00	-	1
Shoaib Khan	7	12	1	101*	284	25.81	1	1
Shahid Anwar	16	31	3	104*	720	25.71	2	-
Yasir Arafat	17	30	6	76*	612	25.50	-	3
Sohail Jaffar	6	9	1	81	204	25.50	-	1
Asif Ali	10	18	1	126	433	25.47	1	3
Mujahid Hameed	5	10	1	73	228	25.33	-	2
Asif Mahmood	6	10	1	84	227	25.22	-	1
Shoaib Malik	8	13	1	130*	300	25.00	1	1
Mohammad Usman	4	8	0	81	199	24.87	-	2
Naveed-ul-Hassan	17	26	3	70	566	24.60	-	2
Atiq-uz-Zaman	18	28	4	104*	586	24.41	1	3
Waqar Ahmed	5	9	1	69	194	24.25	-	1
Rafatullah	15	27	2	91*	600	24.00	-	3
Ijaz Mahmood	14	25	3	79*	521	23.68	-	2
Rizwan Malik	8	13	0	156	304	23.38	1	-
Naveed Ashraf	13	23	0	78	535	23.26	-	2
Haroon Raheem	5	9	1	68	185	23.12	-	2
GA Hick	5	8	0	85	185	23.12	-	1
Naseem Khan	5	9	1	76	183	22.87	-	1
Faisal Afridi	9	14	3	95	246	22.36	-	1
Kamran Hussain	17	27	2	84	554	22.16	-	3
Salman Butt	5	8	0	60	174	21.75	-	1
Fahad Khan	6	8	0	50	173	21.62	-	1
Naeem Akhtar	13	22	1	64	450	21.42	-	2
Imran Qadir	6	11	0	69	235	21.36	-	1
Mohammad Nawaz	12	22	1	109	448	21.33	1	1
Iftikhar Hussain	7	12	0	51	256	21.33	-	1
Farooq Iqbal	9	15	3	53	255	21.25	-	1
Intikhab Alam	12	23	0	77	485	21.08	-	2
Tariq Rasheed	4	8	0	47	165	20.62	-	-
Asadullah Butt	7	14	0	60	275	19.64	-	1
Asif Hussain	5	10	0	100	194	19.40	1	-
Bilal Khilji	12	20	2	46	346	19.22	-	-
Azam Khan	6	11	1	63	192	19.20	-	1
Kashif Siddique	6	9	0	64	172	19.11	-	1
Arshad Khan	10	14	0	57	263	18.78	-	1
Ahmed Zeeshan	15	24	2	57	411	18.68	-	1
Ali Hussain	5	10	2	92	145	18.12	-	1
Nadeem Hussain	7	11	1	45	179	17.90	-	-
Ashar Zaidi	8	15	0	56	268	17.86	-	2
Saleem Mughal	8	13	1	57	211	17.58	-	1
Saeed Anwar, jr	13	24	0	66	418	17.41	-	2
Inamullah Rashid	8	11	0	44	190	17.27	-	-
Azhar Shafiq	16	26	0	122	439	16.88	1	1
Hamaj Mukhtar	5	9	1	29	135	16.87	-	-
Sajid Shah	14	24	4	78*	329	16.45	-	1
Akram Raza	7	13	0	46	211	16.23	-	-
Wasim Yousafi	9	16	1	55	235	15.66	-	2
Zulfiqar Jan	9	15	2	56	202	15.53	-	1
Mohammad Haroon	5	8	0	34	123	15.37	-	-
Majid Jahangir	6	10	0	48	151	15.10	-	-

8 completed innings, average 15.00

BOWLING

Bowling	Overs	Mds	Runs	Wkts	Av	Best	10m	5/inn
Aleem Moosa	138.2	28	415	37	11.21	7-39	2	3
Wasim Haider	95.1	28	194	17	11.41	4-14	-	-
Shakeel Ahmed, sr	308.2	113	621	39	15.92	6-33	-	3
Mohammad Sami	233.5	49	746	44	16.95	6-72	-	3
Waqar Ahmed	225.3	45	717	42	17.07	7-86	1	2
Arshad Khan	272	75	646	37	17.45	7-66	-	2
Akram Raza	148.5	27	426	24	17.75	3-40	-	-
Shahid Iqbal	140.4	32	346	19	18.21	4-44	-	-
Naeem Akhtar	370	114	803	44	18.25	6-18	-	3
Kashif Raza	351	72	1089	59	18.45	6-59	-	6
Sajid Shah	313.3	60	971	52	18.67	6-34	-	1
Mohammad Altaf	239.5	66	488	26	18.76	4-17	-	-

FIRST-CLASS AVERAGES

BOWLING

Bowling	Overs	Mds	Runs	Wkts	Av	Best	10m	5/inn
Farooq Iqbal	202.5	76	378	20	18.90	5-16	-	1
Tahir Khan	143.2	39	343	18	19.05	4-44	-	-
Iftikhar Anjum	275.1	58	820	43	19.06	6-82	2	4
Hasnain Kazim	155.3	34	498	26	19.15	6-46	-	2
Shabbir Ahmed	286.4	56	847	42	20.16	6-51	-	3
Nauman Habib	59	10	203	10	20.30	5-11	-	1
Nadeem Iqbal	342.3	85	876	43	20.37	7-53	-	5
Shoaib Malik	153.2	31	449	22	20.40	7-81	-	1
Mohammad Akram	186.1	38	659	32	20.59	4-18	-	-
Mohammad Hussain	303.1	100	809	39	20.74	5-54	-	3
Fazal Akbar Shah	162.5	28	593	28	21.17	5-25	-	2
Nadeem Afzal	153.2	37	425	20	21.25	5-85	-	1
Asadullah Butt	105	27	281	13	21.61	5-67	-	1
Saeed Anwar, jr	116.5	23	325	15	21.66	4-25	-	-
Naveed-ul-Hassan	590.5	110	1823	84	21.70	7-86	-	5
Mohammad Javed	239.2	46	634	29	21.86	6-50	-	2
Mohammad Zahid	458.5	111	1097	50	21.94	6-58	-	3
Shahid Anwar	96.4	23	220	10	22.00	3-42	-	-
AF Giles	244.3	74	553	25	22.12	5-75	-	1
Danish Kaneria	527.1	141	1354	61	22.19	7-39	-	3
Aqeel Ahmed	401.4	78	1206	54	22.33	7-115	1	5
Naveed-ul-Hassan	590.5	116	1863	84	22.41	7-86	-	5
Sarfraz Ahmed	241	71	609	27	22.55	5-36	-	2
Kabir Khan	170.3	30	526	23	22.86	5-42	-	2
Stephen John	435.1	67	1352	59	22.91	6-32	1	3
Bilal Asad	122	43	278	12	23.16	5-32	-	1
Mohammad Zahid, jr	216.2	34	721	31	23.25	7-71	-	2
Ali Gauhar	222.3	53	700	30	23.33	7-41	1	2
Asif Mujtaba	238.4	79	420	18	23.33	3-37	-	-
Ali Naqvi	129.5	35	376	16	23.50	5-65	-	1
Rauf Akbar	142.4	32	473	20	23.65	7-27	1	1
Faisal Afridi	175.1	34	569	24	23.70	4-45	-	-
Rao Iftikhar	215	42	712	30	23.73	5-55	-	3
Fahad Masood	224.5	44	698	29	24.06	4-47	-	-
Abdur Rehman	266.2	73	700	29	24.13	5-144	-	1
Zahid Saeed	170.4	24	632	26	24.30	4-68	-	-
Shahid Nazir	362	73	1168	48	24.33	6-58	-	2
Jaffar Nazir	491.2	90	1570	64	24.53	7-46	-	2
Yasir Arafat	530	88	1798	73	24.63	6-9	-	2
Abdur Razzaq	159.4	29	447	18	24.83	6-79	1	1
Kamran Hussain	471.2	90	1577	63	25.03	6-53	-	3
Mohammad Sarfraz	261.5	40	844	33	25.57	5-43	-	2
Salman Fazal	256.2	78	595	23	25.86	6-45	-	1
Waqas Ahmed	443	84	1428	55	25.96	7-45	-	2
Shahid Afridi	196.3	49	520	20	26.00	4-58	-	-
Usman Tariq	193	21	643	24	26.79	5-113	-	1
Azhar Shafiq	237.5	56	702	26	27.00	4-19	-	-
Aqib Javed	210.3	57	554	20	27.70	5-139	-	1
Imran Tahir	240	51	703	25	28.12	5-57	-	1

FIRST-CLASS AVERAGES

BOWLING

Bowling	Overs	Mds	Runs	Wkts	Av	Best	10m	5/inn

The following players took 10 wickets in fewer than 8 innings:

Bowling	Overs	Mds	Runs	Wkts	Av	Best	10m	5/inn
Irfan Fazil	423.2	59	1620	57	28.42	6-100	-	5
Mubashir Nazir	474.1	88	1546	54	28.62	6-56	-	3
Maqsood Rana	155	25	525	18	29.16	4-23	-	-
Qaisar Abbas	189	61	415	14	29.64	4-16	-	-
C White	140.2	27	393	13	30.23	4-54	-	-
Naved Latif	97	21	304	10	30.40	2-8	-	-
Tanvir Ahmed	259.4	37	988	31	31.87	6-81	1	2
Tabish Nawab	305.2	61	893	28	31.89	7-64	-	1
Hakim Butt	112	29	357	11	32.45	4-42	-	-
Ahmed Hayat	227.2	29	872	25	34.88	5-62	-	1
Aamer Nazir	266.3	34	1030	29	35.51	5-88	-	1
Faheem Ahmed	173.3	34	543	15	36.20	6-127	-	1
MJ Hoggard	67.3	24	132	17	7.76	5-62	-	1
Faisal Irfan	71.1	22	161	16	10.06	6-19	1	1
Pervez Iqbal	61	20	150	10	15.00	4-59	-	-
Athar Laeeq	82	22	217	12	18.08	3-28	-	-
Adnan Malik	121.4	34	297	15	19.80	5-47	-	1
Wasim Akram	103.5	34	226	11	20.54	6-36	-	1
Shoaib Akhtar	67.5	10	238	11	21.63	5-75	-	1
Maqbool Hussain	68.2	17	217	10	21.70	4-26	-	-
D Gough	129.1	25	373	16	23.31	3-30	-	-
Saqlain Mushtaq	203.2	52	435	18	24.16	8-168	-	1
Saboor Ahmed	110	22	268	11	24.36	4-58	-	-
Ashfaq Ahmed	108	33	292	11	26.54	2-17	-	-
Asim Iqbal	86	13	310	10	31.10	6-90	-	1
Ata-ur-Rehman	147.5	34	508	15	33.86	4-38	-	-
Fazl-e-Akbar	101.2	22	351	10	35.10	5-54	-	1
Kashif Shafi	197.2	30	614	17	36.11	4-68	-	-

Qualification: 10 wickets in 8 innings

FIELDING

76 – Atiq-uz-Zaman (70ct,6st); 69 – Kamran Akmal (67ct,2st) 48 – Humayan Farhat (45ct,3st); 44 – Ahmed Zeeshan (41ct,3st); 32 – Inamullah Rashid (27ct,5st); 30 – Mohammad Shahbaz (25ct,5st), Wasim Yousafi; 28 – Nadeem Abbasi (26ct,2st), Rashid Latif (25ct,3st); 27 – Mohammad Salman (26ct,1st), Nadeem Hussain; 25 – Zulfiqar Jan (21ct,4st); 24 – Hafiz Khalid (23ct,1st); 20 – Aamir Bashir, Mohammad Shafiq; 19 – Naumanullah, Naved Latif; 18 – Aamer Iqbal, Hasan Raza; 17 – Azhar Shafiq; 16 – Shahid Afridi; 15 – Nasir Ali (14ct,1st); 14 – Rafatullah, Zahid Umar (13ct,1st); 13 – Asif Mujtaba, Imran Abbas, Mohammad Masroor, Mohammad Wasim, Rehan Rafiq; 12 – Ali Raza, Ijaz Mahmood, Imran Nazir, Naseer Ahmed, AJ Stewart (9ct,3st), Younis Khan; 11 – Ijaz Ahmed, jr, PA Nixon, Pervez Aziz, Taufiq Umar, Yasir Arafat; 10 – Asfar Nawaz, Ghaffar Kazmi, Imran Farhat, Intikhab Alam, Iqbal Imam, Mohammad Hafeez, Shahid Mahmood, GP Thorpe, Zahoor Elahi

Qualification: 10 catches or more

SRI LANKA

England in Sri Lanka
India in Sri Lanka
Sri Lanka Domestic First-Class Season
Sri Lanka Domestic One-Day Season
First-Class Averages

ENGLAND IN SRI LANKA
by Jonathan Agnew

Sri Lanka Colts XI v. England XI
5–6 February 2001 at De Zoysa Stadium, Moratuwa
England XI 252 (ME Trescothick 100) and 24 for 2
Sri Lanka Colts XI 232 for 8 dec. (M Pushpakumara 54, WMSM Perera 50)
Match drawn

Agentle warm-up exercise for England after a six-week layoff produced a century for Marcus Trescothick – he retired, diplomatically – and a rumpus between Darren Gough and a young fielder, MSP Peiris. This was blown out of all proportion when the Sri Lankan Board became involved. Gough responded, verbally, to the fielder's successful appeal for a catch – when Gough had not touched the ball – and this was followed by a mouthful from the youngster to see the old campaigner on his way! A two-day match was never likely to yield a result, but the Colts at least had the satisfaction of dismissing Atherton cheaply twice.

Sri Lanka Board President's XI v. England XI
8–11 February 2001 at P Saravanamuttu Stadium, Colombo
England XI 329 (N Hussain 81, C White 63, MP Vaughan 57) and 261 for 9 dec.
(GA Hick 75, D Hettiarachchi 5 for 84)
Sri Lanka Board President's XI 265 (TM Dilshan 122) and 160
England XI won by 165 runs

A heartening result for the tourists, made all the more pleasing by a return to a semblance of form by Hussain. He scored 81 in the first innings as he opened with Atherton, who also found some touch in the second with a knock of 47. Dilshan scored a century for the President's XI as Croft took three wickets, but the home team was dismissed for only 160 in its second innings with Gough and Giles claiming four wickets apiece.

Sri Lanka Board President's XI v. England XI
15–18 February 2001 at Uyanwatte Stadium, Matara
Sri Lanka Board President's XI 253 (MRCN Bandaratilleke 73, HGJM Kulatunga 54,

Previous page: After losing the first Test of the series at Galle, it was a superb achievement for England to win the three-match series.

M Pushpakumara 52) and 234 for 7 (TM Dilshan 115*)
England XI 418 for 7 dec. (C White 85*, MA Atherton 85, GP Thorpe 57)
Match drawn

Another unsavoury incident clouded England's final warm-up match before the Test series. Craig White and Ruchira Perera had an angry exchange of words as White's undefeated 85 gave England a commanding 165-run lead. This resulted in a formal letter of complaint being written by the England management to their hosts and fuelled speculation that the Test series would be acrimonious. Ashley Giles picked up a calf strain but was able to bowl on the final day as three wickets for Michael Vaughan gave England a brief glimpse of an unlikely victory. The home team was rescued by a second century in ten days by Tillikeratne Dilshan – an innings that secured his place in the Sri Lanka side for the first Test.

FIRST TEST
22–26 February 2001 at Galle International Stadium

Our worst fears were confirmed during five days of histrionic appealing, poor umpiring and disciplinary action by the referee, Hanumant Singh. The entire Sri Lankan team was officially warned, four Sri Lankans were fined and their captain, Sanath Jayasuriya, was reminded of his responsibilities. Graeme Hick was served with a suspended one-Test ban for showing dissent when he was adjudged caught behind by umpire Peter Manuel, which was just one of a catalogue of umpiring errors. The setting at Galle, with its imposing 18th century Dutch fort dominating one end of the ground, is magnificent, but the manner in which the cricket was played was depressingly ugly.

The pitch was clearly prepared with Sri Lanka's spinners in mind. Dry and crusty, the ball turned increasingly sharply as the match progressed and, having won an important toss, the home batsmen quickly seized the initiative.

Marvan Atapattu, who had endured a miserable series in South Africa, defended as if his life – never mind his career – depended upon it. Ticking along at barely a run per over, his unbeaten double century was a study of concentration. He lost his opening partner, Jayasuriya, in the fifth over, when the captain carved a short ball from Darren Gough to White in the gully, but Kumar Sangakkara, the young wicketkeeper preferred to Romesh

Kaluwitharana, added 92 before driving Croft to short extra cover.

With Atapattu retreating further into his shell, the Sri Lankan innings needed urgency, and this was provided by Aravinda de Silva. By the close of the first day, the little right-hander had almost caught his partner, and the following morning, in a blur of twinkling feet and sumptuous drives, de Silva completed a beautiful hundred. With the score on 340 for two, both batsmen suddenly found themselves at the same end, and Gough's arrow-like throw from mid off beat de Silva's frantic attempt to reach safety. His 106 contained ten fours and a six.

Even from our distant view from the ramparts of

Even Sri Lanka's opening batsman Marvan Atapattu struggled with the heat and humidity at Galle, where dreadful umpiring did little to help England's cause.

FIRST TEST – SRI LANKA v. ENGLAND
22–26 February 2001 at Galle International Stadium, Galle

SRI LANKA

	First innings	
MS Atapattu	not out	201
ST Jayasuriya (capt)	c White, b Gough	14
*K Sangakkara	c White, b Croft	58
PA de Silva	run out (Gough)	106
DPM Jayawardene	run out (Thorpe)	61
WPUJC Vaas	c White, b Giles	8
RP Arnold	not out	1
TM Dilshan		
RD Fernando		
M Muralitharan		
HDPK Dharmasena		
	b9, lb2, nb10	21
	(for 5 wickets dec.)	470

	First innings			
	O	M	R	W
Gough	26	3	95	1
Caddick	30	13	46	-
White	30	6	80	-
Giles	48	8	134	1
Croft	32	6	96	1
Hick	4	0	8	-

Fall of Wickets
1-18, 2-110, 3-340, 4-451, 5-468

ENGLAND

	First innings		Second innings	
MA Atherton	lbw b Vaas	33	c Sangakkara, b Vaas	44
ME Trescothick	c Sangakkara, b Vaas	122	c Sangakkara, b Jayasuriya	57
N Hussain (capt)	lbw b Muralitharan	3	lbw b Muralitharan	1
GP Thorpe	c Dilshan, b Muralitharan	7	lbw b Dharmasena	12
*AJ Stewart	lbw b Jayasuriya	19	not out	34
RDB Croft	c Jayawardene, b Jayasuriya	9	(10) lbw b Jayasuriya	2
GA Hick	c Sangakkara, b Vaas	5	(6) c Jayawardene, b Jayasuriya	6
C White	c Sangakkara, b Jayasuriya	25	(7) lbw b Muralitharan	3
AF Giles	c Dilshan, b Muralitharan	4	lbw b Muralitharan	1
AR Caddick	c Jayawardene, b Jayasuriya	0	(8) b Jayasuriya	1
D Gough	not out	0	b Muralitharan	0
	b2, lb3, nb21	26	b11, lb6, nb11	28
		253		189

	First innings				Second innings			
	O	M	R	W	O	M	R	W
Vaas	24	7	53	3	15	6	29	1
Muralitharan	54.3	14	79	3	42.3	14	66	4
Dharmasena	22	6	51	-	16	6	21	1
Fernando	2	0	10	-	4	0	10	-
Jayasuriya	27	9	50	4	32	13	44	4
de Silva	3	2	5	-				
Arnold					1	0	2	-

Fall of Wickets
1-83, 2-93, 3-117, 4-197, 5-206, 6-217, 7-239, 8-253, 9-253
1-101, 2-105, 3-121, 4-145, 5-167, 6-176, 7-182, 8-183, 9-188

Umpires: PT Manuel & AV Jayaprakash
Toss: Sri Lanka
Test debuts: nil

Sri Lanka won by an innings and 28 runs

the fort – the BBC was barred from entering the ground over a rights dispute – we could see that England's bowlers were toiling. Each delivery was creating a cloud of dust as the ball landed on the pitch, but the Sri Lankans are well at home in these conditions. Mahela Jayawardene added 111 with Atapattu before becoming the second victim to a run out – this time it was Graham Thorpe's perfect kick from backward point that defeated the scrambling batsman: to leave his side on 451 for four.

Sri Lanka might easily have batted on into the third morning, but after Chaminda Vaas – promoted to have a slog – holed out at long off to give Ashley Giles his only wicket of the innings – Jayasuriya called his men in to give England's openers eight uncomfortable overs before the close.

271 runs were needed for England to avoid the follow-on and Atherton and Trescothick, who put on 83 for the first wicket, set them well on course. Atherton rode his luck – he might well have been out leg before on 19 and was dropped on 28 – before Vaas finally trapped him with the third ball after lunch for 33. Hussain fell immediately, leg before to Muralitharan for three and Thorpe was caught in the gully for seven, but Stewart – who is never at his most comfortable when confronted by spin bowling – grafted uncharacteristically for two hours and 20 minutes before he fell victim to the worst lbw decision imaginable.

Jayasuriya, bowling left arm over the wicket, pitched a ball at least a foot outside the leg stump, Stewart missed a pull shot and was so amazed to be despatched by umpire Manuel (although Jayasuriya had no business even asking for it) that he departed the scene without so

Graeme Hick is about to be caught by Jayawardene as Jayasuriya claimed four wickets in England's second innings.

much as a sideways look. It really was atrocious.

England were lifted by Trescothick's first century – a magnificent effort under the circumstances – but avoiding the follow-on was now becoming a challenge. This intensified when Trescothick edged Vaas to Sangakkara in the second over of the fourth day. Hick was on the wrong end of another poor decision and was adjudged caught behind for five, and although White made 25, England lost their last six wickets for 51 as the spinners ran through the tail. The visitors were soon following on, 217 runs behind.

Once again, the openers did their best. This time Atherton and Trescothick posted 101 before, in the second over of the final day, umpire Jayaprakash from India, got in on the action. He fired out Atherton, leg before to Vaas for 44, and followed that by giving Trescothick out caught behind, although the ball only made contact with the batsman's arm. England's chances in their battle for survival now seemed remote and amidst the most appalling scenes of mass-appealing and fielders charging the umpires, further incompetent decisions accounted for Hussain, White and – although it was

now too late – Croft. England lost their last six wickets for 22 runs and were dismissed 45 minutes after lunch, but a shattered window in their dressing room only partly illustrated their feeling of injustice.

Muralitharan and Jayasuriya shared the spoils and, in the aftermath, England's cricketers and media were accused of being high-handed and bombastic in their outrage at the standard of umpiring and the pressure applied to officials by Jayasuriya's team. The truth is that Sri Lanka, in scoring 470, deserved their victory, but in losing four of their top-seven batsmen to poor decisions in the second innings, England were never given the opportunity to compete on level terms.

Sri Lanka Colts XI v. England XI
3 March 2001 at Welagedera Stadium, Kurunegala
Sri Lanka Colts XI 249 for 7 (50 overs) (SI de Saram 62)
England XI 250 for 2 (ME Trescothick 85, N Hussain 73)
England XI won by eight wickets

SECOND TEST
7–11 March 2001 at Asgiriya Stadium, Kandy

If the Galle Test match had been ill-tempered and ruined by umpiring errors, it was a cakewalk compared to the second match in the series. Amidst the hills of central Sri Lanka, the ineptitude of the home umpire, BC Cooray, managed to achieve the impossible by surpassing the efforts even of his predecessors, Messrs. Manuel and Jayaprakash. This resulted in further bad sportsmanship and acrimony, which forced the referee, the apparently tireless Hanumant Singh, to threaten the Sri Lankan captain, Sanath Jayasuriya, with a six-month suspension. Mike Atherton and Kumar Sangakkara were also severely reprimanded for a very obvious fall-out – it was 23-year-old Sangakarra's fourth appearance of the series in the referee's room – and Mr Cooray had to be given a police escort from the ground amidst unsubstantiated rumours that his house had been ransacked by furious Sri Lankan supporters.

The pitch at the Asgiriya Stadium again appeared to be dusty and dry. It was here, 15 years ago, that the left-arm spinner Norman Gifford – then the 45-year-old England 'B' team coach – was forced out of retirement to play in one of the 'Tests' because the strip was so obviously a spinner's paradise, so winning the toss – once again – seemed to be an urgent priority.

For the eighth time in nine Tests, Hussain lost. Conversely, Sri Lanka had now won their last eight on home soil and Jayasuriya's decision to bat first would have been instantaneous. Hussain must have dreaded breaking the news to his team-mates, but, instead, found them determinedly strapping on their bowling boots. This attitude was taken with them onto the field.

Thanks to some inspired seam bowling, Sri Lanka soon found themselves on 93 for four at lunch. The first bad decision of a host in the match had already been given – the South African, Rudi Koertzen, mistakenly believed that the ball had made contact with Sangakkara's bat handle before lobbing into the gully when, in fact, it had come full off the arm guard. Sangakarra's almost obligatory bad sportsmanship earned him another rebuke from the referee.

The afternoon session was a joy to watch as Mahela Jayawardene and Russel Arnold batted throughout, scoring 123 in only 31 overs. It was magnificent entertainment with Jayawardene making 101 in three hours, but Gough returned with the second new ball to restore England's supremacy. Sri Lanka lost five wickets for 20 runs in five overs as, roared on by three-and-a-half thousand England supporters, Gough and Caddick reduced Sri Lanka from 221 for four to 297 all out.

Atherton was nipped out early on the second day for seven – again leg before to Vaas – and when Trescothick was caught, top-edging a sweep, for 23, England were 37 for two. Finally, however, after the most difficult and, personally, unrewarding year of his career, Nasser Hussain returned to form. He required the most outrageous luck – he should have been given out by Mr Cooray, caught at silly point on 53 and 62 – but no-one who has seen Hussain battle against poor decisions and indifferent form this past year could begrudge him his good fortune one bit.

With three quarters of an hour to go on the second day, Hussain was bowled for 109 as he aimed a swipe at Muralitharan when he really should have been looking to playing for the close. This might have spared Hick from one of the most atrocious ducks there can ever have been – he even appeared to face his own hat-trick ball! First, he drove a return catch to Murali, which was given not out by Cooray, and he was then plumb in front to the next delivery, which Cooray turned down. Finally, to spare him any further torture, Cooray despatched Hick in the following Muralitharan over, although the ball would comfortably have missed the leg stump! It was already becoming a lottery.

It was vital for England's prospects that they secured a first-innings lead and, on the third morning, Stewart and White took them from a deficit of 48 to a 26-run advantage. Once again, Stewart showed admirable concentration, defying the spinners for three-and-three-quarter hours before prodding a catch to silly point for 54. However, the real impetus and, as it turned out, match-winning contribution came from the last wicket pair of Gough and Croft who added 41 in an hour, extending the lead from 49 to a now-imposing 90.

Sri Lanka collapsed, with the help of some desperate umpiring. Atapattu was clearly caught behind off Gough – who had his tail up – in the first over, but the dismissal of Jayasuriya in the next was appalling. Aiming a drive at Caddick, the Sri Lankan captain edged the ball into the ground and into a diving Thorpe's outstretched left hand at third slip. The umpires conferred but, sadly, despite the fielders around the bat knowing that the catch was not deliberate, England indulged in celebrations and high-fives. After their experience at Galle, they felt that anything was justified.

With no referral possible to the third umpire, and a complete lack of sportsmanship on the field, BC

Cooray raised the finger just as television replays were showing the ball bouncing en route to Thorpe. Jayasuriya was outraged, throwing his gloves and helmet onto the ground before being booed off by the English contingent in the crowd. Moments later he was followed by de Silva, legitimately caught in the gully although Sangakkara's intervention at the non-striker's end started an argument with Atherton. Croft nipped out Arnold and Dilshan to leave Sri Lanka only eight runs ahead at the close of the fourth day with four wickets in hand. Sangakkara, however, was still at the crease and, next morning, he steadily increased the lead with the help of Dharmasena, who was clearly caught at silly point on 19 – apart from in the mind of BC, that is. As the tension mounted, and with everyone in the ground gripped, Sangakkara appeared to be coasting to his first Test century when, inexplicably, he charged at Croft and was stumped for 95. The lead was 91 and although Vaas was reprieved by Cooray on 0, his 36 and Dharmasena's 54 set England 161 to win.

With the real threat of a suspension hanging over him, Jayasuriya was notably becalmed in the field

Nasser Hussain lived dangerously at Kandy, where umpiring had become such a lottery. He should have been given out on 53 and 62, but went on to score 109.

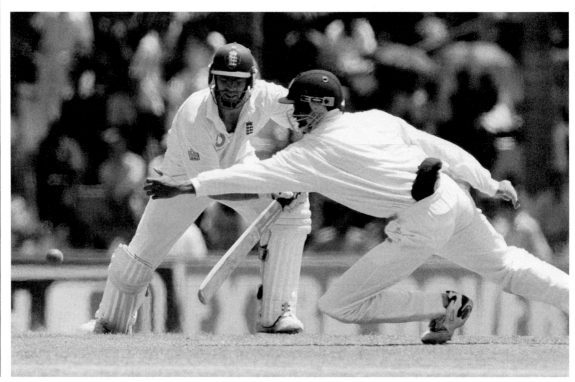

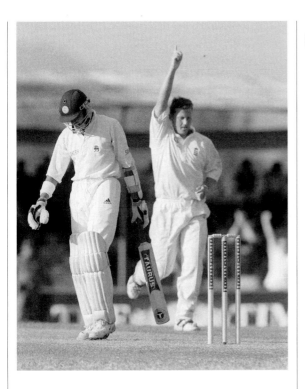

Despite the heat, Darren Gough bowled whole-heartedly and finished with match figures of eight for 123.

and so were his colleagues. England lost their first wicket on 24 when Atherton edged low to Sangakkara and in the next over, Trescothick was adjudged lbw by Mr Cooray, although the delivery would have missed the leg stump. Thorpe and Hussain – who was hindered by a groin strain – added 60 before Thorpe, on 46, was caught behind off Muralitharan and, just before stumps, Hussain was also caught by Sangakkara off Vaas for 15.

So the final day was gloriously set up, with England needing a further 70 to win with six wickets in hand. Stewart and the nightwatchman, Croft, took the score to 99 when Stewart was leg before to Vaas for 11. The stage seemed to be set for Graeme Hick, who responded by scoring 16 from 34 balls, but was then bowled by Jayasuriya with 39 runs required. The nerves were jangling all around the ground as White and Croft added a further 20 but, after an hour and 50 minutes of defiance, Croft played around a straight one from Dharmasena and was lbw for 17.

Nineteen runs required to square the series, and the tail-enders were exposed! Lunch was taken with England wanting just nine to win and, 20 minutes after the break, White forced Jayasuriya through the

SECOND TEST – SRI LANKA v. ENGLAND
7–11 March 2001 at Asgiriya Stadium, Kandy

SRI LANKA

	First innings		Second innings	
MS Atapattu	b Gough	16	c Stewart, b Gough	2
ST Jayasuriya (capt)	c Giles, b Caddick	9	c Thorpe, b Caddick	0
*K Sangakkara	c Trescothick, b White	17	st Stewart, b Croft	95
PA de Silva	c & b White	29	c White, b Gough	1
DPM Jayawardene	c Thorpe, b Caddick	101	b White	18
RP Arnold	c White, b Gough	65	lbw b Croft	22
TM Dilshan	c Atherton, b Gough	36	c Hick, b Croft	0
HDPK Dharmasena	c Thorpe, b Gough	1	c Hick, b Gough	54
WPUJC Vaas	c Thorpe, b Caddick	2	c Croft, b White	36
DNT Zoysa	c Stewart, b Caddick	0	c Hick, b Gough	0
M Muralitharan	not out	10	not out	6
	b1, lb3, nb7	11	b2, lb3, nb11	16
		297		**250**

	First innings				Second innings			
	O	M	R	W	O	M	R	W
Gough	14	1	73	4	22	5	50	4
Caddick	20	3	55	4	18	5	55	1
Giles	15	2	47	-	15	3	58	-
White	17	3	70	2	12.1	3	42	2
Croft	20	2	48	-	22	11	40	3

Fall of Wickets
1-21, 2-29, 3-69, 4-80, 5-221, 6-277, 7-279, 8-282, 9-286
1-2, 2-2, 3-3, 4-42, 5-81, 6-88, 7-181, 8-234, 9-242

ENGLAND

	First innings		Second innings	
MA Atherton	lbw b Vaas	7	c Sangakkara, b Vaas	11
ME Trescothick	c Sangakkara, b Dharmasena	23	lbw b Vaas	13
N Hussain (capt)	b Muralitharan	109	c Sangakkara, b Vaas	15
GP Thorpe	c Dilshan, b Jayasuriya	59	c Sangakkara, b Muralitharan	46
*AJ Stewart	c Dilshan, b Jayasuriya	54	lbw b Vaas	7
GA Hick	lbw b Muralitharan	0	(7) b Jayasuriya	16
C White	st Sangakkara, b Jayasuriya	39	(8) not out	21
AF Giles	b Muralitharan	5	(9) not out	4
RDB Croft	not out	33	(6) lbw b Dharmasena	17
AR Caddick	b Muralitharan	7		
D Gough	lbw b Vaas	10		
	b16, lb20, w1, nb4	41	b1, lb8, nb2	11
		387	(for 7 wickets)	**161**

	First innings				Second innings			
	O	M	R	W	O	M	R	W
Vaas	23	7	39	2	18	4	39	4
Zoysa	10	2	35	-	2	0	16	-
Muralitharan	63	21	127	4	27	7	50	1
Dharmasena	27	4	74	1	8	0	25	1
Jayasuriya	34	10	76	3	16.1	6	22	1

Fall of Wickets
1-16, 2-37, 3-204, 4-232, 5-236, 6-323, 7-330, 8-336, 9-346
1-24, 2-25, 3-86, 4-89, 5-97, 6-122, 7-142

Umpires: BC Cooray & RE Koertzen
Toss: Sri Lanka
Test debuts: nil

England won by three wickets

covers to complete a remarkable victory.

It was as ill-tempered a match as there can ever have been in recent times. Stewart said afterwards that, in 107 Tests, he had never known such acrimony and England left Kandy with Hussain suggesting that he and Jayasuriya needed to get together for a peace summit before the start of the final Test in only four days' time.

THIRD TEST
15–17 March 2001 at Sinhalese Sports Club Ground, Colombo

When Sanath Jayasuriya won Sri Lanka's third successive toss, few of the thousands of England supporters in the ground could possibly have imagined the dramatic events that would unfold before the weekend was out. Not only did England win the game in the final over of scheduled play on the third day, but they clinched the series as well – and that from having lost the opening Test in Galle. This was a truly outstanding achievement.

The two captains, as promised, held a meeting before the match in order to iron out the differences between the teams. Jayasuriya promised better, more sporting behaviour from his players. Hussain immediately claimed the high ground with a similar pledge, to which he added the rider that, as far as he was concerned, England's players were not overstepping the mark. Given that Jayasuriya himself had only recently been the victim of one of England's more grotesque appeals in Kandy, the Sri Lanka captain might have been forgiven for raising an eyebrow at that observation.

Sri Lanka's openers strode to the wicket knowing that they had messed up a similar opportunity in the previous Test. The pitch at the Sinhalese Sports Club appeared to be full of runs with the promise of spin later and, clearly, a first-innings total of 500 was the primary

target. Atapattu, however, aimed a casual flick at Caddick in the second over and was bowled for a duck. Gough roared in, but could not enforce a further breakthrough as Jayasuriya and Sangakkara enjoyed both the conditions and a lightning-fast outfield. They added 86 until Sangakkara again paid for his natural impetuosity by carving Gough to Vaughan at point for 45. His captain played a similar stroke and perished to Croft, also for 45 and, already, Sri Lanka's grip on the game was slipping.

This was compounded by a sudden change to the manner in which the pitch behaved. From playing

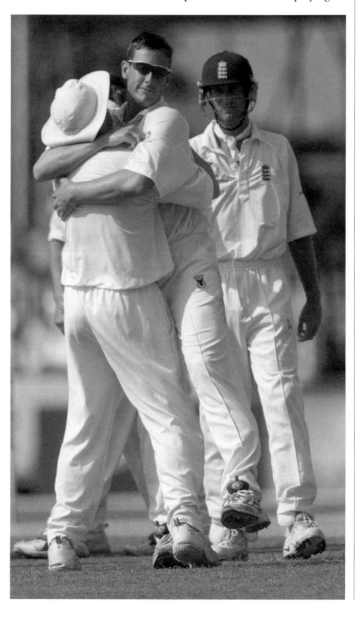

Ashley Giles demolished Sri Lanka in their second innings at Colombo, taking four for 11 off just nine overs.

flawlessly before lunch, the ball began to grip and hold as all the pace evaporated under a baking sun. Croft discovered both turn and bounce as he produced a spell as valuable as he has ever produced in an England shirt. Under his influence, Sri Lanka suffered a dreadful final session in which they lost four wickets for 63 runs and closed the opening day on 221 for seven, and that after having been 205 for three. With the new ball still up their sleeve for the morning, England were already in control and, when play resumed, the last three wickets were wrapped up for the addition of only 20 runs. Croft claimed four for 56 from 32 overs and, in doing so, suggested that Muralitharan would be a handful.

In fact, the master off spinner managed only a single wicket in England's first innings as the blunting tactics employed so successfully in Kandy by the visitors continued to frustrate him. Simply speaking, Murali was spinning the ball so much from wide of the off stump that a firm, defensive thrust of the pad – and some faith in a much-improved, all-round umpiring performance – made it extremely difficult for him to threaten, unless a batsman went on the offensive.

From 45 without loss, England slid to 66 for three. Atherton was undone by Vaas again – in fact, the left armer was to dismiss the opener in all but one innings of the series – Trescothick was 'caught' by the short leg fielder for 23 as he dived for cover to give Hettiarachchi his first Test wicket and Hussain, hindered by his leg injury, drove loosely to extra cover for eight. This dismissal followed an extraordinary incident in which Hussain edged Hetteriachchi to slip and clearly saw that the ball had not carried. Correctly, the umpire in the middle, David Orchard, referred it to the third umpire, BC Cooray who, in a flash, appeared to give the England captain out! Hussain refused to go and, after a short delay, Cooray changed his mind! It was not easy to blame Hussain for this since, in Sri Lanka's first innings, De Silva had edged Giles directly to slip, refused to walk and was given not out by umpire Orchard! Despite the pre-match meeting between the captains, it was clear that the gloves were already off.

At 91 for four, when Stewart fell to Muralitharan, England were wobbling and Sri Lanka had their chance to fight back. Michael Vaughan who, finally, had been preferred to Graeme Hick, walked out to join Thorpe having not batted for a month. If ever the young Yorkshireman's temperament was put to the test, this was it and, assisted nobly and unselfishly by Thorpe, Vaughan passed with flying colours.

THIRD TEST – SRI LANKA v. ENGLAND
15–17 March 2001 at Sinhalese Sports Club, Colombo

SRI LANKA

	First innings		Second innings	
MS Atapattu	b Caddick	0	c Croft, b Gough	0
ST Jayasuriya (capt)	c White, b Croft	45	lbw b Gough	23
*K Sangakkara	c Vaughan, b Gough	45	c Stewart, b Caddick	0
PA de Silva	c Vaughan, b Giles	38	c Thorpe, b Caddick	23
DPM Jayawardene	c Stewart, b Croft	71	lbw b Giles	11
RP Arnold	lbw b Giles	0	c Hussain, b Croft	0
TM Dilshan	lbw b Croft	5	b Giles	10
WPUJC Vaas	not out	19	c Atherton, b Giles	6
RD Fernando	c Trescothick, b Croft	2	c Giles, b Gough	5
D Hettiarachchi	b Gough	0	not out	0
M Muralitharan	b Caddick	1	lbw b Giles	1
	b4, lb4, w1, nb6	15	nb	2
		241		**81**

	First innings				Second innings			
	O	M	R	W	O	M	R	W
Gough	14	5	33	2	6	1	23	3
Caddick	11.1	1	40	2	8	2	29	2
White	10	1	45	-				
Giles	34	13	59	2	9.1	4	11	4
Croft	32	9	56	4	5	0	18	1

Fall of Wickets
1-2, 2-88, 3-108, 4-205, 5-209, 6-216, 7-219, 8-225, 9-240
1-21, 2-24, 3-24, 4-57, 5-59, 6-59, 7-69, 8-76, 9-80

ENGLAND

	First innings		Second innings	
MA Atherton	lbw b Vaas	21	c & b Fernando	13
ME Trescothick	c Arnold, b Hettiarachchi	23	c Sangakkara, b Jayasuriya	10
N Hussain (capt)	c Jayasuriya, b Hettiarachchi	8	(7) c Arnold, b Jayasuriya	0
GP Thorpe	not out	113	not out	32
*AJ Stewart	b Muralitharan	3	c Dilshan, b Jayasuriya	0
MP Vaughan	c Sangakkara, b Vaas	26	(3) b Muralitharan	8
C White	c Sangakkara, b Vaas	0	(6) c Jayawardene, b Jayasuriya	8
AF Giles	c Jayawardene, b Vaas	0	not out	1
RDB Croft	run out (Atapattu)	16		
AR Caddick	c Jayasuriya, b Vaas	0		
D Gough	c Jayawardene, b Vaas	14		
	b10, lb9, nb6	25	lb1, nb1	2
		249	(for 6 wickets)	**74**

	First innings				Second innings			
	O	M	R	W	O	M	R	W
Vaas	27.5	6	73	6	3	0	11	-
Fernando	5	0	26	-	2	0	7	1
de Silva	3	1	2	-				
Muralitharan	41	9	73	1	8	1	26	1
Hettiarachchi	24	6	36	2	3	1	5	-
Jayasuriya	9	1	20	-	8.3	0	24	4

Fall of Wickets
1-45, 2-55, 3-66, 4-91, 5-177, 6-177, 7-181, 8-209, 9-223
1-23, 2-24, 3-42, 4-43, 5-63, 6-71

Umpires: EAR de Silva & DL Orchard
Toss: Sri Lanka
Test debut: D Hettiarachchi (Sri Lanka)

England won by four wickets

Their partnership of 86 stretched into the third morning and, bearing in mind the extraordinary events that were to unfold, it is worth recording that at the start of play, England were 175 for four in their first innings! By the close, 22 wickets had fallen for 229 runs and the match was over.

In fact, England were still batting at lunch. Thorpe had reached a superb century in five hours in which he had masterfully controlled the strike by scampering quick singles. Having lost Vaughan for 26, Thorpe was helped first by Croft's 16, and then by Gough, who thumped 14 before becoming Vaas' sixth victim and leaving Thorpe undefeated on 113. England's lead, though, was only eight runs.

There were shades of Karachi in the mayhem that followed. Sri Lanka, weighed down by local expectation, panicked completely. Rather than accepting that, with half of the match still to play, they had the opportunity to bat themselves into a commanding position, they appeared to have no idea of how they should be playing. Jayasuriya flung the bat for 23 but he had already lost Atapattu for a second duck in the match (Atapattu managed only 18 runs in four innings after his double century in Galle) and Sangakkara, also without scoring. England's bowlers were rampant – they had been here before and now knew how to press home the advantage. Gough and Caddick claimed the first four wickets before the spinners came into their own and seven wickets fell for 24. Giles took four for 11 as, within 29 overs, the Sri Lankan second innings was over. It had been an utter shambles from start to finish, but the huge, vociferous and partisan English crowd clearly helped to lift the visitors to new heights of ruthlessness and passion.

England needed only 74 runs to win both the match and take the series, and the only question was whether or not the runs could be scored before the end of the day. Wickets fell at regular intervals but, in truth, England were never troubled as Thorpe, with 32, steered them home in the final over the day to spark scenes of riotous celebration matched only by those in Barbados in 1994. England had now

As in Karachi, Thorpe was there at the end to steer England to their second series win of the winter.

won their last four series, previously beating Zimbabwe, West Indies and Pakistan – no wonder the Barmy Army broke into a chant of 'bring on the Aussies!'

Sri Lanka Board President's XI v. England XI
21 March 2001 at Colombo CC
England XI 279 (47.4 overs) (GA Hick 100, MP Vaughan 97)
Sri Lanka Board President's XI 228 for 9 (50 overs) (RP Arnold 62, TT Samaraweera 51*, AR Caddick 5 for 31)
England XI won by 51 runs

TEST MATCH AVERAGES
Sri Lanka v. England

SRI LANKA

Batting	M	Inns	NO	HS	Runs	Av	100	50	c/st
MS Atapattu	3	5	1	201*	219	54.75	1	-	-
DMP Jayawardene	3	5	0	101	262	52.40	1	2	6
K Sangakkara	3	5	0	95	215	43.00	-	2	12/1
PA de Silva	3	5	0	106	197	39.40	1	-	-
RP Arnold	3	5	1	65	88	22.00	-	1	2
ST Jayasuriya	3	5	0	45	91	18.20	-	-	2
WPUJC Vaas	3	5	1	36	71	17.75	-	-	-
TM Dilshan	3	4	0	36	51	12.75	-	-	5
M Muralitharan	3	4	2	10*	18	9.00	-	-	-

Also batted: HDPK Dharmasena (2 Tests) 1, 54; RD Fernando (2 Tests) 2, 5 (1ct); D Hettiarachchi (1 Test) 0, 0*; DNT Zoysa (1 Test) 0, 0.

Bowling	Overs	Mds	Runs	Wkts	Av	Best	10w	5w
ST Jayasuriya	126.4	37	236	16	14.75	4-24	-	-
WPUJC Vaas	110.5	30	244	16	15.25	6-73	-	1
M Muralitharan	236	66	421	14	30.07	4-66	-	-

Also bowled: RP Arnold 1-0-2-0; PA de Silva 6-3-7-0; HDPK Dharmasena 73-16-171-3; RD Fernando 13-0-53-1; D Hettiarachchi 27-7-41-2; DNT Zoysa 12-2-51-0.

ENGLAND

Batting	M	Inns	NO	HS	Runs	Av	100	50	c/st
GP Thorpe	3	6	2	113*	269	67.25	1	1	5
ME Trescothick	3	6	0	122	248	41.33	1	1	2
AJ Stewart	3	6	1	54	117	23.40	-	1	4/1
N Hussain	3	6	0	109	136	22.66	1	-	1
MA Atherton	3	6	0	44	129	21.50	-	-	2
RDB Croft	3	5	1	33*	77	19.25	-	-	2
C White	3	6	1	39	96	19.20	-	-	7
D Gough	3	4	1	14	24	8.00	-	-	-
G Hick	2	4	0	16	27	6.75	-	-	3
AF Giles	3	6	2	5	15	3.75	-	-	2
AR Caddick	3	4	0	7	8	2.00	-	-	-

Also batted in one Test: MP Vaughan 26, 8 (2ct).

Bowling	Overs	Mds	Runs	Wkts	Av	Best	10w	5w
D Gough	82	15	274	14	19.57	4-50	-	-
AR Caddick	87.1	24	225	9	25.00	4-55	-	-
RDB Croft	111	28	258	9	28.66	4-56	-	-
AF Giles	121.1	30	309	7	44.14	4-11	-	-

Also bowled: GA Hick 4-0-8-0; C White 69.1-13-237-4.

ONE-DAY INTERNATIONALS

Sri Lanka exacted a measure of revenge for their defeat in the Test series by white-washing England 3–0 in the one-day tournament that followed. While it is true to say that England's relative inexperience in this form of the game was exposed once again, many of the players had one eye on the aeroplane home rather than the limited overs cricket, coming as it did at the end of a long, tiring winter away.

Muttiah Muralitharan revelled in the spinners' conditions at the new Rangiri Stadium in Dambulla.

The opening venue was the latest to join the ever-increasing list of grounds that have staged international cricket. The brand-new Rangiri Stadium in Dambulla is a good four-hour drive from Colombo and was only cleared for this match following an inspection by Cammie Smith on behalf of the ICC. It is a delightful spot, with a large lake to one side, although the two elephants, deliberately tethered to the spot to provide a nice camera shot, was going a bit too far!

Being a new pitch, no-one knew how it would play, but it was soon clear that England's total of 143 would never test the Sri Lankans. Graham Thorpe, who was leading England in the absence of the injured Nasser Hussain, scored 62 of those and could only watch as Muralitharan, spinning the ball

Romesh Kaluwitharana smashed an unbeaten 102 as Sri Lanka cruised to a ten-wicket victory in the third one-day international in Colombo.

sharply, grabbed four for 29. Caddick removed Kaluwitharana immediately, but once Jayasuriya and Atapattu had lifted the score to 50 for the second wicket, Sri Lanka were able to coast to victory with nearly ten overs to spare.

Next, it was back to Colombo for a day/night affair at the Premadasa Stadium. This time Sri Lanka batted first and, thanks to an unbeaten century from Jayawardene, set England 227 to win. A good start was essential, but while Stewart soldiered on to make 55 in 36 overs, wickets fell regularly at the other end. Vaughan scored 26, but it was all too late by then and England were bowled out for only 160 with five overs remaining.

With the end of the tour in sight, England returned to the scene of their greatest triumph of the tour – the Sinhalese Sports Club, but not even memories of their Test victory there could spur them into action. In fact, this was the worst display of the lot as Sri Lanka cruised to a ten-wicket win! England managed to post only 165 for nine from their 50 overs with Hick scoring 46 from 166 balls and then it was one-way traffic as Sri Lanka's openers, Kaluwitharana and Atapattu romped to victory in less than 34 overs. All in all, it had been a disappointing effort by England, but one that should not overshadow their memorable achievements during the winter.

Match One
23 March 2001 at Dambulla International Stadium
England 143 (48.5 overs) (GP Thorpe 62*)
Sri Lanka 144 for 5 (40.5 overs)
Sri Lanka won by five wickets
Man of the Match: M Muralitharan

Match Two
25 March 2001 at R Premadasa Stadium, Khetterama (floodlit)
Sri Lanka 226 for 6 (50 overs) (DPM Jayawardene 101*, MS Atapattu 57)
England 160 (45 overs) (AJ Stewart 55)
Sri Lanka won by 66 runs
Man of the Match: DPM Jayawardene

Match Three
27 March 2001 at Sinhalese Sports Club, Colombo
England 165 for 9 (50 overs)
Sri Lanka 166 for 0 (33.5 overs) (RS Kaluwitharana 102*, MS Atapattu 53*)
Sri Lanka won by ten wickets
Man of the Match: RS Kaluwitharana
Man of the Series: MS Atapattu

INDIA IN SRI LANKA
By Charlie Austin

FIRST TEST
14–17 August at Galle International Stadium

Sri Lanka's mauling in South Africa and their shock home defeat by England precipitated a change of approach for India's three-Test tour in August. Sri Lanka coach Dav Whatmore identified pace bowling on lively wickets as the key to breaking a 16-month spell without a Test series victory.

Dilhara Fernando has genuine pace and claimed five for 42 as Sri Lanka defeated India in Galle.

FIRST TEST – SRI LANKA v. INDIA
14–17 August 2001 at Galle International Stadium

INDIA

	First innings		Second innings	
SS Das	c Jayasuriya, b Vaas	40	c ASA Perera, b PDRL Perera	23
S Ramesh	c Jayasuriya, b Muralitharan	42	b PDRL Perera	2
M Kaif	b Fernando	37	c Tillakaratne, b Muralitharan	14
R Dravid	c Arnold, b Muralitharan	12	not out	61
SC Ganguly (capt)	c Sangakkara, b Fernando	15	b Fernando	4
HK Badani	c Sangakkara, b Fernando	6	c Sanhakkara, b Muralitharan	5
*SS Dighe	c Sangakkara, b Fernando	9	c Arnold, b Muralitharan	3
J Srinath	retired hurt	0	absent injured	
Harbhajan Singh	b Fernando	4	(8) c & b Muralitharan	12
Z Khan	not out	0	(9) c Arnold, b Jayasuriya	3
BKV Prasad	b Muralitharan	0	(10) lbw b Muralitharan	20
	b4, lb3, w2, nb13	22	b12, lb8, nb13	33
		187		**180**

	First innings				Second innings			
	O	M	R	W	O	M	R	W
Vaas	22	10	38	1	16	2	45	–
Fernando	25	9	42	5	17	4	35	1
PDRL Perera	12	4	25	–				
Muralitharan	24.3	8	41	3	26.4	10	49	5
ASA Perera	12	0	34	–				

Fall of Wickets
1-79, 2-105, 3-124, 4-155, 5-161, 6-176, 7-181, 8-185, 9-187
1-15, 2-37, 3-53, 4-64, 5-73, 6-81, 7-104, 8-180

Srinath retired hurt at 177 for six

SRI LANKA

	First innings		Second innings	
MS Atapattu	c Badani, b Singh	33	not out	0
ST Jayasuriya (capt)	c Dravid, b Khan	111	not out	6
+K Sangakkara	not out	105		
DPM Jayawardene	c Dighe, b Srinath	28		
RP Arnold	c Kaif, b Prasad	20		
HP Tillakaratne	lbw b Srinath	11		
ASA Perera	lbw b Srinath	1		
WPUJC Vaas	c Ramesh, b Khan	13		
CRD Fernando	c Srinath, b Khan	3		
PDRL Perera	c Dighe, b Srinath	0		
M Muralitharan	c Kaif, b Srinath	8		
	b1, lb6, w8, nb14	29		
		362	**(for 0 wicket)**	**6**

	First innings				Second innings			
	O	M	R	W	O	M	R	W
Srinath	24.5	5	114	5	1	1	–	–
Prasad	24	4	83	1				
Khan	26	3	89	3	0.5	0	6	–
Harbhajan Singh	33	12	69	1				

Fall of Wickets
1-101, 2-171, 3-211, 4-274, 5-292, 6-296, 7-316, 8-340, 9-342

Umpires: EAR de Silva & SA Bucknor
Toss: Sri Lanka
Test debuts: nil

Sri Lanka won by ten wickets

Nevertheless, Galle International Stadium was a strange place to start Sri Lanka's brave new world. The square is maintained by a former left-arm spinner and is historically friendly to the slower bowlers. This time, though, when the covers were rolled off, the crazy paving like surface had been transformed by a generous grass covering.

Sri Lanka selected an unprecedented four fast bowlers and went on to register an emphatic ten-wicket victory in just ten sessions of play, as India recorded their two lowest-ever Test scores against Sri Lanka and duly lost their first Test against their

Sanath Jayasuriya was Man of the Match for his first–innings score of 111.

South Asian neighbours for 16 years. India were weakened by injuries to key players – Sachin Tendulkar (toe), V.V.S. Laxman (knee), Anil Kumble (shoulder) and Ashish Nehra (groin) – but it was still a woeful performance.

India's openers battled hard after having been put into bat, but progress was painfully slow in the face of tight bowling. They scored just 16 runs in 20 overs before lunch and by tea had crawled to 95 for one after 56 overs. However, just when they looked to have weathered the storm, India slipped up in an extended evening session when they lost four wickets. The turning point was the second new ball, taken in fading light moments before the close, when rookie fast bowler Dilhara Fernando beat Mohammad Kaif for sheer pace and induced a frenetic slash from Hemang Badani. India ended the day on 166 for five.

Fernando carried on in the second morning where he had left off the previous evening. Single-handedly he dismantled the lower order in a memorable spell of hostile fast bowling: Ganguly jerked his head out of the way of a short ball, but the ball was adjudged to have brushed his glove; Harbhajan Singh was cleaned up, as he backed away to leg; and Sameer Dighe was athletically caught by Kumar Sangakkara behind the stumps. To round it off, Fernando forced Javagal Srinath to retire hurt after a painful blow to his left hand that forced him to miss the next two Tests. India had been bowled out for 187, having lost their last six wickets for 32 runs.

Indian coach John Wright summed up his side's performance in the field well when he said: 'There is not a lot a captain can do when his bowlers keep feeding the best square cutter in the world.' Twelve months after his last Test fifty, Jayasuriya capitalized on wayward bowling to score his eighth Test century off just 105 balls. By the end of the second day, Sri Lanka were almost out of sight, with a lead of 77 and with seven wickets remaining.

On the third day, number three wicket-keeper batsman Kumar Sangakkara also regained his batting form, as he grafted hard for a marathon six-hour maiden Test century, which ensured Sri Lanka a healthy lead of 175.

India were 26 for one by tea time, but once again collapsed in the final session, when they lost seven wickets for just 104 runs. This time it was Muttiah Muralitharan who posed the problems, picking up his 25th five-wicket haul in the process. By now the wicket was turning and the mysterious off spinner prayed upon the timidity of the inexperienced batsmen. Only Rahul Dravid provided any resistance

with an assured 61. After 50 minutes of defiance on the fourth morning, India were bowled out for 180 and Man of the Match Jayasuriya quickly knocked off the handful of runs required.

SECOND TEST
22–25 August at Asgiriya Stadium, Kandy

Sri Lanka, so cocksure and accomplished in Galle, became timorous and diffident in the second Test in Kandy. India grabbed their opportunity and, thanks to a timely return to form by captain Saurav Ganguly and a masterful innings by Rahul Dravid, they surged to a memorable seven-wicket triumph.

Sri Lanka's shock failure in front of a capacity crowd was the third time in successive home series that they had lost in Kandy and squandered series-winning opportunities. The locals called it the Kandy hoodoo, but captain Sanath Jayasuriya believes it was just 'bad cricket'.

After the first two days India looked destined to lose. Sri Lanka had cobbled together a competitive 274 in their first innings thanks to a classy 104 from Mahela Jayawardene, the 24-year-old's sixth Test century, and an aggressive 42 from Chaminda Vaas, playing in his 50th Test. The home side had established a lead of 94 by the end of day two, having bowled out the tourists for 232.

It was a case of déjà vu at Kandy where Venkatesh Prasad took five wickets as India levelled the series.

It could have been even worse for India had off spinner Harbhajan Singh not clubbed an entertaining 44 from 32 balls to rescue his side, who had slumped to 154 for six after some incisive seam bowling from Chaminda Vaas, Dilhara Fernando and Ruchira Perera. Singh added 64 priceless runs for the sixth wicket with wicket-keeper Sameer Dighe and the match had started to turn.

Day three was one of the great days in Test cricket. Fast bowlers Zaheer Khan and Venkatesh Prasad finally responded to coach John Wright's call for greater discipline and the pair diligently dismantled Sri Lanka's second innings. Khan probed

Indian captain, Saurav Ganguly, ended a run of 13 innings without a fifty. His unbeaten 98 in the second innings was made under difficult circumstances.

SECOND TEST – SRI LANKA v. INDIA
22–25 August 2001 at Asgiriya Stadium, Kandy

SRI LANKA

	First innings		Second innings	
MS Atapattu	b Khan	39	c Dighe, b Prasad	45
ST Jayasuriya (capt)	run out (Harvinder Singh/ Dighe/Prasad)	3	b Khan	6
*K Sangakkara	c Ramesh, b Ganguly	31	c Dighe, b Khan	13
DPM Jayawardene	c Dighe, b Prasad	104	c Badani, b Khan	25
RP Arnold	c Dravid, b Khan	5	(6) lbw b Khan	4
HP Tillakaratne	c Dighe, b Prasad	10	(5) lbw b Prasad	16
ASA Perera	lbw b Ganguly	18	c Badani, b Prasad	15
WPUJC Vaas	b Harvinder Singh	42	lbw b Prasad	4
M Muralitharan	b Harvinder Singh	5	c Ramesh, b Harbhajan Singh	67
CRD Fernando	c Dighe, b Khan	4	b Prasad	4
PDRL Perera	not out	0	not out	6
	lb7, w1, nb5	13	b4, lb7, nb5	16
		274		**221**

	First innings				Second innings			
	O	M	R	W	O	M	R	W
Khan	22	6	62	3	23	4	76	4
Harvinder Singh	14.3	1	62	2	8	1	25	-
Prasad	18	4	52	2	21	7	72	5
Ganguly	17	5	69	2	10	4	21	-
Harbhajan Singh	7	1	22	-	4.3	2	16	1

Fall of Wickets
1-18, 2-78, 3-82, 4-101, 5-138, 6-189, 7-232, 8-245, 9-274
1-20, 2-52, 3-84, 4-108, 5-116, 6-137, 7-140, 8-153, 9-157

INDIA

	First innings		Second innings	
SS Das	lbw b Vaas	8	b Muralitharan	19
S Ramesh	c Sangakkara, b Fernando	47	c Jayasuriya, b Fernando	31
R Dravid	lbw b Vaas	15	c Arnold, b Muralitharan	75
SC Ganguly (capt)	c Tillakaratne, b PDRL Perera	18	not out	98
M Kaif	c Atapattu, b Fernando	17	not out	19
HK Badani	c Fernando, b PDRL Perera	16		
*SS Dighe	lbw b Vaas	28		
Harbhajan Singh	b Vaas	44		
Z Khan	c Tillakaratne, b Muralitharan	0		
BKV Prasad	not out	1		
Harvinder Singh	b Muralitharan	6		
	lb7, w2, nb23	32	b4, lb2, nb16	22
		232	(for 3 wickets)	**264**

	First innings				Second innings			
	O	M	R	W	O	M	R	W
Vaas	21	3	65	4	20.4	9	42	-
Fernando	14	2	66	2	16	4	64	1
PDRL Perera	7	2	23	2	9	2	26	-
Muralitharan	20.1	5	62	2	25	2	96	2
ASA Perera	2	0	9	-	3	0	11	-
Jayasuriya					3	0	12	-
Arnold					2	0	7	-

Fall of Wickets
1-11, 2-36, 3-68, 4-120, 5-123, 6-154, 7-218, 8-223, 9-223
1-42, 2-103, 3-194

Umpires: TH Wijewardene & SA Bucknor
Toss: India
Test debuts: nil

India won by seven wickets

away at the Sri Lankan batsmen's off stump and picked up four for 76, his best ever Test figures, whilst Prasad swung the ball in overcast conditions and was rewarded with his seventh five-wicket haul in Test cricket. Sri Lanka slumped from 52 for one to 157 for nine.

Cue Muttiah Muralitharan, a local idol, but an unlikely batting hero. His batting has always been comic, but has never provided such feature-length amusement. In a crazy 76-minute, last-wicket partnership he scythed his way to 67 off 65 balls, his maiden first-class fifty. Ganguly panicked, posting eight fielders on the boundary in a vain effort to keep Muralitharan off strike, but the ploy backfired spectacularly and a vocal crowd hooted derisively, as Muralitharan threaded the ball between the outfielders. When he was finally dismissed, Sri Lanka's lead had been extended to what looked like a match-winning 263.

India had not scored more than 232 in the previous three innings of the series, but they had one great hope: Rahul Dravid. In the final analysis he may have been overshadowed by Ganguly's unbeaten 98, but Dravid was the true match winner with a three-hour 75. He skilfully blunted the major threat of Muralitharan and scored freely off Sri Lanka's profligate seam bowlers, who wilted under the pressure.

Ganguly joined his vice captain after Sadogoppan Ramesh obligingly wafted a catch to first slip and the pair doused the home team's hopes with a 91-run partnership for the third wicket. Then, when Dravid offered a simple catch to silly point, Ganguly hurried his side to victory with a string of languid strokes, to end a 13-innings sequence without a Test fifty.

THIRD TEST
29 August–2 September at Sinhalese Sports Club, Colombo

With the impeccable timing that only true stars possess, Muttiah Muralitharan waited until he was needed most before bowling his deadliest spell, to halt Sri Lanka's depressing slide down memory lane and crush India's hopes of a first overseas series win in eight years in the decisive third Test in Colombo.

Sri Lanka's brittle confidence had been knocked in Kandy, so much so that it looked like they had settled for a draw when the curator ordered his helpers, unusually armed with scissors, to cut the dry SSC pitch bare. The result was a surface so bland that a tame draw seemed inevitable.

Muttiah Muralitharan had been largely blunted by England's batsmen, but he took 11 wickets in the final Test against India to give Sri Lanka a 2–1 victory in the series.

Indeed, two hours after Saurav Ganguly had won the toss and jumped at an opportunity to bat, the scribes were predicting a run glut and a 1–1 series stalemate, as India's openers Shiv Sunder Das and Sadogoppan Ramesh cruised to 91 without loss at the lunch interval. Three-and-a-half astonishing hours later, though, Muralitharan had spun his side into the ascendancy.

The indefatigable Muralitharan bowled unchanged for five hours in enervating heat to claim eight wickets for 87, which *Wisden* rated as the second-best performance ever achieved by a spinner in the first innings of a match behind Abdul Qadir's nine for 56 for Pakistan against England at Lahore in 1987–88.

From the time Das was clean bowled for 59 soon

after lunch, to end a 97-run opening partnership, India's batsmen capitulated, losing ten wickets for 137 runs, to be bowled out for 234 in 81.1 overs. Rahul Dravid compiled a patient 36 and Hemang Badani scored an entertaining, and career-best, 38, but the rest had no answer to Muralitharan's relentless accuracy and beguiling mix of spin, bounce and dip.

Ramesh (46) squirted into the gully, Ganguly (one) was controversially trapped leg before whilst padding away, Rahul Dravid and Badani were snapped up at bat-pad, Sameer Dighe (0) opted to play no stroke to a ball homed in on middle stump, Zaheer Khan (0) edged to slip and leg-spinner Sairaj Bahutule (18) was stumped. Chaminda Vaas chipped in with the wickets of Mohammad Kaif (14), to give him 150 Test wickets, and Harbhajan Singh (two), who he trapped leg before.

India would have hoped that their own spin assassin, Harbhajan Singh, could replicate Muralitharan's menace, but he proved uninspiring and predictable in comparison, finishing with a disappointing two for 185 and with just four wickets in the series.

Sri Lanka's batsmen went on a run spree with four batsmen scoring centuries, including debutante all-rounder Thilan Samaraweera, who scored an unbeaten 103. Sri Lanka piled up 610 for six, as opener Marvan Atapattu returned to form with a five-hour 108, Mahela Jayawardene scored a sparkling 139, his second consecutive hundred, and veteran left-hander Hashan Tillakaratne saved his Test career with a career best 136 not out.

India, trailing by 376 and needing to bat for seven sessions to save the series, needed to muster a Herculean performance. Like they had done in the first innings, the openers started well, adding 107 for the first wicket. Muralitharan, however, eventually had Das (68) caught at silly point and then bowled Ramesh (55) with a wonder ball pitching outside leg stump that turned square to flick the batsman's off bail.

India's resistance was then ended after two inexcusable run outs on the fourth evening. Dravid (36) was dismissed by a direct hit from an alert Atapattu and Kaif (five) was left in no man's land after a moments indecision from

Ganguly (30). The captain promptly edged a Samaraweera off break to slip and Bahultule (0) played on to leave India on 217 for six at the close of the penultimate day.

A run-a-ball 45 from Zaheer Khan enlivened a quiet second morning, but Sri Lanka still wrapped up the tail 50 minutes before lunch to secure an innings and 77-run victory. It was their first series win for 16 months and only their first series win against India for 16 years. Unsurprisingly, Muralitharan was named Man of the Match for his 11 wickets, the sixth time in his 65-Test career that he had taken ten wickets in a game.

Hashan Tillakaratne, the veteran Sri Lankan, saved his Test career with a Test-best score of 136 not out in the third Test in Colombo.

THIRD TEST – SRI LANKA v. INDIA
29 August–2 September 2001 at Sinhalese Sports Club, Colombo

INDIA

	First innings		Second innings	
SS Das	b Muralitharan	59	c Tillakaratne, b Muralitharan	68
S Ramesh	c Jayawardene, b Muralitharan	46	b Muralitharan	55
R Dravid	c Tillakaratne, b Muralitharan	36	run out (Atapattu)	36
SC Ganguly (capt)	lbw b Muralitharan	1	c Jayawardene, b Samaraweera	30
M Kaif	c Sangakarra, b Vaas	14	run out (Sangakarra)	5
HK Badani	c Tillakaratne, b Muralitharan	38	lbw b Vaas	11
*SS Dighe	lbw b Muralitharan	0	(8) run out (Atapattu)	4
SV Bahutule	st Sangakarra, b Muralitharan	18	(7) b Jayasuriya	0
Harbhajan Singh	lbw b Vaas	2	c Atapattu, b Vaas	17
Z Khan	c Jayawardene, b Muralitharan	0	c Atapattu, b Muralitharan	45
BKV Prasad	not out	10	not out	4
	b2, lb3, w2, nb3	10	b8, lb5, w2, nb9	24
		234		**299**

	First innings				Second innings			
	O	M	R	W	O	M	R	W
Vaas	24	7	60	2	27	9	62	2
Liyanage	9	2	32	-	5	0	12	-
Fernando	12	2	38	-	17	3	59	-
Muralitharan	34.1	9	87	8	46.5	19	109	3
Samaraweera	2	0	12	-	8	4	10	1
Jayasuriya					21	10	34	1

Fall of Wickets
1-97, 2-115, 3-119, 4-146, 5-192, 6-192, 7-207, 8-210, 9-213
1-107, 2-147, 3-186, 4-196, 5-210, 6-211, 7-221, 8-221, 9-269

SRI LANKA

	First innings	
MS Atapattu	c Das, b Singh	108
ST Jayasuriya (capt)	b Prasad	30
*K Sangakarra	c Badani, b Prasad	47
DPM Jayawardene	lbw b Bahutule	139
RP Arnold	b Prasad	31
DK Liyanage	c Dighe, b Singh	3
HP Tillakaratne	not out	136
TT Samaraweera	not out	103
WPUJC Vaas		
CRD Fernando		
M Muralitharan		
	lb4, w4, nb5	13
	(for 6 wickets dec.)	**610**

	First innings			
	O	M	R	W
Khan	27	3	134	-
Prasad	34	8	101	3
Harbhajan Singh	53.3	6	185	2
Ganguly	12.3	3	44	-
Bahutule	31	5	101	1
Badani	8	2	17	-
Ramesh	5	0	24	-

Fall of Wickets
1-48, 2-119, 3-252, 4-310, 5-321, 6-416

Umpires: EAR de Silva & DL Orchard
Toss: India
Test debut: TT Samaraweera (Sri Lanka)

Sri Lanka won by an innings and 77 runs

TEST MATCH AVERAGES
Sri Lanka v. India

SRI LANKA

Batting	M	Inns	NO	HS	Runs	Av	100	50	c/st
DMP Jayawardene	3	4	0	139	296	74.00	2	-	3
K Sangakarra	3	4	1	105*	196	65.33	1	-	6/1
HP Tillakaratne	3	4	1	136*	173	57.66	1	-	6
MS Atapattu	3	5	1	108	225	56.25	1	-	3
ST Jayasuriya	3	5	1	111	156	39.00	1	-	3
M Muralitharan	3	3	0	67	80	26.66	-	1	1
WPUJC Vaas	3	3	0	42	59	19.66	-	-	-
RP Arnold	3	4	0	31	60	15.00	-	-	4
ASA Perera	2	3	0	18	34	11.33	-	-	1
CRD Fernando	3	3	0	4	11	3.66	-	-	1

Also batted: DK Liyanage (1 Test) 3 ;PDRL Perera (2 Tests) 0, 0*, 6*;
TT Samaraweera (1 Test) 103*.

Bowling	Overs	Mds	Runs	Wkts	Av	Best	10m	5/inn
M Muralitharan	177.2	51	444	23	19.30	8-87	1	2
CRD Fernando	101	24	304	9	33.77	5-42	-	1
WPUJC Vaas	130.4	40	312	9	34.66	4-65	-	-

Also bowled: RP Arnold 2-0-7-0; DK Liyanage 14-2-44-0; ST Jayasuriya 31-13-56-2; ASA Perera 17-0-54-0; PDRL Perera 36-9-95-4; TT Samaraweera 10-4-22-1.

INDIA

Batting	M	Inns	NO	HS	Runs	Av	100	50	c/st
R Dravid	3	6	1	75	235	47.00	-	2	2
S Ramesh	3	6	0	55	223	37.16	-	1	4
SS Das	3	6	0	68	217	36.16	-	2	1
SC Ganguly	3	6	1	98*	166	33.20	-	1	-
M Kaif	3	6	1	37	106	21.20	-	-	1
BKV Prasad	3	5	3	20	35	17.50	-	-	-
Harbhajan Singh	3	5	0	44	79	15.80	-	-	-
HK Badani	3	5	0	38	76	15.20	-	-	4
Z Khan	3	5	1	45	48	12.00	-	-	-
SS Dighe	3	5	0	28	44	8.80	-	-	8/-

Also batted in one Test: SV Bahutule 18, 0; Harvinder Singh 6; J Srinath 0rh (1ct).

Bowling	Overs	Mds	Runs	Wkts	Av	Best	10m	5/inn
J Srinath	25.5	6	114	5	22.80	5-114	-	1
BKV Prasad	97	23	308	11	28.00	5-72	-	1
Z Khan	98.5	16	367	10	36.70	4-76	-	-
Harbhajan Singh	98	21	292	4	73.00	2-185	-	-

Also bowled: HK Badani 8-2-17-0; SV Bahutule 31-5-101-1; SC Ganguly 39.3-12-134-2; Harvinder Singh 22.3-2-87-2; S Ramesh 5-0-24-0.

SRI LANKA DOMESTIC FIRST-CLASS CRICKET
By Charlie Austin

Nondescripts Cricket Club (NCC) won their first domestic title for seven years when they won the Premier League in April, but the health of Sri Lanka's first-class championship continued to be the source of considerable debate in 2000–01.

With young players finding it increasingly hard to bridge the gap between club and international cricket, there were increasing calls for a radical overhaul of the domestic structure. Unfortunately, in a situation not dissimilar to the County Championship in England, the voting power of individual clubs represents a formidable barrier to change.

In fact, the clubs are so powerful that the two clubs earmarked for relegation after the 1999–2000 season, Matara Sports Club and Singha Sports Club, were allowed to stay up in the premier division after threats of legal action.

The result was an unwieldy tournament with 18 teams and over 404 players. Contests were one-sided and the quality of cricket was generally poor – during one week the top players opted to play in an annual six-a-side tournament, rather than play first-class cricket. No wonder then that the Board of Control for Cricket in Sri Lanka (BCCSL) was unable to find a sponsor.

The highlight of the tournament was the second stage when the 18 teams were split into two divisions: the Super Eight and Plate competition. The main clubs all qualified for the Super Eight – NCC, BRC, SSC, Colts, CCC, Bloomfield, Panadura and Tamil Union – which was dominated by NCC and BRC.

Indeed, BRC were the surprise package of the year. They may have bounced along the bottom of

Hashan Tillakaratne forced his way back into the Test side thanks to his astonishing average of 110 for NCC.

the Premier League last year, but were a revelation in 2000–01, mainly because of slow left-arm spinner Sajeewa Weerakoon, who was the highest wicket taker of the season with 80 wickets in all and four ten-wicket hauls.

NCC were well captained by 34-year-old Hashan Tillakaratne, who forced his way back into the Test side after a two-year absence thanks to an average of 110.83. Indeed, it was Tillakaratne who rescued NCC in the crucial penultimate week.

NCC were in pole position, but, taking on second-placed BRC in a top-of-the-table clash, they started badly, slipping to 14 for five on the first morning before Tillakaratne rescued his side with a marathon, unbeaten 185. Well supported by Aravinda de Silva (55), who made sporadic appearances throughout the season, NCC finished on 372 for eight before bundling out BRC for 132 in their first innings to secure an all-important first-innings victory.

There was also tension in the final week, when NCC were bowled out for 245 by CCC, two runs short of a first-innings victory which would have guaranteed them the title. Suddenly, BRC had a chance, if they could defeat Tamil Union on a turning pitch at P. Saravanmuttu Stadium. NCC came surging back into their game though, as experienced off spinner Ruwan Kalpage grabbed seven wickets to leave them needing 143 runs with the clock running out, which they achieved in 24.3 overs.

Crumbling slow pitches predominated, despite calls for quicker surfaces after Sri Lanka's drumming in South Africa, and that meant that spin dominated the tournament, a fact highlighted by the statistics – the top-four wicket takers were all spinners (S. Weerakoon 80; R. Herath 71; S. Chandana 70; and A.W. Ekanayake 67). Nevertheless, three young fast bowlers demanded attention: Dinusha Fernando (62 wickets) with his snappy wrist action; Akalanka Ganegama (41) for his probing accuracy; and Ishara Amarasinghe (36) for his slippery pace.

Several batsmen took the eye – H. Weerasiri (1,105 at 35.64), H. Wickramaratne (830 at 51.87), Pradeep Hewage (784 at 60.3), Sukitha Peiris (777 at 51.8), H. Tillakaratne (665 at 110.83) and Jevantha Kalatunga (663 at 60.27) – but none was able to make an impression in the 'A' team. SSC left-hander Hemantha Wickramaratne and Pradeep Hewage were both unlucky not to be included in the 30-man 'A'-team training squad.

Next year the BCCSL will reduce the number of sides to 16 and four teams were thus relegated this year – Matara SC, Singha SC, Navy SC, Police SC – though the prospect of further legal disputes looms. Ragama CC and Chilaw Marians have been promoted from the second division.

SRI LANKA DOMESTIC ONE-DAY COMPETITION

A star-studded Sinhalese Sports Club won the Premier League limited overs tournament after narrowly defeating Colombo Cricket Club in the semi-final before trouncing defending champions Colts Cricket Club in the final.

The Cricket Board had valiantly tried to boost interest in the one-day tournament by playing the later stages under lights at Premadasa International

Although SSC lost two wickets in the first over as they chased 215, Marvan Atapattu led them to victory over Colts CC in the final of the Premier League limited overs tournament.

Stadium, but slow crumbling pitches limited the entertainment, as the side batting first could only post scores of 174, 182 and 214 in the semi-finals and final.

The SSC side, however, was well balanced and suited to the conditions. Their slow bowlers – off spinner Thilan Samaraweera and slow left-arm spinner Ranil Dhammika – consistently put the brakes on the opposition, whilst the batting was packed full of international talent – Avishka Gunawardene, Mahela Jayawardene, Marvan Atapattu and Arjuna Ranatunga.

Colts Cricket Club won the first semi-final after they managed to defend a total of just 174, bowling out Tamil Union for 130 thanks to a miserly performance by their four fast bowlers and four wickets by left-arm spinner Dinuk Hettiarachchi.

The second semi-final was the best game of the three as SSC squeezed through to the final. SSC ground their way to 184 after a workmanlike unbeaten 49 from Hemantha Wickramaratne and 36 from Arjuna Ranatunga, who had opted to play one final season of domestic cricket after his international retirement in August 2000. CCC batsmen Roshan Mahanama (42) and Anushka Polonowita (46) then carried their side to within striking distance of SSC's total, but the 15-run, last-over target proved to be two runs too many.

The final was played on a better wicket and Romesh Kaluwitharana gave Colts CC a perfect start with a belligerent 49 from 44 balls. The innings was then held together by former international Dulip Samaraweera, who scored an unbeaten 81 off 115 balls, to set what looked to be a competitive 215-run target. SSC, however, won with ease, despite losing two wickets in the first over, as Marvan Atapattu scored 113 not out and captain Mahela Jayawardene 83 not out in a 214-run partnership for the third wicket.

FIRST-CLASS AVERAGES

BATTING

	M	Inns	NO	HS	Runs	Av	100	50
HP Tillakaratne	11	13	3	185*	755	75.50	3	1
PR Hewage	11	15	2	200*	784	60.30	1	5
SKL de Silva	9	11	1	164*	603	60.30	2	4
HGJM Kulatunga	10	14	1	175	717	55.15	2	5
HDPK Dharmasena	4	5	0	157	275	55.00	1	1
DPMD Jayawarden	4	6	0	101	319	53.16	1	3
GP Thorpe	5	9	2	113*	366	52.28	1	2
RPAH Wickramaratne	11	16	0	139	830	51.87	5	1
TT Samaraweera	9	13	5	74	414	51.75	-	3
DP Samaraweera	9	12	2	177*	512	51.20	1	2
MS Atapattu	5	6	1	201*	244	48.80	1	-
CM Bandara	12	13	6	63	335	47.85	-	2
JSK Peiris	11	20	3	136	797	46.88	3	4
A Ranatunga	6	8	1	86	326	46.57	-	2
GRP Peiris	6	11	0	134	487	44.27	2	2
DN Hunukumbura	10	13	0	116	550	42.30	2	2
WMG Ramyakumara	11	18	3	108	629	41.93	1	3
SI Fernando	9	13	2	140	456	41.45	1	1
ME Trescothick	4	7	0	122	286	40.85	1	1
C White	5	9	2	85*	283	40.42	-	2
S Kalavitigoda	11	15	1	119	564	40.28	1	4
WMPN Wanasinghe	6	12	3	101*	356	39.55	1	1
RHS Silva	12	19	2	155	671	39.47	1	4
PA de Silva	7	10	0	106	394	39.40	1	2
UA Fernando	6	8	0	128	315	39.37	1	1
A Rideegammanagedera	11	17	1	120	611	38.18	1	4
TA Weerappuli	7	9	1	83*	305	38.12	-	2
MN Nawaz	12	17	3	97	530	37.85	-	5
GAS Perera	11	18	2	115*	603	37.68	1	3
SI de Saram	5	9	0	86	336	37.33	-	3
S Ranatunga	8	13	1	131	443	36.91	1	3
AS Polonowita	11	15	2	86	477	36.69	-	3
SD Abeynayake	11	17	2	152	545	36.33	1	2
WMB Perera	10	14	1	80	472	36.30	-	4
MMDPV Perera	9	14	4	72*	354	35.40	-	2
WN de Silva	11	5	0	107	524	34.93	1	3
TM Dilshan	8	13	1	122	414	34.50	2	-
HSSMK Weerasiri	13	25	2	107	784	34.08	1	5
BSM Warnapura	11	17	2	138	505	33.66	2	2
HM Madhuwantha	13	25	4	93	701	33.38	-	4
MG Vandort	8	11	0	102	362	32.90	1	1
PB Ediriweera	9	11	1	112*	318	31.80	1	-
MA Atherton	5	9	0	85	283	31.44	-	1
MDK Perera	9	16	0	105	503	31.43	1	2
BMTT Mendis	11	13	2	66*	344	31.27	-	1
PK Siriwardene	13	23	0	87	718	31.21	-	5
ASA Perera	8	11	3	78	249	31.12	-	1
WMSM Perera	12	22	3	129	589	31.00	1	4
K Sangakarra	5	8	0	95	248	31.00	-	2
UC Hathurasinghe	5	7	0	56	217	31.00	-	2
GVS Janaka	6	8	2	58*	184	30.66	-	1
OC Warnapura	9	13	2	57	330	30.00	-	2
NRG Perera	12	17	0	113	508	29.88	1	2
CP Mapatuna	9	12	2	104	295	29.50	1	-
KD Gunawardene	4	6	0	62	177	29.50	-	1
BCMS Mendis	12	19	0	126	551	29.00	2	2
EFMU Fernando	12	19	2	164	488	28.70	1	1
WSH Fernando	5	7	0	63	198	28.28	-	2
DA Gunawardene	5	8	2	69	169	28.16	-	1
RGD Sanjeewa	11	15	1	77	390	27.85	-	2
WR Fernando	10	17	1	79	441	27.56	-	3
BC Jeganathan	6	9	2	58	192	27.42	-	2
RN Weerasinghe	8	15	0	86	408	27.20	-	3
WP Wickrama	10	19	2	91	458	26.94	-	3
GI Daniel	9	17	2	106	404	26.93	1	-
KADJ Siriwardene	11	15	0	89	403	26.86	-	2
TKD Sudarshana	13	26	1	102	668	26.72	1	3
KSC de Silva	12	14	6	74	213	26.62	-	1
HSS Fonseka	13	25	2	97	606	26.34	-	2
M Pushpakumara	4	6	0	69	158	26.33	-	2
CN Liyanage	13	24	2	108	579	26.31	1	3
PRT Fernando	11	20	1	99*	500	26.31	-	3

FIRST-CLASS AVERAGES

BATTING

	M	Inns	NO	HS	Runs	Av	100	50
KADM Fernando	12	16	3	59*	341	26.23	-	2
AS Wewalwala	8	15	1	125	367	26.21	1	1
MCR Fernando	12	15	3	92	313	26.08	-	2
ICD Perera	13	21	3	80	469	26.05	-	2
MI Thahir	8	15	3	71	312	26.00	-	1
KRRK Wimalasena	12	21	2	97	493	25.94	-	3
RR Tissera	12	16	0	56	414	25.87	-	3
CU Jayasinghe	11	16	1	107*	387	25.80	1	1
PB Dassanayake	6	8	1	72*	180	25.71	-	1
MS Sampan	13	22	3	61	486	25.57	-	3
WRD Dissanayake	13	22	0	85	555	25.22	-	2
HWM Kumara	13	25	1	67	605	25.20	-	2
GSP Dharmapala	5	10	3	41	176	25.14	-	-
N Hussain	5	9	0	109	226	25.11	1	1
BARS Priyadharshana	11	20	1	99	474	24.94	-	4
KAS Jayasinghe	6	11	0	91	274	24.90	-	1
CM Withange	13	26	3	108*	567	24.65	1	2
RDB Croft	5	8	3	33*	123	24.60	-	-
YMWB Ekanayake	11	22	0	77	539	24.50	-	3
HAHU Tillekeratne	12	21	1	75	489	24.45	-	2
NG Peiris	12	18	1	89	415	24.41	-	2
WAL Chaturanha	12	21	2	71	463	24.36	-	2
MNR Cooray	13	19	1	86	438	24.33	-	3
WNM Soysa	12	22	0	155	532	24.18	1	1
PSAN Shiroman	12	21	0	93	507	24.14	-	2
HMS Jayawardene	10	19	0	90	457	24.05	-	3
S Jayantha	10	19	0	86	455	23.94	-	2
AJ Stewart	5	9	1	54	191	23.87	-	1
NHV Chinthaka	13	24	1	95	546	23.73	-	2
RSA Palliyaguruge	10	14	0	81	331	23.64	-	1
WT de Silva	6	12	1	79	260	23.63	-	1
J Mubarak	9	13	1	77	282	23.50	-	2
SWK Shantha	8	14	4	46*	235	23.50	-	-
MK Gajanayake	12	19	1	69	418	23.22	-	3
RR Jaymon	12	16	0	100	369	23.06	1	1
GE Randiligama	8	12	0	47	275	22.91	-	-
MC Mendis	8	11	1	80	228	22.80	-	1
DK Liyanage	11	13	3	73*	227	22.70	-	1
PARC Karunasena	7	11	1	48*	227	22.70	-	-
SM Ramzan	13	22	1	112	476	22.66	1	2
ASSPA Attanayake	10	11	2	62	204	22.66	-	1
CR Kumarage	6	10	1	54	203	22.55	-	1
GN Silva	4	6	1	57	111	22.20	-	1
DMGS Dissanayake	11	16	0	108	355	22.18	1	2
NS Bopage	7	12	0	75	265	22.08	-	2
SC Gunasekera	8	13	1	71	265	22.08	-	2
TR Peiris	3	6	0	34	132	22.00	-	-
HPK Rajapakse	8	16	1	98*	329	21.93	-	1
RH Sureshchandra	11	22	1	63	459	21.85	-	1
IC Soysa	10	19	1	100*	392	21.77	1	1
SEDR Fernando	13	22	0	93	478	21.72	-	2
RHTA Perera	8	16	0	95	346	21.62	-	3
MRCN Bandaratilleke	8	11	1	73	215	21.50	-	1
LPC Silva	10	20	1	61	407	21.42	-	3
DD Wickremasinghe	13	20	3	67*	355	20.88	-	2
WC Labrooy	9	11	3	68*	166	20.75	-	1
MP Vaughan	3	5	0	57	103	20.60	-	1
DK Ranaweera	5	7	0	43	142	20.28	-	-
DHS Pradeep	8	9	1	56	162	20.25	-	1
WDDS Perera	9	12	0	64	242	20.16	-	2
DWAND Vitharana	11	15	1	52	281	20.07	-	2
WMJ Wannakuwatta	7	13	2	61	220	20.00	-	1
CP Handunnettige	8	11	0	80	219	19.90	-	1
DF Arnolda	7	10	0	79	199	19.90	-	1
YSS Mendis	7	10	0	76	198	19.80	-	2
HPA Priyantha	12	21	0	59	411	19.57	-	1
GA Hick	3	6	0	75	117	19.50	-	1
SALJ Fernando	11	14	0	62	272	19.42	-	2
EMI Galagoda	9	13	1	59*	231	19.25	-	1
GVKC Dissanayake	3	6	1	31*	96	19.20	-	-
DN Jayakody	11	16	0	62	305	19.06	-	2
MFA Farhath	6	8	0	67	152	19.00	-	1

FIRST-CLASS AVERAGES

BATTING

	M	Inns	NO	HS	Runs	Av	100	50
HSGS Silva	10	19	1	75	338	18.77	-	1
DPS Jayaratne	9	12	1	53	206	18.72	-	1
A Rizan	10	15	2	45	238	18.30	-	-
GST Perera	12	18	0	82	329	18.27	-	2
KPPB Seneviratne	5	7	1	34	109	18.16	-	-
AKIN Perera	13	25	0	74	446	17.84	-	2
LHD Dilhara	12	19	4	61	267	17.80	-	1
CK Hewamanna	10	17	2	71	265	17.66	-	1
TCB Fernando	9	16	2	81	246	17.57	-	1
PCVB de Silva	10	19	4	39	262	17.46	-	-
KADC Silva	13	24	0	81	418	17.41	-	2
S Rodrigo	9	13	1	68	209	17.41	-	1
SA Wijeratne	11	20	0	52	347	17.35	-	1
HHMNC Silva	13	23	2	75*	362	17.23	-	2
NI Liyanage	4	8	2	24*	103	17.16	-	-
S Chandana	13	23	5	32	308	17.11	-	-
MR Porage	5	10	0	38	171	17.10	-	-
CPH Ramanayake	12	18	0	100	307	17.05	1	1
CI Bandaratilleke	5	8	1	64*	119	17.00	-	1
ST Jayasuriya	4	7	0	45	119	17.00	-	-
GL Hewage	13	25	2	73*	390	16.95	-	2
NNN Nanayakkara	7	10	3	29*	118	16.85	-	-
CPL Gamage	10	16	2	45	235	16.78	-	-
KEA Upashantha	8	9	0	39	149	16.55	-	-
RC Galappathy	6	11	0	48	181	16.45	-	-
WCR Tissera	13	22	3	39	312	16.42	-	-
PCL Perera	6	6	1	32	82	16.40	-	-
B de Silva	11	15	2	48	213	16.38	-	-
RS Kaluwitharana	5	8	0	40	130	16.25	-	-
WIMC Boteju	11	17	2	59	243	16.20	-	1
JWHD Boteju	11	16	1	61	241	16.06	-	1
MTT Mirando	11	21	2	75	304	16.00	-	1
SWND Chinthaka	8	15	0	46	240	16.00	-	-
HPW Jayawardene	6	10	0	70	160	16.00	-	1
RMAR Ratnayake	7	9	1	31	128	16.00	-	-
ARMS Ranaweera	9	16	3	46*	207	15.92	-	-
WJU Perera	7	13	1	52	191	15.91	-	1
RATD Perera	5	10	5	32	78	15.80	-	-
MKGCP Lakshitha	12	20	2	45	283	15.72	-	-
KDDHN Perera	9	16	0	69	249	15.56	-	2
KR Pushpakumara	7	8	0	43	124	15.50	-	-
BMSN Mendis	4	7	0	32	107	15.28	-	-
KKK Gangodawila	10	13	1	61*	183	15.25	-	1
ID Gunawardene	11	18	0	57	271	15.05	-	2
RP Mapatuna	6	11	1	33	150	15.00	-	-

Qualification: 5 completed innings, average 15.00

BOWLING

	Overs	Mds	Runs	Wkts	Av	Best	10m	5/inn
RS Kalpage	87.1	28	155	16	9.68	7-27	-	1
S Weerakoon	424.4	125	1037	80	12.96	7-51	4	7
AW Ekanayake	441.1	146	891	67	13.29	8-93	-	7
HMRKB Herath	517	198	947	71	13.33	6-32	2	5
NC Komasaru	198.2	63	404	29	13.93	5-11	-	2
MM Perera	231.3	37	681	48	14.18	6-40	-	1
DGR Dhammika	109.2	30	258	18	14.33	5-47	-	1
MNR Cooray	145.5	32	394	27	14.59	4-9	-	-
SD Dissanayake	95.5	19	284	18	15.77	6-51	-	1
MMDPV Perera	202.1	46	588	37	15.89	6-46	1	3
KLSL Dias	233.1	55	606	38	15.94	6-47	-	2
SHSMK Silva	332.4	98	709	43	16.48	7-52	-	2
HSH Alles	267.5	67	762	46	16.56	5-23	-	2
KSC de Silva	285.4	82	692	41	16.87	5-16	-	3
WCA Ganegama	224.4	41	705	41	17.19	5-34	-	3
KADM Fernando	346.1	50	1137	63	18.04	7-67	2	5
MAP Salgado	257.2	65	598	33	18.12	6-24	-	1
I Dilshan	153.4	29	384	21	18.28	5-71	-	1
JWHD Boteju	197.4	54	551	30	18.36	5-35	-	1
NRG Perera	242.1	25	830	45	18.44	8-24	-	2

FIRST-CLASS AVERAGES

BOWLING

	Overs	Mds	Runs	Wkts	Av	Best	10m	5/inn
MKDI Amerasinghe	253.4	59	673	36	18.69	5-34	-	1
KA Jayasinghe	89	19	230	12	19.16	3-34	-	-
RSA Palliyaguruge	130.5	26	369	19	19.42	4-25	-	-
SI Fernando	366.1	97	822	42	19.57	7-37	1	2
MCR Fernando	436	115	1025	52	19.71	5-86	-	2
MKGCP Lakshitha	287.5	62	851	43	19.79	6-41	-	2
PN Ranjith	193.2	48	555	28	19.82	5-42	-	1
KG Perera	509.3	162	1058	53	19.96	6-14	-	3
GP Wickremasinghe	108.4	31	300	15	20.00	5-22	-	1
JAMW Kumara	253	82	642	32	20.06	4-26	-	-
RADC Perera	193.4	36	603	30	20.10	5-41	-	2
CM Bandara	316.4	74	906	45	20.13	5-58	-	3
SM Ramzan	210.3	44	584	29	20.13	4-72	-	-
PA de Silva	94.4	28	202	10	20.20	5-53	-	1
PKRP Fernando	123.4	31	285	14	20.35	3-22	-	-
NS Rupasinghe	373.3	108	797	39	20.43	5-50	-	1
ID Gunawardene	180.4	29	494	24	20.58	5-28	-	1
HDPK Dharmasena	121.3	38	247	12	20.58	4-10	-	-
WRS de Silva	178	25	643	31	20.74	6-23	-	3
WRD Dissanayake	238.5	51	644	31	20.77	4-18	-	-
DK Liyanage	257.3	66	792	38	20.84	5-34	-	2
S Jayantha	294.2	74	628	30	20.93	5-54	-	2
TT Samaraweera	264.4	53	797	38	20.97	6-55	-	1
CRB Mudalige	243.3	60	713	34	20.97	5-48	-	1
HGSP Fernando	138.4	24	401	19	21.10	6-37	-	1
PIW Jayasekera	215.4	52	531	25	21.24	6-85	1	3
NH Tennakoon	134.5	23	495	23	21.52	6-65	-	1
S Chandana	522.4	115	1527	70	21.81	8-85	2	6
JSK Peiris	80.4	17	210	10	21.90	4-35	-	-
MAM Aslam	152.2	26	593	27	21.96	5-50	-	1
B de Silva	187.2	42	486	22	22.09	4-28	-	-
RMAR Ratnayake	113.3	19	423	19	22.26	4-42	-	-
TCB Fernando	182.2	33	580	26	22.30	5-43	-	1
WMG Ramyakumara	199.1	56	513	23	22.30	6-24	-	1
WMPN Wanasinghe	133.1	20	451	20	22.55	5-29	-	1
PDRL Perera	154.4	22	542	24	22.58	7-40	-	1
WCR Tissera	140.5	26	457	20	22.85	7-89	-	1
JT Samaratunga	127.4	32	344	15	22.93	4-33	-	-
GAS Perera	349.1	84	967	42	23.02	7-45	-	2
WT Abeyratne	313.2	70	807	34	23.73	5-76	-	2
MDK Perera	270.1	53	796	34	23.41	5-42	-	1
PLU Irandika	199.3	56	451	19	23.73	6-28	-	1
KR Pushpakumara	124	24	387	16	24.18	3-60	-	-
MNTH Kumara	150.4	26	484	20	24.20	5-66	-	1
HM Madhuwantha	241	69	660	27	24.44	5-98	-	1
BSM Warnapura	101	28	247	10	24.70	4-40	-	-
HPA Priyantha	197.4	42	496	20	24.80	3-35	-	-
ASA Perera	96.2	19	301	12	25.08	3-36	-	-
MRCN Bandaratilleke	272.1	56	653	26	25.11	6-97	-	1
BWDMM Dissanayake	208.2	32	730	29	25.17	5-29	-	1
KADC Silva	170.5	46	378	15	25.20	3-15	-	-
MGS Dissanayake	235.4	62	560	22	25.45	5-16	-	1
BARS Priyadharshana	275.3	51	918	36	25.50	5-30	-	2
WC Labrooy	137	31	411	16	25.68	3-38	-	-
MHRM Fernando	70	15	265	10	26.50	3-35	-	-
ARMS Ranaweera	285.1	43	854	32	26.68	7-70	-	1
HP Tillakaratne	141.3	29	375	14	26.78	3-54	-	-

FIRST-CLASS AVERAGES

BOWLING

	Overs	Mds	Runs	Wkts	Av	Best	10m	5/inn
A Rideegammanagedera	258.1	76	569	21	27.09	5-8	-	1
HGD Nayanakantha	176.3	23	626	23	27.21	5-38	-	1
RGD Sanjeewa	116.2	31	273	10	27.30	3-41	-	-
BMTT Mendis	117.4	29	328	12	27.33	3-29	-	-
WIMC Boteju	128	25	524	19	27.57	3-88	-	-
NS Rajan	147.3	22	471	17	27.70	4-65	-	-
DPS Jayaratne	88.2	12	333	12	27.75	3-20	-	-
CPH Ramanayake	241	52	642	23	27.91	4-53	-	-
KCA Weerasinghe	188.4	30	775	27	28.70	4-52	-	-
TAVHK Ranaweera	137.1	18	548	19	28.84	5-36	-	1
MJ Sigera	180	35	578	20	28.90	3-31	-	-
PK Siriwardene	103.4	17	392	13	30.15	5-49	-	1
MTT Mirando	240.4	39	765	25	30.60	5-40	-	1
KEA Upashantha	171	22	653	21	31.09	3-28	-	-
D Hettiarchchi	264.4	51	751	24	31.29	6-80	-	2
AAI Dinuka	110.5	14	407	13	31.30	4-64	-	-
WNM Soysa	225.5	37	599	19	31.52	5-62	-	1
HK Karunaratne	188.3	63	386	12	32.16	3-18	-	-
IC Soysa	95	10	387	12	32.25	3-34	-	-
WPA Ariyadasa	90.1	15	323	10	32.30	2-35	-	-
LHD Dilhara	253.2	40	873	27	32.33	3-34	-	-
WMB Perera	115	22	388	12	32.33	4-41	-	-
PTS Fernando	151.4	17	500	15	33.33	4-77	-	-
RCRP Silva	88	8	351	10	35.10	6-65	-	1
AKIN Perera	231	35	813	23	35.34	4-32	-	-
MI Abdeen	138.2	34	427	12	35.58	4-44	-	-
H Rajapakse	158.3	24	519	14	37.07	3-31	-	-
KGAS Kalum	203.1	35	687	16	42.93	8-76	-	1
DDMR Alwis	190.3	24	581	11	52.81	2-15	-	-

Qualification: 10 wickets in 8 innings

The following bowlers took 8 wickets in fewer than 8 innings:

	Overs	Mds	Runs	Wkts	Av	Best	10m	5/inn
PW Gunaratne	46.2	9	109	11	9.90	7-25	-	1
MPGDP Gunatillake	66.4	21	183	13	14.07	4-41	-	-
WPUJC Vaas	110.5	30	244	16	15.25	6-73	-	1
ST Jayasuriya	133.4	40	260	16	16.25	4-24	-	-
MS Villavarayan	91.2	17	292	16	18.25	5-35	-	2

FIELDING

48 – MKPB Kularatne (42ct,6st); 46 – RR Tissera (42ct,2st); 42 – GST Perera (37cct,4st); 34 – ASSPA Attanayake (30ct,4st); 32 – WN de Silva (29ct,3st); 29 – YMWB Ekanayake (26ct,3st), YSS Mendis (26ct,3st), WMSM Perera (22ct,7st); 28 – DWAND Vitharana (22ct,6st); 27 – WAL Chaturanga (22ct,5st), EFMU Fernando (18ct,9st), HAPW Jayawardene(24ct,3st); 22 – WMB Perera, MS Sampan (19ct,3st); 21 – RS Kaluwitharana (18ct,3st); 20 – SKL de Silva (17ct,3st), LVV Silva (17ct,3st); 19 – SMAS Kumara; 18 – NHV Chinthaka, PK Siriwardene; 17 – HGJM Kulatunga; 16 – DT Ariyadasa (13ct,3st), PB Dassanayake (14ct,2st), WR Fernando (15ct,1st), PN Udawatta; 15 – PCVB de Silva, EMI Galagoda (13ct,2st), RMK Mahinda (14ct,1st), K Sangakkara (14ct,1st); 13 – WT de Silva (10ct,3st), DMGS Dissanayake, DN Hunukumbura, BCMS Mendis (12ct,1st), MDK Perera, MMDNRG Perera, HPK Rajapakse, DK Ranaweera, A Rizan; 12 – PB Ediriweera, MM Perera, ICD Perera, WDDS Perera, RHS Silva, BSM Warnapura; 11 – HGSP Fernando, MCR Fernando, DPS Jayaratne, HW Kumara, GAS Perera, MMDPV Perera, DP Samaraweera, PSAN Shiroman, HSGS Silva (10ct,1st), AJ Stewart (9ct,2st), RH Sureschandra; 10 – WT Abeyratne, SWND Chinthaka, PRT Fernando, MK Gajanayake, CP Mapatuna, BMTT Mendis, CRB Mudalige, RHTA Perera (9ct,1st), AS Polonowita, ARMS Ranaweera, KADJ Siriwardene, KRRK Wimalasena

Qualification: 10 catches or more

AUSTRALIA

West Indies in Australia
Carlton One-Day Series
Australia Domestic First-Class Season
Australia Domestic One-Day Season
First-Class Averages

WEST INDIES IN AUSTRALIA
By Jim Maxwell

FIRST TEST
23–25 November 2000 at Woolloongabba, Brisbane

Aiming to equal the West Indies proud record of 11 consecutive Test victories, Australia began the series in a confident mood. Both teams made noises about getting on with the playing of the game, following the distressing allegations of match fixing, which continued to hover over cricket like Nixon over Watergate.

A virulent newspaper campaign in the Australian press called for both Lara and Mark Waugh to be stood down by their respective boards, 'in the interests of the game.' Unsubstantiated allegations from Mr Gupta, an Indian bookmaker, had fingered Lara and Waugh as recipients of 'match' payments. The campaign was ill founded, as no proof had been forthcoming, and as subsequent events unfolded Mr Gupta himself was reluctant to be cross examined.

Initially Australia named a squad that included four fast bowlers, but Gillespie, whose chequered record totted up more games missed than played, withdrew with a hamstring injury. Local reveller Andy Bichel was the in-form replacement.

The West Indies tour form had been ordinary. Losses to Western Australia and Victoria were reminders that in their last eight Test innings the highest score they had achieved was 172. In the selection wash up, Sarwan and Ganga were preferred to Hinds, and Trinidadian fast bowler Marlon Black was named alongside Dillon, McLean and Courtney Walsh, who needed 17 wickets to achieve the unique milestone of 500 Test wickets.

The refurbished Gabba was enveloped in 1960–61 nostalgia as Steve Waugh and Jimmy Adams met for the toss. A reunion of the surviving Benaud/Worrell rivals had been heralded by the release of ABC Television's documentary on the momentous events of the first series to produce a tied result. Entitled *Calypso Summer*, the programme may have inspired the combatants, if they had any sense of history.

Steve Waugh certainly had, and he encouraged his players to research their baggy green antecedents, often inveigling them to make presentations at team meetings. The West Indies players may have been aware of their rich history and calypsonian spirit, but Brian Lara's drooping shoulders, a lone figure

Previous page: The victorious Australian team that white-washed the once invincible West Indies.

Brett Lee made as much of an impression with the bat as with the ball, smashing 62 not out of 80 balls.

returning from net practice, suggested that the spirit had already been broken.

Seeing the despondent mood and vulnerability of his opponents, Waugh had no hesitation in bowling first after winning the toss. First impressions were that the pitch, a dropped-in version following Olympic Games' football, was slow, maybe two paced, but not awkward. Backing his hunches, Waugh tossed the ball to MacGill, and after being struck for two fours, the leg-spinner had a prodding Campbell taken by Mark Waugh at slip. Campbell crossed with the drinks cart, which could have been laden with champagne, or at least the local brew, if the drinks waiters had any sense of anticipation. McGrath had a leaden footed Lara caught behind for a duck – it was his 11th Test match eclipse of the erratic genius, and the West Indies struggled through to lunch at 45 for two.

The West Indies major tour sponsor was a well-known cooker of chooks. Well any thoughts of expanding the menu to include waddling cousins would have been blown away after the finger-lickin' interlude.

McGrath started the rout when Chanderpaul edged to Gilchrist, Ponting held on at slip to shift a stubborn Ganga, and, comically, absurdly, Sarwan was run out attempting an ambitious second run to Ponting retrieving a leg bye deflection. McGrath was twice on a hat-trick, as a blur of snicks and misses produced five ducks, and an inept collapse to 82 all out, the lowest Test score at the Gabba for 50 years. Jimmy Adams was stranded, nonplussed, on 16 not out. McGrath, who was more accurate than hostile, bagged six for 17 from 20 frugal overs, and, as a swaggering Queensland grazier told it, 'mate, they didn't even bat their 50 overs.'

Slater and Hayden took a first innings lead before stumps, with Hayden run out in a misunderstanding with his ebullient partner. The crowd of 19,878 was the best for a Gabba first day since 1960–61. The Caribbean partygoers were momentarily inspired on the second morning when Trinidad's incredible hulk, Marlon Black, pitched up, swung rapid outswingers and had Slater caught off the first ball of the day. Nightwatchman Bichel and Langer also edged Black's swing, and Australia staggered to lunch at 158 for four.

Dillon worked hard, denying Australia the batting rhythm of quick runs. He dismissed the Waugh twins, and when Black had Ponting caught chasing an outswinger, Australia were 220 for seven. The tail wagged demoralisingly for the West Indies, with an aggressive Gilchrist, and a belligerent Lee going at the bowling. Lee's innings was struck from 80 balls, as he top scored with 62 not out. Walsh looked either short of, or past his best, and with a deficit of 150, there was nowhere to hide for the West Indies batsmen.

McGrath removed Campbell and Lara in the last hour of the second day, Lara dispatching a four, and then top edging a pull. Like the groggy boxer on the ropes, the West Indies staggered into lunch on day three at 81 for six. Ganga had been stumped charging at MacGill, speedster Lee snared Adams off an edge and bowled Sarwan, with Chanderpaul defying the bowling despairingly.

Another local wag offered this morsel of

As always, Brian Lara's is the key wicket. Glenn McGrath had him caught behind in both innings for a total of only four runs in the course of his ten-wicket haul.

FIRST TEST – AUSTRALIA v. WEST INDIES
23–25 November 2000 at Woolloongabba, Brisbane

WEST INDIES

	First innings			Second innings	
SL Campbell	c ME Waugh, b MacGill	10		c Gilchrist, b McGrath	0
D Ganga	c Ponting, b Bichel	20		st Gilchrist, b MacGill	8
BC Lara	c Gilchrist, b McGrath	0		c Gilchrist, b McGrath	4
S Chanderpaul	c Gilchrist, b McGrath	18		not out	62
JC Adams (capt)	not out	16		c Gilchrist, b Lee	16
RR Sarwan	run out (Ponting/Gilchrist)	0		b Lee	0
*RD Jacobs	c ME Waugh, b McGrath	2		c ME Waugh, b Bichel	4
NAM McLean	lbw b McGrath	0		lbw b Lee	13
M Dillon	c Gilchrist, b McGrath	0		b McGrath	0
MI Black	c MacGill, b McGrath	0		c Gilchrist, b McGrath	2
CA Walsh	c Langer, b Lee	9		c McGrath, b MacGill	0
	lb6, nb1	7		b8, lb3, nb4	15
		82			**124**

	First innings				Second innings			
	O	M	R	W	O	M	R	W
McGrath	20	12	17	6	13	9	10	4
Lee	11.1	5	24	1	18	9	40	3
MacGill	5	1	10	1	16	5	42	2
Bichel	13	3	25	1	11	4	21	1

Fall of Wickets
1-21, 2-25, 3-53, 4-59, 5-60, 6-63, 7-63, 8-67, 9-67
1-0, 2-10, 3-29, 4-62, 5-66, 6-81, 7-98, 8-117, 9-119

AUSTRALIA

	First innings	
MJ Slater	c Campbell, b Black	54
ML Hayden	run out (Sarwan/Jacobs)	44
AJ Bichel	c Jacobs, b Black	8
JL Langer	c Jacobs, b Black	3
ME Waugh	c & b Dillon	24
SR Waugh (capt)	c Campbell, b Dillon	41
RT Ponting	c Jacobs, b Black	20
*AC Gilchrist	c Jacobs, b Dillon	48
B Lee	not out	62
SCG MacGill	run out (Campbell)	19
GD McGrath	b Walsh	0
	lb5, nb4	9
		332

	First innings			
	O	M	R	W
Walsh	31.4	7	78	1
Black	28	5	83	4
Dillon	25	8	79	3
McLean	25	5	79	-
Adams	5	2	8	-

Fall of Wickets
1-101, 2-111, 3-112, 4-117, 5-179, 6-186, 7-220, 8-281, 9-331

Umpires: DJ Harper & DB Cowie
Toss: Australia
Test debut: MI Black (West Indies)

Australia won by an innings and 126 runs

ignominy: 'Can they lose a wicket during the lunch break?' Somehow they lasted until 47 minutes before tea, McGrath swooping on the tail as Chanderpaul ran out of pals on 62. McGrath's Man of the Match ten for 27, another controlled and disciplined exhibition, was the best ten-wicket haul in Test history. So Australia equalled the record with their 11th consecutive Test victory, which meant that the West Indies had lost 14 of their last 16 Tests away from home. For Australia it was an overwhelming start to a very predictable series.

SECOND TEST
1–3 December 2000 at WACA Ground, Perth

Australia had never beaten the West Indies in five Tests at the WACA Ground in Perth.

In the intervening six days between Australia's crushing win in Brisbane, the West Indies lamentable position worsened with the news that their talented middle-order batsman, Shivnarine Chanderpaul, had succumbed to a stress fracture in his left toe. The decision to replace him was left until the 11th hour, in the hope that his fragile condition may improve. It did not, and Wavell Hinds, a stand-and-deliver left-hander from Jamaica, took over at number three.

Brett Lee routed the West Indies on the third and final day at the WACA, claiming the last three wickets for no runs,

In the meantime, Brian Lara's batting slump was being blamed on an 18-year-old English model, Lynnsey Ward. The West Indies team management had banned wives and girlfriends from coming on tour, and Lara not only had special dispensation to travel with his 'Millennium Babe', but also took a taxi to the team hotel while the rest of the team travelled from airports by bus. At best, Lara's commitment was conditional, and his preferential treatment would never have been tolerated in an Australian team environment.

Following the formalities at the toss, the West Indies batted. Or Australia bowled. Déjà vu. Ganga was sent packing on a marginal leg before decision in Lee's first over, and when Campbell edged a lively McGrath delivery to Ponting at first slip in the ninth over, McGrath took his 299th Test wicket. Lara's arrival, and the customary semi-circle of slip catchers, heightened tension and expectation. The first ball to Lara was perfectly pitched near the off stump, forcing an instinctive jab, and the ball flew straight to MacGill at fourth slip. He juggled, then triumphantly clutched the hiccup. McGrath takes his 300th Test scalp, and the prized one of Lara for a 13th time. McGrath joins the 300 Club at number six, achieving the landmark in his 64th Test behind only Dennis Lillee, who wrote before the match that McGrath should be the first bowler to take 600 Test wickets, Hadlee and Marshall (61), and Warne and Donald (63).

Nineteen for three, and while the Australians and the crowd were still in rapture, Adams took guard. In Brisbane, McGrath was twice on a hat-trick, and missed out. First up to Adams a short pitched ball was too quick and bouncy for a controlled reaction, and Adams' parry lobbed gently to the exultant Langer at short leg. More pandemonium, McGrath's hat-trick was the tenth by an Australian, and the first by a New South Welshman since Fred Spofforth against England in 1878–79. The other eight hat-tricks all fell to bowlers from Victoria.

Hinds rode his luck with some off side dashes and drives, reaching 50 as the West Indies recovered from 22 for five. Hinds' concentration faltered against MacGill, and an ambitious attempted drive was snugly held by Mark Waugh at slip. Nixon Alexei McNamara McLean must have had all those celebrated voices ringing in his brain when his attempt to hit MacGill into the Swan River resulted in an embarrassing stumps shamble, leaving the resourceful Ridley Jacobs to sustain a brave counterattack. Dillon could have been that marshal at 'OK Corral' as he deflected the pace trio's

Mark Waugh was in languid touch at Perth where he scored his 18th Test century.

firepower, until Gillespie hit the off stump zone and Hayden tidied up at third slip. Black followed suit, and Walsh almost lasted long enough to help Jacobs reach his maiden Test century, but succumbed to Gillespie. Remarkably McGrath did not add to his hat-trick, and he'd bowled as well as in Brisbane where he took ten match wickets.

A record first day crowd at the WACA, 11,791, enjoyed Hayden's aggressive approach, as Australia went to stumps at 72 for two. His momentum was jarred on the second morning by the inability of nightwatchman Gillespie to rotate the strike.

Walsh was forced to leave the field after dropping a sharp return catch from Hayden, but the miss was not expensive, with Black bowling the statuesque left-hander via an inside edge for 69. Gillespie lasted for over an hour, too long with eager batsmen stewing in the rooms.

McLean found the line and bounce for a slip catch to Lara, and the West Indies bowlers were showing that they were a handful, as Steve Waugh had predicted before the series. Critically Ganga dropped a tough chance off Mark Waugh in the

SECOND TEST – AUSTRALIA v. WEST INDIES
1–3 December 2000 at WACA Ground, Perth

WEST INDIES

	First innings			Second innings	
SL Campbell	c Ponting, b McGrath	3	c Gillespie, b Lee	4
D Ganga	lbw b Lee	0	c Hayden, b Gillespie	20
WW Hinds	c ME Waugh, b MacGill	50	(4) b MacGill	41
BC Lara	c MacGill, b McGrath	0	(5) b MacGill	17
JC Adams (capt)	c Langer, b McGrath	0	(6) not out	40
RR Sarwan	c Slater, b Lee	2	(7) c Gilchrist, b Lee	1
*RD Jacobs	not out	96	(8) run out (MacGill/Gilchrist)	24
NAM McLean	b MacGill	7	(9) b Lee	11
M Dillon	c Hayden, b Gillespie	27	(3) c Gilchrist, b McGrath	3
MI Black	c Hayden, b Gillespie	0	b Lee	0
CA Walsh	c Gilchrist, b Gillespie	1	lbw b Lee	0
	lb3, nb7	10	b1, lb8, nb3	12
		196		**173**

	First innings				Second innings			
	O	M	R	W	O	M	R	W
McGrath	19	2	48	3	18	7	26	1
Lee	15	5	52	2	15	2	61	5
Gillespie	12	2	46	3	12	4	26	1
MacGill	15	2	47	2	17	6	37	2
Hayden	2	0	9	–				
ME Waugh	2	1	5	–				

Fall of Wickets
1-1, 2-19, 3-19, 4-19, 5-22, 6-97, 7-117, 8-172, 9-178
1-7, 2-16, 3-42, 4-78, 5-95, 6-96, 7-150, 8-173, 9-173

AUSTRALIA

	First innings	
ML Hayden	c Campbell, b Dillon	19
MJ Slater	b Black	69
JL Langer	c Sarwan, b McLean	5
JN Gillespie	c Lara, b McLean	23
ME Waugh	c Adams, b Dillon	119
SR Waugh (capt)	c Campbell, b Walsh	26
RT Ponting	b Black	5
*AC Gilchrist	c McLean, b Walsh	50
B Lee	not out	41
SCG MacGill	not out	18
GD McGrath		
	b2, lb10, w2, nb7	21
	(for 8 wickets dec.)	**396**

	First innings			
	O	M	R	W
Walsh	31	10	74	2
Black	18	2	87	2
Dillon	29	4	130	2
McLean	22	3	78	2
Adams	8	3	15	–

Fall of Wickets
1-52, 2-62, 3-111, 4-123, 5-188, 6-208, 7-303, 8-348

Umpires: PD Parker & JH Hampshire
Toss: Australia
Test debuts: nil

Australia won by an innings and 27 runs

gully from Dillon's bowling on 21. Waugh pressed on elegantly, and at times evasively on the bouncy surface, to his 18th Test hundred, helped by Gilchrist and Brett Lee. Lee's all-round effort included a demoralising clout for six over mid off from Black, and after some cheerful slapping about with MacGill, Waugh declared – cheekily, and confident of a quick West Indies demise. In a replay of the last hour on day two at the Gabba, Australia hunted out two wickets, including nightwatchman Dillon, who was probably unlucky to be given out, caught off his right elbow.

Brett Lee unleashed his fastest balls on the third and final day. He blasted out four of the last five wickets, after Lara's brief, promising innings folded in a terrible premature pull shot against MacGill. Hinds swashbuckled again, and, unsurprisingly, had a huge swipe at a MacGill floater and was bowled by the penultimate ball before lunch. Adams, stranded like the captain of the *Titanic*, was 40 not out when Lee took the last three wickets for none, Walsh just avoiding the hat-trick.

Another rout inside three days, and the West Indies wonderful record of 11 consecutive wins had been overtaken by an Australian side that now seemed certain of winning the next three Tests just as decisively as they had won the first two.

THIRD TEST
15–19 December 2000 at Adelaide Oval, Adelaide

For the first time on tour the West Indies management was, almost, talking up their chances going into the Adelaide Test. Brian Lara had at last found form, smashing 231 from Australia 'A's bowlers on a flat Bellerive pitch. Curiously, and perhaps irrelevantly, his innings coincided with the return to England of girlfriend Lynnsey Ward. And in the Australian camp several injuries had the potential to upset a winning rhythm.

Steve Waugh was nursing a left buttock strain, and Brett Lee had suffered a recurrence of a lower back strain, and, as a precaution, was rested.

Waugh's absence elevated Adam Gilchrist to the captaincy. Gilchrist joined a short list of Australian wicketkeeper captains – Barry Jarman in 1968, and the hirsute Jack Blackham, who wore gauntlets that would not pass for gardening gloves today when he led Australia in eight Tests in the 1880s.

Australia plumped for spin in Lee's absence, calling on Colin Miller, who had linked up with MacGill when Australia won the deciding Test in Antigua in 1999. Damien Martyn, the long suffering attendant in waiting, replaced Waugh. For the West Indies, 19-year-old Marlon Samuels, Chanderpaul's replacement, made his debut on the back of seven first-class matches, joining a growing list of young West Indian debutants.

Lara's appearance stuttered in the style of Gordon Greenidge – a muscle tear, a hamstring twinge – which normally equates to fear the wounded batsman. On a firm pitch the West Indies began promisingly, threatened by Gillespie's ability to move the ball. He bowled Ganga off an inside edge as he belatedly withdrew his bat, and trapped the perennially shuffling, creasebound Campbell leg before. Hinds followed after lunch, deflecting to Ponting in the slips. Lara began sedately, knocked awry by a McGrath bouncer that zeroed in on his helmet.

A pull shot cued the reflex touch and placement, lambasting MacGill's under-pitched deliveries. With

Brian Lara finally hit form at Adelaide, but his majestic 182 still could not prevent a third Australian victory.

THIRD TEST – AUSTRALIA v. WEST INDIES
15–19 December 2000 at Adelaide Oval, Adelaide

WEST INDIES

	First innings		Second innings	
SL Campbell	lbw b Gillespie	18	c Gilchrist, b McGrath	8
D Ganga	b Gillespie	23	lbw b Miller	32
WW Hinds	c Ponting, b Gillespie	27	c Martyn, b MacGill	9
BC Lara	c Waugh, b Miller	182	c Langer, b Miller	39
JC Adams (capt)	c Gilchrist, b Gillespie	49	c Martyn, b Miller	15
M Dillon	c Waugh, b Gillespie	9	(9) lbw b McGrath	19
MN Samuels	lbw b Miller	35	(6) c Hayden, b MacGill	3
*RD Jacobs	c Langer, b Miller	21	(7) c Ponting, b Miller	2
NAM McLean	lbw b Miller	0	(8) c Hayden, b Miller	0
MI Black	not out	1	not out	3
CA Walsh	lbw b Miller	0	c Gilchrist, b McGrath	0
	b8, lb12, nb6	26	b6, lb3, w1, nb1	11
		391		**141**

	First innings				Second innings			
	O	M	R	W	O	M	R	W
McGrath	36	14	83	-	9.5	1	27	3
Gillespie	32	9	89	5	13	5	18	-
Miller	35.5	13	81	5	17	6	32	5
MacGill	24	5	118	-	12	2	55	2
Ponting	1	1	-	-				

Fall of Wickets
1-45, 2-52, 3-86, 4-269, 5-280, 6-354, 7-376, 8-382, 9-391
1-26, 2-36, 3-87, 4-96, 5-109, 6-109, 7-109, 8-116, 9-137

AUSTRALIA

	First innings		Second innings	
MJ Slater	c sub (RR Sarwan), b Samuels	83	(2) c Jacobs, b Dillon	1
ML Hayden	run out (Campbell/Jacobs)	58	(1) c Jacobs, b Walsh	14
JL Langer	c Lara, b Samuels	6	c Jacobs, b Dillon	48
ME Waugh	lbw b Dillon	63	c Jacobs, b Dillon	5
JN Gillespie	lbw b Walsh	4		
RT Ponting	c Jacobs, b Walsh	92	(5) lbw b Walsh	11
DR Martyn	not out	46	(6) not out	34
*AC Gilchrist (capt)	c Jacobs, b McLean	9	(7) not out	10
SCG MacGill	c Jacobs, b Dillon	6		
CR Miller	c Campbell, b McLean	1		
GD McGrath	b Dillon	1		
	b5, lb13, w5, nb11	34	b3, lb1, nb3	7
		403	(for 5 wickets)	**130**

	First innings				Second innings			
	O	M	R	W	O	M	R	W
Walsh	32	7	73	2	14	4	39	2
Black	18	1	75	-	3	0	12	-
Dillon	24.4	2	84	3	12	3	42	3
McLean	21	6	69	2	5	1	9	-
Adams	13	2	35	-	3	0	7	-
Samuels	19	6	49	2	6	1	17	-

Fall of Wickets
1-156, 2-160, 3-169, 4-187, 5-310, 6-369, 7-386, 8-397, 9-398
1-8, 2-22, 3-27, 4-48, 5-111

Umpires: SJ Davis & S Venkataraghavan
Toss: West Indies
Test debut: MN Samuels (West Indies)

Australia won by five wickets

Adams, his 1999 Jamaican shadow, the partnership raced on to 183. Twice Lara exquisitely drove and cut for three boundaries in an over from McGrath and Gillespie. His only blemish was a sharp chance that only Mark Waugh could have taken from MacGill's googly at slip; but he did not.

The second new ball encouraged more Gillespie edginess, and Adams obliged. Lara found second day support from new boy Samuels, who, in the manner of all talented novices, had that extra split second to adjust, and play late. Another double hundred loomed when Lara fell to Miller's off stump spin, and a touch of extravagance. This time Mark Waugh did not miss. The rest was as predictable as another wedding party arriving on Saturday arvo in the adjacent parklands. Miller took the last five wickets for a collective 37 runs. 391 was competitive, but could Lara repeat his performance in the second innings?

Meanwhile Slater and Hayden reminded us how well they can score on a true pitch when the bowling tends to be too attacking. They whistled past 150 in even time. A run out reawakened the West Indies, and Marlon Samuels was the surprise packet, claiming Langer, caught at slip, and Slater, cutting to point, in the last half hour.

Nightwatchman Gillespie followed quickly to the persevering Walsh on day three, and at 187 for four, Australia's chances of equalling the West Indies total looked remote. Mark Waugh and Ponting composed

a partnership, which should have been broken at 260 when Lara spilt a straightforward snick from Ponting, then on 41, off Dillon. Walsh denied Ponting a century with a perfect legcutter, and the tail folded around the cool Martyn, who was on 46 not out. MacGill's dismissal did not please him, and replays suggested the deflection was from his helmet, but as he left the field he appeared to deliberately barge into 12th man Sarwan as Sarwan was coming down the race onto the ground. MacGill had a reputation for short fusing, and he was reprimanded by match referee Alan Smith. MacGill was adamant that the collision had been accidental, but appeared contrite in offering Sarwan an apology.

The tension of a close contest snapped on the fourth morning when Lara and Ganga were building a partnership following the disappointment of losing two early wickets, particularly Hinds who was caught at cover from a MacGill full toss. Just before lunch a tumultuous appeal for a catch by Gilchrist off Miller from Ganga's prod was turned down by umpire Venkat. The Australians' angry reaction encouraged Lara to intervene from the bowler's end. He motioned to the close in fielders to keep quiet, and as the session concluded, Ponting hurled the ball back to Gilchrist, narrowly missing a ducking Ganga. It was not the first time, nor the last, that Ponting lost control during the summer, and he should have been reprimanded.

Lara was scoring quickly, taking 20 from a MacGill over, but a quicker Miller delivery clipped the inside edge to pad, and Langer's short leg celebration was understandable. The rest of the batting capitulated, Miller taking five for eight in 52 balls, as the West Indies folded for 141, losing their last eight wickets for just 54 runs.

Miller's second five-wicket haul meant that Australia required only 130 to win. On a pitch that was starting to produce some variable bounce, the veteran Walsh charged in, supported by a fiery Dillon. Three catches to Jacobs, and a Ponting leg before, and Australia looked wobbly, without the steely presence of Steve Waugh. Langer dug deep, and with the

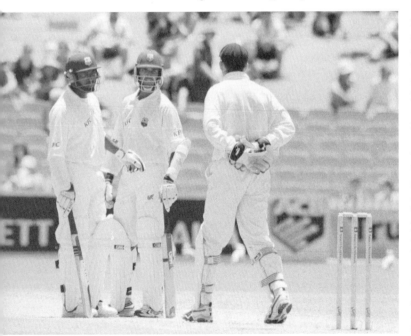

Tempers became frayed on the fourth day at Adelaide and Brian Lara, who intervened at the bowler's end, asked Australia's fielders to keep quiet.

composed Martyn, they carried the innings to 98 for five at stumps.

The West Indies lacked the backup variety for Walsh and Dillon, and Black was obviously carrying an injury. Dillon had Langer caught by Jacobs on the fifth morning, but a flurry of shots ended in an embrace between Martyn and stand-in captain Gilchrist, as Australia won by five wickets. Gilchrist described the match as the hardest of his career, which now read, played 12, won 12. Australia's 13th straight Test win had clinched the Frank Worrell Trophy.

FOURTH TEST
26–29 December 2000 at Melbourne Cricket Ground, Melbourne

Steve Waugh returned to the scene of his Test debut in 1985. Waugh had been recovering from a left buttock strain in Sydney, allowing Gilchrist the space and independence to lead the side in Adelaide. Musing over Australia's performances, Waugh had come to the conclusion that the nightwatchman policy should be abandoned. Australia had used stopgaps in the first three Tests. Waugh's decision was another example of challenging orthodoxies – why continue to do something just for the sake of doing it?

The chastened West Indies introduced Guyanese fast bowler Colin Stuart, who replaced Marlon

Black. MacGill, who had taken some licks from Lara in Adelaide, made way for Andy Bichel. Local knowledge suggested that seam and pace bowling was more effective than spin at the MCG, and the initial appearance of the drop-in pitch seemed to support this view. The grass had a solid mat, dry but deeply textured.

And MacGill would have been mindful of Warne's potential recovery when the blond bomber received his accolade for breaking Dennis Lillee's Australian Test wicket taking record before the match. Facing the crowd at the Richmond end, Warne was presented with a trophy that featured the ball with which he took his 356th wicket in Auckland in March. In the spirit of Boxing Day's festive celebratory mood, the large crowd of 73,233 watched Warne's moment, and a lunchtime motorcade showing off every surviving Victorian-born Test cricketer. Young fans would have struggled to put names to some of the ancient faces, like George Thoms, who played one Test against the West Indies in 1951–52, but the vaudevillian Merv Hughes and his whiskers did not require the cue of an introduction.

The first day was challenging for batting. Adams thought the West Indies' best chance was to bowl first, and at 149 for five, Australia were in the marginal 200 all out zone. Campbell's early miss of Slater on nine did not appear to be expensive, but the dismissal would have kept pressure on the

middle order with a new ball. Dillon's lift and leg cut kept Jacobs jumping with occasional glee, but the tail wagged around a steadfast, counterattacking Steve Waugh.

Gilchrist and Gillespie stuck with him, and he raised his bat for his 23rd Test century after five determined hours of application. With Gillespie the partnership was worth 81, and Miller swung his bat like a New York Yankee, clobbering 29 via two dropped catches. When McGrath was eventually caught by Jacobs, the Antiguan equalled the world record of seven dismissals in an innings. Steve Waugh remained undefeated, a sign that his hunger was not satisfied.

The rain that pushed the tea break back half an hour was not heavy enough to delay another West Indies batting catastrophe.

After missing the third Test through injury, Steve Waugh returned at Melbourne and, typically, responded with a century.

Exploiting the pitch's bounce and movement, Gillespie and Bichel aimed consistently at the off stump. The result – 90 minutes of carnage. Ganga nicked one, so did Hinds, Lara, and Adams, while Campbell prodded Miller's off spin to silly point. At 28 for five the innings was headed for oblivion. The exciting Samuels showed his temperament, and Jacobs the natural dogfight resilience to resuscitate the corpse.

A one-handed Mark Waugh screamer in the slips removed Jacobs for 42, and when Walsh arrived after another Bichel/Gillespie blitz on the tail, eight runs were required to avoid the follow-on. Samuels tried to garner the strike, but with two runs needed Walsh's inventiveness lobbed the ball over cover. They ran two, and in a scene from Monty Python, Walsh was ludicrously run out attempting a suicidal third, his legs and bat flailing about like 'an octopus on de herb'.

Australia batted as aggressively as the moving pitch would allow. Langer at last found touch, Mark Waugh accumulated, Miller had another bash and Steve Waugh declared, leaving 11 overs and two days to finish off the West Indies.

By stumps their second innings was wrecked. Gillespie hit Ganga on the pads, had Hinds caught at fourth slip, and bowled Lara without offering a stroke. Lara's off stump uncertainty had bedevilled

Yet another early breakthrough for Australia as Slater catches Hinds off Gillespie.

him, trying to cope with the relentless attack on his outside edge. The 'knowing when to leave' policy is always dangerous against the moving missile, and Lara's duck chalked an ignominious 24th for his team in the series.

Gillespie mowed down three more victims the next morning, and at 23 for six, another all-time low was likely. Samuels batted defiantly again, his composure lasting until three quarters of an hour after lunch, when, running out of partners he skied to Gillespie off Miller and Australia had prevailed by 352 runs. Steve Waugh said the West Indies inexperience reminded him of Australia's plight in 1985. He noted that the West Indies had recently won the Under 15 World Cup, and that fresh faces like Marlon Samuels pointed to a brighter future. Four down with one to play, that futuristic optimism seemed as distant as Australia winning football's World Cup.

FIFTH TEST
2–6 January 2001 at Sydney Cricket Ground, Sydney

The occasion was billed as the Centenary of Federation Test match, celebrating the birth of the Australian nation on 1 January 1901. Cricket's influence in that late eighteenth-century sense of nationhood was a powerful unifying force. Long before the beginnings of national structures in government, industry and politics, cricket created the

FOURTH TEST – AUSTRALIA v. WEST INDIES
26–29 December 2000 at Melbourne Cricket Ground, Melbourne

AUSTRALIA

	First innings		Second innings	
MJ Slater	c Jacobs, b McLean	30	(2) c Lara, b Dillon	4
ML Hayden	c Jacobs, b Walsh	13	(1) c Hinds, b McLean	30
JL Langer	c Jacobs, b Stuart	31	c Ganga, b Adams	80
ME Waugh	c Adams, b Dillon	25	not out	78
SR Waugh (capt)	not out	121	c Jacobs, b Stuart	20
RT Ponting	c Hinds, b McLean	23	(7) not out	26
*AC Gilchrist	c Campbell, b Stuart	37		
AJ Bichel	c Jacobs, b Dillon	3		
JN Gillespie	c Jacobs, b Walsh	19		
CR Miller	c Jacobs, b Dillon	29	(6) st Jacobs, b Adams	11
GD McGrath	c Jacobs, b Dillon	11		
	lb4, w1, nb17	22	b5, lb4, w1, nb3	13
		364	(for 5 wickets dec.)	**262**

	First innings				Second innings			
	O	M	R	W	O	M	R	W
Walsh	33	6	62	2	18	3	46	–
Dillon	21	2	76	4	17	1	68	1
McLean	27	5	95	2	9	1	30	1
Stuart	15	4	52	2	15	2	66	1
Samuels	14	0	56	–				
Adams	4	0	19	–	18	8	43	2

Fall of Wickets
1-41, 2-47, 3-101, 4-105, 5-149, 6-210, 7-225, 8-306, 9-347
1-8, 2-49, 3-165, 4-212, 5-228

WEST INDIES

	First innings		Second innings	
SL Campbell	c Hayden, b Miller	5	c Ponting, b Gillespie	6
D Ganga	c Gilchrist, b Gillespie	4	lbw b Gillespie	0
WW Hinds	c Slater, b Gillespie	0	c Bichel, b Gillespie	4
BC Lara	c ME Waugh, b Bichel	16	b Gillespie	0
JC Adams (capt)	c Gilchrist, b Bichel	0	(6) c ME Waugh, b Gillespie	0
MN Samuels	not out	60	(7) c Gillespie, b Miller	46
*RD Jacobs	c ME Waugh, b Bichel	42	(8) c Gilchrist, b Miller	23
NAM McLean	b Bichel	17	(9) run out (Bichel)	1
M Dillon	b Gillespie	0	(10) b Miller	15
CEL Stuart	b Bichel	1	(5) lbw b Gillespie	4
CA Walsh	run out (McGrath/Bichel)	4	not out	0
	lb5, nb11	16	lb1, nb9	10
		165		**109**

	First innings				Second innings			
	O	M	R	W	O	M	R	W
McGrath	13	7	15	–	12	6	10	–
Gillespie	18	6	48	3	17	5	40	6
Bichel	13.3	2	60	5	6	0	18	–
Miller	13	5	37	1	14.3	2	40	3

Fall of Wickets
1-5, 2-6, 3-28, 4-28, 5-28, 6-103, 7-144, 8-150, 9-157
1-1, 2-6, 3-7, 4-17, 5-17, 6-23, 7-77, 8-78, 9-108

Umpires: SJA Taufel & S Venkataraghavan
Toss: West Indies
Test debut: CEL Stuart (West Indies)

Australia won by 352 runs

FIFTH TEST – AUSTRALIA v. WEST INDIES
2–6 January 2001 at Sydney Cricket Ground, Sydney

WEST INDIES

	First innings		Second innings	
SL Campbell	c & b MacGill	79	c Gilchrist, b Gillespie	54
WW Hinds	b MacGill	70	b McGrath	46
JC Adams (capt)	lbw b McGrath	10	lbw McGrath	5
BC Lara	c ME Waugh, b MacGill	35	c Gilchrist, b Miller	28
MN Samuels	c Langer, b MacGill	28	lbw b Gillespie	0
RR Sarwan	lbw b MacGill	0	c Gilchrist, b McGrath	51
*RD Jacobs	st Gilchrist, b MacGill	12	lbw b ME Waugh	62
MV Nagamootoo	c Slater, b Miller	12	c Hayden, b Miller	68
NAM McLean	lbw b MacGill	0	c ME Waugh, b Miller	15
CEL Stuart	not out	12	lbw b Miller	4
CA Walsh	c Hayden, b Miller	4	not out	1
	b4, lb4, nb2	10	b5, lb10, nb3	18
		272		**352**

	First innings				Second innings			
	O	M	R	W	O	M	R	W
McGrath	19	7	43	1	24	4	80	3
Gillespie	16	4	44	–	21	5	57	2
MacGill	37	11	104	7	30	7	88	–
Miller	30.1	8	73	2	32.5	3	102	4
ME Waugh	9	3	10	1				

Fall of Wickets
1-147, 2-152, 3-174, 4-210, 5-210, 6-235, 7-240, 8-240, 9-252
1-98, 2-112, 3-112, 4-112, 5-154, 6-239, 7-317, 8-347, 9-351

AUSTRALIA

	First innings		Second innings	
MJ Slater	c Samuels, b Nagamootoo	96	(2) not out	86
ML Hayden	c Lara, b Walsh	3	(1) lbw b Stuart	5
JL Langer	c Jacobs, b McLean	20	lbw b Walsh	10
ME Waugh	run out (Campbell/Jacobs)	22	c Adams, b McLean	3
SR Waugh (capt)	b Nagamootoo	103	lbw b Samuels	38
RT Ponting	lbw b Stuart	51	not out	14
*AC Gilchrist	c Lara, b Stuart	87		
JN Gillespie	c Hinds, b Nagamootoo	2		
CR Miller	not out	37		
SCG MacGill	run out (sub: KCB Jeremy/ Nagamootoo)	1		
GD McGrath	run out (Stuart/Adams)	13		
	b1, lb5, nb11	17	b3, lb7, w1, nb7	18
		452	(for 4 wickets)	**174**

	First innings				Second innings			
	O	M	R	W	O	M	R	W
Walsh	25	4	74	1	15	5	35	1
Stuart	23	4	81	2	7	0	40	1
Nagamootoo	35	3	119	3	9	1	28	–
McLean	20	2	81	1	8	1	35	1
Adams	16.4	2	54	–				
Samuels	16	5	37	–	5.5	0	26	1

Fall of Wickets
1-17, 2-55, 3-109, 4-157, 5-289, 6-360, 7-374, 8-408, 9-410
1-5, 2-38, 3-46, 4-148

Umpires: DB Hair & RE Koertzen
Toss: West Indies
Test debuts: nil

Australia won by six wickets

cooperation between colonies that led to England's recognition of a team that called itself Australia.

Spectators who watched those early Test matches thought of themselves as Australians, even though, by law, they were resident British citizens. Recognizing the significance of the moment, the Centenary organizers created special caps and commemorative coins to present to the Australian players prior to the start of the match.

The Sydney Cricket Ground played a prominent role in the Federation festivities. Banked by a sloping cycling track, the ground hosted exhibitions of baseball, lacrosse, maypole dancing, ball throwing contests, and a Sheffield Shield match between NSW and South Australia. NSW compiled a record 918 to win by an innings, with five batsmen scoring centuries.

A century on, and the new millennium SCG had been revamped especially for this occasion. New seats, new turf and a re-laid pitch awaited the fans and the combatants.

An hour after lunch on the opening day, watched by a crowd of 40,880, the West Indies were 147 for none, and Australia were looking ragged. A New Year hangover, or simply a West Indies resolution to 'hit de ball, man?'

Campbell, who had been in out-of-season hibernation for two months, attacked. His new opening partner, Wavell Hinds, responded excitedly, and with Lara to come, 400 beckoned. Cue MacGill, who had not played since Adelaide. Campbell sent him a dolly catch, Hinds played over a floater, and after making an impressive 35, Lara departed to another swift pickup by Mark Waugh at slip. Old-fashioned values – Waugh's nod confirming to Lara that he had made a fair catch, in two fingers and a left thumb, along the turf. No technology required. MacGill, like an entwining python that terminally consumes its prey, devoured the rest. In a whirl of bat-pads, leg-befores and a lightning Gilchrist stumping, the West Indies were 256 for nine at stumps.

Courtney Walsh could not stop laughing. He was about to face Colin Miller at the start of the second day when he noticed that Miller had gone

Another farewell for Courtney Walsh who received a standing ovation from both the Sydney crowd and the Australian players.

Stuart MacGill returned to Australia's ranks in Sydney and took seven for 104 in the first innings but remained wicketless in the second.

blue. Miller's number two haircut had been rinsed overnight in a 'Federation' blue, and Walsh's paroxysm invoked laughter from the crowd. Walsh was probably still cackling when Hayden caught him off Miller at silly point.

But Hayden's celebration was short-lived, because the indefatigable Walsh quickly had him snaffled up by Lara at slip. Wicket number 493 on Walsh's steadying climb to that landmark 500th. Langer also appeared to be caught by Lara, but stood firm, the umpires deferring to the video evidence, which, as you may have guessed, was inconclusive.

Slater got going belligerently, and after running

out Mark Waugh, tried to get to his hundred with another big boundary. Premeditation and/or nervous nineties, he looped the ball to cover, becoming the first player to be dismissed nine times in the nineties. Steve Waugh and Ponting ensured an Australian lead. Gilchrist, dropped from his first ball edging straight to Adams in the gully, turned on the licks. Top-spinner Nagamootoo was the best West Indies bowler, but not even his variation and bounce threatened Gilchrist's savagery. Waugh's 24th hundred and Miller's innovative swats took the lead to 180.

Campbell and Hinds started confidently again, this time adding 98. Proving that teams under pressure are only a wicket away from calamity, McGrath bowled Hinds with the penultimate ball of the third day, after the left-hander had not offered a stroke. MacGill loomed as the fourth day threat, but it was McGrath and Miller who whittled through, after Gillespie claimed wickets with successive balls.

Samuels' first Test duck meant that the West Indies had achieved the unwanted record of 28 noughts in a series. Lara had a let off when Miller could not hold a skier at mid on, a lapse that precisely coincided with the tale on ABC radio of Miller's framed photo award being dropped in a lift. Miller made amends when Gilchrist held an edge, and for once the tail wagged with Sarwan, and two left-handers, Jacobs and Nagamootoo, flailing freely. Walsh was given a standing ovation, and a guard of honour when he came out for his final innings in Australia.

Set 171 to win, Australia's early decline to 46 for three included Walsh's 494th wicket, a strong effort after he had left the field in the first innings with ankle soreness. Aged 38 he had struggled for success during the series, taking 11 wickets in five Tests.

Another Slater attack, charging and cutting and hooking, rushed Australia towards the target. Ponting hit the winning runs to complete the 5–0 whitewash, concluding the most entertaining match of the series.

In the awards wash up, Steve Waugh won the Sir Garfield Sobers Award for most outstanding batsman, his twin brother Mark took the Joe Solomon Award for best fielder, and Jason Gillespie claimed the Alan Davidson Award for best bowler, with 20 wickets. McGrath's match figures of ten for 27 in Brisbane won the Norm O'Neill Award for the outstanding performance of the series. These awards were inspired by the deeds of the 1960–61 teams. In his admiration for Australia's play, Jimmy Adams must have wondered when a West Indies team would again compete with their most formidable rivals.

TEST MATCH AVERAGES
Australia v. West Indies

AUSTRALIA

Batting	M	Inns	NO	HS	Runs	Av	100	50	c/st
SR Waugh	4	6	1	121*	349	69.80	2	–	–
MJ Slater	5	8	1	96	373	53.28	–	4	3
ME Waugh	5	8	1	119	339	48.42	1	2	11
AC Gilchrist	5	6	1	87	241	48.20	–	2	19/2
RT Ponting	5	8	2	92	242	40.33	–	2	5
ML Hayden	5	8	0	69	236	29.50	–	2	8
CR Miller	3	4	1	37*	78	26.00	–	–	–
JL Langer	5	8	0	80	203	25.37	–	1	5
SCG MacGill	4	4	1	19	44	14.66	–	–	3
JN Gillespie	4	4	0	23	48	12.00	–	–	2
GD McGrath	5	4	0	13	25	6.25	–	–	1

Also batted: AJ Bichel (2 Tests) 8, 3 (1ct); B Lee (2 Tests) 62*, 41*; DR Martyn (1 Test) 46*, 34* (2ct).

Bowling	Overs	Mds	Runs	Wkts	Av	Best	10m	5/inn
B Lee	59.1	21	177	11	16.09	5-61	–	1
GD McGrath	183.5	69	359	21	17.09	6-17	1	1
AJ Bichel	43.3	9	124	7	17.71	5-60	–	1
CR Miller	143.2	37	365	20	18.25	5-32	1	2
JN Gillespie	141	40	368	20	18.40	6-40	–	2
SCG MacGill	156	39	501	16	31.31	7-104	–	1

Also bowled: ML Hayden 2-0-9-0; RT Ponting 1-1-0-0; ME Waugh 11-4-15-1.

WEST INDIES

Batting	M	Inns	NO	HS	Runs	Av	100	50	c/st
MN Samuels	3	6	1	60*	172	34.40	–	1	1
BC Lara	5	10	0	182	321	32.10	1	–	5
RD Jacobs	5	10	1	96*	288	32.00	–	2	20/1
WW Hinds	4	8	0	70	247	30.87	–	2	3
JC Adams	5	10	2	49	151	18.87	–	–	3
SL Campbell	5	10	0	79	187	30.35	–	2	6
D Ganga	4	8	0	32	107	13.37	–	–	1
M Dillon	4	8	0	27	73	9.12	–	–	1
RR Sarwan	3	6	0	51	54	9.00	–	1	1
CEL Stuart	2	4	1	12*	21	7.00	–	–	–
NAM McLean	5	10	0	17	64	6.40	–	–	1
CA Walsh	5	10	2	9	19	2.37	–	–	–
MI Black	3	6	2	3*	6	1.50	–	–	–

Also batted in one Test: S Chanderpaul 18, 62*; MV Nagamootoo 12, 68.

Bowling	Overs	Mds	Runs	Wkts	Av	Best	10m	5/inn
M Dillon	128.4	20	479	16	29.93	4-76	–	–
CEL Stuart	60	10	239	6	39.83	2-52	–	–
MI Black	67	8	257	6	42.83	4-83	–	–
CA Walsh	199.4	46	481	11	43.72	2-39	–	–
NAM McLean	137	19	476	9	52.88	2-69	–	–

Also bowled: MV Nagamootoo 44-4-147-3; MN Samuels 60.5-12-185-3; JC Adams 67.4-17-181-2.

CARLTON ONE-DAY SERIES: AUSTRALIA, WEST INDIES AND ZIMBABWE
by Jim Maxwell

Australia dominated the series, becoming the first team to win every match since the day/night triangular concept originated during World Series Cricket in 1978. Their closest contest was a final ball, one-run win against Zimbabwe in the last preliminary match.

By then the West Indies had already advanced to the finals, so the result had no bearing on qualification. It could have, had Zimbabwe eclipsed the West Indies' 178 in the penultimate game, but they slumped to 134 all out.

The one-sidedness of the series ensured that the only interest was who would Australia play in the finals. And there was a lingering feeling that the triangular concept had run its course. That speculation did not deter the fans, however, who seemed to enjoy watching a champion team exhibiting their prowess.

Mark Waugh batted superbly, scoring three centuries, including the Australian record for the highest innings, 173, in the second final. Everyone was dismayed when Brian Lara was named Player of the Series, a judgment that did not include the finals. Lara was moved to apologise to the crowd for the apparent absurdity of this decision. It was the only award Australia did not win. Again the match-by-match voting system was ridiculed. In part, Australia's rotation policy contributed to the outcome, although any retrospective judgment would have produced an Australian winner.

Australia's athleticism, versatility and confidence were insuperable. Waugh's men set the tone from the start, scoring a potent 267 for six in 39-degree MCG heat. The West Indies were always struggling to keep pace, strangled by near flawless outcricket. Symonds took three wickets in one over as the total nose-dived to 193 for seven.

Playing their first international match in Australia for six years, Zimbabwe lost a nailbiter at the

Gabba. Anchored by Alistair Campbell's 81, a total of 240 for nine looked competitive, given the West Indians batting fragility. From a shaky 155 for six in the 32nd over, Ricardo Powell hit out sensibly, his 83 not out steering his team to a one-wicket win with eight balls remaining.

Australia won the next three matches comfortably. At the MCG, Gilchrist and Mark Waugh thrashed a double century stand from 38 overs for a nine-wicket win over the West Indies, and despite a 116-run Lara cameo at the SCG, Australia won a Duckworth/Lewis contrivance by 28 runs. The rotation policy gave Darren Lehmann the chance to open against Zimbabwe, and he obliged with a rapid 92 not out as Australia galloped home by eight wickets.

Zimbabwe's hopes flickered in Sydney when they bowled the West Indies out for 91 on a dubious pitch, to win by 47 runs. Skipper Heath Streak's double of 45 and four for eight was inspirational. On a good surface in Adelaide, an achievable target of 236 seemed likely at 137 for three, but a de-Flowering triggered a collapse to 175 all out.

Australia kept winning, by ten wickets over the West Indies, who managed only 123, by 86 runs over Zimbabwe in Sydney, and re-emphasizing their

'Australia's athleticism, versatility and confidence were insuperable.'

quality, by six wickets and six overs in Hobart, chasing the Zimbabweans competitive 279 for six.

In Perth another referral to the third umpire showed up both the inadequacy of the technology, and the prevaricating indecision of the men in the middle. A lobbed catch to mid on from Ganga looked fairly taken by Streak, who was only ten yards from umpire Hair. Once upon a time a nod of confirmation from fieldsman to batsman would have sufficed, but in this era of 'replay it is' the integrity of the game has been dehumanized and defiled.

Zimbabwe's best batting effort came too late for the finals. Chasing a healthy 302 for five, of which Martyn made a rotational 144 not out, Stuart Carlisle and Grant Flower kept pace in a stand of 187.

Needing 15 from McGrath's last over, Marillier improvised with two flicks from outside off to fine leg. Down to three for victory off the last ball, they could manage only one. A satisfying conclusion left Heath Streak exasperated about why his spirited team could not produce better batting earlier in the series.

The best-of-three finals were predictably all over in two. A keen West Indies attack made sure that McGrath had to bat for the first time in nine matches, but, from none for two, another horrendous demise confirmed Australia's bowling and fielding strength.

Sensing another fizzer, only 31,915 fans turned out for the Second Final at the MCG. Sent in again, Australia were roused by Mark Waugh's brilliance, with half century help from both Ponting and Bevan.

Their highest total at home, 338 for six, eclipsed the record set in the corresponding match against Pakistan the previous season. Powell and Hinds made a lively 54-run opening stand, but Lara went for a duck. Jacobs and Samuels kept flowing and they needed nine an over from the last eight. Australia always appeared to have control, and won by 39 runs. McGrath and Warne stitched them up, and Australia won in the final over by 38 runs.

The finals win was Australia's first over the West Indies in 22 years of triangular competition, and impressively their 15th over the West Indies in both Tests and one-dayers for the summer.

Match One – Australia v. West Indies
11 January 2001 at Melbourne Cricket Ground (floodlit)
Australia 267 for 6 (50 overs) (RT Ponting 73, ME Waugh 51)
West Indies 193 for 7 (50 overs) (MN Samuels 57)
Australia (2 pts) won by 74 runs
Man of the Match: RT Ponting

Match Two – West Indies v. Zimbabwe
13 January 2001 at Woolloongabba, Brisbane (floodlit)
Zimbabwe 240 for 9 (50 overs) (ADR Campbell 81)
West Indies 241 for 9 (48.4 overs) (RL Powell 83*)
West Indies (2 pts) won by one wicket
Man of the Match: RL Powell

Match Three – Australia v. West Indies
14 January 2001 at Woolloongabba, Brisbane (floodlit)
West Indies 234 for 8 (50 overs) (WW Hinds 54)
Australia 236 for 1 (43.4 overs) (ME Waugh 112*, AC Gilchrist 98)
Australia (2 pts) won by nine wickets
Man of the Match: ME Waugh

Match Four – Australia v. West Indies
17 January 2001 at Sydney Cricket Ground (floodlit)
Australia 277 for 4 (50 overs) (RT Ponting 93, ME Waugh 58)
West Indies 211 for 8 (42.4 overs) (BC Lara 116*)
Australia (2 pts) won by 28 runs (DL Method: West Indies needed to have 240 runs at 42.4 overs when rain stopped play.)
Man of the Match: BC Lara

Match Five – Australia v. Zimbabwe
21 January 2001 at Melbourne Cricket Ground (floodlit)
Zimbabwe 223 for 9 (50 overs) (GW Flower 51)
Australia 226 for 2 (36.5 overs) (DS Lehmann 92*, RT Ponting 68)
Australia (2 pts) won by eight wickets
Man of the Match: DS Lehmann

Match Six – West Indies v. Zimbabwe
23 January 2001 at Sydney Cricket Ground (floodlit)
Zimbabwe 138 (47.2 overs)
West Indies 91 (31.5 overs)
Zimbabwe (2 pts) won by 47 runs
Man of the Match: HH Streak

Match Seven – West Indies v. Zimbabwe
25 January 2001 at Adelaide Oval (floodlit)
West Indies 235 for 6 (47 overs) (BC Lara 70, MN Samuels 68)
Zimbabwe 175 (40.2 overs) (A Flower 50)
West Indies (2 pts) won by 77 runs (DL Method: Zimbabwe target 253 runs from 47 overs)
Man of the Match: MN Samuels

Match Eight – Australia v. West Indies
26 January 2001 at Adelaide Oval (floodlit)

West Indies 123 (35.1 overs)
Australia 124 for 0 (22.5 overs) (DR Martyn 69*, DS Lehmann 50*)
Australia (2 pts) won by ten wickets
Man of the Match: B Lee

Match Nine – Australia v. Zimbabwe
28 January 2001 at Sydney Cricket Ground (floodlit)
Australia 291 for 6 (50 overs) (MG Bevan 74*, AC Gilchrist 63)
Zimbabwe 204 (47.5 overs)
Australia (2 pts) won by 86 runs
Man of the Match: MG Bevan

Match Ten – Australia v. Zimbabwe
30 January at Bellerive Oval, Hobart
Zimbabwe 279 for 6 (50 overs) (ADR Campbell 124, A Flower 51)
Australia 282 for 4 (44 overs) (ME Waugh 100*, SR Waugh 81, A Symonds 60)
Australia (2 pts) won by six wickets
Man of the Match: ADR Campbell

Match Eleven – West Indies v. Zimbabwe
2 February 2001 at WACA Ground, Perth (floodlit)
West Indies 178 (47.2 overs)(BC Lara 83*)
Zimbabwe 134 (42.3 overs)
West Indies (2 pts) won by 44 runs
Man of the Match: BC Lara

Match Twelve – Australia v. Zimbabwe
4 February 2001 at WACA Ground, Perth
Australia 302 for 5 (50 overs) (DR Martyn 144*)
Zimbabwe 301 for 6 (50 overs) (SV Carlisle 119, GW Flower 85)
Australia (2 pts) won by 1 run
Man of the Match: DR Martyn

First Final – Australia v. West Indies
7 February 2001 at Sydney Cricket Ground (floodlit)
Australia 253 for 9 (50 overs)
West Indies 119 (37.2 overs)
Australia won by 134 runs
Man of the Match: IJ Harvey

Second Final – Australia v. West Indies
9 February 2001 at Melbourne Cricket Ground (floodlit)
Australia 338 for 6 (50 overs) (ME Waugh 173, RT Ponting 63, MG Bevan 58)
West Indies 299 (49.3 overs) (MN Samuels 63, WW Hinds 60, RD Jacobs 59)
Australia won by 39 runs
Man of the Match: ME Waugh
Man of the Series: BC Lara

Mark Waugh's 173 in the second final, the highest Australian one-day score, was one of his three centuries of the series, but it was not enough to be named Man of the Series.

AUSTRALIA DOMESTIC FIRST-CLASS CRICKET

PURA CUP 2000–01

Queenslanders agonized over winning the famous Sheffield Shield for 68 years, and were mightily relieved when their team grabbed hold of it at the end of the 1994–95 season.

In 1999–2000 they won the Pura Milk Cup, the trophy that controversially replaced the Sheffield Shield, mid-season, after 106 years of competition. That win was not as historically significant as their first triumph in 1994–95, but a further name change last season meant that Queensland would be the first and only Pura Milk Cup winners; and now they hold the Pura Cup, following victory in 2000–01, celebrating their fourth domestic first-class success in seven seasons. Six outright wins, four of them at home, pushed the rampaging Bulls to top position on the table, from where they made sure of winning the final by four wickets over the hapless Victorians, who had not won in Brisbane for 17 years.

Underpinned by the batting stability of Jimmy Maher, Martin Love and Stuart Law, Queensland were only dismissed twice over ten matches. Maher scored over a thousand runs, more than adequately covering for the prolific Hayden, and Love, forced to miss two matches with a hand injury, scored over 900 runs at an average of 75.83.

The bowling depended on the exceptional work of a pace triumvirate; Andy Bichel, Joe Dawes and Adam Dale. Bichel, who missed three games, shared the leading role with Dawes, taking 49 wickets apiece. Aged 30, Dawes, a burly Brisbane detective and perennial fringe dweller, covered the absence of Kasprowicz (who was recuperating from a shoulder operation and played only once) with sustained pace, defying the discomfort of shin splints. Dale's accuracy and persistence created a swag of 46 wickets, wearing down the opposition. Tyro paceman Ashley Noffke was Man of the Match in the final, taking five for 41 in Victoria's first innings. He was later called up to replace the injured Nathan Bracken on the Ashes tour.

Victoria scored points in every match after losses in their first two games of the season. Opener Matthew Elliott, who missed the first four games with a knee injury following a prolific season with Glamorgan, was overshadowed by Brad Hodge and Jason Arnberger, who both made over a thousand first-class runs. Paul Reiffel, the phlegmatic captain and experienced pace bowler, took 30 wickets,

Stuart Law's 814 runs at an average of 62.61 underpinned the strength of Queensland's batting.

supported by the lively left armer, Matthew Inness, with 43 wickets.

Reiffel passed Alan Connolly's record of 297 career wickets for Victoria, but his hard-working season ended in frustration when he was fined $200 for dissent in the Cup Final. Under a newspaper headline, 'Reiffel fought the Law and the Law won,' the story of Reiffel's out of character contretemps with the Queensland captain was revealed. Law survived a disputed catch decision off Reiffel from his first ball in the Queensland second innings. Abetted by inconclusive television replays and demurring umpires, Law, who made 47 not out, was subsequently caught off a no ball, and then dropped twice before hitting the winning runs.

Tasmania, who won their last three matches to finish third, were magnificently served by their

Jimmy Maher scored four centuries in the course of a prolific season for Queensland.

strength for the first three matches, they took valuable points, but the South Australian match was totally washed out. Then the batting failed, as the selectors used 26 players in a search for talent. Mark Higgs and Greg Mail scored big hundreds, but too much was expected of Michael Bevan, who underachieved with 557 runs at 50.63. In between Tests, Stuart MacGill bowled spasmodically, and Nathan Bracken's left arm promise was rewarded with selection in the one-day squad. Wicketkeeper batsman Brad Haddin again impressed, subbing for Gilchrist in one limited overs match.

The talented Western Australians disappointed, their season upset by coach Wayne Clark, and captain Tom Moody deciding to accept English county appointments. Moody's last match was his 300th, completing a marvellous career record of 21,001 runs at an average 46.75, and 361 wickets at 30.70.

Standing above his inconsistent team-mates, Simon Katich batted plunderously, hitting six hundreds, to head the aggregates with 1,282 runs at 71.22. Joe Angel and Brendon Julian carried the attack, with erratic contributions from Matthew Nicholson. Watch out for the deeds of another Marsh, Shaun, son of Geoff, who made his debut aged 17.

South Australia's injury plagued bowling attack could only dismiss the opposition twice in two matches. They lost left arm spinner Brad Young and paceman Paul Wilson to injuries, throwing the burden on Mark Harrity and Peter McIntyre. Greg Blewett scored heavily, but Darren Lehmann managed only one century. Their best bowler is Jason Gillespie, but between rest, injury and Australian commitments he played in only one game.

On a night that was Australian cricket's equivalent to the Oscars in Hollywood, the Australian Cricket Board honoured its stars with a nationally televised awards presentation. The award for the country's best cricketer over the previous 12 months was won by Steve Waugh, by one vote from twin brother Mark. Steve won the Allan Border Medal. Colin Miller, aged 37, was the surprise Test Player of the Year, and Glenn McGrath the best in one-day internationals. Darren Lehmann, in recognition of his 1999–2000 season, was judged best State player and Nathan Bracken was named Best Young Cricketer.

captain Jamie Cox. He scored twice as many runs as any other batsman, and topped the umpires' votes as Pura Cup Player of the Year. With over a thousand runs and five season centuries, Cox passed David Boon as Tasmania's leading runscorer. Ponting made a superb 233 against Queensland, but was absent thereafter, and the bowling looked ordinary around the veteran wheeling down from 34-year-old David Saker and Shaun Young.

All-round Queensland immigrant Shane Watson shone promisingly, but a dearth of local talent continued to be disturbing.

New South Wales improved to fourth from their disastrous last placing in 1999–2000. Steve Rixon's return from New Zealand as coach and Shane Lee's captaincy produced some improvement. At full

AUSTRALIA DOMESTIC ONE-DAY CRICKET

MERCANTILE MUTUAL CUP

The format was expanded to include home and away matches for the first time. With every state contracting players, the need for more cricket was obvious. The cup competition continued to be innovative, introducing bonus points for quick scoring and penalties for slow over rates. The bonus points enlivened the occasional straightforward run chase, and rewarded teams that took wickets, which was a pleasing throwback to 'real' cricket.

Previous innovations, including only three fieldsmen allowed outside the circle between overs 16 and 30, and the one bouncer per over regulation, were retained.

Five teams were in the running for the semi-finals up to the last round, with the top two emerging as finalists. In the final the Western Australian Warriors were favoured to beat New South Wales at home, but a typically decisive innings from Michael Bevan delivered the Blues their first one-day title for seven years. He was badly missed at mid on on 59 and carried on to 135 not out in a six-wicket win with ten balls to spare.

Bevan was a consistent scorer throughout the competition, with former Zimbabwean Murray Goodwin leading the aggregates totalling 534 at 76.28, and creating the record for the highest individual innings, 167. Refreshingly, a leg-spinner was the most productive bowler. Stuart MacGill equalled the record for the most domestic one-day wickets in a season, taking 18.

NSW fast bowler Don Nash smashed the fastest 50 in the history of the cup, whacking three fours and five sixes in a 24-ball blitz against Western Australia at the SCG.

Darren Lehmann and the veteran Tasmanian all-rounder Shaun Young shared the umpires' award for Best Player, with Victoria's Ben Oliver named Best Young Talent.

Not surprisingly, Michael Bevan excelled in Australia's domestic one-day tournament. NSW beat Western Australia to give 'the Blues' their first title for seven years.

FIRST-CLASS AVERAGES

BATTING

	M	Inns	NO	HS	Runs	Av	100	50
RT Ponting	7	12	3	233	726	80.66	2	3
ML Love	10	15	3	172*	910	75.83	3	5
SM Katich	12	23	5	228*	1282	71.22	6	3
GS Blewett	9	18	1	260*	1162	68.35	3	6
DR Martyn	8	15	4	122	746	67.81	2	4
J Cox	11	21	3	160	1170	65.00	5	4
JP Maher	12	21	3	175	1142	63.44	4	3
SG Law	11	15	2	161	814	62.61	2	4
ME Waugh	7	11	1	152	590	59.00	2	3
AC Gilchrist	8	11	2	109*	531	59.00	2	3
BJ Hodge	13	23	3	134rh	1129	56.45	5	3
MG Bevan	8	13	2	119	557	50.63	2	2
SR Waugh	6	9	1	121*	394	49.25	2	-
MJ Slater	7	11	1	100	491	49.10	1	4
JL Arnberger	12	22	1	173	1006	45.04	2	7
A Symonds	9	13	1	133	558	46.50	1	2
DS Lehmann	8	16	2	146	645	46.07	1	3
BC Lara	7	13	0	231	591	45.46	2	-
ML Hayden	8	13	1	118*	537	44.75	1	3
JM Vaughan	5	10	2	131*	350	43.75	1	2
MA Higgs	7	11	1	181*	413	41.30	1	-
MTG Elliott	7	14	1	98	524	40.30	-	5
DJ Marsh	9	16	3	110	514	39.53	1	3
RD Jacobs	7	13	1	131	472	39.33	1	2
CT Perren	6	9	1	112	304	38.00	1	1
GJ Mail	7	12	0	176	435	36.25	1	2
SP Kremerskothen	9	13	1	81	435	36.25	-	2
IJ Harvey	8	14	0	100	481	34.35	1	2
SA Deitz	9	18	0	114	608	33.77	2	2
S Young	10	17	4	83*	433	33.30	-	3
S Lee	8	11	0	114	365	33.18	1	2
MP Mott	12	22	1	154	695	33.09	1	3
ME Hussey	11	21	1	137	605	30.25	1	1
JL Cassell	8	13	1	136	352	29.33	1	1
WW Hinds	6	11	0	70	322	29.27	-	2
BJ Haddin	9	15	1	93	397	28.35	-	3
M Klinger	9	15	2	99*	358	27.53	-	3
MJ di Venuto	10	18	1	86	466	27.41	-	5
TM Moody	9	14	2	57	324	27.00	-	2
MJ Nicholson	8	11	2	54	241	26.77	-	1
BA Johnson	5	10	0	68	260	26.00	-	2
DA Fitzgerald	7	14	0	107	356	25.42	1	2
MJ North	6	11	0	54	277	25.18	-	2
SL Campbell	8	15	0	119	372	24.80	1	2
BP Julian	9	16	1	78	367	24.46	-	2
JL Langer	8	13	0	80	313	24.07	-	2
PR Reiffel	11	17	3	70	337	24.07	-	2
DF Hills	9	17	0	120	395	23.23	1	2
AJ Bichel	10	13	1	61	278	23.16	-	1
WA Seccombe	11	14	2	52	270	22.50	-	1
CJ Richards	5	9	1	69	177	22.12	-	2
DA Nash	9	14	1	46	255	19.61	-	-
RJ Campbell	5	9	0	35	167	18.55	-	-
AC Dale	11	12	4	45*	139	17.37	-	-
JC Adams	8	15	2	49	213	16.38	-	-
CR Miller	8	11	3	37*	128	16.00	-	-
JA Dykes	4	8	0	32	125	15.62	-	-
SG Clingeleffer	10	14	1	50	203	15.61	-	1
MJ Walsh	8	14	1	50	195	15.00	-	1
DS Berry	10	17	1	61	230	14.37	-	1
GA Manou	9	16	2	53	200	14.28	-	1
BP van Deinsen	5	9	0	29	125	13.88	-	-
SAJ Craig	5	8	0	35	102	12.75	-	-
DJ Saker	10	14	3	34*	133	12.09	-	-
MW Goodwin	7	13	0	59	145	11.15	-	-
D Ganga	7	13	0	32	145	11.15	-	-

Qualification: 8 completed innings, average 10.00

FIRST-CLASS AVERAGES

BOWLING

	Overs	Mds	Runs	Wkts	Av	Best	10m	5/inn
GD McGrath	207.5	77	425	23	18.47	6-17	1	1
JH Dawes	358.3	101	1003	49	20.46	7-98	1	3
BJ Hodge	106.1	27	266	13	20.46	4-17	-	-
B Lee	133	40	411	20	20.55	5-42	-	2
JN Gillespie	175	37	463	22	21.04	6-40	-	2
P Wilson	179.3	62	406	19	21.36	4-23	-	-
TM Moody	189	61	455	20	22.75	5-26	-	1
AJ Bichel	400.3	99	1144	49	23.34	5-60	-	3
AC Dale	570.3	226	1076	46	23.39	5-37	-	2
J Angel	333.3	109	867	37	23.43	5-78	-	1
NW Bracken	240.1	65	688	29	23.72	5-22	-	2
CR Miller	377.1	104	998	40	24.95	5-32	1	2
MWH Inness	403.2	126	1077	43	25.04	6-26	-	2
S Young	203.3	63	532	21	25.33	4-33	-	-
SR Watson	74	13	289	11	26.27	2-22	-	-
DG Wright	192.1	42	593	22	26.95	4-54	-	-
S Lee	151.5	40	463	17	27.23	4-43	-	-
PR Reiffel	325.1	84	824	30	27.46	4-50	-	-
IJ Harvey	172.2	54	474	17	27.88	4-19	-	-
BP Julian	266.2	46	935	32	29.21	4-87	-	-
SCG MacGill	453.4	98	1390	46	30.21	7-104	-	3
BA Swain	195.3	44	521	17	30.64	4-96	-	-
MJ Nicholson	289	86	773	25	30.92	4-119	-	-
MA Harrity	243.3	62	728	23	31.65	4-55	-	-
PE McIntyre	322.2	67	927	28	33.10	5-102	-	1
ML Lewis	246.2	52	772	23	33.56	5-57	-	1
M Dillon	195.4	33	683	20	34.15	4-76	-	-
AG Downton	161.5	42	548	16	34.25	4-51	-	-
AA Noffke	152	29	527	15	35.13	5-41	-	1
CA Walsh	232.4	61	547	15	36.46	4-66	-	-
DA Nash	243.2	56	730	20	36.50	4-57	-	-
GG Swan	223	52	673	18	37.38	3-31	-	-
CEL Stuart	129.3	19	499	13	38.38	3-84	-	-
DJ Marsh	216	44	720	18	40.00	4-80	-	-
DJ Saker	350	66	1080	26	41.53	5-98	-	1
JM Davison	194.1	61	488	10	48.80	4-90	-	-
NAM McLean	164	27	566	11	51.45	2-69	-	-

Qualification: 10 wickets in 8 innings

The following bowlers took 10 wickets in fewer than 8 innings:

BJ Oldroyd	142.2	37	410	13	31.35	4-90	-	-
MI Black	142.2	26	494	12	41.16	4-83	-	-

FIELDING

58 – WA Seccombe (57ct,1st); 37 – DS Berry (36ct,1st); 36 – MJ Walsh (33ct,3st);
32 – AC Gilchrist (29ct,3st); 29 – BJ Haddin (26ct,3st); 25 – SG Clingeleffer (21ct,4st);
21 – RD Jacobs (20ct, 1st); 20 – GA Manou (19ct,1st); 16 – JP Maher; 15 – MJ di Venuto,
MP Mott; 13 – GS Blewett, ME Hussey, ME Waugh; 12 – JL Arnberger, SM Katich, ML Love,
DJ Marsh; 10 – RJ Campbell, ML Hayden, SG Law, DR Martyn

Qualification: 10 catches or more

INDIA

Zimbabwe in India
Australia in India
India Domestic First-Class Season
India Domestic One-Day Season
First-Class Averages

ZIMBABWE IN INDIA
By Qamar Ahmed

FIRST TEST
18–22 November 2000 at Feroze Shah Kotla Ground, Delhi

India took a 1–0 lead in a brief two-match series as they won the first Test by a convincing margin of seven wickets. Rahul Dravid's undefeated double century (200 not out) in the first innings was followed by another useful unbeaten innings of 71 in the second innings, and Javagal Srinath's haul of nine for 141 wickets in the match made the task easier as Saurav Ganguly's India emerged triumphant only nine days after winning the one-off Test against Bangladesh.

Javagal Srinath was simply too good for Zimbabwe at Delhi. The quick bowler took nine wickets in the match.

Previous page: The end of one of the most astonishing series in recent years: India celebrate as they beat the mighty Australia in Chennai.

FIRST TEST – INDIA v. ZIMBABWE
18–22 November 2000 at Feroz Shah Kotla, Delhi

ZIMBABWE

	First innings		Second innings	
GW Flower	b Srinath	0	c Dahiya, b Srinath	0
GJ Rennie	c Dahiya, b Srinath	13	c Ganguly, b Srinath	0
SV Carlisle	c Joshi, b Tendulkar	58	c Ganguly, b Joshi	32
ADR Campbell	c Laxman, b Srinath	70	c Dravid, b Srinath	8
*A Flower	not out	183	lbw b Agarkar	70
GJ Whittall	c Dravid, b Joshi	0	c Ramesh, b Kartik	29
HH Streak (capt)	c Dravid, b Srinath	25	(8) lbw b Kartik	26
PA Strang	c Ganguly, b Joshi	19	(9) not out	14
BA Murphy	run out (Dravid/Dahiya)	13	(7) c Dahiya, b Srinath	6
BC Strang	lbw b Agarkar	6	c Tendulkar, b Joshi	15
HK Olonga	not out	11	lbw b Srinath	10
	b8, lb10, w4, nb2	24	b4, lb9, w1, nb1	15
	(for 9 wickets dec.)	422		225

	First innings				Second innings			
	O	M	R	W	O	M	R	W
Srinath	35	9	81	4	24.1	6	60	5
Agarkar	35	13	89	1	16	4	48	1
Ganguly	8	1	26	–				
Joshi	46	11	116	2	25	7	68	2
Tendulkar	19	5	51	1	4	1	10	–
Kartik	24	7	40	–	11	2	26	2
Laxman	1	0	1	–				

Fall of Wickets
1-0, 2-15, 3-134, 4-154, 5-155, 6-232, 7-266, 8-312, 9-325
1-0, 2-15, 3-25, 4-47, 5-109, 6-144, 7-171, 8-181, 9-213

INDIA

	First innings		Second innings	
SS Das	lbw b Olonga	58	run out (Murphy)	4
S Ramesh	lbw b Streak	13	c PA Strang, b Streak	0
R Dravid	not out	200	not out	70
SR Tendulkar	c PA Strang, b Murphy	122	c Murphy, b PA Strang	39
SC Ganguly (capt)	c A Flower, b Olonga	27	not out	65
VVS Laxman	not out	18		
*V Dahiya				
SB Joshi				
AB Agarkar				
J Srinath				
M Kartik				
	b2, lb10, w2, nb6	20	b9, lb1, w1, nb1	12
	(for 4 wickets dec.)	458	(for 3 wickets)	190

	First innings				Second innings			
	O	M	R	W	O	M	R	W
Streak	30	9	78	1	5	2	18	1
BC Strang	28	9	95	–	3	0	20	–
Murphy	36	5	90	1	11	0	56	–
Olonga	20	3	79	2	6	0	26	–
PA Strang	15	1	52	–	4.2	0	26	1
GW Flower	13.4	3	52	–	1.4	0	10	–
Rennie					3.3	0	19	–
Campbell					3	1	5	–

Fall of Wickets
1-27, 2-134, 3-347, 4-430
1-3, 2-15, 3-80

Umpires: S Venkataraghavan & JH Hampshire
Toss: Zimbabwe
Test debut: V Dahiya (India)

India won by seven wickets

Not the most memorable stroke from one of the game's more graceful batsmen, but Rahul Dravid plundered the Zimbabweans for a double century.

Dravid (70) and Ganguly (65), who hit three sixes and seven fours in his belligerent innings.

Zimbabwe's massive 422 in the first innings was helped by dropped catches – with Indian captain, Saurav Ganguly, being the main culprit in the slips. Stuart Carlisle scored 58 and Alistair Campbell hit 70, containing nine fours, to share 119 runs for the third wicket after the visitors had lost two wickets for 15 having won the toss and decided to bat. Campbell reached 2,000 Test runs during the course of his innings, but it was Andy Flower who dominated the Indian bowlers with a brilliant 183 not out – his eighth Test hundred. He hit 24 boundaries and two sixes in eight hours batting, during which he faced 351 balls.

He put on a record 97 runs for the last wicket with Henry Olonga (11) before Zimbabwe declared on the second day before stumps. By close of play on the third day, India had scored 275 for two as Dravid hit form. He made a career best 200, with 37 fours, adding 107 with Shiv Sunder Das (58) for the second wicket, and then 213 with Sachin Tendulkar for the third. Additional landmarks included Dravid reaching 3,000 runs in Tests while this was Tendulkar's 23rd Test century. India declared at 458 for four on the fourth afternoon.

India, having declared their first innings closed at 458 for four in reply to Zimbabwe's 422 for nine, had only a slender first-innings lead of 36. However, the bowlers – spearheaded by Srinath – bowled magnificently in the second innings to bowl Zimbabwe out for 225. Srinath took five for 60 and India, needing 190 for a win, reached the target with 57 balls to spare on the final day.

The run chase was made possible through an unbroken fourth-wicket stand of 110 between

Zimbabwe tottered to 119 for five in the second innings by stumps on the fourth day and added 106 more on the final day before being dismissed for the second time, leaving India a target of 190 in 47 overs.

'With six batsmen in the side, I knew we could get whatever target Zimbabwe set us,' said Ganguly, while Heath Streak, Zimbabwe's captain, regretted his spinners' inability to exploit a good wicket.

SECOND TEST
25–29 November 2000 at Vidarbha CA Ground, Nagpur

After being made to follow on 227 runs behind, Zimbabwe were saved by a determined, unbeaten 232 by their experienced left-hander Andy Flower. He managed to stretch the innings through the fifth and final day enabling Zimbabwe to finish on 503 for six and earn a respectable draw. When the match was called to a close, Flower was left 34 runs short of Zimbabwe's highest best individual score of 266, scored by David Houghton against Sri Lanka at Bulawayo in 1994.

Flower batted for nine hours for his ninth Test hundred and in the process saved the humiliation of another defeat. His double century contained 34 fours and two sixes, and he put on 209 for the fourth wicket with Alistair Campbell and 113 with Dirk Viljoen for the sixth wicket. Campbell's 113 was his first century after 47 Tests. The off spinner Sarandeep Singh claimed four for 136 in the second

It can only be Sachin Tendulkar, proving that whatever Dravid can do, he can do better!

innings to finish with six wickets on his Test debut.

After winning the toss, India made 306 for two on the first day with Shiv Sunder Das hitting 110, his maiden Test century. He shared 155 runs for the second wicket with Dravid and hit 19 fours in his 252-minute innings. Dravid made 162 and Sachin Tendulkar an unbeaten 201 as the pair then added 249 for the third wicket, allowing India to declare on the second afternoon on 609 for six. Dravid's eighth Test hundred contained 20 fours and a six and Tendulkar's 24th Test hundred was studded with 27 fours.

Zimbabwe did well to reply with 382 with the help of 84 by Guy Whittall, 51 by Stuart Carlisle, 55 by Andy Flower and 106 by Grant Flower who, in his sixth Test century, hit 12 fours and three sixes. At close on the fourth day and following on they were 238 for three. Andy Flower batted on into the final day for his 232 to dash any hopes that India may have had of beating them for the second time.

A marathon, unbeaten 232 from Zimbabwe's prolific Andy Flower helped the visitors to a draw in the second Test.

SECOND TEST – INDIA v. ZIMBABWE
25–29 November 2000 at Vidarbha CA Ground, Nagpur

INDIA

	First innings	
SS Das	c Campbell, b Murphy	110
S Ramesh	run out (Streak)	48
R Dravid	c A Flower, b Streak	162
SR Tendulkar	not out	201
SC Ganguly (capt)	c Streak, b GW Flower	30
AB Agarkar	c Streak, b Murphy	12
SB Joshi	c Murphy, b GW Flower	27
*V Dahiya	not out	2
J Srinath		
Z Khan		
Sarandeep Singh		
	lb11, w4, nb2	17
	(for 6 wickets dec.)	609

	First innings			
	O	M	R	W
Streak	31	7	87	1
Olonga	24	4	98	–
Nkala	22	2	86	–
Murphy	40.5	2	175	2
Viljoen	14	2	51	–
GW Flower	24	0	101	2

Fall of Wickets
1-72, 2-227, 3-476, 4-535, 5-564, 6-601

ZIMBABWE

	First innings		Second innings	
GJ Whittall	c Dravid, b Singh	84	c Tendulkar, b Singh	11
GJ Rennie	run out (Agarkar)	19	c Ganguly, b Singh	37
SV Carlisle	c & b Agarkar	51	c Tendulkar, b Singh	8
ADR Campbell	c Ramesh, b Singh	4	c Joshi, b Khan	102
*A Flower	c Dahiya, b Agarkar	55	not out	232
GW Flower	not out	106	c Ganguly, b Joshi	16
DP Viljoen	c Dahiya, b Khan	19	c Ganguly, b Singh	38
HH Streak (capt)	lbw b Srinath	16	not out	29
ML Nkala	c Dahiya, b Srinath	6		
BA Murphy	c Das, b Joshi	0		
HK Olonga	b Srinath	0		
	b6, lb12, w1, nb3	22	b12, lb14, nb4	30
		382	(for 6 wickets)	503

	First innings				Second innings			
	O	M	R	W	O	M	R	W
Srinath	28.1	7	81	3	15	5	53	–
Khan	21	3	78	1	17	5	48	1
Joshi	25	7	69	1	41	5	153	1
Agarkar	23	7	59	2	14	3	29	–
Sarandeep Singh	22	7	70	2	49	10	136	4
Tendulkar	1	0	7	–	11	3	19	–
Ramesh					3	0	14	–
Dravid					7	0	15	–
Ganguly					1	0	3	–
Das					3	0	7	–

Fall of Wickets
1-43, 2-144, 3-165, 4-166, 5-262, 6-324, 7-359, 8-371, 9-372
1-24, 2-60, 3-61, 4-270, 5-292, 6-405

Umpires: AV Jayakaprash & RS Dunne
Toss: India
Test debut: Sarandeep Singh (India)

Match drawn

TEST MATCH AVERAGES
India v. Zimbabwe

INDIA

Batting	M	Inns	NO	HS	Runs	Av	100	50	c/st
R Dravid	2	3	2	200*	432	432.00	2	1	4
SR Tendulkar	2	3	1	201*	362	181.00	2	–	3
SC Ganguly	2	3	1	65*	122	61.00	–	1	6
SS Das	2	3	0	110	172	57.33	1	1	1
S Ramesh	2	3	0	48	61	20.33	–	–	2

Also batted: AB Agarkar (2 Tests) 12 (1ct); V Dahiya (2 Tests) 2* (6ct); SB Joshi (2 Tests) 27 (2ct); VVS Laxman (1 Test) 18* (1ct).
Did not bat: J Srinath (2 Tests); M Kartik, Z Khan and Sarandeep Singh played in one Test without batting.

Bowling	Overs	Mds	Runs	Wkts	Av	Best	10m	5/inn
J Srinath	102.2	27	275	12	22.91	5-60	–	1
Sarandeep Singh	71	17	206	6	34.33	4-136	–	–
SB Joshi	137	30	406	6	67.66	2-68	–	–

Also bowled: AB Agarkar 88-27-225-4; SS Das 3-0-7-0; R Dravid 7-0-15-0; SC Ganguly 9-1-29-0; M Kartik 35-9-66-2; Z Khan 38-8-126-2; VVS Laxman 1-0-1-0; S Ramesh 3-0-14-0; SR Tendulkar 35-9-87-1.

ZIMBABWE

Batting	M	Inns	NO	HS	Runs	Av	100	50	c/st
A Flower	2	4	2	232*	540	270.00	2	2	2/-
ADR Campbell	2	4	0	102	184	46.00	1	1	1
GW Flower	2	4	1	106*	122	40.66	1	–	–
SV Carlisle	2	4	0	58	149	37.25	–	2	–
HH Streak	2	4	1	29*	96	32.00	–	–	2
GJ Whittall	2	4	0	84	124	31.00	–	1	–
GJ Rennie	2	4	0	37	69	17.25	–	–	–
HK Olonga	2	3	1	11*	21	10.50	–	–	–
BA Murphy	2	3	0	13	19	6.33	–	–	2

Also batted in one Test: ML Nkala 6; BC Strang 6, 15; PA Strang 19, 14* (2ct); DP Viljoen 19, 38.

Bowling

ADR Campbell 3-1-5-0; GW Flower 39.2-3-163-2; BA Murphy 87.5-7-321-3; ML Nkala 22-2-86-0; HK Olonga 50-7-203-2; GJ Rennie 3.3-0-19-0; BC Strang 31-9-115-0; PA Strang 19.2-1-78-1; HH Streak 66-18-183-3; DP Viljoen 14-2-51-0.

ONE-DAY INTERNATIONALS
By Qamar Ahmed

After coming into the fifth and final one-day international at Rajkot with an unassailable lead of three matches to one, India's victory in the final match by 39 runs made their win in the series even more convincing.

Ajit Agarkar's 67 with four sixes and seven fours in only 25 balls was the fastest 50 by an Indian in one-day games. It helped India make 301 for six in 50 overs. His three for 26 later helped to restrict Zimbabwe to only 262 runs. With captain Saurav Ganguly suspended for one match by the match referee for excessive appealing in the previous game, young left-hander Hemang Badani more than compensated for his absence with a controlled 77.

Zimbabwe were 146 for three after 25 overs chasing the tall target and, needing 56 from the last five overs, were eventually bowled out for 262.

Sachin Tendulkar scored 146 out of India's 282 at Jodhpur, but, amazingly, Zimbabwe won by one wicket.

Badani also helped India with an unbeaten 58 in the first match at Cuttack as the home team chased 254 runs to win. They got to the target with ten balls and three wickets to spare, despite having an over docked by the match referee for their slow over rate. In Zimbabwe's 253 for seven, Stuart Carlisle's unbeaten 91 and 68 by Alistair Campbell was a big effort. The two had added 115 for the second wicket.

At Ahmedabad, in the second match, Ganguly hit 144 off 152 deliveries in India's 61-run win. Zimbabwe, facing a target of 307 to win, were restricted to 245 for eight. India had scored 306 for five and a crowd of nearly 40,000 watched Ganguly go berserk as he hit his 16th one-day hundred. Dravid made 62 in a second wicket stand of 175 with his captain. The asking rate for Zimbabwe rose to 14 runs an over in the end, and although Andy Flower and Heath Streak chipped in with 51 runs each, their valiant attempt was in vain.

Zimbabwe's only victory came at the new venue of Jodhpur, where they won by one wicket with a ball to spare. India, in their 283 for eight, were rallied by

India captain Saurav Ganguly may have been suspended from the final match, but he was still voted Man of the Series.

Sachin Tendulkar's 146. Zaheer Khan scored an unbeaten 32 in 11 balls. Zimbabwe were 52 for three, but were helped by the Flower brothers, Andy and Grant, who shared 158 for the fourth wicket. Mluleki Nkala hit a quickfire 36 before being run out. A tie was a possibility as Travis Friend was bowled in the last over by Agarkar, but Henry Olonga managed to scramble a single on the fifth delivery of the over to secure a Zimbabwe victory.

Match One
2 December 2000 at Barabati Stadium, Cuttack
Zimbabwe 253 for 7 (50 overs) (SV Carlisle 91*, ADR Campbell 68)
India 255 for 7 (47.2 overs) (HK Badani 58*)
India won by three wickets
Man of the Match: HK Badani

Match Two
5 December 2000 at Sardar Patel Stadium, Ahmedabad
India 306 for 5 (50 overs) (SC Ganguly 144, R Dravid 62)
Zimbabwe 245 for 8 (50 overs) (HH Streak 51*, A Flower 51)
India won by 61 runs
Man of the Match: SC Ganguly

Match Three
8 December 2000 at Barkatullah Khan Stadium, Jodhpur
India 283 for 8 (50 overs)(SR Tendulkar 146)
Zimbabwe 284 for 9 (49.5 overs) (A Flower 77, GW Flower 70)
Zimbabwe won by one wicket
Man of the Match: GW Flower

Match Four
11 December 2000 at Green Park, Kanpur
Zimbabwe 165 (45.4 overs) (SC Ganguly 5 for 34)
India 166 for 1 (25 overs) (SC Ganguly 71*, SR Tendulkar 62)
India won by nine wickets
Man of the Match: SC Ganguly

Match Five
14 December 2000 at Racecourse Ground, Rajkot
India 301 for 6 (50 overs) (HK Badani 77, AB Agarkar 67*, RS Sodhi 53*)
Zimbabwe 262 (47.4 overs) (TN Madondo 71)
India won by 39 runs
Man of the Match: AB Agarkar
Man of the Series: SC Ganguly

AUSTRALIA IN INDIA
By Jim Maxwell

FIRST TEST
27 February–1 March 2001 at Wankhede Stadium, Mumbai

As a mark of respect for Sir Donald Bradman, players from both teams wore black armbands throughout the match. The news of the Don's demise reached India by way of an early morning call on the day before the match, and the response in the local press was immediate, with a Bradman special edition produced by the Mumbai local newspaper.

Steve Waugh revealed his own statesmanlike qualities when he reflected on Bradman's contribution to the game. He said that his death would serve as a wake-up call for the future of cricket. Bradman, in Waugh's words, 'had played cricket for the right reasons,' not, in a reference to the ongoing corruption allegations, just for himself. And he had been humble about his achievements. Waugh, Tendulkar and Warne, spoke warmly of their once-in-a-lifetime meeting with the Don, and, by the end of the series, Waugh himself may have been mulling on the legend's words about the game becoming tougher to play once you've gone past the age of 30.

In the spirit of Bradman's positive approach, and perhaps in celebration of his phenomenal deeds, the match produced some dazzling batting in an action-packed three days.

India had not played in a Test match since December, whereas Australia were fresh from an annihilation of the West Indies – a 5–0 whitewash in the Test series and an unbeaten run in the three-way one-day series that also included Zimbabwe.

Sensing that India might be under-prepared and vulnerable, Steve Waugh opted for three pace bowlers and one spinner, and like the hustler on a roll with the dice, he made the right call at the toss. India were sent in on a pitch that looked both grassy and bouncy.

McGrath soon sorted out Ramesh. His eye moving faster than his feet while attempting a hook, the opener gloved to Gilchrist. Swapping ends, Fleming's first delivery had Dravid nicking a perfect outswinger, and Das, a diminutive right-hander in the well-organized style of Gavaskar, miscued an attempted drive off the bowling of Gillespie into Hayden's sure hands at fourth slip. With Ganguly falling to Warne in the 23rd over, and with the score at 55 for four, India again looked to the local deity, Sachin Tendulkar, for salvation. He disdainfully flicked Fleming for four from around off to backward square to get off the mark, and then settled into an innings of watchful guidance with Laxman his partner until lunch.

The chanting crowd were baying for Aussie blood, and a section of the partisan support threw up a banner with the provocative warning, 'Beware Kangaroos, our Tigers are wounded.' Tendulkar responded in style, carving Warne's first ball after lunch through the off side, and raced on to 50 with both off- and straight-driven strokes that were both amazingly timed and well-placed. The reintroduction of McGrath, however, broke the flow. In successive overs from the paceman, Laxman was caught in the slips by Ponting for 20, and Tendulkar edged a fuller-length delivery on the off stump to the grateful hands of Gilchrist. This cued a collapse: including another duck for Agarkar, his sixth in succession against Australia, and a bag of four wickets for Warne. McGrath was supreme, and his immaculate control was rewarded with three for 19 off as many overs including an incredible 13 maidens.

Being bowled out for 176 went some way to allaying the pre-match speculation about the pitch being prepared to suit the home team. However, an hour into the second day, and with Australia having plummeted to 99 for five with the ball both spinning and bouncing sharply, the speculation returned. Slater had lost his middle stump just before the close of play to a full-pitched ball from Agarkar. On resumption, the Australians continued their uncertain battle with the pitch. Langer aimed indiscriminate sweeps at Harbhajan's serious off breaks, while Hayden waited for the right length to power slog sweep shots. Langer was caught at slip by Ganguly, and Mark Waugh instinctively turned his first ball to the brilliant clutches of the Indian captain at leg gully. Steve Waugh got the moral adjudication, driving at a huge Sanghvi left-arm turner, that missed everything, but on the sound of Waugh's bat scrape, and with Dravid

collecting the ball at slip, David Shepherd had enough evidence to be convinced of a snick and Australia's captain was given his marching orders. In the next over, Ponting thrust forward, and squirted a catch to Das at silly mid on. The Australians were in trouble.

Fearing that the left-handed combination of a fresh Gilchrist and an established Hayden might take to Sanghvi, Ganguly went with Tendulkar's off spin to support Harbhajan. It may have been a tactical error, the more so when Tendulkar lost his length. Mindful of supporting Hayden, Gilchrist took 15 balls to open his account, and then unleashed a spectacular assault, racing past 50 in

Matthew Hayden's punishing first-innings century (119) set up Australia's victory in the opening Test in Mumbai.

just 55 balls. Cuts, drives, pulls and old-fashioned hoicks thrashed the bowling in perhaps the cleanest display of hitting since Botham's 1981 epics.

Substitute Badani dropped a skier running in from deep square, as, in one purple patch, the left-handers went at eight runs an over. Gilchrist, who had given Hayden a 47-run start, reached his century from 84 balls, with the second 50 coming from just 29. Hayden's controlled aggression and judgement had been a revelation to those who recalled his prior leaden footedness against spin. Before he edged a ball from Srinath to Mongia, his hundred had helped the partnership to 197 runs in just 32 overs. Warne further deflated the spinners with 39 from 37 balls.

Gilchrist was eventually stumped, fortuitously for India off Mongia's pads. From 112 balls, the brilliantly belligerent Gilchrist had struck 15 fours and four sixes, and the ball was still turning and jumping!

Australia led by 173, and India's openers had an hour and a half to weather the hostility of McGrath and Gillespie. Das fended off an unplayable Gillespie lifter to Steve Waugh at gully, while a manic Ramesh, à la Wavell Hinds, flung his claymore, until the inevitable edge found Ponting at second slip. Nightwatchman Mongia, protecting Tendulkar, was forced to retire hurt when another Gillespie missile whacked into his finger, meaning Tendulkar had to face the last salvos of the day.

A huge crowd gathered on the third morning, in expectation of a local sideshow. Holding a banner that read, 'We miss you, Sir Bradman,' a terrace posse was soon swept up by Tendulkar's glorious shots. A flick, a drive, a ferocious pull, and Dravid carefully supported the master's dissection.

Approaching the lunch break, Fleming, in the guise of Colin Miller, resorted to bowling fast off breaks. Dravid attempted a pull, miscuing towards midwicket, where Slater dived forward and claimed a catch. Unsighted or unsure, the umpires deferred to their video colleague, who gave the green light after examining several inconclusive replays. Slater erupted, remonstrating with umpire Venkat, and admonishing Dravid, for not accepting his word. Sadly, Steve Waugh did not intervene to muzzle the dissenting Slater, who was later reprimanded by the match referee Cammie Smith. He was lucky. The outburst demanded severer punishment.

The partnership patiently lingered beyond lunch, with Warne alternating from around to over the wicket without success. Steve Waugh reverted to brother Mark's off spin, and with success. As

FIRST TEST – INDIA v. AUSTRALIA
27 February–1 March 2001 at Wankhede Stadium, Mumbai

INDIA

	First innings		Second innings	
SS Das	c Hayden, b Gillespie	14	c SR Waugh, b Gillespie	7
S Ramesh	c Gilchrist, b McGrath	2	c Ponting, b McGrath	44
R Dravid	c Gilchrist, b Fleming	9	b Warne	39
SR Tendulkar	c Gilchrist, b McGrath	76	(5) c Ponting, b ME Waugh	65
SC Ganguly (capt)	c Hayden, b Warne	8	(6) run out (Slater/Warne)	1
VVS Laxman	c Ponting, b McGrath	20	(7) c Gilchrist, b ME Waugh	12
*NR Mongia	not out	26	(4) c Gilchrist, b Gillespie	28
AB Agarkar	c & b Warne	0	b ME Waugh	0
J Srinath	c ME Waugh, b Warne	12	(11) b McGrath	0
Harbhajan Singh	c SR Waugh, b Warne	0	(9) not out	17
RL Sanghvi	c Gilchrist, b Gillespie	2	(10) b Gillespie	0
	b2, lb3, w1, nb1	7	b4, lb1, nb1	6
		176		**219**

	First innings				Second innings			
	O	M	R	W	O	M	R	W
McGrath	19	13	19	3	17.1	9	25	2
Fleming	15	3	55	1	15	1	44	–
Gillespie	15.3	4	50	2	19	8	45	3
Warne	22	7	47	4	28	11	60	1
ME Waugh					15	5	40	3

Fall of Wickets
1-7, 2-25, 3-31, 4-55, 5-130, 6-139, 7-140, 8-165, 9-166
1-33, 2-57, 3-154, 4-156, 5-174, 6-174, 7-193, 8-210, 9-216

AUSTRALIA

	First innings		Second innings	
MJ Slater	b Agarkar	10	(2) not out	19
ML Hayden	c Mongia, b Srinath	119	(1) not out	28
JL Langer	c Dravid, b Singh	19		
ME Waugh	c Ganguly, b Singh	0		
SR Waugh (capt)	c Dravid, b Sanghvi	15		
RT Ponting	c Das, b Singh	0		
*AC Gilchrist	st Mongia, b Singh	122		
SK Warne	c Tendulkar, b Sanghvi	39		
JN Gillespie	c Mongia, b Srinath	0		
DW Fleming	c Srinath, b Agarkar	6		
GD McGrath	not out	0		
	b9, lb7, nb3	19		
		349	(for 0 wicket)	**47**

	First innings				Second innings			
	O	M	R	W	O	M	R	W
Srinath	16	3	60	2	2	0	17	–
Agarkar	12	1	50	2	1	0	8	–
Harbhajan Singh	28	3	121	4	2	0	11	–
Sanghvi	10.2	2	67	2	2	1	11	–
Tendulkar	7	1	35	–				

Fall of Wickets
1-21, 2-71, 3-71, 4-98, 5-99, 6-296, 7-326, 8-327, 9-349

Umpires: S Venkataraghavan & DR Shepherd
Toss: Australia
Test debut: RL Sanghvi (India)

Australia won by ten wickets

Tendulkar leapt on to a short-pitched ball from the spinner, Langer instinctively tried to evade the plundering hit. The ball cannoned from his back, and ricocheted towards midwicket, where Ponting ran to his left and dived full length to pull off a superb catch. Tendulkar's grief was palpable. Again his dismissal triggered an Indian collapse. Ganguly was ludicrously run out on an indecisive call, Dravid was bowled around his legs by Warne, Laxman edged a whopping bouncing off break from Waugh, and Agarkar, with a stroke of absolute hopelessness, was bowled, swiping, for a duck; number seven against Australia. The match ended after tea when Srinath, who was batting one handed to avoid another bump on his damaged right index finger, was bowled by McGrath. Post Tendulkar, India had lost seven for 65. Australia galloped to their target in only seven overs, recording their 16th consecutive Test victory. Gilchrist, who, according to the defeated captain Ganguly had played the best innings he had ever seen under pressure, was voted Man of the Match.

SECOND TEST
11–15 March 2001 at Eden Gardens, Calcutta

The greatest match in the history of Test cricket? It was surely the most amazing recovery to win a Test, inspired by V.V.S. Laxman's flawless, commanding 281. The heroic deeds of Laxman and Punjabi off spinner Harbhajan Singh enabled India to win a match that they seemed likely to lose on the third day, when they were bowled out in just 58 overs for 171, and were forced to follow-on, 274 runs behind.

Australia had taken the initiative after winning the toss and building what appeared to be an insurmountable total of 445. Hayden and Langer were going at a merry clip, Hayden tucking into Harbhajan's off spin with relish, and racing to 97 at the tea break. A single boundary would have sufficed on resumption, but Hayden loosely lofted to deep midwicket, rather than adjusting his stroke for a solid single. By the close, Australia had lost another six wickets. Harbhajan straightened one on Ponting for leg before, had Gilchrist playing back to his first ball, and Warne pushing to short leg to complete the first hat-trick by an Indian in 338 Tests. Steve Waugh, at the bowler's end, looked bemused when umpire Bansal called for the eye in the sky to confirm Warne's dismissal.

Everyone could see that Ramesh had taken the deflection cleanly; repetitious replays revealed it was probably a bump ball. Gillespie's long reach and

SECOND TEST – INDIA v. AUSTRALIA
11–15 March 2001 at Eden Gardens, Calcutta

AUSTRALIA

	First innings		Second innings	
MJ Slater	c Mongia, b Khan	42	(2) c Ganguly, b Singh	43
ML Hayden	c sub (HK Badani), b Singh	97	(1) lbw b Tendulkar	67
JL Langer	c Mongia, b Khan	58	c Ramesh, b Singh	28
ME Waugh	c Mongia, b Singh	22	lbw b Raju	0
SR Waugh (capt)	lbw b Singh	110	c sub (HK Badani), b Singh	24
RT Ponting	lbw b Singh	6	c Das, b Singh	0
*AC Gilchrist	lbw b Singh	0	lbw b Tendulkar	0
SK Warne	c Ramesh, b Singh	0	(9) lbw b Tendulkar	0
MS Kasprowicz	lbw b Ganguly	7	(10) not out	13
JN Gillespie	c Ramesh, b Singh	46	c Das, b Singh	6
GD McGrath	not out	21	lbw b Singh	12
	b19, lb10, nb7	36	b6, nb8	14
	Penalty runs	5		
		445		**212**

	First innings				Second innings			
	O	M	R	W	O	M	R	W
Khan	28.4	6	89	2	8	4	30	-
Prasad	30	5	95	0	3	1	7	-
Ganguly	13.2	3	44	1	1	0	2	-
Raju	20	2	58	-	15	3	58	1
Singh	37.5	7	123	7	30.3	8	73	6
Tendulkar	2	0	7	-	11	3	31	3

Fall of Wickets
1-103, 2-193, 3-214, 4-236, 5-252, 6-252, 7-252, 8-269, 9-402
1-74, 2-106, 3-116, 4-166, 5-166, 6-167, 7-173, 8-174, 9-191

Harbhajan Singh recorded a hat-trick (Ponting, Gilchrist & Warne)

INDIA

	First innings		Second innings	
SS Das	c Gilchrist, b McGrath	20	hit wicket b Gillespie	39
S Ramesh	c Ponting, b Gillespie	0	c ME Waugh, b Warne	30
R Dravid	b Warne	25	(6) run out (SR Waugh/ Kasprowicz)	180
SR Tendulkar	lbw b McGrath	10	c Gilchrist, b Gillespie	10
SC Ganguly (capt)	c SR Waugh, b Kasprowicz	23	c Gilchrist, b McGrath	48
VVS Laxman	c Hayden, b Warne	59	(3) c Ponting, b McGrath	281
*NR Mongia	c Ponting, b Kasprowicz	2	b McGrath	4
Harbhajan Singh	c Ponting, b Gillespie	4	(9) not out	8
Z Khan	b McGrath	3	(8) not out	23
SLV Raju	lbw b McGrath	4		
BKV Prasad	not out	7		
	lb2, nb12	14	b6, lb12, w2, nb14	34
		171	(for 7 wickets dec.)	**657**

	First innings				Second innings			
	O	M	R	W	O	M	R	W
McGrath	14	8	18	4	39	12	103	3
Gillespie	11	0	47	2	31	6	115	2
Kasprowicz	13	2	39	2	35	6	139	-
Warne	20.1	3	65	2	34	3	152	1
ME Waugh					18	1	58	-
Ponting					12	1	41	-
Hayden					6	0	24	-
Slater					2	1	4	-
Langer					1	0	3	-

Fall of Wickets
1-0, 2-34, 3-48, 4-88, 5-88, 6-92, 7-97, 8-113, 9-129
1-52, 2-97, 3-115, 4-232, 5-608, 6-624, 7-629

Umpires: SK Bansal & P Willey
Toss: Australia
Test debuts: nil

India won by 171 runs

Little was known about V.V.S. Laxman before the Calcutta Test which India seemed destined to lose on the third day.

excellent temperament aided the combative Waugh to add a record 133 for the ninth wicket, extending the innings past lunch and helping Waugh to his 25th Test century and Australia to a dominant total of 445 on the second day. The Bengalis applauded generously, appreciating Waugh's indomitable skill, and his humanity in supporting his 'daughters', the leprosy sufferers at Udaiyan, whom he had visited prior to the match.

After Ramesh had edged Gillespie's third ball to the waiting hands of Ponting for a duck, a brilliant Gilchrist catch off McGrath further ignited a swarming Australian effort in the field, inspiring McGrath's dismissal of Tendulkar, plumb leg before to an inswinger. India capitulated. They were 128 for eight at stumps, briefly reviving thanks to Laxman, who was the last man out for 59. In the follow-on he was promoted to number three, in place of the out-of-form Dravid, and joining Das at 52 for one, he began with a stirring off-driven four. Das, pushed back by Gillespie's pace, trod on his wicket, and an unsettled Tendulkar wafted edgily to Gilchrist, leaving India in deep trouble at 115 for three, and facing the prospect of their third consecutive loss to Australia inside three days.

Laxman counterattacked, without any hint of risk. His driving was powerful and decisive. Seventy per cent of his first hundred runs were scored through the on side, many from Warne, whose around the wicket tactic was confounded by the best footwork that Warne could remember. In support Ganguly survived a mocking bowling tactic from Kasprowicz. Steve Waugh placed every fieldsman on the off side, an act that smacked of contempt, and of Waugh's belief that Ganguly was sure to play another 'I-don't-want-to-be-here' stroke. Ganguly, the local favourite, or prince of Bengal, had not impressed the Australians. They reckoned his haughtiness was pure arrogance. The body language at the toss was obvious. Ganguly kept Waugh waiting at the appointed hour, and, after a belated arrival in the middle, kept his distance in the manner of a chastened child. This became a recurrent theme, played out more often than the contentious calls to the third umpire. Waugh's comment on returning to Australia when asked of his opinion of Ganguly was typically blunt: 'He's a p***k, and that's paying him a compliment.'

On the third day in Calcutta Ganguly was defiant, alongside the swashbuckling, yet controlled, Laxman. They added 117, until McGrath's around-the-wicket perseverance produced a Ganguly snick. Dravid, easily bowled by Warne in the first innings, looked determined to make amends. He saw Laxman through to his century, and stumps, at 254 for four, still 20 in arrears.

The Australians were confident that one breakthrough would suffice to create a collapse. And they had a second new ball to almost guarantee that wicket. Almost. Not quite! Neither Laxman nor Dravid offered a chance. I counted three miscues from the Hyderabadi stylist; two inside edges, and one snick to a vacant second slip. A measure of

Laxman's ability to hit fours, taking occasional leisurely singles was his 200 subscript: 35 fours, 31 singles. Waugh tried nine bowlers, and Ponting bowled as well as any of them, going within a centimetre of claiming an lbw verdict against Dravid in the last over before lunch. And Dravid's support was magnificent, finding his confidence to produce a range of piercing shots, as the partnership reached 357 at stumps on the fourth day. Both batsmen laboured with cramp in the final session, but they were committed, and driven by a boisterous, regaling crowd that touched 70,000 on each day.

Laxman raced past Sunil Gavaskar's record score of 236, and as he and Dravid recovered on saline drips at day's end, a revitalized Ganguly was pondering over the timing of a declaration.

The haunting sound of Calcutta's 9am siren – clocking on time for the city's workforce – blasted forebodingly on the final morning. Australia were set an improbable 384 to win from 75 overs when Ganguly closed at 657 for eight, a total that precisely equalled the highest by a team forced to follow-on; Pakistan at Bridgetown in 1957–58. Aiming for his 43rd four, Laxman was caught at point after almost 11 hours of wonderful batting, and a partnership of 376 – the highest for the fifth wicket by any team against Australia.

A draw was the most likely result, as Hayden and Slater established themselves in an opening stand worth 74. Off spinner Harbhajan hit Slater in the chest with one viciously bouncing delivery: a portent of the trouble ahead. Ganguly then grabbed a close-in catch to remove Slater, Langer's sweeping tactics failed, and Mark Waugh fell leg before to Raju's arm ball; the first of five leg before decisions given by umpire Bansal, who was standing in his last Test.

Ganguly spilt a chance from Steve Waugh at 127 for three, but when Badani snapped up another offering just after tea, Waugh's departing solemnity looked fatalistic. Ponting surrendered meekly, Gilchrist swept prematurely, completing a king pair, Hayden missed a fuller delivery on his favourite sweep shot, and Warne failed to read Tendulkar's wrong 'un. The last pair, Kasprowicz and McGrath, resisted stubbornly, until Harbhajan was switched to umpire Bansal's end, and McGrath padded up once too often. Eden Gardens erupted, many fans lighting pieces of paper and waving them around like Olympic torches at an opening ceremony. India had won, astonishingly, by 171 runs with 5.3 overs to spare. Harbhajan, who took 13 match wickets, applauded Laxman when he was named Man of an unforgettable Match.

THIRD TEST
18–22 March 2001 at MA Chidambaram Stadium, Chapauk, Chennai

The shock of losing in Calcutta could have crushed Australia, who had only three days respite between Tests. Physically exhausted by three days in the field, the bowlers were relieved when Steve Waugh won the toss and batted on a pitch that all the pundits said would spin. Australia brought in off spinner Colin Miller for Kasprowicz. John Buchanan, Australia's coach, told the media that he thought Warne's position could be in jeopardy, citing lack of fitness, and his obvious poor form. Steve Waugh hinted at a serious difference of opinion in the team's power play, when he suggested that Buchanan's comments were best kept off camera. One loss after 16 wins was not going to panic the tenacious Australian captain, and Warne, as well as the hopelessly out-of-touch Ponting, were retained.

India played three frontline spinners, including debutant leggie Bahutule, and tall left armer, Kulkarni. Dighe replaced the injured Mongia behind the stumps. Mongia had been cracked on the nose on the last day in Calcutta, and after being declared unfit the day before Chennai, changed his mind on the morning of the match, only to be overlooked as Ganguly again tested the limits of punctuality at the toss.

The opening session was electrifying. Hayden and Langer flayed the combination of pace and spin, racing to 67 in the 12th over, whereupon Langer cut too close to his body and edged to Dravid at slip: last man 35 from 35 balls. Hayden's footwork destroyed Harbhajan's attack. Using his feet to come down the pitch, he drove into the stands over both long off and long on, hitting four of the six sixes clouted before lunch. And he swept on length, either square or fine, then occasionally over and beyond midwicket. Slater had left in the first over, loosely edging an angled ball from left arm quick Zaheer Khan down Laxman's throat at second slip. Mark Waugh prospered, and the session ended pulsatingly at 140 for two, with 100 of those runs coming in boundaries.

Hayden's aggression and Waugh's deft touches were worth 150, when Bahutule lured Waugh into a lofted drive that he miscued into the hands of Badani running in from long off. By the close Hayden and Steve Waugh had put their team into a virtually unassailable position at 326 for three. Hayden countered the varied spin with a commanding exhibition of defence and bludgeoning attack. Waugh gathered his runs efficiently, and almost as discreetly as the lone figure of a worker heading home that was spotted traipsing across the roof from the main scoreboard to the mini board carrying his gladstone bag.

Australia's innings was cruising 40 minutes into the second day. Then, in the way of a flash flood or an accident when the road seems deserted, Steve Waugh was out freakishly. Attempting to sweep a ball from Harbhajan, Waugh heard an appeal for leg before. The ball ballooned in the air, bounced and spun towards the stumps. Hayden who had seen the danger, yelled, 'look out,' and Waugh, who had removed his right hand from the bat, instinctively

gloved the ball away. The Australian captain knew his fate before umpire Jayaprakash had raised the finger of denouement. He was out for 47.

Like lemmings over a cliff, the Australian lower order succumbed quickly. Ponting was stumped for a first ball duck, as Harbhajan ripped out five wickets while Hayden continued to plunder. McGrath survived long enough for Hayden to achieve his double century, then, aiming for his seventh six, he was caught by Ganguly at long off. Harbhajan's persistence fired out seven victims, as Australia lost seven for 51 from the moment of Waugh's aberration.

Inspired by their remarkable comeback, India began the reply aggressively. Das and Ramesh luxuriated on the front foot, emphasizing the fact that batting is easier against full-length, new-ball bowling, when the ball does not deviate. Warne and Miller also floundered, and the partnership had reached 123 when Ramesh prodded to short leg. Laxman's confidence ensured India's impressive momentum was maintained, with Das looking totally assured on 84 at stumps and the score on 211 for one.

Battling a stomach upset, McGrath bowled magnificently on the third morning. His first ball swung into Das' pads, Laxman soon edged to second slip, and, returning after lunch, he had Ganguly waving terminally to Gilchrist. At the other end, Tendulkar made busy with focussed application. As the news of Malcolm Speed's appointment to the ICC top job filtered through, Tendulkar accelerated, punishing the under-pitched Australian spin. On 82, Slater missed him badly rushing in from deep midwicket. The hapless Miller suffered again when Tendulkar raised his 25th Test hundred with a majestic on drive for six.

Dravid lent excellent support, and the sense of desperation was best expressed by former Australia international, Greg Matthews, when he exhorted the Australians from the ABC commentary box to 'drop the ego, and stop the boundaries'. In another magnificent effort, Gillespie, defying the oppressive heat, responded to the assault, having Dravid and Tendulkar caught behind during a spell of two for 15 in seven overs.

Harbhajan Singh claimed a hat-trick at Calcutta before routing Australia in the final Test at Chennai.

THIRD TEST – INDIA v. AUSTRALIA
18–22 March 2001 at MA Chidambaram Stadium, Chennai

AUSTRALIA

	First innings		Second innings	
MJ Slater	c Laxman, b Khan	4	(2) c Laxman, b Singh	48
ML Hayden	c Ganguly, b Singh	203	(1) c Khan, b Kulkarni	35
JL Langer	c Dravid, b Singh	35	(4) c Laxman, b Bahutule	21
ME Waugh	c sub (HK Badani), b Bahutule	70	(5) c Dravid, b Singh	57
SR Waugh (capt)	handled the ball	47	(6) c Das, b Singh	47
RT Ponting	st Dighe, b Singh	0	(7) c Dravid, b Singh	11
*AC Gilchrist	lbw b Singh	1	(3) lbw b Singh	1
SK Warne	c Das, b Singh	0	lbw b Singh	11
JN Gillespie	c Ganguly, b Singh	0	c Dravid, b Singh	2
CR Miller	c Bahutule, b Singh	0	lbw b Singh	2
GD McGrath	not out	3	not out	11
	b8, lb10, nb10	28	b8, lb6, nb4	18
		391		**264**

	First innings				Second innings			
	O	M	R	W	O	M	R	W
Khan	15	5	57	1	4	0	13	-
Ganguly	2	1	11	-	1	0	8	-
Singh	38.2	6	133	7	41.5	20	84	8
Kulkarni	23	5	67	-	30	11	70	1
Bahutule	21	3	70	1	9	0	32	1
Tendulkar	16	1	35	-	12	0	43	-

Fall of Wickets
1-4, 2-67, 3-217, 4-340, 5-340, 6-344, 7-374, 8-376, 9-385
1-82, 2-84, 3-93, 4-141, 5-193, 6-211, 7-241, 8-246, 9-251

INDIA

	First innings		Second innings	
SS Das	lbw b McGrath	84	c & b McGrath	9
S Ramesh	c Ponting, b Warne	61	run out (Ponting/Gilchrist)	25
VVS Laxman	c ME Waugh, b McGrath	65	c ME Waugh, b Miller	66
SR Tendulkar	c Gilchrist, b Gillespie	126	c ME Waugh, b Gillespie	17
SC Ganguly (capt)	c Gilchrist, b McGrath	22	c ME Waugh, b Gillespie	4
R Dravid	c Gilchrist, b Gillespie	81	c SR Waugh, b Miller	4
*SS Dighe	lbw b Warne	4	not out	22
SV Bahutule	not out	21	c Warne, b Miller	0
Z Khan	c & b Miller	4	c ME Waugh, b McGrath	0
Harbhajan Singh	c ME Waugh, b Miller	2	not out	3
NM Kulkarni	lbw b Miller	4		
	b19, lb2, w1, nb5	27	lb3, nb2	5
		501	**(for 8 wickets)**	**155**

	First innings				Second innings			
	O	M	R	W	O	M	R	W
McGrath	36	15	75	3	11.1	3	21	2
Gillespie	35	11	88	2	15	2	49	2
Miller	46	6	160	3	9	1	41	3
Warne	42	7	140	2	6	0	41	-
Ponting	2	1	2	-				
ME Waugh	3	0	8	-				
Hayden	1	0	7	-				

Fall of Wickets
1-123, 2-211, 3-237, 4-284, 5-453, 6-468, 7-470, 8-475, 9-477
1-18, 2-76, 3-101, 4-117, 5-122, 6-135, 7-135, 8-151

Umpires: AV Jayaprakash & RE Koertzen
Toss: Australia
Test debuts: SV Bahutule and SS Dighe (India)

India won by two wickets

TEST MATCH AVERAGES
India v. Australia

INDIA

Batting	M	Inns	NO	HS	Runs	Av	100	50	c/st
VVS Laxman	3	6	0	281	503	83.83	1	3	3
R Dravid	3	6	0	180	338	56.33	1	1	6
SR Tendulkar	3	6	0	126	304	50.66	1	2	1
SS Das	3	6	0	84	173	28.83	-	1	5
S Ramesh	3	6	0	61	162	27.00	-	1	3
NR Mongia	2	4	1	28	60	20.00	-	-	5/1
SC Ganguly	3	6	0	48	106	17.66	-	-	4
Harbhajan Singh	3	6	3	17*	34	11.33	-	-	-
Z Khan	2	4	1	23*	30	10.00	-	-	-

Also batted in one Test: AB Agarkar 0, 0; SV Bahutule 21*, 0 (1ct); SS Dighe 4, 22* (1st); NM Kulkarni 4; BKV Prasad 7*; SLV Raju 2, 0; RL Sanghvi 2, 0; J Srinath 12, 0 (1ct).

Bowling	Overs	Mds	Runs	Wkts	Av	Best	10m	5/inn
Harbhajan Singh	178.3	44	545	32	17.03	8-84	2	4

Also bowled: AB Agarkar 13-1-58-2; SV Bahutule 30-3-102-2; SC Ganguly 17.2-4-65-1; Z Khan 55.4-15-189-3; NM Kulkarni 53-6-137-1; BKV Prasad 33-6-102-0; SLV Raju 35-5-116-1; RL Sanghvi 12.2-3-78-2; J Srinath 18-3-77-2; SR Tendulkar 48-5-151-3.

AUSTRALIA

Batting	M	Inns	NO	HS	Runs	Av	100	50	c/st
ML Hayden	3	6	1	203	549	109.80	2	2	3
SR Waugh	3	5	0	110	243	48.60	1	-	4
GD McGrath	3	5	4	21*	47	47.00	-	-	1
MJ Slater	3	6	1	48	166	33.20	-	-	3
JL Langer	3	5	0	58	161	32.20	-	1	-
ME Waugh	3	5	0	70	149	29.80	-	2	8
AC Gilchrist	3	5	0	122	124	24.80	1	-	13/-
JN Gillespie	3	5	0	46	54	10.80	-	-	2
SK Warne	3	5	0	39	50	10.00	-	-	-
RT Ponting	3	5	0	11	17	3.40	-	-	7

Also batted in one Test: DW Fleming 6; MS Kasprowicz 7, 13*; CR Miller 0, 2 (1ct).

Bowling	Overs	Mds	Runs	Wkts	Av	Best	10m	5/inn
GD McGrath	136.2	60	261	17	15.35	4-18	-	-
JN Gillespie	126.3	31	394	13	30.30	3-45	-	-
CR Miller	55	7	201	6	33.50	3-41	-	-
SK Warne	152.1	31	505	10	50.50	4-47	-	-

Also bowled: DW Fleming 30-4-99-1; ML Hayden 7-0-31-0; MS Kasprowicz 48-8-178-2; JL Langer 1-0-3-0; RT Ponting 14-2-43-0; MJ Slater 2-1-4-0; ME Waugh 36-6-106-3.

When Australia began their second innings 110 in arrears on the fourth day, the excitable Tamil crowd flung up a sign that read 'Can we bang the Kangaroos again'. Hayden and Slater did most of the banging, though, adding 82 before the fast-moving Zaheer Khan completed a fine catch at deep midwicket off the bowling of Kulkarni. Out for 35, Hayden had contributed 549 runs for the series, a remarkable effort for someone who had no reputation against spin. The promoted Gilchrist failed to read Harbhajan's arm ball, and the hungry fan whose placard read, 'I didn't bring lunch today because Harbhajan promised me some wickets,' was sated, when Slater soon followed Gilchrist, edging to slip, his team still 17 runs adrift. The Waughs resisted superbly, grinding out a modest lead.

Harbhajan's awkward bounce was always threatening, and Mark Waugh fell to a brilliant diving, grappling catch at leg slip from Dravid. Enter Ponting, who popped up his first ball, then lifted Harbhajan for six. On 11 he pushed an off break straight to Dravid, and wandered off, shattered, 17 runs squeaked in five innings. Warne all but held on with Steve Waugh, misjudging the last ball of the day for the plumbest of leg befores.

241 for seven represented a moderate advantage of 131. Asked how many was enough to win, the optimistic Gillespie said, 160. He, too, was caught by Dravid, as Australia squeezed out another 23 runs in just over an hour of anxious batting against their nemesis, Harbhajan. He bagged eight innings wickets, 15 for the match, totalling 32 for the series. So much for Kumble's absence.

Needing 155 to win from 70 overs, India lost Das on a miscued lobbed catch to McGrath. Laxman took charge, flinging boundaries off the spinners with Warne again taking a mauling. Ramesh's run out at 76 for two broke the flow, and once more Gillespie bent his back tellingly, shifting Tendulkar and Ganguly, both via the sure hands of Mark

Waugh in the slips. Dravid's loose drive to Steve Waugh at mid off hinted at Indian panic, as they went into tea at 132 for five. In a bold move Waugh persisted with Miller, who had Laxman brilliantly caught by Mark Waugh at midwicket off a pulled long hop, and then urged an edge from Bahutule to slip. As Dighe picked off a few telling fours, McGrath returned, and Mark Waugh thrillingly held his sixth catch of the match to leave India on a nervous 151 for eight. The harbinger of India's success, Harbhajan Singh, survived a run out chance, and rapturously struck the winning runs off McGrath, to give India a wonderful victory.

Australia had been glorious in their narrow defeat. It was defeat, nonetheless, and the dream of winning in India for the first time since 1969 was destroyed. The Indian team rejoiced. Harbhajan and Hayden were named Men of a Series that hopefully rekindled the passion for Test cricket in India.

After enduring the disgrace of match-fixing and betting scandals, this was the moment the Indian public fell in love with cricket once again. Was this the greatest Test series of all time?

ONE-DAY INTERNATIONALS

A combination of Australia's resilience and the continuation of Matthew Hayden's remarkable batting form were the main reasons for the final 3–2 winning margin achieved by Steve Waugh's team.

And in the deciding match, Michael Bevan showed why he has such an awesome reputation in the limited overs game. His unbeaten 87, carried Australia to an impressive four-wicket win. Bevan tested the wits of the opposition with intimidating running, and well-selected boundary hits. His record in this form of the game is remarkable, averaging over 57 from more than 150 matches.

For India, Tendulkar became the first player in history to pass 10,000 one-day international runs with a typically savage innings of 139 at Indore. Laxman maintained his excellent form from the Calcutta epic, and the left-handed Badani batted impressively in Pune.

An exhausted group of players moved from Chennai to Bangalore to start the series of five one-day matches, just three days after the drama of a tough, mentally draining Test match. A week off would have been perfect. Jason Gillespie, who had survived three matches without any recurrence of back problems, was immediately sent home on suspicion of breakdown. This preventive decision reflected the Australia's smart man-management philosophy.

India's bowling stocks looked threadbare around Harbhajan, and they recalled both Agarkar and Srinath in Bangalore. In a blazing start India passed 100 in the 15th over, and were all out in the final over for an imposing 315. All-

Sachin Tendulkar passed 10,000 one-day international runs during the tight five-match series which Australia won 3–2.

rounder Shewag slammed 58 off 54 balls around Dravid's 80, and neglected wicketkeeper Dahiya's rapid half-century off just 39 balls. Australia chased solidly until Bevan fell to a sharp catch by substitute Robin Singh, and Hayden (who had been belatedly added to the squad after his outstanding Test series) was leg before to Shewag on 99. The momentum faded, and Shewag's fine performance with both bat and ball took the award in an Indian win that halted Australia's winning one-day sequence at ten. Alas for Shewag, he'd fractured a finger, and did not play again in the series.

In Pune, Australia easily ran down India's 248 for nine with five overs in hand, via Mark Waugh's 18th one-day international century. Ganguly, who again failed with the bat, clearly dissented the umpire's decision when a mix up resulted in the run out of Darren Lehmann. Ganguly gestured angrily believing the batsmen had not crossed, and therefore Steve Waugh should have been given out. Match referee, Cammie Smith, who had fined both Gilchrist and McGrath for abusive language and dissent in Bangalore, took no action.

At Indore, Australia's rotation policy and Waugh's insertion decision backfired mightily, when Tendulkar pulverized the bowling and completed his 28th one-day hundred; 139 from 125 balls. As the bounce became more uncertain, Australia, who had rested Matthew Hayden and were missing Mark Waugh with a fractured finger, succumbed by 118 runs.

Jumping back to the east coastal fishing city of Vishakhapatnam, Hayden's maiden one-day hundred in a revelling 219-run partnership with Ponting, who had rediscovered his form, rushed Australia to a match-winning 338 for four. Tendulkar threatened for a time, clobbering 62 from 38 balls. Left armer Bracken had him caught by Steve Waugh in the gully, and with Harbhajan swinging at the death, Australia won by 93 runs to square the series.

In the decider at the ubiquitous Nehru Stadium, this one in Fatorda, near Goa, Ganguly celebrated his early arrival at the toss by both winning it, and making runs: 74 from 83 balls, while Laxman serenely moved to his maiden one-day century. Chasing 266 for six, Gilchrist rampaged to 50 from just 28 balls. A middle-order slump did not include Bevan's vital wicket, though, and from 202 for six in the 40th over, Harvey struck robustly to help Bevan finish off the task with two overs to spare.

Hayden's Indian summer continued, claiming another Man of the Series award as Australia triumphed 3–2.

Match One

25 March 2001 at M Chinnaswamy Stadium, Bangalore (floodlit)
India 315 (49.5 overs) (R Dravid 80, V Shewag 58, V Dahiya 51)
Australia 255 (43.3 overs) (ML Hayden 99)
India won by 60 runs
Man of the Match: V Shewag

Match Two

28 March 2001 at Nehru Stadium, Pune
India 248 for 9 (50 overs) (HK Badani 100, VVS Laxman 51)
Australia 249 for 2 (45.1 overs) (ME Waugh 133*, ML Hayden 57)
Australia won by eight wickets
Man of the Match: ME Waugh

Match Three

31 March 2001 at Nehru Stadium, Indore
India 299 for 8 (50 overs) (SR Tendulkar 139, VVS Laxman 83)
Australia 181 (35.5 overs) (AC Gilchrist 63)
India won by 118 runs
Man of the Match: SR Tendulkar

Match Four

3 April 2001 at Indira Priyadarshini Stadium, Visakhapatnam
Australia 338 for 4 (50 overs) (ML Hayden 111, RT Ponting 101)
India 245 (45 overs) (SR Tendulkar 62)
Australia won by 93 runs
Man of the Match: ML Hayden

Match Five

6 April 2001 at Nehru Stadium, Fatorda
India 265 for 6 (50 overs) (VVS Laxman 101, SC Ganguly 74)
Australia 269 for 6 (48 overs) (MG Bevan 87*, AC Gilchrist 76)
Australia won by four wickets
Man of the Match: MG Bevan
Man of the Series: ML Hayden

INDIA DOMESTIC FIRST-CLASS SEASON
by Qamar Ahmed, Ghaus Mohammad & R. Mohan

India's domestic season offered great variety. There were a number of surprises and reputations were either made or marred. In the Ranji Trophy particularly, there was a refreshing departure from the past as Mumbai, Tamil Nadu, Hyderabad and Karnataka, semi-finalists the season before, all failed to make it to the last four. It was a true reflection of the progress made by the other teams.

Instead the final featured Railways, who were appearing in the Ranji Trophy final for the first time. They may have lost out in the final – a match marred by poor umpiring – but the winners, Baroda, were a deserving winner. They had played the most consistent cricket throughout the season to record their first Ranji Trophy success since 1957–58.

In the league phase, Punjab were the best side, winning all their matches, a rare feat in Ranji Trophy. They defeated Delhi, Haryana, Services, Jammu and Kashmir and Himachal Pradesh quite convincingly to top the group. To have won all their matches was Punjab's way of showing the progress they had made. Some superb captaincy by Vikram Rathore gave the right guidance to a side which gave three players to the national team during the course of the season – R.S. Sodhi, Dinesh Mongia, Yuvraj Singh, not to forget Harbhajan Singh. The other two teams to qualify from the North Zone were Delhi and Jammu and Kashmir. It was a great moment for Jammu and Kashmir, who made the grade for the first time in the history of the Ranji Trophy.

Mumbai qualified from the West Zone along with Baroda and Maharashtra while Orissa, Bengal and Assam made it from the East Zone. From Central, the line up was completed by Railways, Madhya Pradesh and Uttar Pradesh, while Tamil Nadu, Karnataka and Hyderabad qualified from South. There were no real surprises here.

The final of the Ranji Trophy was a fantastic contest with Railways scoring 394 runs after restricting Baroda to 243. But Baroda hit back by scoring 373 with Satyajit Parab hitting 141 and then skittling out Railways for 201 with Zaheer Khan claiming five for 43. The victory target was 223. It was a deserving victory for Baroda, but then poor umpiring left a bad taste.

In the semi-finals, Railways had knocked out the mighty Punjab in a keen contest and Baroda had shut out Orissa at home in a keen match, too.

The Irani Cup at Mumbai pushed Railways left-

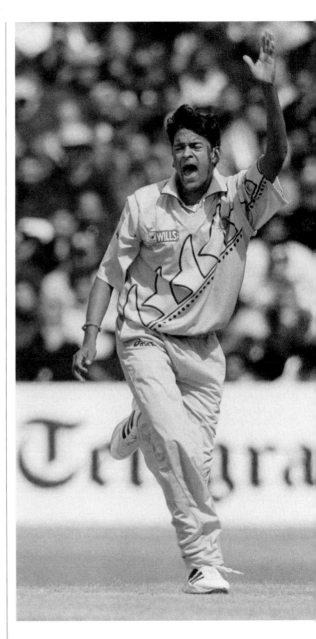

Debashish Mohanty enjoyed a remarkable domestic season in the Duleep Trophy. The swing bowler claimed 23 wickets in only three games.

Right: North batsman and former Test player Vikram Rathore scored 881 runs at an average of 48.94, including a knock of 203, as his side triumphed in the Duleep Trophy.

arm spinner Murali Kartik into the limelight. Javagal Srinath pulled out from the match, but Rest of India were still strong enough to defeat Mumbai inside three days by ten wickets. It was a rare humiliation for the Mumbai side who did well to score 260 with Wassim Jaffer hitting 56. Murali Kartik claimed four for 73. Then V.V.S. Laxman knocked a stylish 167 to help Rest of India take a big lead. In the second innings, Mumbai crashed to Kartik who took nine for 70 and Rest of India then knocked off the runs to win by ten wickets.

Yere Gowda of Railways, hailing from Karanataka, topped the list of run-makers with 901 runs at an average of 75.08 while Test reject pace bowler Dodda Ganesh of Karnataka was the leading wicket taker with 59 at an average of 21.68.

The Duleep Trophy was won by North Zone and it came as no surprise. North dominated the tournament throughout and had already claimed the title before the last round of matches could be completed. Once again the tournament was robbed of its glamour when the stars stayed away in most of the matches.

South Zone were a big disappointment, finishing last. To be fair, South were handicapped by the absence of most of their established players for most of their matches. The runners-up spot went to Central Zone while West Zone finished third and East Zone fourth. This was not the finish one would have imagined. The tournament was once again played on a league basis after the knock-out format last year came in for criticism.

Dinesh Mongia, Virender Sehwag, Vikram Rathore, Akash Chopra and Yuvraj Singh were the star batsmen for North while Ashish Nehra consistently excelled with the ball. He was the tournament's best bowler even though it was Debashish Mohanty who stunned one and all with a remarkable haul of 23 wickets in just three matches, including all ten East Zone wickets in the first innings of the match. It was a performance which saw Mohanty make a comeback to the national side.

The Indian domestic season again focussed on the batsmen because the pitches hardly helped the bowlers, leading to criticism of the Board for not giving any thought to the playing surface. But the panoply of surprises more than made up for any other disappointments.

INDIA DOMESTIC ONE-DAY SEASON
by Ghaus Mohammad

The one-day scene continued to be exciting. The trend was set by a well-contested Challenger Series in Chennai where India Seniors defeated India 'B' by 30 runs. In the final, the Seniors were reeling at 96 for five after 18 overs when Hemang Badani and Virender Sehwag produced some sensational batting. Badani cracked an unbeaten 104 and Sehwag whipped a sizzling 94 off 95 balls as the two added 168 in just 25 overs.

The Deodhar Trophy was also exciting. The title was shared by Central Zone and South Zone after a tie in the final at Lucknow. It was a fitting end to a tournament which had seen some excellent batting and bowling performances. West Zone and East Zone may not have had much to offer, but Central Zone took the cake – led by skipper Amay Khurasiya who was in great form, treating all the reputed bowlers with utter disdain.

The zonal one-day leagues also produced good competitive cricket. Punjab remained unbeaten in North Zone, the only team to maintain a clean record in the entire competition. From West, Mumbai won the right to play the Wills Trophy, while Railways made the grade from Central. In East, Orissa qualified for the first time ever and Tamil Nadu pipped Karnataka in the race despite sharing the honour with eight points each.

Sadly, the Deodhar Trophy was neglected by the selectors and the same fate befell the zonal one-day league. The Challenger Series may have attracted the attention of the selectors, but then it was not as competitive as the Deodhar Trophy.

FIRST-CLASS AVERAGES

BATTING

	M	Inns	NO	HS	Runs	Av	100	50
R Dravid	7	12	2	200*	1024	102.40	4	3
VVS Laxman	11	17	2	281	1420	94.66	5	5
SR Tendulkar	7	12	1	201*	978	88.90	5	2
Y Goud	10	16	3	221*	1093	84.07	3	5
HH Kanitkar	11	14	2	190	912	76.00	3	5
D Mongia	12	16	2	308*	1041	74.35	3	3
P Dharmani	9	12	1	176	812	73.81	3	4
A Chopra	9	16	3	222	915	70.38	4	4
RR Parida	11	18	3	220	1026	68.40	2	7
ML Hayden	6	12	1	203	709	64.45	2	2
P Mullick	7	10	2	191	515	64.37	2	2
SR Waugh	6	10	2	110	509	63.62	3	-
AV Kale	9	13	2	222	674	61.27	2	2
GK Khoda	8	12	1	300*	661	60.09	2	1
VG Kambli	7	11	1	203*	591	59.10	2	3
S Sharath	6	9	1	224	466	58.25	2	1
V Shewag	11	15	2	162*	757	58.23	3	3
SS Parab	8	14	0	141	809	57.78	4	4
Kanwaljit Singh (J&K)	6	12	3	117*	520	57.77	1	5
M Kaif	10	12	2	119*	571	57.10	1	5
JJ Martin	14	21	2	121	1030	54.21	3	6
RS Gavaskar	9	14	2	146	630	52.50	4	1
S Sriram	11	16	0	150	820	51.25	2	4
RS Sodhi	11	16	2	137	715	51.07	2	4
BM Rowland	7	11	2	100*	459	51.00	1	4
Yuvraj Singh	7	12	1	135	560	50.90	2	2
AR Khurasiya	10	15	1	118*	711	50.78	3	4
PK Das	5	8	0	118	397	49.62	1	2
JP Yadav (MP)	10	15	0	177	737	49.13	1	4
VS Rathore	12	18	0	203	881	48.94	2	3
VR Mane	6	10	0	97	489	48.90	-	6
DS Manohar	6	9	0	82	438	48.66	-	5
HS Sodhi	6	10	2	87	380	47.50	-	5
S Mahesh	7	12	4	77*	377	47.12	-	3
Wasim Jaffer	11	18	3	97	702	46.80	-	7
LNP Reddy	5	8	0	138	370	46.25	1	1
NR Mongia	13	21	5	181	737	46.06	1	6
R Nayyar	6	10	2	121	353	44.12	1	1
CC Williams	11	20	1	116	835	43.94	1	5
SK Sahu	8	12	2	122	433	43.30	1	2
AA Pagnis	11	18	1	143	736	43.29	1	6
RR Powar	8	11	3	113*	337	42.12	1	1
SV Bahutule	10	14	4	67	418	41.80	-	4
SS Raul	11	18	1	134	702	41.29	3	1
SS Dighe	6	10	1	98	371	41.22	-	4
SB Bangar	8	14	0	89	551	39.35	-	4
J Arun Kumar	7	11	0	82	422	38.36	-	5
NK Patel	7	11	1	87	380	38.00	-	4
D Bundela	8	11	0	144	409	37.18	1	2
SS Das	15	26	1	178	925	37.00	2	5
A Sharma (HP)	5	8	0	120	295	36.87	1	1
YV Rao	5	8	0	82	291	36.37	-	3
RJ Kanwat	8	12	1	88	400	36.36	-	4
M Sharma	7	9	0	131	326	36.22	1	2
TB Arothe	8	14	0	86	506	36.14	-	7

FIRST-CLASS AVERAGES

BATTING

	M	Inns	NO	HS	Runs	Av	100	50
ND Modi	4	8	0	104	289	36.12	1	1
S Ramesh	10	16	1	101	541	36.06	1	3
Abhay Sharma	11	18	1	188	608	35.76	1	3
TP Singh	7	13	1	80	421	35.08	-	3
RT Ponting	6	11	1	102*	348	34.80	2	2
R Kumar	5	8	0	82	275	34.37	-	2
Nikhil Doru	5	9	1	121	275	34.37	1	1
P Jayachandra	9	14	2	101*	411	34.25	1	2
V Dahiya	9	10	2	81	272	34.00	-	3
SZ Zuffri	7	12	0	82	407	33.91	-	4
SV Carlisle	4	8	0	61	271	33.87	-	3
N Gaur	5	8	0	101	269	33.62	1	2
RS Ricky	8	12	0	113	403	33.58	1	2
A Nandakishore	8	12	0	128	388	32.33	1	2
B Akhil	6	10	2	79	257	32.12	-	2
S Verma	5	10	2	116	256	32.00	1	-
Harbhajan Singh	11	16	4	84	383	31.91	-	2
Tanveer Jabbar	5	10	0	116	319	31.90	1	1
AP Bhoite	7	12	0	78	379	31.58	-	5
JL Langer	6	11	0	115	346	31.45	1	1
VST Naidu	11	15	1	122	433	30.92	1	2
D Dasgupta	7	12	1	89	337	30.63	-	2
S Badrinath	7	12	0	100	363	30.25	1	-
R Puri	5	8	0	89	240	30.00	-	2
SB Saikia	5	8	0	52	238	29.75	-	1
S Medappa	4	8	0	116	235	29.37	1	-
GJ Rennie	4	8	0	79	235	29.37	-	2
A Gupta	6	10	1	56*	259	28.77	-	1
SC Ganguly	7	12	1	65*	315	28.63	-	1
MR Beerala	7	12	1	73	311	28.27	-	1
HK Bhaskar	4	8	0	82	225	28.12	-	2
RP Rane	5	10	1	75	253	28.11	-	1
AA Muzumdar	7	11	0	81	305	27.72	-	2
HR Jadhav	8	14	0	165	386	27.57	1	1
S Dasgupta	4	8	0	62	216	27.00	-	1
KS Parida	10	13	1	84	313	26.08	-	1
D Ganesh	10	11	3	41	208	26.00	-	-
A Dani	5	9	1	54	207	25.87	-	1
D Mahajan	7	11	1	65	250	25.00	-	2
MJ Slater	6	12	1	48	270	24.54	-	-
PK Amre	4	8	0	66	188	23.50	-	1
V Kolambkar	5	10	0	48	233	23.30	-	-
RV Bhardwaj	8	13	0	50	299	23.00	-	2
S Singh (Assam)	9	15	3	68*	272	22.66	-	1
S Ganesh Kumar	5	8	0	50	178	22.25	-	1
VN Buch	9	13	3	50*	220	22.00	-	1
V Bhaskar	6	12	0	62	260	21.66	-	1
SK Sanwal	7	10	2	50*	171	21.37	-	1
S Singh (Serv)	5	10	0	79	213	21.30	-	2
KK Dixit	4	8	0	57	170	21.25	-	1
Jasvir Singh	5	8	0	68	167	20.87	-	1
SU Harbade	4	8	0	42	166	20.75	-	-
SR Paul	7	12	0	46	242	20.16	-	-

Qualification: 8 completed innings, average 20.00

FIRST-CLASS AVERAGES

BOWLING

	Overs	Mds	Runs	Wkts	Av	Best	10m	5/inn
GD McGrath	168.2	70	338	21	16.09	4-18	-	-
DS Mohanty	375.5	109	944	58	16.27	10-46	2	5
A Nehra	298.1	62	931	54	17.24	7-14	3	5
Gagandeep Singh	248.1	73	580	32	18.12	6-14	-	2
Harbhajan Singh	457.4	106	1275	70	18.21	8-84	2	6
Sukbinder Singh	236.1	63	675	36	18.75	6-57	1	3
GD Dutta	108.3	28	310	16	19.37	5-42	-	1
J Das	140.3	47	365	18	20.27	4-28	-	-
D Bundela	129	18	451	22	20.50	6-37	1	2
MA Khan	106	22	350	17	20.58	4-24	-	-
A Qayoom	188.2	48	574	27	21.25	5-42	-	2
SC Ganguly	78.2	21	221	10	22.10	6-46	-	1
GK Pandey	114	36	244	11	22.18	5-49	-	1
AW Zaidi	161.4	38	425	19	22.36	5-84	-	1
J Srinath	192	40	594	26	22.84	6-32	-	2
RS Sodhi	250.5	73	608	26	23.38	5-40	-	1
T Yohannan	172.3	43	456	19	24.00	6-117	-	2
IK Pathan	118.2	30	363	15	24.20	5-55	-	1
AP Bhoite	135.2	12	509	21	24.23	5-22	-	1
WD Balaji Rao	199	57	542	22	24.63	4-60	-	-
SK Sanwal	174.5	43	495	20	24.75	5-82	-	1
S Mahesh	168.2	45	422	17	24.82	5-57	-	1
SV Bahutule	352.5	72	1019	41	24.85	6-49	-	3
TP Singh	263.2	53	701	28	25.03	6-95	1	2
SS Raul	200.1	43	569	22	25.86	3-24	-	-
NP Singh	183.2	37	602	23	26.17	5-39	-	1
Sarandeep Singh	271.3	62	789	30	26.30	6-38	-	2
JP Yadav (MP)	337	67	960	36	22.66	8-80	1	2
SV Ghag	233.1	47	710	26	27.30	8-122	1	2
KN Ananthapadmanaban	150	40	330	12	27.50	4-79	-	-
D Ganesh	378.2	86	1213	44	27.56	6-87	1	3
RB Patel	345.4	58	1188	43	27.62	6-37	-	2
KS Parida	384.3	113	914	32	28.56	5-33	-	1
RL Sanghvi	335.3	91	914	32	28.56	6-71	-	2
RV Bhardwaj	119.2	18	292	10	29.20	3-44	-	-
SK Satpathy	251	65	736	25	29.44	4-25	-	-
S Sharma (Raj)	186	48	501	17	29.47	5-84	-	1
S Sriwastava	311.2	65	931	31	30.03	4-62	-	-
V Sharma	120.3	15	452	15	30.13	5-98	-	1
PL Mhambrey	213	47	608	20	30.40	5-77	-	1
RP Rane	90.1	6	305	10	30.50	3-31	-	-
A Mishra	277.3	82	673	22	30.59	6-138	-	2
Harvinder Singh	219	43	709	23	30.82	5-66	-	2
A Sharma (Servs)	170	36	432	14	30.85	4-45	-	-
VN Buch	361.4	68	1188	38	31.26	6-54	-	1
Z Khan	317.3	74	942	30	31.40	5-43	-	1
AB Agarkar	192	47	522	16	32.62	5-22	-	1
Surendra Singh	302.3	76	979	30	32.63	5-115	-	1
T Kumaran	124.3	33	392	12	32.66	3-57	-	-
P Jayachandra	105	22	327	10	32.70	3-27	-	-
SR Saxena	170.5	37	496	15	33.06	3-72	-	-
IR Siddiqui	341.5	72	1073	32	33.53	5-116	-	1
SK Vadiaraj	232	58	571	17	33.58	4-88	-	-
V Shewag	124	31	372	11	33.81	2-16	-	-
U Chatterjee	388.5	137	838	24	34.91	5-60	-	1
NM Kulkarni	187.5	47	498	14	35.57	4-39	-	-
SK Warne	192.4	40	642	18	35.66	7-56	-	1
M Kartik	299	62	882	24	36.75	9-70	1	1
KS Sahabuddin	206.4	59	588	16	36.75	6-63	-	2
J Zaman	232.3	48	708	19	37.26	5-99	-	1

FIRST-CLASS AVERAGES

BOWLING

	Overs	Mds	Runs	Wkts	Av	Best	10m	5/inn
SB Bangar	179.1	31	570	15	38.00	3-55	-	-
RV Pawar	166.1	42	502	13	38.61	6-109	-	1
ND Hirwani	308.4	58	984	25	39.36	6-90	-	2
LR Shukla	123	25	480	12	40.00	4-119	-	-
SLV Raju	373.2	90	1043	26	40.11	5-16	-	1
SS Paul	174.5	39	562	14	40.14	3-64	-	-
AR Kapoor	332.1	61	1047	26	40.26	7-59	1	1
M Diwakar	152.5	29	627	15	41.80	3-61	-	-
SB Joshi	367.2	80	1133	27	41.96	4-38	-	-
RR Powar	257.5	62	757	18	42.05	5-77	-	1
S Ganesh Kumar	118.5	19	428	10	42.80	5-67	-	1
A Barick	212	40	801	18	44.50	3-48	-	-
MV Sane	190	32	588	13	45.23	3-99	-	-
A Bhandari	176.5	40	593	13	45.61	3-72	-	-
AR Yalvigi	173	31	590	11	53.63	3-92	-	-
RJ Kanwat	276.2	64	763	14	54.50	3-52	-	-

Qualification: 10 wickets in 8 innings

The following bowlers took 10 wickets in fewer than 8 innings:

	Overs	Mds	Runs	Wkts	Av	Best	10m	5/inn
B Bhushan	80.2	23	219	11	19.90	7-51	-	1
S Subramaniam	89.2	18	268	13	20.61	5-36	-	2
R Singh, jr	115.5	31	295	14	21.07	5-61	-	1
F Ghyas	84.4	16	243	11	22.09	5-63	-	1
SR Nair	106.4	26	226	10	22.60	3-20	-	-
JS Yadav	118.3	23	364	15	24.26	7-70	-	1
M Ghose	119.3	34	338	13	26.00	5-97	-	1
MV Rao	112	25	326	12	27.16	3-65	-	-
N Kalekar	98	13	305	11	27.72	5-39	-	1
YS Ranganath	141.5	32	374	13	28.76	4-59	-	-
HA Majumdar	145.5	24	461	16	28.81	6-74	-	1
SS Lahiri	123.4	28	378	13	29.07	4-63	-	-
JN Gillespie	145.3	39	449	15	29.93	3-45	-	-
SA Khalid	149.5	30	413	13	31.76	5-63	-	1
L Patel	167.3	23	577	18	32.05	5-72	-	2
CR Miller	156.4	34	504	15	33.60	6-90	-	1
SV Aradhye	163.5	36	444	13	34.15	4-75	-	-
Kanwaljit Singh (Hyd)	177	28	513	15	34.20	5-100	-	1
V Jain	112	18	408	11	37.09	3-111	-	-
AI Aware	143.1	28	461	12	38.41	5-92	-	1
H Watekar	151	31	465	11	42.27	3-22	-	-
N Madhukar	131	23	428	10	42.80	3-116	-	-
A Sharma (HP)	137.4	18	474	11	43.09	3-98	-	-
RK Panta	122	27	441	10	44.10	2-17	-	-
PV Gandhe	171.4	22	548	12	45.66	4-58	-	-
P Thakur	264.2	75	601	11	54.63	5-107	-	1

FIELDING

31 – NR Mongia (26ct,5st); 27 – G Gopal (23ct,4st), Abhay Sharma (23ct,4st); 26 – D Dasgupta (23ct,3st); 23 – VST Naidu (19ct,4st); 22 – SB Bangar; 21 – A Ratra (17ct,4st); 20 – V Dahiya (18ct,2st), AC Gilchrist (18ct,2st), RB Jhalani (17ct,3st), VB Kamaruddin; 19 – SS Dighe (16ct,3st), VS Rathore (18ct,1st); 17 – D Mongia; 16 – RR Parida, SR Paul (13ct,3st); 15 – SM Kondhalkar (15ct), Sarabjit Singh (14ct,1st); 14 – H Jagnu (11ct,3st), VVS Laxman, JJ Martin, M Maveda (14ct), VR Samant (13ct,1st),CC Williams; 13 – B Akhil, RV Bhardwaj, AA Muzumdar, RT Ponting 12 – A Bhagwat (10ct,2st), SS Das, R Dravid, SC Ganguly; 11 – P Chawla (9ct,2st), A Chopra, S Karim (10ct,1st), V Shewag; 10 – M Mudgal (8ct,2st), SS Raul, RS Ricky, D Sharma (9ct,1st), Yuvraj Singh, M Srinivas (8ct,2st), JP Yadav (MP)

Qualification: 10 catches or more

NEW ZEALAND

ZIMBABWE IN NEW ZEALAND
By Bryan Waddle

Canterbury v. Zimbabweans
19 December 2000 at Jade Stadium, Christchurch (floodlit)
Canterbury 236 for 9 (50 overs) (GR Stead 56)
Zimbabweans 239 for 6 (49.3 overs) (ADR Campbell 72, TN Madondo 52)
Zimbabweans won by four wickets

Chasing a respectable 237 for victory after winning the toss and inserting the home side, the Zimbabweans got their tour off to a winning start by scraping home with three balls to spare. Inspired by an opening stand of 109 between Alistair Campbell and Trevor Madondo, captain Heath Streak hammered 17 off 11 balls to see his side home.

Canterbury v. Zimbabweans
21–23 December 2000 at Jade Stadium, Christchurch
Canterbury 330 for 5 dec. (GR Stead 100*, GJ Hopkins 50*) and 122 for 0 dec. (HTG James 65*, RM Frew 52*)
Zimbabweans 150 (DA Marillier 73, SE Bond 5 for 51) and 38 for 2
Match drawn

Rain and some slow first-day batting by Canterbury ensured that a draw would be the only outcome in the warm up to the Wellington Test.

Sent into bat on a pitch tinged with green, Canterbury, without many regular first-choice players, managed just 185 from the 90 overs on the first day.

Canterbury finally declared on 330 after 134 overs of batting and soon had Zimbabwe on the backfoot, although Doug Marillier gave the total some respectability with a knock of 73, but they had little reason to be over concerned as the time available meant that they had little chance to achieve a result.

ONLY TEST
26–30 December 2000 at Basin Reserve, Wellington

While the majority of Test matches played around the world are competitive and entertaining, the Boxing Day Test between New Zealand and Zimbabwe did little to advance the cause of Test cricket as an exciting spectacle. It didn't help that

Previous page: New Zealand's bowlers stormed back to level the Test series with Pakistan at Hamilton.

the Basin Reserve offered up a docile pitch, devoid of grass and that Wellington experienced strong, gusty nor'westers for the duration of the game.

Both sides may have been depleted by injury, but they gave the impression that they were adopting a conservative, play-not-to-lose philosophy rather than creating the opportunity for a positive result.

The New Zealanders were without experienced key players, Chris Cairns, Dion Nash and Daniel Vettori, while Zimbabwe lost two important players with Grant Flower and Dirk Viljoen both sustaining broken fingers in the build-up to the Test.

Despite reasonable weather in the capital, the pitch was barren and lacking in pace, which prompted New Zealand to include two spinners, expecting it to crumble.

There were periods when the game was lifted above the mediocrity that marked the first day as

Nathan Astle is best known for his attacking batting, but his century at Wellington took him nine hours.

New Zealand struggled to 190 for the loss of four wickets. Nathan Astle and Craig McMillan pumped some adrenalin through the body of the innings on the second day, completing a record fifth-wicket stand of 222.

McMillan was the key ingredient, dominating the partnership in reaching his fourth Test hundred from 168 balls. The normally aggressive Astle spent 301 deliveries before recording his sixth Test century. The attitude of both might have resulted from a pre-Test challenge laid down by selection convenor, Sir Richard Hadlee, that both players, despite their record, were playing for their places.

When McMillan was out for 142, equalling his previous Test best, Astle continued painstakingly to 141, an innings of monumental patience and concentration that lasted nine hours.

New Zealand's decision to bat into the third day didn't help to set up a positive result and with only 29 overs available because of rain and bad light they were forced to declare before achieving the 500 total they desired.

The fate of the Test was settled on the fourth day when Zimbabwe's middle-order batsmen comfortably progressed, enjoying a pitch that gave no sign of the deterioration expected prior to the game.

Gavin Rennie and the stylish Andy Flower gave the innings its substance with a fourth-wicket stand of 130 as Zimbabwe cruised towards the follow-on mark.

Pace bowler Chris Martin offered New Zealand some hope with the new ball, dismissing Flower for 79. In the process the classy left-hander passed the 1,000-run mark in the calendar year 2000 finishing with an impressive 1,045 at an average of 80.38 for the 12-month period. Only Inzamam-ul-Haq with 1,090 exceeded Flower's outstanding total.

Rennie followed the lead of the New Zealand top order on the first day, spending six-and-half-hours to compile his highest Test score, which took Zimbabwe to within 50 of the follow-on mark.

New Zealand made a token effort to score quickly, teasing the small crowd that a meaningful run chase was on the cards, declaring at 153 for four.

The target of 301 off 43 overs was a pointless challenge to any side, and the umpires took pity on the players and spectators when Zimbabwe had crawled to 60 for two.

Both sides blamed the other for failing to liven up the final day, but in truth both sides seemed happy to play negative cricket for most of the first four days making it unlikely that they would change their approach on the last in pursuit of a contrived result.

TEST MATCH – NEW ZEALAND v. ZIMBABWE
26–30 December 2000 at Basin Reserve, Wellington

NEW ZEALAND

	First innings		Second innings	
MH Richardson	run out (Olonga/Flower)	75		
MJ Horne	c Flower, b Streak	1	(1) c Flower, b Streak	0
MS Sinclair	lbw b Strang	9	(2) c Flower, b Murphy	18
SP Fleming (capt)	run out (Whittall/Strang)	22	(3) run out (Olonga)	55
NJ Astle	c Carlisle, b Strang	141	(4) not out	51
CD McMillan	b Murphy	142	(5) c Madondo, b Strang	10
*AC Parore	not out	50	(6) not out	3
BGK Walker	c Olonga, b Strang	27		
PJ Wiseman	not out	0		
SB O'Connor				
CS Martin				
	b1, lb8, w5, nb6	20	b5, lb5, nb6	16
	(for 7 wickets dec.)	487	(for 4 wickets dec.)	153

	First innings				Second innings			
	O	M	R	W	O	M	R	W
Streak	37	10	74	1	5	1	18	1
Strang	46	16	116	3	11	2	25	1
Olonga	30	2	105	-	2	0	12	-
Murphy	46	9	128	1	18	0	86	1
Whittall	22	6	55	-	4	3	2	-

Fall of Wickets
1-5, 2-22, 3-67, 4-145, 5-367, 6-426, 7-487
1-4, 2-44, 3-103, 4-126

ZIMBABWE

	First innings		Second innings	
GJ Whittall	b Martin	9	c Parore, b O'Connor	6
GJ Rennie	c Parore, b McMillan	93	c Parore, b Wiseman	37
SV Carlisle	c Horne, b Martin	0	not out	16
ADR Campbell	lbw b Martin	24	not out	0
*A Flower	c Parore, b Martin	79		
TN Madondo	not out	74		
DA Marillier	c Parore, b Martin	28		
HH Streak (capt)	not out	19		
BA Murphy				
BC Strang				
HK Olonga				
	b3, lb9, nb2	14	lb1	1
	(for 6 wickets dec.)	340	(for 2 wickets)	60

	First innings				Second innings			
	O	M	R	W	O	M	R	W
Martin	32.5	11	71	5	5	2	6	-
O'Connor	16	7	29	-	8	4	8	1
Wiseman	54	13	131	1	6	2	15	1
Walker	22	1	68	-	11	1	30	-
McMillan	9	4	22	1				
Astle	5	2	7	-				

Fall of Wickets
1-21, 2-23, 3-66, 4-196, 5-237, 6-295
1-26, 2-57

Umpires: RS Dunne & BC Cooray
Toss: New Zealand
Test debut: DA Marillier (Zimbabwe)

Match drawn

ONE-DAY INTERNATIONALS

Zimbabwe captain Heath Streak has seldom hit the headlines for his performances with the bat, but it was his explosive hitting in the deciding one-day match of the three-match series against New Zealand that gave his side an historic first-ever series victory on foreign soil.

Streak slammed 79 off 67 balls, hitting a six into the No. 1 Stand at Eden Park for a victory with eight balls to spare after being set what seemed like a defendable target for the home side of 274.

On reflection, Zimbabwe deserved the series win, although, New Zealand should have settled the series early in the deciding match after Zimbabwe had been reduced to 64 for five in the 16th over.

But not for the first time, Andy Flower played a match-saving innings that ultimately became a match-winning effort with 81 from 86 balls, adding 82 with Dirk Viljoen and then 42 with Streak as the target became more achievable.

After Flower had been dismissed by the ever-reliable Nathan Astle, Streak accepted the support of rookie pace bowler, Travis Friend, to add 61 for the eighth wicket, which was to prove to be the final nail in New Zealand's coffin as Zimbabwe reached their target with eight balls to spare.

Faced with Streak's frantic assault, the New Zealand bowling lacked experience and direction, but those problems had been exposed in the previous two games.

In the first match at the holiday resort town of Taupo, New Zealand were set a massive target of 300, with Andy Flower, the unanimous Man of the Series, crafting a polished 80 off 88 balls. Stuart Carlisle added 75, while Streak ended the innings thumping 30 from 18 deliveries.

Chris Cairns, returning after a two-month injury break, bowled only three overs for 24 runs, and pace bowlers Chris Martin and James Franklin, in their first one-day international, learned some harsh lessons about bowling at the top level.

Chasing 301 from 50 overs was a tough task, but a rain interruption during dinner provided the confusing Duckworth/Lewis system with a chance to make the chase even tougher, 281 from 43 overs.

The flamboyant umpire, Billy Bowden, concentrates hard as Zimbabwe win their first ever one-day international series overseas.

New Zealand captain Stephen Fleming raced to 64, but his side never looked capable of pulling off an unlikely victory and fell 71 runs short of the revised target.

The second game in Wellington was a complete role reversal and provided New Zealand with a win, every bit as convincing as the Zimbabwe success in Taupo. Despite Alistair Campbell's innings of 111, Zimbabwe only managed 236 for six against a New Zealand attack that was more accurate and demanding than in the first game. It was the experienced duo, Nathan Astle and Craig McMillan, who were responsible for containing the tourists adequately. Astle, and new opening partner Mathew Sinclair fashioned a match-winning stand of 153 as New Zealand ultimately reached the target in the 46th over.

Having lost the one-day series between the two sides in Zimbabwe the previous September, New Zealand had confidently predicted a 3–0 series whitewash.

It may have been the batting of Heath Streak that left the New Zealanders speechless and motionless on Eden Park at the end of the final game, but it was more likely the realization that the first series of 2001 had been lost 2–1, which produced the muted response as Zimbabwe celebrated.

Match One
2 January 2001 at Owen Delany Park, Taupo (floodlit)
Zimbabwe 300 for 7 (50 overs) (A Flower 80, SV Carlisle 75)
New Zealand 210 (40 overs) (SP Fleming 64)
Zimbabwe won by 70 runs (DL Method: New Zealand target 281 from 43 overs)
Man of the Match: A Flower

Match Two
4 January 2001 at WestpacTrust Stadium, Wellington (floodlit)
Zimbabwe 236 for 7 (50 overs) (ADR Campbell 111)
New Zealand 237 for 2 (45.2 overs) (NJ Astle 89*, MS Sinclair 85)
New Zealand won by eight wickets
Man of the Match: MS Sinclair

Match Three
7 January 2001 at Eden Park, Auckland
New Zealand 273 for 9 (50 overs) (CD McMillan 75*)
Zimbabwe 274 for 9 (48.4 overs) (A Flower 81, HH Streak 79*)
Zimbabwe won by one wicket
Man of the Match: HH Streak

SRI LANKA IN NEW ZEALAND
By Bryan Waddle

ONE-DAY INTERNATIONALS

Both New Zealand and Sri Lanka had completed gruelling, unsuccessful tours of South Africa before they came together for a five-match, one-day series.

After losing the one-day series to Zimbabwe 2–1, the home side were heading for an ignominious 5–0 whitewash before they produced their best form to snatch the final match of the series.

Since winning the ICC Knock-Out Trophy, New Zealand had an abysmal one-day record. They had played 16 one-day internationals and recorded just three wins – it seemed as though the ICC champions had lost the art of winning in the shortened form of the game.

Sri Lanka had deservedly won the series with four emphatic victories, but in the final match New

Sanath Jayasuriya blazed a century at Auckland as Sri Lanka imposed a second one-day series defeat on New Zealand.

Zealand rediscovered the missing component by applying the basics of disciplined, thoughtful batting.

At 2.01 metres tall, Jacob Oram is built more like an All Black forward with some raw power to match the bulk. His batting in the last match, reaching 59 from 57 balls gave the New Zealand innings its momentum as they reached 282 for six.

Sri Lanka's awkward off spinning duo, Kumar Dharmasena and Muttiah Muralitharan had reigned supreme in the previous four games, conceding less than three runs per over and stifling the New Zealand batting. But Oram and, later in the innings Chris Harris and Lou Vincent, showed little respect for either spinner in achieving their best total in eight one-day internationals.

Youthful talent was also the essential ingredient in defending the massive total. 20-year-old left arm seamer James Franklin and 22-year-old Darryl Tuffey shared five of the ten wickets as Sri Lanka made a spirited bid to complete a whitewash.

A New Zealand win under the lights at Jade Stadium, Christchurch, saved the home side the embarrassment of a 5–0 series whitewash.

The final match success, however, could not hide the many shortcomings that had been exposed in New Zealand's first four encounters. They should have won the opening match of the series at Napier's McLean Park soon after Sri Lanka's arrival from South Africa. Daniel Vettori returned to international cricket with an encouraging performance of three for 21 from his ten overs to restrict the tourists to a modest 213. New Zealand never looked like threatening the target, losing by 61 runs through a combination of inexperience and a lack of intelligence at the crease.

Things deteriorated for New Zealand as the series progressed with the balanced Sri Lankan attack efficiently sapping their confidence. Nuwan Zoysa and Dilhara Fernando bowled with hostility and unerring accuracy while Dharmasena, Muralitharan,

Aravinda de Silva and Sanath Jayasuriya all exploited the tentative footwork and timid stroke play of the home side.

In Wellington, the Sri Lankan attack restricted New Zealand to 205, although they made heavy weather of the chase and reached the target with just three balls to spare. In a rain-reduced match in Auckland, captain Sanath Jayasuriya displayed his sublime batting skills with a scintillating century off only 76 balls. The target from 47 overs was 182 and it was reached in just the 29th over.

Rain made the fourth match in Hamilton a 35-over-a-side lottery that was decided more by the toss than in the middle. It was ambitious to schedule a

35-over game that was due to end at 8.30pm without the benefit of lighting and, when poor light forced a finish soon after 8pm, Duckworth/Lewis had the final say. New Zealand had struggled to 182 for nine in their 35 overs and Sri Lanka responded with 155 for five – the victory being set up by a rollicking opening stand of 94 in just 14 overs between Jayasuriya and Romesh Kaluwitharana.

Match One
31 January 2001 at McLean Park, Napier (floodlit)
Sri Lanka 213 for 8 (50 overs) (RP Arnold 50)
New Zealand 152 (42.5 overs) (M Muralitharan 5 for 30)
Sri Lanka won by 61 runs
Man of the Match: M Muralitharan

Match Two
3 February 2001 at WestpacTrust Stadium, Wellington (floodlit)
New Zealand 205 for 8 (50 overs) (CZ Harris 56)
Sri Lanka 206 for 7 (48.3 overs) (RP Arnold 78*)
Sri Lanka won by three wickets
Man of the Match: RP Arnold

Match Three
6 February 2001 at Eden Park, Auckland
New Zealand 181 (45.4 overs) (CD McMillan 61)
Sri Lanka 182 for 1 (29.5 overs) (ST Jayasuriya 103, MS Atapattu 59*)
Sri Lanka won by nine wickets
Man of the Match: ST Jayasuriya

Match Four
8 February 2001 at WestpacTrust Park, Hamilton
New Zealand 182 for 9 (SP Fleming 67)
Sri Lanka 155 for 5 (31 overs) (ST Jayasuriya 52)
Sri Lanka won by 3 runs (DL Method: Sri Lanka needed to have 153 runs from 31 overs when rain stopped play)
Man of the Match: ST Jayasuriya

Match Five
11 February 2001 at Jade Stadium, Christchurch
New Zealand 282 for 6 (50 overs) (JDP Oram 59, CZ Harris 52*)
Sri Lanka 269 (49.2 overs) (MS Atapattu 76, RP Arnold 51)
New Zealand won by 13 runs
Man of the Match: JDP Oram

With an economy rate of less than three runs per over, Muttiah Muralitharan was one of the true stars for Sri Lanka during their successful one-day series.

PAKISTAN IN NEW ZEALAND
By Bryan Waddle

ONE-DAY INTERNATIONALS

Controversy is seldom far from the Pakistan team: it seems to hover in the shadows like another member of the squad. So it came as no surprise that the 2001 Pakistan tour of New Zealand should attract its fair share of attention, and, it was almost from the outset.

Despite management denials, there was certainly no indication that Moin Khan's team were a happy side, and this was reflected, in the major personnel changes through the tour. It started with one of the most potent bowling attacks in world cricket, Wasim Akram, Waqar Younis, Shoaib Ahktar, the youthful

Mohammed Sami, Abdur Razzaq, Azhar Mahmood, Saqlain Mushtaq and Mushtaq Ahmed. By the end of the tour, only Waqar, Sami, Saqlain and Mushtaq had survived, as players were shuttled back and forth: it really was an airline's dream!

Shoaib was first to hit the headlines in the opening one-day international at Eden Park. In a devastating two-over spell, he reduced New Zealand's innings from 142 for five to 149 all out, taking five for 19 in 6.3 overs, hitting the stumps four times.

Television was quick to highlight his bowling action and at the post-match press conference Shoaib, who was named Man of the Match, passionately defended his action. He denied throwing, claimed he had made no changes to his action after previously being reported and pleaded to be able to bowl without being placed under intense scrutiny. Whether it was the simmering controversy or a lack of match fitness, Shoaib failed to play a significant part in the rest of the series.

In Napier, the venue for the second match, Pakistan's batting was equally as inept as New Zealand's had been in Auckland three days earlier. Dismissed for 135 with Abdur Razzaq offering a painstaking 50 off 113 balls, New Zealand reached the target in the 30th over. Shoaib lasted only nine balls of the innings, conceding 16 runs before leaving with an injured thigh muscle.

The topsy-turvy nature of the series gave Pakistan its second victory in Wellington by 28 runs.

The New Zealanders saved their best cricket until the final two matches and it was no coincidence that they won on the two best pitches in the country.

At Christchurch, Craig McMillan underlined his class with his first one-day hundred, lifting off spinner Saqlain Mushtaq over the fence for six off the last delivery of the 50th over to bring up his century off just 75 balls. He was almost denied his personal milestone when he lost the strike with two balls remaining. Inexplicably, though, Saqlain bowled two no balls to allow McMillan back on strike. That incident was later highlighted by coach Javed Miandad when he returned home, as highly suspicious, suggesting that some players had let the team down. Pakistan never threatened the target after sliding to 15 for four in the seventh over and lost by 139 runs.

After such a convincing win in the fourth match, it was a confident New Zealand side that found itself

Shoaib Akhtar took five for 19 in six overs, but television replays again doubted the legality of his bowling action.

Craig McMillan followed his 64 at Wellington with a century at Christchurch.

chasing a massive 286 to win the series. Shahid Afridi had given the tourists a rollicking start with 65 off 55 balls and after 15 overs they had 90 on the board for the loss of Saeed Anwar. The run rate stayed above five an over for the full 50 overs.

Yousuf Youhana played another accomplished innings of 68, Razzaq was thorough in compiling 41, while the lower order, Imran Farhat and Moin Khan, ensured that New Zealand would have no easy target.

However, Pakistan's fielding was no match for their batting and with openers Fleming and Astle both dropped by Ahktar inside the first ten overs, they rode their luck and plundered a record 193-run opening stand which laid the foundation for victory.

Astle reached his ninth one-day hundred. It was not his most attractive innings, but one of the most valuable he has ever played for his country, which frustrated a Pakistan side that became increasingly inept in the field the longer the innings progressed.

Match One
18 February 2001 at Eden Park, Auckland (floodlit)
New Zealand 149 (35.3 overs) (Shoaib Akhtar 5 for 19)
Pakistan 150 for 4 (45 overs)
Pakistan won by six wickets
Man of the Match: Shoaib Akhtar

Match Two
20 February 2001 at McLean Park, Napier (floodlit)
Pakistan 135 (50 overs) (Abdur Razzaq 50)
New Zealand 136 for 4 (30.3 overs)
New Zealand won by six wickets
Man of the Match: DR Tuffey

Match Three
22 February 2001 at WestpacTrust Stadium, Wellington (floodlit)
Pakistan 243 for 9 (50 overs) (Saeed Anwar 57)
New Zealand 215 (48.2 overs) (CD McMillan 64)
Pakistan won by 28 runs
Man of the Match: Saqlain Mushtaq

Match Four
25 February 2001 at Jade Stadium, Christchurch
New Zealand 284 for 5 (50 overs) (CD McMillan 104*, NJ Astle 71)
Pakistan 146 (47 overs) (Moin Khan 50)
New Zealand won by 138 runs
Man of the Match: CD McMillan

Match Five
28 February 2001 at Carisbrook, Dunedin (floodlit)
Pakistan 285 (49.3 overs) (Yousuf Youhana 68, Shahid Afridi 65)
New Zealand 290 for 6 (48.1 overs) (NJ Astle 119, SP Fleming 60)
New Zealand won by four wickets
Man of the Match: NJ Astle

After losing the one-day series 3–2, the Pakistan side looked on the verge of self-destruction as they prepared for the three-Test series. The team was vastly different from the side first chosen for the tour and even the arrival of the experienced Ijaz Ahmed and stylish batsman Younis Khan did little to help them in the three-day warm up to the first Test.

New Zealand 'A' v. Pakistanis
3–5 March 2001 at Bert Sutcliffe Oval, Lincoln
Pakistanis 100 and 124 (Imran Farhat 51)
New Zealand 'A' 278 (JDP Oram 88, L Vincent 57)
New Zealand 'A' won by an innings and 54 runs

A good, old-fashioned green seamer greeted a troubled touring party at Lincoln and coupled with Test prospects Chris Drum, Andrew Penn and Kyle Mills, eager to push for Test places and then losing the toss, Pakistan's attitude didn't improve much. The first innings lasted just 49 overs with only the classy Yousuf Youhana offering a modicum of application in compiling the top score of the innings, 26. Test selection was a carrot for the New Zealand batsmen, too, and captain Jacob Oram and Lou Vincent established strong claims with a fifth-wicket stand of 106, which restored the shaky innings. Oram was eighth out at 251, but by then New Zealand 'A' were well on their way to an overall lead of 178.

Pakistan fared little better in their second innings, with opener Imran Farhat the lone exception scoring 51, as the 'A' seamers shared eight of the ten wickets between them.

FIRST TEST
8–12 March 2001 at Eden Park, Auckland

Loyal fans have accused New Zealand cricket in the past of being too accommodating to touring teams, preparing pitches to suit their strengths. The same charge might have fairly been levelled even before the first Test had started.

In an endeavour to develop Test strips for multi-purpose sport venues, New Zealand has been experimenting with portable pitches to combat the pressure on grounds posed by rugby. Sadly, the experiment seemed a failure as the Eden Park 'portable', after only ten weeks' preparation, produced a lacklustre pitch that created an air of suspicion and apprehension in the home camp and helped the tourists to take a step back from the chasm into which their tour seemed to be heading.

Fleming may have won the toss, but his decision to bowl first was ultimately the wrong one as New Zealand struggled to cope with the quality spin of Saqlain Mushtaq and the lively pace and swing of Waqar Younis and Mohammad Sami. New Zealand

Younis Khan was one of the young batsmen drafted in after Pakistan's defeat by England. He responded by scoring a century in the second innings at Auckland.

might have fared better had they taken the chances that were offered on the first day when they had reduced Pakistan to 138 for four. They recovered well to reach 346 helped by some attractive middle-order batting from Younis Khan, Faisal Iqbal on debut, and Moin Khan.

Saqlain and Sami kept New Zealand's innings under a tight rein, allowing Pakistan to take a 94-run, first-innings lead, which with the help of some lavish strokeplay rapidly became a lead of 430 on

FIRST TEST – NEW ZEALAND v. PAKISTAN
8–12 March 2001 at Eden Park, Auckland

PAKISTAN

	First innings		Second innings	
Imran Farhat	c Parore, b Martin	23	c & b Wiseman	63
Salim Elahi	c Parore, b Tuffey	24	c Wiseman, b Tuffey	7
Misbah-ul-Haq	c Sinclair, b McMillan	28	c Parore, b Tuffey	10
Yousuf Youhana	c Parore, b Martin	51	c Astle, b Franklin	42
Younis Khan	c McMillan, b Tuffey	91	(6) not out	149
Faisal Iqbal	c Fleming, b Tuffey	42	(7) not out	52
*Moin Khan (capt)	c Parore, b Tuffey	47		
Saqlain Mushtaq	c Fleming, b Martin	2	(5) c Parore, b Tuffey	2
Waqar Younis	lbw b Martin	4		
Mushtaq Ahmed	c Parore, b Franklin	19		
Mohammad Sami	not out	0		
	b2, lb7, nb6	15	b4, lb6, nb1	11
		346	(for 5 wickets dec.)	**336**

	First innings				Second innings			
	O	M	R	W	O	M	R	W
Tuffey	34	13	96	4	17	3	43	3
Martin	22	1	106	4	12	2	65	-
Franklin	21	6	55	1	18	2	59	1
Wiseman	7	0	35	-	36	6	107	1
McMillan	14	5	34	1	7	0	27	-
Astle	8	3	11	-	13	6	25	-

Fall of Wickets
1-46, 2-52, 3-130, 4-138, 5-270, 6-271, 7-286, 8-294, 9-346
1-21, 2-59, 3-97, 4-110, 5-189

NEW ZEALAND

	First Innings		Second innings	
MH Richardson	b Mohammad Sami	1	c Imran Farhat, b Saqlain Mushtaq	59
MD Bell	c Moin Khan, b Waqar Younis	0	run out (Younis Khan/ Saqlain Mushtaq)	28
MS Sinclair	c Imran Farhat, b Mohammad Sami	34	(4) c Yousuf Youhana, b Mohammad Sami	10
SP Fleming (capt)	b Saqlain Mushtaq	86	(5) lbw b Saqlain Mushtaq	5
NJ Astle	b Mushtaq Ahmed	0	(6) b Saqlain Mushtaq	1
CD McMillan	c Younis Khan, b Waqar Younis	54	(7) c Saqlain Mushtaq, b Mohammad Sami	0
*AC Parore	not out	32	(8) not out	0
JEC Franklin	lbw b Saqlain Mushtaq	0	(9) b Mohammad Sami	0
PJ Wiseman	lbw b Saqlain Mushtaq	9	(3) b Mohammad Sami	8
DR Tuffey	b Saqlain Mushtaq	2	b Mohammad Sami	0
CS Martin	b Mohammad Sami	0	b Saqlain Mushtaq	0
	b8, lb20, nb6	34	b12, lb7, nb1	20
		252		**131**

	First innings				Second Innings			
	O	M	R	W	O	M	R	W
Waqar Younis	22	8	44	2	11	2	31	-
Mohammad Sami	31.4	11	70	3	15	4	36	5
Saqlain Mushtaq	20	3	48	4	25.4	12	24	4
Mushtaq Ahmed	23	8	62	1	8	2	21	-

Fall of Wickets
1-1, 2-1, 3-82, 5-194, 6-217, 7-217, 8-237, 9-251
1-91, 2-105, 3-121, 4-126, 5-127, 6-130, 7-130, 8-130, 9-130

Umpires: DB Cowie & RB Tiffin
Toss: New Zealand
Test debuts: JEC Franklin (New Zealand), Faisal Iqbal, Imran Farhat, Misbah-ul-Haq and Mohammad Sami (Pakistan)

Pakistan won by 299 runs

the fourth day when Moin declared.

An opening stand of 91 gave New Zealand some hope of at least saving the game if they could not win it, but, on the final morning, Sami produced a stunning spell in his debut Test to lead his team to victory. New Zealand lost nine wickets for 26 runs in a woeful batting display that drew comparisons with the record low total in Tests compiled on the same ground 46 years previously. Sami finished with five for 36 off 15 overs, ending the Test with eight for 106 to win the Man of the Match award.

Mohammad Sami, on his Test debut, propelled Pakistan to victory with five for 36 in New Zealand's second innings.

SECOND TEST
15–19 March 2001 at Jade Stadium, Christchurch

On a portable pitch that was as flat as a newly laid stretch of State Highway One, the second Test was as tedious as the first was unpredictable – to the batsman's benefit. Neither side had a bowling attack capable of extracting much from the benign strip, and the ultimate result became obvious from early on. The novice opening pair of Matthew Bell and Mark Richardson delivered on the potential the selectors had observed with the first of two century partnerships in the series.

The early foundation was the platform Mathew Sinclair needed to record his second double century and his third 150-plus Test innings. He continued on remorselessly till the innings ended – it was a commanding contribution, as he finished unbeaten on 204 from 348 balls. It served as an invitation for

Mathew Sinclair enjoyed the portable pitch at Christchurch. He scored the second double century of his brief Test career as the second Test ended in a draw.

SECOND TEST – NEW ZEALAND v. PAKISTAN
15–19 March 2001 at Jade Stadium, Christchurch

NEW ZEALAND

	First innings		Second innings	
MH Richardson	b Saqlain Mushtaq	46	not out	73
MD Bell	c Faisal Iqbal, Saqlain Mushtaq	75	lbw b Younis Khan	40
MS Sinclair	not out	204	not out	50
SP Fleming (capt)	run out (Younis Khan/ Moin Khan)	32		
NJ Astle	c Moin Khan, b Waqar Younis	6		
G Bradburn	c Imran Farhat, b Fazl-e-Akbar	0		
CD McMillan	c Younis Khan, b Fazl-e-Akbar	20		
*AC Parore	lbw b Saqlain Mushtaq	46		
DR Tuffey	lbw b Fazl-e-Akbar	13		
CJ Drum	c Moin Khan, b Waqar Younis	4		
CS Martin	b Waqar Younis	0		
	b2, lb17, w1, nb10	30	b15, lb4, nb14	33
		476	(for 1 wicket dec.)	**196**

	First innings				Second innings			
	O	M	R	W	O	M	R	W
Waqar Younis	34	6	114	3	8	1	18	-
Mohammad Sami	36	4	107	-	11	3	32	-
Fazl-e-Akbar	32	6	87	3	7	0	26	-
Saqlain Mushtaq	48	11	134	3	24	5	44	-
Younis Khan	6	1	15	-	21	6	47	1
Yousuf Youhana					1	0	3	-
Faisal Iqbal					1	0	7	-

Fall of Wickets
1-102, 2-163, 3-248, 4-276, 5-282, 6-327, 7-428, 8-449, 9-468
1-69

PAKISTAN

	First Innings	
Imran Farhat	c Drum, b Martin	4
Ijaz Ahmed	hit wicket b Drum	11
Faisal Iqbal	c Fleming, b McMillan	63
Inzamam-ul-Haq	c Fleming, b Martin	130
Yousuf Youhana	c & b Richardson	203
Younis Khan	c Parore, b Tuffey	0
*Moin Khan (capt)	c Martin, b Bradburn	28
Saqlain Mushtaq	not out	101
Waqar Younis	c Parore, b Tuffey	12
Fazl-e-Akbar	not out	0
Mohammad Sami		
	b5, lb8, nb6	19
	(for 8 wickets dec.)	**571**

	First innings			
	O	M	R	W
Tuffey	49	13	152	2
Martin	41	9	153	2
Drum	8	1	21	1
Bradburn	42	10	124	1
McMillan	31	13	47	1
Astle	30	12	45	-
Richardson	9	0	16	1

Fall of Wickets
1-5, 2-25, 3-157, 4-259, 5-260, 6-304, 7-552, 8-569

Umpires: DM Quested & DJ Harper
Toss: Pakistan
Test debut: CJ Drum (New Zealand)

Match drawn

threatened to produce from the start. Saqlain played his part, ecstatic at reaching a maiden Test match hundred, but it had taken seven hours and six minutes.

While New Zealand had conceded a 95-run, first-innings lead to the Pakistanis, they were never in danger of succumbing easily as they posted 196 for one before the umpires finally pronounced the match dead. It might have been Test matches like this that prompted American comedian Robin Williams to quip: 'Cricket is baseball on valium.' Had he been among the small crowd that attended he might well have deduced it had overdosed!

Wellington v. Pakistanis

22–24 March 2000 at Basin Reserve, Wellington
Pakistanis 175 (Younis Khan 73, MDJ Walker 5 for 29) and 340 for 7 (Faisal Iqbal 82, Humayun Farhat 74, Misbah-ul-Haq 51)
Wellington 343 for 8 dec. (SJ Blackmore 74, CJ Nevin 67, GT Donaldson 60)
Match drawn

Pakistan took the belated opportunity to give their batsmen some quality practice, but they waited until the second innings of the match after Wellington had established a lead of 168. Faisal

Yousuf Youhana to display his quality strokeplay after a disastrous start to the innings.

Yousuf and Inzamam brought stability to the early innings recovery; Inzamam powerful and dominating, Yousuf more sedate but controlled and solid spending almost nine hours compiling his first Test double hundred. By the time Saqlain joined Yousuf at 304 for six the innings, and with it the match, had lapsed into the tedium that it had

Iqbal produced a classy innings and Humayun Farhat gave a hint of his attacking potential with a lusty knock of 74 from 61 balls to ensure that there was no disastrous defeat prior to the final Test. While the match ended in a draw, there were strong rumours that the rift within the Pakistan squad was coming to a head, with reports that veteran Ijaz Ahmed and coach Javed Miandad had not spoken to each other since Ijaz joined the tour.

THIRD TEST
27–30 March 2001 at WestpacTrust Park, Hamilton

Despite autumnal rains that threatened to wash out more than the one day lost in the deciding Test, New Zealand salvaged something from the season with an emphatic victory over Pakistan to square the series at 1–1. The innings and 185 run win in the third Test was the largest winning margin New Zealand has recorded in all its 46 Test victories, and it took just over two days of playing time to complete in 188 overs.

It was a triumph for New Zealand and for Craig McMillan, whose innings of 98 was one of the most exhilarating Test innings of the New Zealand summer, including a world record 26 from one over.

New Zealand captain Stephen Fleming's lack of success with the toss in previous matches had been costly, and winning it in the decider allowed his bowlers to have first use of a hard, well-grassed pitch with more bounce than the portable pitches used in the first two Tests.

While the seamers were rewarded with encouraging movement and bounce, it wasn't as pronounced as Pakistan's pitiful first innings of 104 from just 26.5 overs might suggest.

In fact Tuffey and Martin were both wayward early on, conceding 28 runs from their first five overs. When they assumed greater control and consistency the wickets started to fall at an alarming rate, aided by some rather cavalier strokeplay from the Pakistan top order. Younis Khan and Humayun Farhat ensured that they reached three figures with a 51-run stand for the sixth wicket in just nine overs.

New Zealand's opening pair of Matthew Bell and Mark Richardson soon showed there were few terrors in the pitch with a quality opening partnership of 181, which belied their lack of experience. They had shared only 18 Test matches between them prior to the Hamilton Test, but in five innings as an opening pair they had compiled four

Craig McMillan led New Zealand's dash for victory at Hamilton. He moved from 50 to 98 off only 17 balls, which included a world record 26 from one over.

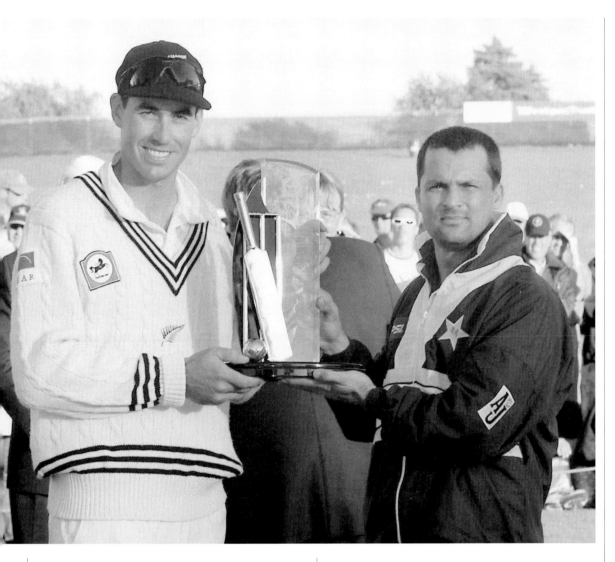

successive half-century partnerships and two of those exceeded one hundred. After such a magnificent start, Bell and Richardson gave the New Zealanders the springboard they needed to develop a winning position, although rain and bad light pushed their partnership into the third day. Both compiled their maiden Test hundreds, Bell from an impressive 153 balls with Richardson's coming from a more sedate 269 balls.

McMillan and Fleming's timing was perfect in recording their best partnership of the series, adding 147 in the two hours up to lunch, Fleming scoring 51 while McMillan's world record 26 runs came from an over by the hapless Younis Khan. McMillan was relatively slow through the first 50, in fact he was overtaken by his captain on the way to their 50s,

Honours shared: New Zealand's Stephen Fleming and Pakistan's Moin Khan, who was replaced as Pakistan's captain after a drawn series in which there were numerous reports of unrest in the visitors' dressing room.

but with some spectacular strokeplay he went from 50 to 98 in the space of just 17 balls. Just as McMillan seemed certain to reach his fifth Test century, he was caught by Waqar Younis who brilliantly grasped an overhead catch on the boundary that seemed headed for McMillan's fourth six of the innings.

Pakistan put up slightly more of a fight in the second innings that occupied 48.5 overs, but four wickets for Franklin helped New Zealand to settle the Test with a day to spare.

THIRD TEST – NEW ZEALAND v. PAKISTAN
27–30 March 2001 at WestpacTrust Park, Hamilton

PAKISTAN

	First innings			Second innings	
Imran Farhat	c Astle, b Martin	24		c McMillan, b Tuffey	1
Ijaz Ahmed	c Parore, b Martin	5		c Parore, b Franklin	17
Faisal Iqbal	c Bell, b Martin	0		c Bradburn, b Tuffey	5
Inzamam-ul-Haq (capt)	lbw b Martin	5		c Tuffey, b Franklin	20
Yousuf Youhana	c Parore, b Tuffey	0		c Parore, b Martin	16
Younis Khan	c Richardson, b Tuffey	36		c Astle, b Tuffey	4
*Humayan Farhat	c Parore, b Tuffey	28		c Bradburn, b Martin	26
Saqlain Mushtaq	run out (Franklin)	0		c Martin, b Franklin	14
Waqar Younis	c Fleming, b Franklin	0		c Parore, b McMillan	4
Fazl-e-Akbar	c Parore, b Tuffey	0		not out	0
Mohammad Akram	not out	1		c & b Franklin	4
	lb3, nb2	5		lb2, nb5	7
		104			**118**

	First innings				Second innings			
	O	M	R	W	O	M	R	W
Tuffey	10.5	2	39	4	19	5	38	3
Martin	10	3	52	4	15	2	48	2
Franklin	6	2	10	1	9.5	3	26	4
McMillan					5	3	2	1
Astle					1	0	2	–

Fall of Wickets
1-28, 2-28, 3-29, 4-34, 5-38, 6-89, 7-89, 8-91, 9-103
1-10, 2-20, 3-43, 4-54, 5-69, 6-71, 7-97, 8-114, 9-114

NEW ZEALAND

	First Innings	
MH Richardson	c Imran Farhat, b Fazl-e-Akbar	106
MD Bell	lbw b Waqar Younis	105
MS Sinclair	c Waqar Younis, b Fazl-e-Akbar	27
CD McMillan	c Waqar Younis, b Fazl-e-Akbar	98
SP Fleming (capt)	not out	51
NJ Astle		
*AC Parore		
GE Bradburn		
JEC Franklin		
DR Tuffey		
CS Martin		
	lb10, nb10	20
	(for 4 wickets dec.)	**407**

	First innings			
	O	M	R	W
Waqar Younis	31	2	98	1
Fazl-e-Akbar	27.2	6	85	3
Mohammad Akram	22	1	106	–
Saqlain Mushtaq	31	6	82	–
Younis Khan	1	0	26	–

Fall of Wickets
1-181, 2-239, 3-260, 4-407

Umpires: RS Dunne & DJ Harper
Toss: New Zealand
Test debut: Humayan Farhat (Pakistan)

New Zealand won by an innings and 185 runs

TEST MATCH AVERAGES
New Zealand v. Pakistan

NEW ZEALAND

Batting	M	Inns	NO	HS	Runs	Av	100	50	c/st
MS Sinclair	3	5	2	204*	325	108.33	1	1	1
AC Parore	3	3	2	46	78	78.00	–	–	16/-
MH Richardson	3	5	1	106	285	71.25	1	2	2
SP Fleming	3	4	1	86	174	58.00	–	2	5
MD Bell	3	5	0	105	248	49.60	1	1	1
CD McMillan	3	4	0	98	172	43.00	–	2	2
DR Tuffey	3	3	0	13	15	5.00	–	–	1
NJ Astle	3	3	0	6	7	2.33	–	–	3

Also batted: GE Bradburn (2 Tests) 0*, (2ct); CJ Drum (1 Test) 4 (1ct); JEC Franklin
(2 Tests) 0, 0 (1ct); CS Martin (3 Tests) 0, 0, 0 (2ct); (PJ Wiseman (1 Test) 9, 8 (2ct).

Bowling	Overs	Mds	Runs	Wkts	Av	Best	10m	5/inn
JEC Franklin	54.5	13	150	7	21.42	4-26	–	–
DR Tuffey	129.5	36	368	16	23.00	4-39	–	–
CS Martin	100	17	424	12	35.33	4-52	–	–

Also bowled: NJ Astle 52-21-83-0; GE Bradburn 42-10-124-1; CJ Drum 8-1-21-1;
CD McMillan 57-21-110-3; MH Richardson 9-0-16-1; PJ Wiseman 43-6-142-1.

PAKISTAN

Batting	M	Inns	NO	HS	Runs	Av	100	50	c/st
Younis Khan	3	5	1	149*	280	70.00	1	1	2
Yousuf Youhana	3	5	0	203	312	62.40	1	1	1
Inzamam-ul-Haq	2	3	0	130	155	51.66	1	–	–
Faisal Iqbal	3	5	1	63	162	40.50	–	2	1
Saqlain Mushtaq	3	5	1	101*	119	29.75	1	–	1
Imran Farhat	3	5	0	63	115	23.00	–	1	4
Ijaz Ahmed	2	3	0	17	33	11.00	–	–	–
Waqar Younis	3	4	0	12	20	5.00	–	–	2

Also batted: Fazl-e-Akbar (2 Tests) 0*, 0, 0*; Humayun Farhat (1 Test) 28, 26; Misbah-ul-Haq (1
Test) 28, 10; Mohammad Akram (1 Test) 1*, 4; Mohammad Sami (2 Tests) 0*; Moin Khan (2 Tests)
47, 28 (3ct); Mushtaq Ahmed (1 Test) 19; Salim Elahi (1 Test) 24, 7.

Bowling	Overs	Mds	Runs	Wkts	Av	Best	10m	5/inn
Saqlain Mushtaq	148.4	37	332	11	30.18	4-24	–	–
Mohammad Sami	93.4	22	245	8	30.62	5-36	–	1
Fazl-e-Akbar	66.2	12	198	6	33.00	3-85	–	–
Waqar Younis	106	19	305	6	50.83	3-114	–	–

Also bowled: Faisal Iqbal 1-0-7-0; Mohammad Akram 22-1-106-0; Mushtaq Ahmed 31-10-83-1;
Younis Khan 28-7-88-1; Yousuf Youhana 1-0-3-0.

NEW ZEALAND DOMESTIC FIRST-CLASS COMPETITION

There's nothing like the prod of some good-natured ridicule to produce the best in an under-performing team. The tag of 'chokers' or 'bridesmaids' had not sat comfortably with the Wellington side since they last won the domestic first-class title, the Shell Trophy, in the 1989–90 season.

Despite boasting sides in the interim that included a number of well-performed international players, Wellington had failed to deliver either of the major trophies to the cabinet, a cause for concern in the capital. So it came as a major surprise that a team of relative no-names should secure the prestigious title when it was least expected.

New Zealand Cricket acceded to the wishes of the players and many officials by extending the first-class season to two full rounds to give it greater meaning and significance. The argument had been that too much one-day cricket, and not enough of the first-class game, had lessened both the player depth and the quality of first-class cricket.

While that appeared to have little effect on the public during the 2000–01 season, with little signs of an increase in the number of spectators, there were encouraging signs that the first-class game had renewed the relevance for the players.

Wellington had to wait until the second last day of the ten-round competition to confirm the title by virtue of a first-innings win over Northern Districts, the only side likely to head them. Even in that game the maturity that had developed in the Wellington side was evident as they knocked off the substantial target of 316 to complete their victory.

Much of the credit for Wellington's success should go to opening batsman Matthew Bell, who not only finished the series as second-top run-scorer with 844 runs including five centuries, but who also had the added burden of captaincy.

At 23, and already a Test match reject, Bell proved to be a determined leader who inspired his young side with superb individual performances. He revealed at the end of the season that he had deliberately pushed himself forward as captain in the belief that it would be good for his personal game and would help him to regain the Test spot he had lost after the 1999 tour of India.

Bell and former Aucklander Richard Jones, who was third behind Bell and Central Districts English professional, Ben Smith, in the run stakes, developed a formidable opening partnership, which allowed Wellington to dominate the majority of their matches.

Smith displayed all his professional class in amassing 939 runs at 58.68 from 17 innings including two centuries and seven fifties that helped to prop up a weak and inexperienced Central side.

The batting success of top players, who took a full or limited part in the Shell Trophy, underlined the success of the competition. Ten players averaged 50 or more – of those Mathew Sinclair, Mark Richardson and Bell were in the Test team by the end of the summer and former Test players, Chris Harris, Roger Twose and Craig Spearman were in the top ten.

With some Test players taking only a limited part in the domestic season, a number of new bowlers came to the fore, although worryingly for New Zealand cricket's future, no obvious successor to Daniel Vettori emerged from the spin bowling ranks.

Newcomer Ian O'Brien's 41 wickets for Wellington topped the season list, and, at 17.87 per wicket marked him as a new-ball bowler of considerable promise. How he performs in a second full season will gauge his future potential.

Central District seamer, Brent Hefford, who was initially only included in the one-day side, was belatedly picked by his provincial selectors and went on to prove that they had made the right decision. Big and strong and with the ability to extract awkward bounce, Hefford was such a success in that competition that he had an irresistible claim to the new-ball role.

Spearman, Smith and aggressive opener, David Kelly, were the consistent run scorers for Central Districts, the defending champions, but their success in the Shell Cup one-day final was the major focus of their season.

Chris Gaffaney, Craig Cumming and Test players Mark Richardson and Matt Horne all scored over 500 runs for Otago, who, after climbing to second place midway through the competition, slumped in the second half.

A former left-arm spinner, Richardson's form through an incredible 12 months earned him New Zealand's Cricketer of the Year award. A passion for playing big innings, coupled with commendable patience and a sound technique, helped Richardson accrue 2,672 first-class runs at an average of 66.8.

Otago and second-placed Northern Districts featured in the season's most bizarre and controversial match. In an effort to hasten an outright result after serious rain interruptions, Otago, with first-innings points opted to use part-time bowlers delivering deliberate full tosses, half volleys and long hops while the fielders made no serious attempt to prevent boundaries. The outcome was 22 overs and four balls in 76 minutes in which Northern scored 285 for six declared.

Both sides defended their actions by saying they were trying to achieve a positive result, although the match ended in a draw. Cricket officials did not hide their displeasure at the farcical nature of the game, however, although they took no action apart from saying that they would actively discourage such an approach in the first-class competition.

Auckland made the strongest charge for the title in the latter part of the season, moving from fifth to third with three outright results in five games.

It was a case of getting some stability in their batting and consistency and continuity in their selection. Pace bowler Kyle Mills made an impact as a potential all-rounder as his figures with the bat were better than those with the ball as he amassed 606 runs while taking only 14 wickets.

Mills, fellow paceman Chris Drum and all-rounders Tama Canning and Andre Adams hit form a little too late for Auckland to maintain their threat to Wellington.

Canterbury were the major disappointment, unable to register an outright win from ten games, taking first-innings points in only three, and finishing a distant last for the second successive year.

In Gary Stead and Jarrod Englefield they had consistent run scorers at the top of the order, but struggled to be the force they have been in previous years.

Matthew Bell, who took on the burden of captaincy in a bid to regain his Test place, flourished under the pressure and Wellington thrived under his command.

NEW ZEALAND DOMESTIC ONE-DAY COMPETITION

Central Districts produced one of the biggest upsets in recent seasons by swapping the Shell Trophy of the previous season for the one-day Shell Cup.

It might have been because of the decline in Canterbury cricket, the influence of the wily Dipak Patel, or simply the enthusiasm and attention to the basics of one-day cricket by an unfancied team that enabled Central to create the season's second surprise title winner.

Canterbury had taken ownership of the Shell Cup, and winning seven titles in nine years made them instant favourites even before the competition started. This preference was confirmed when they reached the best-of-three finals as the top qualifiers.

They were on target to continue their dynasty after winning the first final at Central's home ground, McLean Park, Napier. One-day specialist Chris Harris had led the recovery after a poor start. At 71 for six, Harris found Carl Anderson as a useful ally as they added 67 for the seventh wicket, but they were still defending a modest total of 174.

Central could only manage 161, and, trailing 1–0, they went to Christchurch for a double header with few believing they could win two successive matches away from home. However, the Central players had faith in their ability to topple the champions.

In what turned out to be a low scoring final series, Central Districts successfully defended their total of 173 that had been reached after Glen Sulzberger and Andrew Schwass added 49 in 11.4 overs at the end of the innings.

Sulzberger and the rapidly developing Brent Hefford then took three wickets apiece as Canterbury were dismissed for 128.

To beat Canterbury once away from home was a major upset, but to achieve it a second time was unheard of in the history of Cup final matches.

The title was secured with class and style as Mathew Sinclair, Craig Spearman and Ben Smith punished Canterbury's attack to reach the winning target of 176 in 38 overs.

The three-match final highlighted the many shortcomings in New Zealand's one-day game. The national side had a negative win/loss ratio and while scores in excess of 250 have become the benchmark for success, too many games had been decided by ball dominating bat rather than the other way round.

New Zealand's administrators signalled their concern at the end of the season – outgoing Chief Executive, Chris Doig, highlighted inconsistent form by batsmen and inadequate venues as contributing factors.

Poor pitches have often been a complaint from the leading players, and the season's results confirmed the argument, but the desire to take one-day cricket to the holiday public and the ultimate financial return won out over the use of the best venues.

While the final may have produced some close, dramatic finishes, it was seldom the case through the previous ten rounds, but the end of Canterbury's ten-year dominance offered up another side, in Central Districts, with the potential to assume that supremacy.

FIRST-CLASS AVERAGES

BATTING

	M	Inns	NO	HS	Runs	Av	100	50
KD Mills	8	13	6	117*	606	86.57	1	6
MS Sinclair	8	13	3	204*	724	72.40	2	3
MH Richardson	11	19	2	166	1035	60.88	2	8
RG Twose	4	6	1	108	298	59.60	1	2
BF Smith	10	17	1	168	939	58.68	2	7
CD McMillan	4	6	0	142	324	54.00	1	2
MD Bell	13	21	0	134	1092	52.00	6	3
CM Spearman	7	12	0	130	611	50.91	1	5
SP Fleming	4	6	1	86	251	50.20	-	3
Yousuf Youhana	4	7	0	203	348	49.71	1	1
GR Stead	12	20	2	121*	875	48.61	3	5
Younis Khan	5	9	1	149*	383	47.87	1	2
GP Sulzberger	8	12	1	103	525	47.72	1	4
RA Jones	12	19	0	188	860	45.26	3	3
CD Cumming	10	19	5	125*	626	44.71	2	2
NJ Astle	5	6	1	141	216	43.20	1	1
GJ Hopkins	11	19	7	100*	517	43.08	1	3
CJ Nevin	12	17	4	99	554	42.61	-	4
Faisal Iqbal	4	7	1	82	255	42.50	-	3
MW Douglas	10	16	2	134	583	41.64	2	1
DP Kelly	10	18	2	212*	617	38.56	1	3
JI Engelfield	10	19	0	172	724	38.10	2	3
SB Doull	9	10	1	59	342	38.00	-	2
MG Croy	8	13	5	78	301	37.62	-	1
MN Hart	8	13	2	80	411	37.36	-	4
MDJ Walker	8	10	2	98	289	36.12	-	2
CB Gaffaney	11	18	3	99	541	36.06	-	6
MJ Horne	11	20	2	110	642	35.66	2	4
SJ Blackmore	8	13	1	86*	426	35.50	-	3
WA Wisneski	5	6	1	58*	175	35.00	-	1
AJ Penn	8	10	5	53*	165	33.00	-	1
GE Bradburn	12	18	3	104	494	32.93	1	3
NR Parlane	5	9	1	89	263	32.87	-	2
TG McIntosh	10	18	1	182	553	32.52	2	2
AJ Hore	9	14	1	100	408	31.38	1	2
RM Frew	10	20	1	111	593	31.21	1	4
L Vincent	7	10	0	78	303	30.30	-	3
DJ Nash	10	16	1	100	452	30.13	1	2
GT Donaldson	9	15	2	66	379	29.15	-	4
CJ Anderson	9	16	2	65	403	28.78	-	4
AJ Redmond	9	14	1	80	368	28.30	-	1
RT King	10	18	0	98	498	27.66	-	3
SR Mather	5	8	0	107	214	26.75	1	-
PJ Wiseman	10	10	3	75*	186	26.57	-	1
MA Sigley	7	10	3	71*	184	26.28	-	1
JAF Yovich	10	17	5	43	314	26.16	-	-
ME Parlane	8	14	0	105	366	26.14	1	1
JPD Oram	6	7	0	88	181	25.85	-	1
BA Pocock	10	18	1	123	432	25.41	1	1
BGK Walker	8	12	4	69*	199	24.87	-	1
AR Adams	8	14	0	62	339	24.21	-	2
CJ Drum	12	15	7	60*	193	24.12	-	1
MHW Papps	8	15	1	68	335	23.92	-	1
Humayan Farhat	3	6	0	74	141	23.50	-	1
BP Martin	9	12	5	51	164	23.42	-	1
HJH Marshall	7	13	0	83	304	23.38	-	1
Saqlain Mushtaq	4	7	1	101*	137	22.83	1	-
Imran Farhat	5	9	0	63	203	22.55	-	2
TK Canning	8	12	1	72	244	22.18	-	1
GW Aldridge	7	9	3	37	133	22.16	-	-
HTG James	4	8	1	65*	152	21.71	-	1
MD Bailey	10	17	1	76	340	21.25	-	1
MN McKenzie	6	11	0	76	228	20.72	-	2
CR Pryor	10	12	1	61	209	19.00	-	1
JS Patel	11	9	2	58*	133	19.00	-	1
MR Jefferson	7	8	1	71*	128	18.28	-	1
JAH Marshall	10	18	0	29	287	15.94	-	-
JM Aiken	7	12	0	85	185	15.41	-	1
RG Hart	10	13	3	27	154	15.40	-	-
Salim Elahi	3	6	0	24	89	14.83	-	-
NL McCullum	4	5	0	38	74	14.80	-	-
SJ Cunis	7	13	3	39	143	14.30	-	-

FIRST-CLASS AVERAGES

BATTING

	M	Inns	NO	HS	Runs	Av	100	50
SE Bond	7	8	1	66*	87	12.42	-	1
BB McCullum	3	6	0	45	66	11.00	-	-
WC McSkimming	7	9	2	27	74	10.57	-	-
Mushtaq Ahmed	3	5	0	20	52	10.40	-	-

Qualification: 5 completed innings, average 10.00

BOWLING

	Overs	Mds	Runs	Wkts	Av	Best	10m	5/inn
BE Hefford	202.5	74	438	24	18.25	5-50	-	1
CJ Drum	342.5	99	888	48	18.50	5-65	-	1
DR Tuffey	248.5	78	630	34	18.52	7-12	1	2
IE O'Brien	319.1	81	806	41	19.65	6-55	-	3
JEC Franklin	204.5	40	623	31	20.09	5-39	-	1
AM Schwass	169	45	457	22	20.77	5-53	-	2
MDJ Walker	193.4	69	387	18	21.50	5-29	-	1
TK Canning	243.5	75	585	27	21.66	4-36	-	-
WC McSkimming	226.5	75	585	26	22.50	6-39	-	1
CR Pryor	255.1	66	684	19	23.58	5-28	-	2
CD Cumming	106.2	29	308	13	23.69	3-31	-	-
AR Adams	216.4	52	626	26	24.07	4-12	-	-
AJ Penn	291.5	79	794	32	24.81	4-28	-	-
MR Gillespie	126.5	38	380	14	27.14	4-34	-	-
DG Sewell	283.4	82	799	29	27.55	6-70	-	1
JAF Yovich	332.4	95	938	34	27.58	7-64	-	1
KD Mills	169	36	442	16	27.62	4-57	-	-
MR Jefferson	192.1	49	498	18	27.66	4-84	-	-
SE Bond	187.4	52	536	19	28.21	5-51	-	1
GL West	146	32	407	14	29.07	4-62	-	-
SJ Cunis	217.4	65	556	19	29.26	5-59	-	2
EP Thompson	214.4	36	658	22	29.90	4-83	-	-
GE Bradburn	342.1	107	781	25	31.24	5-114	-	1
BE Scott	116	32	348	11	31.63	6-48	-	1
CS Martin	196.5	46	689	21	32.80	5-71	-	1
BGK Walker	217.2	62	599	17	35.23	5-71	-	1
MJ Mason	214.1	59	568	16	35.50	5-44	-	2
MJ Haslam	178.5	56	371	10	37.10	3-29	-	-
SB Doull	200.2	52	533	14	38.07	3-25	-	-
GW Aldridge	184.1	41	622	16	38.87	5-50	-	1
CJ Anderson	260	79	696	16	43.50	4-97	-	-
JS Patel	329.2	82	942	20	47.10	5-48	-	1
BP Martin	294.2	84	719	15	47.93	5-104	-	1
AJ Redmond	222.4	51	692	14	49.42	4-114	-	-
PJ Wiseman	419.5	111	992	20	49.60	4-102	-	-
GP Sulzberger	283.3	84	841	16	52.56	4-79	-	-

Qualification: 10 wickets in 8 innings

The following bowlers took 10 wickets in fewer than 8 innings:-

	Overs	Mds	Runs	Wkts	Av	Best	10m	5/inn
RG Morgan	79	29	203	11	18.45	5-44	-	1
KR O'Dowda	82	11	276	12	23.00	4-67	-	-
Saqlain Mushtaq	161.4	41	377	15	25.13	4-24	-	-
Mohammad Sami	112.4	24	318	10	31.80	5-36	-	1
TR Anderson	123.3	24	422	13	32.46	6-37	-	1
WA Wisneski	153	30	491	12	40.91	7-151	-	1
RD Burson	127.4	21	464	10	46.40	4-78	-	-

FIELDING

50 – CJ Nevin; 33 – L Vincent; 26 – MG Croy (25ct,1st); GJ Hopkins (24ct,2st); 21 – AC Parore, MA Sigley (20ct,1st); 18 – RG Hart; 15 – GE Bradburn; 14 – RA Jones; 12 – JAH Marshall; 11 – MD Bailey, MJ Horne, CM Spearman, RA Young; 10 – AJ Hore, DP Kelly, RT King, CR Pryor, GP Sulzberger

Qualification: 10 catches or more

SOUTH AFRICA

New Zealand in South Africa
Sri Lanka in South Africa
South Africa Domestic First-Class Season
South Africa Domestic One-Day Season
First-Class Averages

NEW ZEALAND IN SOUTH AFRICA
By Telford Vice and Marcus Prior

ONE-DAY INTERNATIONALS
By Marcus Prior

When New Zealand arrived in South Africa a few days after winning the ICC Knock-Out Trophy in Nairobi, few would have predicted the sorry showing which saw them fail genuinely to make the hosts struggle in all but two of six one-day internationals. South Africa won the series 5–0, with one washout.

In Kenya, the Black Caps had looked inspired, in South Africa they were quite the reverse. It was almost as if they conceded their inferiority before the series was won and lost. Yes, they had injury problems, but this New Zealand side had won a reputation for a backs-to-the-wall, 'we'll-fight-our-way-out-of-this-together' spirit that seemed on this occasion to be absent.

Match one in Potchefstroom was an ominous warning of what was to come. The tourists were surely the more relieved when a cataclysmic downpour brought South Africa's rollicking innings to a halt. At that stage they were 191 for two and Nicky Boje had just posted his maiden one-day international hundred off just 89 balls.

New Zealand's batsmen were given a chance to familiarize themselves with local conditions in match two at Benoni, but could manage only 194 for eight with Roger Telemachus taking one for 16 from his ten overs.

Although South Africa suffered the odd wobble in reply, Gary Kirsten (57) and Boje (64) saw them home with 20 balls to spare.

The sight of Boje at the crease must have been painful enough for the Kiwis by match three at Centurion, but it was only to get worse. The young left-hander struck his second hundred in three matches (129) as South Africa amassed a colossal 324 for four, which also included 94 from Kirsten.

After a brief thunderstorm the New Zealand target was adjusted to 304 off 43 overs, but they were bowled out for 189 with almost ten overs remaining, Telemachus picking up three wickets.

The series was decided when South Africa won match four in Kimberley after successfully chasing 288 on a flat wicket. Roger Twose (89), Stephen

Fleming (85) and Chris Nevin (68) looked to have given the visitors a decent chance, but a South African-record second-wicket stand of 172 between Kirsten (101) and Jacques Kallis (93) put the home side in the hunt.

With 32 needed off the last four overs, Boje – who else? – and Mark Boucher smashed South Africa to victory with an over to spare.

The rain did its best to stop the South African momentum in Durban, but Lance Klusener's 41 off 18 balls saw the home side to their revised target of 153 with two overs to spare – with Klusener himself hitting the winning runs with his third six.

The final humiliation was reserved for match six in Cape Town as New Zealand posted 256 for nine – a record score at Newlands – and were still

Nicky Boje, the young South African all-rounder, hammered two centuries in three matches as New Zealand were swamped in the one-day series. Boje was Man of the Match on three occasions.

Previous page: Allan Donald is congratulated during South Africa's 5–1 success in the one-day series against the West Indies. All in all it was a successful year for the Springboks.

Gary Kirsten who, with Jacques Kallis, added a record 172 for the second wicket at Kimberley.

Match Two
22 October 2000 at Willowmoore Park, Benoni
New Zealand 194 for 8 (50 overs) (NJ Astle 58)
South Africa 197 for 4 (46.4 overs) (N Boje 64, G Kirsten 57)
South Africa won by six wickets
Man of the Match: N Boje

Match Three
25 October 2000 at Centurion Park, Centurion (floodlit)
South Africa 324 for 4 (50 overs) (N Boje 129, G Kirsten 94)
New Zealand 189 (33.4 overs)
South Africa won by 115 runs
Man of the Match: N Boje

Wearing his trademark 69, Lance Klusener bludgeoned the required eight runs to win from the last two balls of the innings in the final match of the series in Cape Town.

overhauled. And it was the manner of the defeat that left Kiwi captain Fleming all but speechless at the post-match presentation.

Roger Twose struck a superb maiden one-day century and, with good support from the half-fit Chris Cairns (84), looked to have put the tourists in control.

That impression was only reinforced when South Africa were reduced to 65 for four, but Boucher (46) and Jonty Rhodes (69) steadied things and with 11 needed off the final over from Shane O'Connor and eight runs from the last two balls, Klusener (59) thumped them both to the boundary. Game, set and match.

Match One
20 October 2000 at North West Stadium, Potchefstroom (floodlit)
South Africa 191 for 2 (38 overs) (N Boje 105*, HH Dippenaar 57)
New Zealand did not bat
Match abandoned

Match Four

28 October 2000 at De Beers Diamond Oval, Kimberley
New Zealand 287 for 6 (50 overs) (RG Twose 90, SP Fleming 85, CJ Nevin 68)
South Africa 289 for 5 (48.5 overs) (G Kirsten 101, JH Kallis 93)
South Africa won by five wickets
Man of the Match: G Kirsten

Match Five

1 November 2000 at Kingsmead, Durban (floodlit)
New Zealand 114 for 5 (32.4 overs)
South Africa 158 for 4 (30.3 overs) (JH Kallis 50*)
South Africa won by six wickets (DL Method: South Africa target 153 runs from 32 overs)
Man of the Match: JH Kallis

Match Six

4 November 2000 at Newlands, Cape Town
New Zealand 256 for 9 (50 overs) (RG Twose 103, CL Cairns 84)
South Africa 258 for 7 (50 overs) (JN Rhodes 69, L Klusener 59*)
South Africa won by three wickets
Man of the Match: L Klusener
Man of the Series: N Boje

FIRST TEST

17–21 November 2000 at Goodyear Park, Bloemfontein
By Telford Vice

Allan Donald's 300th Test wicket and career-best performances by Jacques Kallis and Makhaya Ntini added to the lustre of South Africa's victory. The match ended midway through the final session on the fifth day when South Africa, needing 101 to win, reached 103 for five.

South Africa had declared their first innings on 471 for nine, to which New Zealand replied with 229. The visitors then followed-on and were dismissed for 342.

Underpinned by Kallis' 153 not out, South Africa scored 270 for three before bad light forced the close 35 minutes early on the first day. It was Kallis' seventh Test century, and it improved on his previous highest score, the undefeated 148 he made against the same opponents in Christchurch in 1998–99.

Shaun Pollock won the toss and elected to bat, but without a run on the board Boeta Dippenaar edged Shayne O'Connor's second ball of the match low to second slip. However, the limited and

---

FIRST TEST – SOUTH AFRICA v. NEW ZEALAND

17–21 November 2000 at Goodyear Park, Bloemfontein

SOUTH AFRICA

	First innings		Second innings	
G Kirsten	c Astle, b O'Connor	0	(2) lbw b O'Connor	1
HH Dippenaar	c Astle, b Martin	31	(1) c Parore, b Tuffey	27
JH Kallis	c Parore, b O'Connor	160	lbw b Martin	13
DJ Cullinan	b Walker	29	lbw b Tuffey	22
ND McKenzie	c Parore, b Martin	55	not out	13
*MV Boucher	lbw b Walker	76	(7) not out	22
L Klusener	b O'Connor	9	(6) c McMillan, b Tuffey	4
N Boje	c Tuffey, b Astle	43		
SM Pollock (capt)	c Sinclair, b Martin	25		
AA Donald	not out	21		
M Ntini				
	b5, lb7, nb10	22	nb1	1
	(for 9 wickets dec.)	471	(for 5 wickets)	103

	First innings				Second innings			
	O	M	R	W	O	M	R	W
O'Connor	30	4	87	3	7	0	28	1
Tuffey	26	6	96	–	8	1	38	3
Martin	22.1	4	89	3	5	3	18	1
Walker	27	4	92	2	6.3	2	19	–
Astle	24	5	57	1				
McMillan	13	2	38	–				

Fall of Wickets
1-0, 2-97, 3-164, 4-279, 5-304, 6-330, 7-409, 8-429, 9-471
1-3, 2-16, 3-55, 4-69, 5-75

NEW ZEALAND

	First innings		Second innings	
MH Richardson	b Donald	23	lbw b Donald	77
CM Spearman	c Klusener, b Pollock	23	c McKenzie, b Ntini	15
MS Sinclair	c Cullinan, b Pollock	1	c Klusener, b Donald	20
SP Fleming (capt)	b Boje	57	c Kirsten, b Donald	99
NJ Astle	c Kallis, b Ntini	37	b Ntini	8
CD McMillan	c Boucher, b Donald	16	c Kirsten, b Kallis	78
*AC Parore	lbw b Pollock	11	(8) c Kallis, b Ntini	12
BGK Walker	not out	27	(7) c Boucher, b Ntini	10
DR Tuffey	b Pollock	0	b Ntini	6
SB O'Connor	lbw b Donald	15	b Ntini	0
CS Martin	c Boucher, b Kallis	7	not out	0
	b1, lb7, w2, nb2	12	b2, lb10, w1, nb4	17
		229		342

	First innings				Second innings			
	O	M	R	W	O	M	R	W
Donald	21	4	69	3	28	14	43	3
Pollock	22	10	37	4	25	11	47	–
Ntini	14	4	48	1	31.4	12	66	6
Kallis	13	5	30	1	23	4	88	1
Boje	16	4	35	1	40	14	61	–
Klusener	3	2	2	–	10	3	25	–

Fall of Wickets
1-28, 2-29, 3-72, 4-151, 5-153, 6-176, 7-183, 8-185, 9-213
1-33, 2-93, 3-145, 4-175, 5-247, 6-285, 7-325, 8-340, 9-341

Umpires: DL Orchard & AV Jayakaprash
Toss: South Africa
Test debuts: CS Martin and BGK Walker (New Zealand)

South Africa won by five wickets

inexperienced New Zealand attack struggled to settle and Kallis and Gary Kirsten were able to see off the new ball under little pressure, although attacking shots were few.

They shared a stand of 97 runs for the second wicket before Kirsten drove at what became the last ball before lunch from debutant Chris Martin and edged it to Nathan Astle at second slip. Kallis and Cullinan then added 67 runs for the third wicket

Makhaya Ntini has had his fair share of personal problems in the past, but he took a career best six for 66 to condemn New Zealand to defeat in the first Test at Bloemfontein.

before Cullinan dragged a wide delivery from Brooke Walker, the first specialist leg-spinner to bowl in a Test for New Zealand in 28 years, onto his stumps.

Overnight rain delayed the start of the second day's play by 90 minutes, and, 25 minutes after the start, Kallis lunged forward defensively to O'Connor and was caught behind for 160. He was at the crease for 15 minutes short of six hours, faced 289 balls and hit 26 fours. That ended a partnership of 115, and his partner, Neil McKenzie, was then caught behind off Martin three balls before lunch – his maiden half-century, 55, the product of just more

Jacques Kallis in action at Bloemfontein, where he scored 160 in South Africa's imposing first-innings total of 471 for nine.

than three hours at the wicket.

Mark Boucher and Nicky Boje shared an aggressive partnership of 79 for the seventh wicket, which ended 30 minutes before tea when Boje slashed Nathan Astle to mid-on. Fifteen minutes later, Boucher attempted to sweep Walker and was trapped in front for 76, an innings of close on three hours.

Pollock declared at the fall of his own wicket, caught in the gully off Martin, and the tourists were left to face 29 overs before the close. They were 54 for two when bad light ended proceedings 8.4 overs early.

The innings ended at tea on the third day with New Zealand dismissed 43 runs shy of avoiding the follow-on. Stephen Fleming and Astle added 79 runs for the fourth wicket, a fluent partnership that ended when Boje bowled Fleming through the gate for a two-and-half hour 57, with his fifth delivery of the match.

However, New Zealand struggled to put together any other meaningful partnerships as Pollock, who took four for 37, and Donald, with three for 69, bowled with purpose and were well supported by the rest of the attack.

Donald became the first South African, and the 15th cricketer in the history of the game, to take 300 Test wickets when he trapped O'Connor leg before for his highest Test score of 15. An armoured car on the boundary boomed news of the feat far beyond Bloemfontein.

Following-on, Mark Richardson scored a defiant 50 not out as New Zealand reached the close, brought forward by 2.4 overs by poor light, on 82 for one – still 160 runs short of avoiding an innings defeat.

The slow-but-steady second-wicket stand grew to 60 before, in the seventh over of the fourth day, Mathew Sinclair was brilliantly caught, one-handed, by

Lance Klusener in the gully off the bowling of Donald.

Richardson and Fleming took New Zealand to lunch on 145 for two, and seven balls into the second session the partnership was ended at 52 when Richardson was trapped in front by a yorker from Donald for 77 after spending more than four hours at the wicket.

Fleming was at the crease for four-and-a-half hours, during which time he had shared 72 runs with Craig McMillan for the fifth wicket and had nursed his team into a five-run advantage, before he fended a vicious bouncer from Donald to Kirsten at gully to be dismissed for 99. It was the third time that Fleming, who was hoping to score his third Test century, had been dismissed in the 90s in 25 Tests. He was the sixth captain to be out for 99 in a Test, three of whom – England's Mike Atherton and Salim Malik of Pakistan were the others – had fallen to South Africa since the country's readmission to Test cricket in 1992.

Bad light hastened the close of play by six overs, which came with New Zealand on 260 for five, for an overall lead of 18. They were dismissed in the seventh over after lunch on the final day with the tireless Ntini maintaining a relentless line and length and taking six for 66.

The sixth wicket fell in the 17th over of the day when Walker slashed at a wide delivery from Ntini and was caught behind. An hour later, South Africa claimed the key wicket of McMillan when he drove uppishly at a slower ball from Kallis and was caught at mid-on for a 78 that was four-and-a-half hours in the making.

Ntini needed 16 deliveries after lunch, taken at 332 for seven, to end the innings by inducing Daryl Tuffey to play on, having Adam Parore caught at second slip with a peach of an away-swinger, and bowling O'Connor, who offered no stroke.

South Africa's victory chase started poorly when Kirsten was out leg-before to O'Connor in the third over, followed in the eighth over by Kallis who suffered a similar fate at the hands of Martin. Dippenaar and Cullinan put on 39 before Dippenaar was caught behind off Tuffey for a bright 27 that included five fours.

Tea was taken at 63 for three, and in the second over of the final session Cullinan was trapped in front by Tuffey for 22. In his next over, Tuffey had Klusener caught at deep square leg.

However, McKenzie and Boucher finished the job with an unbroken stand of 28. Boucher swept Walker for three consecutive fours to end the match.

SECOND TEST
30 November–4 December 2000 at Crusaders Ground, St George's Park, Port Elizabeth
By Marcus Prior

The home side recorded a resounding win which confirmed their superiority over the New Zealanders and decided the series in their favour, the victory giving them an unassailable 2–0 lead in the three-match series.

St George's Park was also the stage for the latest young South African to come of age in the Test arena. After Makhaya Ntini's match-winning six for 66 in the New Zealand second innings of the first Test in Bloemfontein, it was batsman Neil McKenzie's turn to play his hand, and he did so with a maiden century.

McKenzie's first-innings hundred was a taste of the qualities that had made him such a highly rated player on the South African domestic scene. With his fabled superstitions left (almost) entirely in the pavilion, the 25 year old drove exquisitely through the offside and was even more punishing with his trademark pulls cracked to the midwicket fence.

Neil's father, Kevin, was a feature of the Transvaal 'Mean Machine' which dominated South African cricket from the late 1970s well into the 1980s. He, too, was famous for the relish he took in dispatching the short delivery, and his son is considered very much a chip off the old block.

After being put into bat by Shaun Pollock, the New Zealand first innings effort was dominated by a fine 150 from Mathew Sinclair, the first time the unorthodox right-hander had reached three figures since scoring 214 on his debut against the West Indies in Wellington almost a year previously. Even his captain, Stephen Fleming, admitted afterwards that Sinclair had thrown in a few unusual strokes, but a magnificent eye and the patience to wait for the bad ball and then punish it more than compensated for Sinclair's uncommon lack of footwork.

With such a large contribution at the top of the order, the New Zealanders might well have been expected to post a more imposing first-innings total than their 298. That they came up short was largely because Sinclair was a man alone, watching wickets fall around him as he ploughed his own furrow.

Only Craig McMillan (39) and another patient and mature innings at number nine from Shane O'Connor (20) were able to partner him for any length of time, as the South African bowlers maintained a disciplined line and length.

SECOND TEST – SOUTH AFRICA v. NEW ZEALAND
30 November–4 December 2000 at St George's Park, Port Elizabeth

NEW ZEALAND

	First innings			Second innings		
MH Richardson	b Ntini	26		c Boucher, b Pollock	60	
CM Spearman	c Kirsten, b Donald	16		lbw b Donald	0	
MS Sinclair	c Kirsten, b Donald	150		lbw b Boje	17	
SP Fleming (capt)	c & b Pollock	14		c Cullinan, b Boje	8	
NJ Astle	lbw b Pollock	2		c Boucher, b Ntini	18	
CD McMillan	c Ntini, b Pollock	39		lbw b Pollock	0	
*AC Parore	c Boucher, b Donald	2		c Kirsten, b Ntini	5	
BGK Walker	c Cullinan, b Pollock	3		lbw b Klusener	19	
SB O'Connor	b Kallis	20		b Klusener	8	
KP Walmsley	c Cullinan, b Donald	5		lbw b Klusener	0	
CS Martin	not out	5		not out	0	
	b4, lb5, w2, nb5	16		b6, lb3, nb4	13	
		298			**148**	

	First innings				Second innings			
	O	M	R	W	O	M	R	W
Donald	26.3	2	69	4	7	1	16	1
Pollock	32	15	64	4	15	4	44	2
Kallis	21	8	44	1	7	2	17	-
Ntini	22	7	59	1	16	6	24	2
Klusener	6	2	8	-	9.3	5	8	3
Boje	19	5	45	-	15	2	30	2

Fall of Wickets
1-43, 2-55, 3-95, 4-101, 5-172, 6-194, 7-203, 8-276, 9-291
1-4, 2-54, 3-64, 4-111, 5-111, 6-115, 7-122, 8-147, 9-147

SOUTH AFRICA

	First innings			Second innings		
G Kirsten	c Parore, b Walmsley	49		(2) not out	47	
HH Dippenaar	lbw b Martin	35		(1) lbw b O'Connor	0	
JH Kallis	c Parore, b Astle	12		c O'Connor, b Martin	23	
DJ Cullinan	b Walker	33		b Walmsley	11	
SM Pollock (capt)	c Spearman, b Martin	33				
ND McKenzie	c Spearman, b McMillan	120		(5) not out	7	
*MV Boucher	b O'Connor	0				
L Klusener	c Parore, b Martin	6				
N Boje	c Parore, b O'Connor	51				
AA Donald	lbw b Martin	9				
M Ntini	not out	0				
	b7, lb4, w2	13		lb1	1	
		361		(for 3 wickets)	**89**	

	First innings				Second innings			
	O	M	R	W	O	M	R	W
O'Connor	26.4	8	68	2	8	4	9	1
Martin	29	8	104	4	12	3	32	1
Walmsley	13	2	40	1	5	2	7	1
Walker	23	5	61	1	7.1	1	32	-
Astle	36	18	46	1	2	0	8	-
McMillan	17	6	31	1				

Fall of Wickets
1-81, 2-96, 3-114, 4-151, 5-181, 6-184, 7-209, 8-345, 9-361
1-4, 2-53, 3-71

Umpires: RE Koertzen & ID Robinson
Toss: South Africa
Test debuts: nil

South Africa won by seven wickets

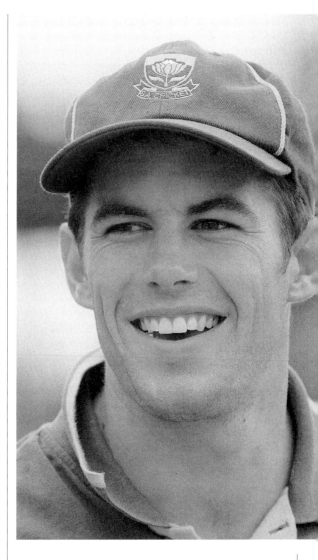

Neil McKenzie followed his half century at Bloemfontein with 120 at Port Elizabeth. He and Boje added a crucial 136 for the eighth wicket.

McMillan's demise was one of the more memorable of the South African summer. The gutsy right-hander, never short of a word or two for the opposition, but more often than not with a wicked smile on his face, was the victim of one of the finest catches ever seen at St George's Park.

Loving the hook and pull as he does, McMillan tried to get after a short delivery from Pollock. His top edge soared high into the ever-blue Port Elizabeth sky, and, after an initial misjudgement and a late 30-metre sprint, Makhaya Ntini threw himself full-length to scoop the ball cleanly only inches from the turf. It was the kind of catch only a true athlete could take, and there is no fitter player in South African cricket.

Pollock finished with four wickets, three of them coming lower down the order after he had bowled well enough to make inroads much earlier in the innings. There were four wickets for Allan Donald as well, fresh from taking his 300th in the first Test.

McKenzie's innings would prove to be crucial in the context of the game as he and Nicky Boje (51) shared an eighth-wicket partnership of 136 in South Africa's reply. Instead of facing a first-innings deficit, which had look distinctly possible at 209 for seven, the home side eked out a lead of 63 that proved to be decisive. The contribution of Boje was just as impressive, the left-hander sacrificing his usual attacking instincts as the circumstances demanded, both to see McKenzie to his personal milestone and to ensure as large an advantage as possible.

Earlier Gary Kirsten and Boeta Dippenaar had given South Africa's reply a solid foundation with a partnership of 81 for the first wicket, but when Dippenaar (35) fell to the increasingly impressive Chris Martin, New Zealand started to make inroads. Jacques Kallis (12) and Daryll Cullinan (33) both made confident starts but could not capitalize, and Pollock's decision to use himself as nightwatchman – a coveted position in a fiercely competitive batting line-up – only just failed to come off.

Pollock made no secret of his disgust when he was out flashing at Martin for 33 on the third morning. South African nightwatchman, Mark Boucher and Nicky Boje in particular, have made something of a speciality of going on to make big scores. Pollock's time with the bat would come, however, only not until the end of the summer.

There were no repeat heroics from Sinclair – or any other New Zealander – in the second innings, however, as New Zealand stumbled to 148 all out, with only Mark Richardson (60) providing any real resistance. Pollock, Ntini and Boje each picked up two wickets, Ntini in particular looking a real handful as he went for less than two runs per over.

The loudest cheer from the St George's Park crowd was reserved for Lance Klusener. The all-rounder had been short of runs and wickets in recent matches – there had even been talk of the player being left out of the starting XI – but three raucously acclaimed New Zealand scalps to wrap up the tail were a timely reminder of his value to the side.

Afterwards, Fleming admitted that his team's inept second-innings display was the most disappointing aspect of a Test in which they briefly threatened South Africa's obvious supremacy. It was to prove all too fleeting.

The South African run-chase was academic. As we had seen in Bloemfontein, small hiccups are a matter of course when chasing small totals, and Kallis, Dippenaar and Cullinan all lost their wickets before the curtain was drawn on a second South African victory.

It was left to the watchful Kirsten to guide his team home with an unbeaten 47, the winning runs coming from the left-hander with a typically crisp drive to the cover boundary off the leg-spin of Brooke Walker.

THIRD TEST
8–12 December 2000 at New Wanderers Stadium, Johannesburg
By Marcus Prior

This was a match that was dominated by the weather, and marred by a meaningless final day that produced a maiden Test century for Boeta Dippenaar, but also revealed some of the inadequacies of the law book.

Torrential rain in the Johannesburg area turned the Wanderers' outfield into a temporary water-skiing facility and ruled out three full days play. By the time South Africa emerged to resume their first innings at 18 for one on the final day, only an extremely brave piece of captaincy from both skippers could have discovered a result lurking somewhere under the covers.

Considering the fall-out from the last time the result of a Test match was contrived, only a few miles up the road against England at Centurion less than a year earlier, it was no surprise that Shaun Pollock, in particular, was keen to play nothing but the most transparent of hands.

Between the downpours, the presence of a familiar figure – mobile phone in hand – just yards from the players' changing rooms, perhaps supported Pollock's decision to pursue the 'safety-first' route. The figure in question, Marlon Aronstam, had made a name for himself as a sharp-talking figure of fun at the King Commission earlier in the year, but it was also he that handed money and a leather jacket to Hansie Cronje at Centurion for his help in trying to force a result.

The game left other unanswered questions, too. Should dead rubbers be played to their conclusion? Should a mechanism not be available to captains and umpires within the laws of the game to allow a meaningless day such as we had at the Wanderers to be called to a premature halt? Should cricket try and move indoors?

There is no doubt that the laws are framed with the intention of preserving the integrity of the sport, but there was no escaping the feeling at the Wanderers that the game of cricket itself had been brought into disrepute by the astounding futility of the final day.

As it was, South Africa batted well into the final session, before the tedium was finally brought to a merciful close about 40 minutes before the scheduled close. Surely the captains should have had some dispensation earlier in the day that would have allowed them to shake hands on a draw that will only be of interest to the statisticians?

Dippenaar will surely disagree, though, as no-one will ever be able to take his hundred from him. He batted quite beautifully, particularly strong on the front foot driving through cover and mid-off, but his dismissal two balls after reaching his century was a lesson worth learning too. He admitted as much afterwards and will be keen to score another hundred for his country in more competitive circumstances as soon as possible.

Jacques Kallis boosted his average with an undefeated, but eye-poppingly tedious, 79 – at one stage after tea he and Daryll Cullinan added just nine runs in 14 overs. Fortunately for cricket, there was only a sprinkling of spectators to witness the torpor. Television sets had surely long been switched off.

Despite the loss of the first day to the elements, the match got off to an absorbing start. All eyes were on new fast bowler, Mfuneko Ngam, a raw talent from the rural Eastern Cape, but maturing fast and with serious pace. He is a bowler with that priceless ability to rattle batsmen through speed alone. The excitement of the Saturday crowd when they realized South Africa had its own Brett Lee was tangible.

Ngam was brought into the side in place of Allan Donald, the first South African into the 300-Club suffering the first of a string

Shaun Pollock would not be tempted into a Cronje-like declaration at Johannesburg, despite the presence of bookie Marlon Aronstam.

THIRD TEST – SOUTH AFRICA v. NEW ZEALAND
8–12 December 2000 at Wanderers Stadium, Johannesburg

NEW ZEALAND

	First innings		Second innings	
MH Richardson	c Boucher, b Ngam	46		
*AC Parore	c McKenzie, b Ntini	10		
MS Sinclair	c Klusener, b Pollock	24		
SP Fleming (capt)	b Ntini	14		
NJ Astle	c Kallis, b Ntini	12		
CD McMillan	c Klusener, b Kallis	4		
HJH Marshall	not out	40		
BGK Walker	lbw b Klusener	17		
DR Tuffey	c Boucher, b Ngam	8		
SB O'Connor	c Kallis, b Pollock	9		
CS Martin	b Kallis	0		
	b2, lb9, w1, nb4	16		
		200		

	First innings				Second innings
	O	M	R	W	
Pollock	26	9	41	2	
Ngam	19	8	34	2	
Kallis	15.5	4	26	2	
Ntini	18	9	29	3	
Klusener	12	2	43	1	
Boje	3	0	16	–	

Fall of Wickets
1-37, 2-83, 3-83, 4-112, 5-113, 6-117, 7-148, 8-174, 9-199

SOUTH AFRICA

	First innings	
HH Dippenaar	b O'Connor	100
G Kirsten	c Richardson, b Martin	10
N Boje	c Sinclair, b Martin	22
JH Kallis	not out	79
DJ Cullinan	not out	31
ND McKenzie		
*MV Boucher		
L Klusener		
SM Pollock (capt)		
M Ntini		
M Ngam		
	lb17, w2	19
	(for 3 wickets dec.)	**261**

	First innings			
	O	M	R	W
O'Connor	15	5	52	1
Martin	15	4	43	2
Tuffey	19	4	60	–
Astle	26	15	31	–
McMillan	17	5	41	–
Marshall	1	0	4	–
Sinclair	4	0	13	–

Fall of Wickets
1-18, 2-87, 3-187

Umpires: DL Orchard & G Sharp
Toss: South Africa
Test debuts: M Ngam (South Africa) and HJH Marshall (New Zealand)

Match drawn

TEST MATCH AVERAGES
South Africa v. New Zealand

SOUTH AFRICA

Batting	M	Inns	NO	HS	Runs	Av	100	50	c/st
ND McKenzie	3	4	2	120	195	97.50	1	1	2
JH Kallis	3	5	1	160	287	71.75	1	1	4
MV Boucher	3	3	1	76	98	49.00	–	1	8/-
N Boje	3	3	0	51	116	38.66	–	1	–
G Kirsten	3	5	1	49	138	34.50	–	–	5
HH Dippenaar	3	5	0	100	162	32.40	1	–	–
DJ Cullinan	3	5	1	33	126	31.50	–	–	4
L Klusener	3	3	0	9	19	6.33	–	–	4

Also batted: AA Donald (2 Tests) 21*, 9; M Ntini (1 Test) 0* (1ct); SM Pollock (3 Tests) 25, 33 (1ct). M Ngam played in one Test but did not bat.

Bowling	Overs	Mds	Runs	Wkts	Av	Best	10m	5/inn
M Ntini	101.4	38	226	13	17.38	6-66	–	1
AA Donald	82.3	21	197	11	17.90	4-69	–	–
SM Pollock	120	49	233	12	19.41	4-37	–	–
JH Kallis	79.5	23	205	5	41.00	2-26	–	–

Also bowled: N Boje 93-25-187-3; L Klusener 40.3-14-86-4; M Ngam 19-8-34-2.

NEW ZEALAND

Batting	M	Inns	NO	HS	Runs	Av	100	50	c/st
MH Richardson	3	5	0	77	232	46.40	–	2	1
MS Sinclair	3	5	0	150	212	42.40	1	–	2
SP Fleming	3	5	0	99	192	38.40	–	2	–
CD McMillan	3	5	0	78	137	27.40	–	1	1
BGK Walker	3	5	1	27*	76	19.00	–	–	–
NJ Astle	3	5	0	37	77	15.40	–	–	2
CM Spearman	2	4	0	23	54	13.50	–	–	2
SB O'Connor	3	5	0	20	52	10.40	–	–	1
AC Parore	3	5	0	12	40	8.00	–	–	7/-
CS Martin	3	5	3	7	12	6.00	–	–	–
DR Tuffey	2	3	0	8	14	4.66	–	–	1

Also batted in one Test: HJH Marshall 40*; KP Walmsley 5, 0.

Bowling	Overs	Mds	Runs	Wkts	Av	Best	10m	5/inn
CS Martin	83.1	22	286	11	26.00	4-104	–	–
SB O'Connor	86.4	21	244	8	30.50	3-87	–	–

Also bowled: NJ Astle 88-38-142-2; CD McMillan 47-13-110-1; HJH Marshall 1-0-4-0; MS Sinclair 4-0-13-0; DR Tuffey 53-11-194-3; BGK Walker 63.4-12-204-3; KP Walmsley 18-4-47-2.

of injuries that would plague him for the rest of the South African summer. Ngam toured with the South African 'A' squad in the West Indies in 2000 where he received rave reviews; his languid approach and spectacular delivery stride prompting some there to compare him to Michael Holding.

Ngam himself admits to a more obvious role model – a man he spent hours and hours in a concrete net attempting to emulate. Allan Donald.

With so much moisture in the air, it was no surprise that Pollock put the New Zealanders in after winning his third toss of the series. What was astonishing was the sight of Daryll Cullinan spilling two routine chances at first slip inside the first six overs – both off a bemused and disappointed Ngam.

The 21 year old would not have to wait long for his first Test wicket though, as Mark Richardson edged a sharp rising delivery to Mark Boucher in the first over after lunch to depart for 46. Richardson, who began his first-class career as a spinner batting at number 11, was one of the few New Zealanders to emerge from the series with credit. Always positive but blessed with patience too, his 46.40 series average was just reward for several years of grafting his batting skills to their current robust state.

Richardson's departure was the spark for the by-now-familiar New Zealand collapse. From 83 for one, they folded to 200 all out. A gritty undefeated 40 from their own debutant, Hamish Marshall, was the difference between a disappointing total and a hugely embarrassing one. Perhaps the most impressive feature of Marshall's innings was the manner in which he refused to be intimidated after receiving a clanging blow to the helmet from Makhaya Ntini when he was yet to get off the mark.

Ngam finished with two wickets, with the rest shared around. Once again, though, Ntini underlined the rapid progress he made during the series, bowling accurately and aggressively as he picked up three top-order victims. He would be rewarded for his efforts at the end of the game with the Man of the Series award, richly deserved and widely applauded.

A more controversial decision, although applauded by some, was to award the Man of the Match award to groundsman, Chris Scott, and his staff for their efforts in doing everything humanly possible to get any play at all underway. While no-one could deny that they had worked overtime, Boeta Dippenaar in particular might have wondered whether his efforts deserved some formal recognition.

SRI LANKA IN SOUTH AFRICA
By Telford Vice, Marcus Prior and Grant Shimmin

FIRST TEST
26–30 December 2000 at Kingsmead, Durban

A match of milestones was stymied by rain, which claimed the entire fourth day and, in all likelihood, prevented South Africa from taking an early series lead. When bad light ended play eight overs before the scheduled close on the fifth day, the visitors had scored 149 for six in search of their academic victory target of 345.

South Africa totalled 420 in their first innings, to which Sri Lanka replied with 216. The home side

Gary Kirsten's first-innings century set up the prospect of a South African win, only for rain to obliterate the fourth day at Kingsmead, Durban.

Dilhara Fernando produced his first five-wicket haul in Test cricket in the first Test in Durban.

declined to enforce the follow-on and declared their second innings closed on 140 for seven.

Muttiah Muralitharan, who went into the match with 291 victims, claimed match figures of 11 for 161, his fifth ten-wicket haul in Test cricket, to become the first Sri Lankan, and the 17th cricketer in the history of the game, to take 300 Test wickets. He reached the mark in the second fewest matches, 58, after Dennis Lillee. In the following innings, Shaun Pollock became the second South African to reach 200 Test scalps after Allan Donald. The third record came in the shape of Gary Kirsten, who scored 180, his 11th century, to temporarily regain a share of the record for the most Test centuries by a South African, held with Daryll Cullinan. The other significant achievement was a partnership of 168 runs between Kumar Sangakkara and Mahela

Jayawardene, the highest third-wicket stand for Sri Lanka against South Africa.

Pollock won the toss and chose to bat on an unusually characterless Kingsmead pitch. South Africa reached 230 for three by the first day's close, which came 10.4 overs early due to bad light and with Kirsten on 112 not out. The left-hander's typically fuss-free innings was the cornerstone of the home side's solid foundation, laid in partnerships of 55 with Jacques Kallis for the second wicket, and 108 with Cullinan for the third. Cullinan scored 59, his 13th half-century, in more than two hours at the crease.

South Africa suffered their only loss of the morning session in the ninth over when Boeta Dippenaar's footwork let him down and he gently edged Dilhara Fernando to Kulawitharana for 11. Kirsten and Kallis showed few inhibitions and attacked the mediocre Sri Lankan bowling. Their stand was ended in the second over after lunch when Kallis, on 21, top-edged a mistimed hook to square leg to give Fernando his second wicket.

Muralitharan was brought into the attack at the southern Old Fort Road End 20 minutes before lunch. He struck half-an-hour after tea when Cullinan flicked a full toss to mid-wicket to terminate another aggressive partnership.

South Africa batted positively on the second morning and were rewarded with 101 runs in the first session. Muralitharan snapped up Neil McKenzie and Mark Boucher in the opening hour by way of close catches. While the wiry master bowler obtained significant drift and sharp turn, Kirsten and Lance Klusener attacked him regardless. With his match-winner entrenched at one end, Sanath Jayasuriya delayed taking the new ball until the 100th over.

However, the seamers failed to make an impression and Muralitharan was back in action in the new ball's 11th over. The change bore fruit when Klusener skied Muralitharan to mid-off for 50, scored in more than two hours and ending a partnership of 89. Kirsten was out 15 minutes before tea when he failed to avoid a short-pitched delivery from Fernando and fended it to wicketkeeper Romesh Kaluwitharana. He was at the crease for nine-and-a-half hours, faced 461 deliveries and hit 20 fours.

The South Africans were eventually dismissed in the third over of the final session. The wickets were shared between Fernando, who took five for 98, his maiden five-wicket haul in Test cricket, and Muralitharan, whose five for 122 was his 23rd.

In the second over of Sri Lanka's reply and without a run on the board, Marvan Atapattu was run out by the swooping Makhaya Ntini's direct hit

FIRST TEST – SOUTH AFRICA v. SRI LANKA
26–30 December 2000 at Kingsmead, Durban

SOUTH AFRICA

	First innings		Second innings	
HH Dippenaar	c Kaluwitharana, b Fernando	11	lbw b Muralitharan	22
G Kirsten	c Kaluwitharana, b Fernando	180	c Arnold, b Muralitharan	34
JH Kallis	c Muralitharan, b Fernando	21	b Muralitharan	15
DJ Cullinan	c Atapattu, b Muralitharan	59	(9) not out	2
ND McKenzie	c Dilshan, b Muralitharan	9	(7) lbw b Muralitharan	13
*MV Boucher	c Arnold, b Muralitharan	17	c Vaas, b Muralitharan	10
L Klusener	c Sangakkara, b Muralitharan	50	(8) not out	11
N Boje	b Muralitharan	32	(5) c Sangakkara, b Fernando	8
SM Pollock (capt)	c Kaluwitharana, b Fernando	2	(4) c Dilshan, b Muralitharan	11
M Ntini	b Fernando	8		
M Ngam	not out	0		
	b5, lb10, w1, nb15	31	b4, lb3, nb7	14
		420	(for 7 wickets dec.)	**140**

	First innings				Second innings			
	O	M	R	W	O	M	R	W
Vaas	26	1	84	-	9	1	25	-
Zoysa	20	3	62	-	5	0	21	-
Fernando	34	4	98	5	10	0	48	1
Muralitharan	58.3	16	122	5	10	1	39	6
Arnold	14	3	39	-				

Fall of Wickets
1-31, 2-86, 3-194, 4-238, 5-269, 6-358, 7-401, 8-410, 9-420
1-46, 2-75, 3-91, 4-92, 5-108, 6-114, 7-132

SRI LANKA

	First innings		Second innings	
MS Atapattu	run out (Ntini)	0	c Boucher, b Boje	20
ST Jayasuriya (capt)	c McKenzie, b Ngam	0	c Cullinan, b Ngam	26
K Sangakkara	c Kirsten, b Boje	74	st Boucher, b Boje	17
DPM Jayawardene	c Boucher, b Klusener	98	c Boucher, b Ntini	7
RP Arnold	b Boje	3	c Dippenaar, b Pollock	30
TM Dilshan	b Ngam	6	not out	28
*RS Kaluwitharana	c Boucher, b Ntini	16	c Boje, b Pollock	1
WPUJC Vaas	c Boucher, b Pollock	2	not out	3
DNT Zoysa	c Ngam, b Pollock	3		
RD Fernando	not out	5		
M Muralitharan	c Boucher, b Pollock	0		
	nb9	9	b4, lb7, nb6	17
		216	(for 6 wickets)	**149**

	First innings				Second innings			
	O	M	R	W	O	M	R	W
Pollock	20.4	7	40	3	16	5	35	2
Ngam	12	0	59	2	13	3	34	1
Ntini	16	5	36	1	10	4	18	1
Kallis	9	3	17	-	6	1	14	-
Boje	19	4	44	2	24	12	30	2
Klusener	11	5	20	1	5	1	7	-

Fall of Wickets
1-0, 2-2, 3-170, 4-184, 5-184, 6-201, 7-208, 8-208, 9-215
1-41, 2-69, 3-80, 4-80, 5-132, 6-140

Umpires: DL Orchard & Riazuddin
Toss: South Africa
Test debuts: nil

Match drawn

on the striker's stumps from mid-on. In the fourth over, Jayasuriya, on nought with the total two, cut an express delivery from Mfuneko Ngam to point, where McKenzie plucked a stinging catch out of the air. Sangakkara and Jayawardene reacted with impressive defiance and Sri Lanka reached the close on 62 for two, still 358 runs in arrears and 158 away from avoiding the prospect of following-on.

They continued in similar vein on the third morning to ensure a wicketless session. However, South Africa wasted a chance to break the partnership when Sangakkara, on 42 and with 116 scored, drove Kallis to short cover where Pollock dived but dropped a difficult catch.

The fast bowlers struggled to beat the bat on the steadily flattening pitch, and Nicky Boje was brought into the attack five overs before lunch. An hour after the interval, Boje broke the partnership when Sangakkara lifted another drive to short cover to be dismissed for his then-highest Test score of 74. He was at the crease for four-and-a-half hours.

That started a slide that saw Sri Lanka lose their last eight wickets for 46 runs in the space of 20 overs and they were dismissed five overs after tea. Three overs after Sangakkara was dismissed, Jayawardene was caught behind off Klusener for 98 having batted for four-and-a-half hours. Pollock went into the match with 198 wickets, and took his 200th when Nuwan Zoysa pulled to long on to be caught for three. His 201st (Muralitharan) followed two balls later.

Pollock gave Durban's humidity and the fact that there was only a day's break between the second and third Tests as his reasons for not enforcing the follow-on. South Africa were 47 for one, a lead of 251, when bad light forced the close 10.3 overs early. Persistent drizzle led to the abandonment of the fourth day's play, and South Africa attacked the bowling to score 93 runs in the 21.3 overs they faced before the declaration came 50 minutes before lunch on the final day.

Their aggressive approach aided Muralitharan's cause, and his 300th victim was Pollock, caught at silly point for 11. Sri Lanka dwindled to 85 for four at tea, but Russel Arnold and Tillekeratne Dilshan stopped the rot with a fifth-wicket stand that endured for 111 minutes before Arnold pulled Pollock to Dippenaar at square leg.

In his next over, Pollock induced Kaluwitharana to drive a full toss to mid-on. However, Dilshan, who batted for two-and-a-half hours for his undefeated 28, and Chaminda Vaas saw Sri Lanka to safety.

SECOND TEST
2–4 January 2001 at Newlands, Cape Town
By Marcus Prior

Were Sri Lanka really that bad? Or were they simply made to look so completely inept? This was the worst defeat in Sri Lankan Test history – it was also South Africa's most emphatic. So one-sided was the game that there was not even one session that the tourists could justifiably claim to have won.

It was a magnificent all-round performance by the South Africans. They were controlled, accurate and aggressive with the ball on a pitch that offered enough extra pace and bounce to unsettle the Sri Lankan top order, and they were clinically professional with the bat.

Man of the Match, Shaun Pollock, admitted afterwards that his luck began when he lost the toss on the first morning and his opposite number, Sanath Jayasuriya, decided to bat. Shortly afterwards Sri Lanka were 13 for four, a position from which they never recovered, with all four wickets falling to Pollock.

While the South African batsmen would later say that batting on the Newlands strip was never easy, it was also never tricky enough for Sri Lanka to have any excuse for crumbling to 95 all out an hour after lunch. They might perhaps have pointed to Pollock, who was rewarded for a nagging line on-or-around off-stump, generating just enough movement to take the edge.

His six for 30 in the Sri Lankans' first innings was the best ever return by a South African captain, and he was superbly backed up by young speedster, Mfuneko Ngam. The 21 year old picked up a career-best three for 26 in his third Test as the Sri Lankans struggled to cope with deliveries consistently approaching 150 km/hour.

Kumar Sangakkara (32) was the only batsman to make a decent start, and although Avishka Gunawardene reached 20 and Nuwan Zoysa ten, the rest failed to reach double figures. Gunawardene had been brought into the team in place of out-of-form Romesh Kaluwitharana, but the burly left-hander never quite managed to throw off the impression that he was born for the one-day game. His shot selection was decidedly random.

Jayasuriya would later admit that his players' inability to cope with the rising ball was the main reason for the woeful demise of the top order and

Muttiah Muralitharan was one of the senior players to suggest Sri Lanka could only benefit from greater exposure to the kind of unfamiliar conditions the team encountered in South Africa.

Another worry for Jayasuriya was his own form, along with that of his opening partner, Marvan Atapattu. Normally such a devastating combination on home soil, neither gave any indication in Cape Town that they had worked out a way of coping with the South African pace attack. With such a fragile spearhead to the batting line-up, it was hardly surprising their team-mates came under such pressure. You had to feel for the Sri Lankans and their coach Dav Whatmore – sometimes it felt as though they were trying to get the ball away with a cotton-bud.

Before the game, the local media spotlight had fallen squarely on Herschelle Gibbs. The opening batsman had been recalled to the South African side just hours after his ban, for agreeing to sell his wicket cheaply in India in March 2000, had come to an end. His return was the subject of enormous debate.

Although the sight of Gibbs striding to the crease was unanimously welcomed by his home crowd at

Shaun Pollock lost the toss, but took the first four wickets as Sri Lanka were routed for 95 at Newlands.

Newlands, his cause was not helped by the fact that he displaced Boeta Dippenaar as opener, the man who only two Tests previously had scored his maiden Test century. Innings of 11 and 22 in the first Test in Durban were certainly no headline-grabbers, but hardly amounted to a case for his exclusion.

Whatever the rights and wrongs of Gibbs wearing national colours again, his second-ball duck, caught at the wicket off Chaminda Vaas, will have smacked to many of poetic justice. It was also the last time the Sri Lankans had any real cause for celebration.

Gibbs apart, the South African top and middle order gorged themselves under the Cape Town sun. Daryll Cullinan struck a South African record 12th Test century, edging him ahead of Gary Kirsten, who also passed 50. Cullinan loves batting at Newlands and the stunning setting was an appropriate backdrop to a majestic display of stroke-making from South Africa's most naturally gifted batsman.

Cullinan's decision to retire from one-day cricket appeared all to his benefit as he concentrated on what he does best. His form against New Zealand earlier in the summer had been disturbingly short of his best, but here was a reminder of just how difficult he will be to replace when he does eventually decide to walk from the middle one last time.

Both Mark Boucher and Lance Klusener should have made hundreds but fell in the nineties, and when the declaration came at 504 for seven before lunch on day three, South Africa's first-innings lead of 409 was the fifth-highest in Test history by a side batting second.

When Ngam removed Jayasuriya without scoring and Kumar Sangakkara for 11 to have Sri Lanka 18 for two at the start of their reply, it was simply a question of whether the game would make it into a fourth day.

That it did not was the result of more poor batting from the tourists and some fine left-arm spin from Nicky Boje, whose four wickets ripped the heart out the Sri Lankan middle order. Mahela Jayawardene underlined his undoubted talent with an enjoyable 45, but good starts by Russel Arnold and Tillekeratne Dilshan were both undone by Boje.

The crowd, which had been healthy if not capacity on all three days, were treated to one final cameo. Chaminda Vaas struck six fours and two sixes in his 26-ball 38, but it was a bravura innings made possible only by the futility of Sri Lanka's position.

Ngam wrapped things up with his sixth wicket of the match and South Africa were 1–0 up. It was all too easy.

SECOND TEST – SOUTH AFRICA v. SRI LANKA

2–4 January 2001 at Newlands, Cape Town

SRI LANKA

	First innings		Second innings	
MS Atapattu	c Kallis, b Pollock	5	lbw b Pollock	13
ST Jayasuriya (capt)	c Boucher, b Pollock	8	c Pollock, b Ngam	0
*K Sangakkara	c Cullinan, b Ngam	32	c Boucher, b Ngam	11
DPM Jayawardene	c Kallis, b Pollock	0	lbw b Boje	45
RP Arnold	c Kirsten, b Pollock	0	c Gibbs, b Boje	26
TM Dilshan	c Pollock, b Kallis	5	c Boucher, b Boje	17
DA Gunawardene	c Kallis, b Ngam	24	b Ntini	13
WPUJC Vaas	c Pollock, b Ngam	7	c & b Boje	38
DNT Zoysa	c & b Pollock	10	c Klusener, b Ntini	0
RD Fernando	not out	0	c Boucher, b Ngam	5
M Muralitharan	c Ntini, b Pollock	0	not out	1
	w1, nb3	4	lb6, w1, nb4	11
		95		**180**

	First innings				Second innings			
	O	M	R	W	O	M	R	W
Pollock	13.4	6	30	6	9	3	29	1
Ngam	13	2	26	3	8.2	1	36	3
Kallis	6	2	19	1	7	1	29	-
Ntini	6	2	20	-	11	2	52	2
Boje					10	3	28	4

Fall of Wickets

1-12, 2-13, 3-13, 4-13, 5-33, 6-66, 7-84, 8-95, 9-95
1-4, 2-18, 3-53, 4-99, 5-112, 6-119, 7-131, 8-135, 9-172

SOUTH AFRICA

	First innings		Second innings
G Kirsten	c Dilshan, b Muralitharan	52	
HH Gibbs	c Sangakkara, b Vaas	0	
JH Kallis	c Jayawardene, b Fernando	49	
DJ Cullinan	run out (Vaas)	112	
ND McKenzie	c & b Arnold	47	
*MV Boucher	c Jayawardene, b Arnold	92	
L Klusener	c Jayasuriya, b Arnold	97	
N Boje	not out	31	
SM Pollock (capt)			
M Ntini			
M Ngam			
	lb5, w1, nb18	24	
	(for 7 wickets dec.)	**504**	

	First innings				Second innings
	O	M	R	W	
Vaas	32	6	109	1	
Zoysa	26	6	80	-	
Fernando	25	2	105	1	
Muralitharan	43	11	99	1	
Jayasuriya	7	1	28	-	
Arnold	24.2	4	76	3	
Jayawardene	1	0	2	-	

Fall of Wickets

1-1, 2-97, 3-130, 4-231, 5-317, 6-411, 7-504

Umpires: IL Howell & EA Nicholls
Toss: Sri Lanka
Test debuts: nil

South Africa won by an innings and 229 runs

THIRD TEST
20–22 January 2001 at SuperSport Park, Centurion
by Grant Shimmin

If the final one-day international between the two sides, played three days before the start of this Test, had ended South Africa's bid for a piece of history (a 6–0 series whitewash), it presaged another, though one more of the individual variety for home captain, Shaun Pollock. It also robbed Sri Lanka of the two main weapons in a limited bowling arsenal, record wicket-taker Muttiah Muralitharan and left-arm seamer Chaminda Vaas, who both picked up groin injuries in the narrow victory at the Wanderers.

Pollock, who had drifted to number nine in the South African batting order after a lean spell with the bat, had given an indication of just what a clean and destructive hitter he could be with his three sixes in a losing cause in Johannesburg and he was called into action in the third session at Centurion, to telling effect.

Jayasuriya had surprised everyone by putting the South Africans in when he was without his two best bowlers, but on balance that didn't seem like too bad a decision when the home side reached tea on 204 for seven, although the scoring rate – with Sri Lanka significantly behind the required 15 overs to the hour – would have been a worry for the tourists.

After tea, taken when debutant Justin Kemp was run out by Kumar Sangakkara, Pollock joined Neil McKenzie, who had already compiled a patient 66. Picking up from where he had left off at the Wanderers, the skipper unleashed a barrage, slamming his first 50 off just 35 balls, five short of the fastest in Test history, before going to his maiden Test century off just 95 deliveries, an achievement that brought a sudden flood of tears, coming 51 Tests into his career. In all, he faced 106 balls for his 111, hitting 16 fours and three sixes.

Pollock had gone into the match well up the list of those who had made the most runs in Tests without recording a century and, as he admitted afterwards, had been the subject of a fair bit of ribbing from his team-mates. The top seven in the South African batting order all had centuries to their name, with only the relative newcomers, McKenzie and Boeta Dippenaar, not having at least two tons.

McKenzie rectified that statistic as he made a polished 103, playing the perfect anchor role as he contributed just 37 to a record eighth-wicket stand

for South Africa of 150 with Pollock. As a result, the home side moved to 378 off just 91.3 overs.

The only bright spot for the islanders was the personal achievement of wicketkeeper Romesh Kaluwitharana in taking five catches, one short of the Sri Lankan record, including the one to dismiss Makhaya Ntini that wrapped up the innings early on the second morning.

The tourists were on the back foot from the moment they started their reply. Marvan Atapattu was run out for three after going for a single that simply was not there. After just 36.5 overs, they were back in the hut for a paltry 119, stands of 21 for the eighth and tenth wickets the best of the innings. Kaluwitharana top-scored with 32 off 30 balls, before becoming one of Ntini's four victims.

In the follow-on innings, enforced by Pollock with

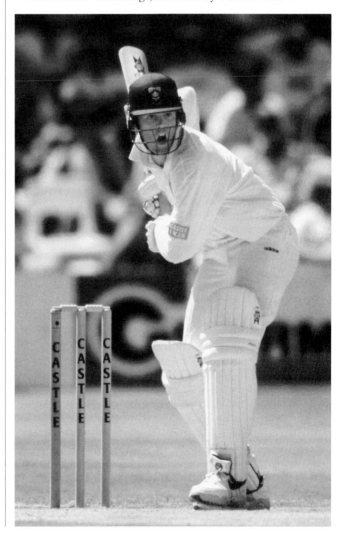

Shaun Pollock got in the act with the bat at Centurion, scoring his maiden Test century, 111 off just 106 balls.

the visitors 259 runs behind, Sri Lanka promoted Sangakkara to open, a decision presumably prompted by Jayasuriya's poor form with the bat – he made just 16 in the first innings. The decision met with some success. After the early losses of Atapattu and Mahela Jayawardene, Sangakkara and fellow left-hander Russel Arnold (71 off 82 balls with 13 fours) added 113 for the third wicket, and the tourists reached the close on 184 for three, with Sangakkara unbeaten on 64.

In the second over of the third morning, Aravinda de Silva was caught at third slip by a diving Pollock off the bowling of Kallis for 22. Although there was some conjecture as to whether the ball had been taken by the captain on the bounce, the batsman walked without waiting for a decision from umpire Rudi Koertzen. Pollock himself was adamant after the match that he had taken a clean catch.

From that moment on, it was simply a question of how long the islanders could hold on, and whether Sangakkara could reach a maiden century and carry his bat through a completed innings. Should he have done so, it would have meant the last three batsmen to do so in Tests were all Sri Lankans – with Atapattu and Arnold having managed it in Zimbabwe a year earlier.

However, he was pulled up short of both milestones when Peter Willey gave him out leg before to a delivery from Ntini that clearly pitched outside leg stump. Sangakkara had held firm for more than five-and-a-half hours for his 98 and he was last man out with the total at 252, leaving the tourists seven short of making South Africa bat again.

Despite taking just a single wicket in the encounter, it was not a surprise when Pollock was named Man of the Match for his game-breaking century. He also picked up the Man of the Series award after his six for 30 in the first innings of the second Test had set up the first of his team's back-to-back innings victories.

With Klusener on the sidelines, Kemp, who had played the last two one-day internationals, was drafted into the Test side as well. While he scored just two runs, he was much more successful with the ball, taking two for 19 in the first innings and following that up with three for 33 off 13 overs in the second.

The tireless Ntini, the Man of the Series against New Zealand, again played a significant role, with six wickets in the match at a cost of 90 runs. It was a somewhat difficult return for Allan Donald, who had been out for a month with a stomach strain, and he took two for 28 in the first innings, but bowled just seven overs in the second for a return of one for 39.

THIRD TEST – SOUTH AFRICA v. SRI LANKA
20–22 January 2001 at SuperSport Park, Centurion

SOUTH AFRICA

	First innings		Second innings
HH Dippenaar	c Kaluwitharana, b Perera	20	
HH Gibbs	c Kaluwitharana, b Zoysa	1	
JH Kallis	c Arnold, b Fernando	7	
DJ Cullinan	c Kaluwitharana, b Wickremasinghe	48	
ND McKenzie	c Wickremasinghe, b Zoysa	103	
*MV Boucher	c Kaluwitharana, b Zoysa	38	
N Boje	c Jayasuriya, b Arnold	6	
JM Kemp	run out (Sangakkara)	2	
SM Pollock (capt)	c Sangakkara, b Zoysa	111	
AA Donald	not out	10	
M Ntini	c Kaluwitharana, b Wickremasinghe	10	
	b4, lb2, w1, nb15	22	
		378	

	First innings				Second innings
	O	M	R	W	
Zoysa	22	8	76	4	
Perera	19	3	73	1	
Fernando	16	1	107	1	
Wickremasinghe	12.3	3	51	2	
Arnold	14	2	50	1	
Jayasuriya	6	3	10	-	
de Silva	2	1	5	-	

Fall of Wickets
1-17, 2-31, 3-54, 4-115, 5-168, 6-185, 7-204, 8-354, 9-359

SRI LANKA

	First innings		Second innings	
MS Atapattu	run out (Gibbs/Dippenaar)	3	c Cullinan, b Pollock	0
ST Jayasuriya (capt)	c McKenzie, b Donald	16	(6) b Donald	16
K Sangakkara	b Donald	3	(2) lbw b Ntini	98
PA de Silva	c Gibbs, b Kallis	5	(5) c Pollock, b Kallis	22
DPM Jayawardene	c Boucher, b Ntini	17	(3) c Dippenaar, b Kallis	23
RP Arnold	b Ntini	13	(4) c Pollock, b Boje	71
*RS Kaluwitharana	c Boucher, b Ntini	32	c Boucher, b Kemp	10
DNT Zoysa	c Kallis, b Ntini	1	c & b Kemp	2
GP Wickremasinghe	c Gibbs, b Kemp	21	c Boucher, b Ntini	1
RD Fernando	lbw b Kemp	0	c Kallis, b Kemp	1
PDRL Perera	not out	1	not out	0
	lb3, w3, nb1	7	lb2, w2, nb4	8
		119		**252**

	First innings				Second innings			
	O	M	R	W	O	M	R	W
Donald	9	2	28	2	7	0	39	1
Pollock	7	3	15	-	17	5	43	1
Kallis	5	1	15	1	14	1	39	2
Ntini	11	5	39	4	19.3	5	51	2
Kemp	4.5	1	19	2	13	2	33	3
Boje					11	2	45	1

Fall of Wickets
1-6, 2-24, 3-25, 4-40, 5-54, 6-71, 7-76, 8-97, 9-98
1-9, 2-43, 3-156, 4-187, 5-212, 6-234, 7-242, 8-243, 9-248

Umpires: RE Koertzen & P Willey
Toss: Sri Lanka
Test debut: JM Kemp (South Africa)

South Africa won by an innings and 7 runs

TEST MATCH AVERAGES
South Africa v. Sri Lanka

SOUTH AFRICA

Batting	M	Inns	NO	HS	Runs	Av	100	50	c/st
G Kirsten	2	3	0	180	266	88.66	1	1	2
L Klusener	2	3	1	97	158	79.00	-	2	1
DJ Cullinan	3	4	1	112	221	73.66	1	1	3
ND McKenzie	3	4	0	103	172	43.00	1	-	2
SM Pollock	3	3	0	111	124	41.33	1	-	6
MV Boucher	3	4	0	92	157	39.25	-	1	14/1
N Boje	3	4	1	32	77	25.66	-	-	2
JH Kallis	3	4	0	49	92	23.00	-	-	5
HH Dippenaar	2	3	0	22	53	17.66	-	-	2

Also batted: AA Donald (1 Test) 10*; HH Gibbs (2 Tests) 0, 1 (3ct); JM Kemp (1 Test) 2 (1ct); M Ngam (2 Tests) 0* (1ct); M Ntini (3 Tests) 8, 10 (1ct).

Bowling	Overs	Mds	Runs	Wkts	Av	Best	10m	5/inn
JM Kemp	17.5	3	52	5	10.40	3-33	-	-
SM Pollock	83.2	29	192	13	14.76	6-30	-	1
N Boje	64	21	147	9	16.33	4-28	-	-
M Ngam	46.2	7	155	9	17.22	3-36	-	-
M Ntini	73.3	23	216	10	21.60	4-39	-	-

Also bowled: AA Donald 16-2-67-3; JH Kallis 47-9-133-4; L Klusener 16-6-27-1.

SRI LANKA

Batting	M	Inns	NO	HS	Runs	Av	100	50	c/st
K Sangakkara	3	6	0	98	235	39.16	-	2	4
DPM Jayawardene	3	6	0	98	190	31.66	-	1	2
RP Arnold	3	6	0	71	143	23.83	-	1	4
TM Dilshan	2	4	1	28*	56	18.66	-	-	3
WPUJC Vaas	2	4	1	38	50	16.66	-	-	1
RS Kaluwitharana	2	4	0	32	59	14.75	-	-	8/-
ST Jayasuriya	3	6	0	26	66	11.00	-	-	2
MS Atapattu	3	6	0	20	41	6.83	-	-	1
RD Fernando	3	5	2	5*	11	3.66	-	-	-
DNT Zoysa	3	5	0	10	16	3.20	-	-	-

Also batted: PA de Silva (1 Test) 5, 22; DA Gunawardene (1 Test) 24, 13; M Muralitharan (2 Tests) 0, 0, 1* (1ct); PDRL Perera (1 Test) 1*, 0*; GP Wickremasinghe (1 Test) 21, 1 (1ct).

Bowling	Overs	Mds	Runs	Wkts	Av	Best	10m	5/inn
M Muralitharan	111.2	28	260	12	21.66	6-39	1	2
RD Fernando	85	7	358	8	44.75	5-98	-	1

Also bowled: RP Arnold 52.2-9-165-4; PA de Silva 2-1-5-0; ST Jayasuriya 13-4-38-0; DMP Jayawardene 1-0-2-0; PDRL Perera 19-3-73-1; WPUJC Vaas 67-8-218-1; GP Wickremasinghe 12.3-3-51-2; DNT Zoysa 73-18-239-4.

ONE-DAY INTERNATIONALS
By Marcus Prior

The Sri Lankan salad days of World Cup glory are fading slowly into the history books, and although they remain a genuine force in the one-day game, South Africa – as they did in the Test series that ran concurrently – exposed their raw underbelly when they play away from the subcontinent.

Sri Lanka won just one match of the six, ending South Africa's one-day winning streak at ten in the final match at the Wanderers, albeit a game curtailed

Trademark Kallis: South Africa won the first five one-day internationals until Messrs. Duckworth and Lewis helped Sri Lanka to clinch the sixth.

by yet more rain in one of the damper highveld summers on record. The one-sided nature of the series came as a major disappointment to the South African public, particularly after New Zealand had failed to win a match earlier in the season.

The tone was set in match one at Port Elizabeth after Sri Lanka had recorded a decent total of 221 all out on a St George's Park pitch on which batting is never straightforward. 55 from Romesh Kaluwitharana and Kumar Sangakkara's 84 were the highlights of the innings in which Shaun Pollock took four wickets.

At 91 for four after 19 overs, South Africa had not made the best of starts to their reply. Crucially, Gary Kirsten was still there, though, and although he went for 58 in the 27th over, Rhodes (61 not out) and Lance Klusener (27 not out) saw them home with 15 balls to spare.

Match two in East London was a South African cakewalk. The home side posted a mammoth 302 for seven after winning the toss and batting, including a maiden one-day hundred for Neil McKenzie and another run-a-ball 50 from Rhodes.

Needing six runs an over from the outset, the Sri Lankans were never in the hunt, with only Mahela Jayawardene (59) getting set as South Africa won by 95 runs.

After a three-week hiatus for the first two Test matches, Sri Lanka's miserable form continued in Paarl near Cape Town, where a competitive 247 for four (Sanath Jayasuriya 66, Kaluwitharana 83, Marvan Atapattu 51 not out) was comfortably overhauled by an immaculate South African batting performance.

Jacques Kallis hit a boundary to move to his sixth one-day century and win the match with seven balls to spare. Boeta Dippenaar (65) and Rhodes (75 not out) were again the men who partnered Kallis so effectively.

The series was wrapped up at Newlands two days later when South Africa amassed a record score at the ground, with Kallis (83) once again leading the way. In the process he became the fastest man to reach 4,000 runs and 100 wickets in one-day internationals, needing just 118 games to do so.

With 77 from Dippenaar and a South African-record, fifth-consecutive 50 from Rhodes, South Africa had set an imposing target. It proved far too much for the visitors, with only Kaluwitharana looking comfortable as Makhaya Ntini continued his impressive summer with a return of five for 37.

Bloemfontein was another South African stroll after the Sri Lankans posted just 206 in the face of

Makhaya Ntini rounded off an excellent Test series with the Man of the Match award in the one-day international at Newlands, taking five for 37.

some disciplined South African bowling. Shaun Pollock's men made it 5–0 with fully eight overs to spare, with Herschelle Gibbs (79) making his first decent score since returning from his ban.

Finally to the Wanderers and a Sri Lankan win at last. It was by a squeak (just four runs) and with the use of the Duckworth/Lewis method, but it was well deserved. A decent batting performance, including 55 from Atapattu left South Africa chasing a recalculated 209 to win.

The home side were always behind the rate, and although Nicky Boje (46) and McKenzie (47) gave some impetus to the innings in the middle order, not even three sixes at the death from Pollock could change the equation in their favour.

Match One

15 December 2000 at St George's Park, Port Elizabeth (floodlit)
Sri Lanka 221 (49.5 overs) (K Sangakkara 84, RS Kaluwitharana 55)
South Africa 223 for 6 (47.2 overs) (JN Rhodes 61*, G Kirsten 58)
South Africa won by four wickets
Man of the Match: JN Rhodes

Match Two

17 December 2000 at Buffalo Park, East London
South Africa 302 for 7 (50 overs) (ND McKenzie 120*, MV Boucher 55, JN Rhodes 50)
Sri Lanka 207 for 6 (50 overs) (DPM Jayawardene 59)
South Africa won by 95 runs
Man of the Match: ND McKenzie

Match Three

9 January 2001 at Boland Bank Park, Paarl (floodlit)
Sri Lanka 247 for 4 (50 overs) (RS Kaluwitharana 83, ST Jayasuriya 66, MS Atapattu 51*)
South Africa 250 for 2 (48.5 overs) (JH Kallis 100*, JN Rhodes 75*, HH Dippenaar 65)
South Africa won by eight wickets
Man of the Match: JH Kallis

Match Four

11 January 2001 at Newlands, Cape Town (floodlit)
South Africa 290 for 7 (50 overs) (JH Kallis 82, HH Dippenaar 77, JN Rhodes 53)
Sri Lanka 191 (42.2 overs) (RS Kaluwitharana 74, M Ntini 5 for 37)
South Africa won by 99 runs
Man of the Match: M Ntini

Match Five

14 January 2001 at Goodyear Park, Bloemfontein
Sri Lanka 206 (49.2 overs)
South Africa 207 for 5 (42 overs) (HH Gibbs 79)
South Africa won by five wickets
Man of the Match: HH Gibbs

Match Six

17 January 2001 at New Wanderers, Johannesburg (floodlit)
Sri Lanka 214 for 6 (42 overs) (RP Arnold 65*, MS Atapattu 55)
South Africa 204 (42 overs)
Sri Lanka won by 4 runs (DL Method: South Africa target 209 from 42 overs)
Man of the Match: RP Arnold
Man of the Series: JH Kallis

SOUTH AFRICAN DOMESTIC FIRST-CLASS COMPETITION

For the third time in as many summers, Border had the championship in their sights. And for the third time they fell at the final hurdle.

On this occasion, Western Province denied Border by winning the five-day Supersport Series final at Newlands by an innings and 26 runs with a day to spare. The season before it was Gauteng, and the season before that Province again.

What keeps going wrong for Border? Their attack, spearheaded by Vasbert Drakes, the superb West Indian professional, has been the best in the country for several seasons, and they are among the better fielding sides in a competition over endowed with quality in that department.

But mastering just two of the three disciplines is not enough to win a first-class championship in most countries, let alone in South Africa. So Border's luck is unlikely to change until they discover at least one batsman of the highest quality below Test level, lest he be whisked away in the national interest.

For Province, though, the season was an unmitigated triumph. They finished at the bottom of the standings in 1999–2000, and their emphatic resurgence was accomplished by virtually the same players who had endured the nadir of the previous summer. The notable differences were Neil Johnson, who gave up his Test career in Zimbabwe to return to the more lucrative South African provincial arena, and Graeme Smith, the former Gauteng batsman.

Smith's move was part of an exodus of quality players from the Wanderers, whose desolate stands were all but the only witnesses as the reigning champions dwindled to the bottom of Pool A before finishing last in the Shield Series – the consolation prize contested by the three teams that did not make it into the Super Eight competition reserved for the top-four teams in each pool.

Gauteng, then, were officially the worst team in the country after winning the championship the season before. Boardroom strife of a political hue was the root cause, and it inevitably wormed its way onto the field.

Good news, for some, came with the mid-summer resignation of the controversial general manager of the board, Ziggy Wadvalla, and it is to be hoped that this dramatic development will prove to be a step on Gauteng's road to rehabilitation as one of South Africa's premier unions.

The final itself was a grinding affair. Province captain H.D. Ackerman inserted Border, and after the first hour they were 19 for two on their way to being dismissed for 252 early on the second morning.

Province's reply of 469 was anchored by opener Smith's 183. It also featured disciplined bowling by off-spinner, Geoff Love, who improved his career best figures to seven for 116.

Tragically for Border, Drakes had Smith caught off a no ball on 19. The significance of that blunder grew as the innings wore on, and the upshot was that the visitors spent more than 13 hours in the field and followed-on 217 runs in the red.

Slow left-arm bowler Claude Henderson showed relentless accuracy in taking five for 62 as Border were dismissed in fading light for 191, of which a defiant Laden Gamiet scored 80.

Graeme Smith moved from Gauteng during the off-season, and tasted Supersport Series success first time round with his new team, Western Province.

SOUTH AFRICAN DOMESTIC LIMITED OVERS COMPETITION

A team that could barely put a foot right in the first-class game won South Africa's domestic limited overs competition, the Standard Bank Cup. The Kwazulu-Natal Dolphins rescued their season with a hard-fought three wicket win over Northerns in the final, but although the trophy will look good in the cabinet, it was paper over some very wide cracks in an otherwise disappointing year.

Despite finishing top of the league stage of the competition, the Dolphins were extremely fortunate to make the final. It would not be toying with the truth to suggest that only an act of god saved them from elimination at the semi-final stage.

After the first two games of the three-leg play-off against Eastern Province had been shared, the Dolphins bowling attack were blasted all over Kingsmead in the third. Eastern Province had piled on 253 for two from just 41.2 overs (Robin Peterson 94 from 73 balls, James Bryant 77 not out and Justin Kemp 57 not out from 47 balls), when rain brought the game to a premature close.

Chasing a total in the region of 280 would probably have been beyond the Dolphins, but instead they made light work of a far easier target the very next day, when the match was replayed in its entirety.

Rain again played a part, this time the Duckworth/Lewis system being called into action after Eastern Province totalled 210 all out before a 90-minute interruption. A revised target of 165 off 33 overs was comfortably negotiated for the loss of just three wickets and with nine balls to spare. It was genuinely rough justice for Eastern Province, who had come back well after a nine-wicket defeat in the first game.

Northerns did pull off a fine comeback in their semi-final series against a strong Border side, winning matches two and three away from home. First they made a robust Border total of 271 look decidedly flimsy, winning with 16 balls to spare (Jacques Rudolph 89, Martin van Jaarsveld 76) and then they skittled their hosts for 85, allowing the smoothest of passages to the final.

Somewhat bizarrely, although the semi-finals were played as a best-of-three contest, the final was a one-off in Durban. Kwazulu-Natal captain, Dale Benkenstein, won a useful toss and put Northerns in to bat.

The Dolphins' attack had a distinctly useful look about it, with both Shaun Pollock and Lance

Klusener back from international duty, although West Indian import Eldine Baptiste (two for 27 from his nine overs) was the pick of an impressive bunch as Northerns could manage only 214 for three from their 45 overs. Were it not for a smash-and-grab 50 not out off 37 balls from Kruger van Wyk, Northerns would have struggled to make it passed 200.

A partnership of 75 for the second wicket between the promising Wade Wingfield (61) and Ashraf Mall (40) laid a firm foundation for the Dolphins' run-chase, and although the middle order imploded, John Kent's 29 off 27 balls and 25 not out from wicketkeeper Errol Stewart took the home side to the trophy.

FIRST-CLASS AVERAGES

BATTING

	M	Inns	NO	HS	Runs	Av	100	50
MH Richardson	6	9	1	173*	500	62.50	1	2
ND McKenzie	9	14	3	123	672	61.09	3	3
SG Koenig	7	13	0	155	789	60.69	3	4
JH Kallis	8	13	1	160	671	55.91	1	4
G Kirsten	6	10	1	180	496	55.11	1	2
AG Prince	8	14	4	120*	539	53.90	1	2
MS Sinclair	6	11	2	150	461	51.22	1	2
DPM Jayawardene	5	9	1	98	378	47.25	-	3
N Boje	7	9	1	105	375	46.87	1	2
HD Ackerman	9	16	3	128	606	46.61	3	2
CM Spearman	5	10	1	115	416	46.22	2	2
GFJ Liebenberg	8	13	0	202	595	45.76	1	4
DN Crookes	8	16	1	117	671	44.73	1	5
JC Kent	7	13	3	178*	435	43.50	1	2
LJ Wilkinson	9	15	0	169	642	42.80	1	3
MV Boucher	8	11	3	92	341	42.62	-	2
GC Smith	9	16	0	183	676	42.25	2	3
JL Ontong	9	15	2	131*	546	42.00	1	4
JM Henderson	8	15	1	98	584	41.71	-	5
JM Kemp	7	11	0	188	455	41.36	1	2
AC Thomas	10	18	5	106*	531	40.84	1	2
AG Puttick	7	12	1	153*	441	40.09	1	2
DJ Cullinan	7	11	2	112	359	39.88	1	1
MI Gidley	10	17	1	151	636	39.75	1	4
AM Bacher	8	15	1	190	552	39.42	1	3
LJ Koen	8	14	0	97	546	39.00	-	5
AJ Seymore	7	14	0	174	543	38.78	1	4
PC Strydom	10	18	0	86	693	38.50	-	7
G Dros	6	10	2	100*	308	38.50	1	-
JF Venter	9	15	2	112*	494	38.00	1	3
NC Johnson	9	15	2	84	490	37.69	-	5
PJR Steyn	8	15	1	188*	527	37.64	1	2
JA Rudolph	9	17	0	144	638	37.52	2	2
CC Bradfield	8	16	1	91	558	37.20	-	3
LL Bosman	7	12	2	115*	371	37.10	1	2
M van Jaarsfeld	9	17	0	132	630	37.05	1	5
ELR Stewart	9	15	4	79	405	36.81	-	2
PPJ Koortzen	10	17	1	127	578	36.12	2	2
MJR Rindel	7	14	0	91	504	36.00	-	4
R Niewoudt	5	9	1	98	287	35.87	-	1
DJ Watson	9	17	2	81	532	35.46	-	5
ML Bruyns	9	17	1	102*	548	34.25	1	3
SC Pope	10	19	0	125	647	34.05	2	3
GD Elliott	10	17	0	125	577	33.94	1	3
GH Bodi	9	12	2	104	326	32.60	1	2
MJ Strydom	9	16	2	124	454	32.42	1	1
N Pothas	8	14	1	93	418	32.15	-	4
P de Bruyn	8	16	2	83	447	31.92	-	4
TL Tsolekile	9	12	0	95	382	31.83	-	3
K Sangakkara	5	9	0	98	281	31.22	-	2
Z de Bruyn	8	14	1	66	404	31.07	-	3
DM Benkenstein	8	15	2	86	399	30.69	-	2
H Davids	6	12	1	124	336	30.54	1	1
MJ Lavine	9	16	0	113	477	29.81	1	1
W Bossenger	10	17	2	74*	439	29.26	-	3
AI Gait	8	13	0	112	374	28.76	1	2
S Elworthy	7	11	3	75*	224	28.00	-	1
I Mitchell	9	17	1	83	446	27.87	-	3
W Wiblin	10	19	2	88	470	27.64	-	3
MW Creed	8	14	1	47	351	27.00	-	-
Ashraf Mall	6	10	0	64	270	27.00	-	1
J Brooker	5	8	0	77	216	27.00	-	2
JG Strydom	4	8	0	73	216	27.00	-	1
ZA Abrahim	9	14	4	57	267	26.70	-	1
HH Gibbs	7	12	0	91	316	26.33	-	2
AG Botha	7	14	4	59	259	25.90	-	1
GM Hewitt	8	14	0	62	357	25.50	-	1
HH Dippenaar	6	10	0	100	243	24.30	1	-
IJL Trott	9	18	2	93	385	24.06	-	3
VC Drakes	9	16	1	53	360	24.00	-	1
GL Brophy	8	12	2	40	238	23.80	-	-
DJ Callaghan	9	16	1	129	347	23.13	1	-

FIRST-CLASS AVERAGES

BATTING

	M	Inns	NO	HS	Runs	Av	100	50
JDC Bryant	9	18	2	70	363	22.68	-	2
RJ Peterson	8	15	2	96*	289	22.23	-	1
DW Murray	9	15	2	58*	289	22.23	-	1
MR Benfield	8	16	1	93	329	21.93	-	2
LL Gamiet	10	18	0	80	383	21.27	-	1
PJ Botha	6	11	0	50	229	20.81	-	1
D Jordaan	5	10	0	75	206	20.60	-	1
JA Morkel	7	12	0	117	241	20.08	1	-
CFK van Wyk	9	15	2	59	256	19.69	-	1
GA Roe	8	14	5	66	175	19.44	-	1
CB Sugden	10	19	0	54	367	19.31	-	2
HC Bakkes	7	9	1	54*	154	19.25	-	1
U Abrahams	4	8	0	51	150	18.75	-	1
C Light	9	16	0	101	299	18.68	1	-
S Abrahams	7	11	0	85	204	18.54	-	1
RP Arnold	5	8	0	71	148	18.50	-	1
GT Love	10	17	7	30	183	18.30	-	-
BT Player	7	12	2	73	172	17.20	-	1
AG Lawson	9	18	1	64	289	17.00	-	3
JH Louw	5	8	0	50	132	16.50	-	1
MN van Wyk	7	11	0	49	179	16.27	-	-
WM Dry	6	11	0	80	176	16.00	-	1
SJ Palframan	7	11	0	31	174	15.81	-	-
EG Poole	10	18	0	50	284	15.77	-	1
FC Brooker	6	10	1	31	135	15.00	-	-
A Jacobs	7	13	0	33	193	14.84	-	-
GJ Kruis	10	16	1	59	212	14.13	-	1
MS Atapattu	5	9	1	42	110	13.75	-	-
D Jennings	8	16	2	53	188	13.42	-	1
ST Jayasuriya	5	9	0	38	118	13.11	-	-
G Toyana	5	9	0	42	114	12.66	-	-
DL Makalima	8	15	1	42*	167	11.92	-	-
HM de Vos	6	11	0	35	130	11.81	-	-
GE Flusk	8	13	2	31*	126	11.45	-	-
MC Venter	7	12	1	44rh	116	10.54	-	-

Qualification: 8 completed innings, average 10.00

BOWLING

	Overs	Mds	Runs	Wkts	Av	Best	10m	5/inn
GA Roe	291.1	92	631	40	15.77	7-47	-	3
CK Langeveldt	125.4	33	359	21	17.09	5-19	-	1
PJ Botha	152.3	54	375	21	17.85	4-48	-	-
KCG Benjamin	190.4	51	549	29	18.93	6-73	-	1
JM Kemp	241.2	68	552	29	19.03	6-56	-	2
SM Pollock	253.2	98	515	27	19.07	6-30	-	1
M Ntini	268.2	89	688	36	19.11	6-59	-	2
DJ Callaghan	156	50	355	18	19.72	5-24	1	3
AA Donald	127.4	32	341	17	20.05	4-69	-	-
CS Martin	121.5	34	392	19	20.63	4-104	-	-
A Nel	154	38	361	17	21.23	5-43	-	2
AC Dawson	238.2	74	583	27	21.59	5-51	-	1
HS Williams	245.1	70	629	29	21.68	6-40	-	4
CM Willoughby	298.5	107	683	31	22.03	5-26	-	1
PV Mpitsang	268.1	61	733	33	22.21	5-24	-	3
CW Henderson	400.3	138	801	36	22.25	5-6	-	3
GJ Kruis	433	119	1083	46	23.54	5-50	-	2
N Boje	220.1	71	448	19	23.57	5-67	-	1
S Elworthy	243.2	65	711	30	23.70	5-41	-	2
G Dros	116.3	29	332	14	23.71	3-32	-	-
VC Drakes	368	101	975	41	23.78	5-80	-	1
D Pretorius	276.3	62	881	37	23.81	4-51	-	-
CA Copeland	145.4	25	515	21	24.52	8-101	1	2

FIRST-CLASS AVERAGES

BOWLING

	Overs	Mds	Runs	Wkts	Av	Best	10m	5/inn
R Telemachus	168.5	34	552	22	25.09	6-54	-	1
PC Strydom	233.5	64	579	23	25.17	3-29	-	-
JC Kent	174	36	555	22	25.22	6-77	-	1
P de Bruyn	105.4	21	306	12	25.50	4-34	-	-
AG Botha	244.2	80	614	24	25.58	6-106	-	1
GE Flusk	195	36	618	24	25.75	5-55	-	1
GJP Kruger	166.5	42	491	19	25.84	4-49	-	-
GH Bodi	239.3	47	750	29	25.86	6-63	-	1
JE Bastow	145.1	42	364	14	26.00	4-46	-	-
F van der Merwe	157.1	42	522	20	26.10	5-62	-	2
DH Townsend	239.2	64	761	29	26.24	5-49	-	1
M Ngam	189.2	38	552	21	26.28	4-78	-	-
NC Johnson	115	24	322	12	26.83	2-5	-	-
L Klusener	107.1	31	269	10	26.90	4-111	-	-
DR Tuffey	134	31	410	15	27.33	5-69	-	1
JF Venter	289.2	66	858	31	27.67	6-90	-	2
AC Thomas	292	84	788	28	28.14	6-26	-	1
ZA Abrahaim	273.1	58	790	28	28.21	5-22	-	1
GJ Smith	330.4	87	870	30	29.00	5-25	-	1
T Henderson	196.1	55	525	18	29.16	6-56	-	1
BGK Walker	120.5	27	350	12	29.16	3-13	-	-
NM Carter	255.4	53	839	28	29.96	6-63	-	2
JH Kallis	200.5	57	528	17	31.05	3-77	-	-
HC Bakkes	221.3	65	625	20	31.25	6-108	-	1
PR Adams	203.3	54	582	18	32.33	3-33	-	-
JA Morkel	199.2	50	621	19	32.68	4-36	-	-
DJ Terbrugge	166.5	46	363	11	33.00	5-39	-	1
MJ Lavine	322	79	995	30	33.16	6-53	1	3
JH Louw	121.4	22	414	12	34.50	3-25	-	-
GT Love	372	100	979	28	34.96	7-116	-	1
EW Kidwell	167.3	20	603	17	35.47	4-71	-	-
BT Player	189.4	58	431	12	35.91	5-26	-	1
A Pringle	170.3	35	486	13	37.38	4-49	-	-
RJ Peterson	329.5	79	919	24	38.29	5-87	-	1
JL Ontong	201.1	25	658	17	38.70	4-120	-	-
GD Elliott	146	37	390	10	39.00	2-18	-	-
GM Gilder	155.2	34	527	13	40.53	3-55	-	-
M Hayward	214.3	24	774	19	40.73	3-69	-	-
CR Tatton	236	64	651	15	43.40	5-80	-	1

Qualification: 10 wickets in 8 innings

The following bowlers took 10 wickets in fewer than 8 innings:

M Muralitharan	145.3	41	310	18	17.22	6-39	1	2
RE Bryson	51	10	193	10	19.30	5-33	-	1
SB O'Connor	116.2	34	309	16	19.31	5-51	-	1
MW Pringle	109.1	31	235	10	23.50	4-32	-	-
JJ van der Wath	127.3	21	411	15	27.40	5-59	-	1
OD Gibson	162.3	41	443	16	27.68	6-53	-	1
NA Fusedale	143.1	27	438	15	29.20	5-170	-	1
JT Mafa	85.5	17	352	11	32.00	6-62	-	1
CRD Fernando	126	17	517	15	34.46	5-98	-	1

FIELDING

40 – D Jennings (38ct,2st); 39 – W Bossenger (38ct,1st); DW Murray; 37 – CFK van Wyk (35ct,2st), EG Poole; 34 – MV Boucher (32ct,2st), I Mitchell (32ct,2st); 31 – TL Tsolekile (30ct,1st); 29 – GL Brophy (27ct,2st); 27 – ELR Stewart (26ct,1st); 26 – SJ Palframan (23ct,3st); 23 – NC Johnson; 17 – LJ Koen, GC Smith; 16 – JL Ontong, AC Parore (14ct,2st), M van Jaarsveld; 15 – GD Elliott, N Pothas, MN van Wyk; 14 – RS Kaluwitharana (12ct,2st); 13 – W Wiblin; 11 – CC Bradfield, M de Kock (10ct,1st), HH Gibbs, A Jacobs, JH Kallis; 10 – HD Ackerman, ML Bruyns, DN Crookes, JC Kent, MJ Lavine, GFJ Liebenberg, BT Player, LJ Wilkinson

Qualification: 10 catches or more

WEST INDIES

South Africa in the West Indies
West Indies Domestic First-Class
Cricket (including England 'A')
West Indies Domestic
One-Day Cricket
First-Class Averages

SOUTH AFRICA IN THE WEST INDIES
By Tony Cozier

In spite of their abysmal overseas record (18 defeats in their previous 20 Tests), the West Indies could at least boast that their home defences had only been breached once in a Test series in 27 years as South Africa arrived for their first full tour of the Caribbean in March 2001.

Since Ian Chappell led his audacious Australians to a 2–0 triumph in 1973, only their successors under Mark Taylor in 1995 had managed a repeat, regaining the Frank Worrell Trophy 2–1.

If these statistics were not 'damned lies', as Mark Twain once observed of all such figures, they were clearly misleading. In the two preceding seasons, only Brian Lara's incredible batting against Australia, a blatant umpiring error and Saqlain Mushtaq's shocking fumbles on two run out chances against Pakistan that allowed the West Indies to squeak home by one wicket had denied the opposition series-clinching results.

Their luck was due to run out, however, and the super-fit, efficient South Africans ensured that it did. They won the second and fourth Tests to claim the new Sir Vivian Richards Trophy before the West Indies had the understandable joy of recording their first victory in 14 Tests in the last match of the series at Sabina Park.

South Africa's dominance was even more evident in their 5–2 winning margin in the one-day internationals that followed, making them the first team to triumph in both forms of the game on a West Indies tour.

They batted more consistently, bowled more effectively and, above all, fielded and caught on a different level to their opponents who dropped more than a dozen chances and bore no comparison on the ground. The failure of Lance Klusener and wicket-keeper Mark Boucher with the bat meant that their lower-order lost some of its usual mastery, but captain Shaun Pollock's form at number eight was usually enough to stave off trouble.

In a significant variation from what was once the norm, South Africa relied mainly on five pace bowlers while the West Indies bowled leg-spinner Dinanath Ramnarine more than anyone else. Indeed, they used a second spinner, the orthodox left-armer Neil McGarrell, in the fourth Test, the first time in two decades that their attack had carried such a balance.

Previous page: Another swansong for Courtney Walsh, who finished his final Test series with a haul of 25 wickets.

Given the circumstances, however, the West Indies were not disgraced as they had so often been of late. And they could glory in the remarkable performance of the evergreen Courtney Walsh who, in his farewell series after 17 years of Test cricket, claimed 25 wickets at under 20 apiece, among them the one-time unimaginable 500th.

The clean sweep in both Tests (5–0) and one-day internationals (6–0) inflicted by Steve Waugh's Australians on the preceding tour down-under should have softened up an already delicate opposition for the South Africans only a few weeks later. As it was, the South Africans arrived to find West Indies cricket in a familiar state of chaos.

Several reputations had been shattered in Australia, not least that of captain Jimmy Adams – to such an extent that it was deemed he could no longer justify a place in the team. So, for the fourth time in five years, it was clear there would be a new skipper.

The eventual appointment of Carl Hooper, a week prior to the first Test, generated even more passionate debate than when Walsh was replaced by Lara three years earlier. At 34, and almost two years after he suddenly announced his retirement prior to the World Cup in England, Hooper returned from his new home in Adelaide eager to regain his place in the West Indies team. He emphatically accomplished his mission with 954 runs (at an average of 95.4) in the Busta International Series.

Chief selector Mike Findlay described him as 'the only logical choice' as captain and his experience and all-round quality certainly made a difference. But it was not a view shared by everyone. Michael Holding, the great fast bowler turned television guru, was so incensed that 'the prodigal son' had been given the highest position in the team, he abandoned his broadcasting assignment in protest.

It was hardly the best environment for the West Indies to start the series, yet they carried every Test well into the fifth day, where only three of their previous nine had made it into the third day and one not even that far.

South Africa had to call on all their experience and resilience more than once to pull themselves out of tight corners. Pollock, whose all-round performance (302 runs at an average of 75.5 and 20 wickets at 23.2) gained him the Man of the Series award, described it as 'the most difficult tour I've ever been involved in'.

On mainly slow, featureless pitches that demanded special care and attention from the batsmen, the tempo of the cricket was invariably slow and the scoring low. There was only one total over 400 compared to three under 250 and three under 200. The overall rate was 2.37 runs an over and the third day of the fourth Test yielded just 132 runs from the 89.1 overs bowled. Still, the balance repeatedly shifted one way then the next, and the contest was seldom less than intense.

As had been the case in England the previous summer and in Australia subsequently, when they were routed for such all-out totals as 54, 61, 125, 82, 125 and 109, the West Indies were betrayed by their batting when it mattered most.

Set a winning target of 232 in the second Test, the 50th at the Queen's Park Oval in Port-of-Spain, they began the last day needing 200 more with nine wickets intact. It was a position encouraging enough to attract an unusually large crowd of around 12,000, but they were to leave disappointed as their team capitulated for 162, their last five wickets tumbling for only 19 runs.

Wicket-keeper Ridley Jacobs' maiden Test hundred, the only one for the West Indies, seemed to have rendered safe the fourth Test in Barbados. But another sudden second-innings collapse late on the last day might have brought another defeat had Ramnarine and Merv Dillon, their eighth-wicket pair, not indulged in blatant time-wasting tactics.

The fourth Test in St John's presented a genuine opportunity for the West Indies to take the initiative as South Africa found themselves on 148 for seven by tea on the first afternoon. They could not seize the chance, however, raising a meagre 130 in reply to South Africa's modest first-innings total of 247. They were never in it after that, in spite of Brian Lara's explosive 91, the left-hander's highest score of the series.

With both the series and the impressive new Sir Vivian Richards Trophy safely secured, South Africa relaxed to such an extent that five of their squad (Paul Adams, Herschelle Gibbs, Andre Nel, Roger Telemachus and physio Craig Smith) celebrated with a little marijuana in one of their hotel rooms that evening.

Initially kept quiet before it became public knowledge weeks later, it was an embarrassing episode for which those involved were each heavily fined.

The same mellowness from the South Africans seemed to carry over to the last Test as the West Indies played their best all-round cricket of the season. However, it was not long before normal service was resumed in the one-day series.

FIRST TEST
9–13 March 2001 at Georgetown, Guyana

A featureless, easy-paced pitch negated any possibility of a decisive result to a closely-fought encounter.

It was an encouraging start for the West Indies following their disastrous tour of Australia. They totalled over 300 in each innings for the first time in 16 Tests and contained South Africa to 332 by despatching the last six wickets for 58, after Kirsten's marathon 150 that occupied seven-and-a-half hours.

The home side had the satisfaction of making a second-innings declaration after Sarwan's polished 91 on his home ground, but there was never any realistic chance that South Africa would falter over the final two-and-a-half sessions. Gibbs, out cheaply in the first innings, helped himself to an unbeaten 83 before the captains agreed to end the stalemate.

Hooper's first act as captain seemed vital. He won the toss on the Bourda ground where he had played since he was a boy, and depended on his batsmen to make the most of an encouraging pitch and fast, parched outfield.

They didn't fulfil his expectations. Although they repeatedly laid the foundations for a sizeable total, each promising partnership was ended before it could develop into something substantial.

From the dominant position of 101 for one at lunch, an effort laced with 14 boundaries, the West Indies fell to 232 for seven on the opening day. They were kept in check by purposeful South African bowling, in which Klusener's accurate, medium-paced off-cutters were essential, and were finally undermined by Donald's two wickets with successive balls late in the day.

The tall, left-handed Gayle, playing in his first Test for nine months, provided the early momentum for the West Indies with 81 off 159 balls that featured thumping off-side strokes, mainly off the back foot, that brought the majority of his 14 fours.

He shared promising early stands with his fellow Jamaicans, adding 43 for the first wicket with Hinds and 88 for the second with Samuels who, batting at number three for the first time, confirmed the impression he had made during his debut tour to Australia.

Once they were gone, Lara joined Gayle for another left-handed partnership, with the innings at the crossroads at 131 for two.

Gayle's commanding innings was ended by Kallis to a wicket-keeper's catch 25 minutes before tea and, when Lara tried to break free of Klusener's tight grip, he lashed four fours for 21 off 16 balls before skying a catch to mid-off attempting another.

Donald quickly capitalized on the breakthrough, yorking the struggling Sarwan and claiming Jacobs leg before with a full toss with successive balls. Klusener dismissed McLean in the closing overs, leaving Hooper with only three bowlers for company the next morning. But, as Hooper took command, much to the delight of the adoring crowd, Dillon stayed with him for almost two hours to add 62 important runs. When Hooper was last out, sweeping Boje to deep square-leg, the total had squeezed past 300.

Dillon returned to provide the West Indies with the early wicket of Gibbs, a shin-high skidder, but Kirsten and Kallis carefully built the foundations of a strong South African position, and they were 130 for one when the second day closed. Even though the left-handed Kirsten moved from his overnight score of 80 to a typically tenacious 150 the next day, South Africa could only gain a marginal lead of 28. Gayle and Hinds then erased the deficit with a volley of nine boundaries, scoring 50 off the 15 overs available to them before close.

Carl Hooper crowned his debut Test in charge of the West Indies with a vital 69 in the first innings.

Two partnerships involving Kirsten seemed to be guiding South Africa to a commanding position when the West Indies restored the balance with a cluster of wickets.

Kirsten and Kallis extended their second-wicket partnership to 146 over the first hour and a half before the West Indies had a lucky break. Kirsten had advanced to his 12th Test hundred in his 69th Test and Kallis had followed to his 50 when umpire Hampshire ruled Kallis leg before off an inside-edge to McLean's off-cutter.

Soon, Cullinan and McKenzie, both with known fallibility to good leg-spin, were gone to Ramnarine to even matters once more and leave the South Africans on 198 for four. The balance tilted again as Kirsten, by now well entrenched, and Boucher added 76 for the fifth wicket.

The pair forced Ramnarine out of the attack, but the second new ball initiated another South African slide either side of tea that proved decisive. Kirsten's tired, top-edged cut provided Walsh with his 495th Test wicket, Klusener was leg before to McLean and Walsh collected his next scalp in the following over, Boucher, again lbw.

The three wickets had fallen for 13 from just 25 deliveries and, for once, South Africa's formidable tail did not wag.

The West Indies had been involved in so many second-innings collapses that their batting on the fourth day came as a relief. They saved themselves from the defeat they had endured in their previous seven Tests and, by close, were hurrying towards a declaration.

The West Indies had eked out 44 runs off the 28 overs before lunch on day four, losing Hinds and Gayle. Lara then threatened to take control, scoring 45 in a stand of 69 with Samuels, before Ntini had him caught at short extra-cover, and when the 20-year-olds, Samuels and Sarwan, struggled to make progress in a stand of 63, the contest seemed destined for stalemate.

Samuels spent four hours 40 minutes for 51 before Kallis plucked out his middle-stump, but then Hooper entered to up the tempo and Sarwan followed his captain's lead.

Hooper and his young fellow Guyanese, Sarwan, took 76 off the last 19 overs – 62 off the last 11 – so that the West Indies could start the last day 258 ahead and were able to dictate terms, a rare situation.

Sarwan overcame an uncertain start to end the fourth day unbeaten on 71 with ten boundaries, while Hooper got the better of what little doubt

FIRST TEST – WEST INDIES v. SOUTH AFRICA
9–13 March 2001 at Bourda, Georgetown

WEST INDIES

	First innings		Second innings	
WW Hinds	c Boje, b Pollock	13	c Boucher, b Donald	14
CH Gayle	c Boucher, b Kallis	81	c Boucher, b Boje	44
MN Samuels	b Boje	40	b Kallis	51
BC Lara	c Donald, b Klusener	47	c Pollock, b Ntini	45
RR Sarwan	b Donald	7	run out (Gibbs)	91
CL Hooper (capt)	c Klusener, b Boje	69	c Cullinan, b Boje	35
*RD Jacobs	lbw b Donald	0	not out	18
NAM McLean	b Klusener	6	lbw b Boje	0
D Ramnarine	run out (Gibbs)	5		
M Dillon	c Cullinan, b Ntini	9		
CA Walsh	not out	2		
	b2, lb12, w2, nb9	25	b10, lb10, w2, nb8	30
	Penalty runs	5		
		304	(for 7 wickets dec.)	333

	First innings				Second innings			
	O	M	R	W	O	M	R	W
Donald	23	9	43	2	20	8	51	1
Pollock	18	2	54	1	17	4	51	-
Ntini	12	2	48	1	20	5	50	1
Kallis	17	2	33	1	15	2	36	1
Klusener	35	13	56	2	8	1	27	-
Boje	19.1	6	56	2	37	13	93	3

Fall of Wickets
1-43, 2-131, 3-165, 4-206, 5-221, 6-221, 7-228, 8-238, 9-300
1-51, 2-78, 3-147, 4-210, 5-299, 6-333, 7-333

SOUTH AFRICA

	First innings		Second innings	
G Kirsten	c Jacobs, b Walsh	150	c Hinds, b Ramnarine	24
HH Gibbs	b Dillon	8	not out	83
JH Kallis	lbw b McLean	50	lbw b McLean	30
DJ Cullinan	c Jacobs, b Ramnarine	7	not out	4
ND McKenzie	b Ramnarine	4		
*MV Boucher	lbw b Walsh	52		
L Klusener	lbw b McLean	5		
N Boje	c Hinds, b Dillon	15		
SM Pollock (capt)	not out	17		
AA Donald	c Lara, b Ramnarine	2		
M Ntini	c Jacobs, b Dillon	11		
	b4, lb5, nb2	11	b1	1
		332	(for 2 wickets)	142

	First innings				Second innings			
	O	M	R	W	O	M	R	W
Walsh	28	7	56	2	10	3	19	-
Dillon	27	5	64	3	5	1	21	-
McLean	22	0	75	2	10	3	25	1
Ramnarine	41	9	105	3	27.3	14	46	1
Hooper	8	0	21	-	14	8	23	-
Samuels	1	0	2	-	2	0	3	-
Sarwan	1	0	4	-				

Fall of Wickets
1-25, 2-171, 3-186, 4-198, 5-274, 6-285, 7-287, 8-310, 9-315
1-66, 2-134

Umpires: EA Nicholls & JH Hampshire
Toss: West Indies
Test debuts: nil

Match drawn

there was from local umpire Nicholls on a first-ball leg-before decision off Kallis to finish the day on 31.

As this was Hooper's first Test as captain, he understandably took no chances with his declaration on the last day. He let the innings run for another hour before he felt it was safe enough to close at 333 for seven.

It left South Africa with 306 to win off a minimum of 76 overs in a match in which the batsmen chugged along at an average of two-and-a-half runs an over. The possibility of the West Indies bowlers despatching ten wickets in the time available was equally remote. Alarm bells might have rung for the South Africans with an early wicket or three, but the West Indies squandered an immediate chance. Hooper, as safe a slip catcher as there is, missed a straightforward catch at second slip that would have removed Gibbs to Dillon's fifth ball.

Gibbs made the most of his luck after that and the match was called off as a draw bang on 4.30 pm.

The day was notable only for the disappointment of Sarwan's run out that left him nine short of his first Test hundred. The graceful little Guyanese batsman had endured a chastening tour of Australia and had fallen cheaply in the first innings, so his rehabilitation revealed character. Sent back by Jacobs on a stroke to square-leg, his full-stretch dive back failed to beat Gibbs' sharp return.

SECOND TEST
17–21 March 2001 at Port-of-Spain, Trinidad

The 50th Test at the Queen's Park Oval – designated the 'Golden Test' – produced a gripping, slow-scoring contest that prompted the South Africa captain, Shaun Pollock, to call it 'the most intense Test I've played in'.

Neither team held the decisive advantage until the West Indies, needing the lowest total of the match to take the lead in the series, lost their last five wickets for just 19 runs on either side of tea on the final afternoon.

It was a disappointing climax to a special match in which Courtney Walsh claimed his 500th Test wicket, a feat marked by spontaneous celebrations around the ground and a special presentation at the end of the day.

In spite of Cullinan's first-day hundred, South Africa's vaunted lower-order collapsed with the loss of the last five wickets for 30 and the West Indies led on first innings for the first time in the eight Tests between the teams, mainly as a result of Jacobs' unbeaten 93. When South Africa's lower-order again folded for 34 in the second innings, the West Indies began the last day requiring 200 more runs with nine wickets in hand on a sluggish but still reliable pitch. It was enough to attract the largest last-day crowd in several years to the Oval, estimated at 12,000, but the result was not what they came to see.

Cullinan disregarded the regular fall of wickets at the other end on the opening day to compile his 13th Test hundred, as South Africa fell from 219 for four an hour after tea to 286 all out.

He came in ten minutes after lunch after Kirsten and Gibbs had fallen in successive overs following a testing morning session after Pollock had won the toss. Cullinan and Kallis immediately mounted a calculated assault, especially on Ramnarine, with a 99-run-a-minute start.

The course of the innings was changed by Hinds, a player who had never previously bowled in a Test match. Trundling right-arm medium-pace, he removed Kallis with his third ball, snaring a stiff return catch so low that the batsman waited for confirmation it was clean from the television replay. When he later returned for a second spell to dismiss Boucher, Walsh had already accounted for McKenzie to Gayle's swooping second-slip catch.

It was the cue for Hooper to bring back Ramnarine. His googlies claimed Klusener and Boje and ended Cullinan's crucial innings to a top-edged slog that skewed to mid-on. It was an ugly end to an innings lasting three hours 25 minutes that contained 14 fours.

McLean completed the West Indies comeback with the wickets of Donald and Ntini, leaving the openers with one over to see out the day.

Donald's four timely wickets on the second day gave South Africa a slight, but significant, advantage. Every time the West Indies were batting themselves into a favourable position, he returned to deal a decisive blow.

Umpire Darrell Hair raises his finger to take Courtney Walsh to a unique milestone: his 500th Test wicket – Jacques Kallis, lbw for no score.

Hinds and Samuels had provided the home side with a solid base after Pollock had claimed Gayle for the only wicket to fall before lunch. Donald separated them with his fourth ball after the interval, removing Samuels to a slip catch. Three-quarters of an hour later he got the benefit of umpire Hair's decision for a keeper's catch against Hinds.

Ntini silenced the crowd of 20,000 by sending back Lara to a slip catch by Kallis off a flailing drive as the innings faltered at 123 for four. For the next hour and 35 minutes, Hooper and Sarwan built an attractive stand of 75 that seemed likely to earn the West Indies the initiative, but Donald came back yet again to snuff out the resistance, removing both to leave the West Indies at 250 for seven at the end of the day and the balance even.

Jacobs' typically robust, unbeaten 93 and his stand of 71 with Dillon earned the home team a useful lead of 56 on the third day, but it was Walsh's achievement in becoming the first bowler in the history of the game to take 500 Test wickets that took centre stage.

Playing in his 129th Test, he dismissed Kallis second ball, to a dubious leg before decision by Hair, 25 minutes before tea, one of at least eight blatant umpiring errors that affected both sides equally. Television replays showed that the ball took the inside edge of the bat, but it was immaterial to the 11 West Indians on the field and the 5,000 or so around the ground who immediately broke into the customary wild West Indian celebrations. Two balls earlier, Walsh had got to within one of his milestone with the wicket of Kirsten.

The West Indies players formed a guard of honour for their hero as the teams left the field at tea and the first man to greet Walsh at the steps to the pavilion was Donald, the only South African with over 300 wickets. At a ceremony immediately after play, the West Indies Cricket Board (WICB) presented Walsh with a trophy to mark the achievement.

After Walsh had claimed his history-making wickets, the adventurous Gibbs and Cullinan settled things with an unbroken partnership of 92, and at the close South Africa were 74 runs to the good.

The West Indies regained the initiative on the fourth day with bowling of such tight control and slick ground fielding that South Africa could only score 22 off the first 22 overs after lunch.

Inevitably, Walsh set the example, adding four wickets to his two overnight scalps, the first time he had taken more than five wickets in an innings at Queen's Park.

SECOND TEST – WEST INDIES v. SOUTH AFRICA
17–21 March 2001 at Queen's Park Oval, Port-of-Spain

SOUTH AFRICA

	First innings		Second innings	
HH Gibbs	b Walsh	34	c sub (S Chanderpaul) b Walsh	87
G Kirsten	c Hooper, b McLean	23	c Jacobs, b Walsh	22
JH Kallis	c & b Hinds	53	lbw b Walsh	0
DJ Cullinan	c Dillon, b Ramnarine	103	c Lara, b Ramnarine	73
ND McKenzie	c Gayle, b Walsh	9	c Jacobs, b Dillon	25
*MV Boucher	c Hooper, b Hinds	16	(7) b Dillon	38
L Klusener	c Jacobs, b Ramnarine	15	(6) c Gayle, b Dillon	5
N Boje	c Jacobs, b Ramnarine	3	c Jacobs, b Walsh	9
SM Pollock (capt)	not out	15	b Walsh	8
AA Donald	c Jacobs, b McLean	0	lbw b Walsh	1
M Ntini	c & b McLean	7	not out	5
	nb8	8	b1, lb4, nb9	14
		286		**287**

	First innings				Second innings			
	O	M	R	W	O	M	R	W
Walsh	21	5	47	2	36.4	13	61	6
Dillon	17	2	74	-	28	8	58	3
McLean	16.5	2	60	3	18	1	76	-
Ramnarine	18	6	57	3	35	8	64	1
Hooper	9	1	25	-	13	3	23	-
Hinds	5	0	23	2				

Fall of Wickets
1-62, 2-62, 3-161, 4-189, 5-221, 6-256, 7-264, 8-265, 9-266
1-38, 2-38, 3-187, 4-198, 5-204, 6-253, 7-264, 8-276, 9-278

WEST INDIES

	First innings		Second innings	
WW Hinds	c Boucher, b Donald	56	lbw b Kallis	2
CH Gayle	lbw b Pollock	10	c Boucher, b Pollock	23
MN Samuels	c Klusener, b Donald	35	(4) c Kallis, b Donald	9
BC Lara	c Kallis, b Ntini	12	(5) lbw b Ntini	0
RR Sarwan	c Cullinan, b Donald	34	(6) c Boje, b Kallis	39
CL Hooper (capt)	lbw b Donald	53	(7) not out	54
*RD Jacobs	not out	93	(8) run out (Gibbs)	4
NAM McLean	c Ntini, b Pollock	3	(9) c Boucher, b Kallis	2
D Ramnarine	b Pollock	2	(3) c Kallis, b Donald	11
M Dillon	b Ntini	21	lbw b Kallis	0
CA Walsh	run out (Ntini/Pollock)	0	b Pollock	0
	b9, lb4, w3, nb7	23	b7, lb4, nb7	18
		342		**162**

	First innings				Second innings			
	O	M	R	W	O	M	R	W
Donald	30	6	91	4	15	4	32	2
Pollock	28	11	55	3	23.1	8	35	2
Ntini	16	4	56	2	16	4	22	1
Kallis	21	10	44	-	16	6	40	4
Boje	19	2	65	-				
Klusener	11	5	18	-	10	5	22	-

Fall of Wickets
1-24, 2-94, 3-118, 4-123, 5-198, 6-235, 7-242, 8-250, 9-321
1-20, 2-35, 3-50, 4-50, 5-51, 6-143, 7-150, 8-159, 9-159

Umpires: B Doctrove & DB Hair
Toss: South Africa
Test debuts: nil

South Africa won by 69 runs

Gibbs and Cullinan batted through the first hour and a half with few problems until Cullinan again paid the price for a wild swing at Ramnarine. He and Gibbs had put on 149 and, after they were separated, the West Indies regained the edge as South Africa's lower-order folded – the last five wickets falling for only 34 runs.

After five hours, 50 minutes for 87, Gibbs' patience ran out when he pulled Walsh straight to square leg. Klusener again fell cheaply (for five) and Walsh and Dillon wrapped up the innings with the second new ball.

By the close of play on the fourth day, the West Indies had cleared 32 of the 232 set for victory, for the loss of Hinds who fell to Kallis' second ball. There was an understandable sense of anticipation as spectators poured in next morning.

As it turned out, South Africa encountered resistance from only one partnership, a 92-run stand for the sixth wicket between Hooper and Sarwan, as they completed victory with 20.5 overs to spare.

The West Indies slipped to 51 for five after Lara fell leg before to Ntini for his first Test duck on his home ground – even though television replays showed that the ball had pitched well outside leg-stump. They were given renewed hope over the next two-and-three-quarter hours as Hooper and Sarwan got together, but once Sarwan was caught off an ill-advised hook off the third Kallis bouncer in the penultimate over to tea, the eager South Africans could not be denied victory.

They swept aside the last five wickets for 19 runs in the final session to take the lead in the series with Hooper left stranded and helpless after three hours and 50 minutes of flawless batting for 54.

THIRD TEST
29 March–3 April 2001, Kensington Oval, Bridgetown, Barbados

The balance shifted one way and then the other throughout until the likelihood of an improbable defeat crept up on the West Indies so quickly in the final session that their eighth-wicket pair, Ramnarine and Dillon, resorted to obvious and demeaning time-wasting tactics to stave it off.

With the top-seven batsmen gone for 82, the stipulated minimum overs complete and another 25 minutes remaining on a worn pitch, Ramnarine summoned physio Ronald Rogers onto the ground for lengthy service to a supposed hamstring injury, while Dillon changed his boots. Ramnarine adopted other blatant methods to consume time, drawing an

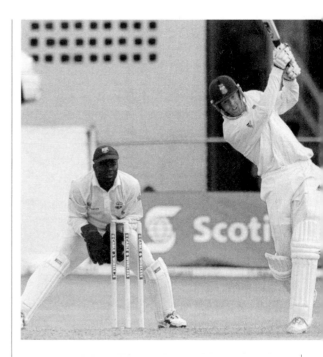

South Africa captain Shaun Pollock hits out on his way to an unbeaten 106 in the third Test at Barbados.

official warning from umpire Bucknor, but he held out for 14 balls, and Dillon for 22 balls, while left-arm spinner Boje and Klusener, from a shortened approach, were confined to five overs in the period.

ICC match referee Mike Denness, the former England captain, summoned both players, manager Skerritt, captain Hooper and coach Harper afterwards, but decided to take no action. Hooper and Skerritt excused the tactics, but Pollock revealed that some senior West Indian players had apologized to him. Percy Sonn, president of the South Africa board, one of several officials in Barbados for the match, called it 'a disgrace'. Alloy Lequay, president of the Trinidad and Tobago board, said it was 'a blatant disregard for the spirit of the game'.

It was a pity it had to end that way for it had been a fascinating contest.

Sent in, and aided by four missed catches, shoddy ground fielding and ineffective bowling, South Africa recovered from the loss of their first three wickets for 58 to reach their highest total against the West Indies.

Kirsten deflected Walsh's third ball of the match to third slip and was followed by Gibbs and Kallis before lunch, both to Dillon. The West Indies' dominance, however, stopped there.

Cullinan compiled another hundred, 134 runs that stretched into the second day and occupied just over six hours, adding a restorative 149 for the fourth wicket with McKenzie. Hinds' speculative medium-pace once more proved a partnership breaker as McKenzie pulled a catch to square-leg and the West Indies did well to come back into contention when Klusener was eighth out at 315 just after lunch on the second day.

Unlike the first two Tests, they could not complete the job, though, as Donald joined Pollock in a frustrating, record eighth-wicket partnership of 132. Pollock gave the lead, shielding his lesser batting colleague at first but giving him his head once he had settled in.

Dropped at slip off Walsh on 45, Pollock was within one run of his second Test hundred when Donald finally fell to the last ball of a Walsh over for 37, his highest Test score. The captain duly tapped a single off Ramnarine next ball to reach the landmark after three hours and 55 minutes.

The openers survived four overs late at the end of the second day, but the home team looked to be in a precarious position at 102 for four when, for the first time in the series, Lara and Hooper batted together. They had to repair the innings after their young colleagues had faltered – Hinds and Samuels the first two of the lively Kallis' six eventual victims, the aggressive Gayle and Sarwan to Ntini.

The West Indies' finest and most experienced batsmen entertained a packed Kensington Oval Saturday crowd with typically flambouyant strokeplay in a stand of 116. They combined to hit 24 fours, but neither player carried on to three figures, placing the pressure on the lower-order.

Not for the first time, Lara was out to a miscued pull to mid-on. When Hooper fell at the start of the fourth day, in an over twice interrupted and spanning 50 minutes while repairs were carried out to the bowlers' footholds, the West Indies were still two runs short of avoiding the follow-on.

It left Jacobs to see what he could manage to do with the tail. Once more, the doughty wicket-keeper rose to the challenge, scoring all but 28 of the 135 runs added by the last four wickets that brought the West Indies to within 67 of South Africa's total.

Typically bold in his approach, the left-hander had useful support from Dillon, who stayed with Jacobs for an hour and 55 minutes while 56 runs were

added, and Ramnarine, who contributed six in over an hour while another 37 were scored. Still, Jacobs was 11 away from his elusive maiden Test hundred when joined by number ten Cuffy.

Recognizing the urgency of the situation, Jacobs lashed two of his four sixes, the second sailing off the top edge into the top tier of the Hall and Griffith Stand at fine-leg to carry him to three figures for the first time in his 29th Test. Had any South African chosen to appeal the ball before, he would have again fallen three short for television replays showed he touched a catch to Boucher off Ntini. As it was, he remained unbeaten on 113 after four-and-a-quarter hours when the innings ended.

As South Africa went to the close on the fourth day with Kirsten (for his first 'pair' in Tests), Gibbs and McKenzie all gone for 52 and when they lost Kallis, Klusener and Boucher in the first hour the next morning, their lead was only 164 with four wickets left. The West Indies seemed to have a sniff of a chance of a stunning victory, but it was only a sniff.

Cullinan and Pollock once more stood in their way with a partnership of 70. Pollock declared when Ramnarine dismissed Cullinan and Donald with successive balls for his first five-wicket haul in Tests.

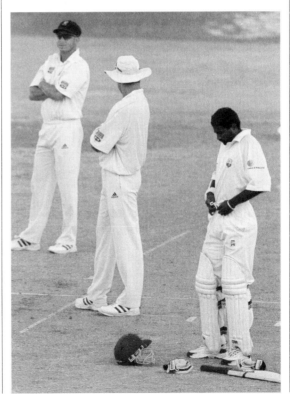

Obvious time-wasting tactics from Dinanath Ramnarine and Merv Dillon brought censure from the match referee, but undoubtedly saved the West Indies from defeat in Barbados.

THIRD TEST – WEST INDIES v. SOUTH AFRICA
29 March–2 April 2001 at Kensington Oval, Bridgetown

SOUTH AFRICA

	First innings		Second innings	
G Kirsten	c Gayle, b Walsh	0	(2) c Samuels, b Cuffy	0
HH Gibbs	c Hooper, b Dillon	34	(1) c Sarwan, b Hooper	19
JH Kallis	c Jacobs, b Dillon	11	(5) c Sarwan, b Hooper	20
DJ Cullinan	c & b Dillon	134	c Lara, b Ramnarine	82
ND McKenzie	c Dillon, b Hinds	72	(3) c Jacobs, b Ramnarine	12
*MV Boucher	c Jacobs, b Cuffy	3	(7) c Jacobs, b Ramnarine	0
N Boje	c Ramnarine, b Dillon	34	(9) not out	9
L Klusener	b Walsh	1	(6) c Cuffy, b Ramnarine	4
SM Pollock (capt)	not out	106	(8) c Hooper, b Walsh	40
AA Donald	c Hooper, b Walsh	37	lbw b Ramnarine	0
M Ntini	c & b Ramnarine	0		
	b6, lb4, w2, nb10	22	lb3, nb8	11
		454	(for 9 wickets dec.)	197

	First innings				Second innings			
	O	M	R	W	O	M	R	W
Walsh	45	15	87	3	14	3	28	1
Dillon	35	1	154	4	4	2	7	–
Cuffy	29	7	64	1	10	4	28	1
Ramnarine	33.1	6	86	1	31.5	10	78	5
Hooper	18	5	31	–	34	12	49	2
Hinds	10	5	13	1				
Samuels	2	0	6	–	2	1	4	–
Gayle	1	0	3	–				

Fall of Wickets
1-0, 2-53, 3-58, 4-207, 5-230, 6-306, 7-307, 8-315, 9-447
1-2, 2-31, 3-36, 4-80, 5-95, 6-97, 7-167, 8-197, 9-197

WEST INDIES

	First innings		Second innings	
WW Hinds	c Boucher, b Kallis	2	(2) c Cullinan, b Boje	8
CH Gayle	c Cullinan, b Ntini	40	(1) c Boucher, b Kallis	48
MN Samuels	c McKenzie, b Kallis	6	c Cullinan, b Boje	3
BC Lara	c Boje, b Kallis	83	b Klusener	8
RR Sarwan	c Gibbs, b Ntini	16	b Kallis	0
CL Hooper (capt)	c Boucher, b Kallis	74	c Boucher, b Boje	5
*RD Jacobs	not out	113	c McKenzie, b Boje	1
M Dillon	b Boje	14	not out	2
D Ramnarine	lbw b Boje	6	not out	0
CE Cuffy	lbw b Kallis	4		
CA Walsh	b Kallis	4		
	b4, lb9, nb12	25	b8, lb1, nb4	13
		387	(for 7 wickets)	88

	First innings				Second innings			
	O	M	R	W	O	M	R	W
Donald	14	7	30	–				
Pollock	35	11	84	–	5	0	25	–
Kallis	36	17	67	6	8	1	34	2
Ntini	28	7	93	2				
Boje	28	7	67	2	16.4	10	17	4
Klusener	10	3	33	–	9	7	3	1

Fall of Wickets
1-37, 2-49, 3-57, 4-102, 5-218, 6-252, 7-316, 8-353, 9-381
1-34, 2-59, 3-63, 4-64, 5-72, 6-82, 7-82

Umpires: SA Bucknor & DB Hair
Toss: West Indies
Test debuts: nil

Match drawn

Since a minimum of 36 overs, or two-and-a-quarter hours, remained, a draw seemed certain, especially when the West Indies reached 59 from 14 overs before losing their second wicket.

Yet nothing is certain with the West Indies and they proceeded to collapse as they had done with such frequency of late.

Gayle's explosive 48, containing 11 fours off 39 balls, seemed indicative of the laid-back attitude in the dressing room. They were in for a rude shock.

Boje, with controlled spin from out of the rough, Kallis, using the new ball instead of the injured Donald, and Klusener, triggered such panic in the West Indies' ranks that six wickets tumbled for 24 runs in just 19.4 overs, prompting Ramnarine and Dillon into their desperate measures.

FOURTH TEST
6–10 April 2001 at St John's, Antigua

Victory for South Africa by 82 runs in another low-and slow-scoring match secured them the series and the imposing Sir Vivian Richards Trophy that went with it. It was a tribute to their discipline, all-round strength and self-belief, for the West Indies had previously fallen only once in a home series in 28 years – to Australia in 1995.

The changed face of West Indies cricket was revealed when they chose two specialist spinners and only two fast bowlers in their XI for the first time since Kerry Packer enticed the great fast bowlers of the day to his World Series Cricket in 1978.

McGarrell, the orthodox left-armer from Guyana, joined Ramnarine to make his Test debut, aged 28, after six years of first-class cricket. Chief groundsman at the Antigua Recreation Ground, Keith Frederick, greeted them with the promise that 'as a true West Indian' he had prepared a spinners' pitch, an assertion that, at one time, would have cost him his job.

As it turned out, the pitch had little influence on the outcome of the game, although it did contribute to the tedious tempo. Nor was the reason for the West Indies' defeat their new-look bowling. It was, yet again, the frailty of their batting.

Given the team selection, Hooper's decision to bowl after winning the toss seemed perverse. Yet South Africa fell to 148 for seven just before tea on the opening day before Pollock arrived to check the West Indies' advance. As he had done twice in the previous Test, the South African captain led the recovery in an eighth-wicket partnership of 75 with the left-handed Boje that was not broken until the second morning.

Herschelle Gibbs' adventurous 85 was the mainstay of South Africa's first innings.

For the first two sessions of the match, the West Indian spinners took the initiative. McGarrell dismissed Kirsten in his fourth over, Kallis was bowled off his inside-edge by Dillon and Cullinan edged Ramnarine to slip, all before lunch.

McGarrell maintained the pressure with his control and variation on a bare pitch offering turn and claimed three of the four wickets South Africa lost for 28 runs in the last three-quarters of an hour before tea. Hooper had taken the other as Gibbs' gloved sweep was acrobatically caught by Jacobs to end an adventurous innings of 85, containing two sixes and 12 fours.

Pollock and Boje then put things right, batting through to the close with the kind of application missing from the earlier batsmen. Boje, badly dropped by Lara at slip off Walsh with the new ball the previous afternoon, fell to the veteran early on the second morning, but Pollock was left unbeaten yet again, two short of his 50. South Africa were dismissed for a modest 247, with their last three wickets adding 37 on the second morning.

It provided the West Indies with a wonderful chance to build a significant first-innings lead that they would need as the team batting last. Instead, they handed the initiative back to South Africa with a succession of unsuitable attacking shots against controlled bowling and dazzling fielding.

They finished the second day tottering at 130 for six and could raise only another ten runs the next morning. Their last six wickets fell for 14 from 15.5 overs, and subjected them to a virtually irretrievable position.

That was where the West Indies lost the match. Their failure was typified by Sarwan's dismissal. At a critical stage on the last day of the second Test, Kallis had carefully set a trap and Sarwan was immediately ensnared, hooking the third bouncer of an over to square-leg. He would be conned by the same ruse again.

When Kallis bounced his first ball of a new spell, Sarwan took the bait. His hook shot just cleared Boje alongside the umpire at square-leg on its way to the boundary. Kallis pounded his second ball into the pitch, but it sailed over Sarwan's back.

Undeterred, Kallis set Boje – the very man who had caught Sarwan in Port-of-Spain – a few yards deeper and bounced again. Once more, the batsman hooked and this time deposited the catch into the fielder's waiting lap.

Sarwan was the most extreme example of such unsuitable strokeplay, but Gayle, Hinds and Lara had all already succumbed cheaply to extravagant strokes to create early trouble. Twice, the West Indies seemed on course to recovery as Chanderpaul shared stands with Sarwan and Hooper but, by close of the third day, he and nightwatchman Dillon were also gone. Hooper was first out next morning and South Africa were batting again by lunch with a winning lead of only 107.

Even with more than half of the match remaining, the West Indies now played for time, and used defensive tactics so effectively that South Africa crawled to 122 for three off 76 overs by the close – the day yielded only 132 runs off 89.1 overs.

They were pinned down mainly by Ramnarine in a lengthy spell in which he pitched his leg-breaks from round the wicket into the rough outside the right-handers' leg-stump.

In a second-wicket partnership of 78, occupying 47 overs and three hours 20 minutes, Gibbs and McKenzie countered more with pad than bat against an attack diminished by the absence after three balls of Dillon, one of the two fast bowlers, with a sprained right thumb.

South Africa fell to 156 for seven before lunch on

FOURTH TEST – WEST INDIES v. SOUTH AFRICA
6–10 April 2001 at Antigua Recreation Ground, St John's

SOUTH AFRICA

	First innings		Second innings	
G Kirsten	c Dillon, b McGarrell	8	(2) c Sarwan, b Walsh	9
HH Gibbs	c Jacobs, b Hooper	85	(1) c Gayle, b Ramnarine	45
JH Kallis	b Dillon	5	(6) not out	30
DJ Cullinan	c Lara, b Ramnarine	4	(5) c Gayle, b McGarrell	28
ND McKenzie	c Jacobs, b McGarrell	35	(3) b Walsh	44
L Klusener	lbw b McGarrell	0	(7) c Hinds, b Walsh	1
*MV Boucher	c Gayle, b McGarrell	1	(8) c Jacobs, b Walsh	3
SM Pollock (capt)	not out	48	(9) not out	41
N Boje	lbw b Walsh	36	(4) c sub (SC Joseph), b Hooper	0
JM Kemp	b Dillon	16		
M Ntini	b Dillon	0		
	b2, lb5, nb2	9	b6, lb3, w4, nb1	14
		247	(for 7 wickets dec.)	215

	First innings				Second innings			
	O	M	R	W	O	M	R	W
Walsh	31	14	45	1	38	13	56	4
Dillon	18.2	4	47	3	0.3	0	3	-
McGarrell	43	19	72	4	15	3	41	1
Ramnarine	20	6	45	1	42	24	55	1
Hooper	10	2	31	1	24	7	37	1
Hinds	3.3	0	14	-				

Fall of Wickets
1-29, 2-35, 3-53, 4-120, 5-126, 6-136, 7-148, 8-223, 9-247
1-17, 2-95, 3-96, 4-123, 5-135, 6-146, 7-156

WEST INDIES

	First innings		Second innings	
CH Gayle	c Pollock, b Kallis	11	c McKenzie, b Boje	12
WW Hinds	c Boucher, b Pollock	9	c Kirsten, b Boje	29
S Chanderpaul	c Cullinan, b Kemp	40	lbw b Boje	16
BC Lara	c McKenzie, b Kemp	19	(5) c McKenzie, b Kallis	91
RR Sarwan	c Boje, b Kallis	25	(6) c Boucher, b Pollock	26
CL Hooper (capt)	c Kirsten, b Klusener	17	(4) c McKenzie, b Klusener	21
M Dillon	b Klusener	0	(9) c Cullinan, b Boje	1
*RD Jacobs	not out	3	(7) c Kirsten, b Pollock	0
NC McGarrell	lbw b Klusener	0	(8) c Kemp, b Pollock	6
D Ramnarine	run out (McKenzie)	2	c Kirsten, b Kallis	9
CA Walsh	lbw b Pollock	4	not out	4
	b3, lb3, nb4	10	b18, lb3, nb4	25
		140		240

	First innings				Second innings			
	O	M	R	W	O	M	R	W
Pollock	22.1	11	25	2	19	5	41	3
Kallis	17	8	24	2	15.4	6	23	2
Ntini	6	2	27					
Kemp	8	2	17	2	6	3	7	-
Boje	12	4	26	-	45	9	118	4
Klusener	11	4	15	3	14	6	30	1

Fall of Wickets
1-13, 2-21, 3-50, 4-88, 5-126, 6-127, 7-132, 8-134, 9-136
1-36, 2-56, 3-86, 4-89, 5-138, 6-138, 7-155, 8-176, 9-229

Umpires: EA Nicholls & S Venkataraghavan
Toss: West Indies
Test debut: NC McGarrell (West Indies)

South Africa won by 82 runs

the fourth morning. It was perhaps already enough to press for victory, but Kallis and Pollock made such an assurance doubly sure, allowing the captain to declare an hour into the second session. It left the West Indies requiring 323 to win, a bold challenge on the ground where Lara had scored his record Test score of 375 and where he had since scored two hundreds, even given the worn pitch.

Lara was once more in scintillating form hitting four sixes, all off Boje, and eight fours in his 91. But it only delayed the inevitable and South Africa completed their series-clinching triumph before tea on the last day.

West Indies' hopes were effectively dashed when Hooper top edged a catch to mid-on off Klusener and Chanderpaul was leg before on the back foot to Boje within eight balls and three runs of each other, inside the last half-hour of the fourth day which they ended on 101 for four.

It left Lara with only Sarwan, Jacobs and the four bowlers to try to salvage at least some pride on the final day.

A shower that delayed play for 40 minutes and Lara's partnership with Sarwan that occupied the first 22.1 overs raised their hopes. But once Pollock dispatched Sarwan to a keeper's catch and Jacobs with a slower ball in the same over, the only consolation for the crowd was the sight of Lara in full flight.

He escaped on Ntini's embarrassing deep-field miss at 64 when he was assaulting Boje and was finally ninth out to the second new ball. He spooned a catch to McKenzie at extra-cover off Kallis who then formalized the result with the wicket of Ramnarine.

FIFTH TEST
19–23 April 2001 at Kingston, Jamaica

A long-overdue victory for the West Indies was more than simple consolation. It was hard fought, comprehensive and through a team effort in which the bit players contributed as much as the established stars, ending a sequence of 13 Tests and almost a year without a victory. In contrast, it was South Africa's first loss in the same number of Tests.

The result was an appropriate parting gift for Courtney Walsh, who ended his celebrated career as he began it, 17 years and 132 Tests earlier against Australia at Perth, with a West Indies triumph. His six wickets in the match, including two of the last three, carried his return in his final series to 25 at an average of just below 20. It was no wonder captain

Hooper pleaded with him to remain on for the later tour of Zimbabwe.

Although the West Indies' squad had been announced with no changes, Garrick's unbeaten 174 in Jamaica's two-day match against the South Africans influenced the selectors into calling him in so late that he only arrived on the evening before the match to make his debut in place of Hinds. Next morning, after Hooper had won the toss, the little right-hander was out to the first ball of the match, cutting Donald hard to gully. The South African Jimmy Cook was the only other batsman to suffer such an indignity on debut, to India's Kapil Dev at Durban in 1992.

Prior to the match, the West Indies management revealed that a system of fines for slack play had been introduced and some of their batsmen had to immediately pay up.

The most culpable was Hooper, who entered the fray in the first over after lunch with the West Indies already in strife at 54 for four. For an hour and 25 minutes, he and Lara added 53 and raised the spirits of a small Sabina Park crowd following the cheap loss of the three young Jamaicans, Garrick, Gayle and Samuels, and Chanderpaul.

Concerned by the growing partnership, Pollock set a deep square-leg back and simply challenged his rival captain to hook. Hooper could not resist the temptation and sent the ball sailing into Kirsten's safe grasp. It may have been reminiscent of Sarwan's fall in earlier Tests, but it was an unbecoming way

for a batsman in his 85th Test to be out.

Jacobs fell in Pollock's next over, so Lara was left with the bowlers to see what they could make of the last half of the innings. That they exactly doubled the total was due first to Lara's skilfully compiled 81 that occupied three hours 50 minutes and 156 balls, and then to spirited batting by Dillon and Ramnarine mixed with a little luck that saw Dillon offering two chances.

The West Indies' 225 seemed an inadequate return on a pitch described by Pollock as the best of the series. But their fast bowlers, maintaining pressure with their control and well supported in the field, struck back by dismissing South Africa for 141 – their lowest total in 11 Tests between the teams.

The South Africans could not recover from the loss of their first four wickets for 51. The only threatening partnership was 40 for the seventh wicket between McKenzie and Pollock. But once Pollock was the second of Dillon's four victims, the last four wickets tumbled for four runs off 21 balls. By the end of the second day, Garrick and Gayle had extended the lead to 118.

The West Indies entered the third day in a strong position, but they were losing ground until Samuels, in his first Test in his native Kingston, and Jacobs, with later help from Dillon and Ramnarine, reclaimed it.

Samuels and Jacobs came together when Hooper could only parry Kallis' sharp bouncer to third slip.

The West Indies had crawled to 126 for five from 68 overs by then – 92 off 51 on the day – and were faltering. They were only 210 ahead with four wickets standing.

Samuels and Jacobs changed the tempo of the game and rebuilt the innings, adding 58 runs in just over an hour. After Samuels played on in Pollock's second over with the second new ball, Jacobs, first with Dillon, and then with Ramnarine, further strengthened his team's position. The final session of the third day brought 107 runs for two wickets off 32 overs, contrasting sharply with the first two sessions that had yielded 114 off 57 overs.

The normally free-scoring Gayle

Ridley Jacobs' innings of 85 in the fifth and final Test helped the West Indies on the road to a morale-boosting victory.

FIFTH TEST – WEST INDIES v. SOUTH AFRICA
19–23 April 2001 at Sabina Park, Kingston

TEST MATCH AVERAGES
West Indies v. South Africa

WEST INDIES

	First innings		Second innings	
LV Garrick	c Pollock, b Donald	0	c Boucher, b Donald	27
CH Gayle	c Kemp, b Donald	25	b Pollock	32
S Chanderpaul	c Boucher, b Kallis	7	c Cullinan, b Kemp	7
BC Lara	c Kallis, b Pollock	81	b Adams	14
MN Samuels	c Boucher, b Donald	3	b Pollock	59
CL Hooper (capt)	c Kirsten, b Pollock	25	c Pollock, b Kallis	5
*RD Jacobs	c Boucher, b Pollock	0	c McKenzie, b Klusener	85
M Dillon	c Boucher, b Donald	24	c Gibbs, b Pollock	13
D Ramnarine	not out	35	c Cullinan, b Pollock	9
CE Cuffy	c Boucher, b Pollock	3	not out	13
CA Walsh	c Adams, b Pollock	4	c Kirsten, b Adams	3
	b4, lb12, w2	18	b14, lb13, w4, nb3	34
		225		**301**

	First innings				Second innings			
	O	M	R	W	O	M	R	W
Donald	25	5	54	4	20	8	54	1
Pollock	26.5	17	28	5	34	8	66	4
Kallis	16	5	38	1	28	10	56	1
Kemp	16	3	45	–	18	9	30	1
Adams	11	1	43	–	21.5	7	54	2
Klusener	2	1	1	–	8	3	14	1

Fall of Wickets
1-0, 2-21, 3-50, 4-54, 5-107, 6-113, 7-167, 8-188, 9-203
1-47, 2-55, 3-77, 4-103, 5-126, 6-184, 7-229, 8-255, 9-287

SOUTH AFRICA

	First innings		Second innings	
HH Gibbs	c Jacobs, b Cuffy	18	(2) b Ramnarine	51
G Kirsten	c Gayle, b Walsh	0	(1) c Jacobs, b Dillon	14
JH Kallis	c & b Dillon	17	(5) b Ramnarine	51
DJ Cullinan	c Lara, b Cuffy	6	lbw b Walsh	18
ND McKenzie	lbw b Ramnarine	45	(3) c Garrick, b Ramnarine	55
L Klusener	b Walsh	13	not out	31
*MV Boucher	c Garrick, b Walsh	13	c Jacobs, b Ramnarine	0
SM Pollock (capt)	c Jacobs, b Dillon	24	c Jacobs, b Dillon	3
JM Kemp	c Walsh, b Dillon	0	lbw b Walsh	0
AA Donald	not out	1	b Walsh	10
PR Adams	c Hooper, b Dillon	3	c Samuels, b Dillon	4
	w1	1	b4, lb13, nb1	18
		141		**255**

	First innings				Second innings			
	O	M	R	W	O	M	R	W
Walsh	18	8	31	3	22	6	62	3
Cuffy	17	6	58	2	10	3	13	–
Dillon	15.1	5	32	4	19	3	59	3
Ramnarine	11	4	20	1	31	6	61	4
Hooper	28	8	43	1				

Fall of Wickets
1-9, 2-24, 3-35, 4-51, 5-77, 6-97, 7-137, 8-137, 9-137
1-37, 2-102, 3-124, 4-190, 5-209, 6-209, 7-235, 8-236, 9-250

Umpires: SA Bucknor & S Venkataraghavan
Toss: West Indies
Test debut: LV Garrick (West Indies)

West Indies won by 130 runs

WEST INDIES

Batting	M	Inns	NO	HS	Runs	Av	100	50	c/st
RD Jacobs	5	10	4	113*	317	52.83	1	2	20/-
BC Lara	5	10	0	91	400	40.00	–	3	5
CL Hooper	5	10	1	74	358	39.77	–	4	6
CH Gayle	5	10	0	81	326	32.60	–	1	7
RR Sarwan	4	8	0	91	238	29.75	–	1	3
MN Samuels	4	8	0	59	206	25.75	–	2	2
S Chanderpaul	2	4	0	40	70	17.50	–	–	–
WW Hinds	4	8	0	56	133	16.62	–	1	4
D Ramnarine	5	9	2	35*	79	11.28	–	–	2
M Dillon	5	9	1	24	84	10.50	–	–	5
CE Cuffy	2	3	1	13*	20	10.00	–	–	1
CA Walsh	5	8	2	4*	21	3.50	–	–	1
NAM McLean	2	4	0	6	11	2.75	–	–	1

Also batted in one Test: LV Garrick 0, 27 (3ct); NC McGarrell 0, 6.

Bowling	Overs	Mds	Runs	Wkts	Av	Best	10m	5/inn
CA Walsh	263.4	87	492	25	19.68	6-61	–	1
NC McGarrell	58	22	113	5	22.60	4-72	–	–
M Dillon	169	31	519	20	25.95	4-32	–	–
D Ramnarine	290.3	93	617	20	30.85	5-78	–	1
NAM McLean	66.5	6	236	6	39.33	3-60	–	–
CL Hooper	158	46	283	5	56.60	2-49	–	–

Also bowled: CE Cuffy 66-20-163-4; CH Gayle 1-0-3-0; WW Hinds 18.3-5-50-3; MN Samuels 7-1-15-0; RR Sarwan 1-0-4-0.

SOUTH AFRICA

Batting	M	Inns	NO	HS	Runs	Av	100	50	c/st
SM Pollock	5	9	5	106*	302	75.50	1	–	4
HH Gibbs	5	10	1	87	464	51.55	–	4	2
DJ Cullinan	5	10	1	134	459	51.00	2	2	10
ND McKenzie	5	9	0	72	301	33.44	–	2	7
JH Kallis	5	10	1	53	267	29.66	–	3	4
G Kirsten	5	10	0	150	250	25.00	1	–	6
N Boje	4	7	1	36	106	17.66	–	–	4
MV Boucher	5	9	0	52	126	14.00	–	1	18/-
L Klusener	5	9	1	31*	75	9.37	–	–	2
AA Donald	4	7	1	37	51	8.50	–	–	1
M Ntini	4	5	1	11	23	5.75	–	–	1
JM Kemp	2	3	0	16	16	5.33	–	–	2

Also batted in one Test: PR Adams 3, 4 (1ct).

Bowling	Overs	Mds	Runs	Wkts	Av	Best	10m	5/inn
JH Kallis	189.4	67	395	20	19.75	6-67	–	1
SM Pollock	228.1	77	464	20	23.20	5-28	–	1
AA Donald	147	47	355	14	25.35	4-54	–	–
L Klusener	118	48	219	8	27.37	3-15	–	–
N Boje	176.5	51	442	15	29.46	4-17	–	–
M Ntini	98	24	296	7	42.28	2-56	–	–

Also bowled: PR Adams 32.5-8-97-2; JM Kemp 48-17-99-3.

typified the West Indies' early struggles. The tall left-hander remained on 27 for an hour before lunch and batted for four-and-a-quarter hours before Pollock baffled him with a change-of-pace yorker that plucked out his middle stump.

The West Indies batted through to lunch on the fourth day, extending their lead to 385 mainly through Jacobs, the doughty left-hander scoring 85 of the 161 runs made in the four hours ten minutes he was at the wicket. He was ninth out, hooking Klusener to McKenzie at deep square-leg.

The West Indies' bowlers were left with five sessions to complete the job and, by close, extended by an hour because of three rain breaks, they had accounted for Kirsten, Gibbs and Cullinan to leave the South Africans on 140. After Kirsten again went cheaply, Gibbs and McKenzie, promoted to number three, kept the opposition waiting for an hour and 40 minutes while they added 65.

Gibbs' patience eventually snapped and he was bowled by Hooper swinging wildly. Walsh, off the field earlier for treatment to a knock on the ankle while batting, struck a crucial blow on his return by claiming Cullinan leg before with his third ball of a new spell.

Earlier in the day, as Walsh walked to the wicket for the last time in Test cricket, the South Africans formed an applauding guard of honour – as the Englishmen did at The Oval last August and the Australians at the SCG last January. It was another touching tribute to a much-admired sportsman – and Walsh duly rose to the occasion by avoiding his 43rd Test duck.

It was not until 20 minutes before lunch on the last day that the West Indies could make a start towards victory. McKenzie and Kallis batted solidly through an hour and 40 minutes before McKenzie prodded forward to Ramnarine's leg-break and was snapped up low by Garrick at silly point.

South Africa still seemed on course for safety reaching lunch at 209 for four, with Kallis entrenched on 51, but Ramnarine changed that within four balls of resumption. Kallis chopped the second back into his stumps and Boucher edged the fourth to Jacobs.

These were match-winning blows and South Africa's resistance crumbled, with the last six wickets falling for 34 runs from 15 overs. Once Klusener and Pollock had batted together for half an hour after Ramnarine's double-strike, Hooper handed Walsh and Dillon the second new ball and they polished things off within five overs for the West Indies' first victory over South Africa since the first, in 1992.

ONE-DAY INTERNATIONALS

South Africa's superiority, evident but not dominant in their hard-fought 2–1 triumph in the Tests, was overwhelming in this series of seven one-day internationals.

The difference between the teams in the basics such as fielding, running between the wickets, variations in bowling pace and in the side's experience was clear cut.

South Africa reeled off five comfortable, successive victories after losing the first at Sabina Park off the last ball, a Donald full toss that Jacobs cut for four.

The West Indies gained a convincing consolation victory in the last match at picturesque Arnos Vale, by the sea in St Vincent, spoiling Jonty Rhodes' 200th one-day international, but this did not mask their glaring deficiencies in the abbreviated game.

South Africa became the first team to win both the Test and the one-day series in the Caribbean, to end yet another proud West Indian record, so many of which have fallen in their sharp decline in recent times.

South Africa's captain Pollock, who had collected the Sir Vivian Richards Trophy after the Test series, had the further satisfaction of receiving the Cable & Wireless 'Bowled Over' Trophy and the Suzuki Vitara vehicle as Man of the Series, an award that covered both Tests and one-day internationals.

The South Africans' fielding was breathtaking, even by the high standards they have set for some time. Rhodes, now retired from Test cricket, made an immediate mark in the first match with two blinding low catches at point to dismiss Gayle and Lara and he and Gibbs presented an almost impenetrable wall on either side of the wicket within the 30-yard zone. Justin Ontong, the 21-year-old Boland all-rounder in his debut appearance, was a gazelle around the boundary and there wasn't a weak link anywhere.

The South Africans saved countless runs not only with their athleticism and anticipation, but by their sheer presence that was a constant threat to the West Indian running. They created eight run outs, whereas the West Indians in contrast created only two.

With such support, the bowlers' strict control of line, length and change of pace throttled the opposition batsmen. The West Indies' highest total was an inadequate 220 for eight in the second match in St John's that was erased with 4.1 overs remaining as Gibbs, with the first of his two hundreds, and Kallis added 179 for the second wicket.

Even when they bowled South Africa out for 200

Herschelle Gibbs was in fine form throughout the one-day series, hitting two centuries.

his second hundred.

The next day, Gibbs was in the headlines again, for the wrong, if not unfamiliar, reasons. The story broke that he, Paul Adams, Justin Kemp, Andre Nel, Roger Telemachus and long-serving physiotherapist Craig Smith had admitted to, and were fined for, smoking marijuana at their hotel in Antigua a month earlier following their series-clinching win in the fourth Test.

Gibbs already had a three-match suspended ban for another earlier social indiscretion in South Africa, but, pointedly, he and the other four players charged were included in the XI for the next match in Port-of-Spain.

in the first match, they only got there by taking 18 off the last two overs.

A packed crowd of 25,000 at the Queen's Park Oval were expectant of a rare victory when South Africa could only raise 190 batting first on a bowler-friendly pitch in the sixth match. But, once Rhodes' direct hit ran out Lara for 41, the last nine wickets tumbled for just 66 runs.

South Africa's most comprehensive wins were in the weekend double-header at the impressive Queen's Park Stadium in Grenada. Based on Kallis' run-a-ball 108, they amassed 287 for four and then bowled the West Indies out for 155 in the first match. In the second, they needed only 46.1 overs and four batsmen to pass the West Indies' total of 200 and were frolicking in their hotel pool well before sunset.

They clinched the series and their second trophy in almost identical fashion three days later at Kensington Oval in Bridgetown, losing three wickets on their way to a target of 200 as Gibbs reeled off

It really didn't seem to matter what combination South Africa chose, everyone knew his role and seldom let his standard drop.

The West Indies tried numerous mixtures of their own, using four pairs of openers, three new-ball combinations and 17 players in all. Chairman of selectors, Mike Findlay, said they were experimenting with the aim of creating a settled team, but it simply amounted to confusion.

It was highlighted when Jeremy, the 21-year-old Antiguan medium-pacer, was picked for the fifth match and was not given a single over by captain Hooper.

Hooper's all-round contributions, not least with his accurate off spin, emphasized what a loss it had been when he withdrew from the last World Cup. But while Lara's value was again obvious with an average of 39.14, he, Hooper and Chanderpaul, the senior batsman, could not provide the necessary middle-order consistency.

Samuels, the gifted 20-year-old Jamaican, batted

and bowled his off spin with the maturity of a seasoned veteran and the resurrection of Cuffy, the tall fast bowler, continued at the age of 31. He was the meanest of the West Indians, as he was in the one-day Carlton Series in Australia in January, and took special delight in gaining the Man of the Match award for his three for 24 spell in front of his home crowd in St Vincent.

But there were too many weaknesses in the West Indies team for it to be seriously competitive against such confident, well-drilled opponents.

Jacques Kallis contributed with both bat and ball as South Africa cruised to a 5–1 series victory.

Match One
28 April 2001 at Sabina Park, Kingston
South Africa 200 (47.4 overs)
West Indies 201 for 7 (50 overs) (BC Lara 54)
West Indies won by three wickets
Man of the Match: NC McGarrell

Match Two
2 May 2001 at Antigua Recreation Ground, St John's
West Indies 220 for 8 (50 overs) (S Chanderpaul 60, CH Gayle 50)
South Africa 221 for 2 (45.5 overs) (HH Gibbs 104, JH Kallis 78*)
South Africa won by eight wickets
Man of the Match: HH Gibbs

Match Three
5 May 2001 at Queen's Park, St George's, Grenada
South Africa 287 for 4 (50 overs) (JH Kallis 107, G Kirsten 50)
West Indies 155 (39 overs)
South Africa won by 132 runs
Man of the Match: JH Kallis

Match Four
6 May 2001 at Queen's Park, St George's, Grenada
West Indies 200 (49.3 overs) (MN Samuels 65)
South Africa 201 for 2 (46.1 overs) (G Kirsten 72, HH Dippenaar 62*)
South Africa won by eight wickets
Man of the Match: AA Donald

Match Five
9 May 2001 at Kensington Oval, Bridgetown
West Indies 199 (49.2 overs) (BC Lara 92)
South Africa 202 for 3 (41.4 overs) (HH Gibbs 107)
South Africa won by seven wickets
Man of the Match: HH Gibbs

Match Six
12 May 2001 at Queen's Park Oval, Port-of-Spain
South Africa 190 (49.5 overs) (ND McKenzie 73)
West Indies 137 (47 overs)
South Africa won by 53 runs
Man of the Match: ND McKenzie

Match Seven
16 May 2001 at Arnos Vale, Kingstown, St Vincent
South Africa 163 for 7 (50 overs) (JH Kallis 69)
West Indies 164 for 4 (44.2 overs) (MN Samuels 54*)
West Indies won by six wickets
Man of the Match: CE Cuffy
Man of the Series: SM Pollock

WEST INDIES DOMESTIC FIRST-CLASS CRICKET (INCLUDING ENGLAND 'A')

It was a year of transition, revolution, innovation and continuing frustration for West Indies cricket.

Carl Hooper controversially replaced Jimmy Adams as the third captain in a year, the fifth in five, and Pat Rousseau resigned as president of the West Indies Cricket Board (WICB) in June after five turbulent years in office.

Australia added another sorry chapter to the West Indies' recent abysmal overseas record, winning all five Tests to retain the Frank Worrell Trophy, and the woes continued back home when South Africa became the first visiting team to the Caribbean to claim both the Test series (2–1) and the one-day internationals (5–2).

Chris Gayle's 945 runs at an average of 63 pushed the opener back into the West Indies team.

The domestic first-class tournament, the Busta Cup and International Shield, introduced England 'A' as the first foreign entrant, a radical change that met initial opposition, but which proved to be a genuine success.

Kenya and Bangladesh, expected to be the overseas teams in 2002, could take heart from the United States' victory over once mighty Barbados in October in the limited-overs Red Stripe Bowl. It was yet another blow to the status of West Indies cricket, even if the Americans were, in fact, mainly ageing, expatriate West Indians.

Rousseau, a 67-year-old Jamaican attorney, quit when the WICB's annual general meeting overturned a decision by him and vice-president Clarvis Joseph to dismiss team manager Ricky Skerritt. It amounted to a virtual vote of no-confidence, leaving them with no alternative but to quit.

Wes Hall, the explosive fast bowler of the 1960s, oftentimes team manager and selector, former Barbados government minister and now an ordained Christian reverend, was chosen to replace Rousseau, reverting to an earlier custom by which the Board was headed by a former Test player.

Hall, 63, proclaimed his immediate priorities to be 'a healing process when the finger-pointing and the internal bickering must stop' and the reversal of the decline of the West Indies team.

As he left, Rousseau pressed for answers to pointed questions on a failed investment of US$3 million he claimed had been made with the brokers Merrill Lynch by chief financial officer Richard Jodhan and secretary Andrew Sealy, without the Board's authorization. The Board's response was that it had 'investigated the matter thoroughly' and was 'completely satisfied that there was no impropriety and specifically no evidence of falsification of Board resolutions'.

There was a little belated encouragement on the field.

Hall's election coincided with success in June and July in Zimbabwe, in the triangular Coca Cola Cup one-day series and the two Tests, and in Kenya in three one-day internationals. The opposition was undeniably weak, but at least it was a start on the road back.

It was Rousseau's style of leadership, rather than its substance, which brought him down. He was always keen on change and stuck to his guns, against widespread scepticism, to bring in England 'A' as 'a major motivational factor to heighten competitiveness' in the Busta Series. A West Indies 'B' team, restricted to Under-23 players not required by their territories and led by former Test captain Richie Richardson, was also added, increasing the field to eight.

The tournament was divided in two, mainly to ensure there was a West Indian champion. The Busta Cup was restricted to the six territorial teams and decided on standings after the round-robin league. The top-four teams then advanced to the semi-finals with the finalists contesting the Busta International Shield.

An ageing Barbados team, reeling off three of their four victories at the end after an indifferent start to the season, claimed the Busta Cup by virtue of more outright wins, four to three, after finishing on equal points with Guyana.

In one semi-final, Barbados were soundly beaten by Jamaica who were appreciably boosted by the inclusion of six players who had returned from the West Indies' tour of Australia. In the other, Guyana, with Hooper at the helm during the course of what for him was a prolific season, inflicted the first defeat on an England 'A' team in 44 matches, stretching over seven overseas tours since 1995.

It ensured that the strongest and best-balanced teams contested the final, with Jamaica securing the inaugural Shield through an 85-run first-innings lead in a drawn match.

Inevitably, the tournament was not free of the controversy that has become an integral part of West Indies cricket. Guyana had two complaints, both subsequently rejected. They wanted to share the Busta Cup with Barbados, as they had the same number of points, 57, and claimed they, not Jamaica, should host the final. The latter argument had to be settled in Antigua by High Court judge Ephraime Georges, who ruled in the WICB's favour. The final was staged in Jamaica, at Sabina Park, after all, but it meant that the match was needlessly delayed for a day.

Jamaica virtually fielded two teams, one pre-Australia, the other post-Australia. They qualified for the Shield semi-finals in fourth place in the Cup, although they might have beaten both Barbados and the Leeward Islands with less defensive declarations. Their only first round loss was to England 'A' in a low-scoring match at Sabina Park.

For the second successive season, their outstanding batsman was Chris Gayle. The tall, 21-year-old left-hander, omitted from the tour of Australia after a disappointing summer in England, compiled 945 runs at an average of 63. His 208 against the fledging West Indies 'B' bowling was matched by an innings of 200 by his little right-handed partner, Leon Garrick, in an unbroken

partnership of 425 that set a new West Indies record first-wicket partnership.

Gayle also had hundreds against Barbados in the Busta Cup and against Jamaica in the Shield final while Garrick's 172 in the Shield semi against Barbados came during a second-wicket stand of 203 with Wavell Hinds, one of the six returnees from Australia.

No other Jamaican managed a score higher than 70 or an average above 30, highlighting the inconsistency that affected every team.

As with most of the others, Jamaica's bowling was based on spin with the contrasting off spinners Gareth Breese and Nehemiah Perry each claiming more than 30 wickets. Ryan Cunningham, the young left-arm spinner, had 22.

Hooper's leadership and batting form that brought him a record 954 runs in ten completed innings, with four hundreds, inspired a basically young Guyana team both to an unbeaten record and to the final. It also helped Hooper to reclaim his place in the Test team, nearly two years after he had announced his retirement, and earned his elevation to the captaincy, an appointment that met with mixed reaction.

No opposition was stronger than Michael

Inspired batting and leadership from Carl Hooper led his side into the Shield final.

Holding's. The great fast bowler of an earlier generation argued that, while Hooper merited his place in the team based on his form, his past record 'disqualified him from the captaincy'. As a mark of protest, he passed up his assignment as television commentator for the series against South Africa.

Guyana's success was not all down to Hooper. Ramnaresh Sarwan, released from the one-day internationals after a traumatic tour of Australia, scored hundreds in both matches against England 'A' and averaged 67.33. Travis Dowlin, a stylish right-hander, also averaged over 50.

Neil McGarrell enjoyed his best season, claiming 32 wickets with his left-arm spin and a call to the Test team. His story contrasted with that of Kevin Darlington, a lively fast bowler who took 26 wickets at less than 20 apiece before he had to give way to Reon King and Colin Stuart on their return from Australia.

While Barbados' selectors stuck to their older players, introducing only three newcomers, their outstanding performances came from Ryan Hinds, the 20-year-old, left-handed all-rounder, whose 15 wickets (nine for 68 and six for 34) against the Leewards in Nevis was an all-time best for Barbados in first-class cricket.

England 'A' came into the tournament with a proud unbeaten record dating back six tours to 1995. They maintained it until the Shield semi-final when, pressed to make up for a first-innings deficit, they were beaten by Guyana.

Left-handed opener Ian Ward of Surrey was their outstanding batsman, his 769 runs (at 64.08) more than double John Crawley's 373 (at 31.08) as the next highest. Ward hit hundreds against Barbados (when he and Warwickshire's Michael Powell added 224 for the first wicket), Guyana and Trinidad & Tobago. Crawley and captain Mark Alleyne were the only others with three-figure innings.

Ryan Sidebottom, whose long hair attracted as much attention beyond the boundary as his left-arm swing did in the middle, Chris Silverwood and Alex Tudor comprised a lively fast attack. Graeme Swann had success with his off spin after arriving as a replacement for Jason Brown (who had been called to the senior team in Sri Lanka), and Chris Schofield gradually found the right line and length for his leg-spin. But Alleyne was not satisfied with the general performance.

'You get the feeling in the last three weeks that a bit of fatigue set in which shouldn't really happen because we play a lot of four-day cricket back home,' he noted.

Prior to their semi-final loss to Guyana, the Leewards had given England 'A' their toughest match. But no team was more inconsistent.

One match the Leewards were overpowering Trinidad & Tobago by 183 runs, the next just holding on for a draw against Guyana. They narrowly avoided defeat against Jamaica, then overwhelmed the Windwards and West Indies 'B' before falling to Ryan Hinds and Barbados by six wickets.

They needed an outright victory over England 'A' to qualify for the semi-finals, but, although they dominated the match, they had to settle for a draw.

Captain Stuart Williams started with hundreds in each innings against Trinidad & Tobago, but only managed one half-century in his eight subsequent innings. They had to wait until the return of Ridley Jacobs from Australia for their only other three-figure innings, 100 against England 'A'. Young fast bowlers Kerry Jeremy and Ricky Christopher, with 26 wickets each, and 18-year-old off spinner Omari Banks, with 21, were their leading bowlers.

It was another disheartening season for Trinidad & Tobago who finished above only West Indies 'B' and winless Windwards. The absence of Brian Lara and Test fast bowlers Merv Dillon and Marlon Black for the entire season and Test opener Daren Ganga for all but one match weakened the team and no one could fill the breach.

Former Test players Suruj Ragoonath, Phil Simmons and Rajindra Dhanraj were called out of retirement, but none completed the season. Ganga showed how much he was missed with 105 against Barbados in his only match on return from Australia. Lincoln Roberts' hard-hitting, unbeaten 102 that gained their only victory over the Windwards was Trinidad & Tobago's only other hundred and their second-innings 307 in a losing cause against Guyana was their only total above 300.

Their leg-spinner, Dinanath Ramnarine, made an emphatic return after a shoulder operation, claiming the most wickets in the tournament, 41. It was enough to gain him reinstatement into the Test team, but both he and the other bowlers were handicapped by the failure of the batting.

The object of the West Indies 'B' team was to give exposure to more young players. As such, it was a qualified success. Results were considered largely immaterial, but victory over the Windwards by 162 runs and a first-innings lead over Jamaica in a match eventually lost were both satisfying.

None of their batsmen managed a hundred or averaged over 30, but Tonito Willett, the 18-year-old son of former Test left-arm spinner Elquemedo

Willett, and Kirk Wilkinson, 19, a stylish Barbadian, showed unmistakeable potential.

Sulieman Benn, a tall, slim left-arm spinner, bowled 114.1 overs more than anyone else and his 26 wickets were earned at an average of just under 25 runs each. But the dearth of fast bowlers that led to Benn and the medium-pacers occasionally sharing the new ball with the pacey Jermaine Lawson was a worrying feature.

The Windwards had realistic expectations of rising from their traditional cellar position following their earlier triumphs in the Under-19 tournament and the limited-overs Red Stripe Bowl. Instead, they were beaten in all seven matches, an inferior performance even by their standards.

Their confidence was shaken when they allowed their opening match to slip from their grasp, as Jamaica moved from 49 for six to 183 for seven and victory. They were then humiliated by West Indies 'B' and there was no comeback after that.

The Windwards' batting was as abysmal as always, passing 300 only once, in the first innings against Guyana, when John Eugene compiled their only hundred. The perennial wicket-keeper, Junior Murray, was their only player with a batting average better than 30.

With Nixon McLean and Cameron Cuffy away in Australia and unavailable for the final match on return, several new bowlers had their moments. Shane Shillingford, a 17-year-old off spinner, enjoyed a sensational debut with seven for 66 against Jamaica, but his action drew wide attention and Test umpire Steve Bucknor called him for throwing, from both square-leg and standing positions, in the match against the Leewards. He had no problems with any other umpire and had 20 wickets all told.

The Windwards' return to their previous lowly rank came only a few months after their captain Rawl Lewis was raising the Red Stripe Bowl in triumph after victory by five wickets over Leewards in the 50-overs-an-innings final at Sabina Park.

The inclusion of the Cayman Islands, where there is a concerted effort to revive interest in a game that has suffered against competition from American sports, further increased the number of teams to ten with ICC North American affiliates Bermuda, Canada and the US again involved.

The quality of the cricket, and the pitches, was such that there were only six totals above 200 in the 23 matches and a solitary individual hundred, an unbeaten 100 by the Windwards' former Test wicket-keeper Junior Murray, who was named the tournament's Most Valuable Player.

FIRST-CLASS AVERAGES

BATTING

	M	Inns	NO	HS	Runs	Av	100	50
CL Hooper	14	22	3	159	1312	69.05	4	8
SM Pollock	7	12	6	106*	391	65.16	1	1
IJ Ward	8	14	2	135	769	64.08	3	4
RD Jacobs	6	12	5	113*	436	62.28	2	2
SC Williams	6	9	0	160	522	58.00	2	1
SL Campbell	3	6	0	86	319	53.16	-	3
CH Gayle	14	27	2	208*	1271	50.84	3	5
RR Sarwan	12	20	3	122	844	49.64	2	5
D Ganga	4	8	1	105	344	49.14	1	1
HH Gibbs	7	14	1	87	598	46.00	-	5
TM Dowlin	9	13	2	116*	487	44.27	1	4
DJ Cullinan	6	12	1	134	503	45.72	2	2
LV Garrick	11	21	1	200*	861	43.05	2	4
MW Alleyne	7	10	1	139	370	41.11	1	1
CM Tuckett	6	10	2	84	326	40.75	-	2
BC Lara	5	10	0	91	400	40.00	-	3
J Eugene	8	15	1	139	536	38.28	2	-
LA Roberts	7	14	1	102*	465	35.76	1	3
VS Solanki	7	10	2	89	281	35.12	-	1
CP Schofield	5	7	1	66	208	34.66	-	2
MJ Powell	6	10	0	96	340	34.00	-	3
ND McKenzie	7	13	1	72	403	33.58	-	3
WW Hinds	7	12	0	101	394	32.83	2	2
RS Morton	7	13	3	65	316	31.60	-	3
IDR Bradshaw	9	14	5	109*	284	31.55	1	1
JR Murray	7	14	1	97*	405	31.15	-	2
JP Crawley	8	14	2	104*	373	31.08	1	2
JA Mitchum	7	14	2	81	364	30.33	-	3
RAM Smith	7	14	0	96	417	29.78	-	2
FL Reifer	6	11	2	64*	264	29.33	-	2
RO Hinds	10	17	3	87	406	29.00	-	3
JH Kallis	6	12	1	53	316	28.72	-	3
RIC Holder	7	14	2	117	339	28.25	1	1
TA Willett	8	16	2	89	392	28.00	-	3
A Jackson	3	6	0	51	167	27.83	-	1
AFG Griffith	8	16	1	84	416	27.73	-	2
RG Samuels	7	11	2	69*	249	27.66	-	1
DA Williams	3	5	0	48	138	27.60	-	-
SH Armstrong	6	11	0	71	295	26.81	-	2
G Kirsten	7	14	0	150	368	26.28	1	1
RN Lewis	7	14	1	74	338	26.00	-	2
FA Adams	7	14	1	75	337	25.92	-	2
KJ Wilkinson	9	17	1	86	408	25.50	-	2
K Mason	7	14	1	82	328	25.23	-	3
PA Wallace	9	18	1	78	424	24.94	-	2
NC McGarrell	10	12	1	56	269	24.45	-	2
GR Breese	8	12	3	54*	220	24.44	-	1
CO Browne	10	13	0	72	317	24.38	-	2
MN Samuels	9	16	2	59	337	24.07	-	2
AJ Tudor	5	7	1	32	144	24.00	-	-
LJ Cush	7	11	1	90	239	23.90	-	1
WW Cornwall	7	12	0	84	285	23.75	-	1
WE Cuff	6	11	0	65	260	23.63	-	1
Usman Afzaal	6	9	1	39	188	23.50	-	-
S Chanderpaul	5	9	2	49*	161	23.00	-	-
NO Perry	9	14	1	59	289	22.23	-	1
A Haniff	11	18	0	62	387	21.50	-	3
S Chattergoon	4	7	0	56	147	21.00	-	1
DS Smith	8	15	0	42	307	20.46	-	-
MV Boucher	7	12	0	56	238	19.83	-	2
N Boje	6	10	2	36	158	19.75	-	-
RS Matthews	6	7	3	27*	79	19.75	-	-
D Mohammed	3	5	0	42	97	19.40	-	-
A Gonsalves	7	13	0	58	247	19.00	-	1
DK Marshall	6	8	4	23*	76	19.00	-	-
D Rampersad	5	10	0	51	189	18.90	-	1
KN Casimir	4	8	0	63	149	18.62	-	1
KF Semple	6	9	0	40	163	18.11	-	-
RB Richardson	7	13	1	49*	216	18.00	-	-
S Ragoonath	4	8	0	59	144	18.00	-	1
CMW Read	5	6	1	29*	90	18.00	-	-
SG Wilson	3	6	1	52*	89	17.80	-	1

FIRST-CLASS AVERAGES

BATTING

	M	Inns	NO	HS	Runs	Av	100	50
KH Hibbert	10	15	0	52	264	17.60	-	1
OAC Banks	6	10	1	43	156	17.33	-	-
N Deonarine	7	14	1	73	221	17.00	-	1
V Nagamootoo	10	11	0	46	185	16.81	-	-
JM Simmonds	6	10	0	54	151	16.77	-	2
L Klusener	7	12	1	60	184	16.72	-	1
HR Bryan	8	11	2	36	148	16.44	-	-
SC Joseph	4	8	1	61	114	16.28	-	1
DE Bernard	7	14	0	43	227	16.21	-	-
NA de Groot	5	8	0	49	129	16.12	-	-
R Dhanraj	5	9	4	28	80	16.00	-	-
GP Swann	4	6	0	49	95	15.83	-	-
DC Butler	6	11	2	54*	142	15.77	-	1
RK Currency	8	15	0	48	233	15.53	-	-
R Griffith	4	7	5	11	31	15.50	-	-
KCB Jeremy	8	13	5	70*	123	15.37	-	1
SJ Benn	7	13	0	47	195	15.00	-	-
J Lawson	5	9	4	25	75	15.00	-	-
E Katchay	4	5	1	28	60	15.00	-	-
I H Jan	6	12	0	33	171	14.25	-	-
CD Cannonier	4	8	0	36	109	13.62	-	-
RA Austin	5	5	0	35	68	13.60	-	-
RL Powell	4	5	1	47	54	13.50	-	-
D Brown	7	14	0	47	188	13.42	-	-
CEL Stuart	6	6	1	33	64	12.80	-	-
G Mahabir	3	5	0	28	64	12.80	-	-
FA Rose	8	12	4	22	102	12.75	-	-
W Phillip	7	14	0	40	177	12.64	-	-
JAR Sylvester	4	8	0	22	96	12.00	-	-
M Ntini	5	6	2	24*	47	11.75	-	-
CC Alexander	5	9	0	40	103	11.44	-	-
K Peters	3	5	1	17	45	11.25	-	-
BA Parchment	4	8	0	23	88	11.00	-	-
CEW Silverwood	5	5	1	16	44	11.00	-	-
IO Jackson	8	15	0	31	155	10.33	-	-

Qualification: 5 innings, averages 10.00
Note: These averages include matches against South Africa 'A' played in September 2000

BOWLING

	Overs	Mds	Runs	Wkts	Av	Best	10m	5/inn
GR Breese	328.4	131	544	36	15.11	7-60	1	3
RO Hinds	292.2	73	654	37	17.75	9-68	1	2
CA Walsh	379	132	691	37	18.67	6-61	-	1
CM Tuckett	107.2	33	226	12	18.83	3-12	-	-
KG Darlington	183.4	48	497	26	19.11	6-25	-	2
L Klusener	142	61	238	12	19.83	3-15	-	-
GP Swann	144.3	48	362	18	20.11	5-27	-	1
JH Kallis	198.4	69	413	20	20.65	6-67	-	1
NO Perry	339.2	106	648	31	20.90	4-39	-	-
OAC Banks	216	62	443	21	21.09	7-70	1	1

FIRST-CLASS AVERAGES

BOWLING

	Overs	Mds	Runs	Wkts	Av	Best	10m	5/inn
RO Cunningham	274.2	101	489	22	22.22	4-62	-	-
RJ Christopher	235.5	51	671	29	23.13	5-32	-	2
CD Collymore	244	63	612	26	23.53	6-109	-	2
KCB Jeremy	253	57	663	28	23.67	6-46	1	-
CEW Silverwood	161.4	42	382	16	23.87	4-45	-	-
AJ Tudor	146	32	454	19	23.89	5-37	-	1
DC Butler	159.5	34	485	20	24.25	4-51	-	-
R Dhanraj	168.1	44	391	16	24.43	6-57	-	2
GT Prince	150.3	33	484	19	25.47	4-75	-	-
SM Pollock	256.1	84	547	21	26.04	5-28	-	1
CEL Stuart	170.2	29	522	20	26.10	4-42	-	-
SJ Benn	297.5	57	836	32	26.12	5-51	-	1
CP Schofield	195.2	43	578	22	26.27	4-72	-	-
N Boje	211.5	60	534	20	26.70	4-17	-	-
M Persad	196	41	489	18	27.16	4-36	-	-
HR Bryan	282.3	64	736	27	27.25	4-45	-	-
S Shillingford	193.1	27	552	20	27.60	7-66	-	1
NC McGarrell	506.2	168	1035	37	27.97	5-82	-	1
AA Donald	165	61	442	16	27.62	4-54	-	-
IO Jackson	262	61	711	25	28.44	8-79	1	1
F Thomas	115.4	28	345	12	28.75	5-53	-	1
MJ Morgan	129.5	30	364	12	30.33	3-38	-	-
CL Hooper	465.3	122	918	30	30.60	5-49	-	1
J Lawson	136.4	21	450	14	32.14	4-79	-	-
RA Austin	150.5	35	388	12	32.33	4-39	-	-
IDR Bradshaw	234	46	731	22	33.22	4-46	-	-
RS Matthews	180	36	507	15	33.80	3-64	-	-
M Ntini	112	25	372	11	33.81	4-31	-	-
RD King	134	27	407	12	33.91	7-89	-	1
DK Marshall	221.1	61	514	15	34.26	5-91	-	1
WW Cornwall	135	20	462	13	35.53	3-65	-	-
D Brown	151.1	22	447	11	40.63	4-80	-	-
FA Rose	177	33	553	13	42.53	2-32	-	-

Qualification: 10 wickets in 8 innings
Note: These averages include matches against South Africa 'A' played in September 2000

The folllowing bowlers took 10 wickets in fewer than 8 innings:-

	Overs	Mds	Runs	Wkts	Av	Best	10m	5/inn
D Mohammed	121	36	231	16	14.43	4-24	-	-
RJ Sidebottom	109.5	31	269	16	16.81	5-31	-	1
JF Brown	119	32	263	10	26.30	4-85	-	-
MV Nagamootoo	162	35	458	17	26.94	6-92	-	1

FIELDING

31 – KH Hibbert (29ct,2st); 24 – MV Boucher (23ct,1st), CO Browne (20ct,4st), RD Jacobs; 22 – VS Solanki; 17 – CL Hooper; 16 – FA Adams, A Haniff; 15 – CH Gayle, JR Murray (12ct,3st); 14 – LV Garrick, V Nagamootoo (12ct,2st); 13 – K Mason (10ct,3st), JM Simmonds (11ct,2st); 12 – TM Dowlin, IH Jan, RS Morton; 11 – DJ Cullinan, W Phillip (10ct,1st), CMW Read (11ct); 10 – RG Samuels

Note: These figures include matches against South Africa 'A' in September 2000

Qualification: 10 catches or more

ZIMBABWE

New Zealand in Zimbabwe
Bangladesh in Zimbabwe
India in Zimbabwe
West Indies in Zimbabwe
Zimbabwe Domestic First-Class Season
First-Class Averages

NEW ZEALAND IN ZIMBABWE
By Bryan Waddle

Zimbabwe Presidents XI v. New Zealanders
1–3 September 2000 at Mutare Sports Club
New Zealanders 339 for 9 dec. (AC Parore 103*,
NJ Astle 57) and 263 for 3 dec. (MS Sinclair 100*, CD
McMillan 57*)
Zimbabwe President's XI 205 (SV Carlisle 92) and
96 for 3
Match drawn

Wicketkeeper Adam Parore saved New
Zealand from embarrassment in the
opening match of their tour with an
unbeaten century in 185 minutes. Parore arrived at
the wicket at 148 for six and helped New Zealand to
a respectable first-innings total. Despite a polished
innings of 92 from Stuart Carlisle, the President's XI
came up 134 runs short on the first innings. New
Zealand used much of the rest of the three-day
match for pre-Test batting practice with Mathew
Sinclair scoring an unbeaten 100. They set a target
of 398 that was unrealistic in the short time
remaining.

Zimbabwe 'A' v. New Zealanders
7–9 September 2000 at Kwekwe Sports Club
New Zealanders 677 for 7 dec. (MH Richardson 306,
MS Sinclair 86, CD McMillan 79, MJ Horne 63) and
137 for 3 dec.
Zimbabwe 'A' 168 (DL Vettori 6 for 43) and 72 for 3
Match drawn

Opener Mark Richardson gave an early preview of
his future Test match prospects with an outstanding
triple century in only his second game for New
Zealand. Amazingly, Richardson started his first-
class career as a left-arm spinner who batted at
number 11, but now he produced his highest first-
class innings – 306 – in a little over 13 hours. Along
the way he broke numerous New Zealand batting
records, notably the longest-ever innings played by a
New Zealand first-class batsman. Daniel Vettori gave
the visitors a stranglehold on the game with six for
43 off 21 overs, which helped to give them a
commanding first-innings lead of 509, and by
batting for a second time without enforcing the
follow-on, they conceded any chance of victory.

Previous page: Andy Flower's inspirational form with the
bat throughout the season saw him rise to the top of the
batting rankings.

FIRST TEST
12–16 September 2000 at Queen's Sports Club, Bulawayo

New Zealand's star all-rounder, Chris Cairns,
appeared only twice throughout an arduous year in
which New Zealand played nine Tests and 27 one-
day internationals, but he made an impact in both as
New Zealand achieved an historic clean sweep in
Zimbabwe – the first time Zimbabwe has been
whitewashed in a Test series.

At the picturesque Queen's Sports Club, Cairns'
mastery with the ball helped New Zealand to a
seven-wicket win that looked more dominant on the
scoreboard than was actually the case. It took until
after tea on the final day for New Zealand to secure
their victory after conceding a slender lead to the
home side on the first innings. The final day
headlines were dominated not only by New

Dion Nash drives during his innings of 62 in the second Test.

Zealand's win but by a controversial final-day decision by umpire Darrell Hair who called Zimbabwe left-arm spinner Grant Flower three times for throwing. Flower was removed from the attack and Gavin Rennie completed the three balls remaining in the over.

The 'throwing' issue was not the only controversy in the Test. Even before the toss had taken place, Zimbabwe's selection panel convened a prolonged meeting near the boundary to settle their playing XI after vice-captain, Guy Whittall, withdrew in an apparent protest over the selection policy. Whittall's withdrawal didn't appear to weaken the top-order batting, however, as Zimbabwe batted painstakingly through five sessions.

The first day produced just 185 runs for four wickets, with Zimbabwe content with occupying the crease without taking a positive approach. Andy Flower tried unsuccessfully to increase the run-rate with a 32-ball innings of 29 which included two fours and two sixes. He eventually fell to the bowling of Cairns, a wicket that lifted Cairns above Danny Morrison as second on the New Zealand all-time Test wicket-taking list, behind Sir Richard Hadlee, with 161.

Finally dismissed for 350, Zimbabwe had New Zealand in trouble at 139 for five and 180 for six, despite Matt Horne's fourth Test hundred. It needed a seventh-wicket partnership of 72 between Cairns and Craig McMillan, and then a ninth-wicket stand of 78 between Daniel Vettori and Adam Parore to get New Zealand within range of Zimbabwe's first innings.

Cairns' innings of 33, made in two hours, played an important part in New Zealand's total, but it was his bowling display in Zimbabwe's second-innings that was to prove decisive.

Cairns started Zimbabwe's second innings slump, removing Gavin Rennie in the seventh over, then Shayne O'Connor and Paul Wiseman picked up wickets to leave Zimbabwe struggling on 23 for three.

At 100 for five by stumps on the fourth day, only Alistair Campbell and Heath Streak stood between New Zealand and a comfortable victory.

Campbell was out without addition to the overnight score and, when Streak departed ten runs later, New Zealand had all but wrapped up the Test. Cairns completed his tenth haul of five wickets in a Test innings, with an impressive five for 31 although his effort wasn't enough to win the Man of the Match award. That went to off spinner Paul Wiseman with match figures of eight for 144.

FIRST TEST – ZIMBABWE v. NEW ZEALAND
12–16 September 2000 at Queen's Sports Club, Bulawayo

ZIMBABWE

	First innings		Second innings	
GW Flower	c Parore, b Vettori	24	c Parore, b O'Connor	3
GJ Rennie	c McMillan, b Wiseman	36	b Cairns	2
SV Carlisle	c Horne, b Wiseman	38	b Wiseman	15
ADR Campbell	lbw b Astle	88	lbw b Cairns	45
*A Flower	c Astle, b Cairns	29	lbw b Astle	22
CB Wishart	c Richardson, b Wiseman	17	c Richardson, b Wiseman	1
HH Streak (capt)	c Parore, b Wiseman	51	c McMillan, b Wiseman	15
PA Strang	c Rishardson, b Wiseman	0	(9) not out	8
ML Nkala	not out	30	(8) c Sinclair, b Cairns	0
BC Strang	c Parore, b O'Connor	10	b Cairns	5
DT Mutendera	b Cairns	10	c Parore, b Cairns	0
	b5, lb4, nb8	17	lb1, w1, nb1	3
		350		**119**

	First innings				Second innings			
	O	M	R	W	O	M	R	W
Cairns	28.2	9	77	2	14.5	5	31	5
O'Connor	30	7	63	1	9	5	8	1
McMillan	9	3	23	-				
Vettori	52	23	79	1				
Astle	11	6	9	1	18	10	24	1
Wiseman	45	16	90	5	25	8	54	3
Richardson					1	0	1	-

Fall of Wickets
1-40, 2-91, 3-120, 4-157, 5-206, 6-282, 7-291, 8-300, 9-323
1-6, 2-23, 3-23, 4-75, 5-86, 6-100, 7-100, 8-110, 9-119

NEW ZEALAND

	First innings		Second innings	
MH Richardson	c Carlisle, b Streak	6	lbw b Rennie	13
MJ Horne	lbw b PA Strang	110		
MS Sinclair	lbw b PA Strang	12	(2) not out	43
PJ Wiseman	lbw b PA Strang	14		
SP Fleming (capt)	c Rennie, b PA Strang	11	(3) lbw b PA Strang	12
NJ Astle	c A Flower, b PA Strang	0	(4) c Nkala, b PA Strang	27
CD McMillan	c A Flower, b PA Strang	58	(5) not out	31
CL Cairns	b Streak	33		
*AC Parore	not out	32		
DL Vettori	c & b PA Strang	49		
SB O'Connor	c Campbell, b PA Strang	4		
	lb1, nb8	9	lb2, w1, nb3	6
		338	(for 3 wickets)	**132**

	First innings				Second innings			
	O	M	R	W	O	M	R	W
Streak	26	9	67	2	5	0	21	-
Nkala	21	7	43	-	2	1	2	-
PA Strang	51.5	11	109	8	20.4	3	49	2
BC Strang	25	7	63	-	2	0	10	-
Mutendera	14	4	29	-				
GW Flower	16	4	26	-	1.3	0	5	-
Rennie					13.3	0	40	1
Campbell					1	0	3	-

Fall of Wickets
1-15, 2-52, 3-109, 4-139, 5-139, 6-180, 7-252, 8-252, 9-330
1-27, 2-43, 3-93

Umpires: RB Tiffin & DB Hair
Toss: Zimbabwe
Test debuts: DT Mutendera (Zimbabwe) & MH Richardson (New Zealand)

New Zealand won by seven wickets

SECOND TEST
19–23 September 2000 at Harare Sports Club

Chris Cairns' all-round effort wasn't enough to win the Man of the Match award in the first Test, but his commanding performance in the second ensured that he outplayed any other contender. It was a well-timed contribution from Cairns: his fourth Test hundred was liberally sprinkled with the belligerent, sparkling strokes that have made him such a consistently dangerous player.

New Zealand were not in desperate trouble when Cairns' innings started at 256 for five on the second morning, but on a placid Harare pitch they were hardly in a dominant position either.

Mark Richardson, Mathew Sinclair and Nathan Astle had all played with admirable commitment after the early loss of Craig Spearman. Richardson's third Test innings ended one short of a deserved century on the last ball of the first day thanks to a disputable lbw decision by Zimbabwean umpire, Ian Robinson.

Cairns' commanding performance occupied much of the second day: 50 off 63 balls and 100 off 144. With Dion Nash, Cairns added 144 for the eighth wicket – a record for New Zealand against all countries – and pushed New Zealand towards a dominant total of 465.

Cairns also played a major part with the ball, grabbing the first two wickets as Zimbabwe struggled to stave off the follow-on and were

Andy Flower connects with another of his favourite sweep shots during Zimbabwe's second Test resistance.

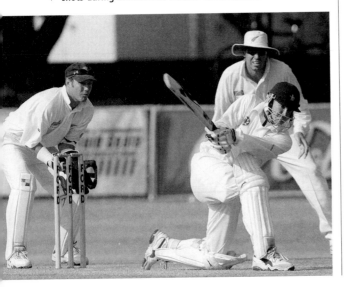

SECOND TEST – ZIMBABWE v. NEW ZEALAND
19–23 September 2000 at Harare Sports Club, Harare

NEW ZEALAND

	First innings		Second innings	
MH Richardson	lbw b Nkala	99	(1) c Rennie, b Streak	2
CM Spearman	c A Flower, b Olonga	2		
MS Sinclair	c Carlisle, b Olonga	44	not out	35
SP Fleming (capt)	c Campbell, b Mbangwa	9	not out	19
NJ Astle	run out (Mbangwa/A Flower)	86		
CD McMillan	lbw b Mbangwa	15		
CL Cairns	st A Flower, b Strang	124		
*AC Parore	c A Flower, b Olonga	4	(2) c Carlisle, b Streak	13
DJ Nash	c GW Flower, b Strang	62		
PJ Wiseman	not out	1		
SB O'Connor	c Whittall, b GW Flower	2		
	lb3, w2, nb12	17	lb2, w1, nb2	5
		465	(for 2 wickets)	**74**

	First innings				Second innings			
	O	M	R	W	O	M	R	W
Olonga	27	5	115	3				
Streak	29	6	74	-	8	2	33	2
Nkala	15	0	60	1	3	0	17	-
Mbangwa	28	10	58	2	4.2	0	22	-
Strang	38	11	80	2				
GW Flower	20.3	6	59	1				
Rennie	3	0	16	-				

Fall of Wickets
1-5, 2-69, 3-91, 4-226, 5-256, 6-302, 7-318, 8-462, 9-462
1-4, 2-42

ZIMBABWE

	First innings		Second innings	
GW Flower	c Parore, b Astle	49	run out (Wiseman/Astle)	10
GJ Rennie	c Spearman, b Cairns	4	c Spearman, b O'Connor	1
SV Carlisle	c Sinclair, b Olonga	31	c Fleming, b Astle	20
ADR Campbell	c Fleming, b O'Connor	0	run out (Sinclair/Parore)	10
*A Flower	lbw b McMillan	48	c Sinclair, b O'Connor	65
GJ Whittall	c Parore, b Cairns	8	not out	188
HH Streak (capt)	c Wiseman, b O'Connor	8	lbw b Cairns	54
ML Nkala	c Parore, b McMillan	0	lbw b O'Connor	0
PA Strang	c Parore, b O'Connor	5	b Cairns	8
HK Olonga	c Parore, b Nash	4	lbw b O'Connor	0
M Mbangwa	not out	0	run out (Nash)	5
	b3, lb3, w1, nb1	8	b4, lb4, nb1	9
		166		**370**

	First innings				Second innings			
	O	M	R	W	O	M	R	W
Cairns	17.1	7	33	2	33	7	80	2
O'Connor	28	9	43	3	45	17	73	4
Nash	17	11	25	1	17.3	8	28	-
McMillan	12.5	2	29	2	20	4	53	-
Astle	14	9	22	2	36	15	73	1
Wiseman	3	0	8	-	27	11	55	-

Fall of Wickets
1-5, 2-76, 3-77, 4-118, 5-146, 6-151, 7-151, 8-157, 9-164
1-1, 2-27, 3-39, 4-48, 5-179, 6-330, 7-335, 8-348, 9-349

Umpires: ID Robinson & DR Shepherd
Toss: New Zealand
Test debuts: nil

New Zealand won by eight wickets

TEST AVERAGES

ZIMBABWE

Batting	M	Inns	NO	HS	Runs	Av	100	50	c/st
A Flower	2	4	0	65	164	41.00	-	1	4/1
ADR Campbell	2	4	0	88	143	35.75	-	1	2
HH Streak	2	4	0	54	128	32.00	-	2	-
SV Carlisle	2	4	0	38	104	26.00	-	-	3
GW Flower	2	4	0	49	86	21.50	-	-	1
GJ Rennie	2	4	0	36	43	10.75	-	-	2
M Nkala	2	4	1	30*	30	10.00	-	-	1
PA Strang	2	4	1	8*	21	7.00	-	-	1

Also batted: M Mbangwa (1 match) 0*, 5; DT Mutendera (1 match) 10, 0; HK Olonga (1 match) 4, 0; BC Strang (1 match) 10, 5; GJ Whittall (1 match) 9, 188*, 1ct; CB Wishart (1 match) 17, 1.

Bowling	Overs	Mds	Runs	Wkts	Av	Best	10m	5/inn
PA Strang	110.3	14	238	12	19.83	8-109	1	1
HH Streak	68	17	195	4	48.75	2-33	-	-

Also bowled: ADR Campbell 1-0-3-0; GW Flower 38-10-90-1; M Mbangwa 32.2-10-80-2; DT Mutendera 14-4-29-0; ML Nkala 41-8-122-1; HK Olonga 27-5-115-3; GJ Rennie 16.3-0-56-1; BC Strang 27-7-73-0.

NEW ZEALAND

Batting	M	Inns	NO	HS	Runs	Av	100	50	c/st
CL Cairns	2	3	1	124	176	88.00	1	-	-
MS Sinclair	2	4	2	44	134	67.00	-	-	2
CD McMillan	2	3	1	58	104	52.00	-	1	3
MH Richardson	2	3	0	99	118	39.33	-	1	3
NJ Astle	2	3	0	86	113	37.66	-	1	1
AC Parore	2	3	1	32*	49	24.50	-	-	10/-
SP Fleming	2	3	0	12	32	10.66	-	-	2

Also batted: MJ Horne (1 match) 110, 1ct; DJ Nash (1 match) 62; SB O'Connor (2 matches) 4, 2; CM Spearman (1 match) 2, 2, 2ct; DL Vettori (1 match) 49; PJ Wiseman (2 matches) 14, 1*, 1ct.

Bowling	Overs	Mds	Runs	Wkts	Av	Best	10m	5/inn
CL Cairns	93.2	28	221	11	20.09	5-31	-	1
SB O'Connor	112	38	187	9	20.77	4-73	-	-
NJ Astle	79	41	128	5	25.60	2-22	-	-
PJ Wiseman	100	35	207	8	25.87	5-90	-	1

Also bowled: CD McMillan 41.5-9-105-2; DJ Nash 34.3-19-53-1; MH Richardson 1-0-1-0; DL Vettori 52-23-79-1.

dismissed for 166 – a deficit of 299.

Zimbabwe's second innings was much more disciplined as Guy Whittall enjoyed his second big total against New Zealand. He followed his double century in the previous home series with a patient, controlled innings of 188 not out, which wiped off the first-innings deficit with only five wickets down.

Whittall, first with Andy Flower, and then with captain Heath Streak, provided the bulk of the runs, 131 for the fifth wicket and 151 for the sixth, which threatened to halt New Zealand's push for a series clean sweep. However, Zimbabwe's tail folded just as it had in the first innings, although Mbangwa and Whittall resisted for 40 minutes until a mix-up resulted in the run out of Mbangwa after a direct hit from Dion Nash.

New Zealand had 18 overs in which to score the required 72 for victory, and the end came spectacularly as Cairns followed a one-handed six off Mbangwa with the winning runs in the 16th over.

ONE–DAY INTERNATIONALS

Zimbabwe staged a dramatic turn around in form to win the three-match one-day series against New Zealand, but they did it the hard way. The revival was led by the former captain, Alistair Campbell, who played two stunning innings to prevent a total demolition job by New Zealand.

The one dayers appeared to be heading the way of the Test series when New Zealand won the opening match in Harare by seven wickets after a dismal batting performance from the home side. Zimbabwe never got out of first gear against the tight bowling of Shayne O'Connor, Nathan Astle and Chris Harris. It required some lusty, lower-order hitting from Paul Strang to make a total that was, at least, challenging. However, it was a breeze for New Zealand with Craig Spearman and Roger Twose slamming 152 in 30 overs after the loss of two early wickets to seal another commanding victory.

New Zealand fired a few shots with the bat in the final two matches, but it was Campbell's masterly batting that settled the series. In the first of a double-header at the Queen's Club in Bulawayo, Campbell scored an adventurous 96, and added 83 in 16 overs with new boy Doug Marillier, to lay the platform for a substantial total.

Spearman, Astle, Twose and Craig McMillan made a strong effort to reach the stiff target, but the Zimbabwe spinners, Paul Strang and Dirk Viljoen, maintained the necessary pressure to unsettle the New Zealand lower-order.

McMillan and Twose played a key role for New Zealand in the deciding match, adding 92 for the fourth wicket to leave them 170 for four after 33 overs. But while they maintained the run-rate at around five an over, their total of 273 did not put Zimbabwe out of the game, in particular when you consider the aggressive strokeplay of Alistair Campbell. The opening partnership savaged the New Zealand seam attack of O'Connor, Harris, Darryl Tuffey and Scott Styris with the first wicket falling at 97 in the 20th over.

The momentum created by that opening stand was enough to restrain New Zealand, as Stuart Carlisle, Andy Flower and Guy Whittall then assisted Campbell towards his century. He remained one short of that personal achievement, but it apparently mattered little to Campbell or his team-mates who joyfully hit off the required runs for a six-wicket victory with 13 balls to spare. It was Zimbabwe's first one-day series win since beating England 3–0 at home four years earlier.

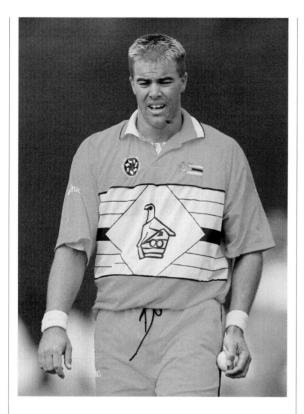

Heath Streak, who led Zimbabwe to a 2–1 victory in the one-day series.

Match One
27 September 2000 at Harare Sports Club
Zimbabwe 183 for 8 (50 overs)
New Zealand 184 for 3 (40.5 overs) (CM Spearman 86, RG Twose 70*)
New Zealand won by seven wickets
Man of the Match: NJ Astle

Match Two
30 September 2000 at Queen's Sports Club, Bulawayo
Zimbabwe 273 for 5 (50 overs) (ADR Campbell 96)
New Zealand 252 (48.5 overs) (RG Twose 64, CM Spearman 62)
Zimbabwe won by 21 runs
Man of the Match: HH Streak

Match Three
1 October 2000 at Queen's Sports Club, Bulawayo
New Zealand 264 for 8 (50 overs) (CD McMillan 78, RG Twose 63)
Zimbabwe 268 for 4 (47.5 overs) (ADR Campbell 99*)
Zimbabwe won by six wickets
Man of the Match: ADR Campbell.

BANGLADESH IN ZIMBABWE
by Telford Vice

ONE-DAY INTERNATIONALS

Only in the third match did Bangladesh provide Zimbabwe with worthy opposition. The first game, in Harare, presented the visitors with an insurmountable obstacle in the form of exaggerated movement off the seam. Raised on pitches that rarely twitched this way or that, the Bangladeshis' gauche batting duly led them to a seven-wicket slaughter.

Naimur Rahman won the toss, elected to bat and kicked himself, as Bangladesh crashed to 15 for four in nine overs before losing the captain himself and Khaled Mashud in the space of three deliveries to leave them dwindling on 49 for six. Akram Khan and Mushfiqur Rahman kept their side's heads above water for the next 19 overs when they shared in a stand of 64 for the seventh wicket.

However, a total of 151 for eight was never going to be enough to hold Zimbabwe, and partnerships of 58 between Guy Whittall and Stuart Carlisle for the second wicket, followed by 66 for the unbroken fourth between Andy and Grant Flower, ensured that there would be no way back for Bangladesh.

The teams returned the next day to find a tamer surface, but again the Asians chased every ball that pitched within sight. Alistair Campbell scored 103 – the same number of runs scraped together by the entire Bangladesh team – as Zimbabwe swept to victory by 127 runs.

Naimur Rahman again won the toss. This time he inserted Zimbabwe – alas, only for his bowlers to let their discipline slip. Campbell and Carlisle took advantage in their second-wicket partnership of 133, which had the Bangladeshis on the hop from the 17th over to the 44th as Zimbabwe totalled 230 for seven.

The only positive aspects of Bangladesh's innings were the batting of Javed Omar, who carried his bat with 33 not out, and Naimur Rahman's 25 off 21 balls with four fours. Mehrab Hossain's 11 was the only other double-figure score.

A Bulawayo pitch that was more familiar to the Bangladeshis helped them supplant their highest total, 257 twice scored against Zimbabwe, with 272 for eight in reply to the home side's overpowering 308 for four to go down, fighting at least, by 36 runs.

But first they had to endure Grant Flower equalling Zimbabwe's highest one-day score, the 142

Dave Houghton made against New Zealand in the 1987–88 World Cup.

Indeed, Zimbabwe's towering total was built around the Flower brothers, who shared a stand of 148 after coming together at 39 for three in the tenth over. Grant Flower scored his runs off 128 balls with ten fours and two sixes, while Andy Flower faced 92 balls and hit five fours in his 81.

Much of the credit for Bangladesh staying in touch with the original required run-rate of 6.18 in the first half of their innings belonged to Javed Omar and Habibul Bashar, who put on 84 runs off 103 balls for the third wicket. Javed Omar's dismissal for 69 in the 27th over heralded the end of Bangladesh's serious challenge and the required run-rate climbed into double figures in the 38th over.

Match One
7 April 2001 at Harare Sports Club
Bangladesh 151 for 8 (50 overs
Zimbabwe 155 for 3 (43.1 overs)
Zimbabwe won by seven wickets
Man of the Match: BC Strang

Match Two
8 April 2001 at Harare Sports Club

More runs for Grant Flower in Bulawayo. His unbeaten 142 led Zimbabwe to a 3–0 series victory.

Zimbabwe 230 for 7 (50 overs)(ADR Campbell 103, SV Carlisle 56)
Bangladesh 103 (30.4 overs)
Zimbabwe won by 127 runs
Man of the Match: ADR Campbell

Match Three
11 April 2001 at Queen's Sports Club, Bulawayo
Zimbabwe 308 for 4 (50 overs)(GW Flower 142*, A Flower 81)
Bangladesh 272 for 8 (50 overs)(Habibul Bashar 74, Javed Omar 69)
Zimbabwe won by 36 runs
Man of the Match: GW Flower
Man of the Series: GW Flower

First Test
19–22 April 2001 at Queen's Sports Club, Bulawayo

Zimbabwe won by an innings and 32 runs with almost five sessions to spare to register their fourth Test victory.

It was a match of solid, though unremarkable, cricket by the victors and a textbook fledgling performance by Bangladesh in their first Test on foreign soil. The visitors bowled well enough, but showed an unfortunate propensity to throw wickets away around breaks in play and fell victim to lapses of concentration in the field.

The match was over in the third over after lunch on the fourth day when Bangladesh, who resumed on 91 for two, were dismissed for 168. Javed Omar maintained what amounted to be a lone vigil at the crease in scoring an unbeaten 85, his second half-century of the match, in more than four-and-a-half hours at the crease – the first time a Test debutant had carried his bat since England's Plum Warner did so for the first time against South Africa in 1898–99.

Heath Streak's decision to field first after winning the toss was prompted by a well-grassed pitch. However, Streak himself was the main reason Zimbabwe did not make earlier inroads, as he bowled wide of the wicket and failed to make the batsmen play enough.

It fell to debutant Andy Blignaut to step into the breach left by his captain and senior bowler. He ventured rather closer to the stumps, refused to budge and was rewarded with four wickets. A catch in the slips and a stunning run out of Akram Khan, which required a sprint from gully to third man, helped to ensure that Blignaut would not be alone in remembering his first day of Test cricket.

That Bangladesh were still batting at the close of

the first day, by which time they had reached 256 for nine, was thanks to Aminul Islam and Javed Omar, who put their heads down in exemplary fashion to share 84 for the third wicket and score 84 and 62 respectively.

Thirteen balls into the second day, Mohammad Sharif edged a drive to first slip to earn Blignaut figures of five for 73, the best return by a Zimbabwean on debut, as Bangladesh managed to add just one run to their overnight score.

Guy Whittall's fourth Test century, 119 in more than four hours, guided Zimbabwe to a lead of 30 runs at stumps, which they reached on 287 for five. Andy Flower's 73 equalled the world record of seven consecutive half-centuries set by West Indian Everton Weekes between 1947 and 1949. Whittall and Flower shared 149 runs for the fourth wicket, but both threw their wickets away after tea without taking full advantage of Bangladesh's limited attack on what had become a sound batting pitch.

However, they helped to rebuild an innings that had stumbled to 66 for three in the 14th over, two of those wickets falling to impressive left-arm seamer Manjural Islam, a debutant.

He went on to improve the best figures by a Bangladeshi to six for 81, but the visitors were not in celebratory mood when bad light forced the close of play nine overs early with them still 109 runs behind and with Khaled Mashud, the only specialist wicket-keeper in the squad, out of the rest of the tour after fracturing his ankle during the warm-up.

Manjural Islam struck half an hour before lunch when he had Streak caught in the covers for his then-highest score of 67. The wicket ended a stabilizing stand of 120 for the sixth wicket between Streak and Grant Flower that began five balls after tea the previous day.

Blignaut came back to earth with a bump when he took guard after Streak's dismissal and sent Manjural Islam's next delivery looping back to the bowler for a first-ball duck. Mluleki Nkala fended off the hat-trick ball.

Six overs into the third session, Flower hooked Hasibul Hossain to fine leg to be dismissed for 68. Nkala became Manjural Islam's sixth victim when his hook shot looped into the welcoming hands of stand-in wicket-keeper Mehrab Hossain. Nkala, whose 47 was his highest Test score, shared 56 runs for the ninth wicket with Murphy.

The innings ended 25 minutes before the scheduled tea interval when Murphy, on 30, also his highest score, was caught at forward short leg off Naimur Rahman, the captain and off spinner, as

Zimbabwe were dismissed for 457.

Bangladesh's problems, on what became the final day, began in the fifth over when Aminul Islam slashed Streak to third man to be dismissed for 11, one of only three double figure scores in a dismal innings.

Only Javed Omar seemed capable of resisting the fatal, injudicious cut shot as Bangladesh lost their last seven wickets for 63 runs, three of them for 37 runs to a relentlessly accurate Streak.

At an impromptu press conference afterwards, the compact opener struggled to curb the tears as he dedicated his defiant unbeaten knock of 85 to his brother, Asif, who had died of a heart attack six years previously. 'I miss him every moment, especially when I'm playing cricket, because he was always motivating me,' Javed Omar said of his brother, also a cricketer. 'If I got a hundred, it would have been for him. But after we lost seven wickets I knew it would be difficult to get my century.'

Unsurprisingly, Naimur Rahman pinned the blame on his batsmen: 'We have to support the guys who

Javed Omar ... a lone vigil and a tearful tribute to his brother who had died six years earlier from a heart attack.

FIRST TEST – ZIMBABWE v. BANGLADESH
19–22 April 2001 at Queen's Sports Club, Bulawayo

BANGLADESH

	First innings		Second innings	
Javed Omar	c Ebrahim, b Murphy	62	not out	85
Mehrab Hossain	c Whittall, b Blignaut	16	b Streak	0
Habibul Bashar	c Murphy, b Blignaut	0	c Murphy, b Watambwa	24
Aminul Islam	c A Flower, b Blignaut	84	c Ebrahim, b Streak	11
Akram Khan	run out (Blignaut/A Flower)	21	c Ebrahim, b Blignaut	8
Naimur Rahman (capt)	c Blignaut, b Watambwa	22	c & b Nkala	6
*Khaled Mashud	c A Flower, b Streak	30	absent injured	
Mushfiqur Rahman	c Streak, b Blignaut	4	(7) c Nkala, b Watambwa	2
Hasibul Hossain	lbw b Streak	1	(8) c GW Flower, b Streak	6
Mohammad Sharif	c Campbell, b Blignaut	0	(9) c Whittall, b Blignaut	8
Manjural Islam	not out	1	(10) c & b Blignaut	6
	lb1, w6, nb9	16	lb2, w6, nb4	12
		257		**168**

	First innings				Second innings			
	O	M	R	W	O	M	R	W
Streak	21	7	47	2	19	5	42	3
Blignaut	23.3	5	73	5	13.3	4	37	3
Watambwa	17	4	38	1	13	3	44	2
Nkala	13	2	45	–	9	0	34	1
Murphy	17	2	53	1	4	1	9	–

Fall of Wickets
1-26, 2-30, 3-114, 4-149, 5-194, 6-226, 7-253, 8-256, 9-256
1-6, 2-61, 3-105, 4-116, 5-129, 6-138, 7-149, 8-160, 9-168

ZIMBABWE

	First innings	
GJ Whittall	c Mohammad Sharif, b Hasibul Hossain	119
DD Ebrahim	c Khaled Mashud, b Manjural Islam	2
SV Carlisle	b Manjural Islam	3
ADR Campbell	c Khaled Mashud, b Mohammad Sharif	19
*A Flower	c Naimur Rahman, b Manjural Islam	73
GW Flower	c Mohammad Sharif, b Hasibul Hossain	68
HH Streak (capt)	c sub (Mohammad Rafique), b Manjural Islam	67
AM Blignaut	c & b Manjural Islam	0
ML Nkala	c Mehrab Hossain, b Manjural Islam	47
BA Murphy	c Habibul Bashar, b Naimur Rahman	30
BT Watambwa	not out	4
	b2, lb10, w1, nb12	25
		457

	First innings			
	O	M	R	W
Hasibul Hossain	30	7	125	2
Manjural Islam	35	12	81	6
Mohammad Sharif	29	3	112	1
Mushfiqur Rahman	20	5	53	–
Naimur Rahman	24.4	7	74	1

Fall of Wickets
1-18, 2-27, 3-66, 4-215, 5-233, 6-353, 7-353, 8-389, 9-445

Umpires: KC Barbour & RE Koertzen
Toss: Zimbabwe
Test debuts: AM Blignaut, DD Ebrahim and DT Watambwa (Zimbabwe); Javed Omar, Manjural Islam, Mohammad Sharif and Mushfiqur Rahman (Bangladesh)

Zimbabwe won by an innings and 32 runs

are already in – we need more application and determination. Javed Omar tried to put up a good show for the team, but we needed to support him.'

Besides Blignaut, Zimbabwe blooded Dion Ebrahim – perhaps unfairly as an opening batsman after he had spent almost all his career until then in the middle-order – and fast bowler Brighton Watambwa, who showed he was keen to back up his considerable pace with a healthy dollop of aggression.

Bangladesh capped medium-pacers Mohammed Sharif and Mushfiqur Rahman, as well as Javed Omar and Manjural Islam.

SECOND TEST
26–30 April 2001 at Harare Sports Club

Bangladesh coach Trevor Chappell prefaced the second Test with the pithy observation that 'some of the players have learned an awful lot, some of them maybe not as much'.

Unfortunately for the tourists the latter were in the majority and Bangladesh made similar blunders to the ones they had made in the first Test. Zimbabwe took full advantage to win by eight wickets an hour after lunch on the fifth day to claim the series 2–0.

That said, Bangladesh did gain the satisfaction of forcing a Test match into the final day for the first time in three attempts, although they were helped in that regard by rain on the third afternoon.

Zimbabwe made one change, excluding leg-spinner Brian Murphy for Ray Price, the orthodox left-arm spinner. Bangladesh also brought in a left-arm spinner, Enamul Haque, in the place of medium pacer Hasibul Hossain. The other change was forced with batsman Al-Sahariar included for wicket-keeper Khaled Mashud, who had fractured his ankle during the warm-up to the first Test. Mehrab Hossain took over the gloves and continued in his primary role of opening the batting.

As in the first Test, Heath Streak inserted Bangladesh upon winning the toss. Movement off the seam justified his decision, as the Bangladeshi openers played and missed a number of times. However, the ball was again not pitched close enough to the bat for Zimbabwe to make the most of their advantage.

Streak took two wickets as Bangladesh slipped to 48 for three at lunch, before Mehrab Hossain and Habibul Bashar embarked on their partnership of 114 – the Asians' first-ever century stand.

It was ended an hour after tea when Price

SECOND TEST – ZIMBABWE v. BANGLADESH
26–30 April 2001 at Harare Sports Club, Harare

BANGLADESH

	First innings		Second innings	
Javed Omar	c Blignaut, b Streak	1	c GW Flower, b Price	43
*Mehrab Hossain	c Carlisle, b Price	71	c Blignaut, b Watambwa	0
Al Sahariar Rokon	c GW Flower, b Streak	11	c Streak, b Watambwa	68
Aminul Islam	c Campbell, b Price	12	lbw b Price	2
Habibul Bashar	st A Flower, b Price	64	c A Flower, b Streak	76
Akram Khan	c Campbell, b Streak	44	c Campbell, b Price	31
Naimur Rahman (capt)	lbw b Price	16	run out (sub: GJ Rennie/ Watambwa)	36
Mushfiqur Rahman	c A Flower, b Streak	2	(9) not out	2
Enamul Hoque	not out	20	(8) c A Flower, b Watambwa	3
Mohammad Sharif	c Carlisle, b Watambwa	0	c Carlisle, b Streak	0
Manjural Islam	c Campbell, b Watambwa	0	c A Flower, b Watambwa	0
	lb8, w3, nb2	13	lb2, w1, nb2	5
		254		**266**

	First innings				Second innings			
	O	M	R	W	O	M	R	W
Blignaut	27	6	67	–	15	6	27	–
Streak	30	12	38	4	21	7	47	2
Watambwa	14.5	3	48	2	21.5	5	64	4
Nkala	19	11	22	–	6	0	19	–
Price	30	9	71	4	30	9	94	3
GW Flower	6	0	13	–				

Fall of Wickets
1-1, 2-23, 3-48, 4-162, 5-171, 6-196, 7-207, 8-253, 9-254
1-2, 2-97, 3-99, 4-127, 5-203, 6-246, 7-264, 8-264, 9-265

ZIMBABWE

	First innings		Second innings	
GJ Whittall	run out (Mohammad Sharif/ Mehrab Hossain)	59	b Enamu Hoque	60
DD Ebrahim	c Akram Khan, b Naimur Rahman	39	run out (Javed Omar/ Mehrab Hossain)	10
SV Carlisle	c Habibul Bashar, b Mohammad Sharif	21	not out	29
ADR Campbell	c Mushfiqur Rahman, b Naimur Rahman	73	not out	0
*A Flower	run out (Javed Omar)	23		
GW Flower	c Mohammad Sharif, b Enamul Hoque	84		
HH Streak (capt)	c Mehrab Hossain, b Mohammad Sharif	87		
AM Blignaut	run out (Mohammad Sharif/ Mehrab Hossain)	15		
ML Nkala	c Mushfiqur Rahman, b Enamul Hoque	7		
RW Price	not out	0		
BT Watambwa				
	b7, lb6	13	lb1	1
	(for 9 wickets dec.)	**421**	(for 2 wickets)	**100**

	First innings				Second innings			
	O	M	R	W	O	M	R	W
Manjural Islam	34	9	113	–	9	2	21	–
Mohammad Sharif	28.4	6	108	2	6	0	36	–
Enamul Hoque	46	15	94	2	3	0	8	1
Mushfiqur Rahman	11	1	33	–	6	1	26	–
Naimur Rahman	28	12	60	2	0.3	0	8	–

Fall of Wickets
1-90, 2-104, 3-164, 4-210, 5-244, 6-377, 7-397, 8-419, 9-421
1-35, 2-92

Umpires: RB Tiffin & DB Cowie
Toss: Zimbabwe
Test debut: Enamul Hoque (Bangladesh)

Zimbabwe won by eight wickets

TEST MATCH AVERAGES

ZIMBABWE

Batting	M	Inns	NO	HS	Runs	Av	100	50	c/st
GJ Whittall	2	3	0	119	238	79.33	1	2	2
HH Streak	2	2	0	87	154	77.00	–	2	2
GW Flower	2	2	0	84	152	76.00	–	2	3
A Flower	2	2	0	73	96	48.00	–	1	6/1
ADR Campbell	2	3	1	73	92	46.00	–	1	5
ML Nkala	2	2	0	47	54	27.00	–	–	2
SV Carlisle	2	3	1	29*	53	26.50	–	–	3
DD Ebrahim	2	3	0	39	51	17.00	–	–	3
AM Blignaut	2	2	0	15	15	7.50	–	–	4

Also batted: BA Murphy (1 Test) 30 (2ct); RW Price (1 Test) 0*; BT Watambwa (2 Tests) 4*.

Bowling	Overs	Mds	Runs	Wkts	Av	Best	10m	5/inn
HH Streak	91	31	174	11	15.81	4-38	–	–
BT Watambwa	66.4	15	194	9	21.55	4-64	–	–
RW Price	60	18	165	7	23.57	4-71	–	–
AM Blignaut	79	21	204	8	25.50	5-73	–	1

Also bowled: GW Flower 6-0-13-0; BA Murphy 21-3-62-1; ML Nkala 47-13-120-1.

BANGLADESH

Batting	M	Inns	NO	HS	Runs	Av	100	50	c/st
Javed Omar	2	4	1	85*	191	63.66	–	2	–
Habibul Bashar	2	4	0	76	164	41.00	–	2	2
Aminul Islam	2	4	0	84	109	27.25	–	1	–
Akram Khan	2	4	0	44	104	26.00	–	–	1
Mehrab Hossain	2	4	0	71	87	21.75	–	1	1/-
Naimur Rahman	2	4	0	36	80	20.00	–	–	1
Mushfiqur Rahman	2	4	1	4	10	3.33	–	–	3
Manjural Islam	2	4	1	6	7	2.33	–	–	1
Mohammad Sharif	2	4	0	8	8	2.00	–	–	3

Also batted in one Test: Al Sahariar Rokon 11, 68; Enamul Hoque 20*, 3; Hasibul Hossain 1, 6; Khaled Mashud 30 (2ct).

Bowling	Overs	Mds	Runs	Wkts	Av	Best	10m	5/inn
Manjural Islam	78	23	215	6	35.83	6-81	–	1

Also bowled: Enamul Hoque 49-15-102-3; Hasibul Hossain 30-7-125-2; Mohammad Sharif 63.4-9-256-3; Mushfiqur Rahman 37-7-112-0; Naimur Rahman 53.1-19-142-3.

whipped through a quicker delivery and Habibul Bashar was stumped for 64. Four overs later, Mehrab Hossain pulled a longhop from Price to short mid-wicket to go for 71, although he had been dropped twice, first off the bowling of Brighton Watambwa, on 12 by Streak at extra-cover, and then on 56 when Watambwa spilled an awkward return catch.

Eight balls before the close, which came with the total on 198 for six, Naimur Rahman attempted to heave Price over mid-wicket and was trapped in front for 16. Price ended the day with four for 47.

The second day turned, and with it the match, on the first 11 balls after lunch which cost Bangladesh three wickets on their way to a total of 254. Mushfiqur Rahman was caught behind off Streak in the sixth over of the morning, but Akram Khan and Enamul Haque batted responsibly to nurse the visitors to lunch on 253 for seven.

Akram Khan edged the third ball after lunch, bowled by Streak, gently to first slip to be out for 44. Six balls later, Mohammad Sharif nicked a delivery from Watambwa to second slip, followed two balls after that by Manjural Islam steering a catch to Campbell at first slip. Streak finished with four for 38, and Price with four for 71.

Guy Whittall and Dion Ebrahim put on 90 in a solid opening stand for Zimbabwe, before hesitation cost Whittall his wicket when he was run out for 59 by Mohammad Sharif's throw from mid-off to the wicket-keeper's end. By the close, Zimbabwe were 110 runs behind on 144 for two. The third day started with a bang when Alistair Campbell sent the first four balls, bowled by left-arm paceman Manjural Islam, speeding to the boundary for four. Campbell pulled the first three deliveries through mid-wicket, and cut the fourth past gully.

Such was the Bangladesh team's displeasure at Manjural Islam's unduly charitable bowling that he was left to retrieve the fourth boundary himself.

Eight balls into the day's play, Stuart Carlisle pushed too firmly at Mohammad Sharif and was caught at short leg for 21 to end a third-wicket stand of 60.

Campbell had reached 73 when, 20 minutes before lunch, he slog-swept a sharply turning off break from Naimur Rahman straight to short mid-

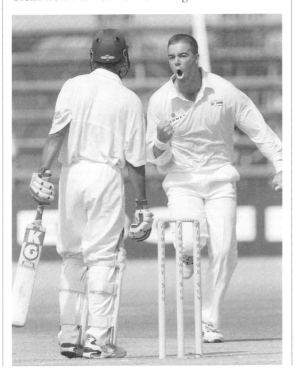

wicket. Grant Flower and Streak then enforced Zimbabwe's dominance with a sixth-wicket stand of 133.

Flower's innings was ended at 84 with what became the last ball of the day, a longhop from Enamul Haque, which he pulled to Mohammed Sharif at mid-wicket. Streak was 65 not out with Zimbabwe on 377 for six – a lead of 123.

Zimbabwe batted briskly for ten overs on the fourth morning, scoring 44 runs in the process before the declaration came with them 167 runs ahead on 421 for nine, when Streak cut at a wide delivery from Mohammed Sharif and was caught behind for 87, his highest Test score.

Streak was 55, and the total 346 for five, when Mehrab Hossain made a hash of a clear stumping chance off Naimur Rahman. Still on 55, Streak seemed to glove a leg-side delivery from Mohammed Sharif to the wicket-keeper, only for umpire Russell Tiffin to give the batsman the benefit of the doubt.

By the close of play on the fourth day, Bangladesh were 219 for five – 52 ahead. They reached lunch on 45 for one, and Price took two wickets in five balls midway through the second session. He had Javed Omar well caught by Grant Flower at second slip for 43 to end a second-wicket stand of 95 scored with Al Sahariar, and four balls later Aminul Islam was adjudged leg-before without offering a stroke. Three overs before tea, Al Sahariar, on 68, miscued a pull shot off Watambwa and sent a looping catch to mid-off.

Habibul Bashar and Akram Khan shared 76 runs in a solid partnership for the fifth wicket until, eight overs from the close, Akram Khan pushed forward to Price and edged to Campbell at slip to be dismissed for 31.

Having made it into the unchartered territory of the final day, Bangladesh promptly collapsed to a total of 266 to leave Zimbabwe to chase a nominal target of 100. The visitors had added just 47 runs to their overnight score and lost their last four wickets for two runs in the space of four overs. Top-scorer Habibul Bashar went in the sixth over of the morning when he edged a Streak away-swinger to be caught behind for 76. Watambwa showed plenty of pace and aggression in taking four for 64.

Guy Whittall scored 60 to guide Zimbabwe to victory. He was out five balls before the winning runs were struck, bowled round his legs by Enamul Hoque.

An early breakthrough for Heath Streak during his first-innings haul of four for 38.

INDIA IN ZIMBABWE
By Craig Ray

FIRST TEST
7–10 June 2001 at Queen's Sports Club, Bulawayo

It took just four days at the Queen's Sports Club for India to accelerate the momentum they had created with their stunning series win over Australia in March. In June it was Zimbabwe, and India claimed their first overseas Test victory for 15 years as they cruised to an eight-wicket win at the Queen's Sports Club.

The Test was also sweet revenge for a 61-run defeat suffered at the hands of Zimbabwe in 1998 – the last time India had toured there. But this was a different Indian side, led by the astute and inspirational Saurav Ganguly and blessed with rare talent in the form of Sachin Tendulkar and off spinner Harbhajan Singh.

Zimbabwe's captain, Heath Streak, won the toss and elected to bat on a pitch that offered bounce to the bowlers, but little lateral movement. On the first morning of the match Zimbabwe made a late change

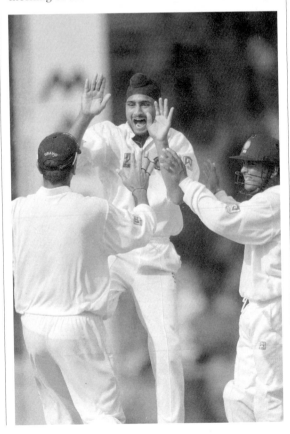

to the starting XI, with seam bowler Henry Olonga coming in at the expense of Travis Friend, who had been set to make his debut. This came to grief when the 23-year-old fast bowler suffered a thigh strain in the nets and could not pass a fitness test in time.

It was not the bowling that concerned Streak on the first day however, but the woeful batting by his side. The hosts scored a paltry 173, which effectively ended their chances of winning the Test on the first day – one in which 13 wickets fell. Zimbabwe went to lunch at 65 for three having lost openers Guy Whittall (six), bowled off an edge by left-arm seamer Ashish Nehra and Dion Ebrahim (12), unluckily run out when a drive from Stuart Carlisle caught the finger of bowler Harbhajan and hit the stumps at the non-striker's end.

Carlisle scored 29, but fell just two overs before lunch after he edged an angled delivery from left-arm fast bowler Zaheer Khan to V.V.S. Laxman at second slip.

After lunch the slide continued, with Alistair Campbell (21) and Grant Flower (five) falling before the home side had reached 100. Left-hander Andy Flower (51) provided the only notable resistance and continued his remarkable form against India as he moved to his fifth half-century against them from just 45 balls. Streak scored 16 and Olonga (16) hit wildly at the end, but the top-order had failed Zimbabwe.

India's response was shaky as they went to the close at 83 for three, having lost openers Shiv Sunder Das (30) and Sadagoppan Ramesh (two) as well as Laxman (28). Javagal Srinath joined Tendulkar as nightwatchman, but fell in the first over of the second morning for one. Ganguly (five) was caught at the wicket by Andy Flower off Streak to leave India reeling at 98 for five. The elegant right-hander Rahul Dravid and Tendulkar steadied the innings and added 80 for the sixth wicket from just 99 balls in 80 minutes.

Tendulkar (74) was brilliantly caught at second slip by Carlisle off the fast-medium pace of Andy Blignaut that offered Zimbabwe some hope in the final session. Dravid scored 44, which left India seven down with 208 on the board, but any thoughts of wrapping the tail up quickly were repressed as Harbhajan and wicket-keeper Samir Dighe contributed another 72 for the eighth wicket. Harbhajan's 66 was a career best and Dighe made

More success for new spin maestro Harbhajan Singh with both bat and ball as India completed an eight-wicket victory in the first Test.

FIRST TEST – ZIMBABWE v. INDIA
7–10 June 2001 at Queen's Sports Club, Bulawayo

ZIMBABWE

	First innings		Second innings	
GJ Whittall	b Nehra	6	c Ramesh, b Srinath	20
DD Ebrahim	run out (Harbhajan Singh)	12	c Dravid, b Srinath	0
SV Carlisle	c Laxman, b Khan	29	c Laxman, b Nehra	52
ADR Campbell	c Dighe, b Singh	21	c Das, b Singh	16
*A Flower	c Das, b Nehra	51	(6) c Ramesh, b Nehra	83
GW Flower	c Dighe, b Srinath	5	(7) run out (Dravid)	71
HH Streak (capt)	run out (Dighe)	16	(8) lbw b Khan	14
AM Blignaut	lbw b Nehra	0	(9) not out	32
BA Murphy	c Dravid, b Khan	7	(5) c Das, b Khan	10
HK Olonga	c Dighe, b Singh	16	b Srinath	0
BT Watambwa	not out	0	run out (Tendulkar/Singh)	0
	lb4, nb6	10	b1, lb17, w2, nb10	30
		173		**328**

	First innings				Second innings			
	O	M	R	W	O	M	R	W
Srinath	15	5	47	1	32.2	11	71	3
Nehra	12	1	23	3	26.4	4	77	2
Khan	11	1	54	2	22	6	44	2
Harbhajan Singh	20.5	6	45	2	37.5	8	92	1
Tendulkar					6	0	23	–
Ganguly					1	0	3	–

Fall of Wickets
1-9, 2-46, 3-65, 4-89, 5-97, 6-137, 7-139, 8-154, 9-165
1-14, 2-34, 3-63, 4-86, 5-134, 6-235, 7-273, 8-308, 9-312

INDIA

	First innings		Second innings	
SS Das	c Ebrahim, b Murphy	30	not out	82
S Ramesh	b Watambwa	2	c Carlisle, b Blignaut	17
VVS Laxman	c Whittall, b Olonga	28	c & b GW Flower	38
SR Tendulkar	c Carlisle, b Blignaut	74	not out	36
J Srinath	c Whittall, b Watambwa	1		
SC Ganguly (capt)	c A Flower, b Streak	5		
R Dravid	c A Flower, b Blignaut	44		
*SS Dighe	c A Flower, b Streak	47		
Harbhajan Singh	c Whittall, b Watambwa	66		
Z Khan	b Streak	0		
A Nehra	not out	0		
	lb4, w1, nb7	12	b4, w1, nb6	11
		318	**(for 2 wickets)**	**184**

	First innings				Second innings			
	O	M	R	W	O	M	R	W
Streak	24	7	63	3				
Watambwa	25.5	6	94	3	15	4	54	–
Blignaut	16	2	68	2	12	3	25	1
Olonga	8	1	35	1				
Murphy	16	3	54	1	18.4	1	78	–
GW Flower					8	0	23	1

Fall of Wickets
1-2, 2-54, 3-81, 4-83, 5-98, 6-178, 7-208, 8-280, 9-280
1-71, 2-132

Umpires: RB Tiffin & DJ Harper
Toss: Zimbabwe
Test debuts: nil

India won by eight wickets

47 before India were finally bowled out for 318 – a commanding lead of 145.

Zimbabwe posted a second-innings score of 328, thanks to the Flower brothers who shared a 101-run sixth wicket stand. India's bowling was hampered by the banning of Nehra, who had been warned by Daryll Harper for running down the wicket on his follow-through. Andy Flower scored 83, the ninth time in 12 innings he had passed 50 against India, which took his tally to 982 runs against them. Meanwhile brother Grant's innings was more patient and he survived until stumps on the third day, only to be run out for 71 on the fourth morning. India needed to score 184 runs to win with five sessions remaining.

Das and Ramesh put on 70 for the first wicket before Ramesh (17) was caught at second slip by Carlisle off Blignaut. Das moved fortuitously to his third Test half-century after being dropped on 18 and 49 as well as clearly edging his second ball to Flower, which was given not out. Laxman (38) was caught and bowled by Grant Flower which brought Tendulkar to the crease. And that was effectively that.

Tendulkar and Das completed the victory in the final session of the fourth day with the former unbeaten on 36 and Das a streaky but vital 82.

SECOND TEST
15–18 June 2001 at Harare Sports Club
By Craig Ray

After losing the first Test so comprehensively, Zimbabwe found the resolve to fight back and claim a four-wicket victory as sensational as it was unexpected, at the Harare Sports Club a week later.

It was a wonderful triumph for the minnows, not least because they lost opening bowler Brighton Watambwa in the seventh over of the first morning to a pulled hamstring.

To bowl India out twice, lacking a genuine wicket-taking bowler for most of the match was a worthy, remarkable achievement.

It was only Zimbabwe's sixth win in 52 Tests, but their second win against India in seven matches.

As well as the home side played, India imploded in typical fashion and failed to win their first Test series outside of the sub-continent for 15 years.

Immediately captain Saurav Ganguly was under pressure due to his own poor batting form and the inability of the team's top-order to carry on to big scores after solid starts.

Ganguly scored just 14 runs in the series and became increasingly irate at questions about the

SECOND TEST – ZIMBABWE v. INDIA
15–18 June 2001 at Harare Sports Club, Harare

INDIA

	First innings		Second innings	
SS Das	c A Flower, b Blignaut	57	lbw b Streak	70
HK Badani	lbw b Watambwa	2	(7) not out	16
VVS Laxman	c Blignaut, b Streak	15	c Murphy, b Friend	20
SR Tendulkar	b Streak	20	c GW Flower, b Streak	69
SC Ganguly (capt)	c Blignaut, b Streak	9	(6) lbw b Blignaut	0
R Dravid	not out	68	(5) c A Flower, b Blignaut	26
*SS Dighe	c GW Flower, b Friend	20	(2) c A Flower, b Blignaut	4
AB Agarkar	c Blignaut, b Friend	6	c A Flower, b Streak	0
Harbhajan Singh	b Murphy	31	c Ebrahim, b Blignaut	5
J Srinath	run out (Murphy)	0	c A Flower, b Streak	3
A Nehra	c Ebrahim, b Murphy	0	b Blignaut	0
	lb2, w6, nb1	9	lb9, w12	21
		237		**234**

	First innings				Second innings			
	O	M	R	W	O	M	R	W
Watambwa	3.4	0	14	1				
Streak	20	4	69	3	27	12	46	4
Friend	20.2	4	48	2	22	4	47	1
Blignaut	20	1	84	1	31.5	14	74	5
Murphy	9.2	3	17	2	10	1	42	–
GW Flower	1	0	3	–	1	0	1	–
Whittall					7	4	15	–

Fall of Wickets
1-7, 2-45, 3-90, 4-103, 5-122, 6-165, 7-172, 8-228, 9-237
1-8, 2-32, 3-150, 4-197, 5-199, 6-202, 7-202, 8-207, 9-226

ZIMBABWE

	First innings		Second innings	
GJ Whittall	c Dravid, b Nehra	0	c Dravid, b Srinath	11
DD Ebrahim	lbw b Singh	49	c Badani, b Singh	20
SV Carlisle	c Badani, b Nehra	3	not out	62
ADR Campbell	b Nehra	8	lbw b Nehra	13
*A Flower	c Das, b Singh	45	(8) not out	8
GW Flower	c Laxman, b Srinath	86	(5) c Laxman, b Agarkar	3
HH Streak (capt)	b Tendulkar	40	(6) c Dighe, b Srinath	8
AM Blignaut	st Dighe, b Singh	35	(7) b Nehra	16
TJ Friend	b Nehra	15		
BA Murphy	b Singh	17		
BT Watambwa	not out	2		
	b4, lb5, w2, nb4	15	b1, lb11, nb5	17
		315	(for 6 wickets)	**157**

	First innings				Second innings			
	O	M	R	W	O	M	R	W
Srinath	29.3	7	82	1	13	1	46	2
Nehra	24	6	72	4	13	1	45	2
Agarkar	24	7	62	–	8	3	22	1
Harbhajan Singh	26	5	71	4	19	6	25	1
Tendulkar	4	0	19	1	1	0	7	–

Fall of Wickets
1-5, 2-9, 3-18, 4-105, 5-110, 6-175, 7-242, 8-271, 9-301
1-25, 2-45, 3-71, 4-89, 5-119, 6-144

Umpires: ID Robinson & EAR de Silva
Toss: India
Test debuts: TJ Friend (Zimbabwe), HK Badani (India)

Zimbabwe won by four wickets

future of his place in the side.

But Zimbabwe played their part and took some fine catches, bowled accurately and with discipline, batted sensibly and ultimately exerted enough pressure on the opposition, to leave them unable to answer the questions asked of their temperament.

Ganguly won the toss and asked Heath Streak to bowl, which proved to be a mistake. Streak admitted afterwards that he would have bowled himself, as the Harare Sports Club wicket traditionally offered the quick bowlers assistance early on.

India were dismissed for 237 on the first day and by the close Zimbabwe were struggling at 31 for three, thanks to an exceptional bowling spell by left-arm seamer Ashish Nehra, who claimed the three Zimbabwean wickets and, mercifully, appeared to

Grant Flower works the ball away during his vital innings of 86 in the second Test.

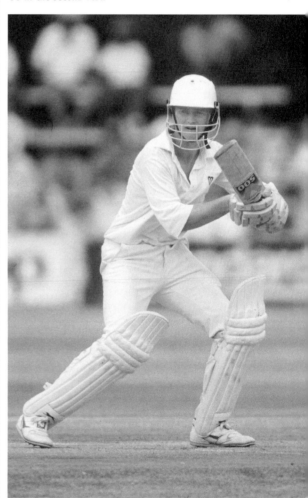

have his follow-through sorted after being banned in the first Test.

Earlier, India opener Shiv Sunder Das continued where he had left off in the first Test, scoring 57 as the top-order folded around him.

The visitors were left reeling at 122 for five after Das was caught at the wicket by Andy Flower off the bowling of right-arm medium-pace Andy Blignaut. Sachin Tendulkar scored a bright 20 and looked set for a big score before he was bowled off the pads by Streak.

Rahul Dravid was the backbone of the innings scoring an unbeaten 68. Dravid and Harbhajan Singh shared a 56-run, eighth-wicket stand that helped India to approach something resembling a decent score.

Harbhajan made 31, which came after a splendid 66 in the first Test, proving that he is more than just a bowler – though still some way short of all-rounder status.

Zimbabwe went to stumps with opener Dion Ebrahim (13) and Andy Flower (five) at the crease. The two then shared an 87-run, fourth-wicket partnership before Harbhajan claimed both their wickets in a three-over spell just before lunch on the second day.

Flower made 45 and Ebrahim fell one agonising run short of his maiden Test half-century. Streak scored a typically aggressive 40, while Blignaut was equally belligerent on his way to 35.

Grant Flower was the steadying influence on the innings and by stumps on the second evening he was unbeaten with 80 along with Brian Murphy (17).

Zimbabwe held a 64-run lead at 301 for eight. But they were dismissed for 315 in just 28 minutes on the third morning to take an overall first-innings lead of 78. Grant Flower was dismissed for 86 as Harbhajan ended with four for 71 and Nehra four for 72.

Most of the third day belonged to the tourists as they amassed 193 for three going into the last over of the day.

Bowling with the new ball, Blignaut claimed the prized (and as it transpired, crucial) wicket of Dravid in the fading light for 26, as India closed at 197 for four and a lead of 119 runs. Das was unbeaten on 68 – his third half-century in the series and his fifth in Test cricket.

Earlier Tendulkar moved to his 28th Test fifty, scoring 69. It was, however, a disappointment for India that he failed to carry on and score a big hundred.

If the third day was all India, the fourth morning belonged to Zimbabwe as India were bowled out for

TEST MATCH AVERAGES
Zimbabwe v. India

ZIMBABWE

Batting	M	Inns	NO	HS	Runs	Av	100	50	c/st
A Flower	2	4	1	83	187	62.33	-	2	8/-
SV Carlisle	2	4	1	62*	146	48.66	-	2	2
GW Flower	2	4	0	86	165	41.25	-	2	3
AM Blignaut	2	4	1	35	83	27.66	-	-	3
DD Ebrahim	2	4	0	49	81	20.25	-	-	3
HH Streak	2	4	0	40	78	19.50	-	-	-
ADR Campbell	2	4	0	21	58	14.50	-	-	-
BA Murphy	2	3	0	17	34	11.33	-	-	1
GJ Whittall	2	4	0	20	36	9.00	-	-	3
BT Watambwa	2	3	2	2*	2	2.00	-	-	-

Also batted in one Test: TJ Friend 15; HK Olonga 16, 0.

Bowling	Overs	Mds	Runs	Wkts	Av	Best	10m	5/inn
HH Streak	71	23	178	10	17.80	4-46	-	-
AM Blignaut	79.5	20	251	9	27.88	5-74	-	1

Also bowled: GW Flower 10-0-27-1; TJ Friend 42.2-8-95-3; BA Murphy 54-8-191-3; HK Olonga 8-1-35-1; BT Watambwa 44.3-10-162-4; GJ Whittall 7-4-15-0.

INDIA

Batting	M	Inns	NO	HS	Runs	Av	100	50	c/st
SS Das	2	4	1	82*	239	79.66	-	3	4
R Dravid	2	3	1	68*	138	69.00	-	1	4
SR Tendulkar	2	4	1	74	199	66.33	-	2	-
Harbhajan Singh	2	3	0	66	102	34.00	-	1	-
VVS Laxman	2	4	0	38	101	25.25	-	-	4
SS Dighe	2	3	0	47	71	23.66	-	-	4/1
SC Ganguly	2	3	0	9	14	4.66	-	-	-
A Nehra	2	3	1	9*	9	4.50	-	-	-
J Srinath	2	3	0	3	4	1.33	-	-	-

Also batted in one Test: AB Agarkar 6, 0; HK Badani 2, 16* (2ct); Z Khan 0; S Ramesh 2, 17 (2ct).

Bowling	Overs	Mds	Runs	Wkts	Av	Best	10m	5/inn
A Nehra	75.4	11	217	11	19.72	4-72	-	-
Harbhajan Singh	103.4	25	233	8	29.12	4-71	-	-
J Srinath	89.5	24	246	7	35.14	3-71	-	-

Also bowled: AB Agarkar 32-10-84-1; SC Ganguly 1-0-3-0; Z Khan 33-7-98-4; SR Tendulkar 11-0-49-1.

234 – adding just 37 runs for the loss of their last six wickets.

Blignaut grabbed three wickets in the session to end with career-best figures of five for 74 in 31.5 overs. Streak, as always, led from the front and completed the innings with four for 46 in 27 overs. It left the hosts with a modest victory total of 157 in a little over five sessions.

Zimbabwe lost six wickets in the chase, but a steady, career-best 62 not out from Stuart Carlisle saw the home side to a famous victory which Streak dedicated to the country's first black international batsman, Trevor Madondo, who had died three days before the match after a sudden attack of cerebral malaria. Das earned the Man of the Series award for scoring 239 runs in the series at an average of 79.66.

WEST INDIES IN ZIMBABWE
By Tony Cozier

FIRST TEST
19–22 July 2001 at Queen's Sports Club, Bulawayo

Wary of complacency, captain Hooper was understandably cautious in his assessment after the West Indies' resounding triumph just after tea on the fourth day.

He called it 'a good victory' and a 'total team effort', but added that it had to be viewed in the context that 'Zimbabwe are not one of the stronger Test teams around'. Yet the West Indies had been brought to their knees so repeatedly in foreign lands over the previous five years that it was a significant result.

Although Zimbabwe had their problems – they were without their one world-class batsman, Andy Flower, through injury; another key batsman, Carlisle, did not bat in their second innings and they might have been distracted by off-field controversies – the West Indies also had to reconstruct their team following their own spate of injuries.

Zimbabwe could not recover from their inadequate first innings of 155 after winning the toss and batting on a true pitch on a bright, cloudless day. Big hundreds by the prolific Gayle, his first in Tests, and Hooper, his ninth and first as captain, were the foundations of the match-winning lead, but

the West Indies were made to fight as Campbell and Ebrahim shared a new first-wicket record partnership of 164 for Zimbabwe.

Campbell, opening for the first time in his 54th Test, scored his second century, but once the openers were separated, Zimbabwe collapsed to the probing pace of Stuart and the left-arm spin of McGarrell, the nine available wickets tumbling for just 64 runs.

The West Indies were obliged to use three bowlers – King, Stuart and the left-arm Collins – who had not played in the preceding series against South Africa, along with McGarrell who had only played in one previous Test. They wrecked Zimbabwe's first innings by the simple strategy of sticking to the basics and not attempting to go beyond their limitations. The home batsmen contributed to their demise with careless batting.

King, pacy but short and wayward in a lengthy opening spell of nine overs, came back strongly after lunch and had four wickets in his first bowl in a Test since the previous August.

Collins, chosen for his first first-class match since May the previous year on the strength of his showing in the nets, kick-started the Zimbabwean woes taking the first two wickets off his first six overs in his first Test since 1999. He had to leave the field with cramp during his second spell, but by that time the damage had been done.

Stuart counted the top-scorers Craig Wishart and Guy Whittall among his three victims, and McGarrell removed Streak in his 12 overs.

King and Stuart dispatched the last three wickets from eight balls without a run being added, allowing the rest of the afternoon for an exhibition of awesome power by

There was a century for skipper Carl Hooper in the first Test – although this sweep shot does not seem to have gone to plan.

Gayle and judicious application by Ganga.

Gayle's three innings leading into the Test were 259 not out, 164 and 99 and he was unbeaten on 52 out of a total of 100 by the close of the first day.

The West Indies continued to dominate on the second day with a ruthlessness seldom seen since their glory days of the 1980s. They consolidated mainly through the power and certainty of the prolific left-handed Gayle's boundary-laden 175 and his opening partnership of 214 with the more sedate Ganga. Gayle's punishing display brought him 34 fours from the 256 balls he received. He scored 123 on the second day from 178 balls with 24 boundaries, and rarely lifted his shots. He survived a close lbw appeal, padding out to Strang within the first half hour, when he was on 56, and was undeniably lucky that Pakistani umpire Riazuddin missed his thin edge to the wicket-keeper off Streak when he was at 96.

Ganga was the ideal foil until he became handicapped after being struck on the calf by a throw from the outfield. He called for a runner, but he drove through the line and chipped the ball back to Price, the left-arm spinner, before he had a chance to use him. His 89, from 248 balls with 11 fours, was his highest score in his ten Tests.

Streak earned Zimbabwe welcome respite with the second new ball, with which he removed Chanderpaul, who clipped a catch to square leg, and Gayle, caught at mid-on from a miscued drive. Sarwan and Hooper tightened the squeeze again, adding 103 over the final hour and a quarter, in which they stroked 18 boundaries as the West Indies ended the day with a lead of 248.

Hooper was 66 at the start of the third day and went on to 149, his tenth Test hundred. He made Streak pay for missing a two-handed, overhead chance off Strang in the third over of the third day when he had added only a single, and added 18 fours and a straight six before Strang finally had his reward.

Sarwan and Samuels both gathered attractive runs before the declaration after which Ebrahim and the left-handed Campbell batted through the remaining 41 overs of the day, trimming the huge deficit by 112.

They kept the West Indies waiting for another 22.4 overs before they finally broke their stand of 164, surpassing the previous best for the wicket of 156 between Gavin Rennie and Grant Flower against New Zealand in Harare almost four years earlier. But once Stuart claimed Ebrahim for 71, the first of four successive lbw victims, the resistance ended.

Campbell, caught at mid-off from a Stuart no ball when he was on 97, had no other blemish in three

FIRST TEST – ZIMBABWE v. WEST INDIES
19–22 July 2001 at Queen's Sports Club, Bulawayo

ZIMBABWE

	First innings		Second innings	
DD Ebrahim	lbw b Collins	0	lbw b Stuart	75
ADR Campbell	c Jacobs, b King	21	lbw b McGarrell	103
SV Carlisle	c Hooper, b Collins	10	absent injured	
CB Wishart	c Chanderpaul, b Stuart	36	lbw b Stuart	4
GJ Whittall	c Gayle, b Stuart	42	not out	10
GW Flower	c Jacobs, b King	6	c Gayle, b McGarrell	2
HH Streak (capt)	c Chanderpaul, b McGarrell	5	c Sarwn, b McGarrell	2
AM Blignaut	c McGarrell, b King	21	c & b McGarrell	9
*T Taibu	c Sarwan, b Stuart	6	(3) lbw b Stuart	4
BC Strang	not out	0	(9) c sub (LV Garrick), b King	7
RW Price	lbw b King	0	(10) c sub (LV Garrick), b King	4
	lb3, nb5	8	lb4, nb4	8
		155		**228**

	First innings				Second innings			
	O	M	R	W	O	M	R	W
King	17	4	51	4	23.4	9	47	2
Collins	13.3	4	29	2	13	1	47	-
Stuart	15.3	3	45	3	19	5	49	3
McGarrell	12	5	22	1	24	9	38	4
Hooper	1	0	5	-	21	6	38	-
Samuels	1	0	5	-				

Fall of Wickets
1-1, 2-31, 3-31, 4-80, 5-105, 6-119, 7-139, 8-155, 9-155
1-164, 2-170, 3-187, 4-193, 5-195, 6-197, 7-211, 8-218, 9-228

WEST INDIES

	First innings	
D Ganga	c & b Price	89
CH Gayle	c Price, b Streak	175
S Chanderpaul	c Whittall, b Streak	7
RR Sarwan	c Blignaut, b Strang	58
CL Hooper (capt)	c Taibu, b Strang	149
MN Samuels	b Price	42
*RD Jacobs	not out	19
NC McGarrell	not out	8
CEL Stuart		
PT Collins		
RD King		
	b1, lb10, nb1	12
	(for 6 wickets dec.)	**559**

	First innings			
	O	M	R	W
Streak	35	8	110	2
Blignaut	30	8	116	-
Strang	45	13	111	2
Price	44	6	157	2
Flower	13	1	52	-
Whittall	1	0	2	-

Fall of Wickets
1-214, 2-261, 3-289, 4-420, 5-520, 6-538

Umpires: ID Robinson & Riazuddin
Toss: Zimbabwe
Test debut: T Taibu (Zimbabwe)

West Indies won by an innings & 176 runs

hours 55 minutes of batting before McGarrell created a misjudgment of line. Campbell was lbw offering no shot, after which the rest of the batting succumbed meekly.

McGarrell took four of the last six wickets and King the other two as the West Indies completed only their second triumph in their last 21 overseas Tests.

SECOND TEST
27–31 July 2001 at Harare Sports Club

The first significant rain of the season denied Zimbabwe the opportunity of pressing for a remarkable victory.

A second-innings hundred by Churchill High School student Hamilton Masakadza, at 11 days short of his 18th birthday the youngest player in Test history to mark his debut with such an achievement, and significant contributions from Campbell, Wishart, Streak and Blignaut, turned the match on its head.

Zimbabwe converted a first-innings deficit of 216 into a lead of 347 that enabled a declaration half an hour after tea on the fourth afternoon. It challenged the West Indies to score as many as they had ever done to win a Test and gave the bowlers a potential 114 overs to complete the job for Zimbabwe.

On a pitch that, against all early indications, became progressively slower and truer, neither outcome was likely. As it was, the weather limited play to just 46.2 overs – 31 on the last day – before the match was abandoned by tea on the fifth day with the West Indies only one wicket down.

It allowed Hooper to receive the new Clive Lloyd Trophy from the most successful of all West Indian captains, after whom it was named. It was the West Indies' first triumph in an overseas series since a similar 1–0 result after two Tests in New Zealand in 1995.

After the thrashing they had administered in the first Test, they prepared themselves for the backlash, but it was late in coming. It was actually just as bad for Zimbabwe over the first two days as it had been in the first Test.

Sent in, they folded for 131. After their spirits were briefly lifted when the prolific Gayle was a single-figure failure, out leg before to Strang, normal service was rapidly restored by Ganga and Chanderpaul in a partnership of 100, containing 18 boundaries.

Ganga fell just before the close of play, but Chanderpaul, all aggression, remained unbeaten on

74, from 84 balls with 13 fours, as the West Indies closed at 126 for two.

Zimbabwe were undermined by McGarrell, who demolished the middle-order with four wickets for one run from 18 balls in his first three overs of left-arm spin immediately after lunch.

By the time Hooper introduced him for the last over before lunch, Zimbabwe already had their backs to the wall at 62 for three. Twenty minutes before lunch, he had them 72 for seven. Wishart was lbw, offering no stroke, Flower caught at the wicket first ball, Streak lbw to another one angled in with the arm and the left-handed Blignaut taken by Browne, in for the suspended Jacobs for his first Test since 1997.

The West Indies could not complete the job quickly as Whittall, rarely troubled, provided the lone resistance with an innings of 43 spread over two hours 35 minutes as the last three batsmen put on 59.

Chanderpaul and Ganga quickly showed that was far from enough and, even after Chanderpaul was removed, without addition, to the sixth ball of the second day to Streak's late away movement, a succession of partnerships involving the fluent Sarwan carried the total to 347, a lead of 216.

Chanderpaul's immediate dismissal brought in Hooper, who set about the bowling with purpose, dominating a stand of 54 with Sarwan. Once Strang, the persevering left-arm medium-pacer and Zimbabwe's best bowler, had him caught at mid-wicket from a miscued drive, Sarwan increased his tempo.

He and Samuels, dropped by wicket-keeper Taibu off Strang when he was on four, gave a glimpse of the future of West Indies batting in a partnership of 79 in an hour-and-a-quarter of handsome batting. But Samuels once again promised much more than the 39 he delivered, as he edged left-arm spinner Price low to slip.

Browne succumbed to Blignaut's outswinger with the second new ball, but Sarwan and McGarrell further frustrated the Zimbabweans with a stand of 50, before Sarwan was run out by Masakadza's direct hit on the bowler's stump from mid-off after an attempt to steal a single.

It was the second time that Sarwan had been stopped short of his first Test hundred by his own misjudgment and an alert fielder. In his native Guyana in April, Herschelle Gibbs ran him out nine away from three figures.

The third day was one of high emotion, history and utmost significance to Zimbabwean cricket.

Masakadza, only the seventh black player to represent his country in Tests, capitalized on slovenly West Indies play to make his mark.

With the help of Campbell, with whom he added 91, and Wishart, whose partnership of 170 was only ended by a bizarre run out when he was on 93, Masakadza turned the match – and Zimbabwean cricket – upside down.

Tall and upright with a strong leg-side bias that the West Indies fed rather than starved, and an obviously unflappable temperament, he batted through the day's six hours. He went to bed unbeaten on 115 as Zimbabwe erased their daunting first-innings deficit of 216 to be 324 for four.

Masakadza was cheered on throughout the day by hundreds of schoolchildren, specially bussed in from the outskirts in an effort to spread the gospel of the game to the majority black population, and by his jubilant mates from Churchill, bedecked in their

The birth of a new star ... Hamilton Mazakadza becomes the youngest player to score a Test hundred on debut.

SECOND TEST – ZIMBABWE v. WEST INDIES
27–31 July 2001 at Harare Sports Club

ZIMBABWE

	First innings		Second innings	
DD Ebrahim	c Browne, b King	19	c Browne, b Stuart	12
ADR Campbell	lbw b Stuart	13	c Gayle, b Hooper	65
H Masakadza	b Stuart	9	c Hooper, b McGarrell	119
CB Wishart	lbw b McGarrell	8	run out (Browne)	93
GJ Whittall	c Ganga, b Black	43	lbw b McGarrell	12
GW Flower	c Browne, b McGarrell	0	c Chanderpaul, b King	15
HH Streak (capt)	lbw b McGarrell	6	not out	83
AM Blignaut	c Browne, b McGarrell	0	b Stuart	92
*T Taibu	c King, b Stuart	9	b Stuart	10
BC Strang	c Sarwan, b Black	20	c Gayle, b McGarrell	13
RW Price	not out	0		
	lb1, w2, nb1	4	b11, lb21, nb17	49
		131	(for 9 wickets dec.)	**563**

	First innings				Second innings			
	O	M	R	W	O	M	R	W
King	16	6	39	1	27	7	80	1
Black	11.1	2	35	2	17	1	93	-
Stuart	13	2	33	3	32	9	99	3
McGarrell	17	7	23	4	60	19	162	3
Hooper	28	7	86	1				
Samuels	3	0	11	-				

Fall of Wickets
1-20, 2-42, 3-43, 4-62, 5-62, 6-68, 7-72, 8-95, 9-116
1-27, 2-118, 3-287, 4-324, 5-333, 6-367, 7-521, 8-535, 9-563

WEST INDIES

	First innings		Second innings	
D Ganga	c Taibu, b Blignaut	43	c Strang, b Streak	5
CH Gayle	lbw b Strang	6	not out	52
S Chanderpaul	c Taibu, b Streak	74		
RR Sarwan	run out (Masakadza)	86	(3) not out	31
CL Hooper (capt)	c Streak, b Strang	39		
MN Samuels	c Campbell, b Price	39		
*CO Browne	c Taibu, b Blignaut	13		
NC McGarrell	c sub (TJ Friend), b Strang	33		
CEL Stuart	lbw b Strang	1		
MI Black	b Price	6		
RD King	not out	2		
	lb2, w2, nb1	5	b4, lb5, w1	10
		347	(for 1 wicket)	**98**

	First innings				Second innings			
	O	M	R	W	O	M	R	W
Streak	22	6	75	1	14.2	3	34	1
Strang	32	13	83	4	14	8	19	-
Blignaut	16	2	92	2	9	3	24	-
Price	35.2	13	81	2	8	3	9	-
Flower	6	3	14	-				
Masakadza					1	0	3	-

Fall of Wickets
1-14, 2-114, 3-126, 4-180, 5-259, 6-283, 7-333, 8-338, 9-345
1-25

Umpires: KC Barbour & AV Jayaprakash
Toss: West Indies
Test debut: H Masakadza (Zimbabwe)

Match drawn

TEST MATCH AVERAGES
Zimbabwe v. West Indies

ZIMBABWE

Batting	M	Inns	NO	HS	Runs	Av	100	50	c/st
ADR Campbell	2	4	0	103	202	50.50	1	1	1
GJ Whittall	2	4	1	43	107	35.66	-	-	1
CB Wishart	2	4	0	93	141	35.25	-	1	-
HH Streak	2	4	1	83*	96	32.00	-	1	1
AM Blignaut	2	4	0	92	122	30.50	-	1	1
DD Ebrahim	2	4	0	75	106	26.50	-	1	-
BC Strang	2	4	1	20	40	13.33	-	-	1
T Taibu	2	4	0	10	29	7.25	-	-	4/-
GW Flower	2	4	0	15	23	5.75	-	-	-
RW Price	2	3	1	4	4	2.00	-	-	2

Also batted in one Test: SV Carlisle 10; H Masakadza 9, 119.

Bowling	Overs	Mds	Runs	Wkts	Av	Best	10m	5/inn
BC Strang	91	34	213	6	35.50	4-83	-	-

Also bowled: AM Blignaut 55-13-232-2; GW Flower 19-4-66-0; H Masakadza 1-0-3-0; RW Price 87.2-22-247-4; HH Streak 71.2-17-219-4; GJ Whittall 1-0-2-0.

WEST INDIES

Batting	M	Inns	NO	HS	Runs	Av	100	50	c/st
CH Gayle	2	3	1	175	233	116.50	1	1	4
CL Hooper	2	2	0	149	188	94.00	1	-	2
RR Sarwan	2	3	1	86	175	87.50	-	2	3
D Ganga	2	3	0	89	137	45.66	-	1	1
NC McGarrell	2	2	1	33	41	41.00	-	-	2
S Chanderpaul	2	2	0	74	81	40.50	-	1	3
MN Samuels	2	2	0	42	81	40.50	-	-	-

Also batted: MI Black (1 Test) 6; CO Browne (1 Test) 13 (4ct); RD Jacobs (1 Test) 19* (2ct); RD King (2 Tests) 2* (1ct); CEL Stuart (2 Tests). PT Collins played in one Test but did not bat.

Bowling	Overs	Mds	Runs	Wkts	Av	Best	10m	5/inn
CEL Stuart	79.3	19	226	12	18.83	3-33	-	-
NC McGarrell	113	40	245	12	20.41	4-23	-	-
RD King	83.4	26	217	8	27.12	4-51	-	-

Also bowled: MI Black 28.1-3-128-2; PT Collins 26.3-5-76-2; CL Hooper 50-13-129-1; MN Samuels 4-0-16-0.

---

a two-handed return catch, low to his right.

He had just passed his hundred with his tenth four, a powerful backfoot stroke past cover off King, when King at deep square-leg dropped his lobbed top-edged sweep off McGarrell.

Wishart had two let-offs, on 29 and on 81, on his way to his highest Test score before his embarrassing dismissal, thrown out by wicket-keeper Browne as he ambled into his crease at the non-striker's end.

Wishart's dismissal was a lucky break for the West Indies and they had success with the last ball as Whittall was leg before on the back foot to McGarrell.

The West Indies started the next day well. Masakadza drove McGarrell tamely to short extra-cover after adding only four to his overnight score and Chanderpaul's two-handed catch to his left at point accounted for Flower after an hour.

It would be two hours 40 minutes and 154 runs before they had another success as Streak and Blignaut demolished them in a run-a-minute stand of 154 that featured four sixes and 17 fours. It led Zimbabwe to their highest total in 54 Tests, surpassing the 544 for four declared against Pakistan on the same ground in the 1994–95 season.

Blignaut was eight away from his maiden first-class hundred when the pacy Stuart bowled him. By then, the main consideration was the timing of the declaration and Streak delayed it until half an hour after tea when he himself was only four short of his Test best.

The clouds were already massing and Zimbabwe had only taken one wicket before the weather took over for good to frustrate them. Gayle ended an outstanding tour with another half-century.

ZIMBABWE DOMESTIC SEASON: 2000–01
LOGAN CUP

Mashonaland won all five of their matches to dominate the competition. Unfortunately, they will be remembered for their on-field tantrums more than for the quality of the cricket they played, which was exemplary.

As the biggest fish in a growing pond, it would have been hoped that Mashonaland would set the example as Zimbabwe strives to improve the standard of its first-class game.

Alas, they did anything but. Australian-style sledging, geared to do nothing more than hasten the dismissal of suitably unsettled batsmen, is deplored in quarters unused to robust competition. However, even that was a pale version of the outright abuse

---

purple and gray blazers. Even at his tender age, he might have recognized the long-term relevance of his achievement.

Another Churchill student, 18-year-old Tatenda Taibu, couldn't join the others in the stands. He made his debut in the first Test in Bulawayo and acclaimed his colleague with the rest of the team from the Zimbabwean area in the pavilion.

Masakadza superseded Salim Malik, the Pakistani now banned from the game for his involvement in match-fixing, in the record books. Salim was already 18 when he scored an unbeaten 100 against Sri Lanka in Karachi in 1960 in his first Test.

Masakadza committed very few errors and got away with the two that should have ended his innings. He was 28, and the left-handed Campbell had just edged Hooper low to first slip an hour and 35 minutes into the day, when McGarrell put down

Eddo Brandes ... a remarkable 21 wickets at 6.95.

Mashonaland's opponents put up with in 2000-01.

At least part of the problem would seem to be the perennially lame-duck administration of the game in the country's premier province. No effort is made to market domestic first-class cricket in Harare, the capital – where the competition is sometimes referred to as the Slogan Cup: the secret Logan Cup.

The contrast in the supposedly lesser lights of Kwekwe and Mutare, where Zimbabwe's socio-economic problems are far more acutely felt than in Harare, couldn't be more blinding. There, officials work long hours spreading the game's gospel and it comes as no surprise to find matches in those towns markedly better attended.

Rain was a major factor in the first half of the season. In all, five days were completely lost to the weather in different matches, while the first-round fixture between Manicaland and Midlands in Mutare was abandoned without a ball being bowled. Still, of the 15 matches scheduled only four were drawn.

FIRST-CLASS AVERAGES

BATTING

	M	Inns	NO	HS	Runs	Av	100	50
CH Gayle	4	7	2	259*	755	151.00	3	2
AC Parore	4	5	3	103*	213	106.50	1	1
MS Sinclair	4	7	3	100*	362	90.50	1	1
CL Hooper	3	4	0	149	332	83.00	1	1
MH Richardson	4	6	0	306	495	82.50	1	1
MJ Horne	3	5	1	110	244	61.00	1	1
SS Das	4	7	1	110	365	60.83	1	3
CD McMillan	4	6	2	79	240	60.00	-	3
DA Marillier	5	10	1	132*	496	55.11	2	4
RR Sarwan	4	7	1	86	323	53.83	-	3
SR Tendulkar	3	6	1	74	243	48.60	-	2
GJ Whittall	9	17	2	188*	725	48.33	2	3
CL Cairns	4	6	1	124	238	47.60	1	-
D Ganga	3	5	0	89	235	47.00	-	2
BG Rogers	7	12	2	86	465	46.50	-	4
Javed Omar	3	6	1	85*	224	44.80	-	2
A Flower	11	18	3	83	671	44.73	-	6
MA Vermeulen	7	12	1	180	483	43.90	1	1
Habibul Bashar	3	6	0	76	254	42.33	-	3
MN Samuels	4	6	0	84	230	38.33	-	2
H Masakadza	10	15	0	119	554	36.93	2	2
VVS Laxman	4	7	0	100	258	36.85	1	-
SV Carlisle	11	19	3	92	579	36.18	-	4
HH Streak	10	17	1	119	576	36.00	1	5
TR Gripper	6	8	0	112	286	35.75	1	1
TJ Friend	7	11	3	115	277	34.62	1	-
CB Wishart	9	17	1	151	552	34.50	1	3
NJ Astle	4	6	0	86	197	32.83	-	2
GW Flower	13	22	1	86	684	32.57	-	6
GB Brent	6	12	3	72*	293	32.55	-	2
Harbhajan Singh	4	6	1	66	160	32.00	-	1
Akram Khan	3	6	0	55	191	31.83	-	1
ADR Campbell	14	24	1	140	732	31.82	2	3
DJR Campbell	6	7	2	65	159	31.80	-	1
CN Evans	6	9	2	78	217	31.00	-	2
ML Nkala	14	21	4	168	508	29.88	1	2
GM Croxford	7	13	2	80	327	29.72	-	1
SS Dighe	4	6	0	87	174	29.00	-	1
PA Strang	10	14	5	81*	260	28.88	-	1
Mehrab Hossain	3	6	0	76	170	28.33	-	2
RW Sims	3	6	0	72	164	27.33	-	1
S Matsikenyeri	5	8	0	70	218	27.25	-	1
DD Ebrahim	14	21	0	90	560	26.66	-	4
S Chanderpaul	4	6	0	74	158	26.33	-	3
NC McGarrell	4	5	1	47	101	25.25	-	-
AM Blignaut	11	16	1	92	355	23.66	-	1
RE Butterworth	5	8	0	113	182	22.75	1	-
DP Viljoen	6	9	1	79	179	22.37	-	2
S Ramesh	3	6	0	52	132	22.00	-	1
DT Mutendera	10	11	3	53	171	21.37	-	1
GJ Rennie	12	21	2	79*	404	21.26	-	2
PK Gada	4	8	0	71	170	21.25	-	1
Aminul Islam	3	6	0	84	119	19.83	-	1
A Maregwede	5	6	1	50	99	19.80	-	1
SP Fleming	4	7	0	30	136	19.42	-	-
LJ Soma	4	7	3	28*	75	18.75	-	-
WT Siziba	5	9	0	48	168	18.66	-	-
Naimur Rahman	3	6	0	36	112	18.66	-	-
GM Strydom	4	7	0	31	127	18.14	-	-
C Delport	5	10	0	55	181	18.10	-	1
T Duffin	5	9	0	74	159	17.66	-	1
BA Murphy	5	7	1	30	106	17.66	-	-
M Kenny	5	7	1	33	105	17.50	-	-
CK Coventry	5	8	0	43	134	16.75	-	-
JA Young	4	7	0	32	115	16.42	-	-
NR Ferreira	4	8	1	49*	114	16.28	-	-
T Taibu	11	14	1	75*	210	16.15	-	1
CA Grant	4	8	0	39	128	16.00	-	-
SC Ganguly	4	6	0	53	96	16.00	-	-
RJ King	5	8	0	54	107	13.37	-	1
MG Burmester	4	7	0	22	93	13.28	-	-
DT Hondo	4	6	1	29*	66	13.20	-	-

FIRST-CLASS AVERAGES

BATTING

	M	Inns	NO	HS	Runs	Av	100	50
IA Engelbrecht	5	5	1	30	52	13.00	-	-
EZ Matambanadzo	7	6	0	39	76	12.66	-	-
C Mahachi	5	6	2	23	50	12.50	-	-
RW Price	6	11	1	56	118	11.80	-	1
GA Lamb	4	4	0	38	47	11.75	-	-
TN Madondo	3	5	0	36	58	11.60	-	-
KPR Went	4	7	2	27*	58	11.60	-	-
NB Mahwire	4	6	0	29	64	10.66	-	-
BM Vaughan-Davies	2	4	0	21	40	10.00	-	-

Note: These averages include matches played against India and West Indies in 2001
Qualification: 4 completed innings, average 10.00

BOWLING

	Overs	Mds	Runs	Wkts	Av	Best	10m	5/inn
EA Brandes	70.4	29	146	21	6.95	6-48	-	3
DR Tuffey	24	9	64	5	12.80	4-48	-	-
Harbhajan Singh	148.1	42	337	21	16.04	6-37	1	1
GB Brent	174.2	46	461	26	17.73	5-44	-	1
CEL Stuart	123.4	33	392	22	17.81	5-58	-	1
IA Engelbrecht	150.5	31	430	24	17.91	6-56	-	1
A Nehra	88.1	13	260	14	18.57	4-72	-	-
MG Burmester	78	23	168	9	18.66	3-34	-	-
PA Strang	288	59	698	35	19.94	8-109	1	1
RD King	112.2	36	281	14	20.07	4-51	-	-
BT Watambwa	264.2	58	768	38	20.21	5-36	-	2
BC Strang	308.4	98	758	37	20.48	5-6	-	2
SB O'Connor	139	51	230	11	20.90	4-73	-	-
CL Cairns	127.2	40	314	15	20.93	5-31	-	1
D Ramnarine	44	12	126	6	21.00	3-28	-	-
AJ Mackay	76	22	191	9	21.22	3-44	-	-
DL Vettori	111.2	41	217	10	21.70	6-43	-	1
JM Lewis	38.5	3	152	7	21.71	4-40	-	-
NJ Astle	86	44	133	6	22.16	2-22	-	-
Z Khan	67	15	205	9	22.77	3-41	-	-
DP Viljoen	131.4	33	409	17	24.05	4-49	-	-
HH Streak	373.2	109	877	36	24.36	4-38	-	-
J Srinath	114.5	34	286	11	26.00	3-9	-	-
RW Sims	55.4	15	157	6	26.16	3-68	-	-
M Mbangwa	161.4	56	344	13	26.46	2-2	-	-
CB Wishart	43.2	5	188	7	26.85	4-50	-	-

FIRST-CLASS AVERAGES

BOWLING

	Overs	Mds	Runs	Wkts	Av	Best	10m	5/inn
NC McGarrell	161	51	395	14	28.21	4-23	-	-
AM Blignaut	300.4	78	900	31	29.03	5-73	-	2
BA Murphy	63	14	175	6	29.16	4-77	-	-
RW Price	390.5	104	1065	36	29.58	5-36	-	2
GA Lamb	85	17	266	9	29.55	3-69	-	-
M Kenny	98.1	16	358	12	29.83	4-47	-	-
PJ Wiseman	123.5	40	304	10	30.40	5-90	-	1
Manjural Islam	102.4	28	291	9	32.33	6-81	-	1
DA Marillier	91	11	353	10	35.30	3-32	-	-
DT Mutendera	187.3	36	681	19	35.84	3-22	-	-
ML Nkala	278.4	60	903	24	37.62	4-46	-	-
EZ Matambanadzo	116.5	19	453	12	37.75	3-38	-	-
Enamul Hoque	70	17	191	5	38.20	2-43	-	-
BG Rogers	126.3	12	506	13	38.92	3-49	-	-
DT Hondo	93.3	20	325	8	40.62	2-21	-	-
C Mahachi	60.3	10	246	6	41.00	2-24	-	-
IM Coulson	97	15	373	9	41.44	4-72	-	-
BA Murphy	150	25	501	12	41.75	4-77	-	-
HK Olonga	95	17	378	9	42.00	3-25	-	-
TJ Friend	149	36	472	11	42.90	3-30	-	-
Naimur Rahman	68.1	20	218	5	43.60	2-60	-	-
LJ Soma	55	5	220	5	44.00	4-35	-	-
JA Young	77	6	312	7	44.57	3-64	-	-
MI Black	57.1	10	260	5	52.00	3-109	-	-
C MacMillan	89.3	13	275	5	55.00	2-28	-	-
Mohammad Sharif	79.4	11	324	5	64.80	2-44	-	-

Note: These averages include matches played against India and West Indies in 2001
Qualification: 5 wickets

FIELDING

34 – T Taibu (31ct,3st); 27 – A Flower (25ct,2st); 18 – ADR Campbell; 15 – RD Jacobs (14ct,1st),
AC Parore (14ct,1st); 14 – SV Carlisle; 12 – SS Dighe (11ct,1st), CB Wishart; 11 – AM Blignaut,
DD Ebrahim; 10 – C Delport, GW Flower, ML Nkala; 9 – DJR Campbell (8ct,1st), CN Evans,
NR Ferreira, GJ Whittall; 7 – W Gilmour, DA Marillier, MA Vermeulen; 6 – SS Das, C Mahachi,
A Maregwede (5ct,1st), Mohammad Sharif, GJ Rennie, BG Rogers, PA Strang; 5 – R Dravid,
SP Fleming, TJ Friend, CH Gayle, VVS Laxman, S Matsikenyeri, EZ Matambanadzo, S Matsikenyeri,
M Mbangwa, MS Sinclair

Note: These figures include matches played against India and West Indies in 2001

Qualification: 10 catches or more

For those who view the glass as half-full, that statistic may seem a glowing advertisement for the virtues of three-day cricket. Others will recognize in it a low standard of skills characteristic of a fledgling first-class structure.

Nothing illustrated the latter perspective better than Matabeleland's second innings in their match against Mashonaland at Harare Sports Club. Murk overhead, a new and spiteful pitch underfoot and humidity all around conspired with the likes of Bryan Strang and Eddo Brandes to dismiss the Matlanders for 19, a record low total.

Strang took five for six and Brandes five for 12 as Mashonaland won by 282 runs. In the process, the shell-shocked Matabeleland batsmen faced just 71 deliveries – nine of which they managed to reach

with their bats. Five of those balls were edged, and ten of the 19 runs came by way of a six and a four.

Individually, Doug Marillier, the exciting Midlands batsman who threw strong hints at the national selectors with his 77 off 47 balls for Zimbabwe 'A' in a first-class tour fixture against Bangladesh, topped the Logan Cup batting averages with 412 runs at 58.85. He scored two centuries and three half-centuries. A resurgent Brandes, all 38 years of him, headed the bowlers with 21 wickets at the stupendous average of 6.95. Strang took 25 at 9.24 and a further 12 wickets in Test matches. Both, obviously, were helped by the Matabele massacre.

The 2000-01 Logan Cup generated reasons to remember it, then. But it also generated reasons to forget.

BANGLADESH

India in Bangladesh
Bangladesh Domestic First–Class Cricket
Bangladesh Domestic One-Day Cricket
First-Class Averages

INDIA IN BANGLADESH
By Qamar Ahmed

INAUGURAL TEST
10–13 November 2000 at Bangabandhu Stadium, Dhaka

Granted the full membership of the International Cricket Council, Bangladesh lost no time in playing their first-ever Test match. They invited India and gave them a scare before losing by nine wickets.

In front of an enthusiastic and exuberant crowd, numbering nearly 60,000 on each day, their inexperienced players dominated the proceedings for the first three days before they suffered a batting collapse on the fourth to concede the match.

India's first win in seven years on foreign soil, and their first under Saurav Ganguly as the captain of his country, owed a lot to left-arm spinner Sunil Joshi who finished the match with a haul of eight wickets (five for 142 and three for 27) for 169 runs.

For the newly-inducted nation the match meant a lot as they piled up 400 runs in the first innings. This was beyond their wildest dreams and expectations. 'We would be happy to last five days and would be very happy if we can draw the match,' said the captain Naimur Rahman before the start. Had they not succumbed in the second innings in only two sessions of the match on the fourth day, they might have done just that.

The feature of Bangladesh's first innings was the batting of their former captain, Aminul Islam, who made 145 and the bowling of their off spinner and captain Naimur Rahman, who had a haul of six wickets for 132 as India took a 29-run first-innings lead.

It was indeed encouraging to see Bangladesh take the strike first after they had won the toss. Having lost Shahriar Hossain for 12 and Mehrab Hossain for four, they recovered remarkably well through the efforts of Habibul Bashar and Aminul Islam to finish the first day's play on a respectable 236 for six. Habibul was caught by Ganguly off medium-pacer Zaheer Khan, but not before he had struck 71 runs with ten fours after having faced 112 deliveries.

On the second day, Bangladesh added 164 more runs before being dismissed for 400. Aminul Islam's 145 (off 380 balls) contained 17 fours in nine hours of batting. He became only the third batsman in Test history to score a century in his country's

Previous page: Mohammed Rafique claimed 21 wickets at an average of 20.23 and forced his way into the Test team.

ONE-OFF TEST – BANGLADESH v. INDIA
10–13 November 2000 at Bangabandhu National Stadium, Dhaka

BANGLADESH

	First innings		Second innings	
Shahriar Hossain	c Ganguly, b Joshi	12	lbw b Joshi	7
Mehrab Hossain	c Karim, b Khan	4	c Kartik, b Khan	2
Habibul Bashar	c Ganguly, b Khan	71	c Khan, b Agarkar	30
Aminul Islam	c Srinath, b Agarkar	145	lbw Agarkar	6
Akram Khan	c Dravid, b Nash	35	(6) c Das, b Joshi	2
Al Sahariar Rokon	lbw b Agarkar	12	(5) c & b Joshi	6
Naimur Rahman (capt)	c Das, b Joshi	15	(8) c Ganguly, b Srinath	3
*Khaled Mashud	c Das, b Joshi	32	(7) not out	21
Mohammad Rafique	c Das, b Tendulkar	22	c Ganguly, b Srinath	4
Hasibul Hussain	not out	28	c Das, b Kartik	0
Ranjan Das	c Ganguly, b Joshi	2	c Das, b Kartik	0
	b13, lb6, nb3	22	b7, lb1, nb2	10
		400		**91**

	First innings				Second innings			
	O	M	R	W	O	M	R	W
Srinath	22	9	47	–	11	3	19	3
Khan	21	6	49	2	5	0	20	1
Agarkar	31	13	68	2	11	4	16	2
Joshi	45.3	8	142	5	18	5	27	3
Kartik	24	9	41	–	1.3	0	1	1
Tendulkar	10	2	34	1				

Fall of Wickets
1-10, 2-44, 3-110, 4-175, 5-196, 6-231, 7-324, 8-354, 9-385
1-11, 2-32, 3-43, 4-53, 5-53, 6-69, 7-76, 8-81, 9-81

INDIA

	First innings		Second innings	
SS Das	b Naimur Rahman	29	not out	22
S Ramesh	b Ranjan Das	58	b Hasibul Hussain	1
M Kartik	c sub (Rajin Saleh), b Naimur Rahman	43		
R Dravid	c Al Sahariar Rokon, b Mohammad Rafique	28	(3) not out	41
SR Tendulkar	c sub (Rajin Saleh), b Naimur Rahman	18		
SC Ganguly (capt)	c Al Sahariar Rokon, b Naimur Rahman	84		
*SS Karim	st Shahriar Hossain, b Naimur Rahman	15		
SB Joshi	c Al Sahariar Rokon, b Mohammad Rafique	92		
AB Agarkar	c Ranjan Das, b Naimur Rahman	34		
J Srinath	c & b Mohammad Rafique	2		
Z Khan	not out	7		
	b13, lb4, w2	19		
		429	(for 1 wicket)	**64**

	First innings				Second innings			
	O	M	R	W	O	M	R	W
Hasibul Hussain	19	2	60	–	6	0	31	1
Ranjan Das	19	3	64	1	3	0	8	–
Naimur Rahman	44.3	9	132	6	4	0	22	–
Mohammad Rafique	51	12	117	3	2	0	3	–
Habibul Bashar	8	0	39	–				

Fall of Wickets
1-66, 2-104, 3-155, 4-175, 5-190, 6-236, 7-357, 8-413, 9-421
1-11

Umpires: SA Bucknor & DR Shepherd
Toss: Bangladesh
Test debuts: All for Bangladesh and SS Das, SS Karim & Z Khan (India)

India won by nine wickets

inaugural Test after Charles Bannerman's 165 for Australia against England in 1876–77 and David Houghton's 121 against India at Harare in 1992–93. Bangladesh's 400 was also the second-highest first-innings total for a debutant country after Zimbabwe's 456 at Harare against India in 1992-93.

India recovered from 190 for five to finish the third day at 366 for seven. A 121-run seventh-wicket stand between Ganguly and Joshi had provided them with the first-innings lead. Ganguly made 84 off 153 balls hitting five fours, but it was Joshi who delighted the crowd with his attacking 92 with nine fours – his first 50 in Tests.

In the second innings, Bangladesh batsmen failed to come to terms with both Javagal Srinath's pace and movement, and Joshi's spin. They claimed three wickets for 19 and 27 runs respectively. Bangladesh lost five wickets in each session after lunch on the fourth day to be skittled out for 91 in their second innings. Only Habibul Bashar and Khaled Masud entered double figures and India, needing 64 runs to win, reached their target without any fuss losing only Sadagoppan Ramesh on the way.

BANGLADESH DOMESTIC FIRST-CLASS SEASON
by Qamar Ahmed & Utpal Shuvro

The realization of a long-cherished dream to attain Test status pushed everything else that happened during the season into the background. After gaining Test status in June 2000, Bangladesh, formerly East Pakistan, played its inaugural Test against India in November at the Bangabandhu National Stadium, which had previously staged seven Tests before Bangladesh gained its independence.

Bangladesh lost, as expected and within four days, but they did have some moments to cheer. In their very first innings, Bangladesh scored exactly 400 runs and Aminul Islam, who had lost the captaincy in between the granting of Test status and the inaugural Test, became only the third batsman to score a century in his country's inaugural Test. The new captain, Naimur Rahman, also performed creditably by grabbing six wickets in India's first innings.

One of the pre-conditions of gaining Test status set by the ICC was to start a domestic first-class structure. The Bangladesh Cricket Board duly launched a tournament named the National Cricket League in the 1999–2000 season with six divisional teams. The tournament had to wait until the next year, however, before it was granted first-class status.

Last season two more teams, namely Bangladesh Biman and Dhaka Metropolis, were added to the competition alongside the existing six divisional teams Dhaka, Chittagong, Khulna, Rajshahi, Sylhet and Barisal.

In the preliminary round, the teams were divided into two groups. The matches were played on a home-and-away basis, and consisted of a three-day match and a 50-over one-dayer. Bangladesh Biman, Chittagong, Dhaka Metropolis and Khulna qualified for the final round by emerging as champion and runners-up in their respective groups.

The final round matches were played over four days and were followed by a one-dayer. For an outright win in the three- or four-day matches, the teams got six points and in the case of a draw, four points were awarded to the team who gained the first-innings lead. Winners of the one-day matches got two points.

The title was decided in the last round, as Bangladesh Biman emerged as the champion with a final total of 50 points. The champions had a star-studded team with a good number of national players, but the most crucial factor in their success proved to be their choice of foreign player.

Each team had the opportunity to include one foreign player in their ranks and Biman played a masterstroke by signing Pakistani youngster Imran Farhat. The Lahore all-rounder didn't play for the whole tournament, as he got the nod from the Pakistani selectors, but in the six first-class matches he played, he was simply irresistible. He scored the highest number of runs (735) at an incredible average of 91.87 (although he still did not top the averages – that accolade went to fellow Pakistani Manzoor Akhter, who came later to play for Biman and averaged 96 in just two matches). Farhat added 23 wickets to his run tally, and also gained the distinction of scoring the first double century in Bangladesh's domestic first-class cricket with a knock of 216 against Chittagong in the very first match of the season. Later in the season, his Biman team-mate, Habibul Bashar, hammered a brilliant 224 against Khulna in the last match to become the highest scorer of the tournament. Hasanuzzaman of the same team scored the highest number of centuries (three).

The bowling honours went to Chittagong's left-arm spinner, Enamul Haque, who claimed 57 wickets at an average of 16.63. But the find of the tournament was 15-year-old pace bowler Mohammed Sharif, who took 49 wickets and within a month was opening the bowling in a Test match in Zimbabwe.

FIRST-CLASS AVERAGES

BATTING

	M	Inns	NO	HS	Runs	Av	100	50
Imran Farhat	6	10	2	216	735	91.87	2	4
Rajin Saleh	5	8	3	115	284	56.80	1	1
Aminul Islam (Biman)	10	15	2	153	704	54.15	3	3
Hasanuzzaman	10	14	3	118	575	52.27	3	1
Sanwar Hossain	10	11	2	116	449	49.88	1	2
Minhajul Abedin	10	13	2	139	531	48.27	1	4
Enamul Hoque	9	10	1	81	394	43.77	–	4
Habibul Bashar	11	17	1	224	695	43.43	1	4
Golam Mortaza	10	13	7	43	256	42.66	–	–
Javed Omar	9	14	0	102	562	40.14	2	3
Naimur Rahman	5	9	1	106	317	39.62	1	1
Ehsanul Haque	10	15	1	101	540	38.57	1	5
Rafiqul Islam	6	12	0	124	461	38.41	1	3
Al Sahariar	9	16	1	128*	575	38.33	1	4
Safaiat Islam	6	11	2	105*	343	38.11	1	–
Faruk Ahmed	5	8	1	68	258	36.85	–	1
Nafis Iqbal	10	16	1	147	550	36.66	1	4
Mehrab Hossain	11	18	0	133	641	35.61	2	3
Sajjadul Hasan	9	17	3	147	491	35.07	1	1
Ahsanullah Hasan	6	11	3	78	259	32.37	–	1
Khaled Mahmud	10	14	1	71	418	32.15	–	2
Jamaluddin Ahmed	10	16	3	50	413	31.76	–	1
Anisur Rahman (Rajshahi)	6	12	0	70	381	31.75	–	3
Mohammad Ashraful	10	19	0	157	585	30.78	2	3
Sajjad Ahmed	10	17	2	117	444	29.60	1	2
Raju Parvez	9	16	1	84	441	29.40	–	3
Parvez Ahmed	6	10	0	91	291	29.10	–	2
Mosaddek Hossain	5	10	2	140	229	28.62	1	–
Hannan Sarkar	6	11	0	100	305	27.72	1	1
Akram Khan	8	11	0	58	298	27.09	–	2
Mizanur Rahman	5	9	0	76	242	26.88	–	1
Manjural Islam Rana	10	15	3	76	299	24.91	–	1
Nahidul Haque	9	17	1	81	396	24.75	–	3
Azam Khan	10	14	2	76	285	23.75	–	3
Imran Ahmed	6	11	0	60	259	23.54	–	1
Niamur Rashid	8	12	2	69	235	23.50	–	2
Mohammad Salim	9	15	1	150	322	23.00	1	–
Khaled Mashud	4	8	1	27	160	22.85	–	–
Asadullah Khan	10	16	1	90	340	22.66	–	2
Nasirul Alam	6	9	1	33	180	22.50	–	–
Rashidul Haque	6	12	0	71	263	21.91	–	2
Ziaur Rashid	7	8	0	49	171	21.37	–	–
Shahid Mahmood	10	15	0	84	308	20.53	–	2
Fahim Muntasir	5	10	0	81	205	20.50	–	1
Halim Shah	10	17	1	71	301	18.81	–	1
Harunar Rashid	5	10	0	66	188	18.80	–	1
Biplab Sarkar	6	11	1	31	176	17.60	–	–
Nuruzzaman	5	10	0	80	172	17.20	–	1
Alok Kapali	6	9	0	76	153	17.00	–	1
Aminul Islam (Rajshahi)	6	10	4	26	97	16.16	–	–
Anwar Hossain	9	12	4	29	128	16.00	–	–
Towhid Hossain	5	8	0	51	124	15.50	–	1
Mohammad Kalim	6	12	0	38	177	14.75	–	–
Mohammad Rafique	6	9	0	53	132	14.66	–	1
Sohel Hossain	4	8	0	50	116	14.50	–	1
Mohammad Sharif	10	12	3	26	130	14.44	–	–
Moinuzzaman	6	11	2	27	127	14.11	–	–
Mazharul Haque	6	12	2	37*	141	14.10	–	–
Tushar Imran	9	15	0	45	207	13.80	–	–
Sohel Islam	9	14	2	51	146	12.16	–	1
Al Amin (Khulna)	5	9	4	16*	59	11.80	–	–
Mohammad Mostadir	6	12	1	25	127	11.54	–	–
Hasibul Hossain	5	8	1	28*	80	11.42	–	–
Saiful Islam	5	10	2	21	88	11.00	–	–
Al Amin	6	9	2	17	73	10.42	–	–
Imran Parvez	6	10	1	21	93	10.33	–	–
Ahmed Kamal	6	9	3	23	60	10.00	–	–

Qualification: 8 innings, average 10.00

FIRST-CLASS AVERAGES

BOWLING

	Overs	Mds	Runs	Wkts	Av	Best	10m	5/inn
Alok Kapali	84	18	190	13	14.61	5-33	–	1
Enamul Hoque	433	130	948	57	16.63	7-74	3	6
Mohammad Sharif	312.5	67	879	49	17.93	6-31	2	5
Manjural Islam Rana	309	81	705	35	20.14	6-24	1	3
Mohammad Rafique	213.5	63	425	21	20.23	4-16	–	–
Imran Farhat	144.2	28	474	23	20.60	7-31	–	2
Jamaluddin Ahmed	259	42	636	30	21.20	5-82	–	1
Iqbal Hossain	95	26	213	10	21.30	3-28	–	–
Hasibul Hossain	120.5	23	349	16	21.81	6-41	1	1
Niamur Rashid	120.4	24	349	16	21.81	3-30	–	–
Al Almin (Khulna)	132	37	361	16	22.56	5-39	–	1
Sharafudoulla	353.4	106	713	31	23.00	6-45	–	2
Aminul Islam (Rajshahi)	139.3	31	416	17	24.47	6-57	–	1
Shahid Mahmood	312	39	1120	45	24.88	5-37	1	3
Ziaur Rashid	156.5	43	353	14	25.21	3-53	–	–
Ahmed Kamal	170.3	58	356	14	25.42	4-40	–	–
Mohammad Ashraful	326	72	994	39	25.48	7-99	–	3
Imran Rahim	137	41	282	11	25.63	4-51	–	–
Imran Parvez	158	29	490	18	27.22	5-82	–	1
Manjural Islam	171	52	411	15	27.40	6-27	–	1
Sohel Islam	215.4	43	576	21	27.41	4-40	–	–
Shahfiuddin Ahmed	233.1	64	575	20	28.75	4-52	–	–
Khaled Mahmud	274.3	68	727	24	30.29	3-19	–	–
Saifullah Khan	141	19	489	16	30.56	3-28	–	–
Shabbir Khan	123.2	20	403	13	31.00	3-18	–	–
Mohammad Mostadir	132.3	21	404	13	31.07	3-21	–	–
Ranjan Das	156.1	25	494	13	38.00	3-64	–	–
Naimur Rahman	184.3	35	610	14	43.57	6-132	–	1

Qualification: 10 wickets in 8 innings

The following bowlers took 10 wickets in fewer than 8 innings:

Mushfiqur Rahman	113	27	304	17	17.88	4-51	–	–
Saiful Islam	135.2	48	342	10	18.00	7-62	–	2
Ahsanullah Hasan	143	40	405	21	19.28	8-76	–	2
Biplab Sarkar	101.1	22	357	13	27.46	4-69	–	–
Ziaul Haque	128.3	24	363	13	27.92	7-63	–	2
Manzoor Akhtar	118.3	20	396	12	33.00	5-91	–	2
Fahim Muntasir	155	31	478	14	34.14	4-57	–	–

FIELDING

24 – Mohammad Salim (21ct,3st); 20 – Anwar Hossain (17ct,3st); 18 – Golam Mortaza (15ct,3st); 13 – Atiar Rahman (12ct,1st), Jamaluddin Ahmed; 12 – Sanwar Hossain; 11 – Enamul Hoque, Mizanur Rahman (9ct,2st); 10 – Ehsanul Haque, Mehrab Hossain, Minhajul Abedin, Raju Parvez, Tushar Imran; 9 – Al Sahariar, Mukhtar Siddique; 8 – Azam Iqbal, Halim Shah, Imran Farhat, Niamur Rashid, Sajjad Kadir; 7 – Akram Khan, Habibul Bashar, AKM Mahmood, Khaled Mahmud, Mafizul Islam, Manjural Islam Rana, Mohammad Mostadir, Sajjadul Hasan, Ziaur Rashid

Qualification: 10 catches or more

OTHER ONE-DAY INTERNATIONAL TOURNAMENTS

ICC Knock-Out, Kenya
CricInfo Women's World Cup

ICC KNOCK-OUT, KENYA, OCTOBER 2000
By Ralph Dellor

And there was always New Zealand...

After the first ICC Knock Out tournament in Dhaka in 1998, when considerable funds were raised for ICC's development programme, Nairobi was selected for the second of these events with a similar objective in mind. In the back of the hosts' minds was the fact that Bangladesh had achieved Test status after the tournament was staged in that country. Kenya are not nearly ready for such elevation, but there was no doubting the effort that went into making the tournament a success.

The ICC poured money into making the Nairobi Gymkhana ground adequate for such a competition. A number of spectator stands were built along with a media centre that was perfectly positioned at straight long-off. It was not an ideal place from which to watch cricket for anyone prone to seasickness, swaying alarmingly as it did, while a serious lack of telecommunications and an intermittent power supply added to the excitement. It also allowed for some extortionate dealings to secure mobile telephones that would operate in the region.

The 1998 tournament had been won by South Africa, captained by Hansie Cronje. Now in their first major international tournament of the post-scandal era, the South Africans were fancied once again. So too were the Australians, on the basis that every time they take to a cricket field, they will be deemed favourites. England were fresh from their renaissance summer, India and Pakistan were fancied. And there was always New Zealand.

The draw was based on the 1999 World Cup results, requiring those sides who had not reached the second phase then to play in the opening round here. As hosts, Kenya got the tournament under way with a match against India. The Kenyans showed just how good a batting surface had been prepared by visiting groundsman Andy Atkinson by going past the 200 mark in their allotted 50 overs. When Sachin Tendulkar was out leg before for 25, Kenyan hopes rose. They were dashed by Saurav Ganguly (66) and Rahul Dravid (68 not out) as India eased through with eight wickets and seven-and-a-half overs to spare.

A stand of 160 for the third wicket in 28 overs

Previous page: The New Zealand team celebrate their country's first major international trophy success.

from Aviska Gunawardena (131) and Mahela Jayawardena (72) posted a Sri Lankan total that was 108 runs more than a dispirited West Indian team could manage. In the third of the qualifying matches, England overwhelmed a Bangladesh side making their first appearance in such elevated company since gaining full member status. Alec Stewart (87 not out) and Nasser Hussain (95) contributed 177 runs towards England overcoming what was a very respectable total by Bangladesh.

Enter the favourites. Australia began against India, and in fewer than 100 overs of cricket were on their way back home. With youngster Yuvraj Singh scoring a most attractive 84 in the middle-order, India had a defendable total. Even so, the Australians were still going well before a brilliant diving catch in the covers accounted for Ian Harvey and an equally astounding direct hit ran out Michael Bevan as he was beginning to motor. In both instances, Yuvraj Singh did the trick. He was named as Man of the Match.

When Pakistan played Sri Lanka, Wasim Akram and Azhar Mahmood, with three wickets each, ripped the heart out of the talented Sri Lankan batting line-up and they were dismissed for under 200. A quality, undefeated innings of 105 from Saeed Anwar did the rest.

England fared even worse against South Africa than Sri Lanka had against Pakistan. Four English batsmen perished on the leg-side boundary before Jacques Kallis and Boeta Dippenaar took South Africa through at the gallop.

And then there was New Zealand. They rattled up far too big a total for Zimbabwe to challenge with Roger Twose (85) in prime form, but with Chris Cairns struggling with a long-standing knee injury. Even with their champion all-rounder crocked, New Zealand took their place in the semi-finals against Pakistan while India met South Africa.

The prospect of India's batting flair against South Africa's pace attack was one to savour. On these pitches, however, there should have been but one winner of that particular battle. In fact, it was hardly a battle at all. Ganguly won the toss, opened with Tendulkar, and in the first 15 overs flayed the South African attack. Tendulkar was out at that point for 39, but there were 66 runs on the board. Dravid joined his captain and as he reached 58, India reached 211 in the 40th over. Yuvraj Singh continued the momentum with 41 and although four wickets fell in the last two overs for the addition of two runs, Ganguly was still there at the end on 141 not out.

His was a marvellous innings that deserved to win the match and it duly did so as the South Africans found the target too great. They needed to preserve wickets while scoring steadily at the outset. Instead, they lost wickets steadily while scoring almost recklessly. Despite the efforts of the lower middle-order, South Africa hardly achieved respectability in being bowled out with nine overs remaining and 95 runs behind.

Pakistan against New Zealand threatened to be one-sided when Pakistan won the toss and got off to a flyer. Led by Saeed Anwar with another century, they were 111 for one in the 24th over and New Zealand had no answer. A mid-order collapse gave the Kiwis hope until Abdul Razzaq and Wasim Akram got flaying. Both were out to Shayne O'Connor's wicket-taking ball – the full toss – and the final total was not as great as it might have been.

New Zealand missed the bowling of the injured

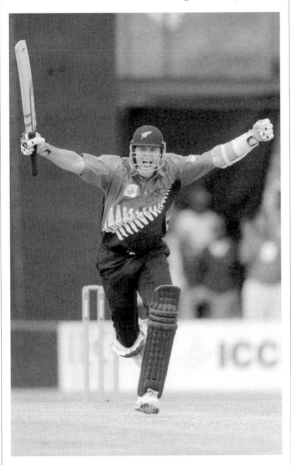

Chris Cairns scampers home to end unbeaten on 102 and to secure ICC Knock-Out Trophy success for New Zealand.

Cairns, and at 15 for two it looked as if his absence from the batting order would be crucial. However, the innings was a case study in timing the accumulation of runs. Nathan Astle missed a half-century by one run, Craig McMillan got one run past his milestone to be not out at the end, after Twose had once more masterminded the middle of the innings with 87 more muscular runs. New Zealand were in the final.

Of course, India began it as favourites. New Zealand had never won a major international tournament, despite having as good a record of reaching semi-finals as anyone. Surely their collective nerve could not hold good here?

A strong nerve was needed as Ganguly and Tendulkar put on 141 without being separated by the 27th over. It was a run out that effected the separation, and another that prematurely ended Dravid's blossoming innings. When Ganguly was third out for another fine knock of 117, a potential total of 300 plus was brought down to more reasonable proportions of 265 to win.

Cairns had shown his fitness by bowling his full ten-over quota, and came to the wicket as New Zealand were sliding into problem areas at 82 for three. At 132 for five and half the overs used, there was a crisis, but the experienced Chris Harris joined Cairns and these two took New Zealand to the brink. Harris was out for 46 in the 49th over with 11 still required, but Adam Parore scampered and Cairns smote.

Cairns was undefeated on 102 as his side recorded a four-wicket victory with all of two balls to spare. The Indian players were inconsolable, as is usually the case when an important match appears to be won but is not. And there was New Zealand – on the winners' podium.

at Gymkhana Club Ground, Nairobi
3 October 2000
Kenya 208 for 9 (50 overs) (RD Shah 60, MO Odumbe 51)
India 209 for 2 (42.3 overs) (R Dravid 68*, SC Ganguly 66)
India won by eight wickets
Man of the Match: A Kumble

4 October 2000
Sri Lanka 287 for 6 (50 overs) (DA Gunawardene 132, DPM Jayawardene 72)
West Indies 179 (46.4 overs)
Sri Lanka won by 108 runs
Man of the Match: DA Gunawardene

5 October 2000
Bangladesh 232 for 8 (50 overs) (Javed Omar 63*)
England 236 for 2 (43.5 overs) (N Hussain 95,
AJ Stewart 87*)
England won by eight wickets
Man of the Match: AJ Stewart

7 October 2000
India 265 for 9 (50 overs) (Yuvraj Singh 84)
Australia 245 (46.4 overs)
India won by 20 runs
Man of the Match: Yuvraj Singh

8 October 2000
Sri Lanka 194 (45.4 overs)
Pakistan 195 for 1 (43.2 overs) (Saeed Anwar 105*)
Pakistan won by eight wickets
Man of the Match: Saeed Anwar

9 October 2000
New Zealand 265 for 7 (50 overs) (RG Twose 85,
CD McMillan 52)
Zimbabwe 201 (42.2 overs) (SV Carlisle 67)
New Zealand won by 64 runs
Man of the Match: RG Twose

10 October 2000
England 182 (44.1 overs) (GA Hick 65)
South Africa 184 for 2 (39.1 overs) (JH Kallis 78*,
HH Dippenaar 65*)
South Africa won by eight wickets
Man of the Match: JH Kallis

First Semi-Final

11 October 2000
Pakistan 252 (49.2 overs) (Saeed Anwar 104,
SB O'Connor 5 for 46)
New Zealand 255 for 6 (49 overs) (RG Twose 87,
CD McMillan 51*)
New Zealand won by four wickets
Man of the Match: SB O'Connor

Second Semi-Final

13 October 2000
India 295 for 6 (50 overs) (SC Ganguly 141*,
R Dravid 58)
South Africa 200 (41 overs) (MV Boucher 60)
India won by 95 runs
Man of the Match: SC Ganguly

FINAL – INDIA v. NEW ZEALAND
15 October 2000 at Gymkhana Club Ground, Nairobi

INDIA

Batting

SC Ganguly (capt)	c Harris, b Astle	117
SR Tendulkar	run out (Styris/Astle)	69
R Dravid	run out (Styris/Allott)	22
Yuvraj Singh	c Twose, b Styris	18
VG Kambli	c O'Connor, b Styris	1
RR Singh	c Spearman, b Allott	13
AB Agarkar	not out	15
*V Dahiya	not out	1
A Kumble		
Z Khan		
BKV Prasad		
	lb2, w4, nb2	8
	(for 6 wickets) 50 overs	**264**

Bowling

	O	M	R	W
Allott	10	0	54	1
O'Connor	5	0	37	–
Cairns	10	2	40	–
Styris	10	0	53	2
Astle	10	0	46	1
Harris	5	0	32	–

Fall of Wickets
1-141, 2-202, 3-220, 4-229, 5-237, 6-256

NEW ZEALAND

Batting

CM Spearman	c Yuvraj Singh, b Prasad	3
NJ Astle	c Singh, b Kumble	37
SP Fleming (capt)	lbw b Prasad	5
RG Twose	st Dahiya, b Kumble	31
CL Cairns	not out	102
CD McMillan	c Ganguly, b Tendulkar	15
CZ Harris	c Singh, b Prasad	46
*AC Parore	not out	3
SB Styris		
SB O'Connor		
GI Allott		
	lb15, w1, nb7	23
	(for 6 wickets) 49.4 overs	**265**

Bowling

	O	M	R	W
Khan	7	0	54	–
Prasad	7	0	27	3
Agarkar	6.4	0	44	–
Kumble	9	0	55	2
Tendulkar	10	1	38	1
Yuvraj Singh	10	0	32	–

Fall of Wickets
1-6, 2-37, 3-82, 4-109, 5-132, 6-254

Umpires: SA Bucknor & DR Shepherd
Toss: New Zealand
Man of the Match: CL Cairns

New Zealand won by four wickets

CRICINFO WOMEN'S WORLD CUP
By Ralph Dellor

The fact that women's sport is taken seriously in New Zealand made it the ideal venue for the seventh women's World Cup tournament. The country, and in particular the host city of Christchurch, did the competition proud. Extensive publicity left no-one in any doubt about the fact that the event was taking place, and when a thrilling final of genuine cricketing quality ended with New Zealand beating Australia, the whole country gloried in the success.

From the outset, it was thought that Australia and New Zealand would be certainties to make the semi-finals, along with two from England, South Africa and India. Sri Lanka, Ireland and the Netherlands were considered to be battling for no more than sixth place and so qualification for the next World Cup. The six previous competitions had gone three apiece to England and Australia, and the fact that every time an Australian side takes the field it is expected to win – male or female, youth or senior – pointed to yet another Australian victory.

That prospect was confirmed in the opening match when the holders took on the hosts. Australia over-powered New Zealand by six wickets to claim an ascendancy that was not to be broken until the final itself. The pre-tournament form line continued with England amassing 256 for three in their 50 overs against the Dutch, with Charlotte Edwards hitting an impressive 139 not out.

The Anglo-Dutch match was played at the main ground at Lincoln University, while news came back from Hagley Park that there were some doubts about the bowling actions of two Indian bowlers – Renu Margrate and Purnima Rau. They caused the first five South African wickets to fall, but also started tongues wagging as India won by eight wickets.

While New Zealand won easily against the Irish, England's batting failed miserably in the first of their crucial matches. Bowled out for just 143, the South Africans overcame a difficult start – after they had fallen to 40 for four with over half their overs gone – to win with something to spare. Two days later, the English girls were in action again in the other vital match against the Indians. Again, the bowlers almost did their job, restricting India to 109 for seven in 42 overs, before an unbroken eighth-wicket partnership between Smitha Harikrishna and Rupanjali Shastri raised another 46 runs inside the final eight overs.

Claire Taylor kept England in the hunt with a combative 60, but all around her England lost their nerve, their wickets and, ultimately, the match. Effectively, they also lost the chance of a semi-final berth.

Meanwhile, with every ball seen live on the Internet, there was increased speculation about the legality of the actions of both the Indian opening bowler Margrate and her off spinner team-mate Rau. Neither action replays on television nor still photographs did much to dispel the idea that they straightened their arms immediately prior to delivery. The problem was that women's cricket did not have the same procedures as the men's game for disciplinary action. Eventually, they were cited, as were Dutch off spinner Caroline

New Zealand captain Emily Drumm hits out during her side's 72-run victory over India

Salomons and, surprisingly, New Zealand's young left-arm spinner Erin McDonald. Women's cricket had wanted to be taken seriously for some time and a throwing controversy may not have been the most desirable publicity, but it did ensure continued media interest – even in the quieter stages of the tournament.

The competition continued along a predictable path. New Zealand captain Emily Drumm disguised and protected a broken finger to take her place in the one side that looked capable of matching the Australian juggernaut. India's problems increased when Mithali Raj, a precocious batting talent, was admitted to hospital with a serious fever. England beat the rest but failed to match the best, and the most cheerful team of all, Ireland, at last had something to celebrate when they beat the Dutch and then saw Sandra Dawson and Barbara McDonald break the world record for the tenth wicket in a women's international. They might only have put on 37, and Ireland may well have gone on to lose the game against South Africa by nine wickets, but it was another excuse to party.

The semi-finals were not competitive. Despite Rau opening the innings and carrying her bat for India, the side only made 117 – a total reached without any difficulty and for only the loss of one New Zealand wicket. In the other semi, South Africa's 180 for eight proved almost as easy for Australia. They were home for the loss of only one wicket in less than two hour's batting.

So to the final. The Lincoln Oval was a picture, the pitch good and a crowd in excess of 3,000 people was held captivated by the quality of the cricket. No longer was it a case of novelty entertainment. Now it was a match that had all the qualities that makes cricket the game it is, and it did not matter whether it was being played by men or women.

New Zealand won the toss and batted. They lost an early wicket, then went on brightly at four an over, before a steady decline saw them trying to survive the full 50 overs. When the last four wickets went for 12 runs in a couple of overs, even that objective was out of reach. The fastest bowler in women's cricket, Cathryn Fitzpatrick, touches 70 mph, and that pace was simply too much for the Kiwi tail.

Lisa Keightley, who was to be Player of the Tournament, went to the fourth ball of the Australian reply and the dangerous Karen Rolton was run out by a direct hit from Helen Watson to make it two for two in the third over. Watson had been included for her fielding, and what an inspired choice the selectors had made.

Belinda Clark steadied the innings in company with Cherie Bambury, putting on 83 runs for the third wicket in 20 overs. Australia were cruising. Until, that is, four wickets fell for the addition of 30 runs in 12 overs. If Australian captain Clark remained, her side would surely win. If she were out, it would become rather more open.

She was out in the 42nd over with another 34 runs required, three wickets in hand and 53 balls to be bowled. Therese McGregor was going well until falling victim to another Watson throw. Fitzpatrick took up the challenge and took off for a run until it was pointed out that a bail had fallen. It took a look at the slow-motion replay to confirm that she had been bowled.

The start of the last over saw more drama. Medium-paced Haidee Tiffen had overs in hand. Off spinner Clare Nicholson was found to have one left, but only after a recount. Drumm backed the experience of Nicholson to bowl the last six balls of a World Cup final with one wicket to fall and only five runs needed for victory. Charmaine Mason had scored 11 runs from 13 balls and was facing. The first ball got an edge, Rebecca Rolls, standing up, just held onto the catch, and the field was invaded by as joyous a crowd as has ever swarmed onto a cricket pitch. A marvellous moment for New Zealand cricket, for women's cricket and, it has to be said, for the game of cricket as a whole.

29 November 2000
at BIL Oval, Lincoln
Australia 167 for 4 (47.3 overs) (EC Drumm 74, TA McGregor 4 for 18)
New Zealand 166 for 9 (50 overs) (KL Rolton 51*)
Australia (2 pts) won by six wickets

30 November 2000
at BIL Oval, Lincoln
England 256 for 3 (50 overs) (CM Edwards 139*, B Daniels 79)
Netherlands 116 for 9 (50 overs) (SV Collyer 5 for 32)
England (2 pts) won by 140 runs

at Hagley Oval, Christchurch
South Africa 128 for 8 (50 overs)
India 129 for 2 (39.4 overs) (M Raj 69*)
India (2 pts) won by eight wickets

1 December 2000
at Hagley Oval, Christchurch
Australia 282 for 3 (50 overs) (KL Rolton 154*,

LM Keightley 56)
Sri Lanka 82 (39 overs)
Australia (2 pts) won by 200 runs

at BIL Oval, Lincoln
Ireland 99 (49.4 overs)
New Zealand 102 for 2 (24.5 overs)
New Zealand (2 pts) won by eight wickets

2 December 2000
at BIL Oval, Lincoln
England 143 (47.5 overs)
South Africa 144 for 5 (46.5 overs) (S Viljoen 54*)
South Africa (2 pts) won by five wickets

at Lincoln Green, Lincoln
India 275 for 4 (50 overs) (A Chopra 69, H Kala 56*, M Raj 51)
Netherlands 121 for 6 (50 overs)
India (2 pts) won by 154 runs

3 December 2000
at Hagley Oval, Christchurch
Ireland 90 (49.3 overs) (ZJ Goss 4 for 10)
Australia 91 for 0 (20.3 overs)
Australia (2 pts) won by ten wickets

at Lincoln Green, Lincoln
New Zealand 210 for 4 (50 overs) (AM O'Leary 91*, HM Tiffen 58)
Sri Lanka 88 (49.3 overs)
New Zealand (2 pts) won by 122 runs

4 December 2000
at Lincoln Green, Lincoln
India 155 for 7 (50 overs)
England 147 (49.2 overs) (SC Taylor 60)
India (2 pts) won by 8 runs

at Hagley Oval, Christchurch
Netherlands 92 (37.1 overs) (LP Lewis 4 for 20)
South Africa 93 for 6 (26.2 overs)
South Africa (2 pts) won by four wickets

5 December 2000
at Lincoln Green, Lincoln
Sri Lanka 129 (47.3 overs) (ADH Abeysinghe 52)
Ireland 119 (49.5 overs)
Sri Lanka (2 pts) won by 10 runs

6 December 2000
at BIL Oval, Lincoln
Australia 223 for 5 (50 overs) (LM Keightley 74,

KL Rolton 61)
India 172 for 8 (50 overs)
Australia (2 pts) won by 51 runs

at Hagley Oval, Christchurch
Netherlands 80 (48 overs)
New Zealand 81 for 2 (16.3 overs)
New Zealand (2 pts) won by eight wickets

7 December 2000
at BIL Oval, Lincoln
Ireland 103 (44.2 overs) (CE Taylor 4 for 25)
England 105 for 2 (29.3 overs)
England (2 pts) won by eight wickets

8 December 2000
at Lincoln Green, Lincoln
Sri Lanka 134 for 9 (50 overs)
South Africa 135 for 4 (45.3 overs) (M Terblanche 53*)
South Africa (2 pts) won by six wickets

9 December 2000
at BIL Oval, Lincoln
New Zealand 224 for 5 (50 overs) (AM O'Leary 89, DA Hockley 53, HM Tiffen 50*)
India 150 for 7 (50 overs) (C Kaul 59*)
New Zealand (2 pts) won by 74 runs

10 December 2000
at Lincoln Green, Lincoln
Australia 190 for 7 (50 overs)
England 136 (47.3 overs)
Australia (2 pts) won by 54 runs

at Hagley Oval, Christchurch
Sri Lanka 139 (47.1 overs)(SARC Silva 53)
Netherlands 113 (39.4 overs)(CR Senevirathne 4 for 23)
Sri Lanka (2 pts) won by 26 runs

11 December 2000
at Hagley Oval, Christchurch
India 199 for 9 (50 overs) (A Chopra 70)
Ireland 169 (47.2 overs)
India (2 pts) won by 30 runs

at Lincoln Green, Lincoln
New Zealand 265 for 5 (50 overs) (EC Drumm 108*)
South Africa 107 (35.4 overs)
New Zealand (2 pts) won by 158 runs

12 December 2000
at BIL Oval, Lincoln

England 242 for 4 (50 overs) (SC Taylor 137*,
J Cassar 63*)
Sri Lanka 137 for 9 (50 overs) (ADH Abeysinghe 57)
England (2 pts) won by 105 runs

13 December 2000
at BIL Oval, Lincoln
South Africa 169 for 8 (50 overs)
Australia 171 for 1 (25 overs) (KL Rolton 107*)
Australia (2 pts) won by nine wickets

14 December 2000
at BIL Oval, Lincoln
New Zealand 238 for 8 (50 overs) (RJ Rolls 65,
EC Drumm 53)
England 145 (47.3 overs)
New Zealand (2 pts) won by 93 runs

at Hagley Oval, Christchurch
Ireland 232 for 6 (50 overs) (CM Beggs 66*, A Linehan
54)
Netherlands 191 for 8 (50 overs) (RC Milburn 71)
Ireland (2 pts) won by 41 runs

15 December 2000
at Lincoln Green, Lincoln
India 230 for 4 (50 overs) (C Kaul 80, A Chopra 68*)
Sri Lanka 89 (49.2 overs)
India (2 pts) won by 141 runs

16 December 2000
at Lincoln Green, Lincoln
Netherlands 107 for 7 (50 overs)
Australia 109 for 0 (24 overs) (LM Keightley 51*)
Australia (2 pts) won by ten wickets

at Hagley Oval, Christchurch
Ireland 176 for 9 (50 overs)
South Africa 177 for 1 (36.1 overs) (L Oliver 101*)
South Africa (2 pts) won by 9 wickets

SEMI-FINALS

18 December 2000
at BIL Oval, Lincoln
South Africa 180 for 8 (50 overs)
Australia 181 for 1 (31.2 overs) (LM Keightley 91*, BJ
Clark 75)
Australia won by nine wickets

20 December 2000
at BIL Oval, Lincoln
India 117 (45.2 overs) (P Rau 67)
New Zealand 121 for 1 (26.5 overs) (AM O'Leary 50*)
New Zealand won by nine wickets

FINAL

23 December 2000
at BIL Oval, Lincoln
New Zealand 184 (48.4 overs)
Australia 180 (49.1 overs) (BJ Clark 91)
New Zealand won by 4 runs
Player of the Match: BJ Clark
Player of the Tournament: LM Keightley

Emily Drumm holds aloft the CricInfo Women's World Cup.
New Zealand won the trophy for the first time to break the
England–Australia stranglehold on the tournament.

FORM CHARTS

Derbyshire
Durham
Essex
Glamorgan
Gloucestershire
Hampshire
Kent
Lancashire
Leicestershire
Middlesex
Northamptonshire
Nottinghamshire
Somerset
Surrey
Sussex
Warwickshire
Worcestershire
Yorkshire

DERBYSHIRE CCC

FIRST–CLASS MATCHES

BATTING

Match	LD Sutton	SD Stubbings	SP Titchard	MJ Di Venuto	RJ Bailey	DG Cork	G Welch	KM Krikken	RK Illingworth	TA Munton	KJ Dean	MP Dowman	CWG Bassano	NRC Dumelow	TM Smith	T Lungley	LJ Wharton	WG Khan	ARK Pierson	P Aldred	AD Edwards	RM Khan	SA Selwood	Extras	Total	Wickets	Result	Points
v. Middlesex	26	1	37	3	10	12	28	10	17	12	1*													–	–	–		
41 (Derby) 25–28 April	198	10																						–	–	–	D	5
v. Pakistanis	26	8	11			27		0				36	17	6	14*	0	0							21	166	10		
(Derby) 8–10 May	34	15	0			15		10*				145*	13	–	–									15	247	5	D	
v. Worcestershire	42	1		108	11		29	8*	6	–		0		5*			1							11	222	8		
(Worcester) 16–19 May	–	–		–																				–	–	–	D	4
v. Hampshire	9	93		22	52		10	24	18	0		3		50*	0									16	297	10		
(Derby) 25–28 May	8	29		52	0		12	0	61*	11		2		14	9									17	215	10	L	5
v. Middlesex	18	35		1	1		18*	9	0	11		7	0	11			0							21	132	10		
(Southgate) 30 May–1 June	15	3		2	21		25	29	4	3*		44	61	2			0*							17	226	10	L	1
v. Durham	15	29		19	26		16	54	13	20		45	25	8*										48	318	10		
(Derby) 6–9 June	13	7		86	24		9	75	6	10		8	8	6*										15	267	10	D	10
v. Sussex	33	67		8	4		32	19*		0		2	4			0			9					19	197	10		
(Arundel) 13–15 June	14	0		9	33		21	3		4		17	2			0			1*					14	118	10	L	3
v. Gloucestershire	13	126		2	36		1	3*				25	186*	–			–			–				31	432	5		
(Derby) 20–22 June	3*	9		43	2		45	1				50	106	21			1*			0				16	297	9	D	9
v. Hampshire (Southampton	21	13		8	8		22	0				35	1				0			24	4*			4	140	10		
Rose Bowl) 29 June–1 July	33	13		10	98		0	23				0	19				0*			12	23			13	244	10	L	3
v. Worcestershire	16	75	39	0	2		7					2	absent	33			1*			0				23	198	9		
(Derby) 5–7 July	14	53	5	136*	21		39					0	absent	7			0			2				18	295	9	L	2
v. Warwickshire	2	27		9	6		2	18		50	18	14					1*			8				10	165	10		
(Edgbaston) 18–21 July	110*	62		109	8		64	8*		33							–			–				41	435	5	D	7
v. Nottinghamshire	0	127		59	3	128	38	93*		3		22		23						35				41	572	8		
(Derby) 28–30 July	–	–		–																–				–	–	–	D	12
v. Durham	14	5		29	5		1	7		0		6	16				0*			3				9	95	10		
(Chester-le-Street) 8–11 August	4	14	111rh		1		10	3		1		70*					–			7*				3	224	6	W	15
v. Sussex	140*	0		8			11	32		1		10	18			19	0			0				24	263	10		
(Derby) 15–18 August	54	1		3			6	4		4		8	0			13	2*			6				16	117	10	L	5
v. Nottinghamshire	10	12		165	2		18	11		18		56		0			0			9				19	320	10		
(Trent Bridge) 22–25 August	1	19		93	17		6	0		20*		28		5			1			14				17	221	10	L	6
v. Gloucestershire		62		61			18	5		0	3	0	0	5*			2					13	18	15	210	10		
(Bristol) 5–7 September		120		4			5	3		15		35	48	7*			0					5	15	19	278	10	L	2
v. Warwickshire		8		36			3	0			14	8	1	0		13	8*						1	14	106	10		
(Derby) 12–15 September		13		33			3	0			23	13	2	8		47	13*						9	30	194	10	L	2

	LD Sutton	SD Stubbings	SP Titchard	MJ Di Venuto	RJ Bailey	DG Cork	G Welch	KM Krikken	RK Illingworth	TA Munton	KJ Dean	MP Dowman	CWG Bassano	NRC Dumelow	TM Smith	T Lungley	LJ Wharton	WG Khan	ARK Pierson	P Aldred	AD Edwards	RM Khan	SA Selwood
Matches	15	17	3	14	14	4	16	14	5	9	8	14	8	9	6	6	12	1	1	8	1	1	2
Innings	27	31	5	25	25	6	29	25	8	13	12	26	14	15	10	11	18	1	2	13	2	2	4
Not Out	3	0	0	1	1	0	2	5	1	1	2	1	2	1	2	4	10	0	1	1	1	0	0
Highest Score	140*	127	39	165	136*	128	64	93*	61*	50	23	145*	186*	61	19	47	13*	1	9	35	23	13	18
Runs	688	1047	92	1082	515	205	511	435	125	145	117	567	523	304	79	108	29	1	10	120	27	18	43
Average	28.66	33.77	18.42	45.08	21.45	34.16	18.92	21.75	17.85	12.08	11.7	22.68	43.58	21.71	9.87	15.42	2.63	1	10	10	27	9	10.75
100s	2	3	–	4	1	1	–	–	–	–	–	1	2	–	–	–	–	–	–	–	–	–	–
50s	1	6	–	5	2	–	1	3	1	1	–	1	2	2	–	–	–	–	–	–	–	–	–

DERBYSHIRE CCC

FIRST-CLASS MATCHES

BOWLING

	DG Cork	G Welch	RK Illingworth	TA Munton	KJ Dean	NRC Dumelow	TM Smith	T Lungley	LJ Wharton	RJ Bailey	P Aldred	Overs	Total	Byes/Leg-Byes	Wickets	Run outs
v. Middlesex (Derby) 25–28 April	9-4-15-0 -	14-5-33-1 -	20-7-37-4 -	16-6-35-0 -	9-3-24-0 -							68 -	146 -	2 -	5 -	- -
v. Pakistanis (Derby) 8–10 May	16-4-34-0 5-2-10-0					22-4-81-4 5-2-10-0	16-3-50-3 5-1-14-1	15.3-1-58-3 3-1-20-0	9-2-36-0 2-0-8-0			78.3 20	262 63	3 1	10 1	- -
v. Worcestershire (Worcester) 16–19 May		6-1-23-0 -	2-1-2-0 -	4-2-5-0 -		3-0-21-0 -						15 -	52 -	1 -	0 -	- -
v. Hampshire (Derby) 25–28 May		35-7-123-2 4-2-7-0	31-12-71-1 3-1-6-0	37-7-107-3 -		12-1-57-1 4-0-22-0		21-6-72-0 -		7.2-3-17-2 -		143.2 15.1	464 49	17 1	10 1	1 -
v. Middlesex (Southgate) 30 May–1 June		31-5-91-0 -	35-6-103-1 -	34-12-91-2 -		25.1-4-103-4 -		21-2-97-3 -		8-3-11-0 -		160.1 -	543 -	30 -	10 -	- A
v. Durham (Derby) 6–9 June		15.2-1-46-3 25-8-65-2	21-8-46-3 17.4-5-57-1	24-4-76-2 23-6-57-1		17-5-46-1 11-2-36-0		14-4-40-1 3-0-28-0		- 4-1-19-1		91.2 84.4	260 280	6 17	10 7	- 2 A
v. Sussex (Arundel) 13–15 June		22.5-2-82-6 -		22-4-57-1 -			12-1-66-0 -		28-6-74-2 5-0-18-0			104.5 -	349 -	8 -	10 -	- A B
v. Gloucestershire (Derby) 20–22 June		29-4-102-0 6-0-33-0		28-6-90-3 -		23-4-82-0 3-0-25-0		37-12-98-1 3-0-17-0	7-1-19-1 3-0-37-0	33-5-129-3 5-0-27-0		163 25	560 177	25 1	8 0	- A C D E
v. Hampshire (Southampton Rose Bowl) 29 June–1 July		26-8-87-2 -		32.1-8-85-5 -				17-3-53-1 1-1-0-0	- 0.1-0-6-0	26-5-104-2 -		114.1 1.1	383 6	14 0	10 0	- F
v. Worcestershire (Derby) 5–7 July	27-5-84-2 -	39-8-132-3 -				8-1-44-1 -		27-7-89-0 -	6-0-22-1 -	31.3-3-102-3 -		138.3 -	496 -	23 -	10 -	- -
v. Warwickshire (Edgbaston) 18–21 July		23-5-53-5 -		19-5-50-2 -	14-2-56-1 -			4-0-9-0 -		11-1-33-0 -		71 -	204 -	3 -	10 -	2 -
v. Nottinghamshire (Derby) 27–30 July	27.2-4-122-4 27-5-69-0	25-1-99-1 18-7-41-1			19-3-106-1 23-5-100-3	15-1-71-0 16-3-63-0			15-4-29-2 11-0-53-0	14-2-64-1 15-1-99-1		118.2 128	526 557	19 21	10 5	1 A - A D G
v. Durham (Chester-le-Street) 8–10 August		15-5-30-6 24-6-87-2		14.2-4-42-4 19-4-73-6		7-0-45-1 1.1-0-4-1				7-2-16-0 8-2-22-1		43.2 52.1	125 193	2 7	10 10	- -
v. Sussex (Derby) 15–18 August		24-9-51-0 22.2-4-58-4		28.3-7-72-4 23-5-70-3		18-3-61-4 12-1-41-1		21-10-30-1 17-9-21-1	4-2-6-0 2-2-0-0	17-5-43-1 10-1-36-0		112.3 86.2	280 230	17 4	10 10	- 1
v. Nottinghamshire (Trent Bridge) 22–25 August		23-4-92-2 19-5-66-1		21-3-89-5 17-3-46-2		12.2-5-50-1 5-1-31-0		12-2-45-1 10.3-2-41-0	- 4-1-8-0	9-3-42-1 3-0-25-0		77.2 58.3	322 223	4 6	10 3	- -
v. Gloucestershire (Bristol) 5–7 September		30-8-144-2 -		38-12-113-3 -	12-4-29-3 -			19-0-110-1 -	24-4-87-1 -			130 -	508 -	5 -	10 -	- E
v. Warwickshire (Derby) 12–15 September		26-3-86-1 -			25-7-107-2 -	12.4-3-54-0 -		15-0-89-3 -	5-0-36-0 -			85.4 -	400 -	10 -	6 -	- E

	DG Cork	G Welch	RK Illingworth	TA Munton	KJ Dean	NRC Dumelow	TM Smith	T Lungley	LJ Wharton	RJ Bailey	P Aldred
Overs	111.2	502.3	126.4	242.1	250.5	185.5	91.3	115.4	217.3	76.3	189.3
Maidens	24	108	39	61	58	34	15	14	58	17	30
Runs	334	1631	316	659	888	723	383	527	644	245	742
Wickets	6	44	10	19	34	14	11	12	8	7	13
Average	55.66	37.06	31.60	34.68	26.11	51.64	34.81	43.91	80.50	35.00	57.07

A   MJ DiVenuto 6-0-17-0; 1-0-1-0; 5-1-16-1; 6-1-15-0; 3-0-16-0; 9-0-59-0
B   ARK Pierson 10-0-28-0
C   CWG Bassano 2-0-11-0
D   SD Stubbings 2-0-11-0; 2-0-25-0
E   MP Dowman 1-0-15-0; 7-3-20-0; 2-0-18-0
F   AD Edwards 13-3-40-0
G   KM Krikken 7-0-27-0

FIELDING

34   KM Krikken (33ct,1st)
15   MJ Di Venuto
9   LD Sutton
8   RJ Bailey
6   SD Stubbings
5   P Aldred, CWG Bassano, DG Cork, TM Smith
4   MP Dowman
3   G Welch
2   KJ Dean, NRC Dumelow, TA Munton
1   ARK Pierson, SA Selwood, LJ Wharton

DURHAM CCC

FIRST–CLASS MATCHES

BATTING

	JB Lewis	MA Gough	JA Daley	PD Collingwood	NJ Speak	N Peng	MP Speight	DR Law	JE Brinkley	N Killeen	SJ Harmison	ML Love	A Pratt	ID Hunter	NC Phillips	SJE Brown	NG Hatch	GD Bridge	GM Scott	GJ Pratt	Extras	Total	Wickets	Result	Points
v. Durham UCCE	110	22	128rh	130	45*	0	23*	–	–	–	–										27	485	4		
(Chester-le-Street) 16–18 April	–	–																			–	–		D	
v. Gloucestershire	32	10	16	22	41		0	5	5	1		61	28*								21	242	10		
(Chester-le-Street) 20–23 April	1	24	28	68	2		24					67	28*								13	255	7	D	8
v. Nottinghamshire	56	34	4	95	7		22	4	0	0*		23	12								27	284	10		
(Trent Bridge) 25–28 April	–																				–	–		D	8
v. Warwickshire	8	13		153		4	4	9	3	17*		52	31	4							31	329	10		
(Edgbaston) 9–12 May	5	8	1			22	0	23	absent	0*		0	37	10*							6	102	9	L	6
v. Middlesex	19	2	26			101	20		1	5		13	8	31	10*						38	274	10		
(Chester-le-Street) 16–19 May	5	41	59	28			36*			5		13	31	11	7*						8	226	6	D	9
v. Nottinghamshire	21	35	91*	7			39	0		9		16	17	0	12						29	276	10		
(Chester-le-Street) 30 May–2 June	112	18	0*									149*									39	318	2	W	17
v. Derbyshire	7	42		34		14	10	0*				54	19	18	30	22					10	260	10		
(Derby) 6–9 June	28	7		90		36	37					40	5	15*	1*						21	280	10	D	
v. Gloucestershire	11	79				21	1	24		2		70	6	24	3	11*					35	278	10		
(Gloucester) 13–16 June	14	10					26*					52*									14	116	2	D	9
v. Hampshire	62	24				15	9	0				78	17	0	1	29	16*				15	266	10		
(Southampton Rose Bowl) 20–23 June	38	9				49	21	7				9	7	0	11*	0	0				12	163	10	L	5
v. Warwickshire	15	17	69	0		21	12					66	6	1		2*	12				10	231	10		
(Chester-le-Street) 29 June–2 July	32	10	21	70			67*	0				45	2	14			0*				23	284	8	D	9
v. Sussex	99	29	34	2		6	4				27	35	51*			24	1				48	360	10		
(Chester-le-Street) 18–21 July	32	0	34	0		31	11				absent	41	22			8*	0				23	202	9	L	5
v. Middlesex	18	0	17	45		4	2		13*			64	13			3	1				7	187	10		
(Lord's) 27–29 July	6	0	22	4		66	27		3*			19	9			3	4				0	163	10	L	2
v. Worcestershire	7	16	5	47		22	64				5	50	2			21*	0				21	260	10		
(Kidderminster) 2–5 August	0	–	38	16*		2*						58									4	118	3	W	17
v. Derbyshire	41	20	0			2	5					7	31	2		0*	5	8			4	125	10		
(Chester-le-Street) 8–10 August	4	3	19			43	0					0	68*	4		17	1	25			9	193	10	L	3
v. Hampshire	18	4	0	12rh			103	65		14		49	0			8*	31				19	323	9		
(Chester-le-Street) 17–20 August	8	2	3	0			42	6		3		52	14			12	39*				21	202	10	L	6
v. Sussex	10	89		0			2	0		9		45	26			5*	22	8			38	254	10		
(Hove) 22–25 August	33	16		2			27	2		3*		82	19			0	7	0			8	199	10	W	17
v. Worcestershire	129		5	103			20	7				26	2		12	0*	11			37	17	369	10		
(Chester-le-Street) 5–8 September	19		31	68			21					62	1		18*		3*			8	6	237	7	D	11

	JB Lewis	MA Gough	JA Daley	PD Collingwood	NJ Speak	N Peng	MP Speight	DR Law	JE Brinkley	N Killeen	SJ Harmison	ML Love	A Pratt	ID Hunter	NC Phillips	SJE Brown	NG Hatch	GD Bridge	GM Scott	GJ Pratt
Matches	17	13	9	13	3	13	8	16	10	4	12	15	16	8	7	4	9	7	1	2
Innings	32	23	16	24	5	23	15	26	13	3	14	29	28	14	11	5	16	13	2	4
Not Out	0	0	1	3	1	2	3	1	2	0	4	2	4	3	4	2	8	2	0	0
Highest Score	129	79	128*	153	45*	101	67*	103	65	5	27	149*	68*	37	30	29	24	39*	25	37
Runs	1000	450	428	1108	95	551	304	586	111	6	97	1364	476	199	87	64	129	125	33	53
Average	31.25	19.56	28.53	52.76	31.66	26.23	25.33	23.44	10.09	2	9.7	50.51	19.83	18.09	12.42	21.33	16.12	11.36	16.5	13.25
100s	3	–	1	3	–	1	–	1	–	–	–	1	–	–	–	–	–	–	–	–
50s	3	1	1	6	–	3	1	1	1	–	–	13	3	–	–	–	–	–	–	–
Ct/St	6	8	1	10	–	8	3/–	11	4	–	–	20	49/7	4	6	1	1	5	1	1

DURHAM CCC

FIRST-CLASS MATCHES
BOWLING

	MA Gough	PD Collingwood	DR Law	JE Brinkley	N Killeen	SJ Harmison	ID Hunter	NC Phillips	SJE Brown	NG Hatch	GD Bridge	Overs	Total	Byes/Leg-Byes	Wickets	Run outs
Durham University CCE (Chester-le-Street) 16-18 April	-		10-8-2-2		6.5-1-11-2		9-4-25-1		11-6-14-3	12-8-9-1		48.5	67	6	10	1
	7.3-3-15-1	1-1-0-0	5-0-22-0	6-4-9-0	6-1-14-1	10-2-25-0						35.3	92	7	2	-
Gloucestershire (Chester-le-Street) 20-23 April	3-1-21-0	7-1-22-0	7-0-40-0	9.5-1-32-6	17-7-35-3	12-4-44-1						55.5	198	4	10	-
	1-0-1-0	1-0-3-0	-		1-1-0-1	2-2-0-0						5	6	2	1	-
Nottinghamshire (Trent Bridge) 25-28 April	12-2-24-1	8-0-34-0	18-4-65-2	20-6-45-1	22-7-69-2	25-6-81-0						105	344	26	6	-
	-	-	-	-	-	-						-	-	-	-	-
Warwickshire (Edgbaston) 9-12 May	-	6-3-19-0	5-2-14-0	13-2-41-2		13-4-43-1	14.3-1-55-4	4-0-22-1				55.3	209	11	10	2
		8-2-22-2	7-0-37-0	-		19-4-55-0	13.5-1-69-1	8-2-32-0				55.5	227	12	3	-
Middlesex (Chester-le-Street) 16-19 May	21-2-66-5	10-6-16-0	5-0-32-0		20-5-50-1	22-5-43-0	19-1-73-0	31.2-4-101-2				128.2	386	5	10	2
	8-0-38-0		-		12-2-40-0	12.3-3-47-2	3-0-21-0	8-0-36-1				43.3	189	7	4	1
Nottinghamshire (Chester-le-Street) 30 May-2 June	6-0-26-0		11-4-26-1	4-0-20-0	13-4-71-1	33-5-100-5	16-2-52-3	24-8-61-0				107	371	15	10	-
	1-0-5-0	-		6-0-28-1	6-1-19-0	17-2-39-2	10-1-37-0	21-4-89-2				61	219	2	5	-
Derbyshire (Derby) 6-9 June	-		5-0-13-0			28-3-83-3	20-4-52-2	36.3-13-64-5	19-5-72-0			108.3	318	34	10	-
		17-4-28-1	8-4-15-1			20-5-65-3	7-1-29-1	31-8-92-4	9-2-23-0			92	267	15	10	-
Gloucestershire (Gloucester) 13-16 June	9-3-21-0		14-1-56-0			25-6-78-1	21-3-68-0	26-5-104-3	22.4-5-70-6			117.4	417	20	10	-
			7-1-18-1			10-3-25-0	4-2-17-1	13-1-52-1	14-4-41-1			48	159	6	4	-
Hampshire (Southampton Rose Bowl) 20-23 June	3-1-6-0		16.3-4-53-6				8-1-36-0	13-2-28-0	18-4-62-2	12-2-55-2		70.3	246	6	10	-
	-		20-4-41-1				10-1-35-0	22-7-70-2	14.2-4-31-3	13-3-42-3		79.2	230	11	10	1
Warwickshire (Chester-le-Street) 29 June-2 July	13-3-37-0	16-6-32-1	21.3-6-58-4					26-5-79-1	18-5-34-2	23-5-60-1		117.3	310	10	10	1
	12-4-39-1	16-3-62-1	15-2-48-2					22-1-109-1	-	15-1-60-1		80	324	6	6	-
Sussex (Chester-le-Street) 18-21 July	11-3-30-0	10-3-40-0	32-4-101-2		35-4-111-6				17-3-64-0	34.3-7-80-1		139.3	442	16	10	1
	3-0-9-3	16-4-35-0	18-3-49-2		5-0-37-0				17-0-64-0	19-3-57-4		78	253	2	9	-
Middlesex (Lord's) 27-29 July	30-8-83-2	16-6-54-0	31.4-8-94-5	29-4-92-0					25-6-82-3	-		134.4	424	19	10	-
									-	-						
Worcestershire (Kidderminster) 2-5 August		8-2-37-0	22-2-78-3		21.3-5-58-3				14-5-48-3	16-1-55-2	-	65.3	227	6	10	1
		4-1-12-0	21-8-52-5		10.2-4-19-3				-	2-1-5-0		53.2	147	4	10	-
Derbyshire (Chester-le-Street) 8-10 August		6-0-22-2					3-0-26-0		8-0-32-2	-		27	95	1	10	-
		3-0-8-0					5.1-0-40-1		17-4-56-3	11-1-35-0		58.1	224	3	6	1 A
Hampshire (Chester-le-Street) 17-20 August		-	14.3-1-48-0	19.3-6-67-4		21-5-61-0			13-3-42-0	35.1-12-84-6		103.1	312	10	10	-
		-	6-1-29-0	8-0-40-0		14-0-53-1			6-0-35-0	18-2-54-2		52	216	5	3	-
Sussex (Hove) 22-25 August			-	12-5-27-3		15-2-52-4			8.4-1-37-2	16-6-22-2		35.4	117	1	10	1
				16-7-33-0		32.2-6-86-3			15-2-50-2			100.2	265	16	10	1
Worcestershire (Chester-le-Street) 5-8 September		5-0-19-0	6-3-13-1			23-3-91-0	16-2-77-2			20-4-69-1	23.2-5-72-2	93.2	356	15	9	3
		-	8-5-10-2			14-4-34-2	11-7-13-1			9-3-16-1	13-11-4-1	55	85	8	7	-
Overs	157.3	165	351	222.1	89	419.5	181.3	285.5	115	248.4	172					
Maidens	34	50	70	61	29	86	27	60	29	43	48					
Runs	449	465	1103	663	222	1262	700	939	333	867	413					
Wickets	14	9	42	31	11	35	16	23	14	26	18					
Average	32.07	51.66	26.26	21.38	20.18	36.05	43.75	40.82	23.78	33.44	22.94					

A GM Scott 3-1-11-0

FIELDING

56	A Pratt (49ct,7st)
20	ML Love
11	DR Law
10	PD Collingwood
8	MA Gough, N Peng
6	JJB Lewis, NC Phillips
5	GD Bridge
4	JE Brinkley, ID Hunter
3	MP Speight
1	SJE Brown, JA Daley, NG Hatch GJ Pratt, GM Scott

ESSEX CCC

FIRST-CLASS MATCHES

BATTING

Match	PJ Prichard	WJ Jefferson	DDJ Robinson	SG Law	RC Irani	SD Peters	JS Foster	RSG Anderson	AP Cowan	MC Ilott	PM Such	N Hussain	BY Hyam	TJ Mason	AC McGarry	AP Grayson	GR Napier	RS Clinton	MK Davies	JE Bishop	TJ Phillips	ML Pettini	ZH Sharif	JB Grant	Extras	Total	Wickets	Result
v. Leicestershire (Leicester) 20–22 April — 1st	1	69	34	20	87	38	2	31	6	2	0*														28	318	10	W
— 2nd																												
v. Northamptonshire (Chelmsford) 25–28 April — 1st	8		61	26	8	19		2	27			15	2	0	0*										38	206	10	
— 2nd	22		0	58	4	56*		19	25*			34	22	3											14	257	8	D
v. Cambridge University CCE (Cambridge) 9–11 May — 1st	111		109		44									19*		127	104								19	533	5	
— 2nd						6	50*	39*																	1	96	1	W
v. Yorkshire (Chelmsford) 16–19 May — 1st	0		16	53	34	49*	21	0	22				17			17	0								20	249	10	D
— 2nd																												
v. Surrey (Oval) 25–28 May — 1st	0		7	153	17	23	4	8	12	9*	0					37									30	300	10	
— 2nd	34		2	57	51*	22*										115									31	312	4	D
v. Kent (Tunbridge Wells) 30 May–1 June — 1st	0		6	99	64	9	33	45	11	2					4*	5									20	298	10	
— 2nd	0		3	4	2	4	27	6	11	0					1*	4									6	68	10	L
v. Glamorgan (Chelmsford) 6–9 June — 1st	6		8	19	22	17		22	4	25			63		0*	6									1	193	10	
— 2nd	19		80	67	66	43			20	18*			23*			189									15	540	7	L
v. Surrey (Ilford) 13–16 June — 1st			25	1	119	4	3	18	29	21*	0					5	36								35	296	10	
— 2nd			66*		0												24	58*							5	153	2	D
v. Lancashire (Old Trafford) 19–22 June — 1st			2	116*	7	5	10	10	7	0						5	25	7							32	226	10	
— 2nd			1	123*	1	18	3	0	9	4						36	38	5							19	257	10	L
v. Australians (Chelmsford) 29 June–1 July — 1st			34		18	74			7	0		16			0*	0	59	0	0						23	231	10	
— 2nd																												
v. Somerset (Taunton) 4–7 July — 1st			1	40	11	2	0	8	0*							1	38	11		4					14	130	10	
— 2nd			24	57	31	0	0	34	4							9	21	15		11*					19	225	10	L
v. Kent (Southend) 18–20 July — 1st			24	0	27	18		2	7*						0	0	19	1		0					9	107	10	
— 2nd			2	0	7	8		7	0						0*		54	13		0	11				12	114	10	L
v. Northamptonshire (Northampton) 27–30 July — 1st			63	12	5	6	79	15*	0							173	35	5			25				12	430	10	
— 2nd			31	48	14	13	16	1	0*							149	9	1			0				15	297	10	L
v. Leicestershire (Chelmsford) 1–4 August — 1st			102	115	2	0	1	26	4*							9	36			16	27				18	356	10	
— 2nd			118*	23	3	19	21									2*	44								6	236	5	D
v. Glamorgan (Cardiff) 15–18 August — 1st			0	91	9	14	57		68	28					4*	13	17				7				19	327	10	
— 2nd			38*													21*									5	64	0	D
v. Lancashire (Colchester) 22–25 August — 1st			13	18	9	26	32	1	21					41*		26	23				5				21	236	10	
— 2nd			0	46	18	3	15	32						2		186*	11				5*				16	334	8	D
v. Somerset (Chelmsford) 5–7 September — 1st			89	30	6	7	14		0*							6	4	0	0		7				9	172	10	
— 2nd			35	66	32	10	2		4							19	56	21	10*		18				9	282	10	L
v. Yorkshire (Scarborough) 12–15 September — 1st			27	33	41	5	4									42	40	0				1	15	1*	41	250	10	
— 2nd			0	51*	15	9	33										7	1				41	2		13	172	8	W

	PJ Prichard	WJ Jefferson	DDJ Robinson	SG Law	RC Irani	SD Peters	JS Foster	RSG Anderson	AP Cowan	MC Ilott	PM Such	N Hussain	BY Hyam	TJ Mason	AC McGarry	AP Grayson	GR Napier	RS Clinton	MK Davies	JE Bishop	TJ Phillips	ML Pettini	ZH Sharif	JB Grant
Matches	7	1	18	13	17	15	12	8	15	10	15	2	6	3	6	16	10	8	2	8	3	1	1	1
Innings	11	1	31	23	29	26	20	11	24	12	20	3	9	5	8	29	16	15	4	12	5	2	2	1
Not Out	0	0	2	3	2	3	0	0	3	1	9	0	2	2	6	3	0	1	1	2	0	0	0	1
Highest Score	111	69	118*	153	119	56*	79	45	68	34	25	34	63	41*	4*	189	104	58*	10*	18	27	41	15	1*
Runs	201	69	955	1311	779	508	462	154	360	186	117	65	150	85	5	1275	506	283	22	74	63	42	17	1
Average	18.27	69	32.93	65.55	28.85	22.08	23.10	14	17.14	16.9	10.63	21.66	21.42	28.33	2.5	49.03	31.62	20.21	7.33	7.4	12.6	21	8.5	–
100s	1	–	3	4	1	–	–	–	–	–	–	–	–	–	–	6	–	–	–	–	–	–	–	–
50s	–	1	4	8	6	1	3	–	2	–	–	–	1	–	–	1	2	1	–	–	–	–	–	–
Ct/St	1	2	11	18	4	6	24/6	2	8	6	7	–	20/1	–	2	7	4	2	–	–	–	–	1	1

ESSEX CCC

FIRST-CLASS MATCHES

BOWLING

Match	RC Irani	RSG Anderson	AP Cowan	MC Ilott	PM Such	TJ Mason	AC McGarry	AP Grayson	GR Napier	JE Bishop	Overs	Total	Byes/Leg-Byes	Wickets	Run outs
v. Leicestershire (Leicester) 20-22 April	8-3-19-0	13-6-21-4	12-2-32-2	16.2-6-27-4	-						49.2	104	5	10	-
	12-5-18-1	20.2-7-50-5	23.1-5-87-2	13.5-7-19-1	6-1-26-0						75.2	205	5	9	-
v. Northamptonshire (Chelmsford) 25-28 April	24-11-43-5	15-4-45-3	16-3-34-1			-	7-0-23-1				62	150	5	10	-
	19-6-40-0	21-3-56-3	17-5-51-2			8-4-11-0	11-1-38-2				76	199	3	7	-
v. Cambridge University CCE (Cambridge) 9-11 May		9-3-21-5	13-5-18-0	14-8-25-1	13-10-5-1	10-5-18-1		5-1-13-0	10-1-24-2		74	128	4	10	-
		5-0-13-1	6-1-25-1	12-4-23-1	5-0-20-0	15-3-40-5		-	6-0-39-2		49	166	6	10	-
v. Yorkshire (Chelmsford) 16-19 May	23-6-70-1	20-4-62-1	23-5-111-3	23-5-57-2				13-3-35-0	12.2-2-61-2		114.2	403	7	9	-
	-										-	-	-	-	-
v. Surrey (Oval) 25-28 May	13.4-2-47-1	29-1-154-4		33-7-127-3	24-4-65-0		22-4-71-2	7-1-19-0			128.4	498	15	10	-
	-	9-1-33-0		5-0-21-0	21-5-81-4		10-2-41-1	7-0-28-0			52	206	2	5	-
v. Kent (Tunbridge Wells) 30 May-1 June	13-4-38-0	28-9-68-2		24-4-78-0	39.1-4-143-1		22-5-77-0	23-3-97-2			149.1	518	17	5	-
	-	-		-	-		-	-			-	-	-	-	-
v. Glamorgan (Chelmsford) 6-9 June	22-6-55-2		24-4-90-0	26.5-6-85-5	12-4-21-0		19-1-77-3	10-4-31-0			113.5	370	11	10	-
	12.5-2-66-0		14-0-62-0	17-2-66-0	18-2-84-3		7-0-33-0	12-0-49-1			80.5	367	7	4	-
v. Surrey (Ilford) 13-16 June	17.5-3-58-5	12-3-38-1	13-2-64-3	6-1-34-1	-			-			49.5	198	4	10	- A
	19-6-56-2	27.5-7-79-5	20-3-70-1	18-2-64-2	10-2-26-0						94.5	306	11	10	-
v. Lancashire (Old Trafford) 19-22 June	21-8-42-0	22-6-59-1	25.4-4-65-3		45-12-124-3			3-1-8-0			150.4	431	12	10	- B
	5-1-25-1	-	3.5-0-18-0		2-1-6-0			-			10.5	53	4	1	-
v. Australians (Chelmsford) 29 June-2 July	8-3-11-0			19-4-83-2	23-3-99-1		11-0-86-0	8-2-42-0	-	18-5-70-2	87	405	14	5	-
	-			13-2-62-0	39-11-131-5		19-2-121-1	13-2-54-0	-	15-0-80-1	120	569	30	9	ACDE
v. Somerset (Taunton) 4-7 July	23-10-38-2		29.1-9-99-2	38-7-116-4	6-0-32-0			8-0-29-0	-	25-4-91-2	129.1	415	10	10	-
	-		-	-	-			-	-	-	-	-	-	-	-
v. Kent (Southend) 18-20 July	-		34-10-78-3	10-2-19-0			20-4-70-0	-		36-8-120-4	116	353	6	7	- F
	-			-			-	-			-	-	-	-	-
v. Northamptonshire (Northampton) 27-30 July	15-3-45-1		26-3-105-0		53-13-182-3			21-2-85-1	14-2-59-0		162	633	13	6	- F
	6-0-43-0		4-0-36-0					1-0-16-0	-		11	96	1	0	-
v. Leicestershire (Chelmsford) 1-4 August	17-5-64-1		40-10-102-1		27-6-86-0			4-0-19-0	14.5-5-55-3	38-10-148-5	153.5	559	28	10	- F
	-		-		-			-	-	-	-	-	-	-	-
v. Glamorgan (Cardiff) 15-18 August	20-2-69-2		31.5-7-112-2	8-0-34-1	29-7-99-1			12-2-49-0	12-0-50-0	25-2-120-2	137.5	546	13	8	-
	-		-	-	-			-	-	-	-	-	-	-	-
v. Lancashire (Colchester) 22-25 August	28.3-5-79-6		30-9-84-0		31-7-71-2	6-1-29-0		-	18-2-77-0	21-3-71-2	134.3	423	12	10	-
	-		-		-	-		-	-	-	-	-	-	-	-
v. Somerset (Chelmsford) 5-7 September	21-6-80-2		34-11-89-3		19-4-38-0			5-1-8-0	12-2-56-2	23.2-4-94-3	118.2	391	6	10	- B
	-		5-0-22-1		-			-	-	4.1-0-34-0	9.1	64	8	1	-
v. Yorkshire (Scarborough) 12-15 September	4-0-15-0		10-5-21-2					-	3-1-15-1	10.3-3-30-2	33.3	104	3	3	- G
	2-0-19-0		8-1-47-1					10-2-20-5	2-0-17-0	8-0-57-1	45	267	3	10	- G H

	RC Irani	RSG Anderson	AP Cowan	MC Ilott	PM Such	TJ Mason	AC McGarry	AP Grayson	GR Napier	JE Bishop
Overs	354.5	231.1	462.4	287	432.1	39	148	162	104.1	224
Maidens	97	54	104	65	98	13	19	24	15	39
Runs	1040	699	1522	921	1358	98	637	602	453	915
Wickets	32	35	33	27	24	6	10	9	12	24
Average	32.50	19.97	46.12	34.11	56.58	16.33	63.70	66.88	37.75	38.12

A   RS Clinton 1-1-0-0; 8-0-30-2
B   MK Davies 34-4-121-3; 4-0-20-0
C   DDJ Robinson 10-0-54-0
D   JS Foster 2-0-6-0
E   N Hussain 1-0-1-0
F   TJ Phillips 16-2-60-0; 33-3-144-1; 13-2-57-0
G   JB Grant 6-0-20-0; 13-0-81-3
H   ZH Sharif 2-0-23-0

FIELDING

39	JS Foster (31ct,8st)
21	BJ Hyam (20ct,1st)
18	SG Law
11	DDJ Robinson
8	AP Cowan
7	AP Grayson, PM Such
6	MC Ilott, SD Peters
4	RC Irani, GR Napier
2	RSG Anderson, RS Clinton, AC McGarry
1	ML Pettini, PJ Prichard, ZH Sharif

GLAMORGAN CCC

FIRST-CLASS MATCHES

BATTING

Match	AW Evans	JP Maher	MJ Powell	MP Maynard	A Dale	K Newell	AD Shaw	RDB Croft	AG Wharf	SD Thomas	SL Watkin	SP James	DA Cosker	OT Parkin	MA Wallace	SP Jones	IJ Thomas	AP Davies	J Hughes	Extras	Total	Wickets	Result	Points
v. Northamptonshire (Northampton) 20–23 April	8	34	106	15	204	103	33*	14*	–	–	–									31	548	6		
	4	34*	23*	–	–	–	–	–	–	–	–									4	65	1	D	11
v. Somerset (Cardiff) 25–28 April	41	29	64	21	64	3	62	23	14*	6	1*									25	353	9		
																				–	–	–	D	9
v. Lancashire (Old Trafford) 16–19 May																				–	–	–		
																				–	–	–	D	4
v. Kent (Swansea) 25–28 May		12	0	16	29		18	20	31	42	20*	1	17							32	238	10		
																				–	–	–	D	8
v. Yorkshire (Swansea) 30 May–1 June		35	0	0	20	14	5		3	12	4*	4	0							7	104	10		
		8	1	10	4	7	17		11	0	21	24	9*							13	125	10	L	3
v. Essex (Chelmsford) 6–9 June		21	1	9	113	17	8			138	13*	1	24	0						25	370	10		
		38	7	90	43*	10*						156								23	367	4	W	19
v. Kent (Maidstone) 13–16 June		6	16	0	41	13				50	38	27	4		80*	2				9	286	10		
		123*								76*										4	203	0	D	9
v. Northamptonshire (Cardiff) 29 June–2 July		150	86	69	54			93		1*		62			26					15	556	7		
																				–	–	–	D	12
v. Leicestershire (Cardiff) 18–21 July		15	31	20	89			4	7	24	0		2		6*	5				8	211	10		
		16	27	89	40			69	0*	13	7	4	2							20	287	10	L	3
v. Somerset (Taunton) 27–29 July		62	21	6	0				0	8	22	21	2*		8	0				19	169	10		
		98	0	80	16				0	21	11	77rh	20*		15	0				26	364	9	L	2
v. Lancashire (Colwyn Bay) 1–4 August		60	5	145	140					13	0	2*	35		6	3	35			35	479	10		
		10	3	35	0					73*		44*	8		10		17			20	220	7	D	12
v. Surrey (Oval) 8–11 August		6	24	31	5				0	57	8				63*	4	13	0		12	223	10		
		2	51	14	15				0	0					18*		59	16*		26	201	7	W	16
v. Essex (Cardiff) 15–18 August		217	108	22	19					68		8*	4				18	40		42	546	8		
																				–	–	–	D	12
v. Yorkshire (Scarborough) 21–24 August		36	28	59	13					9	8*	5	31			4	18	0		12	223	10		
		21	21	45*	30					0	8	6	6			46	21	7		34	245	10	L	3
v. Leicestershire (Leicester) 7–9 September		24	4	0	1				0	7	21	61*	13		4		5			6	146	10		
		100	25	0	32*				1	13	4	17	1		10		17			25	245	10	L	3
v. Surrey (Cardiff) 12–15 September		7	56	13	70*					13	0	17	24		0				38	20	258	10		
		0*													6*				49	14	69	1	D	7

	AW Evans	JP Maher	MJ Powell	MP Maynard	A Dale	K Newell	AD Shaw	RDB Croft	AG Wharf	SD Thomas	SL Watkin	SP James	DA Cosker	OT Parkin	MA Wallace	SP Jones	IJ Thomas	AP Davies	J Hughes
Matches	2	14	15	13	15	7	5	10	5	15	15	9	11	1	10	8	6	4	1
Innings	3	23	25	20	23	11	6	13	4	21	17	15	15	1	16	11	11	7	2
Not Out		2	2	0	3	2	1	2	1	2	7	3	4	0	3	1	1	1	0
Highest Score	41	217	108	145	204	103	62	93	31	138	38	156	35	0	80*	46	59	40	49
Runs	53	1133	681	621	1026	296	143	350	59	562	188	568	175	0	290	83	194	85	87
Average	17.66	53.95	29.6	31.05	51.3	32.88	28.6	31.82	19.66	29.57	18.8	47.33	15.9	–	22.3	8.3	19.4	14.16	43.5
100s	–	4	2	1	3	1	–	–	–	1	–	1	–	–	–	–	–	–	–
50s	–	3	4	3	4	1	1	3	–	4	–	4	–	–	2	–	1	–	–
Ct/St	1	13	12	6	9	5	11/-	6	1	5	5	5	10	1	27/1	–	2	2	–

GLAMORGAN CCC

FIRST-CLASS MATCHES

BOWLING

	A Dale	AJ Wharf	SD Thomas	SL Watkin	RDB Croft	DA Cosker	SP Jones	AP Davies	Overs	Total	Byes/Leg-Byes	Wickets	Run outs
Northamptonshire (Northampton) 20–23 April	10-1-45-0	20-1-92-1	24-3-78-1	24-4-94-3	32-8-84-2				117	446	20	7	– A
	–	–	–	–	–				–	–	–	–	–
Somerset (Cardiff) 25–28 April	6-2-15-0	19.4-2-102-1	32-5-105-1	28-8-78-0	45-13-109-2				133.4	435	23	5	1 A B
	–	–	–	–	–				–	–	–	–	–
Lancashire (Old Trafford) 16–19 May	–	–	–	–	–	–			–	–	–	–	–
	–	–	–	–	–	–			–	–	–	–	–
Kent (Swansea) 25–28 May	6-0-23-0	18-2-66-4	16-3-56-0	16-3-40-2	7-1-15-0	18.5-6-48-4			81.5	252	4	10	–
	–	–	–	–	–				–	–	–	–	–
Yorkshire (Swansea) 30 May–1 June	10-3-17-0	25-6-63-5	23-3-81-1	22.1-7-49-3			19-5-61-1		99.1	280	9	10	–
	4-1-15-0	18-2-57-3	12-2-51-0	21-11-50-2			21-2-88-2		76	277	16	7	–
Essex (Chelmsford) 6–9 June	3-0-23-0		15-2-54-4	12-4-41-1			8.4-2-29-3		51.4	193	1	7	– D
	11-3-27-1		27-4-122-1	37-11-104-2			33-4-100-1		148	540	10	7	A C D
Kent (Maidstone) 13–16 June	11-4-27-0		23-2-67-4	15-3-33-2	34-10-88-2	18-3-72-1			102	304	15	10	1 A C
	2-0-14-0		23-5-84-4	28-5-88-2	35-11-93-3	14.1-3-43-1			108.1	358	12	10	C
Northamptonshire (Cardiff) 29 June–2 July	3-3-0-0	10-2-26-0	16-2-72-3	11-1-32-0	33.3-11-95-5	31-5-109-2			104.3	344	10	10	–
	3-0-6-1	17-4-42-0	15-2-56-0	16-6-36-0	57-25-96-5	29-5-85-1			141	349	18	7	– A E
Leicestershire (Cardiff) 18–21 July	6-1-18-0		20.5-1-117-2	31-6-126-4	36-6-145-3	19-2-68-0	20-1-101-1		132.5	588	13	10	–
Somerset (Taunton) 27–29 July	6-0-35-0		23-2-99-1	22-4-99-3	32-4-137-2	18-3-93-0	26-2-123-2		127	600	14	8	–
Lancashire (Colwyn Bay) 1–4 August	7-2-22-1		14-0-80-0	23-5-74-2		24-4-100-4	18.4-3-104-2		89.4	402	19	9	– C
	5-0-34-3		8-0-52-0	8-2-27-0		12-3-72-2	8-2-35-2		41	225	5	7	–
Surrey (Oval) 8–11 August	4-1-15-1		15-0-69-3	17-4-53-1	5-2-4-1		16-2-52-1	18-4-76-3	75	281	12	10	–
	–		6-2-29-1	17.5-6-28-4	4-1-16-0		16-6-36-3	7-1-24-2	50.5	141	8	10	–
Essex (Cardiff) 15–18 August	3-1-6-0		28-8-68-2	26.4-7-67-6		12-2-29-0	17-3-66-0	24-6-84-2	110.4	327	7	10	–
	–		5-2-12-0	6-2-12-0		–	4-0-19-0	4-0-16-0	19	64	5	0	–
Yorkshire (Scarborough) 21–24 August	6-2-14-0		21-3-93-1	32-8-71-2		60.5-13-168-4	3-2-135-2	21-4-73-0	164.5	580	22	9	– A
	–		–	–		–	–	–	–	–	–	–	–
Leicestershire (Leicester) 7–9 September	–		18.2-2-77-3	25-3-82-2	14-3-40-1		16-2-87-2	12-1-68-2	85.2	372	18	10	–
	–		–	2-0-6-0	–		1.3-0-14-0	–	3.3	20	0	0	–
Surrey (Cardiff) 12–15 September	11-1-54-0		35-3-146-1	32-3-110-2	60-12-176-2	48.3-6-159-4			191.3	701	55	9	– A F
	–		–	–	–				–	–	–	–	–

	A Dale	AJ Wharf	SD Thomas	SL Watkin	RDB Croft	DA Cosker	SP Jones	AP Davies
Overs	117	127.4	420.1	472.4	325.3	423.5	198.2	86
Maidens	25	19	56	113	86	84	29	16
Runs	410	448	1668	1400	917	1390	887	341
Wickets	7	14	33	43	24	33	17	9
Average	58.57	32.00	50.54	32.55	38.20	42.12	52.17	37.88

JP Maher 7-1-33-0; 2-1-1-0; 6-1-27-0; 3-0-10-0; 1-0-4-0; 2-0-13-0
AW Evans 1-0-2-0
K Newell 3-0-19-0; 1-0-2-0; 6-0-24-0; 3-0-3-0
OT Parkin 13-2-45-2; 31-2-131-2
MP Maynard 1-1-0-0
IJ Thomas 3-1-2-0

FIELDING

- MA Wallace (27ct,1st)
- JP Maher
- MJ Powell
- AD Shaw
- DA Cosker
- A Dale
- RDB Croft, MP Maynard
- SP James, K Newell, SD Thomas, SL Watkin
- AP Davies, IJ Thomas
- AW Evans, OT Parkin, AG Wharf

GLOUCESTERSHIRE CCC

FIRST-CLASS MATCHES

BATTING

Match	THC Hancock	RJ Cunliffe	MGN Windows	KJ Barnett	IJ Harvey	MW Alleyne	CG Taylor	JN Snape	JMM Averis	J Lewis	AM Smith	RCJ Williams	MJ Cawdron	DR Hewson	MCJ Ball	RC Russell	MA Hardinges	BW Gannon	AN Bressington	RJ Sillence	Extras	Total	Wickets	Result
v. Durham (Chester-le-Street) 20–23 April	29	0	0	82	36	31	0	6	0	0*	4										10	198	10	
	0	0*	4*	–	–	–	–	–	–	–											2	6	1	D
v. Middlesex (Bristol) 9–11 May	29	24	0	99	41	–	2	1	5*			15	29								27	272	10	
	14	48	106*	18	14	49*	–	–	–												16	265	4	L
v. Hampshire (Southampton Rose Bowl) 16–19 May		37	11	–	20	0	26	8	0	7*		15	0	0							9	133	10	
		1	5		28	19	11	73	4	4*		13	2	89							23	272	10	D
v. Worcestershire (Bristol) 25–28 May	6	–	4	6	1	1	15	69	1	9*		10	4	35							15	175	10	
	9	4	19		23	1	42	7	2			28	7*	6							7	155	10	L
v. Warwickshire (Edgbaston) 31 May–3 June	55	1	32	53	44	10	0	2*				33		30	68						32	360	10	
	25	1	12		15	2	17	2	15*			5		0	2						10	106	10	L
v. Nottinghamshire (Trent Bridge) 6–9 June		0	114		20	196	1	0				26*		36	7	29	22				22	473	10	
		73	45		17	19	21*	–						51	22						17	265	5	W
v. Gloucestershire (Gloucester) 13–16 June		0	14		132	54	53	0				0	8	60*	48	20					28	417	10	
		60*	15		30	13	0*						29								12	159	4	D
v. Derbyshire (Derby) 20–23 June			11		73	136	83	119	7*				10	12*	53	14	–				42	560	8	
			–		72*									100*							5	177	0	D
v. Warwickshire (Bristol) 4–7 July		0	0		9	2	61	2					10	26	13	12	0*				10	145	10	
		14	21		10	33	89	1					4	11	0	91*	1				22	297	10	D
v. Worcestershire (Worcester) 20–22 July		9	54	0	0	50	15	0					5	45	18			10*			16	222	10	
		8	0	13	0	0	25	6					7	4	20			0*			4	87	10	L
v. Sussex (Cheltenham) 28–30 July		22	79	11	1	140	131	0					10	32	32	1*					61	520	10	
		–	21*										1*								1	23	0	W
v. Hampshire (Cheltenham) 1–4 August		91	41	11	12	56	21						5	40	2	0	17*				38	334	10	
		21	93	9	22*	37	5						17	–	28*	–					13	245	6	D
v. Middlesex (Lord's) 8–11 August			123	38	130*	12*	–	–						77			–				20	400	3	W
			–																		–		–	
v. Nottinghamshire (Bristol) 15–18 August		28	174	6*	72	148	100*	–						16	12	16	4				32	608	8	W
		–												–										
v. Derbyshire (Bristol) 5–7 September	49	3	30	34	104	16			0					168	59	24			2*		19	508	10	W
	–	–							–					–							–		–	
v. Sussex (Hove) 12–14 September	14	41	37	71	33		0*			4			0	3					17	0	8	228	10	
	0	27	10	37	5		4*			0				79	0				0	6	5	173	10	L

	THC Hancock	RJ Cunliffe	MGN Windows	KJ Barnett	IJ Harvey	MW Alleyne	CG Taylor	JN Snape	JMM Averis	J Lewis	AM Smith	RCJ Williams	MJ Cawdron	DR Hewson	MCJ Ball	RC Russell	MA Hardinges	BW Gannon	AN Bressington	RJ Sillence				
Matches	6	5	16	14	10	16	12	12	15	5	1	5	6	14	12	10	3	6	5	2				
Innings	11	8	27	25	15	26	20	21	19	8	1	9	9	25	16	12	3	6	5	2				
Not Out	0	1	3	2	2	3	0	3	3	7	0	0	2	2	3	2	0	4	2	0				
Highest Score	55	48	174	114	130*	136	196	131	7*	15*	4	33	29	168	68	91*	22	10*	17*	6				
Runs	230	141	840	1029	532	718	930	868	35	44	4	123	82	816	379	373	56	12	40	6				
Average	20.9	20.14	35	44.73	40.84	31.21	46.5	48.22	2.18	44	4	13.66	11.71	35.47	29.15	37.3	18.66	6	13.33	3				
100s	–	–	3	1	2	2	3	3	–	–	–	–	–	3	–	–	–	–	–	–				
50s	1	–	3	7	1	2	4	5	–	–	–	–	–	4	3	2	–	–	–	–				
Ct/St	7	5	6	10	8	12/1	6	10	3	–	1	16/1	1	6	20	42/2	2	–	2	–				

GLOUCESTERSHIRE CCC

FIRST–CLASS MATCHES

BOWLING

	J Lewis	IJ Harvey	JMM Averis	JN Snape	MW Alleyne	MJ Cawdron	MCJ Ball	MA Hardinges	BW Gannon	AN Bressington	RJ Sillence	Overs	Total	Byes/Leg-Byes	Wickets	Run outs
v. Durham (Chester-le-Street) 20–23 April	24-11-50-4	25.3-10-54-2	17-5-47-1	22-10-27-3	-							107.3	242	5	10	- A B
	22-7-56-3	23-7-59-1	23-7-55-1	14-2-28-0	-							110	255	7	7	- B C
v. Middlesex (Bristol) 9–12 May	26-12-50-3	31-5-96-4	15-5-39-1	7-4-6-0	13-6-14-2	18-10-28-0						110	245	12	10	-
	13-2-57-0	22-1-83-4	15.5-2-50-0	6-0-28-0	14-4-45-1	9-4-22-0						79.5	293	8	5	-
v. Hampshire (Southampton Rose Bowl) 16–19 May	27.2-7-82-1	18-9-45-1	18-3-57-0	6-0-43-0	21-7-58-1	19-6-56-1						109.2	350	9	4	-
	5-0-22-2	-	5-0-26-2	-								10	55	7	6	2
v. Worcestershire (Bristol) 25–28 May	28.2-6-71-5		29-5-98-3	9-2-24-0	22-7-54-1	24-11-39-1						119.2	326	20	10	- A
	25-8-60-3		18-9-31-1	16-3-52-2	13-2-42-1	14-2-56-1						86	256	15	8	-
v. Warwickshire (Edgbaston) 31 May–3 June	5-3-6-0		36-10-104-2	18-2-46-2	37-7-82-2		44-8-131-2					158	448	12	9	- A
	-		-	2-0-8-0	-		1.4-0-14-0					3.4	22	0	0	-
v. Nottinghamshire (Trent Bridge) 6–9 June			19.2-8-52-3	-	14-3-49-1	24-5-79-4	4-1-18-0	15-3-59-2				76.2	267	10	10	-
			22-3-104-2	-	8-4-26-2	22-5-90-3	4-1-17-1	9-3-36-2				65	284	11	10	-
v. Durham (Gloucester) 13–16 June			22.2-5-72-4	-	11-3-44-1	9-1-47-0	33-8-80-4	9-1-32-0				84.2	287	12	10	1
			8-1-25-1	5-2-10-0	-	5-0-17-1	10-2-33-0	4-0-23-0				34	116	2	2	- C
v. Derbyshire (Derby) 20–23 June			25-5-89-0	23-4-48-0	20-3-72-3		34-15-44-0	27-6-90-1	21-3-71-1			156	432	8	5	- C D
			10-2-44-0	3-0-29-0	17-2-57-3		23-2-100-5	9-1-36-1	7-1-23-0			69	297	8	9	-
v. Warwickshire (Bristol) 4–7 July			18-2-49-4	-	20.1-5-50-5	20-6-45-1	5-2-11-0		13-2-45-0			76.1	204	4	10	-
			8.5-1-42-0	-	-	4-0-19-0	4-0-18-1		5-0-26-1			21.5	113	8	2	-
v. Worcestershire (Worcester) 20–22 July		28-14-59-2	22-4-90-2	-	11.5-4-30-4		-		10-1-45-2			71.5	240	16	10	-
		7-1-36-3	1-0-6-0	-	1.4-0-17-0		-		5-0-14-0			14.4	73	0	3	-
v. Sussex (Cheltenham) 28–30 July		18.5-13-13-3	16-4-53-1	-	6-1-9-1		24-10-41-3		11-1-46-1			75.5	167	5	10	1
		23-11-33-5	19-2-114-2	11-4-26-0	22-5-59-1		27-7-70-2		10-1-61-0			112	375	12	10	-
v. Hampshire (Cheltenham) 1–4 August		16-4-48-2	-		12-1-40-2		3-0-27-0		11-0-47-3	14-4-56-3		56	230	12	10	-
		6-1-19-1	-		-		5-2-6-0		4-3-2-0	7-4-13-0		22	40	0	1	-
v. Middlesex (Lord's) 8–11 August		-	17.2-5-55-5	11-1-31-1	12-2-21-2		26.1-9-51-2	6-1-19-0		13-5-36-0		85.3	222	9	10	-
		14.2-7-20-4	5-0-30-0	-	9-2-22-2		10-4-20-2	-		9-3-18-1		47.2	119	9	10	1
v. Nottinghamshire (Bristol) 15–18 August		22-4-72-3	18-3-86-3	-	25-4-83-3		11.4-2-29-1			11-0-38-2		96.4	322	1	10	1
		-	14.3-12-51-3	-	17-4-45-3		12-1-31-1			11-0-38-2		54.3	166	1	10	1
v. Derbyshire (Bristol) 5–7 September		6-0-47-1	12-0-72-0	-	14-4-24-0		18-9-23-6			11.4-4-42-3		61.4	210	2	10	-
		28-5-89-5	13-1-57-1	-	8-1-31-0		33.1-10-67-3			5-0-23-0		87.1	278	11	10	1
v. Sussex (Hove) 12–14 September		-	14-8-23-1	-	26-6-105-0		16-1-45-1			28-5-105-2	28.5-5-97-5	112.5	384	9	10	1
		-		-	-		-			2-0-15-0	1-0-3-0	3	18	0	0	-

		J Lewis	IJ Harvey	JMM Averis	JN Snape	MW Alleyne	MJ Cawdron	MCJ Ball	MA Hardinges	BW Gannon	AN Bressington	RJ Sillence
Overs		175.4	288.4	462.1	153	374.4	168	348.4	79	97	120.4	29.5
Maidens		56	92	112	34	87	50	94	15	12	31	5
Runs		454	883	1621	406	1079	498	876	295	360	397	100
Wickets		21	41	43	8	41	12	34	6	8	11	5
Average		21.61	18.85	37.69	50.75	26.31	41.50	25.76	49.16	47.50	36.09	20.00

A THC Hancock 3-0-13-0; 7-1-20-0; 18-4-67-1
B AM Smith 16-6-46-0; 17-7-24-2
C KJ Barnett 11-2-26-0; 2-1-6-0; 3-1-3-0
D DR Hewson 3-1-7-0

FIELDING

44	RC Russell (42ct,2st)
20	MCJ Ball
17	RCJ Williams (16ct,1st)
13	MW Alleyne (12ct,1st)
10	KJ Barnett, JN Snape
8	IJ Harvey
7	THC Hancock
6	DR Hewson, CG Taylor, MGN Windows
5	RJ Cunliffe
3	JMM Averis
2	AN Bressington, MA Hardinges
1	MJ Cawdron, AM Smith

HAMPSHIRE CCC

FIRST-CLASS MATCHES

BATTING

Match	DA Kenway	GW White	WS Kendall	RA Smith	NC Johnson	JP Stephenson	AN Aymes	AD Mascarenhas	AC Morris	JRC Hamblin	AD Mullally	SD Udal	LR Prittipaul	CT Tremlett	I Brunnschweiler	JEK Schofield	JS Laney	JD Francis	Extras	Total	Wickets	Result	Points
v. Warwickshire (Edgbaston) 20–23 April	23	44	0	4	43	7	3	11	20	5	0*								10	170	10		
	52	0	11	118	0	39	4	11*	25*	–									25	285	7	D	
v. Worcestershire (Southampton Rose Bowl) 9–11 May	12	26	10	4	0	51	3	104	32		1*	23							43	309	10		
	30	9	0	3	11	8	37*	13	20		1	1							26	159	10	W	17.
v. Gloucestershire (Southampton Rose Bowl) 16–19 May	131	17	43	102*	23	21*	–	–	–										13	350	4		
	8	0	13	1	13	2	–	6*	–	–	1*								11	55	6	D	
v. Derbyshire (Derby) 25–28 May	57	3	94	2	53		83*	13	4		36	12	84						23	464	10		
	11	29*	6*	–	–	–													3	49	1	W	
v. Sussex (Southampton Rose Bowl) 30 May–2 June	35	141	32	0	60		1	0	65		3*	39		24					37	437	10		
	–	–	–	–	–		–	–	–		–	–		–					–	–	–	D	
v. Middlesex (Southgate) 13–16 June	58	3	1	64	54		69	0	43			59	23	17*					13	404	10		
	39*	20*	–	–	–		–	–	–			–	–	–					2	61	0	D	
v. Durham (Southampton Rose Bowl) 20–23 June	15	41	2	13	32		41	7	59		7	6	1*						22	246	10		
	20	44	14	1	86*		1	6	9		27	4	1						17	230	10	W	
v. Derbyshire (Southampton Rose Bowl) 29 June–1 July	6	32	26	38	59		73	14	11		8*	81	5						30	383	10		
	6*	0*	–	–	–		–	–	–		–	–	–						0	6	0	W	
v. Sussex (Hove) 6–7 July	18	9	22	7	0		6	8	0		0	2	2*						7	81	10		
	0	5	0	0	19		8	7	0		17	40*	10						2	108	10	L	
v. Nottinghamshire (Southampton Rose Bowl) 18–21 July	25	18	14	49	16		112*	37	12		0	20	26						18	347	10		
	166	15	0	1	49		39	36	16*		10	1*							19	352	8	W	
v. Australians (Southampton Rose Bowl) 28–30 July	70	0	0	113	88			10			4*	15	10	1	0				43	354	10		
	22	8	9	10	37			14				2			10*	1*			21	134	8	W	
v Gloucestershire (Cheltenham) 1–4 August	20	14	19		72		0		6		8	5	9	13			52*		12	230	10		
	17	12*	11	–	–		–	–	–		–	–	–	–			–		0	40	1	D	
v. Warwickshire (Southampton Rose Bowl) 7–10 August	18*	1	4*	–	–		–	–	–			–							3	26	1		
	–	–	–																–	–	–	D	
v. Durham (Chester-le-Street) 17–20 August		31	49	2	27		6	76	52		0	12				21*	18		18	312	10		
		74	54	9*	2*												60		17	216	3	W	
v. Worcestershire (Worcester) 22–25 August	0	17	36	26	103		1	39*	5			4		1			1		14	247	10		
	40	0	31	0	23		28*	5	44			4		2			6		10	194	10	L	
v. Middlesex (Southampton Rose Bowl) 5–7 September	13	6	0	0	16		57*	9	0		4	62						15	9	191	10		
	6	2	38	7	74		0*											29*	10	166	5	W	
v. Nottinghamshire (Trent Bridge) 12–15 September	9	6	27	24	105*			20*										72*	16	258	4		
	5	112	72	0	8													15	13	245	6	D	
Matches	16	17	17	16	17	3	16	15	16	1	13	16	7	7	1	3	4	2					
Innings	30	32	30	26	27	6	19	23	19	1	12	20	9	9	2	5	5	4					
Not Out	3	4	3	2	3	1	5	5	2	–	5	2	–	4	1	2	1	2					
Highest Score	166	141	94	118	105*	51	112*	105	65	5	36	81	84	26	10*	21*	60	72*					
Runs	932	739	638	598	1073	128	572	447	423	5	82	414	165	83	11	25	137	131					
Average	34.51	26.39	23.62	24.91	44.7	25.6	40.85	24.83	24.88	5	11.71	23	18.33	16.6	11	8.33	34.25	65.5					
100s	2	2	–	3	2	–	1	1	–	–	–	–	–	–	–	–	–	–					
50s	4	1	3	1	8	1	4	1	3	–	–	3	1	–	–	–	2	1					
Ct/St	16	17/2	11	4	28	1	43/2	8	10	–	4	5	6	2	5/–	1	8	1					

HAMPSHIRE CCC

FIRST–CLASS MATCHES

BOWLING

v. (Match)	AD Mullally	AC Morris	AD Mascarenhas	NC Johnson	SD Udal	CT Tremlett	JEK Schofield	Overs	Total	Byes/Leg-Byes	Wickets	Run outs	
v. **Warwickshire** (Edgbaston) 20–23 April	37-12-77-3	28-6-72-2	27-9-56-1	21-3-100-0				145.4	455	14	10	–	A B
	–	–	–	–				–	–	–	–	–	
v. **Worcestershire** (Southampton Rose Bowl) 9–12 May	28-9-66-2	17-3-39-4	17-7-26-1	4-0-22-0	15-1-62-2			84	236	9	10	–	B
	13-5-23-2	10.5-2-27-4	5-0-20-0	–	16-6-32-4			44.5	108	6	10	–	
v. **Gloucestershire** (Southampton Rose Bowl) 16–19 May	18.4-6-41-5	8-2-20-0	9-2-22-0	8-4-15-1	9-2-30-3			52.4	133	5	10	1	
	27.1-10-59-3	25-6-74-4	17-5-34-2	7-2-31-0	26-6-60-1			102.1	272	14	10	–	
v. **Derbyshire** (Derby) 25–28 May	26.4-10-52-5	20-6-62-2	21-3-85-1	–	33.5-13-90-2			102.4	297	6	10	–	C
	21-8-46-2	17-5-39-0	17.3-5-43-1	–	38-16-74-7			93.3	215	13	10	–	
v. **Sussex** (Southampton Rose Bowl) 30 May–2 June	28-10-71-1	33-14-73-1	31.3-6-104-1	–	55-8-167-2			166.3	500	13	7	1	C D
	–	6-2-13-0	13-5-27-0	–	15-7-33-0			67	179	8	0	–	C D E F
v. **Middlesex** (Southgate) 13–16 June		22.5-4-62-2	26-5-69-3	6-0-23-0	49-10-117-3	26-6-64-2		133.5	380	25	10	–	C
		–	–	–	–	–		–	–	–	–	–	
v. **Durham** (Southampton Rose Bowl) 20–23 June		16.2-2-53-1	15-1-41-1	12-3-45-2	18-5-75-3	21-8-43-3		82.2	266	9	10	–	
		10-2-34-1	13-5-22-2	6-1-27-2	10-1-38-1	12-5-34-4		51	163	8	10	–	
v. **Derbyshire** (Southampton Rose Bowl) 29 June–1 July	14-3-30-4	11-1-39-1	6-0-18-0	6.3-1-20-4	11-4-29-1			48.3	140	4	10	–	
	21-5-46-1	13-0-38-0	20.3-5-60-6	11-2-30-0	25-4-65-2			90.3	244	5	10	1	
v. **Sussex** (Hove) 6–7 July	20-4-75-3	19-2-68-3	11.3-3-38-2	15-0-49-1	10-1-28-0	7-1-28-1		82.3	302	16	10	–	
	–	–	–	–	–	–		–	–	–	–	–	
v. **Nottinghamshire** (Southampton Rose Bowl) 18–21 July	15-3-45-2	9-1-42-3	10-2-28-1	5.3-0-23-1	3-0-14-0	13-4-47-3		55.3	209	10	10	–	
	19-2-68-5	15-4-40-1	4-0-11-0	3-1-13-1	3-2-1-0	9.5-4-15-3		54.5	152	3	10	–	C
v. **Australians** (Southampton Rose Bowl) 28–30 July	11.4-3-18-5		8-2-117-1	4-0-25-0	1-0-6-1		6-2-25-3	30.4	97	6	10	–	
	8-3-20-0		1.5-0-8-0	16-4-50-2	47.1-10-149-4		28.1-3-106-2	109.1	389	18	9	–	C
v. **Gloucestershire** (Cheltenham) 1–4 August	14-5-43-0	20-1-82-1		20-6-55-3	32-9-76-4	16.3-5-68-2		102.3	334	10	10	–	
	14-4-26-1	13-2-52-0		10.5-1-58-1	25-4-85-3	2-0-15-1		64.5	245	9	6	–	
v. **Warwickshire** (Southampton Rose Bowl) 7–10 August	32-10-90-8	25-8-60-1		20-3-57-0	17-6-50-0	15-3-46-1		109	308	5	10	–	
	–	–		–	–	–		–	–	–	–	–	
v. **Durham** (Chester-le-Street) 17–20 August		22-2-84-4	27-12-56-3	10-0-29-0	12-2-46-0	9-1-41-0	16-2-52-2	96	323	15	9	–	
		20-11-39-5	14-3-46-1	18-5-45-0	13.1-3-33-3	–	12-5-28-1	78.1	202	12	10	–	C
v. **Worcestershire** (Worcester) 22–25 August		12-2-63-1	16-6-37-1	18-3-58-3	26-10-50-3		9-4-23-1	81	247	16	10	1	
		13-1-51-1	18.4-6-45-3	13-0-56-1	18-5-88-1		18-1-51-4	80.4	306	15	10	–	
v. **Middlesex** (Southampton Rose Bowl) 5–17 September	18-9-23-1	9-0-33-2	16-5-26-6	3-1-11-1	4-1-4-0			50	101	4	10	–	
	24.3-7-70-3	22-5-56-1	17-11-21-3	11-2-50-0	18-5-50-3			92.3	253	6	10	–	
v. **Nottinghamshire** (Trent Bridge) 12–15 September	31.3-12-74-5	30-9-108-5	8-2-28-0	4-0-19-0	3-1-10-0			76.3	245	6	10	–	
	5-1-22-1	5-3-5-1	9-2-27-0	–	13-1-48-1			59	314	7	7	–	E F G H

	AD Mullally	AC Morris	AD Mascarenhas	NC Johnson	SD Udal	CT Tremlett	JEK Schofield
Overs	447.1	472	399.3	252.5	566.1	131.2	89.1
Maidens	141	106	112	42	143	37	17
Runs	1085	1428	1015	911	1610	401	285
Wickets	58	51	40	23	54	20	13
Average	**18.70**	**28.00**	**25.37**	**39.60**	**29.81**	**20.05**	**21.92**

A   JRC Hamblin 18-1-88-1
B   JP Stephenson 14.4-3-48-3; 3-0-12-1
C   GW White 1.1-0-2-0; 8-0-29-1; 4-0-17-0; 4-0-20-0; 1-0-1-0; 8-0-38-1; 1-0-2-0
D   LR Prittipaul 11-0-43-0; 14-1-43-0
E   WS Kendall 14-2-32-0; 2-0-4-0
F   AN Aymes 1-0-6-0; 11-0-101-2
G   DA Kenway 8-0-66-1
H   JD Francis 6-0-34-1

FIELDING

45   AN Aymes (43ct,2st)
28   NC Johnson
19   GW White (17ct,2st)
16   DA Kenway
11   WS Kendall
10   AC Morris
8   JS Laney, AD Mascarenhas
6   LR Prittipaul
5   I Brunnschweiler, SD Udal
4   AD Mullally, RA Smith
2   CT Tremlett
1   JD Francis, JEK Schofield, JP Stephenson

KENT CCC

FIRST–CLASS MATCHES

BATTING

	DP Fulton	RWT Key	ET Smith	MJ Walker	PA Nixon	MA Ealham	JB Hockley	MV Fleming	MM Patel	DD Masters	MJ Saggers	JM Golding	MJ McCague	Amjad Khan	BJ Trott	DJ Cullinan	GO Jones	A Symonds	JC Tredwell	Extras	Total	Wickets	Result	Points
v. Cambridge University CCE (Cambridge 16–18 April)	120	1	42	15	55*	13	17	1	0*	–	–									35	299	7		
	–	67	48	4	–	0*	11	11*	–	–										26	167	4	D	
v. Surrey (Oval 20–23 April)	111	101	2	105	22	11	23	35*	27	–	7*									12	456	8		
																							D	12
v. Yorkshire (Canterbury 25–28 April)	31	17	19	12	10	22	13	4	0	2*	1									11	142	10		
	15	98	103*	33	2	0	6	1	27	6	4									23	318	10	L	3
v. Pakistanis (Canterbury 12–14 May)	3	119	0	98	42*	–	0	–	–	–	21*	–	–	–						30	313	5		
	40	21	17	–	–	–	6*	–	–	–										10	94	3	D	
v. Somerset (Taunton 16–19 May)	140	0	48	–	21	–	16	7	0*	0	21					57	5			28	343	10		
																							D	10
v. Glamorgan (Swansea 25–28 May)	78	1	0	112*	0	15	25	0	3	–	–				0	2				16	252	10		
																							D	9
v. Essex (Tunbridge Wells 30 May–1 June)	179	48	12	124	34*	–	–	–	–							63				58	518	5		
																							W	20
v. Yorkshire (Headingley 6–9 June)	24	58	84	9	1	–	0	3	2*	–	3	15			0					13	212	10		
	42	38	42	19	34	–	9	5*	2	–	30	0			0					29	250	10	L	4
v. Glamorgan (Maidstone 13–16 June)	4	97	74	5	16	–	29	10	14	–	27*	0			13					15	304	10		
	45	21	116	53	17	–	0	46	8	–	5	30			1*					16	358	10	D	
v. Leicestershire (Canterbury 20–22 June)	19	28	5	26	12	–	26	29	34	–	1	1			4*					25	210	10		
	107	0	33	26	12	–	26	35	0	–	1	2*			0					11	253	10	L	3
v. Lancashire (Canterbury 4–6 July)	65	13	15	11	82	10	–	23	3	–	61*	–			10			31		24	348	10		
	17	83	59	7	46*	–	1	1	0	–	–				0			10		13	240	10	L	17
v. Essex (Southend 18–20 July)	70	123	7	18	3	44	–	14*	17*	–								33		24	353	7		
																							W	19
v. Leicestershire (Leicester 27–30 July)	21	5	19	120*	31	5	–	59	–	–	2				13			48	10	57	390	10		
	22	36	107	12	29*	14	–	15	–	–	3*							125	–	40	403	7	W	19
v. Somerset (Canterbury 1–4 August)	208*	50	8	81	8	0	–	3*	–	–	16							56		21	451	7		
	104*	20	19	–	–	–	–	–	–	–								59		3	205	3	D	12
v. Northamptonshire (Northampton 8–11 August)	197	20	91	15*	–	–	–	–	–	–								131		10	464	4		
																							D	12
v. Surrey (Canterbury 16–19 August)	25	79	37	4	66*	–	15	38	2	–	–	4			0			0		31	301	10		
																							D	10
v. Northamptonshire (Canterbury 5–8 September)	9	4	0	1	4	2	–	0	32	–	0				11*			23		22	108	10		
	196	1	40	35	17	153*	–	33	30	–	16*							4		51	576	8	D	7
v. Lancashire (Old Trafford 12–15 September)	0	132	7	40	87*	7	–	9	5	–	3				5			43		39	377	10		
																							D	8

	DP Fulton	RWT Key	ET Smith	MJ Walker	PA Nixon	MA Ealham	JB Hockley	MV Fleming	MM Patel	DD Masters	MJ Saggers	JM Golding	MJ McCague	Amjad Khan	BJ Trott	DJ Cullinan	GO Jones	A Symonds	JC Tredwell
Matches	18	18	18	17	18	12	7	17	17	4	17	5	2	1	14	3	1	8	1
Innings	27	28	28	25	24	15	13	23	19	3	20	2	1	–	13	3	1	12	1
Not Out	2	0	1	3	7	2	1	5	3	2	5	2	0	–	3	0	0	0	0
Highest Score	208*	132	116	124	87*	153*	29	59	38	6	61*	30	4	–	13	63	5	131	10
Runs	1892	1281	1054	985	651	299	166	393	247	8	185	90	4	–	57	122	5	563	10
Average	75.68	45.75	39.03	44.77	38.29	23	13.83	21.83	15.43	8	12.33	15	4	–	5.7	40.66	5	46.91	10
100s	9	4	3	4	–	1	–	–	–	–	–	–	–	–	–	–	–	2	–
50s	3	7	4	3	4	–	–	1	–	–	1	–	–	–	–	2	–	2	–
Ct/St	27	7	5	9	44/4	8	6	6	9	2	1	2	–	–	–	3	–	13	–

KENT CCC

FIRST-CLASS MATCHES
BOWLING

	MJ Saggers	DD Masters	MA Ealham	MM Patel	MV Fleming	BJ Trott	JM Golding	A Symonds	Overs	Total	Byes/Leg-Byes	Wickets	Run outs	
v. Cambridge University CCE	13-4-17-1	11-4-14-2	11-5-12-2	23-11-34-3	10.4-6-17-1				77.4	129	10	10	-	A
(Cambridge) 16–18 April	4-2-7-0	7-2-14-0	2.5-0-7-0	11-4-14-1	8-6-5-1				34.5	53	2	2	-	A
v. Surrey	25-3-106-2	22-1-104-0	24-5-80-3	38.3-7-117-4	16-3-55-0				125.3	473	11	10	1	
(Oval) 20–23 April	-								-	-	-	-	-	
v. Yorkshire	33-11-64-3	26-6-52-3	25-7-72-3	3-1-14-0	25-6-67-1				113	285	6	10	-	A
(Canterbury) 25–28 April	10-0-37-2	4-0-25-0	5-2-16-1	9.4-0-46-2	9-0-43-0				-	-	-	-	-	
v. Pakistanis				14-0-83-0		20-4-66-0	12-2-32-0		70.2	307	7	1	-	A B C
(Canterbury) 12–14 May				-		-	-		-	-	-	-	-	
v. Somerset	15.1-3-36-3	10-1-45-1		19-4-29-2	16-4-35-1		10-1-23-3		70.1	184	16	10	-	
(Taunton) 16–19 May	26-4-68-1	11-2-32-1		32-8-67-0	23-3-74-4		28-8-70-1		125	334	9	7	-	D E F
v. Glamorgan	22-6-70-5		12-3-19-0	32-14-38-2	8.2-2-20-2	18-1-65-1			92.2	238	26	10	-	
(Swansea) 25–28 May	-								-	-	-	-	-	
v. Essex	17-8-32-1		18-6-46-0	31-10-77-2	14.1-6-44-1	26-7-65-5			117.1	298	10	10	-	D
(Tunbridge Wells) 30 May–1 June	12-5-30-3		4-2-3-0	13-7-11-0	2-1-5-0	9.5-4-13-6			40.5	68	6	10	1	
v. Yorkshire	34-6-125-1			26.5-5-74-3	21-3-53-4	31-9-98-1	14-3-51-0		126.5	413	12	10	1	
(Headingley) 6–9 June	6-1-30-0			-	-	6-1-22-1	-		12	53	1	1	-	
v. Glamorgan	16-2-60-2			34-10-72-2	16-4-57-3	16-1-61-1	2.3-0-8-1		97.3	286	7	10	-	A
(Maidstone) 13–16 June	10-2-38-0			10-2-39-0	-	8-3-31-0	5-0-28-0		44	203	2	0	-	A G
v. Leicestershire	34-12-94-4			47-8-140-1	23-1-101-0	23-4-96-1	23-3-118-1		162	612	19	8	1	A G
(Canterbury) 20–22 June	-			-	-	-	-		-	-	-	-	-	
v. Lancashire	13-4-33-1		16-2-64-6		3-0-11-0	14-3-58-1	7.2-0-33-2		53.2	214	15	10	-	
(Canterbury) 4–6 July	7-2-20-1		8-3-20-3	4-1-12-0	-	15-3-43-5	-		34	106	11	9	-	
v. Essex	14-5-24-1		14-8-13-5	11-4-22-1	6-0-11-0	13.5-4-27-3	1-0-3-0		59.5	107	7	10	-	
(Southend) 18–20 July	11.1-4-24-5		7-2-13-0	16-5-24-1	2-0-9-1	11-1-32-3			47.1	114	12	19	-	
v. Leicestershire	28.1-5-92-6		17-5-53-0		18-2-66-0	24-4-99-2	19-2-61-0		117.1	425	7	10	-	G
(Leicester) 27–30 July	19-3-85-3		23-9-52-1		11-1-39-0	17-0-64-2	6-1-23-0		98	365	7	7	-	G H
v. Somerset	26-6-72-2		14-2-38-0	43.2-12-119-8	9-1-31-0	11-0-46-0	1-0-13-0		104.2	336	17	10	-	
(Canterbury) 1–4 August	5-0-24-0		-	22-13-25-4	-	8-1-33-1	13-4-28-3		48	113	3	8	-	
v. Northamptonshire	22-3-76-3		9-3-31-0	15-3-36-2	22-4-58-1	23-4-94-3	13-4-38-0		104	355	22	10	1	
(Northampton) 8–11 August	-		-	-	-	-	3-2-4-0		5	13	0	0	-	G
v. Surrey	20.2-4-58-4			20-7-42-1	11-1-46-1	15-4-37-0	10-2-35-3		86.2	258	4	10	-	C
(Canterbury) 16–19 August	15-3-37-3			9-2-30-0	9-1-20-1	16-2-48-3	7-1-21-0		64	193	9	8	-	C
v. Northamptonshire	28-6-98-3		-	13-6-30-0	16-3-39-0	27.4-3-89-5	11-2-38-0		115.4	357	16	10	-	G
(Canterbury) 5–8 September	17-1-77-3		-	27-14-33-1	3.3-1-4-0	13.3-2-37-3	15-5-36-2		76	199	12	9	-	
v. Lancashire	6.4-3-10-1		-	-		6-3-11-0	-		12.4	21	0	1	-	
(Old Trafford) 12–15 September	-		-	-		-			-	-	-	-	-	

Overs	509.3	91	226.5	54.2	304	372.5	94.3	106.2
Maidens	118	16	63	18	59	68	17	23
Runs	1544	286	574	128	891	123	330	333
Wickets	64	7	25	4	22	47	6	10
Average	24.12	40.85	22.96	30.70	41.36	26.27	55.00	33.30

A   JB Hockley 9-1-25-1; 2-1-4-0; 1-0-10-0; 7-0-38-0; 13-5-21-1; 7-1-48-0; 7-0-30-0
B   Amjad Khan 8-2-46-1
C   MJ McCague 9-2-35-0; 10-1-36-1; 8-2-28-1
D   DJ Cullinan 3-2-5-0; 11-4-24-1
E   RWT Key 1-0-5-0
F   GO Jones 1-0-4-0
G   MJ Walker 4-1-17-0; 5-2-14-0; 3-0-9-1; 3-0-8-0; 2-0-9-0; 3-0-12-1
H   DP Fulton 1-0-2-0

FIELDING

48	PA Nixon (44ct,4st)
27	DP Fulton
13	A Symonds
9	MM Patel, MJ Walker
8	MA Ealham
7	RWT Key
6	MV Fleming, JB Hockley
5	ET Smith
3	BJ Trott
2	JM Golding, DD Masters
1	GO Jones, MJ Saggers

LANCASHIRE CCC

FIRST-CLASS MATCHES

BATTING

	RC Driver	MJ Chilton	JP Crawley	A Flintoff	NH Fairbrother	JC Scuderi	WK Hegg	G Chapple	PJ Martin	MP Smethurst	G Keedy	MA Atherton	M Muralitharan	CP Schofield	TW Roberts	KW Hogg	JJ Haynes	G Yates	J Wood	GD Lloyd	Extras	Total	Wickets	Result	Pts
v. Somerset (Taunton) 20–23 April	19	53	14	19	179*	48	6	0	3	7	8										22	378	10		
	-	-	-	-	-	-	-	-	-	-	-										-	-	-	W	1
v. Surrey (Old Trafford) 25–28 April	-	-	-	-	-	-	-	-	-	-	-										-	-	-	D	
v. Leicestershire (Leicester) 9–11 May	1	23	8	45	30	35*	0	0	3			29	14								11	199	10		
	35	11	53	1	15	7	44	5	6			12	1*								14	204	10	L	
v. Glamorgan (Old Trafford) 16–19 May	-	-	-	-	-	-	-	-	-												-	-	-	D	
v. Northamptonshire (Northampton) 30 May–2 June	9	104	20	17	23	23	31	38*				0	4	3							19	291	10		
	2	25	24	14	33	107*	72*					-	15	0							13	305	7	W	1
v. Leicestershire (Old Trafford) 6–9 June		8	0	0	101	46	51	8	8		6*	48	1								15	292	10		
		13	50	43	9*	4*							39								6	164	10	W	1
v. Durham University CCE (Durham Racecourse) 13–16 June	16	16		120					0	0				62	17	19	30	57	15*		20	372	10		
	-	-																			-	-	-	D	
v. Essex (Old Trafford) 19–22 June		9	1	18	19	11	133	12	19		17*	160	14								18	431	10		
		0	21*									24*									8	53	1	W	
v. Surrey (Oval) 29 June–2 July			43	40	1	3	74*	6	11			0		9			57			3	29	276	10		
			84*	34	26*							0					9			-	17	170	2	D	
v. Kent (Canterbury) 4–6 July		35	13	12	39*	0	22		5	0		21					7		25		35	214	10		
		8	3	23	33	absent	3		0	7*		10					0		8		11	106	9	L	
v. Somerset (Old Trafford) 19–21 July		9	8	6	22	8	155	16			20*			58			13		3		6	324	10		
		18	absent	45	0	9	4	0			0*			23			11		8		8	126	9	L	
v. Yorkshire (Headingley) 27–30 July		0	73	12		56	76	33	0		12*	17		55					12	5	27	373	10		
		2	113	21		7	14	0	51*		4	1		34					35	2	32	314	10	L	
v. Glamorgan (Colwyn Bay) 1–4 August	9	0	0	34	158	34	13	64	18*		5*			40							27	402	9		
	2	83	10	68	23	11	14	0*						3*							11	225	7	D	1
v. Yorkshire (Old Trafford) 7–10 August		10	1	52	15	78	35		7	1*				8					3		27	242	10		
		74	8	43	0	26	7		1*	1*				5					3		18	188	10	L	
v. Northamptonshire (Old Trafford) 15–18 August		46	280	38	51	89	75*	2*	-					2							17	600	6		
		30	68	0	44	61*	8	11	-					1				8*			12	243	7	D	1
v. Essex (Colchester) 22–25 August		98	0	18	132	14	13					0		80*			6		15	9					
		-	-	-	-	-	-					-		-			-		-	-				L	2
v. Kent (Old Trafford) 12–15 September	9*	3	9*									-		-			-		-	-				L	

	RC Driver	MJ Chilton	JP Crawley	A Flintoff	NH Fairbrother	JC Scuderi	WK Hegg	G Chapple	PJ Martin	MP Smethurst	G Keedy	MA Atherton	M Muralitharan	CP Schofield	TW Roberts	KW Hogg	JJ Haynes	G Yates	J Wood	GD Lloyd
Matches	5	14	14	14	12	12	13	13	9	5	13	4	7	9	2	1	5	2	8	3
Innings	8	24	24	23	19	17	20	19	12	8	15	8	8	14	3	1	8	2	10	4
Not Out	0	1	2	1	4	2	4	3	3	1	8	1	1	2	0	0	1	1	1	0
Highest Score	35	104	280	120	179*	89	133	155	51*	7	20*	160	21	80*	17	19	57	57	35	9
Runs	93	684	898	686	939	444	782	497	169	29	81	330	70	390	20	19	133	65	127	19
Average	11.62	29.73	40.81	31.18	62.6	29.6	48.87	31.06	18.77	4.14	11.57	47.14	10	32.5	6.66	19	16.62	65	14.11	4.75
100s	-	1	2	1	4	-	2	1	-	-	-	1	-	-	-	-	-	-	-	-
50s	-	4	5	2	1	3	5	2	1	-	-	4	-	-	-	1	1	-	-	-
Ct/St	5	10	4	17	16	2	35/3	3	2	-	6	4	4	8	1	-	7/-	2	-	3

LANCASHIRE CCC

FIRST–CLASS MATCHES

BOWLING

	PJ Martin	G Chapple	MP Smethurst	JC Scuderi	A Flintoff	G Keedy	M Muralitharan	CP Schofield	J Wood	Overs	Total	Byes/Leg-Byes	Wickets	Run outs
v. Somerset	16-3-57-1	17.5-9-46-6	12-3-36-0	10-1-40-1	6-1-18-1	-				61.5	204	7	10	1
(Taunton) 20–23 April	21-7-55-3	17-4-41-1	14-5-32-3	11-3-24-1	5.1-2-7-2	-				68.1	170	11	10	-
v. Surrey	-	-	-	-	-	-				-	-	-	-	-
(Old Trafford) 25–28 April	-	-	-	-	-	-				-	-	-	-	-
v. Leicestershire	13-2-53-1	16.3-4-40-5	15-3-60-2	3-0-25-0			25-10-56-2			72.3	240	6	10	-
(Leicester) 9–11 May	27-9-52-5	15-4-38-1	4-0-21-0	-			37.2-13-56-4			83.2	169	2	10	-
v. Glamorgan	-	-	-	-	-	-				-	-	-	-	-
(Old Trafford) 16–19 May	-	-	-							-	-	-	-	-
v. Northamptonshire	36-9-95-3	23.1-6-77-4			-		49-9-116-2	26-6-86-1		136.1	398	9	10	- A B
(Northampton) 30 May–2 June	15-3-60-2	25-5-60-5			-		33-15-49-3	5-0-9-0		79	194	14	10	-
v. Leicestershire	17.5-9-32-3	18-2-49-3		-	13-1-36-3	3-1-3-0	22-2-75-1			73.5	202	7	10	-
(Old Trafford) 6–9 June	27-9-64-4	5-1-17-0			8-1-45-0	11-1-38-0	40-17-74-6			91	251	13	10	1
v. Durham University CCE			18-4-48-0		9-4-23-0	18.4-9-36-1		18-3-53-3	8.2-2-29-0	104	251	9	10	1 C D E
(Durham Racecourse) 13–16 June			3-0-8-0		-	-		-		6	21	0	0	- C
v. Essex	14-6-37-1	10.5-1-27-1		-	3-1-5-0	38-13-72-2	48-22-53-6			113.5	226	32	10	-
(Old Trafford) 19–22 June	11.5-4-35-2	16-4-55-3		1-0-4-0	10-0-24-0	22-4-52-0	39-14-70-4			99.5	257	17	10	1
v. Surrey	19-3-56-2	15-2-45-2		4-1-5-0	15-2-31-1	7-4-16-0	39.4-12-81-5			99.4	248	14	10	-
(Oval) 29 June–2 July	20.5-5-58-2	9-0-45-1		5-0-15-0	18-6-44-1	19-0-68-1	55-23-72-3			121.5	320	28	9	1
v. Kent		22-1-87-0		20.4-8-48-3	15-3-27-1	3-1-8-0	30-11-69-3		25-4-97-3	115.4	348	7	10	-
(Canterbury) 4–6 July		5-1-30-0		7-2-14-1	11-2-27-2	20-3-59-1	28.5-5-70-6		12-2-24-0	84.5	240	11	10	- E
v. Somerset	21-7-77-1	21-5-60-1			6-1-30-0	34.3-10-73-5		29-5-76-1	15-1-61-1	126.3	385	8	10	1
(Old Trafford) 19–21 July	4-0-19-0	4-0-12-0			-	7-1-21-0		3-1-10-0		18	66	4	0	1
v. Yorkshire	28-4-113-2	22-7-83-5		1-0-15-0	18.2-3-55-2	28-3-103-0		22-6-67-0	15-0-84-1	134.2	531	11	10	-
(Headingley) 27–30 July	5-1-13-0	4-0-23-0		-	7-1-27-0	10.5-1-67-3		5-3-17-0	2-1-10-0	-	-	-	-	-
v. Glamorgan	26-5-93-1	23-7-68-2		5-1-21-0	17-1-79-1	35.2-7-98-5		26-6-83-1		134.2	479	19	10	- A
(Colwyn Bay) 1–4 August	-	13-4-30-2		5-0-15-0	8-2-28-0	29-5-82-3		16-3-55-2	-	71	220	10	7	-
v. Yorkshire		19-1-92-2	10-0-49-2	4-0-18-0	19-2-72-1	23-5-110-4		16-2-69-0	9-1-49-0	100	467	8	9	-
(Old Trafford) 7–10 August		-	-	-	-	-		-		-	-	-	-	-
v. Northamptonshire		19-4-70-0		7-1-40-0	16-4-58-1	33-2-134-2		21-3-72-2	13-1-45-1	128.5	495	11	8	- D
(Old Trafford) 15–18 August		2-0-7-0		-	-	3-3-0-0			3.3-0-6-1	8.3	13	0	1	-
v. Essex		24-6-71-4		18-11-17-2	11-3-12-0	11-1-24-0		18.1-5-37-1	10-2-40-2	97.1	236	17	10	- B
(Colchester) 22–25 August		25-9-65-3		19-5-32-1	19-5-48-3	23-3-53-0		28-7-73-1	14-1-53-0	129	334	8	8	- F
v. Kent		15-2-53-2		-	11-3-40-0	7.5-0-33-1	38-6-130-5	19-2-50-2	13-1-42-0	103.5	377	29	10	-
(Old Trafford) 12–15 September		-		-	-	-	-	-	-	-	-	-	-	-

	PJ Martin	G Chapple	MP Smethurst	JC Scuderi	A Flintoff	G Keedy	M Muralitharan	CP Schofield	J Wood
Overs	322.3	379.2	103	115.4	245.3	387.1	484.5	252.1	139.5
Maidens	86	87	17	33	48	76	159	52	16
Runs	969	1174	371	318	736	1150	971	757	540
Wickets	33	53	7	9	19	28	50	14	9
Average	**29.36**	**22.15**	**53.00**	**35.33**	**38.73**	**41.07**	**19.42**	**54.07**	**60.00**

A   RC Driver; 2-0-15-0; 2-0-18-0
B   NH Fairbrother 1-0-2-0; 5-1-18-1
C   KW Hogg 9-3-17-3; 3-0-13-0
D   G Yates 19-6-23-2; 19.5-4-65-2
E   MJ Chilton 4-0-13-0; 1-0-5-0
F   JP Crawley 1-0-2-0

FIELDING

38	WK Hegg (35ct,3st)
17	A Flintoff
16	NH Fairbrother
10	MJ Chilton
8	CP Schofield
7	JJ Haynes
6	G Keedy
5	RC Driver
4	MA Atherton, JP Crawley, M Muralitharan
3	G Chapple, GD Lloyd
2	PJ Martin, JC Scuderi, G Yates
1	TW Roberts

LEICESTERSHIRE CCC

FIRST–CLASS MATCHES

BATTING

	VJ Wells	ND Burns	IJ Sutcliffe	BF Smith	Aftab Habib	DJ Marsh	DL Maddy	JM Dakin	J Ormond	MJA Whiley	DE Malcolm	DI Stevens	CD Crowe	AS Wright	PAJ DeFreitas	OAC Banks	SAJ Boswell	P Griffiths	TR Ward	Shahid Afridi	RP Davis	Extras	Total	Wickets	Result	Points
v. Essex	19	0	21	15	5	13*	1	16	0	0	1											13	104	10		
(Leicester) 20–22 April	2	21	21	26	absent	61	23	28	4	1	9*											9	205	9	L	3
v. Lancashire	34	9*	22	1	0	71	44	10		0	1	28										20	240	10		
(Leicester) 9–11 May	0	39	29	14	1	50*	20	3		0	0	7										6	169	10	W	16
v. Surrey		45	1	28	33	0	8	69	5		0*	0	42									15	246	10		
(Oval) 16–19 May		7*	10	12	23	15	6	–	–		17*	–										4	94	5	D	8
v. Pakistanis		0	55	7			0				17	2	0	0	0	4	4*					7	96	10		
(Leicester) 24–25 May		28*	38	18			0				24	0	30	1	4	0	1					28	172	10	L	–
v. Somerset	2	0	21	11	138*	15		11		0	63	0						93				33	387	10		
(Leicester) 30 May–2 June	86	33*	58	66	2	1		–		–	14	3*						119				8	390	7	D	11
v. Lancashire	12	25	1	35		28	57*	12	4		4	0						3				21	202	10		
(Old Trafford) 6–9 June	5	2	24	33		38	40	35	20		4*	2						11				37	251	10	L	6
v. Northamptonshire	2	10	1	39		25	9				4*	7	6		15			50				18	185	10		
(Leicester) 13–16 June	–	–	55	7*		–	–				–	–	–		–			160*				11	233	1	W	15
v. Kent	138	51	64	110	55	72	0		34*	1*	–				59*			0				29	612	8		
(Canterbury) 20–22 June	–	–	–	–	–	–	–		–	–	–				–			–				–	–	–	W	20
v. Yorkshire	17	33	40	0	25	4	4	18	2*		8				12							11	174	10		
(Headingley) 29 June–1 July	4	31	9	26	5	0	6	4	1*		1*				2							10	99	10	L	2
v. Surrey	14	45	0	6	3	1	1		14*		3				22			46				10	165	10		
(Leicester) 4–7 July	32	66*	25	179	5	82	0		–		–				3			42				38	472	8	D	7
v. Glamorgan	34	24	203	117	72*		6	6			0				0			109	2			15	588	10		
(Cardiff) 18–21 July	–	–	–	–	–		–	–			–				–			–	–			–	–	–	W	20
v. Kent	1	60	4	111	153		5		42	1*	8							28	5			7	425	10		
(Leicester) 27–30 July	0	64*	5	5	5		111		10*	–	–							110	42			13	365	7	L	8
v. Essex		50*	165	37	124		55	10			1			0	31			25	7			54	559	10		
(Chelmsford) 1–4 August		–	–	–	–		–	–			–			–	–			–	–			–	–	–	D	12
v. Somerset		1	9	28	24		15		5		50	29					16*	20	69			11	277	10		
(Taunton) 7–10 August		–	13	180*	149		6		–		–	28*						11	–			13	400	4	D	9
v. Yorkshire	15*	25	9	2	7		27		1		1	7			8			4				15	121	10		
(Leicester) 15–18 August	133	0	5	2	12		25		39*		16	11			97			0				30	370	10	L	3
v. Northamptonshire	6	69	64	29	74*		1				2				4			2	164	51		18	484	10		
(Northampton) 23–26 August	5	13	17	10	0		10				0*				2			20	6	0		2	85	10	L	8
v. Glamorgan	67	111	9	68	4		25		24		13*	8	18					5				20	372	10		
(Leicester) 7–9 September	–	–	6*	–	–		–		–		–	–	–					14*				0	20	0	W	19
Matches	13	17	17	17	13	9	17	7	11	3	16	8	7	1	9	1	2	1	12	5	1					
Innings	22	28	31	30	21	16	29	11	16	5	21	14	10	2	14	2	3	2	21	7	2					
Not Out	1	7	1	2	2	3	1	0	5	1	7	2	1	0	1	0	1	1	2	0	0					
Highest Score	138	111	203	180*	153	138*	111	69	42	1*	50	63	42	30	97	4	16*	4*	160*	164	51					
Runs	628	862	1004	1222	779	600	521	211	216	2	126	260	73	30	256	4	20	5	872	295	51					
Average	29.9	41.04	33.46	43.64	41	46.15	18.6	19.18	19.63	0.5	9	21.66	8.11	15	19.69	2	10	5	45.89	42.14	25.5					
100s	2	1	2	5	3	1	1	–	–	–	–	–	–	–	–	–	–	–	4	1	–					
50s	2	6	5	2	3	5	2	1	–	–	1	1	–	–	2	–	–	–	2	1	1					
Ct/St	8	65/3	5	19	8	13	15	1	2	–	1	2	4	–	–	–	2	–	7	6	2					

LEICESTERSHIRE CCC

FIRST-CLASS MATCHES

BOWLING

	DE Malcolm	JM Dakin	VJ Wells	J Ormond	DL Maddy	DJ Marsh	CD Crowe	SAJ Boswell	PAJ DeFreitas	Shahid Afridi	RP Davis	Overs	Total	Byes/Leg-Byes	Wickets	Run outs
v. Essex (Leicester) 20–22 April	27-7-54-3	22-5-54-1	12-4-35-0	33.1-11-71-5	5-2-9-0	8-0-23-0						124.1	318	18	10	- A
	-	-	-	-	-							-	-	-	-	-
v. Lancashire (Leicester) 9–11 May	28-6-78-5		17.5-4-69-3	10-2-18-2		7-4-6-0						77	199	3	10	- A B
	19-2-70-2	10.5-1-40-3	12-4-26-1		8-0-26-2	11-2-35-2						60.5	204	7	10	-
v. Surrey (Oval) 16–19 May	18-3-61-1	2-0-13-0			25-10-55-4	1-0-5-0	17-5-47-5					63	190	9	10	1
	-	-			-							-	-	-	-	-
v. Pakistanis (Leicester) 24–25 May					13-4-27-2		10-0-34-1	28.3-5-87-3	18-4-41-2			99.3	294	13	10	- C D E
					-		-	-	-			-	-	-	-	-
v. Somerset (Leicester) 30 May–2 June	26-2-96-4		14-4-28-0	30.2-3-94-3	15-5-30-1	17-4-45-1	20-5-60-1					122.2	374	21	10	-
	22-5-73-3		7-2-19-1	27-5-83-2	9-0-27-1	5-2-9-0	9-3-13-0					83	268	23	8	- E
v. Lancashire (Old Trafford) 6–9 June	13-1-76-1	16-2-53-4	4-0-19-0	27-7-67-3	2-0-16-0	19.2-7-37-2	2-0-17-0					83.2	292	7	10	-
	11-2-39-0	4-2-6-0	-	7-2-28-1		15-1-66-2	5.1-0-21-1					42.1	164	4	4	-
v. Northamptonshire (Leicester) 13–16 June	16.4-3-64-4		8-3-13-0		8-0-28-3	-			16-4-43-3			48.4	159	11	10	-
	16.2-6-46-3		13-1-38-0		21-4-67-5	13-4-33-0	11-6-11-0		19-4-54-2			93.2	257	8	10	-
v. Kent (Canterbury) 20–22 June	23-5-83-4		-	22-8-70-1	4-1-5-0				12.2-2-43-4			61.2	210	9	10	1 A
	12-0-61-1		13-5-36-5	18-2-65-2	10-2-29-1	8-4-17-0			15-3-38-1			76	253	7	10	- A
v. Yorkshire (Headingley) 29 June–1 July	32.2-2-123-5	17-4-60-1	5-2-19-0	28-6-94-1	7-3-22-0	17-3-58-0			27-5-95-3			133.2	500	29	10	-
	-	-	-	-	-				-			-	-	-	-	-
v. Surrey (Leicester) 4–7 July	18-3-63-8		-	12-3-25-0	-	1-1-0-0			7-4-13-2			38	102	1	10	- E
	43-12-124-2		16-2-56-1	30-8-72-2	7-2-21-0	30-11-76-2			23-6-71-2			152	478	54	9	-
v. Glamorgan (Cardiff) 18–21 July	16-5-50-2	13-4-48-1		6-2-20-0				23.3-5-65-6	13-3-22-0			71.3	211	6	10	1
	23-1-98-5	19-1-83-3		4-1-14-0	5-3-13-0			10.1-3-15-2	20-8-52-0			81.1	287	12	10	-
v. Kent (Leicester) 27–30 July	27-6-82-1		7-2-21-1	26.1-6-90-4	13-3-28-1					10-2-48-1		101.1	390	22	10	- E
	10-1-59-0		2-0-2-0	31-7-114-3	22-1-118-3					12-1-53-0		84	403	30	7	1
v. Essex (Chelmsford) 1–4 August	25-3-86-1	0.5-0-1-0			8.1-1-31-0		27-8-74-2		26-6-72-2	30.1-10-84-5		117.1	356	8	10	- E
	17-5-49-2				6-1-30-0		14-3-39-0		12-3-50-1	20-7-45-1		75	236	4	5	-
v. Somerset (Taunton) 7–10 August	10-1-47-1			24-8-71-3	11-0-61-0			17-2-74-3		8-2-31-1		70	298	14	10	2
	-			-	-							-	-	-	-	-
v. Yorkshire (Leicester) 15–18 August	8-2-33-0		18-5-37-3	33-8-66-2	16.5-3-43-3				20-11-41-2	20-3-84-1		96.5	230	10	10	- E
	11-1-43-0		6-1-21-0	45-6-146-5	16.1-1-72-2				27-2-92-0	20-3-92-2		112.1	429	14	8	1 E
v. Northamptonshire (Northampton) 23–26 August	34-5-134-4		-		6.5-1-25-1				34-4-121-2		19-3-88-1	113.5	469	17	10	1
	8-1-27-0		-		3-1-14-0				13-0-80-0		23-4-73-6	67	302	16	8	-
v. Glamorgan (Leicester) 7–9 September	16.5-3-60-3		10-3-24-3	15-4-43-4	8-3-15-0							49.5	146	4	10	-
	15-1-69-3		14-4-52-1	18-5-48-3	12.3-4-47-3	2-0-10-0						61.3	245	19	10	-

	DE Malcolm	JM Dakin	VJ Wells	J Ormond	DL Maddy	DJ Marsh	CD Crowe	SAJ Boswell	PAJ DeFreitas	Shahid Afridi	RP Davis
Overs	546.1	122.3	181	451.4	247.3	152.2	117.1	45.3	303	153.1	41
Maidens	94	23	47	109	45	43	30	7	66	39	7
Runs	1948	427	498	1302	804	410	326	161	934	511	161
Wickets	68	16	18	48	28	9	9	6	34	11	7
Average	**28.64**	**26.68**	**27.66**	**27.12**	**28.71**	**45.55**	**36.22**	**26.83**	**27.47**	**46.45**	**23.00**

A   MJA Whiley 17-4-54-1; 13.1-6-20-0; 16-3-87-1; 7-1-27-0
B   DI Stevens 1-0-5-0; 6-1-23-0
C   P Griffiths 20-7-51-2
D   OAC Banks 9-0-38-0
E   IJ Sutcliffe 1-0-3-0; 4-0-21-1; 3-1-4-0; 2-0-7-1; 6-1-19-1; 1-1-0-0; 1-0-13-0

FIELDING

68   ND Burns (65ct,3st)
19   BF Smith
15   DL Maddy
13   DJ Marsh
8   Aftab Habib, VJ Wells
7   TR Ward
6   Shahid Afridi
5   IJ Sutcliffe
4   CD Crowe
2   SAJ Boswell, RP Davis, J Ormond, DI Stevens
1   JM Dakin, DE Malcolm

MIDDLESEX CCC

FIRST–CLASS MATCHES

BATTING

Match	AJ Strauss	MA Roseberry	SP Fleming	OA Shah	BL Hutton	PN Weekes	DC Nash	SJ Cook	ARC Fraser	PCR Tufnell	TF Bloomfield	JP Hewitt	RMS Weston	AW Laraman	CB Keegan	D Alleyne	MJ Brown	EC Joyce	JWM Dalrymple	Extras	Total	Wickets	Result	Points
v. Oxford University CCE (Oxford) 16–18 April	0	5	2	29	133	55	2	10	5	1	0*									27	269	10		
	3	87	30	56	5*	5*	–	–	–	–	–									24	210	4	D	
v. Worcestershire (Lord's) 20–23 April	125	63	42	48	4	0*	0*													20	302	5		
																				–	–	–	D	9
v. Derbyshire (Derby) 25–28 April	38	21*	3	24	8	15	27*													10	146	5		
																				–	–	–	D	7
v. Gloucestershire (Bristol) 9–12 May	0	7	52	5	47	31	50*	4	25	0	0									24	245	10		
	7	10	121*	57	59	9*	–	6												24	293	5	W	16
v. Durham (Chester-le-Street) 16–19 May	8	17	114	190	1	1	19	–	0	0	0*	3								19	386	10		
	3	46	31*	88	4															7	189	4	D	11
v. Nottinghamshire (Lord's) 25–28 May	20		14	58	2	50	56	93*	9	3	0		29							36	370	10		
	78		42	2	0	2	12	16				10*	1							34	197	8	D	11
v. Derbyshire (Southgate) 30 May–1 June	33	21	0	203	139	40	5	30		6	1*			29						36	543	10		
																				–	–	–	W	20
v. Hampshire (Southgate) 13–16 June	33	30	5		6	13	77	22	25	1			135*		0					33	380	10		
																				–	–	–	D	11
v. Warwickshire (Edgbaston) 20–23 June	18	20	67		36	22	6		12	1	11		19		30*					31	273	10		
	44	10rh	92		30	52	9						100		–					22	359	6	W	13
v. Sussex (Lord's) 29 June–2 July	48	44		11	6	7	50		14	11*	4	7	83							41	326	10		
	26	8		0	36*	0*							34							31	135	4	D	10
v. Nottinghamshire (Trent Bridge) 4–7 July	67		151	144	82	21	6		3	0*	0	2	7							44	527	10		
																				–	–	–	D	12
v. Durham (Lord's) 27–29 July	176	0		38	120	2	1		41	0*	0		13		4					29	424	10		
																				–	–	–	W	20
v. Sussex (Hove) 2–5 August	8	20		5	5	64			4	7*	28		25		2	0				40	208	10		
	51	11		0	4	41	0		0	4			4		4*	8				34	161	10	L	3
v. Gloucestershire (Lord's) 8–11 August	37		10	37	35	37		16	1*	5			18		0	3				23	222	10		
	1		4	1	0	0		3	6*	2			40		1	44				17	119	10	L	2
v. Warwickshire (Lord's) 22–25 August	14		102	17		107	103*	14*									0	104	11	30	502	7		
	29	65	0		21	17*											10	7	0*	18	167	6	D	11
v. Hampshire (Southampton Rose Bowl) 5–7 September	56	14	2		1	1		0	0	0*			6		0			11		10	101	10		
	112*	74	1		15	16		5	2	0			18		0			0		10	253	10	L	3
v. Worcestershire (Worcester) 12–15 September	92	1	0		63	1	37*		0		27		106		4			108*		14	349	10		
	83	55	24		45*								34					4		19	368	4	D	11
Matches	17	11	14	15	14	17	15	10	13	16	16	4	10	1	7	2	1	3	1					
Innings	28	17	23	25	22	27	19	11	12	18	16	5	17	1	10	4	2	6	2					
Not Out	1	2	1	0	2	5	5	3	0	7	4	1	1	0	1	0	0	1	1					
Highest Score	176	87	151	203	139	107	103*	93	41	11*	28	10*	135*	29	30*	44	10	108*	11					
Runs	1210	420	1091	1040	786	719	458	236	149	45	85	22	672	29	45	55	10	234	11					
Average	44.81	28	51.95	41.6	39.3	32.68	32.71	29.5	12.41	4.09	7.08	5.5	42	29	5	–	5	46.8	5.5					
100s	3	–	4	3	3	1	1	–	–	–	–	–	3	–	–	–	–	2	–					
50s	6	2	6	4	2	5	4	1	–	–	–	–	1	–	–	–	–	–	–					
	7	9	22	14	20	15	39/4	3	4	–	2	1	5	1	1	4/–	–	5	2					

MIDDLESEX CCC

FIRST-CLASS MATCHES

BOWLING

	TF Bloomfield	ARC Fraser	PCR Tufnell	SJ Cook	PN Weekes	JP Hewitt	CB Keegan	Overs	Total	Byes/Leg-Byes	Wickets	Run outs	
v. Oxford University CCE	21-8-49-3	16-9-23-1	21.3-7-36-2	13-5-23-3	12-5-19-0			93.3	191	17	10	-	A
(Oxford) 16-18 April	7-4-7-0	5-2-5-0	3-2-1-0	9-6-10-3	-			29	45	3	3	-	A
v. Worcestershire	15-2-61-2	29.1-6-70-3	24-10-44-1	20-5-65-0	19-5-42-1			110.1	301	6	8	1	A
(Lord's) 20-23 April	-	-	-	-	-			-	-	-	-	-	
v. Derbyshire	17-3-47-2	22-12-29-1	29.4-10-42-4	20-4-59-3	10-5-11-0			98.4	198	10	10	-	
(Derby) 25-28 April													
v. Gloucestershire	33-7-97-3	26.2-11-52-2	16-3-38-1	19-2-60-3	6-4-10-1			100.2	272	15	10	-	
(Bristol) 9-12 May	22-4-76-1	24-4-75-2	17-5-34-0	12-1-36-0	15-3-34-1			90	265	10	4	-	
v. Durham	10-0-42-1	26-7-56-2	32.5-15-44-3		15-3-54-2	11-1-58-2		95.5	274	15	10	-	B
(Chester-le-Street) 16-19 May	16-4-45-2	16-2-66-1	26.3-4-74-1		10-2-39-0	-		69.3	226	2	6	2	
v. Nottinghamshire	33.5-3-133-5		31-5-83-2	21-3-73-0	11-1-40-0	16-2-95-3		115.5	467	23	10	-	A
(Lord's) 25-28 May	16-2-64-0		26-8-61-5	8-3-24-1	16-5-69-2	3-0-19-0		69	252	15	8	-	
v. Derbyshire	6-2-10-0		27.4-11-44-6	6-2-24-0	24-11-37-4			63.4	132	17	10	-	
(Southgate) 30 May-1 June	9-2-25-1		34.3-5-89-4	4-1-13-0	29.1-8-70-3			81.3	226	0	10	-	C
v. Hampshire		29-10-89-1	46-8-113-2	13-2-49-1	31.1-4-90-5		16-4-57-1	135.1	404	6	10	-	
(Southgate) 13-16 June		3-0-7-0	7-1-20-0	-	5-0-29-0		6-3-5-0	21	61	0	0	-	
v. Warwickshire	22-3-89-4	29.4-11-64-3	24-8-49-2		-	10-2-42-0		85.4	251	7	10	1	
(Edgbaston) 20-23 June	11-2-48-0	24-7-75-3	26-10-57-4		3-0-7-0	16.5-7-52-3		80.5	252	13	10	-	
v. Sussex	18-2-82-1	26.1-10-47-2	22-5-56-2		17-2-42-2	20-2-72-3		106.1	323	9	10	-	A
(Lord's) 29 June-2 July	12-0-59-0	23-7-53-2	20-4-29-1		42-6-108-2	13-1-52-0		110	315	14	6	1	
v. Nottinghamshire	19-4-75-3	16-4-52-0	30-6-79-3		22.4-5-71-3	10-2-34-1		97.4	314	3	10	-	
(Trent Bridge) 4-7 July	23-6-58-5	19.2-3-66-1	11-2-20-1		1-1-0-0	10-0-56-1		64.2	215	15	8	-	
v. Durham	15-3-31-2	9-3-21-0	19-5-41-3		21-6-45-3		10.5-1-44-2	74.5	187	5	10	-	
(Lord's) 27-29 July	11-3-30-1	11-1-33-0	16.2-4-46-5		10-2-41-2		7-4-13-2	55.2	163	0	10	-	
v. Sussex	23-3-87-2		33-7-96-2	25.1-6-57-2	17-7-46-1		16-1-63-1	114.1	351	2	8	-	
(Hove) 2-5 August	18-2-56-1		19-3-59-1	4-1-17-0	5.5-0-25-4		11-4-35-1	57.5	210	18	7	-	
v. Gloucestershire	17-1-95-1	31-7-100-1	31-4-86-0		16-3-36-0		16-2-79-0	111	400	4	3	1	
(Lord's) 8-11 August	-	-	-		-		-						
v. Warwickshire	20.4-0-111-3	37-8-109-1		20-3-96-2	58-6-163-2			167.4	631	11	9	-	B D
(Lord's) 22-25 August	-	-		-	-								
v. Hampshire (Southampton	15-4-37-2	32-14-66-3	8-3-27-1		-		15.2-2-54-4	70.2	191	7	10	-	
Rose Bowl) 5-7 September	11.1-2-44-1	14-2-46-3	12-1-40-0		8-2-18-1		3-0-12-0	48.1	166	6	5	-	
v. Worcestershire	30-2-111-4		23-5-94-1	21-3-77-2	13-3-47-1		26-5-92-2	113	434	13	10	-	
(Worcester) 12-15 September	8-1-40-0		14-3-45-2	3-0-13-0	2-1-5-0		16-3-40-2	48	179	4	4	-	B E F

	TF Bloomfield	ARC Fraser	PCR Tufnell	SJ Cook	PN Weekes	JP Hewitt	CB Keegan
Overs	479.4	469.4	690	218.1	439.5	83	170
Maidens	79	140	166	47	100	8	38
Runs	1709	1204	1721	696	1198	386	588
Wickets	50	32	60	20	40	10	18
Average	34.18	37.62	28.68	34.80	29.95	38.60	32.66

A   BL Hutton 10-2-24-1; 5-2-19-0; 3-0-13-0; 3-0-20-0; 3-0-15-0
B   OA Shah 1-1-0-0; 2-0-28-0; 2-0-10-0
C   AW Laraman 4.5-1-20-2
D   JWM Dalrymple 30-1-113-1
E   SP Fleming 2-0-19-0
F   AJ Strauss 1-0-3-0

FIELDING

43 DC Nash (39ct,4st)
22 SP Fleming
20 BL Hutton
15 PN Weekes
14 OA Shah
9   MA Roseberry
7   AJ Strauss
5   EC Joyce, RMS Weston
4   D Alleyne, ARC Fraser
3   SJ Cook
2   TF Bloomfield, MJ Brown, JWM Dalrymple
1   JP Hewitt, CB Keegan, AW Laraman

NORTHAMPTONSHIRE CCC

FIRST–CLASS MATCHES

BATTING

	ME Hussey	MB Loye	JW Cook	RJ Warren	AJ Swann	GP Swann	AL Penberthy	D Ripley	JP Taylor	DM Cousins	JF Brown	KJ Innes	TMB Bailey	JAR Blain	LC Weekes	AS Rollins	MR Strong	ME Cassar	MS Panesar	RA White	Extras	Total	Wickets	Result	Points
v. **Glamorgan** (Northampton) 20–23 April	18	25	14	175	21	7	132*	0	26*	-	-										28	446	7		
	-	-			1																-	-		D	10
v. **Essex** (Chelmsford) 25–28 April	21	13	20	33	10	3	20	6	1*	0	-	0									23	150	19		
	3	26	16	55	47	29	6	4*	-	0*	-	-									13	199	7	D	7
v. **Surrey** (Northampton) 9–12 May	75	5	80	0	96		75		12	3*	5	41	34								50	476	10		
	67	167*	52*																		18	304	1	D	11
v. **Yorkshire** (Headingley) 25–27 May	22	14	0	65*	16	6	3	2	11		15		2								39	195	10		
	17	52	0	1	21	31	45	14	7*		40		0								27	255	10	L	3
v. **Lancashire** (Northampton) 30 May–2 June	70	177	23	0	1	33	31	4	6	2*			16								35	398	10		
	82	9	0	12	4	15	24	13*	3	1			1								30	194	10	L	7
v. **Leicestershire** (Leicester) 13–15 June	10	0	7	13	25	0	31		4	0		0			44*						25	159	10		
	45	31	21	55	4	20		1	15*	5		26			18						16	257	10	L	3
v. **Somerset** (Northampton) 20–22 June	12	197	7	64	37	0	80	95	18	27	5*										25	567	10		
	-	-																			-	-		D	12
v. **Glamorgan** (Cardiff) 29 June–2 July	159	73		0	1	47	21	2	2	2*						5	12				20	344	10		
	68	8		77	1	10	60	25*	1*	-						65	-				34	349	7	D	10
v. **Yorkshire** (Northampton) 4–7 July	64	50		27	2	5	18	21*	18		0					24	2				22	253	10		
	122	38		0	8	55	0	17	21		0					1	14*				22	298	10	D	3
v. **Surrey** (Guildford) 18–20 July	15	21		3	0	19	1	0	0*				3			38	0				20	120	10		
	41	14		0	41	5	11	16	5				8			14	12*				26	193	10	L	3
v. **Essex** (Northampton) 28–30 July	329*	52		38		1	101	10*					25			39	-				29	633	6		
	70*	21*		-				-	-				-			-	-				5	96	0	W	19
v. **Kent** (Northampton) 8–11 August	35		84	5	46	77	39	11		0			22			1	1*				34	355	10		
	7*							-		-			-			6*	-				0	13	0	D	9
v. **Lancashire** (Old Trafford) 15–18 August	93	10rh		194		54	17	43	17				11			21	6*				29	495	8		
	10*	-					-	-					3			-	-				0	13	1	D	3
v. **Leicestershire** (Northampton) 23–26 August	232			37	4	9	15	31	34	35*						34	9	10			19	469	10		
	82			52*	113	22	0	7	1	-						1	0	2*			22	302	8	W	19
v. **Kent** (Canterbury) 5–8 September	7		50	104	61	6	73	16	10				0*			2			4		24	357	10		
	23		0	28	2	26	12	62*	11				1*			20			2		12	199	9	D	11
v. **Somerset** (Taunton) 12–15 September	208		13	144	0	16	7	1	33				12*			5		3*			21	463	9		
	48		88	42	0	61	101	16	53				0*			1		-			22	432	9	L	

	ME Hussey	MB Loye	JW Cook	RJ Warren	AJ Swann	GP Swann	AL Penberthy	D Ripley	JP Taylor	DM Cousins	JF Brown	KJ Innes	TMB Bailey	JAR Blain	LC Weekes	AS Rollins	MR Strong	ME Cassar	MS Panesar	RA White
Matches	16	12	9	16	13	15	15	15	12	8	11	4	5	5	1	6	9	1	2	1
Innings	30	21	16	26	22	25	24	26	17	10	12	7	7	9	2	10	13	2	3	2
Not Out	4	3	1	2	0	0	1	6	3	3	5	1	0	4	1	1	4	0	2	0
Highest Score	329*	197	88	194	113	61	132*	95	53	27	35*	40	41	34	44*	65	34	9	10	4
Runs	2055	1003	391	1303	479	543	942	481	273	87	56	86	113	66	62	214	110	9	15	6
Average	79.03	55.72	26.06	54.29	21.77	21.72	40.95	25.31	19.5	12.42	8	14.33	16.14	13.2	62	23.77	12.22	4.5	15	3
100s	5	3	-	4	1	-	3	-	-	-	-	-	-	-	-	-	-	-	-	-
50s	9	4	4	7	2	3	5	2	1	-	-	-	-	-	-	1	-	-	-	-
Ct/St	19	4	5	8	9	9	11	45/3	3	-	2	1	3/-	-	-	3	2	2	-	-

NORTHAMPTONSHIRE CCC

FIRST-CLASS MATCHES
BOWLING

	DM Cousins	JP Taylor	AL Penberthy	JF Brown	GP Swann	KJ Innes	JAR Blain	MR Strong	MS Pancsar	Overs	Total	Byes/Leg-Byes	Wickets	Run outs	
v. Glamorgan (Northampton) 20–23 April	36-4-141-1	31-4-99-2	36-4-129-0	29-7-73-1	20-3-70-1					161	548	13	6	1	A B
	8-1-38-0	6.5-4-25-1	-	-	-					14.5	65	2	1	-	
v. Essex (Chelmsford) 25–28 April	28-8-62-4	12.1-1-52-2	22-8-46-2		7-4-4-1	5-1-18-0				74.1	206	24	10	1	
	20-2-71-1	12.3-1-39-0	15-6-26-1		13-4-41-2	19-3-76-4				79.3	257	4	8	-	
v. Surrey (Northampton) 9–12 May	33-2-127-0		20.5-2-66-4	52-8-172-2		20-4-77-1	27-3-125-2			161.5	607	9	10	-	C
	-		-	-		-	-			-	-	-	-	-	
v. Yorkshire (Headingley) 25–27 May	34.4-5-102-8		22-6-62-1		18-4-41-0	22-5-64-1	24-3-81-0			122.4	374	18	10	-	
	9-2-23-1		2-0-13-1			1.2-0-3-0	8-0-34-4			20.2	77	4	6	-	C
v. Lancashire (Northampton) 30 May–2 June	23-4-79-2		20-3-39-4	18-3-64-2	8-0-33-0		21-2-71-2			90	291	5	10	-	
	28-3-120-7		12-4-27-0	16-2-47-0	110.2-2-35-0		11-0-67-0			77.2	305	9	7	-	
v. Leicestershire (Leicester) 13–15 June	19-4-58-3			10.3-4-17-1	-	8-0-51-3				52.3	185	8	10	-	D
	12-1-60-1			13-2-46-0	9-2-26-0	8.3-2-42-0				53.3	233	3	1	-	D
v. Somerset (Northampton) 20–22 June	26-5-100-4	19.3-3-57-3	19-6-47-1	13-0-52-0	7-4-13-1					95.3	299	13	10	-	B
	31-8-102-3	30-5-92-2	9-3-16-0	29-8-84-2						140	430	24	8	-	A B C E
v. Glamorgan (Cardiff) 29 June–2 July	26-5-93-1	27.2-3-112-1	28-5-77-1		41-7-131-1			31-3-125-2		155.2	556	15	7	1	B C A
	-	-	-		-			-		-	-	-	-	-	
v. Yorkshire (Northampton) 4–7 July		19-1-66-2	-	37-11-85-3	31-6-84-2			24-7-66-2		111	309	8	10	1	
		3.4-1-7-1	-	-	-			4-2-3-0		7.4	10	0	1	-	
v. Surrey (Guildford) 18–20 July		22-3-82-1	19.5-0-75-2	28-6-91-4	-			27-5-104-3		98.5	368	7	10	-	A
		-	-	-	-			-		-	-	-	-	-	
v. Essex (Northampton) 27–30 July		28-4-85-3	16-2-60-3	32-5-101-0	32-10-96-3			24-7-66-1		134	430	8	10	-	A
		13-6-30-1	5-3-6-0	40.2-10-107-5	29-6-82-2			13-3-57-2		100.2	297	15	10	-	
v. Kent (Northampton) 8–11 August		20.1-1-93-2	5-2-21-0	35-8-95-0	16-0-99-0			24-3-130-1		107.1	464	6	4	-	A C
		-	-	-	-			-		-	-	-	-	-	
v. Lancashire (Old Trafford) 15–18 August		31-5-125-1	26.4-6-102-1	32-4-145-1	22-3-96-1			21-1-106-2		135.4	600	11	6	-	A
		8-1-22-0		30-3-89-3	27-5-75-3			19-2-51-1		85	243	6	7	-	A
v. Leicestershire (Northampton) 23–26 August		18-3-64-0	3-2-4-0	36-8-110-3	32-5-101-3			14-2-71-0	35-5-120-4	138	484	14	10	-	
		1-0-7-0	-	23-13-29-1	17.1-7-34-5			1-0-2-0	20-16-11-4	62.1	85	2	10	-	
v. Kent (Canterbury) 5–8 September		12-0-58-3		1-0-2-1		10-3-42-6		2-0-2-0		25	108	4	10	-	
		36-4-118-0		33-4-97-1	23-3-83-1	32-5-132-3		32-8-98-3		171	576	16	8	-	B F
v. Somerset (Taunton) 12–15 September		25-3-100-4	24-4-104-2		12-0-57-0		20-0-121-0	15.3-2-79-2	28-5-120-2	137.3	650	13	10	-	B
		3-0-11-0	-		16-0-85-4		-	5-1-32-0	18.3-2-107-1	42.3	259	15	6	1	

	DM Cousins	JP Taylor	AL Penberthy	JF Brown	GP Swann	KJ Innes	JAR Blain	MR Strong	MS Pancsar
Overs	333.4	379.2	339.2	473.5	422.3	83.5	153	256.3	101.3
Maidens	54	49	70	102	87	15	16	46	28
Runs	1176	1345	1019	1407	1365	331	673	992	358
Wickets	36	29	25	28	30	9	17	19	11
Average	32.66	46.37	40.76	50.25	45.50	36.77	39.58	52.21	32.54

A ME Hussey 2-0-11-0; 3-0-14-1; 2-0-9-0; 2-0-14-0; 5-1-15-1; 3-0-15-0; 1-1-0-0
B JW Cook 7-4-12-0; 11-6-17-1; 4-1-14-0; 12-3-25-0; 13-2-56-0
C AJ Swann 9-2-31-1; 2-1-6-0; 1-0-5-0; 2-1-3-0; 2-0-5-0
D LC Weekes 15-4-51-3; 11-1-56-0
E RJ Warren 1-1-0-0
F RA White 3-0-7-0

FIELDING

48	DJ Ripley (45ct,3st)
19	ME Hussey
11	AL Penberthy
9	AJ Swann, GP Swann
8	RJ Warren
5	JW Cook
4	MB Loye
3	TMB Bailey, AS Rollins, JP Taylor
2	JF Brown, ME Cassar, MR Strong
1	KJ Innes

NOTTINGHAMSHIRE CCC

FIRST-CLASS MATCHES

BATTING

Match	DJ Bicknell	GE Welton	GS Blewett	Usman Afzaal	P Johnson	KP Pietersen	CMW Read	PJ Franks	GD Clough	RJ Logan	GJ Smith	DJ Millns	CM Tolley	MN Malik	AJ Harris	RD Stemp	DS Lucas	JE Morris	BM Shafayat	SJ Randall	JER Gallian	Extras	Total	Wickets	Result	Points
v. Durham	34	0	133	20	30	2	39*	44*														42	344	6		
(Trent Bridge) 25–28 April	-	-	-	-	-	-	-	-														-	-	-	D	10
v. Sussex	14	30	49	29	43	51	50	13	2		3	3*										45	332	10		
(Hove) 9–12 May	17	3	12	5	88*	13	4	24	0		20	4										18	208	10	L	5
v. Warwickshire	167	7	99	61	6	11	7*	2*														42	402	6		
(Trent Bridge) 16–19 May	-	-	-	-	-	-	-	-														-	-	-	D	9
v. Middlesex	38	11	12	43		165*	1	85			11				0	22						57	467	10		
(Lord's) 25–28 May	44	0	76	22		65*	0	6			8*				0							19	252	8	D	12
v. Durham	45	16	3	89	109	38	4	23*			1				2	2						39	371	10		
(Chester-le-Street) 30 May–2 June	-	4	137*	21	15	12	2	20*														8	219	5	L	7
v. Gloucestershire	21	22	22	88	0	10	28		7		0*				2	41						26	267	10		
(Trent Bridge) 6–9 June	15	0	23	9	35	72	15		3		27				20*	28						37	284	10	L	5
v. Sussex	29	15	13	40	25		18		2		44*				6	0	60					28	280	10		
(Trent Bridge) 20–23 June	123	0		7	19		78		8		1*				6	0						37	285	10	L	5
v. Worcestershire	6		0	0	9	103*	2		1						1	5	21	3				9	160	10		
(Worcester) 29 June–2 July	104		134*	88	26*													94				15	461	3	W	15
v. Middlesex	27	0	79		8	37	12		19		32*				11	2		72				15	314	10		
(Trent Bridge) 4–7 July	50	10	3		0	2	76*		0						14*	11		24				25	215	8	D	9
v. Hampshire	0		13		5	2	76*		1		8				4	66		14	4			16	209	10		
(Southampton Rose Bowl) 18–21 July	5		16		0	8	38		28		0*				10	10		2	14			21	152	10	L	4
v. Derbyshire	41	19	31	138		0	23		14	2*					16	170			13			59	526	10		
(Derby) 27–30 July	19	50	52	12		218*	-									136*			11			59	557	5	D	11
v. Warwickshire	4		97	86		71	19*		4*							10	5		23rh			31	350	6		
(Edgbaston) 3–6 August	45		1	14		37	4		0		3*				0	16	8		-			15	141	9	L	7
v. Worcestershire	23		31	0	9	2			8	10	0*				0	51						15	149	10		
(Trent Bridge) 8–11 August	38		108	53	18	86	65		2*	4	3				6							40	423	10	W	15
v. Gloucestershire	50	61	0		149	1	7		13	17	0*					2		5				17	322	10		
(Bristol) 15–18 August	0	30	0	0		13	14		4	0	6*					54		28				17	166	10	L	4
v. Derbyshire	21	42	27		0	150	44		4	0	0*					9		7				18	322	10		
(Trent Bridge) 22–25 August	4	6	106*		65		44									20*		-				22	223	3	W	18
v. Hampshire	4	11	14	91	14	17			29						2*		42	1				14	245	10		
(Trent Bridge) 12–15 September	62	0	1	12	87	21			37*						-		75	8*				11	314	7	D	6

Player	Matches	Innings	Not Out	Highest Score	Runs	Average	100s	50s	Ct/St
DJ Bicknell	16	29	0	167	1050	36.2	3	3	8
GE Welton	12	22	0	61	337	15.31	-	2	5
GS Blewett	16	30	3	137*	1292	47.85	5	5	24
Usman Afzaal	12	22	0	138	928	42.18	1	7	9
P Johnson	13	24	2	149	684	31.09	2	2	7
KP Pietersen	15	26	4	218*	1277	58.04	4	6	15
CMW Read	16	27	5	78	666	30.27	-	5	43/1
PJ Franks	5	8	4	85	217	54.25	-	1	2
GD Clough	4	6	0	37*	22	3.66	-	-	1
RJ Logan	10	15	2	44*	162	12.46	-	-	4
GJ Smith	14	19	9	6	189	18.9	-	-	2
DJ Millns	1	2	1	-	7	7	-	-	1
CM Tolley	1	-	-	20*	-	-	-	-	-
MN Malik	5	6	5	66	12	12	-	-	-
AJ Harris	9	15	2	41	79	6.07	-	1	-
RD Stemp	5	7	0	170	105	15	2	-	1
DS Lucas	5	8	0	75	145	18.12	-	-	-
JE Morris	8	16	2	94	640	45.71	2	4	3
(unidentified)	3	6	0		231	38.5			
(unidentified)	4	7	1		73	12.16			
BM Shafayat	1	1	1	23rh	23	-	-	-	1
SJ Randall	1	2	0	13	18	9	-	-	-
JER Gallian	2	4	0	18	43	10.75	-	-	-

NOTTINGHAMSHIRE CCC

FIRST–CLASS MATCHES

BOWLING

	PJ Franks	GJ Smith	RJ Logan	GD Clough	G S Blewett	Usman Afzaal	KP Pietersen	MN Malik	AJ Harris	RD Stemp	DS Lucas	SJ Randall	Overs	Total	Byes/Leg-Byes	Wickets	Run outs
v. Durham (Trent Bridge) 25–28 April	25-4-74-3	19.3-1-61-2	16-2-69-4	19-3-52-1	4-3-2-0	1-0-11-0	-						84.3	284	15	10	-
	-	-	-	-	-	-	-						-	-	-	-	-
v. Sussex (Hove) 9–12 May	36-8-95-2	36-13-64-5		7-0-23-0	8-0-34-0	12-0-35-1	24-7-52-0						145.1	404	32	10	1 A
	14-3-47-0	18-5-37-5		-	8-0-34-1	30-6-115-2	5-2-21-0						78	298	26	8	- A
v. Warwickshire (Trent Bridge) 16–19 May	-	-	-	-	-	-	-	-					-	-	-	-	-
	-	-	-	-	-	-	-	-					-	-	-	-	-
v. Middlesex (Lord's) 25–28 May	30-9-65-4	21.1-8-61-3			2-0-9-0	12-2-57-0			26-4-87-1	26-8-77-2			117.1	370	14	10	-
	15-3-45-1	14-7-20-1			15-7-19-0	12-7-13-1			21.5-12-43-2	27-11-39-3			104.5	197	18	8	-
v. Durham (Chester-le-Street) 30 May–2 June	17.1-4-57-2	20-3-73-3							18-7-45-2	28-5-88-3			83.1	276	13	10	-
	12-2-46-1	9-1-41-0				4.1-1-21-1	21-4-69-0		15-4-55-0	24-5-72-0			85.1	318	14	2	-
v. Gloucestershire (Trent Bridge) 6–9 June		28-8-71-3		18-2-66-1	21-6-67-2	2-1-9-0	15-0-53-1		30-6-98-2		15-0-95-0		129	473	14	10	1
		9-3-19-0		19-4-69-3	8-1-20-2	2-0-9-0	5-2-25-0		14-1-73-0		9-0-35-0		66	265	15	5	-
v. Sussex (Trent Bridge) 20–23 June		26.4-9-58-2		19-2-72-1	15-3-40-0				34-10-98-6	23-4-68-1			118.4	354	14	10	- B
		14-1-43-0		18-2-71-0	10-1-57-0	8-1-41-0			16-1-56-0	31-3-97-0			97	372	7	0	-
v. Worcestershire (Worcester) 29 June–2 July			20-4-96-5		4-0-20-0				11-2-36-1	3.4-0-9-1	17-1-80-3		55.4	248	7	10	-
			17-6-83-0		5-0-18-0	15-3-44-2			20.5-5-56-4	27-5-74-2	21-2-78-2		105.5	369	16	10	-
v. Middlesex (Trent Bridge) 4–7 July		27.1-9-84-2	34-9-118-5		21-7-53-0		4-2-12-0		29-11-101-2		23-1-135-1		138.1	527	24	10	-
		-	-		-		-		-		-		-	-	-	-	-
v. Hampshire (Southampton) 18–21 July		24-2-62-2	19-2-75-3		-		8-2-24-1		26-6-79-3	27-2-97-1			104	347	10	10	-
		10-0-41-0	24-4-103-4		-		15-1-54-0		17-6-53-1	28-8-86-3			94	352	15	8	-
v. Derbyshire (Derby) 27–30 July		21-2-89-2	24-5-101-1		-		29.1-5-88-3	13-1-49-0			25-3-99-2	36-7-132-2	149.1	572	13	10	- C
		-	-		-		-	-			-	-	-	-	-	-	-
v. Warwickshire (Edgbaston) 3–6 August		24-6-48-4	22-4-94-2		6-2-23-1		6-2-22-0	20-6-67-2	22-7-63-1	8-1-49-0			108	373	7	10	-
		13-1-44-2	10-2-41-0		-		7-0-55-0	3-1-16-0	10-1-54-1	-			48.2	257	4	3	- C D
v. Worcestershire (Trent Bridge) 8–11 August		21.3-6-59-5	16-1-72-2		-		1-1-0-0	13-3-50-0	11-0-65-2				62.3	252	6	10	1
		13.5-2-42-3	18-2-76-2		-	4-1-6-0	16-2-46-2	11-2-48-2	9-1-35-0				71.5	259	6	10	1
v. Gloucestershire (Bristol) 15–18 August		27-4-96-2	37-4-155-3		-		15-0-75-0	25-6-113-1				41-4-147-2	146	608	22	8	- E
		-	-		-		-	-				-	-	-	-	-	-
v. Derbyshire (Trent Bridge) 22–25 August		16-5-47-1	23.1-3-93-6	3-1-6-0			21-6-48-0	12-1-53-0			26-7-64-2		101.1	320	9	10	1
		12.2-4-25-2	24-3-89-3				1-0-8-0	18-3-57-5			8-0-35-0		63.2	221	7	10	-
v. Hampshire (Trent Bridge) 12–15 September		12-2-38-1	14-1-55-1			12-2-46-0	11-5-26-0	14-4-42-1				12-2-44-0	75	259	8	4	1
		9-1-33-0	11-1-55-2			-	12-1-52-2	11-2-51-1				9.1-1-43-1	52.1	245	11	6	-

	PJ Franks	GJ Smith	RJ Logan	GD Clough	G S Blewett	Usman Afzaal	KP Pietersen	MN Malik	AJ Harris	RD Stemp	DS Lucas	SJ Randall
Overs	149.1	446.2	329.1	100	113	149.2	234	104	330.4	244.4	118	132.1
Maidens	33	103	53	13	34	29	52	21	84	51	8	21
Runs	429	1256	1375	353	374	530	767	414	1097	707	571	465
Wickets	13	50	43	6	6	9	9	10	28	16	8	7
Average	33.00	25.12	31.97	58.83	62.33	58.88	85.22	41.40	39.17	44.18	71.37	66.42

A DJ Millns 22.1-3-69-1; 3-1-18-0
B GE Welton 1-0-4-0
C JE Morris 1-0-1-0; 2.2-0-18-0
D CMW Read 3-0-25-0
E P Johnson 1-1-0-0

FIELDING

44	CMW Read (43ct,1st)
24	GS Blewett
15	KP Pietersen
9	Usman Afzaal
8	DJ Bicknell
7	P Johnson
5	GE Welton
4	RJ Logan
3	JE Morris
2	PJ Franks, GJ Smith
1	GD Clough, DJ Millns, SJ Randall, RD Stemp

SOMERSET CCC

FIRST-CLASS MATCHES

BATTING

	J Cox	PCL Holloway	M Burns	PD Bowler	KA Parsons	RJ Turner	GD Rose	KP Dutch	RL Johnson	PS Jones	JP Tucker	ME Trescothick	MN Lathwell	JID Kerr	AR Caddick	PD Trego	JO Grove	MP Bulbeck	ID Blackwell	MJ Wood	Aamir Sohail	Shoaib Akhtar	Extras	Total	Wickets	Result	Points
v. Lancashire	66	4	26	0	35	7	4	6	18	22	5*												11	204	10		
(Taunton) 20–23 April	0	1	8	2	0	15	12	37	4		0*												17	170	10	L	4
v. Glamorgan	95*	78	70	16	0							147											29	435	5		
(Cardiff) 25–28 April																										D	12
v. Yorkshire	35	23	20		38	5	7		9			12	65	10*	0								33	257	10		
(Headingley) 9–12 May	80	85	50		33	1	5					31	1	12*	10*								19	327	10	W	17
v. Kent	11	39	21	42		4	0		1				1	3		32	4*						26	184	10		
(Taunton) 16–19 May	63	13	20	87	0		5*						58	12*		43							33	334	7	D	7
v. Leicestershire	21	15	60	138*	27	10			1				19	7		21	0						35	374	10		
(Leicester) 30 May–2 June	13	85	7	2	34	10*							63	4		17	2*						31	268	8	D	11
v. Surrey	26	15	20	73	9	10	51	15*					99					7	33				19	377	10		
(Oval) 6–9 June	15	11	42	10	22	2	21	29*					13					9	30				30	234	10	L	7
v. Yorkshire	95	5	221		4								98*		4*					71			55	553	5		
(Bath) 13–16 June																										D	10
v. Northamptonshire		9	0	7	5	84	20	11*					0	32				103	9				19	299	10		
(Northampton) 20–22 June		30	20	60	33	23	0*						2	18*				122		90			32	430	8	D	8
v. Essex	47	6	11	39	115*	118	9	5					16				1	26					22	415	10		
(Taunton) 4–7 July																										W	20
v. Australians		0	9	2	38	42								13			6	30	39	50	4*		34	267	10		
(Taunton) 13–16 July		7	59	26*	3	9								0			0	28	51	36	10		11	240	10	L	–
v. Lancashire	46	2	55	65	72	31	3	13*					7					13	64				14	385	10		
(Old Trafford) 19–21 July	39*	23*																					4	66	0	W	19
v. Glamorgan	29		81	164	15		69*	36				26	53	5*					102				20	600	8		
(Taunton) 27–29 July																										W	20
v. Kent	50	20	0	0	29		75*	46	10				63					18	2				23	336	10		
(Canterbury) 1–4 August	24	3	18	26	1		1	8*	3*				9						15				5	113	8	D	9
v. Leicestershire	0	5	10	93	25		68	22					1				1*	16	27				30	298	10		
(Taunton) 7–10 August																										D	9
v. Surrey	76	38	0		29		23	10	6				1				19*		120	24			27	373	10		
(Taunton) 23–26 August	46	70	34		28*								27						67	3			36	311	6	D	11
v. Essex	186	7	18	1	70		0	35*	0					36					4	8			26	391	10		
(Chelmsford) 5–7 September	33*	3*																		20			8	64	1	W	19
v. Northamptonshire	82	1		139	36		12	17	29				92	20*					77				23	650	10		
(Taunton) 12–15 September	86	26		36*	6*		2						14						0				15	250	6	W	20
Matches	15	12	17	14	5	17	3	16	13	16	1	3	13	8	2	3	4	5	11	6	1	1					
Innings	25	21	28	22	8	26	4	22	15	16	2	4	21	12	3	5	5	7	17	10	2	2					
Not Out	3	1	1	2	1	3	0	4	3	5	2	0	1	5	2	1	2	2	0	0	0	1					
Highest Score	186	85	221	164	139	115*	15	118	68	29*	5*	147	99	36	10*	43	19*	18	122	90	50	10					
Runs	1264	567	961	827	254	761	25	530	379	180	5	216	702	167	15	117	30	50	839	342	86	14					
Average	57.45	28.35	35.59	41.35	36.28	33.08	6.25	29.44	31.58	16.36	–	54	35.1	23.85	15	29.25	10	10	49.35	34.2	43	14					
100s	1		1	2	1	1		1				1							1								
50s	9	4	7	4		3		3	2				8						3	3	1						
Ct/St	6	3	13	14	5	59/-		19	3	3		3	9	1				2	3	5	1						

SOMERSET CCC

FIRST-CLASS MATCHES
BOWLING

	RL Johnson	PS Jones	KP Dutch	M Burns	AR Caddick	JID Kerr	JO Grove	ID Blackwell	Overs	Total	Byes/Leg-Byes	Wickets	Run outs
v. Lancashire (Taunton) 20–23 April	35-9-107-5	28-6-86-3	-	-					101	378	8	10	- A B C
	-	-							-	-	-	-	-
v. Glamorgan (Cardiff) 25–28 April	28-1-106-5	24.2-2-83-1	20-4-56-2	-	-	-			107.2	353	7	9	- B C
				5-1-35-0	-				-	-	-	-	-
v. Yorkshire (Headingley) 9–12 May		18.2-8-37-3	-	2-0-11-0	25-7-81-5	14-3-50-1			73.2	231	6	10	- B
		16-0-91-4		-	21-3-92-5	4.4-1-8-1			41.4	192	1	10	
v. Kent (Taunton) 16–19 May		26.5-6-71-3	10-2-31-2	-		17-1-63-1	19-3-85-1		99.5	343	8	10	- D
									-	-	-	-	-
v. Leicestershire (Leicester) 30 May–2 June		23-4-74-1	18-3-77-0	9-2-26-3		17-3-51-3			99.1	280	9	10	- D E
		19-1-100-2	34-6-118-3	-		14-3-57-2			76	277	16	7	- D E
v. Surrey (Oval) 6–9 June	21-3-66-3	25-3-82-3	29.1-5-96-4	4-0-13-0				27-5-91-0	114.1	403	13	10	- E
	9-0-42-0	9-1-41-0	18.3-5-55-3	-				13-2-64-1	49.3	210	8	4	- E
v. Yorkshire (Bath) 13–16 June	35-3-110-2	30-6-104-1	24-6-64-2	13-0-60-0		22-6-66-0			164	589	13	5	- D F G H I
	-	-	-	-		-			-	-	-	-	-
v. Northamptonshire (Northampton) 20–22 June	40.1-2-127-5	36-5-121-4	31-6-98-1	15-4-48-0		27-5-84-0		13-1-72-0	162.1	567	12	10	-
	-	-	-	-		-			-	-	-	-	-
v. Essex (Taunton) 4–7 July	17-6-43-4	17-5-34-3	-	4-3-1-1			4.2-0-46-2	10-9-1-1	42.2	130	6	10	-
	17-8-42-1	18.1-2-66-3	27-6-57-4	4-0-12-0			13-3-40-1		89.1	225	7	10	-
v. Australians (Taunton) 13–16 July				7-1-21-0		17-3-52-1	16-0-96-1	8-0-25-0	74	348	15	3	- C J K
				4-1-8-0		19-0-89-0	14-1-77-0	24-3-88-2	81	335	3	4	- C J
v. Lancashire (Old Trafford) 19–21 July	22-4-77-2	19-3-91-3	11-0-62-1	5-1-19-1				6.2-1-27-1	76.2	324	2	10	- E
	15.1-5-40-4	7-2-22-2						15-4-47-3	44.1	126	4	9	- E
v. Glamorgan (Taunton) 27–29 July	12.1-3-33-4	17-6-45-1	-		18-2-84-5				47.1	169	7	10	- E
	20-3-93-2	20-4-83-3	15-2-45-0	3-0-15-0	24.4-5-62-3			23-8-46-1	105.4	364	20	9	-
v. Kent (Canterbury) 1–4 August	13.5-4-69-0	31-4-115-5	15-2-49-1	12-3-39-0			22-6-56-0		118.5	451	9	7	1 E
	8-0-31-0	7-1-25-0	-	4.4-0-35-1			11-0-63-2		36.4	205	1	3	- E
v. Leicestershire (Taunton) 7–10 August	23-2-69-2	24-3-101-2	-	16.1-2-54-6					69.1	277	9	10	- E
	12-0-52-2	18-4-57-0	25-3-103-2	10-1-66-0				17-3-59-0	97	400	9	4	- E L
v. Surrey (Taunton) 23–26 August	26-8-62-5	20.2-1-98-3	2-1-1-0	8-0-36-0			10-1-55-1	5-2-14-1	71.2	278	12	10	-
	28-8-90-4	19-4-70-1	3-2-4-0	-			12-0-90-0	22-11-29-0	84	294	11	6	1
v. Essex (Chelmsford) 5–7 September	17-5-40-5	15-2-55-1	16.2-6-32-4	-		9-4-33-0			59.2	172	7	10	- C
	21-3-72-3	27-8-78-2	16-3-49-2	3-2-7-0		8-3-26-0		27-11-45-3	102	282	5	10	-
v. Northamptonshire (Taunton) 12–15 September	37-10-90-4	35-8-111-4	21-0-83-1	10-2-33-0		15-4-47-0	9-0-47-0		134	463	19	9	- C
	6-2-13-0	10-1-74-1	31-2-188-3	-		3-0-19-0		39.2-6-122-5	89.2	432	16	9	-

	RL Johnson	PS Jones	KP Dutch	M Burns	AR Caddick	JID Kerr	JO Grove	ID Blackwell
Overs	463.2	560	367	138	88.4	186.4	88.2	291.4
Maidens	89	100	64	23	17	36	8	72
Runs	1474	2015	1268	539	319	645	489	896
Wickets	62	59	35	12	18	9	6	20
Average	23.77	34.15	36.22	44.91	17.72	71.66	81.50	44.80

A JP Tucker 17-2-82-0
B GD Rose 17-4-73-1; 19-8-36-1; 14-3-46-1
C KA Parsons 4-0-22-1; 11-3-30-0; 9-1-42-0; 13-1-61-0; 2-0-5-0; 7-0-33-0
D PD Trego 27-5-85-3; 15-3-71-1; 4-0-30-0; 12-3-57-0
E MP Bulbeck 17-2-70-2; 15-0-77-0; 8-0-42-0; 13-0-46-2; 7-1-13-0; 25-0-114-0; 6-0-50-0; 6-0-44-0; 13-3-45-0
F MJ Wood 7-1-30-0
G MN Lathwell 7-0-37-0
H PCL Holloway 4-0-19-0
I RJ Turner 10-3-29-0
J Shoaib Akhtar 14-0-81-1; 7-3-9-2
K Aamir Sohail 3-0-16-0
L PD Bowler 2-0-9-0

FIELDING

59	RJ Turner
19	KP Dutch
14	PD Bowler
13	M Burns
9	MN Lathwell
6	J Cox
5	ID Blackwell, KA Parsons
3	MPL Bulbeck, PCL Holloway, RL Johnson, PS Jones, ME Trescothick
2	JO Grove, MJ Wood
1	JID Kerr

SURREY CCC

FIRST–CLASS MATCHES

BATTING

	MA Butcher	IJ Ward	MR Ramprakash	AJ Hollioake	AD Brown	BC Hollioake	JN Batty	MP Bicknell	AJ Tudor	IDK Salisbury	ESH Giddins	GP Thorpe	AJ Stewart	RM Amin	Nadeem Shahid	TJ Murtagh	GP Butcher	Saqlain Mushtaq	MA Carberry	GJ Batty	Extras	Total	Wickets	Result	Points
v. Kent (Oval) 20–23 April	0	70	146	49	72	41	59	19	2	0	2*										13	473	10		
	–	–	–	–	–	–	–	–	–	–	–										–	–	–	D	11
v. Lancashire (Old Trafford) 25–28 April	–	–	–	–	–	–	–	–	–	–	–										–	–	–		
	–	–	–	–	–	–	–	–	–	–	–										–	–	–	D	4
v. Northamptonshire (Northampton) 9–12 May	28	79	0	50	122		56	36	33			148	32	0*							23	607	10		
	–	–	–	–	–		–	–	–			–	–	–							–	–	–	D	11
v. Leicestershire (Oval) 16–19 May	26		29	5	2	30	9	16		36*	5				19	2					11	190	10		
	–		–	–	–	–	–	–		–	–				–	–					–	–	–	D	7
v. Essex (Oval) 25–28 May	52	43	3		12	31	38	116	26	4*		32	106								35	498	10		
	72	3	52		33	0		18*					24*								4	206	5	D	12
v. Somerset (Oval) 6–9 June	76	32	143	48		0		7		6	1*			0	65		8				17	403	10		
	24	24	90	17*											27		16*				12	210	4	W	20
v. Essex (Ilford) 13–16 June	0	5	8	77			1	26*		8	1			1	0		36				35	198	10		
	2	22	61	52			0	24		37	9*			0	14		56				29	306	10	D	7
v. Lancashire (Oval) 29 June–2 July	11	12	59	8	19	14	10	50	28	23								0*			14	248	10		
	86	18	35	73	2	10	2	26*	9	13								7*			39	320	9	D	8
v. Leicestershire (Leicester) 4–7 July			0	15	0	0	12	13	15						7		9	5*	23		3	102	10		
			64	5	59	12	85*	86	30*						14		38	4	13		68	478	9	D	9
v. Northamptonshire (Guildford) 18–20 July				–	103	11	39	18	35	42*	8			4			4	46			11	368			
	–	–	–	–	–	–	–	–	–	–	–			–			–	–			–	–	–	W	19
v. Yorkshire (Headingley) 1–4 August				33	4	16	23	32		54	2*				25		3	38	11		37	278	10		
				0	44	68	9	23*		6	0						9	3	46		40	281	10	D	9
v. Glamorgan (Oval) 8–11 August	145*	3	19	0	0		11	27	17	1					26		10				22	281	10		
	2	24	0		1	15		29	29	19	2*				8		4				8	141	10	L	5
v. Kent (Canterbury) 16–19 August		47		3	0	31	40	78	34	0*				0			13	6			6	258	10		
		1		14	8	3	18	110*	0					0			13*	15			11	193	8	D	9
v. Somerset (Taunton) 23–26 August		48		20	7	56	9	34		7	1*						18	34		25	19	278	10		
		4		83	64	56	8*	12*										33		19	15	294	6	D	9
v. Yorkshire (Oval) 5–8 September	90	63	131	18	2	118		36		11			0				11*				36	516	9		
	–	–	–	–	–	–		–		–			–				–				–	–	–	W	20
v. Glamorgan (Cardiff) 12–15 September	230	63		97	115	27		6		23*	0						1		84		55	701	9		
	–	–		–	–	–		–		–	–						–		–		–	–	–	D	12
Matches	10	11	9	13	13	12	10	15	7	15	12	2	5	3	7	1	4	9	6	1					
Innings	15	18	14	20	20	19	16	22	11	21	12	6	4	12	1	8	14	10	2						
Not Out	1	0	0	1	0	0	1	6	1	4	8	0	1	1	0	1	0	5	0	0					
Highest Score	230	79	146	97	122	118	59	110*	116	54	9(	148	106	1	65	2	56	38	84	25					
Runs	844	561	776	758	630	586	239	748	399	440	36	180	196	1	208	2	175	131	311	44					
Average	60.28	31.16	55.42	39.89	31.5	30.84	15.93	46.75	39.9	25.88	6	90	39.2	0.33	17.33	2	25	14.55	31.1	22					
100s	2	–	3	–	3	1	–	1	1	–	–	1	1	–	–	–	–	–	–	–					
50s	5	–	4	4	7	2	4	1	4	1	1	–	–	1	–	1	–	1	–	–					
Ct/St	11	5	4	15	3	18	26/2	5	2	9	2	2	13/1	2	8	–	1	1	6	2					

SURREY CCC

FIRST–CLASS MATCHES

BOWLING

	MP Bicknell	AJ Tudor	BC Hollioake	ESH Giddins	IDK Salisbury	RM Amin	Saqlain Mushtaq					Overs	Total	Byes/Leg-Byes	Wickets	Run outs	
v. Kent (Oval) 20–23 April	20-1-76-0	33-7-105-2	16-3-53-1	32-7-103-2	24-4-72-2							140	456	12	8	-	A B
	-	-	-	-	-							-	-	-	-	-	
v. Lancashire (Old Trafford) 25–28 April	-	-	-	-	-							-	-	-	-	-	
	-	-	-	-	-							-	-	-	-	-	
v. Northamptonshire (Northampton) 9–13 May	38.1-9-129-3	30-6-89-2			39-3-130-4	22-6-59-0						149.1	476	18	10	-	A
	9-1-27-0	5-0-33-0			8-1-45-0	18-3-65-0						72	304	14	1	-	A B C D E F
v. Leicestershire (Oval) 16–19 May	21-5-61-4		9-1-44-0	17.5-6-48-5	15-1-42-1							78.5	246	13	10	-	A B
	7-0-25-3		5-1-17-1	5-2-19-0	-							28	94	2	5	-	C D G
v. Essex (Oval) 25–28 May	29-8-65-4	19-2-65-1	7-1-39-0	25-7-69-2	12.4-1-46-3							94.4	300	14	10	-	D G
	17-8-27-2	19-5-53-1	-	14-3-37-0	38-10-106-1							129	312	15	4	-	D
v. Somerset (Oval) 6–9 June	22.1-5-62-4			20-3-82-0	45-9-115-2	33-11-80-3						130.1	377	23	10	-	A B H
	18-6-47-2			8-3-25-1	35.2-7-95-5	22-5-50-1						87.2	234	9	10	-	H
v. Essex (Ilford) 13–16 June	23.3-6-54-3			29-6-94-3	35-8-74-1	7-3-18-1						106.3	296	23	10	-	A B H
	16-1-60-2			11-1-39-0	3-2-14-0	-						38	153	1	2	-	A B H
v. Lancashire (Oval) 29 June–2 July	20-4-80-1	15-6-36-2	6-2-17-0		18-3-41-1		36.3-7-89-6					95.3	276	13	10	-	
	13-4-23-0	12-2-48-1			16-3-36-0		28-9-44-1					71	170	11	2	-	B
v. Leicestershire (Leicester) 4–7 July	15-4-54-4	11-4-45-2	-				17-4-60-4					43	165	6	10	-	
	23-6-69-1	8-1-52-0	6-0-41-0				52.2-9-172-5					113.2	472	11	8	-	B C H
v. Northamptonshire (Guildford) 18–20 July	11-2-23-1	13-3-54-5		17-9-18-3	-		3-0-15-0					44	120	10	10	1	
	21-6-60-7	13.2-5-38-1	6-1-23-1	15-3-44-1	1-0-7-0		5-2-8-0					61.2	193	13	10	-	
v. Yorkshire (Headingley) 1–4 August	21-4-67-3		10-1-31-0	19-6-50-4	-		11.4-6-23-3					65.4	204	15	10	-	H
	18-5-36-1		9-1-37-0	24-5-66-1	8-1-21-0		26-4-46-0					91.4	244	11	2	-	C H
v. Glamorgan (Oval) 8–11 August	24-9-69-6	20-4-74-2	3-1-10-0	7-2-30-0	5-2-11-0		14.3-4-21-2					73.3	223	8	10	-	
	18-4-48-5	8-1-40-0	-		10-2-44-1		11.2-1-38-1					55.2	201	10	7	-	
v. Kent (Canterbury) 16–19 August	25-7-47-4		15.2-3-39-2	22-4-80-0	17-4-58-2		39-13-60-2					118.2	301	17	10	-	
	-		-	-	-		-					-	-	-	-	-	
v. Somerset (Taunton) 23–26 August	27-5-84-3		6-1-23-0	20-3-79-1	9-2-45-0		42.4-13-107-6					109.4	373	8	10	-	B
	24-6-62-1		10-0-52-1	12-2-25-1	6-0-27-0		41.4-10-114-3					95.4	311	28	6	-	C
v. Yorkshire (Oval) 5–8 September	16-2-43-3		6-2-20-0	19-6-42-1	25.4-5-49-4		48-17-70-2					114.4	235	15	10	-	
	26-9-83-3		2-0-4-0	6-0-21-0	10-1-52-0		25.4-8-58-7					69.4	235	17	10	-	
v. Glamorgan (Cardiff) 12–15 September	14-5-34-2		12-2-56-2	16-3-71-4	17.4-4-44-1		9-2-27-1					74.4	258	4	10	-	A
	5-0-23-0		5-1-24-1		-		-					14	69	6	1	-	

	MP Bicknell	AJ Tudor	BC Hollioake	ESH Giddins	IDK Salisbury	RM Amin	Saqlain Mushtaq
Overs	541.5	206.2	133.2	352.5	396.2	102	411.2
Maidens	132	46	21	83	72	28	109
Runs	1358	732	530	1102	1151	272	952
Wickets	72	19	9	30	27	5	43
Average	21.36	38.52	58.88	36.73	42.62	54.40	22.13

A   MA Butcher 2-0-9-0; 12-1-37-1; 7-0-34-1; 2-0-15-0; 4-1-15-0; 8-1-20-2; 4-1-10-0; 6-1-22-0

B   AJ Hollioake 13-3-26-1; 8-2-14-0; 9-4-10-0; 7-2-19-1; 1-0-2-0; 1-0-8-0; 2-0-8-0; 8-0-51-1; 5-0-27-0

C   AD Brown 11-1-52-0; 3-0-13-0; 2-0-3-0; 3-0-18-0; 2-0-3-0

D   MR Ramprakash 12-3-23-0; 2-0-3-0; 2-0-2-0; 35-11-56-0

E   GP Thorpe 1-0-11-0

F   AJ Stewart 1-1-0-0

G   TJ Murtagh 5-2-13-0; 6-3-15-1

H   GP Butcher 3-0-8-0; 4-1-8-1; 3-1-11-0; 3-0-21-0; 13-3-53-1; 4-0-18-0; 4.4-0-19-0

FIELDING

28   JN Batty (26ct,2st)
18   BC Hollioake
15   AJ Hollioake
14   AJ Stewart (13ct,1st)
11   MA Butcher
 9   IDK Salisbury
 8   Nadeem Shahid
 6   MA Carberry
 5   MP Bicknell, IJ Ward
 4   MR Ramprakash
 3   AD Brown
 2   RM Amin, GJ Batty, GP Butcher, ESH Giddins, Saqlain Mushtaq, GP Thorpe, AJ Tudor

SUSSEX CCC

FIRST-CLASS MATCHES

BATTING

Match	RR Montgomerie	MW Goodwin	CJ Adams	B Zuiderent	PA Cottey	UBA Rashid	RSC Martin-Jenkins	RJ Kirtley	MA Robinson	MJ Prior	JD Lewry	MH Yardy	WJ House	MJG Davis	PM Havell	BV Taylor	NJ Wilton	TR Ambrose	Extras	Total	Wickets	Result	Points
v. Worcestershire (Worcester) 25–28 April	15	94	15rh	0	46	1	26	0	–	25*	14*								19	255	7		
	0	42*	–	6	4*														2	54	2	D	6
v. Nottinghamshire (Hove) 9–12 May	0	9	122	19		55	8	1	0*	36	46	42							66	404	10		
	66	2	22	23		28	8*	11	–	68	0	14*							56	298	8	W	19
v. Cambridge University CCE (Cambridge) 16–18 May	84*		–		20	–				28*				–	–				15	147	1		
	–																					D	
v. Warwickshire (Hove) 25–28 May	36	0	4	4		22	42*	2		0	7	39	6						46	208	10		
	116	4	17	33		13	11	5		35	2*	5	1						11	253	10	L	3
v. Hampshire (Southampton Rose Bowl) 30 May–2 June	56	195	25	45		38	56*	33		15*		8							29	500	7		
	88*	8rh	–							–	–	75*							8	179	0	D	10
v. Worcestershire (Horsham) 6–9 June	12	19		2		1			0*	40	14	4	13	23					8	137	10		
	112	109		8		1			1	5	10	2	21	43*					22	372	10	W	15
v. Derbyshire (Arundel) 13–15 June	0	0	192	58		2	1*	0		66	0	2		16					12	349	10		
	–																					W	18
v. Nottinghamshire (Trent Bridge) 20–23 June	13	115	4	73		16	1	1*		31	12	50		16					22	354	10		
	160*	203*	–	–		–	–	–		–									9	372	10	W	19
v. Middlesex (Lord's) 29 June–2 July	22	69	59	11		0	1	1*		28	40	46		29					17	323	10		
	116	61	21	56		3				10				3*					20	315	6	D	6
v. Hampshire (Hove) 6–7 July	7	9	71	20		15	4	15	6			87*	19	11					38	302	–		
	–																					W	18
v. Durham (Chester-le-Street) 18–21 July	156	36	53	34		106	0	1		17	4*	7		2					26	442	10		
	71	46	90	0		19	0	1		5		5		10*					6	253	9	W	20
v. Gloucestershire (Cheltenham) 27–30 July	33	39	12	11		9	8	0*		7		21		12	0				15	167	10		
	107	12	123	11		0	8	0	1	0				48	24*				36	375	10	L	3
v. Middlesex (Hove) 2–5 August	39	127	16	43		21	36*	2*		7	5	41							14	351	8		
	6	0	54	25*		14	9			2		72							28	210	7	W	19
v. Australians (Hove) 8–10 August	157	105	66*	0*		7					6								21	355	4		
	2	28*	–	6		7				–		21*		1			1		6	86	2	L	
v. Derbyshire (Derby) 15–18 August	19	67	17	21		14	5	5*	31	0	20			52					29	280	10		
	19	11	59	0		22	9*	3	15	6	30			44					12	230	10	W	17
v. Durham (Hove) 22–25 August	24	17	0	0		3	1	3*	38	23	0			7					1	117	10		
	25	65	5	2		94	12	5*	14	0	13			4					26	265	10	L	3
v. Warwickshire (Edgbaston) 7–10 September	0	150	33			4	17*	1	14	12	21			3				26	40	321	10		
	121	0	139			11*	13		–	–	22*			–				52	18	376	5	D	
v. Gloucestershire (Hove) 12–14 September	11	5	11	6			113	51*	10		47	42		44				14	30	384	10		
	11*	7*	–																0	18	0	W	19

	RR Montgomerie	MW Goodwin	CJ Adams	B Zuiderent	PA Cottey	UBA Rashid	RSC Martin-Jenkins	RJ Kirtley	MA Robinson	MJ Prior	JD Lewry	MH Yardy	WJ House	MJG Davis	PM Havell	BV Taylor	NJ Wilton	TR Ambrose
Matches	18	17	15	17	2	14	9	16	14	16	17	17	3	15	1	4	1	2
Innings	33	32	23	27	3	21	15	24	15	24	18	29	4	22	–	3	1	3
Not Out	4	5	2	1	1	1	4	6	7	2	4	6	0	4	–	1	0	0
Highest Score	160*	203*	192	122	46*	106	113	51*	10	66	47	87*	46	52	24*	1	0	52
Runs	1704	1654	1086	619	70	367	524	196	32	433	202	796	80	439	–	35	1	92
Average	58.75	61.25	51.71	23.8	35	18.35	47.63	10.88	4	19.68	14.42	34.6	20	24.38	–	17.5	1	30.66
100s	8	7	3	1	–	1	1	–	–	–	–	–	–	–	–	–	–	–
50s	5	5	7	3	–	–	3	1	–	1	–	5	–	1	–	–	–	1
Ct/St	16	8	28	18	1	1	4	8	1	39/2	7	9	1	6	–	–	–/1	3/–

SUSSEX CCC

FIRST–CLASS MATCHES
BOWLING

	JD Lewry	RJ Kirtley	RSC Martin-Jenkins	MA Robinson	UBA Rashid	CJ Adams	MJG Davis	BV Taylor	Overs	Total	Byes/Leg-Byes	Wickets	Run outs
v. Worcestershire (Worcester) 25-28 April	3.2-0-13-1	3-2-1-0	-	-	-	-			6.2	14	0	1	-
	9-0-37-0	7-0-36-0	12-3-50-3	9-2-34-0	3.1-0-25-1	-			40.1	188	6	4	-
v. Nottinghamshire (Hove) 9-12 May	24.2-4-95-5	21-2-85-1	19-3-66-2		2-0-13-0		25-5-64-2		91.2	332	9	10	-
	15.3-2-65-4	14-2-50-4	11-2-42-2		10-2-23-0		2-0-23-0		52.3	208	5	10	-
v. Cambridge University CCE (Cambridge) 16-18 May	5-1-9-1			6-4-10-2	4-1-19-1			7-1-31-1	31	94	1	5	- A B
	-			-	-			-	-	-			-
v. Warwickshire (Hove) 25-28 May	32-10-101-4	33-13-82-1	29-7-89-1		13-6-20-2	2-0-11-0	35-11-66-2		148	395	9	10	- B
	6-1-18-0	3-0-13-0			4-1-10-0	-	6.3-2-20-2		19.3	70	9	2	- B
v. Hampshire (Southampton Rose Bowl) 30 May-2 June	28-9-59-1	28.5-8-87-2	30-10-77-4		17-6-38-0	-	51-10-148-3		157.5	437	23	10	- B
	-	-	-		-	-	-		-	-			-
v. Worcestershire (Horsham) 6-9 June	16-5-43-1	23.4-4-60-5		14-4-25-3	4-2-7-1		11-1-35-0		68.4	183	13	10	-
	11-4-33-0	17.5-3-49-3		20-8-43-1	10-4-21-0		36-6-116-6		94.5	293	31	10	-
v. Derbyshire (Arundel) 13-15 June	23-7-55-2	19-2-71-2		17.5-6-35-5	-	-	8-4-12-0		74.5	197	11	10	- B
	16-7-28-2	15-3-45-6		7-4-7-0		-	8-2-15-1		50	118	12	10	1 B
v. Nottinghamshire (Trent Bridge) 20-23 June	20-6-70-1	22-0-90-4		19-2-71-2	-	-	25-9-45-2		86	280	4	10	1
	24-1-91-2	28-9-72-3		21-4--70-4	8-2-27-0		6-4-5-0		90	285	13	10	1 B
v Middlesex (Lord's) 29 June-2 July	33-7-103-4	30.2-7-79-3		22-7-54-2	6-0-23-0	4-1-3-0	18-4-43-1		113.2	326	21	10	-
	13-3-31-0	15-7-32-1		12-5-15-2	6-1-13-0	2-0-7-0	8-0-20-0		59	135	17	4	- C D
v. Hampshire (Hove) 6-7 July	15.4-5-37-6	15-5-27-1				2-0-6-1	2-0-5-0	10-8-5-2	44.1	81	1	10	-
	12-2-42-7	12-2-63-2						0.2-0-1-1	24.2	108	2	10	-
v. Durham (Chester-le-Street) 18-21 July	23.2-8-58-1	32-8-127-3		26.2-7-69-1	2-0-6-1	11.2-2-28-4	18-4-46-0		113	360	26	10	-
	10-1-51-1	15-2-71-2		15-1-42-2	9.1-5-9-4		6-2-22-0		55.1	202	7	9	-
v. Gloucestershire (Cheltenham) 27-30 July		34-8-127-2		24-9-91-2	19-5-78-0	10-1-31-3	24-6-90-1	-	138	520	29	10	-
		2-0-7-0		-	-	-	-	1.3-0-15-0	3.3	23	1	0	-
v. Middlesex (Hove) 2-5 August	21-4-64-4	24-10-63-3	10-4-15-0	18-2-56-3	-	-			73	208	10	10	-
	13-3-30-0	11-1-36-1	17-10-18-4	19.3-12-34-4	7-3-20-1	1-0-3-0			68.3	161	20	10	-
v. Australians (Hove) 8-10 August	7-0-22-0			4-0-24-0	-	-	10-1-39-2		21	86	1	2	-
	11-2-52-1			13-1-71-0	10-0-46-0	-	12-1-56-1	16.5-1-93-0	63.5	339	15	2	- D
v. Derbyshire (Derby) 15-18 August	28-9-55-4	17-4-50-1	28-5-94-2	15.5-4-30-3			9-1-16-0		97.5	263	18	10	-
	14-7-18-3	11-1-28-2	5-1-21-0	15-3-38-5		-			45	117	12	10	-
v. Durham (Hove) 22-25 August	30-8-76-1	29-12-48-5	12-2-36-0	18-7-42-1		7-2-17-2	9-2-21-1		105	254	14	10	-
	9-3-31-0	19.1-7-47-5	12-4-36-0	24-7-59-5		1-0-5-0	6-2-17-0		71.1	199	4	10	-
v. Warwickshire (Edgbaston) 7-10 September	16-5-57-2	20.3-5-64-3	25-6-75-4	25-7-46-1	-				86.3	248	6	10	-
	8-2-29-0	12-2-46-0	12-3-33-0	16-6-32-2		-	16-4-42-1		79	240	7	3	- C D
v. Gloucestershire (Hove) 12-14 September	6-0-33-1	18-3-59-4	11-0-64-0	17.1-6-39-4	-		8-2-19-1		60.1	228	4	10	-
	9-0-42-0	14.1-3-34-6	15-3-48-2	17-8-46-2	-				55.1	173	3	10	-

	JD Lewry	RJ Kirtley	RSC Martin-Jenkins	MA Robinson	UBA Rashid	CJ Adams	MJG Davis	BV Taylor
Overs	512.1	566.3	248	415.4	134.2	40.2	349.3	45.4
Maidens	126	135	63	126	38	6	82	11
Runs	1548	1749	764	1083	398	111	956	184
Wickets	59	75	24	56	11	10	24	6
Average	26.23	23.32	31.83	19.33	36.18	11.10	39.83	30.66

A PM Havell 7-3-16-0
B MH Yardy 2-0-8-0; 4-1-17-0; 3-1-5-0; 7-3-13-1; 4-0-11-0; 3-1-7-0
C MW Goodwin 2-2-0-0; 11-1-40-0
D RR Montgomerie 1-1-0-1; 1-0-6-0; 4-0-11-0

FIELDING

41	MJ Prior (39ct,2st)
28	CJ Adams
18	B Zuiderent
16	RR Montgomerie
9	MH Yardy
8	MW Goodwin, RJ Kirtley
7	JD Lewry
6	MJG Davis
4	RSC Martin-Jenkins
3	TR Ambrose
1	PA Cottey, WJ House, UBA Rashid, MA Robinson, NJ Wilton (1st)

WARWICKSHIRE CCC

FIRST-CLASS MATCHES

BATTING

Match	MJ Powell	NV Knight	MA Wagh	DL Hemp	DP Ostler	DR Brown	NMK Smith	KJ Piper	MA Sheikh	VC Drakes	A Richardson	MM Betts	NM Carter	IR Bell	AF Giles	T Frost	CE Dagnall	JO Troughton	JA Spires	TL Penney	Extras	Total	Wickets	Result	Points
v. Hampshire (Edgbaston) 20–23 April	0	140	46	5	119	2	54	4	19	17*	5										44	455	10		
	-																				-			D	12
v. Durham (Edgbaston) 9–12 May	3	1	15	10	3	45	47	37		12*	1	2									29	205	10		
	20	22	104	38*	7*	-	-	-		-	-	-									36	227	3	W	16
v. Nottinghamshire (Trent Bridge) 16–19 May	-	-					-					-									-	-	-		
	-						-														-			D	6
v. Sussex (Hove) 25–28 May	93	46	90	30	22	63	19	2		3*	2	2									23	395	10		
	11	26	20*	4*	-	-	-	-		-	-	-									9	70	2	W	19
v. Gloucestershire (Edgbaston) 31 May–2 June	133	-	1	36	92	1	55		13	-	10*	3*	51								28	448	9		
	-						7*						15*								0	22	0	W	19
v. Oxford University CCE (Oxford) 6–8 June	236		14	35	14	25	-		-	-	-	-	130		0*						27	457	6		
	-	93	100*		23	-		33	-	-	-	-	-		17						12	278	4	D	-
v. Worcestershire (Worcester) 13–16 June	23		16	17	10	32	8	92*	28		19		17	0							15	277	10		
	-					-			-					-							-			D	7.75
v. Middlesex (Edgbaston) 20–23 June	4		10	105	44	0	-	15	0	-	14		0	40*							15	251	10		
	11		77	61	3	7	-	20*	14	0			20	24							15	252	10	L	5
v. Durham (Chester-le-Street) 29 June–2 July	12	75	6	0	121	21	4	34		11	2	10*									14	310	10		
	1	25	112	14	86	67*	5	4*		-	-	-									10	324	6	D	10
v. Gloucestershire (Bristol) 4–7 July	9	13	89	24	3	6	17	3		17	2*	1									20	204	10		
	16	47*	37	5*	-	-	-	-		-	-	-									8	113	2	D	8
v. Derbyshire (Edgbaston) 18–21 July	37	47		38	10	15	11	26*		0	5	0	6								9	204	10		
	-																				-			D	8
v. Nottinghamshire (Edgbaston) 3–6 August	15	0	7	52	104	16	20		13		15*		103								28	373	10		
	9	98*	0	105	-	-	-		-				29*								16	257	3	W	17.75
v. Hampshire (Southampton Rose Bowl) 7–10 August	83	4	4	14	50	0	33		0	0*		5	98								17	308	10		
	-								-												-			D	7
v. Worcestershire (Edgbaston) 15–18 August	5	83	186*		85	11*	21						4				27				25	447	6		
	0	29	8		2*	-	-						28				5*				5	77	4	D	12
v. Middlesex (Lord's) 22–25 August	6	0	315	36	53		40		41	4*			98			1					37	631	9		
	-					-	-		-												-			D	10
v. Sussex (Edgbaston) 7–10 September	0	17	5	16	23	8	13		50	6*	14		80								16	248	10		
	27	59	74*	45	-	-	-		-				22*								13	240	3	D	8
v. Derbyshire (Derby) 12–15 September	1	124	30	3	53*	29*			-				135		-						24	400	6		
	-								-												-			W	20
Matches	17	12	16	17	10	16	14	15	4	14	13	12	6	11	2	1	3	1	1	1					
Innings	24	17	24	25	12	20	14	17	4	13	9	11	4	16	3	2	1	2	-	1					
Not Out	0	2	2	5	1	3	2	5	0	3	4	3	1	3	1	1	0	1	-	0					
Highest Score	236	140	315	186*	121	104	54	92*	33	50	6*	19	5	135	40*	17	1	27	-	1					
Runs	755	744	1277	987	520	666	254	426	66	209	20	92	10	836	64	17	1	32	-	1					
Average	31.45	49.6	58.04	49.35	47.27	39.17	21.16	35.5	16.5	20.9	4	11.5	5.1	64.3	32	17	1	32	-	1					
100s	2	2	3	4	2	1	-	-	-	-	-	-	-	3	-	-	-	-	-	-					
50s	2	3	6	2	2	6	1	2	-	1	-	-	-	4	-	-	-	-	-	-					
Ct/St	14	15	4	12	22	16	2	39/1	-	1	6	9	2	11	4	5/1	-	-	-	3/-					

WARWICKSHIRE CCC

FIRST–CLASS MATCHES

BOWLING

	VC Drakes	A Richardson	MA Sheikh	DR Brown	NMK Smith	MA Wagh	MM Betts	NM Carter	CE Dagnall	AF Giles			Overs	Total	Byes/Leg-Byes	Wickets	Run outs
v. Hampshire	10.5-1-34-2	18-3-55-1	20-7-36-4	14-4-42-3	2-1-1-0	-							64.5	170	2	10	-
(Edgbaston) 20–23 April	26-5-74-2	22-10-32-2	34-15-67-1	23-10-44-2	18-5-40-0	8.1-4-12-0							133.1	285	3	7	- A
v. Durham	27-2-83-4	20-5-61-4		25-4-81-0			16.2-2-57-2						100.2	329	15	10	- A
(Edgbaston) 9–12 May	16-8-19-1	12-1-29-0		8.2-3-15-3	5-2-10-0		14-7-22-5						55.2	102	6	9	-
v. Nottinghamshire	22-1-86-1	11-1-51-0	26.1-10-82-		22-3-74-3	1-0-2-0	21-2-101-1						103.1	402	6	6	-
(Trent Bridge) 16–19 May	-	-	-										-	-	-	-	-
v. Sussex	14-4-45-3			22-10-33-1	17-5-29-2	4-1-4-1	20-8-35-2	6-0-50-1					83	208	12	10	-
(Hove) 25–28 May	27-6-55-2			10-2-25-0	34-6-76-4	14-2-29-3	18-6-47-1	4-1-18-0					107	253	3	10	-
v. Gloucestershire	30-9-83-3			12.4-5-23-1	21-7-59-2	16-5-30-1	26-3-81-2	27-5-76-1					132.4	360	8	10	-
(Edgbaston) 31 May–3 June	19-3-37-5			14-7-29-2	5-2-7-0		8.2-4-17-3	4-0-16-0					50.2	106	0	10	-
v. Oxford University CCE		19-4-56-3	6-2-11-0	2-0-6-0		4-1-6-0		11-2-31-2	7-1-29-0				69.5	210	16	10	- B
(Oxford) 6–8 June		7-5-9-1	4-2-6-1	5-0-14-0		1-0-1-0		14-2-63-1	7-0-36-1				60	182	19	5	-
v. Worcestershire	23.1-5-101-3			17-2-81-1	4-0-25-0		13-2-70-1			19-4-55-2			76.1	347	15	7	-
(Worcester) 13–16 June	-			-	-		-			-			-	-	-	-	-
v. Middlesex	19.3-3-64-1		12-4-25-1	12-4-33-1			22-2-88-5			24-7-54-2			89.3	273	9	10	-
(Edgbaston) 20–23 June	30-8-85-0		7-0-28-0	26.5-5-58-3			11-3-36-0			46-11-132-1			120.5	359	20	6	2
v. Durham	-	29-8-55-1		29-7-74-1	13.2-6-16-3		26-9-78-4						97.2	231	8	10	1
(Chester-le-Street) 29 June–2 July	24.5-4-106-	16-6-27-1		14-3-37-2	24-7-57-2	7-1-14-0	20-7-36-2						105.5	284	7	8	-
v. Gloucestershire	19-8-38-3	19.3-4-40-3		16-6-29-1			11-5-28-3						65.3	145	10	10	-
(Bristol) 4–7 July	31-8-97-1	21-8-40-2		23-10-31-2	24-7-57-3	11.4-2-31-1	10-3-21-1						120.4	297	20	10	-
v. Derbyshire		19.3-9-28-4		9-2-21-1	8-2-22-1		14-0-46-2	16-0-40-2					66.3	165	8	10	-
(Edgbaston) 18–21 July		20-4-75-1		21-4-77-2	20-2-68-0		9-2-19-0	14-0-66-1					126	435	29	5	- A B C D
v. Nottinghamshire	26.5-4-116-1	27-6-66-2		24-5-70-0	20-6-39-1	2-0-15-0	2-0-5-1						109.5	350	15	6	- C
(Edgbaston) 3–6 August	11-3-35-2	9-6-13-0		12-1-39-1	16.4-4-42-3	3-1-3-3	-						51.4	141	9	9	-
v. Hampshire (Southampton Rose Bowl) 7–10 August	3-1-2-0	2.1-0-5-0		-	-	-	-	5-0-18-1					10.1	26	1	1	-
	-	-		-	-	-	-						-	-	-	-	-
v. Worcestershire	31-5-111-0	21-5-56-1		30-3-133-2	5-0-28-0	26.1-2-81-2		19-2-78-5					134.1	524	20	10	- E
(Edgbaston) 15–18 August	9.2-2-42-0	9-4-17-0		6-3-8-0	23-4-67-1	15-0-68-0							69.2	233	6	2	- A
v. Middlesex	31-5-78-1	26.5-5-83-2		19-3-79-1		33-6-93-0			21-4-73-2				153.5	502	14	7	1 F
(Lord's) 22–25 August	10-1-35-2	4-2-13-0				18-8-29-2			4-0-13-0				63	167	4	6	- F
v. Sussex	22.5-6-51-3	31-8-89-5		25-8-50-2	12-2-44-0	-	15-2-71-0						105.5	321	16	10	-
(Edgbaston) 7–10 September	21-5-60-1	30.5-7-77-3		19-2-71-0	13-2-28-0	20-4-55-0	18-1-71-1						121.5	376	14	5	-
v. Derbyshire		1-0-6-0		14.2-8-20-4	-	-	6-1-20-0		21-7-50-6				42.2	106	10	10	-
(Derby) 12–15 September				19-2-60-6	-		7.4-1-30-1		23-4-78-3				49.4	194	26	10	-

	VC Drakes	A Richardson	MA Sheikh	DR Brown	NMK Smith	MA Wagh	MM Betts	NM Carter	CE Dagnall	AF Giles							
Overs	505.2	395.5	109.1	471.2	314	184	308.2	120	83	89							
Maidens	107	111	40	123	75	37	70	12	16	22							
Runs	1537	983	255	1284	813	473	979	456	279	241							
Wickets	42	36	8	42	25	13	37	14	12	5							
Average	36.59	27.30	31.87	30.57	32.52	36.38	26.45	32.57	23.25	48.20							

A MJ Powell 2-0-13-0; 5-1-8-0; 20-0-54-1; 7-1-25-1
B DL Hemp 2-0-9-0; 12-1-28-0
C IR Bell 9-1-16-0; 8-3-24-1
D KJ Piper 1-0-3-0
E JO Troughton 2-0-17-0

FIELDING

40	KJ Piper (39ct,1st)
22	DP Ostler
16	DR Brown
15	NV Knight
14	MJ Powell
12	DL Hemp
11	IR Bell
9	MM Betts
6	T Frost (5ct,1st), A Richardson
4	AF Giles, MA Wagh
3	TL Penney
2	NM Carter
1	VC Drakes

WORCESTERSHIRE CCC

FIRST-CLASS MATCHES

BATTING

	WPC Weston	A Singh	GA Hick	VS Solanki	DA Leatherdale	PR Pollard	SJ Rhodes	AJ Bichel	SR Lampitt	MJ Rawnsley	CG Liptrot	A Sheriyar	Kadeer Ali	Kabir Ali	DJ Pipe	NR Boulton	Extras	Total	Wickets	Result	Points
v. Middlesex	9	36	81	16	93	3	6	33	8*	4*							12	301	8		
(Lord's) 20–23 April	-	-	-	-	-	-	-	-	-	-							-	-	-	D	8
v. Sussex	6	8*															0	14	1		
(Worcester) 25–28 April	78*	20	31	34	0*	-	-	15	-								10	188	4	D	6
v. Hampshire	1	7	120	10	34		0	15	5	5	2	6*					31	236	10		
(Southampton Rose Bowl) 9–11 May	4	33	5	5	4		14	30	0	0	5	0*					8	108	10	L	4
v. Derbyshire	17*	26*															9	52	0		
(Worcester) 16–19 May	-	-															-	-	-	D	4
v. Gloucestershire	83	15	4	30	45		21	76	0	8		0*	4				40	326	10		
(Bristol) 25–28 May	58	0	2	4	41		32*	37	24*	32		-	1				25	256	8	W	18
v. Australians	6	62	19	3	22				8	13*	3	5	11	5			6	163	10		
(Worcester) 1–3 June	22	11	0	15	72				1	4*	5	2	39	8			9	188	10	L	-
v. Sussex	42	0	13	26	1		46	8	0	24		4*	0				19	183	10		
(Horsham) 6–9 June	21	43	13	89	39		41*	2	11	0		0	1				33	293	10	L	3
v. Warwickshire	74	23	124	29	18	0	22*	5	17*								35	347	7		
(Worcester) 13–16 June	-																-	-	-	D	10
v. Durham University CCE	60	128		106		131rh			15*				14	50*	24	47	56	631	6		
(Worcester) 20–22 June	-																-	-	-		
v. Nottinghamshire	5	17	123	5	12		2	24			19*	0	22	0			19	248	10		
(Worcester) 29 June–2 July	192	27	17	15	9		17	40			11	0*	0	21			20	369	10	L	4
v. Derbyshire	17	60	171	109	0		37*	25				4	14	13	7		39	496	10		
(Derby) 5–7 July	-																-	-	-	W	20
v. Gloucestershire	35	42	10	6	9	45	0	13	11	0*			25				44	240	10		
(Worcester) 20–22 July	38*	15	0	12	4*								-				4	73	3	W	16
v. Durham	5	45	0	0	12	45	1	37	42*	6		20					14	227	10		
(Kidderminster) 2–5 August	2	57	12	0	0	28	10	7	23*	1		1					6	147	10	L	7
v. Nottinghamshire	19	88	17	14	25	0	0	53	13	1	0*						22	252	10		
(Trent Bridge) 8–11 August	3	43	22	43	9	22	40*	42		1	6	1					27	259	10	L	5
v. Warwickshire	23	0	201	112	23		28*	42	19	15	9				0		52	524	10		
(Edgbaston) 15–18 August	102*	22	41*	56													12	233	2	D	11
v. Hampshire	30	32	9	27	7	26	32	35	5*	22	2						20	247	10		
(Worcester) 22–25 August	16	0	76	1	25	0	52	78	39	0	0*						19	306	10	W	16
v. Durham	55	9	200*	0	7	3	9	32	17	0	3*						21	356	9		
(Chester-le-Street) 5–8 September	2	0	8	11	14	6	21*	0			1*						22	85	7	D	11
v. Middlesex	71	168	31	0	33		30	0	20*	17	3	38					23	434	10		
(Worcester) 12–15 September	36	17	59*	24	12*		23										8	179	4	D	12
Matches	18	18	17	18	17	10	15	16	10	15	12	16	5	4	3	4					
Innings	31	31	28	29	27	12	20	24	13	21	14	19	8	5	5	5					
Not Out	4	2	3	0	3	1	7	0	5	5	4	8	0	1	0	0					
Highest Score	192	168	201	112	93	131rh	52	78	42*	39	20	20	38	50*	24	47					
Runs	1132	1054	1409	803	570	309	442	627	205	210	128	71	65	138	59	75					
Average	41.92	36.34	56.36	27.65	23.75	28.09	34	26.12	25.62	13.12	12.8	6.45	8.12	34.5	11.8	15					
100s	2	2	6	3	-	1	-	-	-	-	-	-	-	-	-	-					
50s	7	4	3	2	2	-	1	3	-	-	-	-	1	-	-	-					
Ct/St	12	5	19	17	7	5	51/1	5	4	7	4	3	2	-	4/1	1					

WORCESTERSHIRE CCC

FIRST-CLASS MATCHES

BOWLING

	AJ Bichel	CG Liptrot	SR Lampitt	MJ Rawnsley	DA Leatherdale	GA Hick	A Sheriyar	Kabir Ali	Overs	Total	Byes/Leg-Byes	Wickets	Run outs
v. Middlesex (Lord's) 20–23 April	29-9-85-1	17-6-44-2	15-5-51-0	32-9-61-1	5-1-26-0	9-3-12-1			112	302	6	5	- A
	-								-	-	-	-	-
v. Sussex (Worcester) 25–28 April	26-9-84-4	13-2-43-1	4-0-37-0		5-1-21-0	9.4-3-22-1	11-1-43-0		68.4	255	5	7	1
	2-1-5-1	1-0-7-0	6-2-14-1		-	4-0-23-0	2-0-5-0		15	54	0	2	-
v. Hampshire (Southampton) 9–11 May	29.5-9-100-1	16-4-43-0	15-3-45-3	6-2-12-0	2-0-15-0		32-12-85-4		100.5	309	9	10	1
	22-6-55-2	8-3-26-2	10-3-27-2	4-1-14-0			14.5-2-30-4		58.5	159	7	10	-
v. Derbyshire (Worcester) 16–19 May	15-5-51-1	13-2-31-1	15-3-55-1		7-2-23-3		14-3-51-2		69	222	5	8	- A
	-								-	-	-	-	-
v. Gloucestershire (Bristol) 25–28 May	21-6-44-6		12.5-4-22-5	14-6-26-1	-	2-2-0-0	21-7-46-3		70.5	175	9	10	-
	15-5-37-2		11-3-37-0	11-2-25-1	2-0-6-0		18-7-42-3		63	155	1	10	-
v. Australians (Worcester) 1–3 June		17-3-37-3		23-4-90-3	5-0-46-0	-	20-3-86-1	12-2-43-3	87.2	351	16	10	- A
		11-0-74-1		24-3-108-3	-		12-1-78-1	11-1-55-1	67	360	4	8	- A
v. Sussex (Horsham) 6–9 June	15-5-37-2		16-8-22-3	5-0-23-1	-	-	14.3-5-53-4		50.3	137	2	10	-
	30-8-88-3		18-5-51-0	39.5-13-72-3		3-0-15-0	23-5-83-4		131.5	372	12	10	- A
v. Warwickshire (Worcester) 13–16 June	28-5-92-2		23.3-5-58-3	3-1-2-0	11-2-36-1		33-12-76-4		98.3	277	13	10	-
	-								-	-	-	-	- A B C
v. Durham University CCE (Worcester) 20–22 June		32-9-81-3		47-23-55-3			25.4-4-78-4	5-0-12-0	129.4	284	18	10	- A B C
		6-1-25-0		15-4-36-0			6-2-19-0	-	52	164	9	0	- A B C D
v. Nottinghamshire (Worcester) 29 June–2 July	14.4-4-45-5	5-2-20-2	11-2-46-2		-	-	12-0-44-1		42.4	160	5	10	-
	24-2-127-1	14-2-56-0	16-3-61-1			25-8-70-0	27-5-92-1		115.2	461	9	3	- A B D
v. Derbyshire (Derby) 5–7 July	17-2-53-4			18-7-60-2	4-1-4-0	4-3-4-2	8-0-34-0	7-0-28-1	58	198	15	9	-
	21-4-57-1			27-5-74-1	6-2-17-0	5-1-16-0	27-6-68-5	20.4-5-51-2	106.4	295	12	9	-
v. Gloucestershire (Worcester) 20–22 July	20.3-7-54-6		16-0-76-1	3-0-9-0	11-3-39-1	-		18-6-42-2	68.3	222	2	10	-
	12-4-32-4		-	-	6-2-29-1	-		10.2-5-22-5	28.2	87	4	10	-
v. Durham (Kidderminster) 2–5 August	19-1-72-3		6-1-37-1	13-3-33-0	5-2-21-0		18-5-88-6		61	260	9	10	- D
	9-1-40-1		8-2-30-1	2-1-5-1			9-2-38-0		28.2	118	0	3	-
v. Nottinghamshire (Trent Bridge) 8–11 August	15-7-27-2	11-2-29-1		-	9.3-2-31-3	-	16-4-51-4		51.3	149	11	10	-
	27-7-102-1	21-5-84-3		14-2-72-0	17-5-53-1	3-0-8-0	25.1-8-80-4		107.1	423	24	10	1
v. Warwickshire (Edgbaston) 15–18 August	22-6-91-0	27-6-89-2		37-8-88-0	11-1-41-1	11-3-28-0	28-8-94-3		137	447	15	6	- B
	9-2-28-1	8-3-12-3		-	2.1-0-8-0		7-2-28-0		26.1	77	1	4	-
v. Hampshire (Worcester) 22–25 August	23-8-64-3	22-8-43-3		15.1-5-45-1	8-3-10-1	14-5-30-0	15-3-47-2		97.1	247	8	10	-
	13.5-2-62-5	10-7-10-1		11-3-29-2	3-1-15-0	2-0-20-0	12-1-50-2		51.5	194	8	10	-
v. Durham (Chester-le-Street) 5–8 September	22-3-64-1	23-5-85-3		34-11-85-0	20-6-70-4	-	31.3-14-55-2		132.3	369	7	10	- A
	14-2-48-3	11-4-38-1		14.2-4-50-2	3-0-10-0		17-1-60-1		67	237	4	7	- A
v. Middlesex (Worcester) 12–15 September	22-5-73-0	16-6-41-2		11-2-33-0	10-2-44-0	11-1-33-3	24.3-1-121-5		94.3	349	4	10	-
	12-0-52-0	6.4-0-48-1		23-3-104-2	5.2-3-15-0	3-1-6-0	12-1-70-1		75	368	7	4	- A C

	AJ Bichel	CG Liptrot	SR Lampitt	MJ Rawnsley	DA Leatherdale	GA Hick	A Sheriyar	Kabir Ali
Overs	555.5	308.4	203.2	446.2	158	105.4	536.1	84
Maidens	137	80	49	122	39	30	125	19
Runs	1804	966	669	1211	580	287	1795	253
Wickets	66	35	24	27	16	7	71	14
Average	27.33	27.60	27.87	44.85	36.25	41.00	25.28	18.07

A   VS Solanki 5-0-17-0; 5-2-6-0; 10-3-33-0; 9-1-41-2; 18-3-51-0; 14-7-18-0; 4-0-12-0; 4-0-18-0; 2-0-3-0; 7.4-1-27-0; 5-0-39-0

B   NR Boulton 4-1-12-0; 9-2-21-0; 3-1-14-0; 1-0-1-0

C   Kadeer Ali 2-0-10-0; 7-3-20-0; 8-2-27-0

D   WPC Weston 5-0-22-0; 2.2-0-14-0; 0.2-0-5-0

FIELDING

52	SJ Rhodes (51ct,1st)
19	GA Hick
17	VS Solanki
11	WPC Weston
7	DA Leatherdale, MJ Rawnsley
5	AJ Bichel, DJ Pipe (4ct,1st), PR Pollard, A Singh
4	SR Lampitt, CG Liptrot
3	A Sheriyar
2	Kadeer Ali
1	NR Boulton

YORKSHIRE CCC

FIRST-CLASS MATCHES

BATTING

	S Widdup	MP Vaughan	A McGrath	DS Lehmann	D Byas	RJ Sidebottom	MJ Lumb	GM Fellows	RJ Blakey	CEW Silverwood	MJ Hoggard	C White	D Gough	SA Richardson	MJ Wood	JD Middlebrook	ID Fisher	PM Hutchison	GM Hamilton	SP Kirby	RKJ Dawson	AKD Gray	CR Taylor	VJ Craven	SM Guy	Extras	Total	Wickets	Result	Points
v. Kent (Canterbury) 25–28 April	14	71	29	68	27	40*	1	18	1	0	2															14	285	10		
	27	14	2	41	23	–	9	43*	6*	–	–															11	176	6	W	17
v. Somerset (Headingley) 9–12 May	2	79	0	38	3	0		63	0	7		4	11*													24	231	10		
	1	8	5	77	31	3*		29	5	22		4	2													5	192	10	L	4
v. Essex (Chelmsford) 16–19 May			13	7	55			20	41	70				22	29	84	28*	9*								25	403	9		
			–	–	–			–	–	–				–	–	–	–	–								–	–	–	D	12
v. Northamptonshire (Headingley) 25–27 May		133		5		6	50	30	42*	0	4	20		12	44											28	374	10		
		4		26*		6	0	2*				7		0	5											27	77	6	W	19
v. Glamorgan (Swansea) 30 May–1 June			75	63	1*			22	23	2		39		0	1	35				6						13	280	10		
			22	105*	–			61	4			24		5	0	25*				13						18	277	7	W	17
v. Kent (Headingley) 6–9 June			90	3				20	59	25		26		69	90	1		0	11*							19	413	10		
												5*		29*	10			–	–							9	53	1	W	20
v. Somerset (Bath) 13–16 June			187*	20				63	78*			16		68	124			–	–							33	589	5		
														–	–											–	–	–	D	10
v. Leicestershire (Headingley) 29 June–1 July			104	30			122	34	15	7	1*			3	102					0	37					45	500	10		
														–	–											–	–	–	W	20
v. Northamptonshire (Northampton) 4–7 July			29	110*	20	25		2				6		55					14	1	23	0				24	309	10		
								5*						1*	2											2	10	1	D	10
v. Lancashire (Headingley) 27–30 July			0	252	7	0		5	18			23	96	86						15*	0					29	531	10		
			21*	48	14*							19	–	51						–	–					5	158	3	W	20
v. Surrey (Headingley) 1–4 August			11	52	6	8*		27	12					7					25	5	2		14			35	204	10		
			14	106*										85*					–	–	–		15			24	244	2	D	8
v. Lancashire (Old Trafford) 7–10 August			5	26	27			17	0	34*		186		115				11*	6		2					38	467	9		
								1	–	–				–	–											–	–	–	W	20
v. Leicestershire (Leicester) 15–18 August	82		0	20				3	15			3		33				2*	15	15	16					26	230	10		
	47			193	100			0	6*			8		11				–	34	–	3					27	429	8	W	16
v. Glamorgan (Scarborough) 21–24 August	45		29	1	104			54				183		124					1	0	9*					30	580	9		
	–				–									–	–					–	–					–	–	–	W	20
v. Surrey (Oval) 5–8 September	11	116*		24						0				51						2	2	3	7	0	0	19	235	10		
	61	73		4						2				27						0	1	1	18	7	12*	29	235	10	L	10
v. Essex (Scarborough) 12–15 September			5	29	41*			3*						8								0	6	3		9	104	5		
		113	70	5				19				2		0						0	0	0	0	23*		35	267	10	L	3
Matches	2	7	9	13	16	8	4	12	15	8	7	9	2	7	14	4	1	3	8	10	9	3	3	2	1					
Innings	4	13	15	19	24	8	7	17	21	9	6	15	3	11	23	4	1	3	9	10	11	4	6	4	2					
Not Out	0	0	2	2	5	4	0	1	6	1	1	1	1	2	1	1	1	3	0	1	1	0	0	1	1					
Highest Score	27	133	187*	252	110*	40*	122	63	78*	70	4	186	96	69	124	84	28*	11*	34	15*	37	3	18	23*	12*					
Runs	44	673	417	1416	853	78	218	455	405	167	11	567	109	215	1060	145	28	22	114	49	95	4	60	33	12					
Average	11	51.76	32.07	83.29	44.89	19.5	31.14	28.43	27	20.87	2.2	40.5	54.5	23.88	48.18	48.33	–	–	12.66	5.44	9.5	1	10	11	12					
100s	–	3	1	5	4	–	1	–	–	–	–	2	–	–	4	–	–	–	–	–	–	–	–	–	–					
50s	–	3	2	5	2	–	1	3	3	1	–	2	–	2	6	1	–	–	–	–	–	–	–	–	–					
Ct/St	5	6	6	6	38	3	–	4	49/5	2	–	5	–	6	10	2	–	–	1	4	6	2	1	2	–					

YORKSHIRE CCC

FIRST-CLASS MATCHES
BOWLING

Match	CEW Silverwood	MJ Hoggard	RJ Sidebottom	MP Vaughan	GM Fellows	DS Lehmann	D Gough	C White	PM Hutchison	JD Middlebrook	GM Hamilton	SP Kirby	RKJ Dawson	AKD Gray	Overs	Total	Byes/Leg-Byes	Wickets	Run outs
v. Kent (Canterbury) 25-28 April	18.1-3-45-5	12.1-3-32-1	17-7-30-1	14.5-8-23-1	8-3-9-2										70.1	142	3	10	-
	32-6-96-3	-	31.4-8-67-4	19-2-48-0	26-6-69-1	12-4-13-0									124.4	318	15	10	- A
v. Somerset (Headingley) 9-12 May	18-3-57-3		18-3-46-2	6-0-22-0	16-8-19-0	4-1-10-0	22-10-47-2	15-2-51-1							99	257	5	10	2
	11-1-47-0		18-10-32-0	15-1-47-4	10-2-29-0	21-4-53-1	22-3-67-1	18-5-39-0							115	327	13	8	2
v. Essex (Chelmsford) 16-19 May	18-1-67-1				12-5-23-3	5-2-5-1			16-3-59-1	19-4-49-3					83	249	14	10	- B
	-				-										-	-	-	-	-
v. Northamptonshire (Headingley) 25-27 May	21.4-5-58-5	22-8-46-2	17-6-55-1	-	14-5-25-1			-							74.4	195	11	10	1
	17.4-4-37-2	24-7-82-5	18-2-52-0	9-3-25-2	12-3-40-1			-							80.4	255	19	10	-
v. Glamorgan (Swansea) 30 May-1 June	9-5-20-5		10-3-37-2		2-0-5-0					10-3-22-1	8-3-15-2				41.3	104	1	10	-
	10-4-25-0		13-3-49-4		-	0.4-0-0-1				5-1-23-0	9-3-27-5				37.4	125	1	10	-
v. Kent (Headingley) 6-9 June	16-4-38-3	19.2-5-48-4				5-2-24-0		9-4-19-2	7-1-18-0	14-1-44-1	-				73.2	212	9	10	-
	7-3-18-0					11-3-31-2		25-11-34-1	17-4-37-0	26-6-62-0	20-4-50-7				117	250	11	10	-
v. Somerset (Bath) 13-16 June			26-5-82-0			13-1-53-1		14-0-68-1	19-2-59-0	24-2-116-1	24-6-81-1	23-3-79-1			143	553	15	5	-
		-	-			-		-		-		-			-	-	-	-	-
v. Leicestershire (Headingley) 29 June-1 July	9.4-1-33-2	14-6-43-1			2-1-4-0	-						15-4-46-6	10-2-44-1		50.4	174	4	10	-
	7-1-20-1	11-2-43-3			-	-						9.2-1-26-6	1-0-8-0		28.2	99	2	10	-
v. Northamptonshire (Northampton) 4-7 July			16-6-33-2			7-2-12-1					13-5-40-1		12-5-39-0		88.5	253	16	10	1
			17-3-54-1								18-6-47-4	18-5-50-2	26-10-74-1	20-4-63-2	99	298	10	10	-
v. Lancashire (Headingley) 27-30 July			16-5-45-2	2-0-11-0	9-1-35-0		24-4-65-4	15-2-43-0				23.4-4-103-3	18-3-62-1		107.4	373	9	10	-
			15-5-31-1	-	5-3-10-0		20-1-96-1	17.1-3-57-4				12-2-48-2	11-0-62-1		80.1	314	10	10	1
v. Surrey (Headingley) 1-4 August			17-5-39-2		10-1-26-1	6-2-9-0						17.2-0-69-2	20-2-90-4	10-1-34-1	80.2	278	11	10	-
			6-3-6-1		11-3-21-0	4-1-14-0						19-2-66-3	16-5-54-0	36.5-5-98-6	92.5	281	22	10	1
v. Lancashire (Old Trafford) 7-10 August	10-0-71-2				-	7.3-2-13-3		4-0-19-0	11-3-40-2		8-1-41-1		13-0-49-1		53.3	242	9	10	1
	4-1-12-1				2-0-9-0	8-2-23-1		8.2-1-19-1	14-1-51-0		13-3-33-3		17-8-29-4		66.2	188	12	10	-
v. Leicestershire (Leicester) 15-18 August				-	-	7-1-14-0		9-1-33-2	5-2-11-3		6-1-23-1	8-1-20-2	7-1-23-2		35	121	11	10	-
				-	-	-		10-3-41-2	14-6-28-3		15-2-76-1	20-3-82-3	27-8-109-1		93	370	20	10	-
v. Glamorgan (Scarborough) 21-24 August				-		4-0-10-0		14-4-27-1			11-2-27-0	11-4-35-0	30-5-82-6		88.1	223	6	10	- C
				-		9-1-56-3		4-3-4-0			10-2-21-1	20-10-40-4	25-7-62-1		80	245	26	10	-
v. Surrey (Oval) 5-8 September		30-5-99-2		-							21.4-1-104-1	22-7-94-0	39-7-128-4		130.4	516	22	9	- C D
v. Essex (Scarborough) 12-15 September		23.3-6-51-6		-								15-3-81-0	17-4-39-2	12-4-21-1	77.3	250	7	10	- C
		10-3-35-2		-								13-3-38-3	19-3-66-0	9-3-30-3	51	172	3	8	-

	CEW Silverwood	MJ Hoggard	RJ Sidebottom	MP Vaughan	GM Fellows	DS Lehmann	D Gough	C White	PM Hutchison	JD Middlebrook	GM Hamilton	SP Kirby	RKJ Dawson	AKD Gray
Overs	209.1	192	257.5	63.5	156	139.1	88	167.3	60	82	211.2	280.3	315.5	92
Maidens	42	50	73	14	43	33	18	45	11	15	43	60	69	23
Runs	644	561	646	165	398	368	275	410	224	265	672	980	1014	281
Wickets	33	26	27	723.57	12	12	8	16	7	5	26	47	30	10
Average	19.51	21.57	23.92		33.16	30.66	34.37	25.62	32.00	53.00	25.84	20.85		28.10

A MJ Lumb 4-1-10-2
B ID Fisher 13-3-32-1
C A McGrath 2-0-2-0; 8-4-22-2; 7-0-29-1
D VJ Craven 10-1-47-0

FIELDING

54	RJ Blakey (49ct,5st)
38	D Byas
10	MJ Wood
6	RKJ Dawson, DS Lehmann, A McGrath, SA Richardson, MP Vaughan
5	C White, S Widdup
4	GM Fellows, SP Kirby
3	RJ Sidebottom
2	VJ Craven, ADK Gray, JD Middlebrook, CEW Silverwood
1	GM Hamilton, CR Taylor